THE BODY AND T

THE BODY AND THE BLOOD

The Middle East's Vanishing Christians and the Possibility for Peace

Charles M. Sennott

PublicAffairs
New York

Published in the United States by PublicAffairs™,
a member of the Perseus Books Group.

Printed in the United States of America.

PublicAffairs books are available at special discounts for bulk purchases in the U.S. by corporations, institutions, and other organizations. For more information, please contact the Special Markets Department at The Perseus Books Group, 11 Cambridge Center, Cambridge MA 02142, or call (617) 252–5298.

Book Design by Jenny Dossin.

Library of Congress Cataloging-in-Publication Data
Sennott, Charles M.
The body and the blood:
the Middle East's vanishing Christians and the possibility for peace
p. cm.
Includes bibliographical references.
ISBN 1-58648-165-7 (pbk.)
1. Christianity—Middle East.
2. Middle East—Church history—20th century.
I. Title.
BR1070.S45 2001
275.69'083—dc21
00–051789

1 3 5 7 9 10 8 6 4 2

FOR JULIE

CONTENTS

IV
The Passion

PREFACE TO THE PAPERBACK EDITION

In the darkness before dawn, an Israeli attack helicopter swept over the hills around Bethlehem, its searchlight beaming down on the Shepherds' Fields, where tradition holds, an angel heralded the birth of Jesus. A convoy of armored personnel carriers and tanks rumbled through a miserable, drizzling rain. Israeli troops were moving in to surround the West Bank town.

It was Tuesday, April 2, 2002, and by dawn the invasion was underway—an offensive against what the Israelis called the Palestinian Authority's "infrastructure of terrorism." The Israeli operation came in response to a wave of Islamic extremist groups' suicide attacks—including a Hamas bombing that killed twenty-eight people at a Passover seder in Netanya—that had left a death toll of nearly one hundred Israeli civilians and soldiers in the long, bloody month of March. The Israelis were pressing forward not only into Bethlehem but also into Nablus, Jenin, and Ramallah. In Ramallah the Israeli forces had surrounded Palestinian leader Yasser Arafat's headquarters and kept him under a militarily imposed form of house arrest.

On the fringe of Bethlehem's Manger Square, the massive treads of the Israeli Merkeva tanks groaned and creaked as they advanced, rolling across the diplomatic, political, and geographic lines that had been drawn by the now fully eclipsed "peace process." The spree of Palestinian suicide bombings and the subsequent Israeli reoccupation of the pockets of previously Palestinian-controlled territory exposed the depressing reality that the political equation of "land for peace" had been replaced by the biblical axiom of "an eye for an eye."

Captain Michael Aviad, a 32-year-old Israeli Army reservist and head of the Israeli infantry unit known as the Jerusalem Brigade, peered out of the small bullet-proof window of an armored personnel carrier that was rumbling forward from a military base at the Jewish settlement of Neve Daniel. The tanks flanking the personnel carrier slowly plowed forward, smashing parked cars and dumpsters, storefront awnings and feeble Palestinian roadblocks, and anything else that got in its way as the convoy plodded along Pope Paul VI street in Bethlehem.

Ibrahim Abayat, 30, the leader of a local Palestinian militia, saw the Israelis coming. Hailing from a Bedouin tribe on the outskirts of Bethlehem that saw itself as the Muslim protectors of Palestinian land, Abayat was cruising the back streets in his Toyota pickup truck. He was shouting last-minute orders to his ragtag group of fighters, telling them to take up positions throughout the Old City of Bethlehem and to fight the advancing Israeli troops with everything they had, which wasn't much.

Inside the Franciscan monastery at the Church of the Nativity in Manger Square, the Roman Catholic Franciscan brother Raphael Tayim, 23, was rising for the morning prayer services when he heard the first bursts of machine-gun fire echoing in the narrow alleyways of the Old City. He donned the humble brown, hooded robes of his order, tightened the rope of his garments, and made his way down toward St. Catherine's chapel, the Roman Catholic church built inside the sprawling compound of the Church of the Nativity. For Tayim, a Palestinian Christian from the Galilee, this was not the first time he had awoken to machine-gun fire. So he tried to go about the daily ritual of prayer, a continuum practiced inside the church since it was built by the Roman emperor Constantine in the fourth century A.D. to circumscribe the stone grotto that, Christian tradition holds, is the place where Jesus was born.

These three men—a Jewish soldier, a Muslim militant, and a Christian cleric—and the strands of their vastly different personal narratives were all woven together in this moment at one of the holiest sites in Christendom. They would find themselves caught up in the fighting around the Church of the Nativity and ultimately at the center of the long, 38-day standoff that would take place there. Even before the siege began, I had, through several years spent reporting this book, gotten to know the separate stories of these three men.

The Israeli captain, "Mike," was one of the first Israelis I befriended in my neighborhood, and we often shared coffee together. We walked our dogs and strolled with our babies in the same park, and as hard as we tried not to, we almost always ended up talking politics. Like many of the people one meets in the Middle East, he had a complex background that defied the narrow parameters used too often to try to frame the issues. He was a staunch Zionist, a proud Israeli. But he had been born in California, and his father was an Irish Catholic university professor. His mother, Janet Aviad, was a leading Israeli peace activist, and I had interviewed her on several occasions.

The Palestinian militia leader, Abayat, was a member of a Muslim tribe outside Bethlehem whose role in the *intifada* I had been researching since the fall of 2000. I had been in his home and interviewed his mother as well, though she was no peace activist. She was proud of her sons and the men in her extended family for fighting against the Israelis. She felt that any of those who died—and there would be a good number who would—were martyrs who would surely find their way into paradise and make her family proud. The Abayat family was of interest to me because of the pivotal role it played in forming the militia that had first started targeting Israeli civilians and soldiers on the outskirts of Jerusalem in the early phase of the *intifada*. Christian families around Bethlehem had long mistrusted the tribe. There were frictions that dated back to the 1930s, largely over tribal issues. But in this *intifada*, or uprising, the tribal differences between Christians and Muslims were suddenly being recast in religious terms. Many Christian families in Bethlehem feared that the Abayats were intentionally putting the Christian community in the crosshairs of the conflict, and the siege at the Church of the Nativity was the most dramatic example of that.

The Palestinian Christian Franciscan, Tayim, was part of the faith community at the Church of the Nativity that I had explored in researching Bethlehem's Christian community. I had spent time in the small Christian village from which he hailed in the Galilee. Like Aviad, Tayim also had a complex identity. He was a citizen of Israel, but he saw himself as Palestinian. As a Christian, he was a minority within a minority of the Arab community, which constitutes about 19 percent of the total Israeli population. And in taking on a vocation in the priesthood he told me he was trying to help preserve the presence of a disappearing Palestinian Christian community from the land where the faith began.

So when I returned to the West Bank in April 2002 to cover the fighting in Bethlehem for the *Boston Globe*, there was a kind of dizzying convergence of these three stories for me. They became a personal touchstone in trying to understand yet another horrible turning point in the Israeli-Palestinian conflict. It had been one year since I completed the book. And the scenes I was witnessing on this return reporting trip were worse than anything I could have imagined when I left Jerusalem. I had left at the end of the summer of 2001 to take on a new assignment in London. But after the attacks on the United States on September 11, I ended up covering the war in Afghanistan and returning throughout the year to the Middle East. In Israel the relentless wave of Palestinian suicide bombings that targeted Israeli civilians on crowded streets and bus stops and cafés had left a trail of carnage and agony—and ultimately rage. Palestinian civilians, too, were dying as the Israeli offensives pushed into Palestinian refugee camps, towns, and villages. And the heavy-handed Israeli military curfews imposed on the West Bank had cut a wide swath of economic suffering, mass malnutrition among children, and an unprecedented level of despair among the Palestinian people. In the aftermath of 9-11, the Israeli-Palestinian conflict had taken on a horrifying intensity, and in America there was a heightened sense of awareness of it all. For some Americans the tragic images from Israel and the West Bank and the United States' role in that part of the world were now framed by a pervasive question—"Why do they hate us?"

Michael Aviad and his unit entered the narrow, cobblestone streets of the Old City at about 6 A.M. They encountered fire that he believed was coming from the half-constructed Peace Center that was being built adjacent to the Lutheran church. The Israelis returned fire, blowing out windows in the church. The soldiers broke into the church and smashed open the wooden doors of the office of the Lutheran minister, Mitri Raheb. They ransacked the place. Raheb was in his home inside the church compound and confronted the soldiers, informing them that they were violating a place of worship, and denying that any gunmen were stationed near the church. They sat him down at gunpoint and questioned him. Finally, a senior commander arrived, and the troops were told to move on, leaving Raheb and his family in the rubble.

The troops moved on through the winding passages toward Manger Square, exchanging fire with Palestinian fighters on rooftops and alleyways in the maze of Bethlehem's Old City. As they approached the square, Aviad said, shooting again erupted from a church. This time it was the Syrian Orthodox church, and again the Israeli soldiers stormed the church, trying to pursue the Palestinian gunmen. There was more exchange of fire, and to Aviad, there was a pattern emerging.

"The Palestinians were shooting from churches. They were shooting from rooftops and other places too. But it was pretty clear to us that they had taken up positions around the churches and monasteries, which are just about everywhere in the Old City. They knew we would have to be more careful around the churches. They definitely understood that the churches were cover," Aviad said.

If indeed it was a strategy, it seems to have evolved from the leaders of the Abayat tribe. They were a particularly tough group of Bedouins who had produced several generations of shepherds, car thieves, gun runners, and militants. For over a year, the Abayat-led militia, a splinter faction of the Al-Aqsa Martyrs' Brigade, had been sniping at Israeli soldiers and Jewish settlers on the so-called "bypass" roads that lead from Jerusalem into the West Bank. In the first days of this *intifada* in the fall of 2000, Ibrahim's cousin Hussein, a self-styled Palestinian Rambo, had been the leader of the militia. In those early days of the fighting, Hussein Abayat had arranged his undisciplined fighters to launch their attacks from the predominantly Christian village of Beit Jala, on the fringe of Jerusalem, intentionally using the Christian neighborhoods as a base for attacks, according to several of his supporters. Hussein knew that the Israelis were more conscious of the negative public opinion in the Western world when neighborhoods with Christian churches were in the Israeli troops' crosshairs. This strategy, he believed, forced the Israelis to be more restrained in their fighting.

On November 9, 2000, the Israeli military assassinated Hussein on a road in Beit Sahour, near the Shepherds' Fields. Hussein was killed instantly when Israeli attack helicopters slammed three anti-tank missiles into his white Isuzu pickup truck. Ibrahim was traveling with Hussein that morning in a convoy but narrowly escaped death, though he suffered burns on his hands trying to rescue his cousin from the flaming wreckage of his truck. Afterward, Ibrahim assumed the mantle of leadership in the Bethlehem area for the militia.

As the fighting stretched on through 2001 and into 2002, at least a half-dozen members of the Abayat tribe were killed. For the Abayats the battle was now a tribal war in the dry, chalky hills outside Bethlehem as much as it was a military confrontation between Israelis and Palestinians. Their quest for revenge was personal, not just political. On that morning of April 2, the cat-and-mouse tactics of guerrilla warfare—with Palestinian gunmen sniping at Israeli vehicles from the roadside and Israeli troops trying to respond with tanks and attack helicopters from the nearby Jewish settlement of Gilo—had been replaced with an all-out field battle. Israel's modern high-tech military was confronting the Palestinians' ragtag forces in open fighting on the streets.

In just four hours that morning, Aviad's Israeli military unit had essentially cornered the Palestinian fighters in Manger Square. The Palestinian gunmen retreated into the Church of the Nativity with its fortresslike walls. At the orders of Ibrahim Abayat, the Palestinian fighters shot off the locks on the doorway into St. Catherine's chapel. The Franciscan priests and brothers were startled at the invasion of their sacred space. So were the Greek Orthodox clerics and the Armenian monks with whom they shared the church compound. In the chaos and confusion of the fighting, dozens of civilians and Palestinian police officers and officials also retreated to what they saw as the relative safety and sanctuary of the church. The priests and nuns told Abayat and his fighters that the church would provide sanctuary but asked that they put down their guns. Abayat adamantly refused, and his armed militia began breaking apart church pews to barricade the doors.

The Israeli troops stopped short of the basilica, clearly understanding the implications of invading such a holy site in Christendom. "It was made clear to us the church was off-limits," said Aviad, recounting the events later. "The army did not want photographs of people being massacred in front of the Church of the Nativity."

When the hours of wild fighting on that morning had quieted and the two sides were beginning the standoff, Aviad said his thoughts turned to his late father, Thomas O'Dea, who would "probably be rolling over in his grave" if the Israeli troops had invaded the church.

"It felt strange, I have to admit," he said. "I am an atheist. I don't believe in holy places. But I can respect that other people do. We all knew this was a serious place for some people and that if my father were alive it would have been one for him. It may very well have been smarter to say, 'Fuck it, we'll capture them later.' We could have left snipers positioned around the city and been patient and killed the terrorists when they came out. But the siege just took on a life of its own, and then pretty soon the whole media was there and it became a spectacle. We were in it now."

The Israelis surrounded the church, and Aviad and his men set up a headquarters in the Peace Center in Manger Square, surrounding it with sandbags, barbed wire, and tanks. The troops destroyed the offices of the police department in the building's basement; they smashed computers, looted property, and systemically destroyed the Palestinian municipality's vehicles. One member of the press referred to it as "state-sponsored vandalism." The Israeli forces expressed their intention to remain in position until they captured or killed a "most wanted" list of "terrorists," including Ibrahim Abayat and at least three other members of the Abayat tribe. The Israelis established more tank positions and sniper nests. They blasted loud music and shrieking electronic sounds that resembled the wailing cries of wounded animals to try to psychologically tax and frustrate those inside to the point where they would give up. They also erected two industrial cranes and attached to the boom of each a robotic sniper rifle, which allowed them to reach over the compound and shoot down into it. Over the course of the standoff, the Israeli snipers killed eight people in the church compound, including a partially deaf and mildly retarded Palestinian Christian who rang the bells in the tower over the Armenian monastery. They also wounded twenty-two people inside the compound, including an Armenian monk who was merely passing by a window of his living quarters.

"I was with the sniper who shot the bell ringer. Obviously, it was a mistake. I think he was holding a mop or something that looked like a gun," said Aviad. He said he wasn't aware that an Armenian monk had been shot.

Aviad was unrepentant about the snipers killing people inside the church: "If you were holding a gun then you were a terrorist. That was how we saw it. We knew there were civilians in there, and we were very careful."

Both Israeli prime minister Ariel Sharon and Palestinian leader Yasser Arafat sought to capitalize on the crisis in Bethlehem as proof that the other side was incapable of protecting religious sites in the Holy Land. The Christians shrugged their shoulders at the political games both leaders played, and seemed almost resigned to their fate—that they would be caught in the middle of this conflict.

During the fighting, several windows of the sprawling church compound had been shot out. A fire touched off by flares or perhaps a phosphorous tracer bullet had ripped through the community center above the Franciscan chapel. Spent tear-gas canisters littered the ground, and yellow phosphorous stains from stun grenades and light tank rounds streaked the ancient walls, which were left pocked but mostly undamaged.

It wasn't the first time that these thick stone walls had witnessed conflict. There was the Persian invasion in the sixth century A.D., then the Arab Islamic conquest in the seventh century, the battles of the Crusades in the eleventh and twelfth centuries, and on through the Bedouin tribes' marauding, not to mention World War I, when the British set up a garrison in front of the church. And so it has gone, generation after generation of warriors and holy men fighting over the sacred land where Jesus was born. But through the ages, most historians believe, the fighting has always ended at the entrance to the church's central nave, known as the "Door of Humility." It was a portal modified in the 13th century to be low and narrow so as to keep horsemen—both marauding and faithful—out of the church.

At this present turn in history, the fighting had actually entered the church compound, which some biblical historians believe was a first in the church's long history. Israeli snipers were shooting into the courtyards of the compound, and Palestinian fighters were shooting from the rooftop. The reports of the exchanges of gunfire around the cradle of Christianity were being beamed out across the world live on CNN. Those watching could be forgiven if they were perplexed that a place sacred to Christians all over the world was caught in the middle of the Israeli-Palestinian conflict. The presence of the Christian cross in the eye of the TV cameras contravened most Western viewers' perceptions of this conflict. Wasn't this a fight between Jews and Muslims? What role did the Christians play in the land where their faith was born? As one Texas pilgrim to the Holy Land put it to me some years earlier, "We don't got a dog in this fight."

There were nearly two hundred people holed up inside the church during the siege. They included Catholic and Orthodox clergy, Palestinian police officers, a few civilians, and members of several different armed factions. They were a mix of Muslims and Christians. For the fighters their presence in the church was a matter of ruthless guerrilla strategy; for some of the Christian clerics it was a testimony of personal faith; for some civilians it was pure fate; and for still others it was a quest for justice.

On two occasions during the siege I was able, on a mobile phone from Ibrahim Abayat's home, to speak with him inside the church. At first he vowed, "We will never come out to surrender to the Israelis. We will die as martyrs."

Through a translator, I asked him whether—as the Israelis were claiming—he and the other militants were preventing the civilians and clerics from leaving. He said that this was "an Israeli lie" and that there was a strong solidarity among those inside the church; the only fear of coming out was that the Israelis would shoot them. Abayat said, "In Islam, we believe Jesus was a prophet. This place is holy to us as well. We will protect it from the Israelis."

Through interviews on mobile phones with people holed up inside and with dozens of civilians and clerics who did slowly stream out over the days and weeks, the truth about what was going on inside the siege was difficult to discern. It seemed that many of the civilians and Palestinian policemen feared that, if they ventured outside, they would be captured by the Israelis and perhaps imprisoned or shot. But there was also pressure on the inside to stay. Several civilians recounted that the Palestinian governor of Bethlehem, Mohammed Madani, who came into the church on the second day and remained inside, said that, if anyone wanted to go out, he would open the door for them but that they should understand they would be "traitors." In the West Bank and Gaza, to be labeled a traitor was at best to live in fear and at worst to face death at the hands of street justice.

Tayim, the Palestinian Franciscan, would tell me later that he was not a hostage, as the Israelis had been telling everyone on radio and TV. He had stayed in the church because he believed he was fulfilling a sacred duty as a Christian witness during the siege. He had become a scribe, taking meticulous notes of the ordeal. He wrote in small letters on the backs of the shiny souvenir photographs typically sold by peddlers at the entranceway to the church. They were all marked with the date and time and captured a running narrative of the experience—of Muslims praying alongside the Catholic and Orthodox Christians, of collective meals together, and of how the food ran low and they were forced to make a soup out of grass and leaves from the courtyard. The images were of conflict and fear and also of solidarity among Palestinians—Christian and Muslim alike—and perhaps even of some level of reconciliation among the people holed up together. Tayim spent many hours reading St. Augustine and studying theology. He said he prayed the rosary throughout the long siege. "We were all praying every day that it would end," he said. "I was also praying for my life."

This siege reflected the essence of the torturous narrative that is the Israeli-Palestinian conflict—two implacable foes caught in a battle over a sacred land. But because this time the fighting over sacred space centered on a site so clearly Christian, the standoff also came to symbolize the fate of a struggling and dwindling Palestinian Christian presence in the Holy Land. In reporting from Bethlehem, I realized that the themes of my book were all laid bare in the siege itself and in the microcosm that was inside the church.

The Palestinian Christians—and one of their holiest sites—were now clearly caught in the line of fire in this most intractable of modern conflicts. Their sacred space had been violated by both sides—by the Israeli military and by the Palestinian militias—and the Christians' unique role and precarious position seemed starkly exposed. And yet the way this standoff finally ended also offered a glimpse of the pivotal role that the minority of indigenous Christians of the Middle East might offer for a land where two peoples and three faiths have struggled to find a way out of the cycles of revenge and bloodshed, and a way back to the road to peace.

Most dramatically, though, the siege made starkly clear just how imperiled the Christian community felt. In the Bethlehem houses stacked atop each other, with St. George crosses above the doorways, the Christian community saw this siege as more evidence that it was time to get out. As the ordeal dragged on, more and more Christians in the Palestinian controlled areas were trying to get visas to leave the land. The steady hemorrhage documented in this book was now a demographic crisis threatening the Christian community with literal extinction. This was most depressingly clear on the Orthodox Easter Sunday. It was the first week in May, and the usual celebrations of Easter in the Palestinian Christian communities were taking place under the dark cloud of strict Israeli military curfew and the military siege. Families were not permitted to leave their homes.

"It is hard to feel happiness this Easter, but I am praying for a miracle," said Rihan Murad, 58, as she returned from Orthodox Easter services on a back street just off Manger Square. "We need a miracle that could bring the hearts of Jews, Muslims, and Christians together. Here that would be a real miracle."

She and her husband, Sameeh Murad, 60, who was the organist at Bethlehem's Syrian Orthodox Church, were permitted by the Israeli troops to attend services. Their home had been searched by Aviad's unit of Israeli soldiers, and one teenage soldier had smashed the washing machine door with a rifle butt.

There would be no big family celebration this year, they explained, no coloring of the Easter eggs, no baking of the special Easter cookies. Their two children had already emigrated to America, and their extended families had all left, as well. Now they too were preparing to emigrate to Los Angeles to live with their son.

"I have had it. This is our home, but we can not live like this. We are very sad," added Sameeh Murad, a beloved figure in Bethlehem who had taught three generations to play the piano and the accordion.

Herta Jallo, 35, a secretary, was visiting the Murads that day. She had also applied for a visa to emigrate to America. "This is a very sad Easter for us, the saddest in my lifetime," she said. "I blame both sides for this. The Palestinian fighters should have more respect . . . and the Israelis should have never invaded. With all of this, how can any of us hang on here?"

With each day, the images around the church had become a public-relations challenge for Israel, as a growing media pack gathered along the barbed wire on the edge of Manger Square. The Israeli Defense Forces' press office handed out cakes and sodas to reporters—along with a press packet serving up the Israeli message that they were there to root out "terrorists" and to "protect the integrity and sanctity of all holy places in Bethlehem." The IDF press office was keenly aware of the Muslim-Christian tensions in and around Bethlehem and eagerly sought to play this situation to its advantage in the battle for public opinion. Its press packet claimed, for example, that Muslim militants had stolen Christian land—an assertion that infuriated Christian Palestinians as an attempt to divide and rule, some of them angrily pointing out that the only Christian land near Bethlehem that had been "stolen" recently was the land taken by Israel to build the Jewish settlements that ring Bethlehem.

At one press conference along the barbed wire, Israeli military spokesmen were asked how the military could be protecting the "sanctity" of the church when Israeli snipers had targeted and killed seven people (IDF said the bellringer was an "accident") inside the church. Lieutenant Colonel Adir Haruvi, who looked straight out of central casting for the tough Israeli soldier, with his shaved head, thick neck, and harsh cadence, retorted, "Was the church damaged?"

When asked if he was implying that the people inside—even if they were gunmen—were not part of the sanctity of the church, he continued, "The people, they are not Christian, or whatever. They are terrorists. The seven were terrorists."

The Roman Catholic Church was stepping up its public criticism of the siege, as well. To many church leaders, the Israelis were claiming to defend the sanctity of the building's stones but at the same time violating the sanctity of the message of the Son of God, whom Christians believe was born there.

"These shootings are extremely regrettable," said Reverend David Jaeger, a lawyer for the Franciscan Order's "Custody of the Holy Land," the community within the order that is responsible for overseeing holy sites for the Roman Catholic Church. "Within a holy place, acts of violence should not take place, whoever the perpetrators and the victim may be," he said.

The papal nuncio (the Vatican's representative in Jerusalem), Reverend Pietro Sambi, echoed these sentiments. "This basilica represents love, peace, justice, and reconciliation," he said. "The people with guns inside and the military with tanks outside are to be seen as a complete contradiction of what this place is all about."

On Friday, May 10, 2002, the standoff was coming to an end, on its thirty-eighth day. The breakthrough came after intense diplomatic pressure was put on both sides by the powers that be in the West—the Central Intelligence Agency, the Vatican, the European Union, and a host of embassies, institutions, and charities. Finally, an agreement was reached for the Israelis to withdraw and for the Palestinian militants to leave Bethlehem—thirteen of them exiled to various cities in Europe and about twenty others sent to Gaza.

In the morning, the militants were marched out. Ibrahim Abayat left smiling for the cameras and putting up two fingers in a "V" sign, not for peace but victory. He was loaded onto a bus and deported. Before he left, he said in an interview by mobile phone from inside the church, "We think the deportations are a dangerous return to an old Israeli policy, but we have been convinced that for the good of the Palestinian cause we will go."

At high noon, a searing midday sun baked the cobblestones in front of the basilica's Door of Humility. Israeli soldiers ringed the doorway as the Palestinian fighters' guns were removed by U.S. federal agents and loaded into GMC Suburbans with U.S. diplomatic plates.

The Israeli tanks and armored personnel carriers kicked up dust as they rumbled out of Bethlehem, and the Palestinian residents of the town began to emerge hesitantly from their homes. Within hours Manger Square was filled with the citizens of this biblical town where the history of Christianity begins. The siege was over.

Looking back on the siege several months later, Aviad said, "I don't think it did all that much good. What did we accomplish? I still think we should get out, give the West Bank back. Why not? Let them have their state, and we will have our state."

At the conclusion of the siege, a solemn procession started back into the church as the faithful reclaimed their holy site. First, the Greek Orthodox with their long black vestments, then the Franciscans in their brown hooded robes, and then the Armenians with their peaked caps. The three rites share control—often quite contentiously—of the church. And even in this moment in organizing the order of procession, they were following the strict protocols set down by the nineteenth-century Ottoman decree known as the "Status Quo Ante." The decree was set up to keep the three from killing one another over who would control the sacred space. On this day the clerics were bickering over who would proceed first. Cooler heads prevailed, especially with the world media watching, and the Greek Orthodox were allowed in first.

I joined the procession along with the Franciscans as the priests filed into the church to reclaim its sanctity and to assess the damage. As the Franciscans sang a hymn in Latin, we ducked to pass through the Door of Humility. Inside the basilica's cool darkness, the fragrance of holy incense wafted from a censer carried during the procession. The ancient, spiritual scent mingled strangely with the faint smell of gunpowder and cordite and the stench of urine and sweat. The Palestinian militants had left behind piles of garbage and soiled old mattresses lying on the sides of the basilica's central nave.

Out of the damp darkness of the church, Tayim emerged, looking frail and in need of a shave. He was squinting in the sunlight. He hugged his fellow Franciscans, drank a large bottle of fresh water, and was bombarded with questions about the ordeal inside. He explained in a soft voice that he simply believed it was his duty as a Christian to stay in the church, not only because Franciscans are entrusted with the role of caretakers of holy sites but, more important, he said, because his Christian teaching had taught him to do everything he could to stop people from allowing their hatred to lead to violence and vengeance.

"I think in the end our presence and our prayers saved both sides from even more killing, from turning the church into a blood bath," said Tayim. "I think there is something mystical in that. Even if our presence as Christians here is fading, I think the siege showed just how important it is that we hold on. The priests and nuns and all of us who stayed in our church and refused to let the church become a battlefield, were trying to bring the teaching of Jesus, the lessons of nonviolence and forgiveness, into all this. I don't know if anyone heard the message, but I hope they did."

Bethlehem, West Bank
Spring 2002

PROLOGUE

At the first station of the cross on the Via Dolorosa, where tradition holds that Jesus shouldered his heavy wooden burden and stumbled toward his crucifixion, the stones came raining down.

Then the shooting started.

It was half past noon on Friday, October 6, 2000, in Jerusalem's Old City. Thousands of Palestinian Muslims who had just finished their Friday prayer at the central mosque in Jerusalem, known as Al-Aqsa, were setting out on what the Palestinian leadership had declared would be a "Day of Rage" against Israeli occupation. They hurled rocks at Israeli soldiers. And the soldiers opened fire in an escalating sequence of tear gas, rubber-coated steel bullets (which Israel calls "rubber bullets"), and then live ammunition.

It was the end of the first week of what was being called a new *intifada,* or uprising. Palestinian youths were lined up along the Old City's Ottoman-era ramparts, near St. Stephen's Gate (referred to in Hebrew as Lion's Gate), and climbing atop the interior northern wall around the Al-Aqsa mosque, inside what Muslims call Haram al-Sharif, or Noble Sanctuary.

This thirty-five-acre sacred sanctuary houses the shimmering Dome of the Rock, which Muslims revere as the place from which the prophet Mohammed ascended to heaven in the seventh century. It is one of the holiest shrines in Islam, and it has become a central symbol of Palestinian nationalism.

But that same plot of land is also revered by Jews as the Temple Mount, the holy ground where the Second Temple of Judaism stood before it was destroyed by the Romans in A.D. 70, before the Jews were pushed into exile. For Israelis and Jews the world over, the capture of the Old City and the Temple Mount during the Six-Day War in 1967 was a milestone symbolizing the return of the Jewish state after nearly two thousand years of exile.

For most Christians, the Temple Mount has yet another meaning. It is the place where Jesus, as a radical rabbi living under Roman occupation, railed against the priestly caste that ran the Temple. He even overturned the tables of the money changers and those who sold animals for sacrificial offerings to God in the Temple. All of this commercial activity at the Temple, Jesus felt, obscured the point of the Jewish faith, of what it meant to live a life in covenant with God and to truly uphold the Law. According to the gospels, he predicted the Temple's destruction.

This history of overlapping sacred spaces was probably far from the minds of the Muslim youths as they ducked the bullets fired by Israeli soldiers. It is also unlikely that it was on the minds of the Israeli forces dodging the fist-sized rocks and the fiery arches of Molotov cocktails crashing down around them. It wouldn't have been on the minds of the Christian Palestinian shopkeepers on the Via Dolorosa, or of the few Western Christian pilgrims scurrying to get out of the cross fire. But the history was there, as always in this city, this quarry of ancient stone and biblical prophecy, where religion and nationalism have collided again and again.

I crouched inside a doorway near the Ecce Homo arch, caught between the stones and the gunfire. The first-century arch marks the first station of the cross on the Via Dolorosa pilgrimage route. According to tradition, this is the place where Jesus was turned over to his executioners by the Roman procurator in Jerusalem, Pontius Pilate. I realized that the very stones on the pathway where I was crouching were Roman paving stones that dated to the time of Jesus.

The Palestinian youths unleashed a hailstorm of rocks. Then the advancing Israeli forces opened with volleys of tear gas canisters. The explosions of stun grenades echoed off the stones of the Old City.

. . .

On a journalistic pilgrimage retracing the path of Jesus's life through the year 2000—from Christmas 1999 to Easter 2001—I set out to document the dramatically diminishing Christian presence in this land where the faith began. I wanted to examine the historical, economic, and political factors that had contributed to the ongoing exodus of indigenous Christians and had brought their community, which traced its roots back to the origins of the church, perilously close to extinction. But my pilgrimage came to be about more than that, as the events along the path created an increasingly dramatic narrative all their own. The path of Jesus's life, from Bethlehem to Nazareth and finally to Jerusalem, had, by October 2000, become a war zone.

On the first part of my journey, I had been saddened by signs of the fading Christian presence. In one Jerusalem parish, there were not enough young Christian men left to carry a casket at a funeral. In the Galilee, a small stone church was all that was left of the Christian village of Ikrit, which had been destroyed by Israeli forces after 1948; its former residents were allowed to return only once a year, for Christmas. In the sanctuary of an Upper Egypt monastery, Christians cowered in fear of violence from Islamic militants and systematic human rights violations by Egypt's police state. In Lebanon, the empty halls of once-grand Maronite Christian monasteries echoed a long-distant past that was crumbling and disappearing in the aftermath of a devastating civil war—a war in which the Maronites had committed many sins of their own. Even during Pope John Paul II's historic pilgrimage to the Holy Land in February and March 2000, the indigenous Christians were overlooked, pushed aside, and forgotten. In all of these places, I found the Christian community withering, as daily life grew steadily more difficult.

These were the images that made up "the body and the blood" of the Holy Land's Christian community. The "body" was what Paul referred to as the local and universal church. The "blood" of the Eucharist, according to Matthew's gospel, was to be "poured out for many for the forgiveness of sins" (26:28b [NIV]). In some four hundred references throughout the Hebrew Bible and the New Testament, body and blood were a metaphor for the life of the faithful, and when one was taken from the other, the result was death. The body and blood had always implied the mystical union of the physical with the spiritual, creating and sustaining all human life.

I had much to learn about the "body" in this part of the world before I could fully understand how the indigenous Christians are both part of the Arab nation and part of the universal church. Historically, the largest number of Christians in the Middle East have been followers of the Eastern rite—the Orthodox Church. The major churches that make up the Orthodox tradition—including the Greek, Syrian, Coptic, Ethiopian, and Russian—are all independent and self-governing. Yet they all share in a tradition that emerged from the Byzantine Empire, with common cultural and historical roots in Greece. The second-largest group of Christians in the Holy Land—roughly one-third—are members of the Roman Catholic Church (in this part of the world referred to as "Latin Catholic"). The so-called Uniate churches—the Maronite and the Melkite ("Greek Catholic")—also acknowledge the primacy of Rome but have maintained liturgies and rituals distinct from those of Roman Catholicism. In addition to these denominations, there are many indigenous Lutheran, Anglican, Baptist, and evangelical churches throughout the Holy Land. These various manifestations of Christianity make up an ornate tapestry. But sadly, deep divisions—especially the bitter, thousand-year-old schism between Greek Orthodoxy and Roman Catholicism—too often have fractured the Holy Land's Christian community, contributing to its diminution.

In the fall of 2000, as my journey among the Christians of the Holy Land took an unexpected turn, I walked straight into the worst eruption of violence there since 1967. It was a moment of reckoning, a critical turning point in the long Israeli-Palestinian conflict. I had no idea when I set out that the year would have such a dramatic ending, with fighting on the streets of the Old City. I didn't think I would see tanks and attack helicopters firing missiles on villages around Bethlehem. I never guessed that there would be violent clashes in the Galilee and in Nazareth, that Muslims and Christians there would rise up with stones and Molotov cocktails, and that at least thirteen Arab citizens of Israel would be shot dead there by Israeli police. By the end of 2000, the death toll in the West Bank, Gaza, Jerusalem, and all of Israel had climbed into the hundreds.

I never thought that I would have to weigh the possibility of evacuating my family—but so I did, after my pregnant wife and I narrowly avoided a machine gun battle and street riots as we tried to drive to the maternity hospital for an ultrasound examination in the weeks before our baby was due.

In the blazing heat of the Jerusalem summer, the Camp David peace talks had offered inspiring hope that a final settlement was at hand. Then the talks dramatically collapsed. Now, in these first cool nights of autumn, the Middle East was awash in the deceptive grays of dusk—caught between the fading light of peace and the enveloping darkness of war.

. . .

So how did I become enmeshed in the life and death of the small, insular Christian community of the Middle East? I arrived in Jerusalem in 1997 as the *Boston Globe*'s correspondent, and in 1998 I began researching a series of articles on the diminishing Christian presence in the Holy Land. The series became the basis for this book. And even though the narrative of the book covers the path of Jesus through the year 2000, much of my reporting and research actually stretched out over a span of more than two years. Over those years I came to know many Christians in Jerusalem, Bethlehem, Nazareth, the Galilee, Jordan, Egypt, Syria, and Lebanon—all places that I had heard about while I was growing up, in the biblical readings droned out from pulpits on Sundays. I found the stories of these living Middle Eastern Christians unexpectedly compelling.

What has struck me most as a Middle East correspondent is that the themes that resonated in this land during Jesus's time still resonate today. Jesus was a young rabbi, rebellious and idealistic, preaching in an occupied land to an occupied people (primarily, to Jews), many of whom longed for an open revolt against Roman rule. Jesus's message was one of creative nonviolent resistance to occupation. His theology of forgiveness is just as radical and challenging today as it was back then. His message was simple and direct—people must forgive before they can get along. Forgiveness, he argued, is the only way to achieve a lasting peace; there must be forgiveness before there can be justice.

The forces that caused division in Jesus's time are still at the center of today's conflicts in Israel, the West Bank, Gaza, Jerusalem, Jordan, Egypt, and Lebanon: economic injustice, a struggle for self-determination, religious extremism, apocalyptic fervor, terrorism, and a seemingly endless cycle of recrimination. The forces of globalization also were at work in both eras. Two thousand years ago, those forces were embodied in rule by Rome, with its uniform architecture, its global system of taxation, its military legions, and its local kings, such as Herod, who were permitted to rule as long as they ultimately served the purposes of the emperor. Today the forces of globalization are evidenced through the activities of the United States of America, with its global franchises and its high-tech military superiority, and through its strategic allies, including Israel, which are actively supported as long as they serve U.S. interests in the region. The classical arches of Roman architecture have been replaced in the Holy Land by the golden arches of McDonald's. And then, just as now, a battle was under way for Jerusalem, the Holy City. Yet history has shown that no ruling power can ever hold sovereignty over a place revered as the nucleus of salvation for all three Abrahamic faiths—the sacred place where, all three religions hold, God's final redemption will be revealed.

By setting out along the path traveled by Jesus during his lifetime, I sought to open a window for Western Christians into the Middle East conflict, to encourage them to think about the realities of this land, and about what it means if the living presence of Christianity here should wither and die. I wanted to acquaint them with the role Christians have played in the Middle East, with the ways in which the ideas and institutions of Christianity—its school system and hospitals and universities—have shaped or influenced current thinking in this part of the world. What will happen if those ideas and those institutions are abandoned, if they become barren, empty, echoing halls of the past?

As I began to ask myself these questions, I realized that most of the Arabs and Jews, Palestinians and Israelis, I spoke to about my book were responding with either disinterest or disdain. At the close of a millennium that was book-ended by the Crusades and the Holocaust, the disappearance of Christianity was not generating deep concern or sympathy among most Muslims and Jews. Questions about the role Christianity played in this land inevitably ended up back at the darkest and most horrible chapters of Christian history. My desire to study the dwindling Christian presence in the Holy Land immediately prompted the question, whose Holy Land? And how does one define "Holy Land"? Is it the territory of the Hebrew Bible and its prophets, is it the land of Jesus and his ministry, or is it also the shrines of Islam? What are the boundaries of the Holy Land? For the purposes of this book, the path I decided to take through the Holy Land linked the places that according to at least one of the gospels Jesus himself had visited at key moments in his life and ministry. These places include Bethlehem, Egypt, Nazareth, the Galilee, Jordan, Lebanon, and Jerusalem.

It was even harder presenting my ideas for this book to Western

Christians—in part because it seems counterintuitive to Americans and Europeans that Christianity could be imperiled anywhere; after all, their nations—especially the United States—have a powerful Christian culture. Israelis—even those active in interfaith dialogue—were often defensive about the idea of a withering Christian presence and the touchy history it stirred of Israel's role in the displacement of Palestinians. And as citizens of a Jewish state, some felt my line of approach failed to factor in Israel's relatively enlightened treatment of its Christian minority, compared to the treatment of Jewish minorities by various Christian countries throughout history.

Muslims were almost universally suspicious of my focus on the Christian minority, seeing it as yet another Western attempt to divide and rule by diluting the collective Palestinian and Arab identity. Muslims typically mistrusted any concern for local Christians expressed by an American reporter. Christianity, as they saw it, was a Western faith; and it had too often been used as an extension of Western power in the Middle East—a power that many Muslims believe has been exerted through Arab Christians. Even the Arab Christians I spoke with didn't really like the idea of a book about the Christian exodus. They worried that it might become a sensationalistic account pitting them against their Muslim brothers, and that their attitudes and actions might be misconstrued as antinationalist. They also worried that the story might be distorted by the American evangelical churches—which for the most part are stridently pro-Israel—and used to foster an image of the Arab Islamic world as intolerant of Christians. But perhaps even more importantly, they must have understood that within their tribal culture any act that drew attention to their withering presence would only exaggerate their weakness and therefore increase their vulnerability.

. . .

So is this land "holy" to me? Am I religious? Do I go to church? There are no easy answers to these questions, except the last one, which would be "not often." But even that answer should be qualified, since in the course of researching this book I found myself in churches on many Sundays, checking out nearly every denomination of the faith—Roman Catholic, Greek Orthodox, Russian Orthodox, Coptic Orthodox, Ethiopian Orthodox, Syrian Orthodox, Melkite, Anglican, Lutheran, and Baptist, as well as various nondenominational prayer groups among evangelical communities. It has been an enlightening journey about the different personalities and cultures that exist within the faith. Although I do not consider myself particularly religious, I am struck by the enduring stories of the Bible, the archetypal truths they reveal, and the power of Jesus's message.

I grew up in Massachusetts, in what some might call a traditional Irish Catholic home, though it never felt traditional to those of us growing up in it. But looking back, our lives revolved around the spiritual axis of our local parish. My parents had a strong faith, and the church was at the center of life and death. Our extended family gatherings usually began in churches, at baptisms, weddings, and funerals. They ended up at the family home, with coolers full of beer, and a well-stocked bar for my aunts and uncles. My mother's first cousin, Father William Morgan, who was a priest in the Boston archdiocese, presided over and preached with soulful spirituality at all of these family events. I still somehow feel at home with the ritual functions of the Catholic Church, with the work of its institutions on behalf of the poor all over the world, with the generosity and spirit of the priests and nuns I've known.

I still struggle spiritually and intellectually with the mystery of faith. As a child growing up in a Catholic home, I was discouraged from actually reading the Bible. Those who quoted it too literally or too often were viewed with suspicion and assumed to be Protestant. This was far more than a cultural divide—it was a theological fault line between the Reformation and Catholicism. To this day, there aren't many Catholics who go around citing chapter and verse to back up their arguments. The culture of Catholicism had taught them to put more faith in catechism than scripture. The big black leather-bound Bible on the bookshelf just by the front door of my childhood home was not for reading but for storing important documents. My mother stuffed its pages with baptism and confirmation records from our local parish, St. Theresa's. There were prayer cards from Doherty's Funeral Home. There was a deed to the plot where my grandparents were buried, in St. Joseph's Cemetery. She must have known that it was the one book my brothers and sister and I were most likely not to touch. Things stayed safe and sound in the Bible.

But in the course of writing this book, I read the gospels in a way I never had before. I read them as a reporter. For a correspondent here in Jerusalem, the holy books—the Hebrew Bible, the New Testament, and the Koran—cannot just sit on shelves but have to be pored through in order for one to understand what the people on the streets of Jerusalem and Gaza are talking about. When Muslims and Jews start referring to each other's ideas of Abrahamic progeny and land in terms of Isaac and Ishmael—as they do in just about every fortified Jewish settlement in the West Bank and every dusty refugee camp where Islamic militants of Hamas have built a mosque—it is time to hit the holy books.

My wife Julie and I come from different faith backgrounds. She hails from a secular Russian Jewish clan out of New York. Our wedding was a truly intercultural experience that brought together two very different tribes, each of which perhaps learned something about the other in the process. We arrived in Jerusalem when our first son, William, was four months old. A year and a half later came Riley Joseph; and then, on St. Patrick's Day 2000, my wife surprised me with the news that we were expecting another child in December. Waiting for that birth through the long ordeal of conflict that gripped the land in the fall became a kind of metaphor for the year 2000; it was a time of great expectancy, in which the hope was born that after the writhing and the kicking there would be a new life.

. . .

On that Friday in October on the Via Dolorosa, pinned down by the rocks and the gunfire, several other reporters and I took advantage of a momentary lull in the shooting to dash toward St. Anne's Basilica. A French priest let us into the courtyard overflowing with well-tended flower gardens and the beautiful and simple power of the Crusader-era church. The peacefulness of the place stood in bizarre contrast to all that was going on outside the thick, bolted door. Farther inside the courtyard were the ancient remains of the Bethesda pools, where the gospels say Jesus healed a paralytic. The inner courtyard of this monastery embodied for me the Western Christianity implanted on this land. It was a well-groomed garden, tucked away from the violence of the street behind large, wooden doors. Yet it was also on the very land where streets raged with violence that scarred the lives of those who lived there, just as it must have been at the time of Jesus. The basilica was a part of a layered reality I was trying to unearth, digging past the superficial Western Christian presence to find the Eastern church, to see the Christians of this land who are the living links to the origins of the faith, to understand that Jerusalem was "the mother church" of Christianity. From the monastery, I watched Palestinian youths, or *shebab,* furiously stoning and then burning a small Israeli police station near a chapel marked "The Birthplace of Mary," just inside St. Stephen's Gate. As I watched the violence unfold, the smells of the monastery, a fragrant mix of incense and flowers, mingled with the smoke and wisps of tear gas out on the street.

At sunset, the fighting finally quieted. Fire smoldered in the ruined police station. The evening call to prayer sounded over the loudspeakers of the mosques of the Muslim quarter. Church bells echoed from the Christian quarter. The Via Dolorosa was littered with tear gas canisters, shell casings, rocks, and bloody rags. The plaza in front of the Western Wall was carpeted with rocks. Prayer tables and chairs had been knocked over by Jewish worshipers fleeing the violence. In response to the rioting, Israeli police were tightening the seal around the Palestinian territories. The West Bank and Gaza would be placed under strict closure by nightfall and would be kept that way until Monday, which was the end of Yom Kippur, a time of fasting and atonement, the holiest day of the Jewish calendar.

At the end of the day, Ibrahim, a 50-year-old Palestinian shopkeeper, swept up the broken glass, the empty plastic food ration containers discarded by Israeli soldiers, and the scattered tear gas canisters. Inside his store, which specialized in souvenirs for Christian pilgrims, he righted the toppled crucifixes and busts of Jesus and straightened a rack of Holy Land postcards and tourist maps that had been knocked over amid the chaos. Ibrahim was a Christian, a Roman Catholic. He, like most Palestinian Christians, was caught in the middle of this conflict between Palestinian Muslim *shebab* and the soldiers of the Jewish state. His greatest worry about the fighting, he said, was its devastating impact on tourism. With the eruption of violence, more and more tour groups were canceling their plans. Hotels from Nazareth to Bethlehem were emptying at what was supposed to have been the height of the season.

"Do you think any tourists will come to the Via Dolorosa with this going on?" Ibrahim asked, holding up a shell casing that he had picked up off the ancient Roman paving stones in front of his shop.

Ibrahim didn't want to talk much, and he fretted about his name being used. As he collected scattered postcards of Christian holy sites and rearranged them on the rack, he shrugged his shoulders when asked about how Christians felt about this return to violence.

"More Christians will leave," he said, with an air of resignation.

. . .

Is Christianity truly going to die out in the land where it began? Not, Jesus said, as long as "there are two or more gathered in my name." Important international efforts by Christian churches have been gathering strength to counter the trend of emigration. All of us—Christians, Muslims, and Jews—have a stake in their success. The Christian presence in the Holy Land is a potentially important, possibly essential, voice in the dialogue for peace, but it is a voice that has been reduced to a hoarse whisper. Historically, Christianity has provided a kind of leavening in the Middle East, a small but necessary ingredient acting as a buffer between the Arab world's broad Islamic resurgence and the strands within Israel of a rising ultranationalist brand of Judaism. These two fundamentalist movements, which have fused religion with nationalism, increasingly cast the territorial Israeli-Palestinian conflict in religious terms. If the Christians disappear, the Middle East will become that much more vulnerable to this embittered dichotomy.

In the end, the living presence of faith is preserved by drawing itself toward sufficient light so that it does not perish but sustains itself among its people. In this land, Christians are struggling to find that light, to find sustenance as a small minority—just as they did at the time of Jesus.

AUTHOR'S NOTE

In writing this book, I set out to travel the path Jesus followed during his life, although no one knows for certain exactly where that path began and ended.

The idea was to take a journalistic pilgrimage in the year 2000 from Bethlehem to Egypt, Nazareth to Jordan, Galilee to Lebanon, and finally back to Jerusalem. Along the way, I intended to document the modern realities of life for the local inhabitants—specifically, focusing on the reasons for the ongoing exodus of Christians from the land where the faith began.

But in charting this course, I discovered there was little agreement, even among the gospels of the New Testament, on the precise path. The contradictions within the gospels on where the birth narrative of Jesus should begin and where Jesus and the Holy Family traveled require intense historical and theological analysis. There are great bodies of work on the historical Jesus; but they were not the focus of my book, nor did I feel equipped to navigate their academically challenging terrain. My understanding of the life of Jesus, and of how his message fit in with the places where he was born, where he was raised, where he wandered, where he preached, and where he died, was based on the three synoptic gospels, my own personal experiences, and my reading of the Bible, augmented by the work of various scholars. Because I am a journalist and not an academic, my intention was to tell the stories of the Christians I encountered along this path. I should point out that my ideas of how to present these stories were influenced by the reflections of two Palestinian Christian pastors: the Lutheran minister Mitri Raheb and the Anglican Father Naim Ateek.

The works of two scholars at Hebrew University, Marcel DuBois and David Flusser, also informed my perspective. The historical background came largely from Jerome Murphy O'Connor's *The Holy Land;* Robert L. Wilken's *The Land Called Holy: Palestine in Christian History and Thought*; Karen Armstrong's works, especially *Jerusalem: One City, Three Faiths*; Thomas Cahill's *Desire of the Everlasting Hills: The World Before and After Jesus;* and William Dalrymple's *From the Holy Mountain: A Journey Among the Christians of the Middle East.*

The works of biblical historian John Dominic Crossan, especially his book *Jesus: A Revolutionary Biography*, had a most profound effect on my thinking. Crossan's Jesus was a Jewish peasant, a revolutionary living under Roman occupation, and Crossan's scholarship resonated with my own perceptions. I found this view of Jesus the most interesting way to bring the story of his life to bear on my understanding of the modern conflict I was covering. I felt drawn to this Jesus, who was a rebel, a leader of resistance to occupation, through peaceful and nonviolent means; a teacher who challenged accepted notions of tribe and family; a man who was truly of this rugged terrain but who also questioned its focus on progeny and land and opposed its often destructive culture of revenge. There are, of course, many other views of Jesus, which present him and the path he traveled differently. Many scholars, for example, say Jesus was not a peasant but of a more comfortable class of artisans, and that he was most likely a learned rabbinical leader. Others say that the man Christians believe was the messiah should be seen in the tradition of healers and mystics who traveled the land, preaching folk wisdom and opening up Jewish thought to the poor and downtrodden. Where there are important contradictions either in the gospels or among historians and archaeologists, I have tried to point them out in the text or in the source notes.

But not only are there biblical points of contradiction; there are myriad other complexities to grapple with, including a modern map with contested borders and newly carved boundaries that did not exist at the time of Jesus. Place-names are imbued with political and historical meaning. What religious Israelis refer to as the biblical Judea and Samaria, Palestinians call the West Bank. Israelis call Jerusalem the Jewish state's "eternal and indivisible" capital. Palestinians call Jerusalem *Al-Quds* ("The Holy"), and describe it as illegally occupied. One of the more difficult and embattled place-names is *Palestine.* Although today it is roughly defined geographically as the territory coextensive with modern Israel west of the Jordan River, Palestine in ancient times included the lands of Bashan and Gilead, east of the Jordan. Modern Palestinians often use the word *Palestine* to describe the area of a future state that their leadership has vowed to establish on this territory. Many Palestinians also use the phrase *historic Palestine* in reference to the land before it was divided among Israel, Jordan, and Egypt in 1949 (in the settlement following the 1948 war). Many Israelis dismiss "Palestine" as a modern creation of the British, dating it to the period of mandatory government that began after World War I. But the land was known by the Latin form of this same name—*Palaestina*—under ancient Roman imperial rule. Like most Jews of his time, Jesus probably considered this name foreign—a linguistic imposition by the occupying Romans, ephemeral and unrooted in the native tongues spoken in his homeland. Yet modern-day Palestinians often claim that Jesus was Palestinian—an assertion that is packed with political significance, although it is generally viewed as having little basis in historical fact.*

Starting in Part Two, where I set out on my own journalistic pilgrimage in the year 2000, each chapter begins with a brief preface. These passages are intended to help readers see where they are on the path of Jesus's life, and to provide some spiritual context for understanding the modern conflict. It is also important for readers to know that the book is generally chronological in time, and that the narrative is linear, building toward the dramatic collapse of the "peace process" and the outbreak of the *intifada* in the fall of 2000.

Readers should bear in mind that the idea of chronicling a journey this way was born in 1999, at a time when very few observers would have predicted the eruption of violence in the following year (and I was no exception). As I traveled in the footsteps of Jesus and approached the end of the year 2000, I felt a great heaviness in writing the last part of the book, titled "The Passion," as the violence was unfolding on the ancient cobblestone streets of Jerusalem's Old City, in the same place where Jesus met his death. In choosing this narrative structure, I had no intention of comparing the suffering of one party in this conflict—at the expense of another—to the suffering of Jesus on the cross. Rather, I wanted to look at the way in which the vio-

*The preceding discussion of Palestine is based on Robert L. Wilken, *The Land Called Holy: Palestine in Christian History and Thought* (New Haven and London: Yale University Press, 1992), p. 197.

lence that was convulsing this land was in so many ways a Via Dolorosa, a Way of Sorrow, for all of the people who lived it. The Via Dolorosa was to me a metaphor for Arabs and Jews, for Palestinians and Israelis, and for members of all three of the monotheistic faiths of Judaism, Christianity, and Islam, as they stumbled forward in their own agony, trying to find peace, justice, and perhaps salvation. In the end, this metaphor and the narrative structure it imposed became a burden. But it also forced me to reflect on the deeper meanings of current events, and, I hope, to provide a new perspective, a different way of thinking about this land and its people, and of what the fate of the local Christian community may portend for Arabs and Jews.

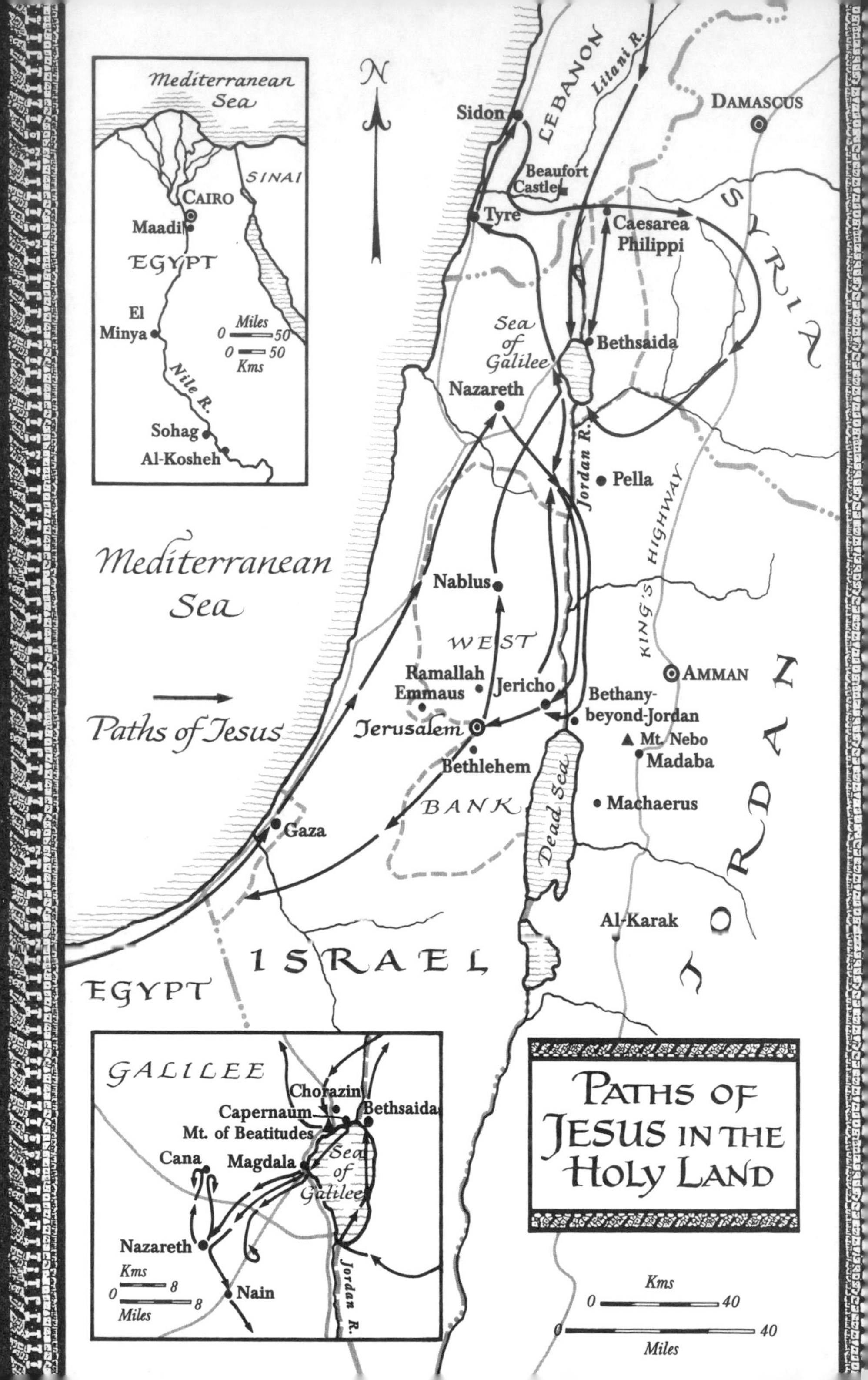

Mediterranean Sea
SINAI
CAIRO
Maadi
EGYPT
El Minya
Miles
0 50
0 50
Kms
Nile R.
Sohag
Al-Kosheh
N
LEBANON
Litani R.
Sidon
DAMASCUS
Beaufort Castle
Tyre
Caesarea Philippi
SYRIA
Sea of Galilee
Bethsaida
Nazareth
Jordan R.
Pella
HIGHWAY
KING'S
Mediterranean Sea
Nablus
WEST
Ramallah
Emmaus
Jericho
AMMAN
Bethany-beyond-Jordan
Paths of Jesus
Jerusalem
Mt. Nebo
Madaba
Bethlehem
BANK
Dead Sea
Machaerus
Gaza
JORDAN
Al-Karak
ISRAEL
EGYPT
GALILEE
Chorazin
Capernaum
Bethsaida
Mt. of Beatitudes
Cana
Magdala
Sea of Galilee
Nazareth
Kms
0 8
8
Miles
Nain
Jordan R.
PATHS OF JESUS IN THE HOLY LAND
Kms
0 40
0 40
Miles

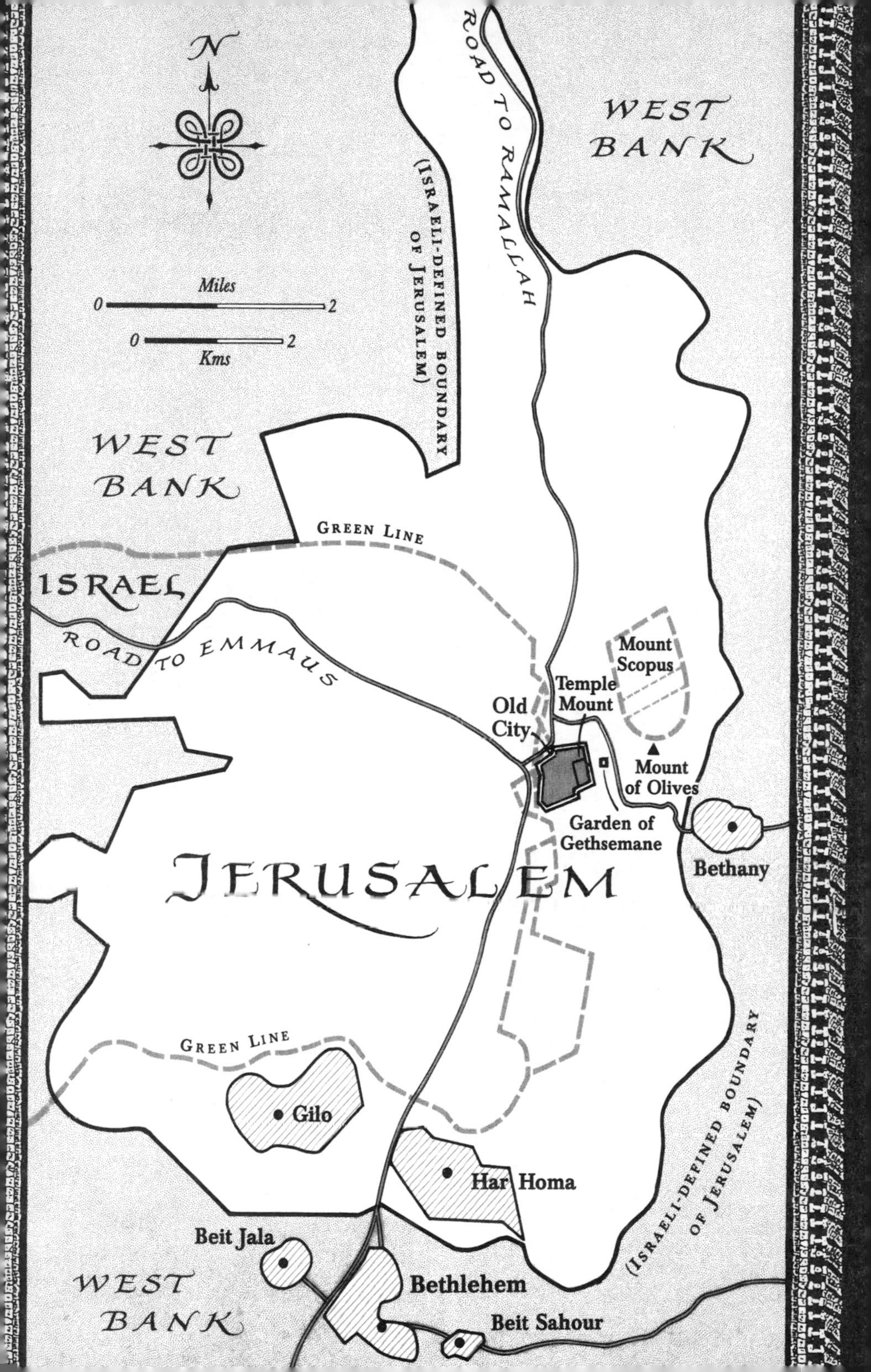

N
Miles
0
2
0
2
Kms
ROAD TO RAMALLAH
(ISRAELI-DEFINED BOUNDARY OF JERUSALEM)
WEST BANK
WEST BANK
GREEN LINE
ISRAEL
ROAD TO EMMAUS
Mount Scopus
Temple Mount
Old City
Mount of Olives
Garden of Gethsemane
Bethany
JERUSALEM
GREEN LINE
Gilo
Har Homa
Beit Jala
Bethlehem
Beit Sahour
WEST BANK
(ISRAELI-DEFINED BOUNDARY OF JERUSALEM)

I

Anno Domini

1

Pilgrimage

Christmas 1999

SUNRISE BRUSHED the desert sky in red over the soft brown folds of the Judean hills as I set out along a ridge of the Kidron valley, heading toward Bethlehem. I stopped at a perch overlooking Mar Saba, a Greek Orthodox monastery that dates back to the fifth century. Considered the greatest of the desert monasteries for both its architecture and its history, Mar Saba is embedded in a sheer cliff face that towers above a trickling river. Its two watchtowers are joined by a massive, saw-toothed wall that plunges downhill, protecting and enclosing the domed chapels, sacristies and cupolas, tombs of martyrs, and glass reliquaries that cradle the skulls of seventh-century monks slain by invading Persians. The Great Laura of Mar Saba (*laura* being the Greek for "monastery") is among the more indelible images of the Holy Land.

Within the ancient rhythm of the ascetic life preserved in this castle of prayer, the monks were just finishing chanting the divine office, as they had every morning for 1,517 years, when the first light of day sliced in on the iconostasis of their Church of St. Nicholas. This community, once a thriving paragon of intellect and theology for Byzantium's 150 desert monasteries, is among the mere handful that still adhere to the austere life of the desert fathers. In the sixth century, as many as 700 monks occupied the cells honeycombing the stone cliffs of Mar Saba's Great Laura. Now there are no more than a dozen, with their black-hooded robes and long white beards, clinging to the life of sacrifice and prayer and meditation—an ancient tradition gradually slipping from grasp. Mar Saba's most famous monk was the brilliant theologian John Damascene, whose efforts to bridge the gap between Christianity and Islam in the early eighth century, during the rule of Caliph Yazid (with whom he had a close friendship), exemplify the role that the Christians of this land historically have played in linking East to West. The frail, tiny community of successors to the habit at Mar Saba struggle today to offer charity to nearby Palestinian villages and at the same time to stave off thieves and toughs from the neighboring tribes, such as the Tamari, among whom Islamic militancy has flourished.

I was hiking with a small group of Palestinians and European tourists and a few expats. As we stopped to ponder the view of Mar Saba in the soft light of a winter dawn, I noticed the flicker of kerosene lamps inside some of the dwellings. The monastery had no electricity. This outwardly solid and imposing structure sheltered a fragile way of life. I was reminded that Christianity is an Eastern religion in its origins, rooted in the desert wilderness and the ferment of the Middle East. Mar Saba presented a searing vision of the end of that culture, the last echo of Byzantium.

Hoping to use the cooler morning hours to keep up the pace and make Bethlehem by midday, we soon moved on. We hiked through valleys that formed natural wheat-threshing floors, and along ancient, terraced aqueducts. On the horizon stood the crumbled remains of the Herodion, a massive circular palace built in the first century B.C. by Kind Herod, inside a volcanic rock formation. Here and there along the rocky pathways were cisterns sealed by huge stones to prevent the theft of what was still the most precious commodity in the desert. A shepherd herded his flock down into a wadi, a gully where water collects in the rainy season. These timeless scenes gave us fleeting glimpses of life as it had been two thousand years earlier.

It was Saturday, December 4, 1999. I had joined up with a group of seven hikers who had been en route for six days and were on the final leg of the "Nativity Trail," which stretches from Nazareth to Bethlehem. They were planning to end up in Manger Square for the official ceremony launching a millennial celebration called Bethlehem 2000. As we made our way along the ridge, we stopped again to take in the panorama of Jerusalem to the north and the hills of Bethlehem to the south, and in the distance to the east, the more jagged, barren shale wilderness that tumbled down to the Dead Sea, the lowest point on earth. We were walking in the footsteps of biblical characters—pilgrims, perhaps, though no one on this hike would have described himself or herself that way. Jumana Ayyad, 22, a smart young professional Palestinian woman from a Catholic family in Bethlehem, summed up her reasons for coming: "I am walking because I want to know my own land better. Is that a pilgrimage?"

Still, as we trod the path of the prophets through the ancient hills, I experienced an overwhelming sense of physical connection to a spiritual realm. In this open desert expanse I felt somehow closer to that realm than in the crowded, bustling cobblestone alleys and pathways of the Old City in Jerusalem, or Manger Square in Bethlehem. These hills seemed so far away from the tourist shops and the idling, air-conditioned buses waiting for armies of pilgrims in matching sun hats to be shuttled to the next site on the package tour. To devout Christians, the Via Dolorosa, with its souvenir stands and T-shirt shops, can seem crassly and depressingly commercial. Along the Way of Sorrow you can buy a glow-in-the-dark Jesus statue for the dashboard of your car, or a genuine handwoven crown of thorns to take home as a gift. Wooden crosses can be rented for just a few Israeli shekels from a man named Jihad, who holds claim to this concession just outside the Crusader doorway of the Holy Sepulcher. Among the keepsakes most prominently displayed by the shops are hologram posters of Jesus. The Lord is featured with solid European good looks, brown hair and blue eyes. And as you walk among the Semitic faces, the Jewish and Arab men who are the residents of Jerusalem and who certainly bear a much closer resemblance to Jesus, this hologram of the handsome, blue-eyed Jesus shifts in the light from eyes open and in smiling glory to eyes closed and in tearful agony. The other two monotheistic faiths have their fair share of kitsch as well. Shelves are lined with plastic replicas of the Second Temple, ceramic seder plates stamped with "Jerusalem 2000," and plastic shofars. There are alarm clocks in the shape of the Dome of the Rock, which resound at the appointed hour with the Muslim call to prayer. But no matter how much this commercial industry of pilgrimage assaults you along the path, it is impossible to stroll the Old City—regardless of which quarter you are in—and not be struck by a profound sense of time, of origins. You are surrounded by the idea of, if not the belief in, God. And in fact, the businesses catering to this human enterprise called pilgrimage are as ancient a tradition as the religions themselves.

After three years of living in Jerusalem, I had learned to resist my instinctive cynicism about pilgrimage and to become more accepting of its tactile spirituality. I had come to see it as a human experience as ancient as man's relationship to God. There was something about putting one's hand on the stones of Jerusalem, about standing within earshot of the place where the first utterances of the existential dialogue between Man and God were heard, or are believed to have been heard.

Through the centuries, believers of Judaism, Christianity, and Islam have ascended the same desert paths that I was walking on my way to Bethlehem; they have climbed Jerusalem's rocky, terraced hillsides to the walled Old City, to visit the holy places of the Hebrew Bible, the New Testament, and the Koran. In a way, the history of these three faiths is a history of pilgrimage and of emigration—the movement of people along a path they feel compelled to follow by economic and political necessity and by the will of God. This is true of the central prophets of all three faiths. In Judaism, Moses led his people out of slavery in Egypt and through the Sinai desert to a hillside just east of the Jordan River, where he pointed them toward the Promised Land. In Christianity, God set Jesus on his path from Bethlehem to Golgotha. In Islam, Jerusalem's central mosque, Al-Aqsa, which takes its name from the Arabic for "farthest place," is revered as the endpoint of the prophet Mohammed's "night journey" from Mecca to Jerusalem. Here he ascended to heaven, according to the Hadith, a collection of Islamic sayings and stories.

From the earliest days of recorded history, Jews went to Jerusalem to stand before God at the Temple. By 300 B.C., throngs from all over the Mediterranean and the Near East regularly converged on the City of David, the Israelite king who had built a resting place for the Ark of the Covenant and surrounded it with protective walls, establishing a religious ideal and a symbol that he hoped would help transcend the jealousies dividing the twelve tribes.

When Jesus entered Jerusalem in the days before his arrest and crucifixion, he too came as a pilgrim. He had traveled there from Galilee, for the feast of Passover. Jerusalem was then under Roman authority and the local rule of the Jewish kings of the Herodian dynasty. Imagine the city at that time, with the massive, Herodian

Temple rising from its center and the smoke from animal sacrifices coiling up into the air. Huge crowds would have been lining up to buy their sacrificial animals, to have them ritually slaughtered and burned on the altar in the Temple's inner chamber. Historians estimate that pilgrimages during feast days in Jesus's time typically tripled Jerusalem's population, which rose from 40,000 to 120,000 as Jewish believers flocked to the Temple Mount (the site of the Second Temple) to pray and make sacrificial offerings before God. Indeed, this overcrowding might explain why Jesus and his disciples reportedly sought lodging outside the city walls, just over the Mount of Olives, in the village of Bethany. Moreover, the disturbance Jesus caused in the Temple during this crowded and emotional holiday must have seemed likely to lead to popular unrest; on some level, Jesus was viewed as a security risk that neither Rome nor the Jewish rulers could tolerate.

After the Roman destruction of the Second Temple in A.D. 70 and the Jewish revolt against Rome ended in A.D. 135, Jews were expelled and the idea of pilgrimage would live on among the exiles in a simple prayer of yearning and promise. This prayer was intoned every year through the centuries at the end of the Passover seder: "Next year in Jerusalem!"

After Constantine made Christianity the religion of the Roman Empire in the early fourth century, the Christian faith flourished and streamed out over the Roman world. Constantine's mother, Queen Helena, set out to "locate" the sacred places where the events of Jesus's life and ministry took place. More than three hundred years after his death and resurrection, Helena identified by imperial fiat most of the holy sites that would set the path for Christian pilgrims from then until now. The elderly dowager, with a huge royal entourage, made her way through the Roman province identifying the cave of the nativity in Bethlehem, Golgotha, the tomb, and even the site of the ascension of Christ on the Mount of Olives. And then her son set about a campaign to build massive shrines and basilicas dedicated to this new understanding of God in the Roman Empire.

Another Roman citizen, the "Anonymous Pilgrim from Bordeaux," who arrived in Jerusalem in A.D. 333, left what is today the oldest pilgrimage diary. This gentleman (his name lost to history) dutifully, although not poetically, chronicled his journey along the Roman road paved with smooth stones, listing each of the staging posts at which he stopped. In Jerusalem, he provided the first glimpse of the destruction on the Temple Mount and the haunting solemnity of Jesus's tomb (which Helena had discovered only a few years earlier). But his descriptions were a catalogue of personal experiences and included hardly a word about the local Christian community.

Other pilgrims of the Byzantine era left more telling accounts of their journeys—for example, the legendary monk John Moschos, who in A.D. 587 set off from the shores of the Bosphorus to the Egyptian desert and the wilderness of Judea before finally entering the Holy Land. Moschos produced a detailed and beautifully written manuscript chronicling his journey, the characters he encountered along the way, and the conversations he had with them. It is replete with anecdotes, aphorisms, and fables about monks and brigands and sorcerers. His pilgrimage diary (in English, titled *The Spiritual Meadow*) chronicles a time when the sun was beginning to set over the Byzantine Empire—when the Persian conquest was unfolding in its violent wrath, before the invading Islamic armies swept through Arabia into Palestine and on to Spain. Moschos's pilgrimage occurred in the twilight between two historical periods: the dusk of the Byzantine era and the dawn of the Islamic conquest.

During the Golden Age of Islam, Muslims flocked to Jerusalem from around the Arab world to visit the Dome of the Rock, a mosque built in the seventh century. Because the prophet Mohammed is believed to have ascended to heaven from this spot, Muslims and all of the Arab world refer to Jerusalem as Al-Quds, "the Holy," and revere it as the third-holiest city in Islam, after Mecca and Medina.

Christian pilgrimage to Jerusalem was fueled by millennial expectations at the turn of the second millennium, as it would be by similar expectations among some fringe Christians at the turn of the third millennium. In the year 1033—one thousand years after the death of Jesus is held to have occurred—a flood of pilgrims from Europe came to Jerusalem anticipating the Second Coming. Instead they found death and famine, and a forbidding earthly Holy City.

By the close of the eleventh century, Christian pilgrimage had been transformed into a military quest in the Crusades. With internecine warfare in Europe threatening to destroy the Holy Roman Empire, Pope Urban II devised this religious campaign as a way to unify the Christian forces of the continent and use them to expand Rome's power. He assembled an "Army of Christ" to "liberate" the Holy Land from Islam and "the reign of the Anti-Christ." In a stirring speech at the Council of Clermont in 1095 he called for a holy war to liberate the tomb of Christ from Islam, and the crowd answered in thundering unison, "Deus hoc volt!" (God wills this!)

The Crusaders carried out bloody assaults on Muslims and Jews (and local Christians of the Eastern Orthodox churches often were not spared), to shouts of "Deus hoc volt!" For three days they systematically slaughtered more than 30,000 inhabitants of Jerusalem—until there was no one left to kill. Crusade chroniclers were not shy about describing the "rivers of blood" spilled in the name of the Lord. Legend has it that tens of thousands of Muslims were slaughtered at Al-Aqsa—perhaps an exaggeration, historians say, but not by much. Jews were crowded into their synagogue and burned alive. The butchery is still seared into the memory of this land, scarring relations between Christianity and the other two religions of Abraham.

Chaucer's *Canterbury Tales,* penned in the fourteenth century, portrayed the ideal Christian life as a "glorious pilgrimage to the celestial Jerusalem." But in later centuries not everyone found pilgrimage to the Holy Land so heavenly. "Lepers, cripples, the blind, and the idiotic assail you on every hand. . . . Jerusalem is mournful, dreary, lifeless. I would not desire to live here," wrote Mark Twain in his 1869 book *The Innocents Abroad.*

The human tide in and out of this land—on trade and pilgrimage routes and on quests both spiritual and colonial—formed the contours of the group that today call themselves Arab Christians and the churches to which they belong. The first people to follow Jesus—his disciples and the first members of his ministry—were Jews living in Roman-occupied Palestine. The message spread among Romans and Greeks, and then Assyrians and Nestorians in what is today Syria, and among Phoenicians in the coastal city-states of modern Lebanon. Armenian Christians came to Palestine as the earliest pilgrims in the fourth century and ever since have been a part of this land. When the Crusaders came, many stayed, and over the ensuing centuries they intermingled, through marriage and concubinage, with other local communities. The Greek and Russian Orthodox churches, the Roman Catholic Church, or Latin Catholic, all brought their clerics to serve in the land. Then came the architects to design the cathedrals that would reflect each church's power, and the stone- and marble-cutters who would give physical substance to their visions. Many of these Christian artisans from the West would stay on. There were also many who came to the Holy Land via trade routes that wove through the Arabian peninsula to Mount Lebanon and into Damascus.

By modern times it had become nearly impossible to divine the intricately laminated ethnic origins of the Christians of the Holy Land; but their given names provide clues. The Greek Orthodox Christian name *Anastas* is derived from the Greek word for "resurrection." Another common Christian name is *Khouri,* an Arabic word derived from the French *curé,* meaning "priest." Some historians believe the latter name can be traced back to warrior Franks who participated in the Crusades. Many local family names were even more obviously of European origin (such as Cannavatti and Giacaman, the names of two prominent Bethlehem clans). Almost all Christians of the Holy Land can be considered the descendants of pilgrims and conquerors of one kind or another; some have simply been around longer than others.

. . .

Our pilgrimage along the "Nativity Trail" came through the West Bank Palestinian village of Beit Sahour into Bethlehem. The timeless, meditative beauty of the desert landscape gave way to modernity, with cars whipping along a road lined with telephone and power lines and Palestinian homes topped with satellite-television dishes. It took us a minute to reorient ourselves to the traffic and crowds of tourists jamming the roads of Bethlehem at the beginning of what was expected to be the busiest year of tourism the Holy Land had ever seen. Still on foot, we walked uphill to the Basilica of the Nativity, situated on Manger Square. The fortress-like fourth-century church was erected on the spot where Jesus was believed to have been born. A hurried renovation of the square had just been completed (or nearly completed), and plaster dust was everywhere. A flurry of new construction had taken place in preparation for what Palestinian government and business leaders hoped would be a millennium-inspired bonanza of Christmas and New Year's Eve tourists. Bethlehem, which was brought under the new Palestinian government's control as a result of the historic 1993 peace agreement, was the beleaguered Palestinians' best hope for cashing in on the anticipated armies of Christian tourists.

The keystone of the renovation of Manger Square was the Peace Center—a building that had all the architectural flair of a south Florida strip mall. It was built on the site of the old Israeli police station, which had long stood as a symbol of the occupation with its barbed wire, machine-gun-toting soldiers, and blue-and-white flags with the Star of David. The barbed wire and the flags had been defiantly torn down in 1994, when Israeli troops withdrew from Bethlehem and turned the town over to the Palestinian Authority, as spelled out in the peace process's so-called interim agreement. The construction of the Peace Center reflected the optimism and the empowerment of the local community at the time. But the Center today also provides a ready metaphor of the precarious peace process: an architecturally flawed structure financed by foreign governments and hastily thrown up amid fears of its possible collapse.

But Bethlehem had been decked out in its holiday best, and an invitation had been issued to the world to come to "the Holy Land, Palestine," as the freshly printed brochures from the Palestinian Authority's Ministry of Tourism proclaimed. For the official ceremony launching Bethlehem 2000, the stage in Manger Square was designed in a way that suggested a huge cradle. In a long procession, the patriarchs and bishops of the thirteen established Christian denominations in the Holy Land marched into the square, led by Scout troops wearing plaid scarves and playing bagpipes—a holdover from the British mandate. Children carried a torch lit from the flame in the grotto of the Basilica of the Nativity—a symbol of the light that came to the world with the birth of Jesus. The church bells of Bethlehem rang out over the hills. The clerical leaders took their places on the dais. The Roman Catholic patriarch was seated together with the leaders of the so-called Uniate Catholic churches—the Greeks, Maronites, Syrians, Armenians, Chaldeans, and Copts. The Greek Orthodox patriarch was seated among the representatives of Orthodox denominations, including the Armenians, Copts, Ethiopians, Romanians, Syrians, "White Russians" (the Russian Church Abroad), and "Red Russians" (the Moscow patriarchate's Russian Ecclesiastical Mission in Jerusalem). Also seated on the dais were the bishops of the Episcopal Church of Jerusalem and the Middle East, and of the Lutheran Church. The leaders' liturgical vestments and their impressive miters reflected the kaleidoscope of cultures and traditions and rites that they represented; each carried traces of the ancient sees of the churches in Rome and Alexandria and Antioch and Constantinople and Jerusalem. Woven into the garments themselves were elements of history and theology that had created so many seams—and tears—between these churches, and also the common elements of faith that ultimately bound them together. There were the classical Latin black cassocks with magenta silk ribbing, the more ornate Orthodox vestments with embroidered chasubles, and the consciously austere vestments of the Episcopal, or Anglican, church. The Gospel proclaiming the birth of Jesus was read in Arabic, English, Latin, Greek, Coptic, and Aramaic.

Three weeks later, on December 24, 1999—Christmas Eve, on the Western calendar—this square was packed with the tourists that the promoters of Bethlehem 2000 had hoped for. A sea of Mylar balloons with Santa Claus faces, and Muslim kids waving Palestinian flags, filled the newly renovated square. Palestinian Christian families dressed in their finest milled about, pushing strollers, as the children ate cotton candy. But most didn't stay long. Christmas is not as big a holiday in the East as it is in the West. The real focus of Christian celebration in this part of the world is Holy Week, which precedes Easter. Some local Christians grumbled that teenage Muslim boys for many years had made Christmas Eve a rowdy night of carousing among Western tourists who came to the square. This sign of tension between the Bethlehem locals was lost on many American tourists, many of whom seemed equally unaware that Bethlehem was under a Palestinian administration.

Indeed, many American tourists I encountered were surprised to learn that some Palestinians are Christians, having made the assumption that all Palestinians are Arabs and therefore Muslims. In their simplified equation, a Palestinian Christian was an impossibility. The same held true for other ethnic groups throughout the Middle East: Western Christians have a hard time imagining Christians in Egypt, Jordan, or Syria. Yet, of course, there are and have been indigenous Christians in these places since the very beginning of the Christian faith.

A Jerusalem Christian—a waiter who had a university degree in English literature—once told me about a tour group from California that had come into the restaurant and noticed he was wearing a cross. Even though this waiter was versed in the works of Shakespeare and the novels of Hemingway, one woman, assuming he spoke little or no English, pointed to his cross and asked him in slow, deliberate voice, "We were just wondering, w-h-e-n d-i-d y-o-u c-o-n-v-e-r-t?"

In Manger Square, thousands of Americans and other Western tourists were enjoying a Christmas concert featuring various orchestras, choirs, and gospel groups. I wandered through the crowd, looking for American Christians who might volunteer their views of this place and its people. I wanted to find some tourists who were exploring the connection between the origins of the Christian faith and the local community of Palestinians. I held out some hope that I had found the right person when I saw a woman with a red, white, and blue scarf waving a small red, black, and green Palestinian flag.

Her name was Leah Mitchel. She was a 50-year-old mother of three from Greenville, South Carolina, a kindergarten teacher and a member of the Methodist church. Shouting over the loud music, I introduced myself and asked her if she was enjoying the evening. "You know, I didn't know they had Santa Claus in Israel," Mitchel shouted back. This was not a conversation that was going to be very enlightening, I feared. Mitchel told me she had come with a tour group to Manger Square, and confessed that she had "not been informed" that when she left Jerusalem and came into Bethlehem she was in a Palestinian-ruled area. I asked whether she realized there were Palestinians who are Christian. "I did not know that!" she gasped, opening her eyes with a theatrical expression of surprise. At first I thought maybe she was kidding—but she wasn't. "That is so nice!" she added, smiling.

I didn't ask Mitchel whether she apprehended the political significance of the event for the Palestinian people, but I felt pretty safe in assuming she didn't. It turned out that the flag had simply been handed to her and she was not sure what it symbolized.

I had met scores of Americans journeying through the Holy Land who had a deep knowledge of and compassion for the complex political situation. Some of the hikers on the Nativity Trail, for example, saw their pilgrimage in social and political terms, as a way of recognizing the local people and of gaining a more intimate knowledge of the land. During their six-day trek, they said, they had learned a lot both about Israelis and about Palestinians. I gained many new insights about the situation, about faith, and about history through the scores of conversations I had with these Christian pilgrims. But in general, a vast ignorance about the politics of the situation seemed to prevail among American Christian tourists. American Jews who came as tourists were much more politically aware of the situation. The issues that affected Israel were, to them, closely intertwined with the concerns of their community, with their faith and their history. Why, I wondered, did Christians seem so removed from the land, so ignorant of the reality of the place?

That the Palestinians counted a minority of Christians among their number was a fairly obscure point that was lost on many well-educated friends and relatives, and on plenty of well-informed foreign journalists, too. But what I found truly baffling was the seeming inability, especially among these American tourists, to comprehend that the birth narrative of Jesus emerged in a real town, where real people continue to live in that tradition of faith. It was as if this little town of Bethlehem had been created just for their video cameras. The place existed in their minds as an ancient stage set that was no longer in use, void of any political, social, or historical reality—like the plastic crèches set up every year at Christmas in front of their parish churches. So many American Christians whom I had encountered over the years approached the land of the Bible as a mythic place—or perhaps more accurately, as a spiritual theme park.

The Rev. Jerome Murphy-O'Connor, a Catholic priest of the Dominican order and a world-renowned biblical historian, in his three decades of living in Jerusalem had observed this Western ignorance and the simultaneous exodus of local Christians. As he put it, "We are talking about the Christian Church in the Middle East becoming a museum church, a Disneyland of faith nearly void of the living community of believers."

At that time, work was under way on such a theme park in Florida. So perhaps future tourists wouldn't even bother to come all this way. They could just visit the "Holy Land Experience," as the exhibit was to be called, and "walk through the time of Jesus," as the promotional brochures promised.

Standing in the crowd on Manger Square, Trent Morgan, 21, of Amarillo, Texas, who had been raised in a Baptist church, seemed a bit puzzled by an Arabic band singing a tune that sounded strangely similar to the Christmas carol "Silent Night" (which it in fact was). "I figured there'd be, like, a situation where we could sing along. Not so much Arabic. I thought it was all for tourists, but there are a lot of locals," said Morgan, a West Texas A&M baseball cap pulled down and the brim folded into a tunnel around his eyes. "I honestly didn't know there were people who celebrate Christmas here. What are they celebrating? I mean do they, like, see Jesus as a prophet or a Messiah, or what?"

. . .

At a beautifully appointed old stone home just down the hill from Manger Square, the Anastas family of Bethlehem was coming together for a Christmas party. This family gathering was part of a continuum that harks back to the beginning of the Christian faith for the residents of the town where their savior was born. But it was a continuum that, for their immediate family, had been broken for nearly three decades by the facts of history. Almost all of the 50 or so members of the extended family had flown in from Europe and the Americas, some for the first time in thirty years, for the holiday. Only a handful still actually lived in their homeland. This situation was, sadly, common among the Christian families of Bethlehem.

The turn of the millennium had provided a unique occasion for the family to come together in a way they had not done since before 1967. From Paris and Philadelphia and California and Latin America they had returned to the town where their savior, and they themselves, had been born. The children of those who had emigrated were speaking Spanish and French and English. Only the older generation spoke Arabic.

They had just finished celebrating an Orthodox mass (the Christmas service in Orthodox tradition is typically held on January 6, but they had arranged to celebrate on December 24 so as to accommodate Western vacation schedules). Olive trees in the garden were strung with blinking Christmas lights. A stereo system piped in Christmas carols sung by Fairuz, the legendary Lebanese Christian singer. A beaujolais nouveau, brought by one of the relatives living in France, was served in crystal wine goblets. A rosewood humidor stacked with the Cohiba Cuban cigars that another relative had brought from Latin America were generously offered.

The Anastases were among Bethlehem's Christian upper class, one of the town's many wealthy, educated, and successful families. The patriarchs of the family were named Mary and Joseph. Joseph was a carpenter. Sounds familiar, right? The family, especially the kids, laugh at the biblical symmetry of it all. The symmetry isn't exact to a Westerner, however: the mother goes by Maryam, which is the Arabic name for Mary, and the father, who had passed away several years earlier, was Yusef, Arabic for Joseph. And the word *carpenter* does not fully capture his highly valued skills as a master craftsman of wood and a licensed structural engineer. Maryam and Yusef were married just after the 1948 Arab-Israeli war broke out. They did their best to bring up their children in the 1950s and 1960s, when Bethlehem was under Jordanian rule and roiling with tension and conflict. At that time, Jordan paid little attention to Bethlehem, which was mired in poverty—a sleepy backwater in a kingdom that was struggling to bring some order to the vast desert wilderness over which it ruled. The wars of 1948 and 1967 pushed Muslims from the neighboring villages into the city of Bethlehem, and soon the Christians were no longer a majority. After the 1967 war came the Israeli occupation and a massive wave of emigration.

Maryam and Yusef had ten children, and they watched seven of them emigrate abroad. Bashir, the civil engineer, and Miranda, with a Ph.D. in mathematics, now had families of their own in California. Alma lived on the Main Line outside Philadelphia. Ayreen, an architect, was in New York. Munir served with a Palestine Liberation Organization (PLO) faction in the war in Lebanon, but escaped to fulfill his dream of being a musician and was now a composer living in Paris. Lucy, like many other Palestinian immigrants, had gone to Latin America, and she was living in Venezuela. Khalil, an architect for a French company, was currently working on a project in Tahiti. Only three children stayed in Bethlehem: Wa'el, the passionate and gifted economist, who worked for the United Nations Development Project; Olivia, a dentist, who was married and raising a family in Bethlehem; and Shibly, an electrical engineer.

The first to leave Bethlehem for new horizons abroad was Alma, who emigrated along with her husband Kamal Hazboun, a scion of one of the largest Roman Catholic clans in Bethlehem. Kamal had left Bethlehem to attend Villanova University in 1966, and ended up following the 1967 war on television. He had no desire to stay in the United States; but after graduating in 1970, he found out he would not be allowed to return home as a resident. He had been in the middle of exams in 1967 when the Israelis occupied Bethlehem and therefore was not available for the census that Israel carried out immediately after its occupation of the West Bank. Palestinians who were absent during the Israeli census were not considered citizens and were prevented by Israel from returning. Kamal was thus left in limbo, with a Jordanian passport but with no hope of obtaining permission to return to his family home in Bethlehem—a beautiful old home that now stood vacant and with its windows broken out.

He did manage to get temporary passes to cross the bridge from Jordan. During one such visit, he met Alma. The two quickly fell in love, and they were married in 1978. Even for their wedding ceremony, Kamal was given only a 40-hour pass by Israeli authorities. After the wedding, the couple flew off to America to start a new life together in Philadelphia. They both had been granted student visas—she, for undergraduate studies at Pennsylvania State University, and Kamal, to complete a master's degree in computer science.

At the time, the United States was relatively lenient in immigration policy toward Palestinians from the occupied territories, especially if they were Christian. There were several reasons why Christians seemed to be favored. The first was because Christians tended to have more family contacts in the United States, which strengthened their case. The second was because it was mostly Christian Palestinians, who tended to be more educated and more fluent in English, who worked at the American consulate in East Jerusalem. The local hires in the consulate helped facilitate the immigration applications of their Christian Palestinian neighbors and made sure they had a leg up in the process. There may also have been a level of cultural bias among the American staff in the visa section, who tended to favor those with backgrounds similar to their own, including attendance at Catholic schools and acceptance to big American universities. These factors help explain why Christians have emigrated at a rate that is more than double that of Muslim Palestinians.

Kamal worked at Penn State for several years and then landed a job with Xerox, where he is now a marketing manager. Alma graduated cum laude and went on to become a financial controller at a large medical apparel company. They have two children—Rana, 16, and Christopher, 2. They are a typical suburban American family, busily trying to balance two children and two careers.

"I have a very respected job at an $18 billion multinational corporation," Kamal said. "I have a U.S. passport. My children are born in America. I pay taxes. I have voted in five presidential elections in America. But I can't return to my homeland. Even though I have a birth certificate from the Church of the Nativity in Bethlehem, even though my parents' house sits vacant, even though we can trace our lineage back hundreds and hundreds of years, none of this is considered proof of citizenship by the Israelis.

"But if you are from New York or Moscow and you are born Jewish, you have the right to become a citizen in Israel the minute you land at the airport. Do you know what that does to you?"

He was referring to the Israeli law of return, which permits anyone with a Jewish grandparent to live in Israel and guarantees them financial assistance in making the move. Actively seeking to bring Jews to

Israel, the country has received more than a million immigrants from the former Soviet Union alone.

Kamal continued: "It is very difficult trying to make Americans, our neighbors and friends, our colleagues at work, our fellow parishioners at church, comprehend these facts. Even the very educated in America just have no idea what is going on here, or the injustices that take place."

But this Christmas, if only temporarily, Alma and Kamal had come home again. They gazed over the stone wall of the patio at the town where they grew up. Beneath the balcony, tourists and pilgrims from Europe and America and all over the world streamed into Manger Square for the celebrations of Bethlehem 2000.

"When you live in America, you learn what freedom means," said Alma, "and I think it makes it impossible to ever think of coming back to this, to the checkpoints, and the humiliation, and the daily outrages of life here. I miss it. This is my home. But we cannot come home."

The experience of the security check on a flight to or from Israel's Ben Gurion International Airport brings all that aggravation sharply into focus, Kamal said. He feels the young Israeli security officers cast sullen stares when they see the place of birth on his U.S. passport. Their questions are thorough; the security concerns in this part of the world demand that. But for Palestinian travelers the process is often humiliating and degrading. On their way to Bethlehem for the Christmas gathering, Alma and Kamal and their two children were taken aside at the airport. Their bags were taken to a back room, where they were opened and the contents emptied out. They were asked to wait to one side of the line, while dozens of other passengers went ahead of them. Finally, they were let through. Kamal was furious.

"All I can think standing in line is that I am an American taxpayer contributing to the billions of dollars in taxes that go to Israel," said Kamal. "I get furious knowing what life is like for our families and friends back home, knowing how brutal this occupation was, and knowing that all these forces of history and economics were pushing our people, including Christians, off of this land, even right here where Jesus was born."

. . .

That Christians of the Holy Land are an almost invisible minority in a land ruled by others and ignored by visitors—and that many have emigrated under the economic and political and religious strain this reality has created—is a phenomenon as old as the faith itself. In some ways, it defined the faith.

The earliest Christians were a tiny, messianic sect of Jews drawn to a rabbi who had conceived a radical theology of forgiveness and economic equality in a land struggling under Roman occupation and heavy-handed taxation. Jesus's message was inherently subversive. And the early Christians' oppression, first under the Roman Empire and, later, other powers, was woven into the fabric of an enduring faith that emphasized spiritual grace in suffering. And Christian emigration, in part to escape this suffering, was in many ways the history of that church.

Immediately after Jesus's execution, the movement went underground. A seedpod of Jewish Christians was planted in the shadows of Jerusalem—a devout community, adhering closely to the observance of Jewish law and at first seen as one of many sects within the Jewish faith. At this time, clashes were frequent and bitter between the Pharisees, the Sadducees, and the Essenes—religious groups that espoused rival streams of rabbinical teaching. The Christian movement quickly ran afoul of the Sadducees, the priestly aristocracy that then controlled the Temple. The apostle James, the brother of Jesus, was the leader of the Jerusalem "mother church." He was known as "the Just," for his devotion to a strict adherence to Jewish law. Most historians believe that he was martyred in Jerusalem around A.D. 60. Stephen, the first deacon in the Christian church and a particularly charismatic speaker, held to the notions that God did not depend on a Temple made by human hands and that Jesus's coming had been prophesied by Moses. He was judged and sentenced for these beliefs by the Sanhedrin—Judaism's supreme court of Justice in Jerusalem at the time of Jesus—and was stoned to death.

Nearly all the apostles emigrated. They feared the violence that awaited them for a theology that rebelled not just against Roman rule but against what they saw as corrupt practices of the Jewish power structure around the Temple. The apostles had witnessed the executions not only of their savior and Lord, Jesus Christ, but also of John the Baptist and a growing list of martyrs for their beliefs. At this time, one of the men carrying out these persecutions was Saul, a member of the Pharisees—the sect from which most scholars believe Jesus emerged, and which he sharply criticized in his own teachings. We know by Saul's own words that as a Pharisee he was actively involved in the persecution of the messianic Jesus movement, expelling believers from synagogues and shunning them in the community. After his conversion to Christianity on the road to Damascus, Saul—now known by his Roman name, Paul—was transformed from a persecutor of believers in Jesus to one of the movement's most powerful advocates. Biblical historians and theologians have made much of Paul as the inventor of Christianity, the organization man who took an unfocused, anti-intellectual grouping led by Galilean peasants and helped shape an inspiring and appealing religion. He gave the Jesus movement an intellectual edge and brought its message westward, into Europe. And there, outside the cultural setting of Judaism, he began to put forward a convincing argument in the fledgling church's first great theological debate, on whether Jewish law should be imposed on Gentile converts. At the First Council of Jerusalem in A.D. 48, Paul passionately asserted that since the Law of Moses was fulfilled in Jesus Christ, Gentiles could gain salvation without following Jewish laws of circumcision, and of observance of the sabbath need no longer be followed. Paul, it is widely believed among scholars, continued to observe the law, as did most of the early leaders of the Jewish Christian church.

In A.D. 70, when the Romans destroyed the temple in Jerusalem to suppress the rising rebellion of the Jewish zealots, the Jewish community died fighting or fled the city. The Jewish Christians fled along with them, as the Romans did not distinguish this Jewish sect from the others. The Jewish Christians ended up across the Jordan River, in the town of Pella.

When a measure of calm had been restored in and around Jerusalem, which the Romans had renamed Aelia Capitolina, the Jewish Christian community returned. The faith struggled to take root in the dry, rocky soil of the Middle East. Eventually it sprouted in the desert monasteries of Egypt and took root in the mountains of northern Phoenicia; and slowly it emerged among Romans posted in the distant fringes of the empire. In the early centuries of the church, Christianity was increasingly defined against its Jewish roots and the Jewish establishment's rejection of Jesus's message. There was an increasing intolerance among Christians of their spiritual predecessors; and eventually they began to equate the triumph of their faith with the degradation of Judaism. The vile weed of anti-Semitism thus sprang up within the garden of Christianity.

Christianity spiraled outward in waves, undulating beneath the persecution of the Roman Empire and cresting to the surface in Rome, where by decree it was recognized as an official religion within the empire in the fourth century. When Christianity has ruled the Holy Land, it has done so through conquering forces from the West—forces that generally cared little for the indigenous Christian population and that at times failed to even distinguish them from other confessions within the local population. And, as a result, Christian rule has often not been looked upon very favorably by the local Christians, even if they tended to side with it in order to survive.

The foreign Christian rulers, throughout the history of the Holy Land, certainly have ranked abysmally low on the scale of tolerance and of what we today know as "human rights." The local church became enmeshed with the ruling Christian powers from the West—the Greeks of Byzantium and the conquering Europeans of the Crusades. Outside the land where the faith began, Christianity has not merely survived but flourished through its powerful appeal as a faith, through military conquest, and through missionary zeal. It spread from Europe to Africa and Asia and the Americas, and today it has some two billion adherents worldwide. But in the Holy Land, according to important historical texts, Christians have been in the minority for nearly two thousand years, except for a relatively brief period under the Byzantine Empire, in the fifth and sixth centuries, when they are believed to have become a majority. But recently some scholars have questioned whether Christians truly represented a statistical majority during this period. If they did, this status was soon reversed by the onset of Islam and the massive conversion of Arab Christians, along with pagan and nomadic tribes, to the religion of the prophet Mohammed, which seemed to resonate so clearly in this land.

After the Islamic conquest, Christianity held on with a solid minority presence for centuries, then steadily but almost imperceptibly diminished. It held its own until the twentieth century, when modern warfare caused an accelerated decline in the Christian population until it reached a perilously marginal existence. By the year 2000, the indigenous Christian community of the Holy Land had dwindled to what in the language of the Hebrew Bible would be called a "remnant."

. . .

According to the census data kept by the Ottoman Empire, the Christian population in 1914 was 24 percent of what we today consider the Middle East, including Israel/Palestine, Egypt, Jordan, Lebanon, Syria, Iraq, and Turkey. Today the Christian presence in the Middle East is no more than 5 percent.

In Israel and the Palestinian-ruled areas of the West Bank and Gaza the decline of the Christian community in the last century has been precipitous. In the early 1900s, the Christian presence was by some estimates as high as 20 percent of the total population. This figure was widely used by the churches, although more official population data, including a census under the British mandate, put the number significantly lower, at about 13 percent. Population figures in a place as politically and religiously charged as the Middle East have always depended greatly on which group gathers the data, for what purpose, and with what methods. But whatever the point of departure—whether 20 percent or some lesser proportion—it is indisputable that today the Christian presence in Israel, the West Bank, Gaza, and Jerusalem has dwindled dramatically, to less than 2 percent. The Israeli Central Bureau of Statistics numbered the "Arab Christian" population living in Israel at 101,000 in the 1995 census, out of a total population of 6.3 million. (The Israeli population figures include the 8,000 Palestinian Christians living in East Jerusalem.) In the West Bank and Gaza, the number was estimated at no more than 32,000 out of a total of nearly 3 million. So in 1995 there were about 133,000 Palestinian Christians in Israel and the Palestinian territories, compared to an estimated 145,000 under the British mandate. The Palestinian Christians are the only demographic group, among the three faiths, that decreased in the intervening years. In contrast, the Muslim and Jewish populations soared—among Muslims, through a high birthrate, and among Jews, due to waves of immigration.

The diminishing Christian presence in the Holy Land is a highly charged issue, and the Israeli government has been emphatic in countering the claims that Israel is in any way responsible for the decline. Israeli officials believe that the Jewish state has shown enlightened leadership in relation to the religious minorities, both Muslim and Christian, who live as citizens within Israel. In a broader sense, the Israeli government insists that the gains of Israel's modern economy and its parallel development of efficient health care and educational opportunities have been shared by all Israeli citizens and have therefore done much to keep the Christian population from leaving. The Israeli officials who have dealt with this issue for years are always quick to point to the fact that Christians in the occupied West Bank are constantly applying, through family reunification and marriage, for Israeli citizenship—a fact that these officials view as evidence of Christians' mistrust of Palestinian rule.

The Palestinian Authority is also defensive about the issue of a disappearing Christian presence. Palestinian leaders typically assert that economic hardships caused by occupation have pushed Christians to emigrate or move to Israeli-administered territory. After Israel undermined Palestinian development and weakened the economy and social structure for thirty-three years Palestinians insist it is unfair to assume the Christian minority was voting with its feet against the Palestinian Authority by preferring the relative economic and social stability of Israel within its pre-1967 boundaries.

Population figures are and always have been explosive in this region. There have been many contradictory claims, mitigating factors, and corrupt accounting practices. Bernard Sabella, a professor at Bethlehem University who has tracked the Christian population in Israel and the West Bank, Gaza, and Jerusalem, said the best way to look at the diminished Christian presence is to project what the population would be with a conservative growth rate of 2 percent. If the Palestinian Christian population had maintained a 2 percent growth rate (which was lower than the average in Israel/Palestine) from its prewar population of about 145,000, by the year 2000 it should have reached about 420,000. That means that some 287,000 Palestinian Christians are living in the diaspora, or more than two times as many as there actually are living in Israel and the Palestinian territories.

Sabella, himself a Palestinian Christian from Bethlehem, said that if the rate of decline continues, the indigenous Christian community could virtually disappear within two generations. Or, as he put it, Palestinian Christians as a demographic category "would represent a fraction of a percent of the population and become statistically unrecognizable."

Both Sabella and a leading Israeli demographer, Yehoshua Ben-Arieh of Hebrew University, believe that a focus on the historical population figures for the major urban areas—such as Jerusalem, Nazareth, Bethlehem, and the West Bank town of Ramallah—offers a clearer understanding of the diminishing Christian presence. Consider, for example, that twice as many Christians from Ramallah now live in Dearborn, Michigan, as live in Ramallah. Three times as many Christians from Bethlehem live in the Palestinian diaspora as in Bethlehem itself.

Nowhere is the wave of Christian emigration more noticeable or more poignant than in Jerusalem. The city had a Christian population of about 30,000 in 1944, under the British mandate. After the war of 1948, when the city was partially under Jordanian rule, the figures dropped precipitously. When the Israelis captured East Jerusalem in the Six-Day War in June of 1967, there were about 12,000 Christians left in the city. By 2000 there were no more than 8,000 Palestinian Christians—or just slightly more than 1 percent of the total population—within the Israeli-defined boundaries of Jerusalem.

The neighborhoods of West Jerusalem that were once predominantly Christian—including the German Colony, Talbiya, and Qatamon—were seized by Israel during the war in 1948. The families that fled the fighting were never permitted to return. After the armistice agreement, their homes were seized by Israel's "Custodian of Absentee Property," and the Jewish Agency turned them over to new Jewish immigrants, who were flooding into the newly founded state. Today these old Arab homes—coveted properties for a wealthy elite of Israelis and some Western journalists—seem almost haunted by this past. The home where we lived in the German Colony was one of them. I had researched the British mandate–era deeds of the building and tried in vain for several years to find the Palestinian family that once lived there. I wondered what had happened to them, where they had gone.

The reasons for the Christian diaspora are layered and complex. Primarily, historians say, the Christians of the Holy Land have left a land torn by war to seek economic opportunity. The Christians' traditional economic strength, higher levels of education (generally, provided by Christian missionary schools), and ties to Western churches have supported their emigration, paving their way to the United States, Latin America, Europe, Canada, and Australia. In this sense it is always difficult to disentangle the roles of class and religion in understanding the waves of Christian emigration from the Middle East.

And it should be emphasized that Christians have been pouring out of the Middle East at least since the late nineteenth century, for reasons that have nothing to do with religion. They were part of a global movement of people seeking a better life, as rail and shipping routes opened access to the New World.

The first significant wave of Christian emigration began in earnest with the demise of the Ottoman Empire, during the closing years of World War I. As the Ottomans, who had allied themselves with the Central Powers of Germany and Austria-Hungary, realized that they were soon to be defeated, they suppressed many local communities. Conditions became especially harsh for the *dhimmi,* the non-Muslim minorities—Jews and Christians—living under their rule. *Dhimmi* were often suspected of conspiring with the Allies (specifically, Great Britain, France, Russia, Belgium, and Serbia). Although the *dhimmi* previously had been exempted from military service, they began to be conscripted as they had been before, during the Balkan war in the late nineteenth century. The conditions in the military were bad to begin with, and they dramatically worsened as the Allies advanced against the Central Powers. Amid a crumbling economy, food shortages, and starvation, many Christians began boarding boats at the newly developed port in Beirut (and to a lesser extent in the old port of Jaffa) to flee. The largest number left for Latin America, because that was where the established shipping routes would take them. A smaller number went to North America and Europe. This early migratory wave established a network of support for future Palestinian Christians immigrating to the Americas and to Europe in the following decades.

After a slowdown in emigration during the years between the two world wars, the second big wave came in 1948, with the Israeli-Arab war. On November 29, 1947, the General Assembly of the United Nations approved the partition of Palestine into separate Jewish and Arab states, as waves of Jews who had survived the Holocaust fled Europe to rebuild their lives in the Holy Land. The Arabs rejected the U.N. partition, and sporadic fighting broke out between the two sides. The British, who had ruled under international mandate as part of the peace settlement of World War I, announced their intention to withdraw troops by May 1948. On May 14, David Ben-Gurion declared the creation of the state of Israel. The surrounding Arab armies attacked.

Israel won the war, not only holding on to the land granted by the United Nations partition but also capturing even more territory. Palestine was divided into three parts, with Israel taking about 70 percent, Jordan taking the West Bank, and Egypt controlling the Gaza

Strip. In the upheaval of war, some 700,000 Palestinians—including 60,000 Christians (about 35 percent of the total Christian population)—fled or were forced to flee their homes, and the Israelis did not permit them to return. The Palestinian refugee crisis was born.

The events of June 1967 set off another wave of emigration. As Arab forces lined up for what Israel feared would be another invasion, the Israeli military struck first. In a stunning victory, the Israeli forces quickly defeated the larger Arab armies of Jordan, Syria, Egypt, and Iraq. During the conflict (which later came to be known as the Six-Day War), the Israelis captured the West Bank, Gaza, the Golan Heights, and East Jerusalem—conquests that some religious Zionists regarded as involving divine intervention (the land, as they saw it, had been promised to the Jews by God). As was the case before, Palestinians who had fled their homes during the fighting or who were forced out by the Israeli army were not permitted to return, although some exceptions were made in the interest of family reunification.

A massive influx of Jewish immigrants from Europe, Russia, and North Africa and a soaring Muslim birthrate among Palestinians made the Christians who stayed in their native villages and cities an ever shrinking minority. Statistics show that most of these Palestinian Christians are elderly, poor, and/or female. Today the median age of Palestinian Christians is 31 years, compared to 18 years for the general Palestinian population. And in the late 1980s, there were 100 females for every 80 males in the Palestinian Christian population. A majority of young Christian men—those able to obtain coveted visas—emigrate. And most of the others dream of following them.

"Now the biggest issue for Christians is the brain drain," said Columbia University professor Edward Said, one of the most provocative and recognizable advocates for the Palestinian cause, himself a Palestinian Christian, and raised in the Anglican church. "The best minds and the most talented young people leave. The ones left behind are increasingly the powerless and the poor."

The pressures that have squeezed Christians out of the Middle East are diverse. They include economic pressures created by the upheaval of war, as well as social pressures created by the demographic earthquake that came with Zionism's effort to bring Jews from all over the world into Israel, and the Muslim population explosion detonating all around them. In Israel, Christians faced discrimination as an Arab minority in a Jewish state. In the West Bank and

Gaza and East Jerusalem, life under occupation was full of difficulties and indignities.

Christians within Arab societies throughout the Middle East have suffered, just as their Muslim neighbors have, under the brutal and corrupt regimes that ruled them. They were squeezed further by the upsurge in Islamic fundamentalism that in the last two decades of the twentieth century dramatically altered the social and political landscape of the Arab world. For Christians, who were a tiny religious minority within Israel and the Arab world, life was becoming untenable.

Christians who were leaving—and those they were leaving behind—described a climate of intolerance within a culture and a political structure increasingly defined as Islamic on the Palestinian side and as religiously Zionist on the Israeli side. These forces at times have caused Christians to feel that they don't belong in the land where the Christian faith began. As a minority within a minority, they have been caught in a cultural no-man's-land where their mere presence evokes suspicion: as Arabs, they are mistrusted by the Israelis; and as Christians, by the overwhelmingly Muslim Palestinians. Although complaints have increased of discrimination against Christians by extremist Muslim and Jewish forces, the overriding feeling—the one causing so many Christians to leave—was simply no longer having a sense of belonging, of mattering. The voices of Muslim and Jewish religious extremism were drowning them out, squeezing them out of the public space.

This is true not just in Israel and the Palestinian-controlled areas but throughout Christian communities of the Middle East, from as far north as Turkey to as far south as the Sudan. The Copts of Egypt are frequent targets of the fiery rhetoric and sustained violence of Islamic militants in the south. In Lebanon, where the ruling Maronite Christians for many decades have practiced their own brand of intolerance (and where, fatefully, the leading political parties sided with Israel in the civil war), a kind of social backlash has taken place that has largely stripped the longtime leaders of power and has given the Shiite Muslims' Hezbollah, or "Party of God," an increasingly dominant voice in the national dialogue.

Secular academics, political leaders, and supporters of interfaith dialogue, including Jews and Muslims, are quick to point out that everyone suffers in a climate of religious intolerance, not just Christians. But many also feel that the resulting exodus of Christians poses grave social and political consequences. The Christian minority, they say, has historically provided a buffer against surging fundamentalism. That is not to suggest that the Christians are neutral. They are not. But as a third leg of faith, they serve to stabilize a land that could too easily topple into all-out religious conflict with only Judaism and Islam to support it.

In a sense, the Christians have served as guarantors of a more secular and pluralistic society. As a minority representing Western values and culture in the Middle East, they also have provided a test of tolerance for the governments that rule them. They are, as one American diplomat in the region phrased it, "canaries in the mine" of the modern Middle East. As this Christian population has steadily vanished, so, many would argue, has a spirit of tolerance, a spirit that was a particularly precious commodity as the region struggled to find a formula for peace and an end to a half century of Arab-Israeli conflict.

. . .

On the Latin Patriarchate Road, just inside Jaffa Gate in Jerusalem's Old City, I met with the Roman Catholic Patriarch Michel Sabbah to discuss the diminishing Christian presence. Sabbah was born in Nazareth and was the president of Bethlehem University during the difficult years of the first *intifada*, from 1987 to 1993, when he was forced to close the campus. Sabbah was considered an unabashed Palestinian nationalist. He was the first Palestinian cleric to rise in the Catholic hierarchy and to be named patriarch—a fact that underscored the Catholic church's efforts to localize its leadership. To his detractors, Sabbah's political views were more pronounced than his pastoral role. But Sabbah knew the injustice that Palestinians, both Muslim and Christian, had suffered, and he had seen the devastating exodus from the parish churches within his fold. To him the Christians' role as an embattled minority in the Holy Land was a beautiful mystery, perhaps even a sacred mission. He believed their thinning presence was the perfect metaphor for the faith. It represented the challenge of balancing the Christian doctrine of not seeking political power with the mandate of siding with and protecting the most weak and downtrodden, of recognizing and resisting injustice.

"In Judaism, religion and politics are closely linked, and it is the same for Islam. We don't, as Christians, come back to the idea that Christians need political power. But we are concerned about political issues that involve injustice. That has to be our pastoring role," he said.

"I understand people are tired. We tell them to endure, to adhere as Christians to the land. It is deeply sad for us to watch them leave," he added. "There is a mystery here. Jesus and his disciples were always a small minority. It is a mystery we live as Palestinian Christians today. I think the Christian community here will always be a small church, reflecting the life of Jesus, one that is small and one that is refused and rejected even in its homeland. There are mysteries in history. You can have much analysis, but ultimately you have to rely on mystery."

II

The End of Days

New Year's Eve, 1999

IN THE LAST DAYS before the year 2000, an Israeli police captain sat wincing over a bitter cup of instant coffee as he scanned a bank of 36 video monitors at the police station just inside the Jaffa Gate in the Old City—the half-mile-square, ancient heart of Jerusalem. The captain's eyes darted from one screen to the next, over a collage of images captured by some 200 surveillance cameras posted throughout the labyrinth of stone and sacred space that is the Old City. Every nine seconds a screen jumped from one camera angle to the next, creating a warm, television-blue montage of flashing images: Narrow alleyways packed with kiosks selling spices and nuts, tourist shops peddling T-shirts and Holy City souvenirs, a freshly butchered goat hanging on a hook outside a meat market, produce piled on vendors' carts, and a crush of humanity trying to push its way through it all. There were Western pilgrims studying tourist maps, Orthodox Jews dressed in traditional black frock coats rushing to prayers, devout Muslims in checkered headscarves and prayer rugs tucked under their arms, and Christian clerics in the brown robes of the Franciscans and the sleeker black vestments of the Greek Orthodox. It was a Jerusalem mosaic, and it all reflected off the captain's polished eyeglasses as he fixed his gaze on the wall of video monitors. This was the Jerusalem command control center of an Israeli police surveillance project dubbed "Watch 2000."

The Israeli police station is located at the western entrance to the Old City—the walled city's most heavily fortified side. The Jaffa Gate is one of seven passageways that lead through the imposing stone ramparts. The spire that guards the entrance, commonly referred to as the Tower of David, is actually the minaret of an Ottoman-era mosque believed to have been built in the fifteenth century. The remains of the citadel beneath date back to Herod the Great in the first century B.C. This is believed to be the site of the praetorium where Pontius Pilate sat in judgment of Jesus. (The location of the First Station on the pilgrimage route of the Via Dolorosa, established around the fourteenth century, reflects the belief that the praetorium was near St. Stephen's Gate; but most biblical historians and archaeologists today maintain that the Tower of David near the Jaffa Gate is the more likely site.) Adjacent to these ruins is a cluster of low-lying, stone and stucco buildings—once an Ottoman military encampment, then a British mandate post, then a Jordanian army base, and now an Israeli police station. Throughout all that history, this corner of the Old City had been a place where rulers watched over the ruled. If they wanted to maintain dominance, they had to be vigilant in this sacred city of plots, revolts, and revolutions. And so it was here, in a basement room of one of the stone buildings in this complex, that the Israeli police captain, with his team of about ten other detectives and computer technicians, leaned forward to focus more intently on his monitors.

He sat at the command chair in front of a desktop computer displaying a map of the Old City's four separate quadrants: the Muslim, Jewish, Christian, and Armenian quarters. The captain, a sixteen-year police veteran and an expert on terrorism, moved the computer's mouse with his right hand and clicked. Each click on the coordinates of the map brought up an image in a window on his desktop and simultaneously appeared on the central monitor's large screen. Then he clicked again, moving the camera in for a zoom focus or pulling back for a wider angle from one corner of the Old City to another. They were grainy color images, an almost voyeuristic glimpse of the sacred space that defined the history of man's relation to God through thousands of years and the deeply personal moments that the prayerful have at these spots—all summoned by the simple click of a mouse on a computer screen.

Click: The Via Dolorosa. The camera moved in on a group of Christian pilgrims—who, gauging by the matching yellow tourist agency caps they all wore, were from Latin America—led by a Franciscan friar in brown robes. They huddled together, carrying a wooden cross along the cobblestone path that links fourteen Stations of the Cross. They stopped and knelt at the second station, some closing their eyes as they mumbled fervent prayers. The camera swiveled and retreated from this intensely personal moment.

Click: The Western Wall. Standing before the massive, gray Herodian stones of the Wall, a crowd of about one hundred Orthodox Jewish men in prayer shawls rhythmically rocked back and forth as they chanted ancient appeals to God. Then a side view of an elderly man with a black felt *kippah* and graying *payos,* or side curls. His face had the same delicate translucency and wrinkles of the yellowed parchment of a Torah scroll. He held out his hand to touch the stone as he bowed his head in prayer—and the unblinking camera politely tilted upward to gaze on the massive stones of the wall.

Click: The Dome of the Rock. At one of the most beautiful shrines of Islam, the camera pulled back for a wide angle on the Muslim Quarter's central artery, El Wad road, and the life flow of tens of thousands of Muslim faithful pumping on this Friday toward gates flanked by armed Israeli police, heading for the Haram al-Sharif, or Noble Sanctuary. The camera shifted back to focus on the open plaza around the Dome of the Rock, where men removed their shoes and rolled open the small rugs they had carried, to kneel and prostrate themselves in prayer at Al-Aqsa.

There were only a few days left in December 1999, and tension was mounting as the year 2000 approached. The captain and his team cut from one camera angle to another like this, zooming in on the shadowy corners and the filtered sun that sliced down on the cobblestones of the Old City. The detective's seasoned eyes scanned each image mechanically: a group of elderly American tourists; a couple of Jewish settlers carrying army-issue Galil assault rifles; several young Palestinian men with dark beards and smoldering eyes. How, I wondered, could any law enforcement agency patrol a plot of earth so sacred, so rich in layers of emotion, and so shaped by hatreds as hard and ancient as the smooth stones that paved its crooked pathways? Buoyed by the expectation that ancient prophecies were soon to be fulfilled, political extremists yearned for violence, and fundamentalists brimmed with apocalyptic visions of a final battle for redemption, especially as the end was approaching. The end, that is, of the calendar year 1999.

The Holy Land had been stung by a millennial panic set in motion by fringe preachers of the End of Days. To keep an eye on all this, the Israeli government had not only implemented Watch 2000 but also dispatched some 12,000 police and military troops to the streets of Jerusalem in the weeks preceding the New Year. It was, the police said, the largest security undertaking in the history of their country, which had lived through at least five wars and numerous insurrections in the fifty-two years of its existence. If the end of the world was really coming, the Israeli police were damned if it was going to happen on their watch.

The press corps was almost giddy with visions of a grand Armageddon scenario, some mass suicide of cult members, a bizarre but big news story that might reveal itself on this turn of the calendar. All across the world, the fear of Y2K computer glitches that could effectively plunge the world into chaos ran rampant.

And some of the fear seemed grounded in reality. On December 15, American and Jordanian security officials revealed that a terrorist attack had been foiled just a few weeks before it was to be carried out. Jordan's security forces arrested a cell of eleven Jordanians, an Iraqi, and an Algerian, who were purportedly linked to Osama bin Laden, the Saudi financier of terrorism. The cell was allegedly planning attacks on tourist sites in Jordan, timed to coincide with New Year's celebrations. On December 22, the U.S. Department of State issued a worldwide warning to American citizens, saying they should "avoid large crowds and gatherings" on Christmas and New Year's Eve.

Terrorism experts worldwide unanimously agreed that the most potentially explosive millennial scenario could unfold in the heart of Jerusalem. The greatest threat, they believed, was posed not by Islamic militants but by Christian and Jewish extremists anxious to restore the Temple, who might try to usher in the messianic age by force, through an attack on the sacred plot of earth revered by Muslims as well as Jews. This rise of land, defined in the Bible as Mount Moriah, today is known to Jews and many Christians as the Temple Mount. Jewish tradition holds that upon this hilltop the biblical patriarch Abraham was called upon to sacrifice his son Isaac; and many believe that the Ark of the Covenant was later housed on this spot, inside the Holy of Holies, the inner sanctum of the ancient Temple of Judaism.

After the Romans destroyed the Second Temple, it was left for centuries as a heap of rubble and then was used as a garbage dump. The Byzantine Christians viewed the ruins as symbolic of the triumph of

Christianity over Judaism. Jews were permitted by Roman (and later Byzantine) rulers to return only once a year to the site of their destroyed Temple. In the seventh century, when the impressive Muslim shrine known as the Dome of the Rock was built atop the rubble, Muslims gave the compound the name *Haram al-Sharif.* To them, the construction of the beautiful shrine over the ruins of the Jewish Temple symbolized Islam's perfect completion and fulfillment of the two older monotheistic faiths. Through the ensuing ages, this overlapping sacred space gradually became linked with beliefs—in a final redemption, in the return of the messiah, and in the "end times"—shared by all three faiths.

At the end of the second millennium, a growing religious extremist subculture—both Christian and Jewish—was flourishing around a fervent belief that the Muslim sanctuary and its mosque, which had stood there for more than 1,300 years, must be replaced by a rebuilt Temple. Believers held that the Third Temple would prepare the way for the messiah. Computer-generated posters for sale in the Old City's tourist shops depicted an image of the rebuilt Temple superimposed over the Dome of the Rock. Institutes and organizations, such as the Temple Mount Faithful and the Temple Institute, were founded and dedicated to restoring the Jewish presence in the form of the Temple.

Among the strongest supporters of this fringe movement—those who come to the museums in the Old City and who contribute donations to their activities—are evangelical Christians. The movement of self-proclaimed Christian Zionists is gathering strength in America. The essential belief of its members is that the restoration of the State of Israel, on what they believe is land promised to Jews by God, is evidence that there is a hope of redemption for the world. The Israeli military victories of 1948 and 1967 are seen as acts of divine intervention to restore Jews to the land before the coming torments of the Apocalypse, at the beginning of which the Christian believers will be "raptured," or taken up to heaven, to be followed by the physical reign of God on this earth. What happens to the Jews in this scenario? They will either have to embrace Jesus as Lord or perish in the final battle. This interpretation of scripture allied the forces of Jerry Falwell and Pat Robertson with the hard right in Israel, especially the former Israeli Prime Minister Benjamin Netanyahu, who actively courted the Christian Zionist movement. Elements of the hard right Likud Party and the Jewish settler movement have embraced the Christian Zionists largely because of the vast funds they have raised in America and funneled into support services for Israel. I once asked David Bar-Illan, one of Netanyahu's chief advisers, about what seemed an awfully cynical alliance. He said, "We worry much less about what goes on in their minds, and focus on what they do on the ground to support us."

From the viewpoint of those on the Jewish and Christian fringes who support the restoration of the Temple, the Muslim shrine stands squarely in the way of redemption. And this is why Israel's security establishment was so fearful that an extremist group would try to hasten the coming of the messiah, at the turn of the millennium, by blowing up the Dome of the Rock.

The idea was not far-fetched. Such an act was nearly attempted by a messianic Jewish extremist group in the early 1980s, which had purchased explosives for the purpose. Their plot was only narrowly thwarted after several years in gestation. In a separate incident in 1982, Alan Goodman, a Baltimore-born immigrant to Israel who had fallen under the influence of the anti-Arab extremist Rabbi Meir Kahane, entered the Noble Sanctuary carrying an M-16 assault rifle. He shot two guards, killing one of them, and then fired randomly, blasting out windows and doors, until he ran out of bullets and was apprehended. And in 1969, an Australian Christian, Dennis Rohan, provoked Muslim riots around the world with his nearly successful attempt to burn down the Al-Aqsa mosque. Faced with an underground that ceaselessly fantasized about such acts, the world's intelligence-gathering communities were not sitting idly by on the cusp of the new millennium.

The FBI had undertaken "Project Megiddo." The project name referred to the biblical site of Har Megiddo, the site in the northern Jezreel valley where the biblical Battle of Armageddon is prophesied to occur. The intention of Project Megiddo was to monitor threats of millennial violence worldwide. In an October 1999 report the FBI stated, "A simple act of desecration, or even a perceived desecration of any of the holy sites on the Temple Mount is likely to trigger a violent reaction."

Israel had formed a special millennial task force uniting police detectives, agents of the domestic secret service known as Shin Bet, and members of the Mossad, Israel's foreign intelligence service. All of them were working in coordination with the FBI and the CIA to monitor the extremists. The Israeli task force was conducting undercover operations and moving to deport those who prophesied a bit too loudly that the millennium was a time when the Holy Land would see "the war to end all wars," as spelled out by the Hebrew Bible's prophet Zechariah and in the New Testament book of Revelation.

So on a warm day at the end of December, I set out from Jerusalem for the roughly two-hour drive northward to the Jezreel valley and the biblical "Armageddon." The place had been fashioned into a tourist attraction. And if indeed the final battle between good and evil was imminent, as some believed, a ticket for admission was going to cost spectators 18 shekels, or about U.S. $4. But the attendants wanted me to know there was plenty of free parking. Six air-conditioned tour buses idled in Armageddon's parking lot, which the attendants told me had recently been expanded to accommodate millennial tourists. For years the site had attracted 200,000 tourists annually, and in the year 2000 Israeli tourism officials expected the number to double.

A steady stream of tour groups from Europe and America shuffled past the ticket booth and made their way up a steep hill to a rocky outcropping, which featured the layered archaeological remains of some two dozen lost civilizations destroyed by one war after another through thousands of years of history. The crowd of curious tourists eager to see one of the most dramatic archaeological sites in Israel were almost all religious pilgrims of mainstream denominations and were primarily interested in the biblical significance of the hilltop. Only a handful were biblical literalists with apocalypticist expectations.

Jim Siske, a Southern Baptist from Iredell, Texas, was walking through the vast site, which includes remnants of prayer altars that date to 3000 B.C., horse stables for the chariots of warriors under King Solomon from about 1000 B.C., and a circular stone silo for grain storage from the same period.

"Yes, I believe in the literal interpretation of the Bible," said Siske, a retired history teacher, "so I believe this is the place where the battle that will end the world will happen. I believe there is a lot that tells us that we are very close to the time when these events will occur. Very close, a matter of days."

Siske was fringe. The mainstream Christian tourists tended to view Revelation, the last book of the New Testament, believed to have been written by the apostle John, as an allegory.

Jim and Florine Postel of Cincinnati, Ohio, were in this larger category. As their two young boys climbed over the rocks and ran through the ruins, they told me they were enjoying touring the site.

"We're on a millennial vacation," said Jim, 41, an architect and a member of an Episcopal church. "We are here out of curiosity, but certainly not for any sense of interpreting the biblical prophecies. . . . No sir, I see that as one big thing we aren't really meant to understand. And I just thought the kids would like this place."

The Rev. Valentino Cottini, a Catholic priest from Verona, Italy, was leading a group of twenty-five nuns from the Order of the Daughters of Charity deep into a 50-yard tunnel that dates back to 1000 B.C. The tunnel was used for gathering water when the ancient settlement of Megiddo was under military siege. Standing in the damp, dark passageway, Cottini explained, "The Book of Revelations and the passage referring to Armageddon has to be seen as a symbol, a metaphor of the battle between good and evil. It is not to be taken literally."

Sister Floria joked as she ascended the steep stone stairs, worn smooth through the ages, that lead out of the tunnel. "You don't have to worry about the world ending, but you should be very careful on these steps."

The hilltop of Megiddo looks out over the fertile plains of the Jezreel valley, one of the classic military theaters of history. The valley's foothills and wheat fields have long stood as silent witnesses to the bloodshed of war. The strategic hill—positioned along the crucial trade routes from Egypt to the south and Mesopotamia to the north—was conquered by the pharaohs of Egypt, the Canaanites, the Persians, and the Israelite kings. It is within that military context that the New Testament book of Revelations (16:16) describes Armageddon as the final battleground between the forces of good and evil. Historians have noted that the fortified city of Megiddo was destroyed and abandoned by the fourth century B.C. Yet it resonated as a place of battles epic enough for John, some five hundred years later, to cast it as the location for mankind's final conflict.

In modern times, the area around Megiddo was the site of World War I battles in which British troops trounced the Ottomans. A bit later, during the 1948 Arab-Israeli war, troops of the new Jewish state defended the land here against attacking Syrian and Iraqi forces.

On this day, the site was quiet—a serene perch from which to view the lush fields of the nearby kibbutz of Megiddo. Despite the serenity, Israeli police said they would post ten officers on the hilltop over the following three days to prevent deranged pilgrims from carrying out an act of millennial violence or perhaps mass suicide. Badran Ismael, the Israeli Parks Department manager of the small museum at the foot of the site, said, "We are afraid of what might happen here, and so the site will have to be guarded for the first time ever."

Vince Duran was the kind of guy they were worried about. He was a drifter, about 50 years old, his arms covered with apocalyptic prison tattoos. He told me he had left his trailer home in New Mexico, where he lived with his mother, to come to Megiddo to see the "spiritual war," as he put it, that he believed would begin the following night. "You are either a child of light or a child of darkness," he said, "and we will find out tomorrow."

But in the past year the Israeli police on the whole had focused less on the small number of believers in the end times who flocked to Megiddo than on the growing community of about one hundred evangelical Christians—mostly Americans—who had taken up residence just outside the Old City, on the Mount of Olives, where they believed Jesus would come to judge the living and the dead. One of their leaders was Brother David, who had come to Jerusalem from his trailer home in Albany, New York, eighteen years earlier, expecting to witness the Second Coming at any moment. In the fall of 1999 he still believed the event was imminent. I had joined the group in their weekly prayer meeting on the Mount of Olives, in a ramshackle Palestinian neighborhood called Al-Ayzariyah, which the Gospels refer to as Bethany, the place where Jesus raised Lazarus from the dead. Brother David, in his early 50s, lean and intense with a jet-black goatee and a thick shock of hair, stood before the group with a microphone and led his followers in prayer and song. Some spoke in tongues. Some danced. They referred to Jesus as "Yeshua," preferring the Hebrew rendering of his name. Brother Raymond, a 27-year-old ex-convict from the California state prison system who had found the Lord, recited his rap poetry full of the fire of sin, the fear of judgment, and the promise of redemption. Raymond was thin and handsome, although the white supremacy prison tattoos that covered his arms and chest gave him an ultimately menacing quality. His girlfriend, Sister Keren, who had been a stripper in Florida before she found Jesus and came to Jerusalem to wait for his return, moved gracefully about on a broken tile floor in a flowing white gown with purple flags, playing a tambourine and offering a fully clothed interpretive dance of the Holy Spirit.

"Hallelujah, the King of Kings is coming here! I believe that!" Brother David told his congregation. "I believe we are very close to the coming of Our Lord. We are in the right place at the right time, praise the Lord! But we can't just stand here. We have a responsibility, every born-again Christian has a responsibility to let the people know, to warn them of what is coming, so they can prepare."

As Brother David's companion, Sister Sharon, put it, "I just feel blessed out of my socks to be here for this!"

But Brother David, Sister Sharon, Brother Raymond, and Sister Keren—who had ripped up their passports and refused to provide their last names even to the Israeli authorities—never made it to the day that they believed was approaching in Jerusalem. A group of about forty Israeli police and soldiers, some clad in full combat gear, raided their homes in the middle of the night and arrested them and about twenty members of their faith community, including four children. Ed Daniels of North Dakota was not sure why he was spared arrest; but from an upper window of his apartment across the street, he watched the people he prayed with every day being hauled away by the Israeli police. The adults were bound in hand and leg irons and taken to Ma'asiyahu and Neve Tirza prisons to await formal deportation proceedings on the charge that they had overstayed their tourist visas and flouted passport control regulations. Israeli police told reporters that the group posed "a threat to public order" and that there was evidence that it was planning some apocalypticist act, perhaps a mass suicide. Brother David called me from prison and denied all of the charges, saying that he simply wanted to be present on the Mount of Olives to witness what he believed would be the final judgment and the return of the Messiah. "I wish you luck, brother," he said. "God willing, you'll be there to see it."

Others were deported along with Brother David and his followers. The most celebrated were the members of the Denver-based sect known as Concerned Christians, whose leader, Monte Kim Miller, had predicted that he would die on the streets of Jerusalem at the end of December 1999 and then be resurrected three days later. Fourteen members of the sect were arrested at two homes in the modern Jerusalem suburb of Mevaseret Tsiyon, where they had been living in preparation for the fulfillment of Miller's prophecy. Israeli police said they had unearthed evidence in their operation "Walk on Water" that the group was plotting to blow up the Dome of the Rock—an action that Israeli terrorism experts had long warned had the potential to literally set off a third world war by bringing one billion Muslims into conflict against Israel.

Another target of the millennium police was a 67-year-old street preacher known as Elijah, who for over a decade had wandered the streets of Jerusalem with his long gray beard, flowing white robes, sandals, and a black attaché case, telling anyone who would listen that he was the biblical prophet Elijah and that he was also one of two witnesses cited in chapter 11 of the Book of Revelation. He had begun to attract a following in the netherworld of "end timers" hanging out at the Petra Hotel, a low-budget hostel inside the Jaffa Gate, in the center of Jerusalem's Christian Quarter. The police picked him up for questioning, and persuaded him to leave the country.

Brother Solomon, 65, who was once Winston Rose, a New York City schoolteacher, led a congregation of about forty people who referred to themselves as Christian Jews and who came out of the Branch Davidian sect of Seventh-Day Adventists. They were co-believers with the followers of David Koresh. Most of Koresh's followers had met a fiery death in 1993, at the group's armed compound in Waco, Texas. Brother Solomon, echoing Koresh's prophecies, told of "a great war" in Jerusalem that would signal the coming of the Lord, and described it as imminent. He too was rounded up and deported soon after Elijah.

Amid this crackdown on the apocalypticist fringe, a group of twenty-six Irish pilgrims, many of them physically and mentally disabled children confined to wheelchairs, landed at the port of Haifa in mid-October. The group hailed from the Pilgrim House Community of Wexford, steeped in the social activism of Dorothy Day and the social justice tradition of the *Catholic Worker*. The leader of the group, Helena O'Leary, complained that they were denied visas and questioned for hours by border police, and that several members were roughed up by Israeli police and treated with utter contempt and suspicion. The group's intention was to bring the disabled young people on a pilgrimage so they could see and feel the spirit of the Bible in the land where the narratives took place. But in the Israeli media's reports, they were dubbed a "Doomsday Cult" of "Concerned Christians" and were linked with Monte Kim Miller's group. None of it was true. These children had never left Ireland before, and many of them had never left their wheelchairs, much less become entangled with some cult in the mountains of Colorado. The Israeli police and media thus revealed their glaring, even insulting, ignorance of Christianity, having failed to distinguish a ministry for the disabled within mainstream Catholicism from a fringe evangelical sect from Denver that sought meaning in the writings of Charles Manson and viewed the pope as the "the whore of Babylon." Whereas most of the other deportees had been people of marginal (and in most cases, ultimately harmless) theology, the Irish pilgrims were not. The Irish ambassador fumed throughout the month of December about the group's shabby treatment by Israeli officials, and demanded unsuccessfully that they be granted visas to return for the millennium celebrations.

The beliefs of Brother David and Elijah and Brother Solomon may seem like the fantasies of a jagged fringe of two-bit preachers and end-times hucksters. But their core belief in the Second Coming is a belief that is also central to mainstream Christianity. It is intoned by one billion Catholics every Sunday, at mass. Protestant church teachings likewise point toward this event with great hope and yearning. But the expectation is most imminent and feverish in evangelical Christianity. Theirs is a more literal interpretation of scripture, and one that is widely accepted in America. A *Newsweek* poll published in November 1999 found that 40 percent of American adults believe that the world will end one day just as described in the Book of Revelation.

The prophecies of doom, and the millennial expectations, have long existed beneath the surface of the American psyche. They came over on the *Mayflower* with the Pilgrims, whose beliefs were supported by the pillars of millennialism and a passionate attention to Old Testament prophecies and the role Jews were to play in the Second Coming. Two popular theological movements in the nineteenth century revived the millennialists' fervent belief that the End was approaching—one headed by William Miller, a Baptist farmer from upstate New York who believed the world would end in 1843; and another led by Englishman John Darby, who did not designate a specific year for the Second Coming but saw the restoration of Jews to the land of Zion as heralding that event. Americans who believed in this eschatology never abandoned their fervent hopes—not even in the late 1960s, when a secularized, hippie version of the millennialist movement emerged, coalescing around the idea of the "Age of Aquarius."

In the 1970s, these widespread yearnings for the end times were reflected in the wild popularity of Hal Lindsey's *The Late Great Planet Earth,* the best-selling book of the decade. It had sold over 30 million copies by the year 1999. Lindsey himself has headed a number of pilgrimage tours to Jerusalem. In the late 1990s, a series of novels by Tim LaHaye and Jerry Jenkins based on Christian prophecies of the

Apocalypse sold more than 9 million copies. Jenkins was a ghostwriter; the ideology was provided by LaHaye, a leader of the Moral Majority, who was virulently anti-Catholic. The first of the novels, *Left Behind: A Novel of the Earth's Last Days,* chronicles the final "rapture" as it is described in the New Testament. In the rapture, the faithful are taken up to heaven while the Lord judges those "left behind" on earth in a final war of all the nations that plays out in Jerusalem after the rebuilding of the Jewish Temple in the heart of the Old City. One of the central narrators of the novel is Buck Williams, a secular reporter for the *Global Weekly,* who is covering the war in the Middle East. Israel wins a miraculous victory through divine intervention, and Buck ultimately comes to believe that these events are a fulfillment of biblical prophecy.

In the real world of the Middle East, the days leading up to the year 2000 featured no war with divine miracles and no reports of "rapture." But some "experts" did see strange things going on. Yair Bar-El, director of the Kfar Shaul Psychiatric Hospital, had become famous for researching a unique psychological affliction that he had dubbed "the Jerusalem Syndrome." According to Bar-El, about a hundred people every year in Jerusalem become overwhelmed by the emotion and passion that the holy places can inspire in susceptible pilgrims and unwitting tourists. A smaller group of sufferers fall victim to a fleeting mental crisis in which they assume the role of a biblical character—Christ or John the Baptist, Mary Magdalene or the Virgin Mary. Bar-El said he believes the syndrome is caused by a psychic break in those disturbed by "the image versus the reality of Jerusalem." The sufferers (typically tourists with no history of mental illness prior to their arrival in the Holy Land) have been known to wrap themselves in white sheets from their hotels and to disrupt prayer services, shrieking about the wages of sin.

A colleague, Larry Kaplow of Cox Newspapers, and I went to see Bar-El, whose name fittingly enough means "Son of God" in Hebrew, at the psychiatric hospital's Jerusalem Syndrome unit. The doctor told us that he expected the problem of "Jerusalem Syndrome" to soar in 2000, amid what was anticipated to be a record 3 million tourists flooding the Holy Land, most of them Christian. The Israeli Psychiatric Society estimated that as many as 3,500 of those visitors would suffer some mild variation of "Jerusalem Syndrome"—not as severe as taking on a biblical identity, but more along the lines of becoming "overwhelmed emotionally" by the city and suffering a form of mental breakdown, or perhaps insisting that they were part of the actual playing out of biblical prophecy.

"Most of the sufferers are Christian, and almost all, Protestant," Bar-El informed us. "This is what our research has found." But as he explained his findings, I couldn't help wondering why this syndrome was exclusively reserved for Christians. What about the Islamic fundamentalists strapping bombs to their waists in the name of defending the al-Aqsa mosque? What about Jewish settlers who arrive from California and New Jersey believing they have a divine right to the West Bank, as spelled out in God's covenant with the Jews? What about the Chabad Hasidim, an ultra-Orthodox Jewish group that clings to a burning expectation of the messiah's imminent arrival—weren't they also fervently acting out biblical prophecies? Weren't they also "overwhelmed emotionally" (as Bar-El put it) by the power of Jerusalem? I was struck by the fact that Bar-El could label Christians who behaved in this way as having a "syndrome." But to the followers of his own religious traditions, with which he was certainly more familiar and had a more nuanced understanding, he found it not so easy to compartmentalize their strange spiritual wanderings into psychology's clinical terms. I thought about how people of different faiths can be tone deaf to each other's music and thus unable to distinguish a discordant and off-pitch sound within a certain melody. As Kaplan and I left the hospital, a young Chabad follower with a flowing white shirt and a rainbow *kippah* was dancing in the street in his own spiritual bliss. It was unclear whether he was a patient on the loose or just another resident of Jerusalem.

Psychological diagnoses notwithstanding, since the beginning of recorded history Jerusalem has had a community that believed it was living out biblical prophecies, especially those related to the end times. The belief is as ancient as the city itself. John the Baptist stood squarely in that apocalypticist tradition, and so, many biblical historians believe, did Jesus. How Jesus understood the end times in the teachings of the Hebrew Bible, in the books of Daniel and Isaiah, is an extremely controversial and vexing debate in theological circles.

The most commonly held belief among theologians of the established Catholic and Protestant churches is that Jesus sought to announce a whole new understanding of "the Time," and he did so in a way that the Jewish Galilean peasants would have understood as the fulfillment of the time they had prayed for, the time when God would show his special love for the Jews by breaking the bonds of servitude and finally, after so many epochs of suffering, exalting them among the nations. The first words Jesus speaks in the Gospel of Mark are: "The time has come: the kingdom of God is near. Repent and believe the good news!" (1:15 [NIV]).

Thomas Cahill, the author of *Desire of the Everlasting Hills: The World Before and After Jesus,* explains the passage as follows:

> Jesus's idea of the Time-That-Has-Come has no suggestion of catastrophe, no smell of fire and brimstone in it. Though present in his announcement is a challenge, his words caress the listener with welcome possibility. He does not threaten or condemn: he opens his arms to invite and encourage. The gentleness of this prophet is as unexpected as his message. . . . They are invited to shake off their worldly preoccupations and "open (their) hearts." The Greek imperative is "metanoeite," which means literally "change your minds." It is usually translated as "repent" or "convert," both more harsh than the Greek. The word certainly refers to a spiritual turnaround, but the change that is looked for here is an openness to something new and unheard of.

. . .

And so it was, with an Israeli police force both nervous and alert, and an Israeli public both indifferent and perhaps a bit curious, that the marking of the end of the second millennium of Christianity was upon Israel. New Year's Eve was a day of no significance on the Jewish or Muslim calendars, and it was of little significance to the local Christians. But because it fell on a Friday, it provided a strange confluence of worship within the three faiths of Jerusalem, where observant Jews were preparing for sabbath, Muslims were celebrating the festive last Friday of the Muslim holy month of Ramadan, and Western Christian tourists were pouring into the city. To watch these three streams of the faithful converge in the streets of the Old City, I took a perch at the Austrian Hospice, one of the great secrets within the ramparts just off the Via Dolorosa. The Hospice, built in the nineteenth century for the medical care of pilgrims to the Holy Land, has since been converted to an affordable hotel for the European pilgrimage crowd. It is secluded behind high walls, with beautiful gardens, and terraces that overlook the chaos of the Old City. The view from the roof is one of the best in Jerusalem. The two perches on the wall were a favorite spot of mine to have coffee and watch the city below on El Wad road, the main thoroughfare from Damascus Gate to the Noble Sanctuary and the Western Wall. Thousands of Orthodox Jews in black wool rushed to prayers at the Wall. And with the Ramadan holiday—one of the most important religious days of the Muslim calendar—some 200,000 Muslims, many in the traditional kaffiyeh and *jalabiya* (loose-fitting robes), thronged to noon prayers at Al-Aqsa. Tens of thousands of pilgrims from all over the world—America and Europe and Asia and Africa—saddled with their maps of the Via Dolorosa and video cameras and water bottles, seemed almost swept up in the wave of humanity that flowed like a river down El Wad road.

As evening set in and the long countdown to midnight began, I walked along the Old City walls down into the Kidron valley, toward the base of the Mount of Olives. There was a candlelight vigil there at the Roman Catholic Church of All Nations, just outside the olive groves of the Garden of Gethsemane, where Jesus suffered in agony before his arrest and crucifixion. Several hundred worshipers, mostly Catholic, had gathered there, along with at least one hundred reporters and photographers.

The streets of Jerusalem were eerily quiet; it was Saturday, and most Jews were observing the sabbath. There were no festive lights, no public concerts, and few open-air celebrations. This reflected the ambivalence that Israelis felt about what the rabbi and theologian Donniel Hartman compared to "hosting a party that is not your own." Perhaps due to this evident indifference to the occasion, a cosmic disappointment hung in the air in Jerusalem in the hours before the clock struck midnight. A little later, however, a bearded, middle-aged British man answered the prayers of those reporters looking for a crazy Christian to liven up their stories. A man who said his name was Richard arrived, yelling and screaming, in front of the Golden Gate, also known as the Gate of Mercy, where Jews and Christians share the belief that the messiah will return in judgment. The gate had been sealed and walled up by Muslims in the thirteenth century, and a cemetery placed in front, in the belief that a Jewish savior would hesitate to stumble over tombs and risk ritual impurity—or at least that's the legend. But a half hour before midnight on this last day of 1999, we all witnessed the coming not of the messiah but of this British fellow Richard, staggering drunk and screaming something about "the whore of Babylon" and "the mark of the beast" and several other apocalyptic prophecies. Quickly, he was dragged away by Israeli police—but not before a small army of photographers and reporters descended upon him.

Just at the stroke of midnight, I walked quickly along Saladin street in predominantly Arab East Jerusalem and over to the Garden Tomb, a small, pleasant forest of pine trees clustered around a cave and a stone burial chamber dating back to the first century A.D. The Garden Tomb was the Protestant answer to the dark and cluttered Church of the Holy Sepulcher, where the different Catholic and Orthodox denominations joust for space on the site where it was believed Jesus was crucified and buried. The Garden Tomb was discovered by the nineteenth-century British explorer Charles Gordon, who noticed a hill north of Damascus Gate that was in the shape of a skull, and theorized that it could well be "the place of the skull," or Golgotha. When he found an ancient rock tomb there, the place was given its current name. Over time, it developed into a place of worship for many Protestant Europeans who were put off by the musty and unruly Holy Sepulcher. The best biblical historians in the world still put their money on the Holy Sepulcher as the spot where the crucifixion happened, but the Garden Tomb seemed somehow truer to the emotional experience of a tomb and of sacred space. It was quiet and reflective there, and it somehow allowed believers to think more about the meaning of Jesus's death and resurrection within the context of their faith.

That night at the Garden Tomb, several hundred evangelical Christians were gathered for a raucous night of singing and prayers ushering in the New Year. Over coffee and cookies after the service, Pastor Wayne Hilsden of Jerusalem's King of Kings Church said: "It seems like the reporters were almost upset that nothing happened. But the only people who I ever heard talking about the new year as the time of the return of the messiah were on television and in newspapers. You do not hear that in churches. There's no theological basis for it."

From there I walked on into the vast darkness in the predawn hours that hung over Jerusalem, descended through the Damascus Gate and into the quiet of the Old City. Other people also were meandering about the lanes of the Old City, but only a handful. There was a strange silence to the place, and I wandered for hours, running into only small pockets of people—some college kids from America and Europe celebrating with a bottle of champagne, and a few religious pilgrims. Quickly, it seemed, dawn was approaching. As always, the first to rise in Jerusalem were the prayerful, then the bakers, and then the garbage collectors. A few Orthodox Jews were shuffling toward their synagogues for the first prayer. There was a warm glow of brick ovens in tiny bakeries that were busily making the morning bread, and the smell of fresh-baked pita and warm sesame wafted through the Old City.

The world had not ended.

The dire predictions of mass suicides and plots to blow up the Muslim shrines on the Temple Mount seemed ridiculous in the quiet morning hours of New Year's Day. Many months later, when I checked back with Bar-El, he informed me that he had not seen a single case of Jerusalem Syndrome on New Year's Eve, New Year's Day, or surprisingly, on any day in the months after. There were no terrorist plots executed at the Dome of the Rock or anywhere else in the world; no Y2K-inspired chaos and no airplanes dropping from the sky as a result of glitches; no power grids knocked out in major cities. Nothing happened. And after the millennial hype, in the quiet of a new day and a new year, January 1, 2000, it seemed more relevant than ever to ask, Two thousand years of what? What precisely did the millennium measure?

The answer in the Holy Land was tangible, it was grounded in the hills of the Galilee near Nazareth and the narrow cobblestone streets of Bethlehem and Jerusalem, and stared you in the face. It was the history of the life of Jesus Christ, born two thousand years earlier, give or take a few, in a grotto on a rocky, terraced hillside in the ancient town of Bethlehem.

But the countdown to midnight—which was still passing from one time zone to the next—had become one of the great technological displays of the television age. Live coverage by the world's networks began at a place dubbed "the Millennium Island," an uninhabited piece of land in the South Pacific in the Republic of Kirbati, where the first stroke of midnight occurred. From there the millennium moved westward, with each stroke of midnight, and the festivities that surrounded it, being beamed back to America by satellite. After it raced past Bethlehem and Jerusalem, it crested with live broadcasts from the Royal Greenwich Observatory and then culminated in the scene of two million revelers waiting for the ball to drop in Times Square in New York City. And through it all, the sleepy, ramshackle town of Palestinian-ruled Bethlehem and the dark grotto where the infant Jesus was born couldn't really hold a candle to the glittering celebrations broadcast on live television.

Perhaps it was just easier to make this celebration secular and inclusive and part of a collective measure of time for the whole world. In globalizing the event, we needed to strip it of its spiritual context. But the fact remained that the chronology of time that brought us this big round number was derived from the Christian calendar. The chronology was established in the sixth century A.D. by Dionysius Exiguus, the first person to mark years from the birth of Jesus, which he fixed as A.D. 1, with the initials standing for *anno Domini,* or "the Year of Our Lord." But Dionysius Exiguus miscalculated, many historians now believe, and the actual birth probably took place four to eight years earlier.

This first Christian calendar also had a built-in error left over from the Julian calendar of ancient Rome (established by Julius Caesar), which led to its losing one day every 128 years. So in 1582, Pope Gregory XIII reformed the calendar by lopping off ten days and refining the system of leap years to avoid the occurrence of discrepancies in the future. So that's how we got where we were on January 1, 2000—on a calendar that was more of an art than a science in dating the exact birth of Jesus.

Although it was immediately adopted by the Roman Catholic countries of Europe, the Gregorian calendar was not immediately accepted by the rest of Christendom. England and its overseas colonies (including the future United States) did not accept it until 1752, and it wasn't until 1918 that Russia came on board. Some churches within the Eastern Orthodox tradition still have not adopted it, which explains why Greek Orthodox Christmas falls on January 6 and Armenian Orthodox Christmas falls on January 19.

This Christian calendar stood out in Jerusalem against the two other religious calendars, the Jewish and the Muslim. On the Jewish calendar, the year was 5760. In other words, regarding the arrival of the third millennium, the Jewish response is "Been there. Done that," in the words of one Israeli writer. The Muslim calendar marks time from the Christian year A.D. 622, commemorating the prophet Mohammed's exodus from Mecca and his arrival in Medina. It was there that Islam declared that the Age of Ignorance had ended. And according to this lunar calendar, which has 354 days to a year, we were in the year 1420. So the third millennium for Muslims was still 580 years away.

Still, in our era, the Gregorian calendar had become the conventional measure of time, leading the *New York Times* to opine, six days before the millennium, "Within this context, 2000 no longer refers to the cyclical, ritual time of a particular faith, but to the more linear chronology of historical time." This comment struck me as puzzling. Just because the world uses the Christian calendar, does that make it no longer a Christian calendar? Perhaps this was putting too fine a point on it. But shouldn't it be viewed as both a Christian calendar, or a ritual time for that specific faith, and a universally accepted chronology of historical time? One need not exclude the other.

The millennial fervor that so gripped the Western media, that entranced a fringe of American and European evangelicals camped out on the Mount of Olives, and that stirred so much anxiety in the security establishment of Israel and in the FBI, meant nothing to the Christians of the Holy Land. The extended Palestinian families of Jerusalem and Bethlehem and Nazareth, who saw themselves as part of a continuous presence of the Christian faith for two thousand years in the land, watched these apocalypticist contortions with amazement; these were bizarre deviations from their faith and from the realities of their often difficult lives. Their community, and its quiet exodus, were far removed from all the noise of the millennium.

The indigenous Christian community is what the apostle Peter referred to as the "living stones" of the church, the living community upon which the faith is built. The steady exodus of these living stones from the Middle East in the past century made for a particularly poignant irony in a millennial year in which some three million Western Christian tourists were expected to flock to the Holy Land to see dead stones, the cathedrals and monasteries featured in their tour books. To indigenous Christians, the phrase "the end of days" had a sharp statistical meaning to it as they saw their local parishes slowly withering away.

. .

This "end of days" was reverberating in the Christian and Armenian quarters of the Old City. After the millennium craze had quieted and the tourists had left and the apocalypticist fringe had sublimated its manic energies, I was taking a stroll through the Old City and stopped in to see the Sandrouni brothers, who own Jerusalem's finest pottery studio, just across from the Armenian Convent of St. James.

The Sandrounis were artists, and their work was a beautiful family tradition.

Inside the shop, the brothers were unusually quiet and seemed weighed down by something. Finally, the news came out that one of the three brothers, George, had made a decision to emigrate with his wife and children to Canada. The impending breakup of a family like the Sandrounis, which had such a successful business and such a strong tradition in Jerusalem, was sending shock waves through the community. One more Christian family gone.

The Armenians are a Christian community with a historical presence of at least 1,600 years in Jerusalem. They represent the intersection between pilgrimage and the living presence since the first wave of Armenians came in the fourth and fifth centuries as pilgrims and never left. They are a classic example of the Christian existence "in the in-between" in Jerusalem. Some stridently assert the Palestinian identity. Others carry Israeli passports and say that they are Israeli. They straddle the divide between the two; and in some ways they have been a critical bridge between the communities at some of the worst moments of Israeli-Palestinian tension. All have a deep attachment also to their Armenian roots.

The origin of the Armenians goes back to the biblical story of Noah's ark. They are an ancient culture that originated in a region that is now divided between northeastern Turkey and the Republic of Armenia. The symbol of Armenia and its people is Mount Ararat, the mountain upon which tradition holds the ark rested when the waters of the Flood receded. The Armenians were the first people to make Christianity a state religion, which they did in A.D. 301.

As early as the late fourth century, Armenian pilgrims began arriving in Jerusalem, and some stayed on, forming a tight-knit local community. Today the majority of their descendants consider themselves Palestinian by nationality and Armenian by birth. The Ottoman Turks conquered Armenia in the sixteenth century and ruled over most of it for the next four hundred years. The Armenians were governed by the patriarchate in Istanbul. In the late nineteenth century a growing nationalist movement by the Armenians was brutally suppressed by the Turks. In 1915, during World War I, the Turks carried out what is commonly referred to as the Armenian massacre, the first genocide of the twentieth century. Some two hundred villages and cities were destroyed and burned, and in the rampage and the subsequent forced marches into the desert, an estimated one million Armenians were killed. This fact of history has given many Armenians a feeling of kinship with Jews: Systematic efforts have been made to wipe out the identity and culture of both peoples. But the Israeli government's refusal to officially recognize the slaughter of Armenians as genocide (largely due to Israel's valued diplomatic ties with Turkey) also has embittered many Armenians toward Israel. George's father, Hagop, survived that genocide and arrived in Jerusalem with a group of orphans. Both of his parents had died in a forced march through the desert. The Armenian story is particularly poignant, and Jerusalem is central to that story—not only for its spiritual significance to Christians but also as a sanctuary where a people found refuge and endured. That the Armenian presence here was dying out was a profound development in the general exodus of Christians.

Later, I stopped in again to visit with George while he waited for a moving truck. At his home in the Armenian Quarter a shipping agency was carrying out of his home a beautiful old piano and artwork, antique pottery, books, children's furniture, and old family photographs that told the story of generations of a family in Jerusalem. It was sad to think of all that culture and heritage and tradition encased in bubble wrap and prepared for a container shipment that would end up in Toronto in about six weeks.

"In this land it is very difficult to feel community in a community as small as ours, and here community is everything. We live very well here, really, in a lot of ways. We get along with the Palestinians and the Israelis. But the problem is the economy, the stress, the insecurity. As a parent, I have a responsibility to my family, to my children. If my daughters stayed here they would not even have a young man from our community to marry. There are more in Canada than here. I don't expect anything from anyone, so why does everyone expect so much from us? Why does everyone want us to stay? I mean you have to do what is right for your family, right?" George asked, looking for approval as the movers loaded the truck.

In the Armenian Quarter, the word was spreading of his departure, and the pressure was extraordinary. This was in part because the Armenian community was truly in danger of disappearing within the next generation. The church claimed there were only 1,500 Armenians left in Jerusalem, but the Armenians themselves said the real number was closer to 800, and many were elderly. (In 1948 there had been 6,000 Armenians in Jerusalem, and by 1967 the number had dropped to 3,000.) There were on average 30 deaths and only 10 births each year. George's two brothers were also considering moving to Canada or America, but they had not yet decided and seemed to be leaning away from it.

In the Sandrounis' shop, the dialogue about the family's exodus was nonstop. Each time a Christian prepared to leave Jerusalem, it was like watching a funeral procession. George Hintlian, a sociologist, translator, and leader of the Armenian community, was in the shop one day when I dropped in, talking to the brothers. He invited me for coffee around the corner so that we could discuss the family's departure in private. "I have had many opportunities to go abroad," he said angrily. "All of us are tempted by that. But we have a responsibility to the living church. This place is not a museum. I think we have an obligation to stay that extends to the world's Christian community, not only to ourselves." Later, in a gentler, more melancholy mood, he confided that he was at times melancholy, perhaps lonely. He had watched almost all of his high school class and most of his neighbors in Jerusalem emigrate; and now the Sandrounis were going. "Every family that leaves is a blow, especially a family like the Sandrounis," he told me. "They are very successful, so their departure cuts to the core, and suddenly everyone feels they should just pack up and leave. I don't like this subject, the decline of Christians. It has become a very important subject and we can't not talk about it anymore. But I don't like it. History does not like losers."

There was a political dialogue that ran parallel to discussions of emigration. And that was that many Armenians are angry at their patriarchate for failing to use the considerable endowment it has built up to provide financial backing to the Armenian community in the form of improved housing and business loans and investments. The often frayed relationships between the Christian communities and the clerical hierarchies is at the core of the debate over why the Christians are leaving the Holy Land.

The patriarchates not only oversee spiritual matters and the administration of churches but they also control vast real estate holdings. The Armenian patriarchate holds about one-sixth of the entire Old City and is considered to have the most open and valuable real estate in this coveted sacred space. The Armenian patriarchate (and even more so the Greek Orthodox patriarchate) has been accused of selling land to Israeli Jewish agencies and entities, which the larger Palestinian community fears is part of a long-term strategy to expand the Israeli influence and increase the Jewish character and presence throughout the Old City. "We are extremely worried about settlers in the Old City. As more people leave, they are waiting so they may attempt to buy up the properties," explained Hintlian.

Militant Jewish settlers in the Old City have carried out dozens of land takeovers, arousing anger and bitterness among their Palestinian neighbors. The organization Ateret Cohanim, which is dedicated to establishing a Jewish presence in the Old City and to rebuilding the Temple, carried out a particularly notorious seizure of St. John's Hospice, a Greek Orthodox property that was being run as a hotel. Ateret Cohanim chose Easter week 1990 to seize the property. About one hundred armed settlers swarmed into the hotel and unceremoniously tossed the Christian artwork and crosses out the window into a heap. They claimed the property had originally been owned by Jews who had been forced out in the 1929 riots. According to lawyers who knew the facts of the deal, Ateret Cohanim had purchased the lease from a protected tenant, thus "reclaiming" the property. The deal was brokered behind the scenes by a shadowy character named Shmuel Evyatar. This thin, bearded former Mossad agent had been stationed in southern Lebanon during the civil war in the mid-1970s, and in the year 2000 he was Mayor Ehud Olmert's adviser for Christian affairs. The takeover became an international incident after Israeli police roughed up the Greek Orthodox patriarch as he led a protest march on Holy Thursday.

Evyatar and the Ateret Cohanim group say they were simply exercising their right to buy land in Jerusalem. But Hintlian and other Palestinian leaders rightly point out that this was no mere private acquisition of land by an individual but a state policy that traditionally has been backed and funded by the Likud Party power structure within the Israeli government. (The funds used to purchase the lease on St. John's were traced to the Israeli Ministry of Housing, which at the time was headed by Ariel Sharon.) The intense competition between Israelis and Palestinians to decide who will own the deeds to the sacred space of the Old City is one of the most raw and contentious in modern Jerusalem. Palestinians who sell their property or transfer their leases to Israelis are killed as collaborators. The Israelis are reported to be offering huge sums of money to the patriarchates in other backroom land deals that are nearly impossible to trace. Many such deals have been struck over the decades.

After coffee with Hintlian, I went back to the Sandrounis' shop to say good-bye to George. The heated discussion was still simmering. Just then a family of three sisters came into the shop. Ani Voskarejian Montgomery lived in Toronto. Her sister, Tina Voskarejian Markey, lived in Reston, Virginia, and Alice Voskarejian lived in Boston. The whole family had been born in Jerusalem but pulled up stakes in 1963. They knew what George Sandrouni was going through, and they were actually exchanging addresses so that they could get together with him and his family when they arrived.

Ani was talking about what it felt like to be in Jerusalem for the first time since the Israeli capture of the Old City, and describing the shock she felt when she saw Israeli police in the Holy Sepulcher actually pushing a crowd of tourists. "That Holy Sepulcher is two thousand years of our history, and what is right there underfoot as you walk through it? That is Armenian mosaic. I think of this ancient connection we have to this history and to think of it disappearing is just overwhelming. It is very sad."

"George, you can't leave," Ani said, turning to him as he wrapped a set of bowls that she had bought. "There are going to be no Armenians left."

"Okay, you move here and I'll take your house," said George with a smile and a laugh, trying to serve a customer and not let the emotion of this topic get the best of him.

But Ani kept pressing, saying, "There is no one left in the churches here on Sunday morning."

Then George, with much more of an edge in his voice, said, "What do you want us to do? Should we stay here so you can come to the shop once every thirty-five years?"

After Ani and her sisters had left with their packages of gifts, George said under his breath, "The only thing I want to do is to jump off this sinking boat as soon as possible."

III

The Vicar of Christ on Earth

March 27, 2000

POPE JOHN PAUL II shuffled forward and reached out across history to touch the Western Wall. His white satin cassock shone in contrast against the massive, yellow-gray Herodian stone—all that remains of the Second Temple, the holiest site in Judaism, and the symbol of yearning for its people from the time of their exile until their return to Jerusalem two thousand years later. He paused. His hand trembled with age as he laid it on the stones and paid respect to Judaism, the faith he referred to as "the older brother" of Christianity. In the history of Christendom, no pope had ever made such a gesture; nor had any other pope, since the apostle Peter's time, even stood in this place. Peter would have passed by this wall (which was actually a retaining structure of the Temple Mount) as he ascended Mount Moriah in the company of Jesus, during the days leading up to the feast of Passover, just before the Last Supper. Forty years later, the Temple would be destroyed at the order of the Roman general Titus.

John Paul II's twenty-two-year papacy had taken him all over the world, but no journey was more important to him personally and spiritually, he said, than this pilgrimage to the Holy Land. He wanted to focus on spiritual renewal for the church, and on what he termed "soul searching on the threshold of a new millennium." To be in the city revered by the three monotheistic faiths was the defining moment of his papacy, the culmination of his theology of reconciliation and interfaith understanding. It was something he had been planning since the start of his papacy in 1978.

Now, frail and stooped, at 79 years of age, he was fulfilling a lifelong dream. Throughout a reign that had changed the face of the world and that had been pivotal in bringing about the most far-reaching political event of the late twentieth century—the collapse of communism and the opening up of the Soviet Union—John Paul II brought a presence, a power, a spirituality, and a grace that resonated at the end of the second millennium of the Christian faith. But as he faced the Wall, he was also confronting the dark history of a Christian millennium that was book-ended by the slaughter of Muslims and Jews in the eleventh-century Crusades and by the genocide against Jews in the twentieth-century Holocaust. These historical atrocities had shaped the destiny of this land. Now the pope had come, in the spirit of humility, to confront the church's failures and to seek forgiveness from, and reconciliation with, the people of the land—Muslim, Jew, and Christian. He was seeking a way forward, at the edge of a new millennium, via a spiritual cleansing of the past.

Following a Jewish tradition, the pope placed a message to God in a crevice of the ancient stone wall. The typewritten words, signed in his hand and sealed with the Vatican stamp, read, "God of our fathers, you chose Abraham and his descendants to bring your Name to the Nations: We are deeply saddened by the behavior of those who in the course of history have caused these children of yours to suffer and, asking your forgiveness, we wish to commit ourselves to genuine brotherhood with the people of the Covenant." (This message was later removed from the Wall by Israeli officials, framed behind glass, and placed in Yad Vashem, the Holocaust memorial.)

The historic sojourn marked what the Vatican had decreed a "Holy Year of the Great Jubilee," an intersection of sacred time and sacred space that celebrated two millennia since the birth of Jesus and the beginning of Christendom. The pilgrimage, the pontiff decreed, was not intended to be political. But this was the Middle East, and he was the pope. Everything about it was political.

In March 2000, the Israeli-Palestinian peace process was at a critical juncture. None of the issues that beset it—especially the nationalist struggles for the earthly Jerusalem—could be avoided on this trip. Although he recognized this fact, the pope preferred to play the role of listener. In doing so, he allowed the two sides of the Israeli-Palestinian divide to tell their own narratives. And that in itself was an important contribution toward reconciliation

But this trip was motivated by practical concerns as well, by a global political dynamic, for this man was the spiritual representative of one billion Catholic souls worldwide. The pope was inextricably pulled into the larger institutional and political concerns of the church in its dealings with the 1.2 billion Muslims of the world and the 14 million Jews in Israel and the diaspora. No issue more consumed the people of these faiths, Islam and Judaism, than the Israeli-Palestinian conflict. How would the Holy See fulfill its commission to seek justice, in a land where the church itself had perpetrated so many injustices for which it needed forgiveness? The political considerations of the Israeli-Palestinian conflict, even the questions of justice, seemed somehow smaller than the pope's abiding concern for the very soul of the church. But both weighed on his visit.

Shouldering all of these heavy counterweights, the pope had little strength left to address another, less prominent issue: the dwindling Christian presence in the land where the faith began. The Palestinian Christians' faint voice would barely be heard in the resonant dialogue and the somber silences and the triumphant symbolism of this historic journey.

. . .

John Paul II completed his pilgrimage in two legs. The first was in Egypt in February, and the second came in March, when he passed through Jordan and on to Israel, and finally Jerusalem. Along the way, he was treading "the path of salvation," as he called it. He was the most traveled pope in history, having made some 90 official trips to more than 120 countries. Some of those travels changed the face of the world, such as his momentous journey in 1979 to his native Poland, which shook the foundations of communism. By some historians' accounts, his blessing of the Solidarity labor movement presaged the collapse of the Soviet Union.

Throughout the years, the pope had spoken out forcefully against unbridled capitalism and child labor. The Catholic left claimed this mercy too often fit within a conservative paradigm that did little to challenge the oligarchies and corporate powers that created the injustices and their attendant suffering. John Paul II was unbendingly conservative on social issues, as signaled by his strict opposition to married clergy, homosexuality, contraception, divorce, priests in politics, and women in the priesthood. But this tall, ruggedly handsome, polyglot Slav persevered in what he believed was the mission of the church. He stood as witness to the sufferings of the former Yugoslavia and Lebanon. He prayed in war zones and quiet chapels. He met with presidents and kings in their palaces and the poor and powerless in their slums. He communed with clerics of all faiths. He took a bullet in 1981, and some believe his survival was a miracle. After recovering, he met with his would-be assassin, an Islamic militant from Turkey who was purportedly inspired by the Russian KGB. He forgave his assailant and then petitioned for his release.

Through all these sojourns, the "pope mobile"—the special Mercedes outfitted with a glass-enclosed bubble—was an important symbol. It reflected and facilitated the pope's desire to reach out to people—for him to see them and for them to see him. John Paul II had waved and cast blessings from this mobile throne to what must have been hundreds of millions of people. It was the perfect vehicle for the first pope to embrace television and to use it to spread his message. In its way, it had become his chariot.

But not in Jerusalem's Old City. Israel had surrounded the pope's visit with a force of 18,000 police and military troops. This surpassed even the millennial security detail in Jerusalem, and, police said, set a new record for the largest security undertaking in the history of the Jewish state. The Israeli security establishment dubbed it "Operation Old Friend." The police insisted that the pope ride in a white GMC Suburban, steel-reinforced against bombs and bullets. It provided better protection than the pope mobile and, equally important, better cornering in the narrow alleyways of the Old City.

As his motorcade lumbered through the streets, John Paul II peered out from behind the tinted windows of the Suburban, his view a narrow, artificially confined one. The streets had been carefully cleaned and the fronts of shops freshly painted. As the cynical local media observed, the fresh paint only reached to a height of approximately six feet—in other words, just as much as the pope would see from his view in the Suburban. And the paint and polish were visible only along the route the pope would take. Beyond that, there was little attempt to clean or revamp the often grim, filthy reality of the Old City's Christian and Muslim quarters.

Again for security reasons, the Israelis had ordered all shops closed and imposed a curfew in the Old City that prevented people whose homes were situated along the pope's path from going outside during much of that day. Understandably, Israel's legitimate security concerns were enormous. But the exacting standards of implementation of security measures meant that John Paul II traveled through a seemingly empty relic of a city full of holy shrines but void of a living community. There was no glimpse of the typically crowded, chaotic Palestinian Christian and Muslim neighborhoods, the spice shops smelling of cardamom, saffron, cinnamon, and Arabic coffee. There was no sense of the heart of their family traditions and ancient observances. There was no sense of their sufferings, of the rampant drug use, the high unemployment, the municipal neglect of the Christian and Muslim quarters. It was as if the Israeli government had fashioned a stage-set designed to create an impression of Jerusalem as a clean, efficient museum of faith.

The pontiff's motorcade made its way toward the Church of the Holy Sepulcher, the Crusader-era church venerated as the site of Golgotha, the outcropping of rock upon which Jesus was crucified and near which his body was placed in a stone burial chamber. I was standing nearby, in an alley ten yards off the Via Dolorosa, with a group of about 150 Palestinians, most of whom were Christians. They were pressing up against metal barricades and craning to catch a glimpse of the pope's motorcade. They were old ladies with shopping bags and young men with slicked hair and shiny silver crosses, elderly gentlemen with red-checked kaffiyeh covering their heads, and couples with baby strollers, all leaning forward, struggling to get into a position to see the spiritual leader of one billion Catholic souls. Israeli police and soldiers forcefully pushed the surging crowd back. As the advance cars of the motorcade arrived, the crowd pressed harder and the soldiers struggled for a minute to hold their ground, then pushed harder, forcing the crowd back into the alley. Curses were hurled at the Israeli soldiers by Palestinian teenagers safely situated near the back of the throng.

And then the white Suburban, its tinted windows reflecting a kaleidoscope of gray stone and the backs of the soldiers' green uniforms, turned the corner. Though it was not possible to see the pope, the crowd was in his presence and realized it. There was a hush. The pushing stopped. Several people crossed themselves. An old woman with black rosary beads twisted in her gnarled hands whispered a Hail Mary in Arabic. There was a stillness after the pope disappeared around the next corner. Just then an Israeli military jeep at the rear of the motorcade missed the sharp turn and smacked into a stone wall that lined Christian Quarter road. The Palestinian crowd released a small cheer and laughed bitterly at the Israeli soldiers. The driver smirked at the crowd, backed up, negotiated the turn, and drove on.

For these indigenous Christians—the Greek Orthodox, Roman (Latin) Catholic, Greek Catholic (or Melkite), Syrian, Armenian, Anglican, Lutheran, and other streams of Christianity—the pope's visit was a powerful witness of their role as a nearly invisible minority. Of course, those who belong to Orthodox and Protestant denominations do not recognize the primacy of the bishop of Rome (the pope's official title). In fact, the historical divisions and petty rivalries among the Catholic and Orthodox, as well as the haughtiness of the Protestants, were legendary in Jerusalem. Still, to most local Christians, the pope's visit was a time to momentarily halt those quarrels. I watched the crowd as they blessed themselves down the line as the pope passed, and it was evident they were a mix of all the denominations of Jerusalem's Christians. The act of blessing oneself in a symbolic reference to the cross was a kind of secret code here that revealed on which side of the Orthodox-Catholic, East-West divide one stood. The Roman Catholics bless themselves from head to chest and then left to right, across the heart. The Greek Orthodox and the Melkites cross themselves from head to chest and then right to left, and do so with the thumb and first two fingers joined, in honor of the trinity. The fourth and fifth fingers are tucked into the palm to honor the two natures of Christ—human and divine—in one person. This interpretation of the nature of Jesus is a central tenet of the Byzantine church, which has insisted, since the earliest councils of Christianity, that the doctrine be proclaimed in word and symbol. This was the theological underpinning of the deep division between Catholics and Orthodox—which had just as much to do with geopolitical and economic realities as with religious interpretations. The worldwide attention focused on the pope's visit must have been a bit awkward for the Greek Orthodox hierarchy, whose insecurity and resentment toward Rome's claims of supremacy were legendary; but all of that history of divisiveness seemed for this moment in history put aside.

This was an especially long-awaited opportunity for solidarity among the entire Palestinian Christian community, which shared a difficult history under modern Israeli rule and a more distant legacy of Muslim domination. These indigenous believers of Christianity were fiercely proud of their roots in the very beginnings of the church—whether they were Catholic or Orthodox or Anglican or another denomination. And when they waved the small yellow-and-white Vatican banners handed out along the way, they were reminding the world, and perhaps themselves, of that.

It has been said that this is a land of tribes with flags. The Israelis have the azure Star of David between two lines of the same hue set against white, in the pattern of the traditional Jewish prayer shawl. The Palestinian nationalists have their red, green, and black flag—outlawed until 1993 in the West Bank and Gaza, and now the symbol of a nascent state. The Islamic movement has a green banner featuring the central prayer of Islam written in Arabic calligraphy. The Palestinian and Islamic flags were often flown together at Palestinian gatherings and rallies. As one Christian from Nazareth told me, "Christians have no flag. But when the pope came, we found we had a flag and we wanted to wave it." Waving that yellow-and-white Vatican banner may also have been a kind of distress signal, a plea to the world to recognize the steady erosion of the local Christian presence. That Palestinian Christians along the motorcade route were held back, kept from a direct view of the pope, was an apt metaphor for the age-old experience of Arab Christians: being overlooked by the powers of Western Christendom, caught in a hinge of history between the East and the West, between the ascendancy of the modern Jewish state and the contemporary rise of political Islam. In this sense the pope's view from his bulletproof Suburban was similar to the vista from the air-conditioned tour buses that ferry around most Western Christian pilgrims to the Holy Land. Through tinted windows and tilted perspectives, the local Christian population was obscured from view.

Many local Christian leaders were profoundly disappointed by the pope's inattention to their community during his visit. They were especially upset that a meeting scheduled that day in Jerusalem with local representation of the Catholic Church had been canceled at the last minute. Efforts to reschedule the meeting were unsuccessful, leaving many in the local clergy feeling slighted.

. . .

The idea of a "Jubilee Year" has roots in the Torah. It was defined as a celebration every fifty years for the people of Israel. When the appointed year arrived, it is written in Leviticus, liberty was proclaimed for Israelites who were in bondage to their own countrymen. (The price of a slave in ancient Israel was based on how close the sale date fell to the Jubilee.) It was to be a time of personal reflection, and a time to leave the land fallow. In one of Jesus's most radical sermons, at the synagogue in Nazareth, he challenged this notion of Jubilee by reemphasizing the universal ideas of human freedom that were enshrined in the prophetic tradition of Judaism. Jesus said that God was announcing not just the Year of Jubilee for the Jewish people but a new and perpetual jubilee that would grant freedom to all, Jews and Gentiles alike, who were held in bondage. It was God's gift of economic and political freedom from all tyranny. Sometimes referred to as "Jesus's Manifesto," this sermon represented the rabbi from Nazareth at his radical best. But by the late thirteenth century, the Church of Rome had distorted this radical theological meditation on freedom as a marketing strategy to increase the contents of its coffers. The scheme was to encourage pilgrimages to Rome by announcing that in the Jubilee Year any such visit would absolve one of sin. It was a kind of spiritual frequent-flier program for the Middle Ages. The tradition was so brazenly exploited through the next centuries that it lost all spiritual meaning. But in the year 2000, the pope sought to restore its true meaning and brought the idea back into consciousness by calling for pilgrimage to Rome and to the Holy Land. Of course, once again it was helping the Vatican coffers, and it was expected to increase tourism revenue in the Holy Land. But more than that, it was intended as an invitation to a spiritual reawakening to the original message of the radical rabbi railing against occupation from a synagogue in Nazareth.

The pope arrived on February 24 for a three-day visit that would take him to Cairo, the city to which tradition holds the Holy Family fled from the wrath of Herod and the "Slaughter of the Innocents" after the birth of Jesus. He presided over an outdoor mass for Egypt's small Roman Catholic population of 150,000. (The overwhelming majority of Egypt's roughly 4 million Christians are Coptic Orthodox.) He also met with the revered sheikhs of Al-Azhar, the oldest and most prestigious theological seminary in Islam. From Cairo the pope traveled through the rugged desert wilderness to St. Catherine's Monastery, at the base of the harsh, red granite peaks of Mount Sinai, where God delivered the Ten Commandments to Moses. The monastic community founded here in the third century still endures as the oldest and longest continually inhabited Christian monastery in the world. The pope had dreamed of holding a historic interfaith meeting here, with Catholic and Orthodox Christians, the chief rabbis of Israel, and the head Islamic clerics of Egypt. But again, church politics and the deep division between the Eastern and Western rites got in the way. The age-old tension between Rome and Constantinople hung heavy in the air as the Greek Orthodox bishop, after receiving John Paul II, left the garden to say a separate mass in the chapel.

The pope spoke alone to the crowd from a stage set in an ancient olive grove and shaded by a single blooming almond tree, in a garden within the Greek Orthodox compound. With a dry wind rushing down from the jagged peaks of Mount Sinai, he said: "In this year of the Great Jubilee, our faith leads us to become pilgrims in the footsteps of God. We contemplate the path He has taken through time, revealing to the world the magnificent mystery of His faithful love for all humankind. Today, with great joy and deep emotion, the Bishop of Rome is a pilgrim to Mount Sinai, drawn by this holy mountain which rises like a soaring monument to what God revealed here." He paused. "God revealed man to man himself," the pope said, his face creased with age, his hands trembling slightly. He stopped and looked out at the crowd of only a few hundred who had managed to make the trek to the remote monastery, a six-hour drive from Cairo through the Sinai desert. And then he repeated, "God revealed man to man himself." He continued, "Sinai stands at the very heart of the truth about man and his destiny." There was an urgency in his tired and often hoarse voice borne on the dry desert breeze.

After Egypt, the pope would return to Rome to prepare for the next stage of his pilgrimage. On March 20, he arrived in Amman, Jordan, where he ascended Mount Nebo, the peak from which Moses looked out toward the Promised Land. Moses himself went no farther; but the pope continued on the path, descending the winding roads from Mount Nebo through the village of Madaba, with its well-preserved sixth-century mosaic map of the Holy Land. Some 400 meters below sea level, in the desert wilderness near the Dead Sea, the pope blessed a newly discovered archaeological site—the remains of a Byzantine shrine believed to mark the site of John the Baptist's ministry. It is, archaeologists believe, the likely spot where John would have baptized Jesus.

On March 21, the pope traversed the same desert (albeit by helicopter) that Joshua had charged across to conquer Jericho, and that Jesus had wandered for forty days after his baptism. He landed in Tel

Aviv, a sprawling, modern Israeli city. John Paul II was the first pope to visit Tel Aviv since 1964, when Pope Paul VI had made a short trip. Paul VI's trip came at a time when Catholic culture was still steeped in wrongful teaching on the Jews and when the church hierarchs were in the process of reexamining their long-held "teaching of contempt." Within this teaching, the logic went, the fact that the Jews had been subject to so much suffering was proof that that they were accursed. Paul VI's predecessor, Pope John XXIII, had sought to change this tenet as part of his radical reorientation of the church through the Second Vatican Ecumenical Council. As papal envoy to Turkey during World War II, the future Pope John had helped save thousands of Jews from the clutches of the Nazis, and this personal experience had driven him to eagerly reappraise the earlier anti-Semitic teachings of the church. After his death in 1963, those teachings were repudiated in a profoundly important Vatican document titled *Nostra Aetate,* which marked the beginning of the thirty-five-year-old Catholic movement toward reconciliation with Judaism. But within the Vatican, the spirit of these changes had yet to take hold when Paul VI made his journey to Israel. Paul VI first visited the holy sites in Jerusalem's Old City, then under Jordanian rule. He then briefly crossed the cease-fire line from the West Bank to travel to the site of Armageddon, which was under Israeli control, before going on to Nazareth. He spent no more than a few hours in the country, never once uttering the words *Israel* and *Jews.* (Instead he referred to Jews as "Children of Abraham's covenant.") He avoided Yad Vashem, the Israeli holocaust memorial, and made no official visits to any Israeli government buildings—for to do so, the Vatican felt, could be construed as recognition of the state of Israel. Just before he left, Paul VI made a speech in which he pointedly praised his mentor, Pope Pius XII, who reigned during World War II. Jews remembered him as a man who turned his back on them and did little to prevent their slaughter by the Nazis.

John Paul II's visit was dramatically different in tone, and his presence embodied the change in the church's relationship to Judaism and the state of Israel. First of all, this pope had devoted a great deal of effort to Jewish-Catholic reconciliation for two decades before he even set foot in the Holy Land. In 1986, the pope had prayed at Rome's main synagogue, during the first recorded visit of any pope to a synagogue. And he had made numerous statements about the common ground between Catholicism and Judaism, and the need to reassess the church's teaching on Judaism and to confront its past anti-Semitism. These efforts were met with sharp criticism by many Jews and some Catholics who perceived them as too little, too late—especially given the pope's insistence on the beatification of Pius XII. But even his harshest critics would agree that John Paul II had done more to redefine relations between Jews and Catholics than any before him, and that his attempts were profoundly important. These efforts culminated in the signing in Jerusalem of the Fundamental Agreement that established full bilateral relations between the Vatican and Israel on December 30, 1993. The preamble of the agreement made clear that this document was much more than a standard diplomatic recognition between states. It was a historic act toward the reconciliation of the Catholic Church with the Jewish people.

To understand just how profound a transformation this was, and how significant the pope's visit would be to Israel, consider the reply of Pope Pius X to Theodor Herzl, the founder of modern Zionism, in January 1904, when Herzl asked for Vatican support of the then fledgling Zionist enterprise. According to Herzl's diaries, the pope had replied: "We are unable to favor this movement. We cannot prevent the Jews from going to Jerusalem, but we could never sanction it. As the head of the Church, I cannot answer you otherwise. The Jews have not recognized our Lord. Therefore, we cannot recognize the Jewish people; and so, if you come to Palestine and settle your people there, we will be ready with churches and priests to baptize all of you."

The Vatican's refusal to establish full diplomatic relations with Israel when the new state was founded in 1948 was about more than theology. It was about political opposition to Israel's occupation and annexation, beyond the U.N partition agreement, of lands including the town of Nazareth and many Christian villages of the Galilee. Israel's declaration of Jerusalem as its capital, the Vatican felt, violated the understandings of the 1947 United Nations partition plan, which proclaimed that Jerusalem, as a city holy to three faiths, should be ruled by an international body. There was also the matter of the dispossession of Palestinians, about half of whom were Catholic.

In 1967, when Israel captured the West Bank and Gaza and East Jerusalem, including the Old City, the Vatican's opposition to the occupation became even more strident. With Israel annexing East Jerusalem, including the Old City which held the Church of the Holy Sepulchre, the Church's political and financial interests were at stake. The Church also had communities, institutions, large property holdings, and other assets in various Arab countries throughout the Middle East, and the Holy See feared that a rapprochement with Israel would jeopardize these interests. The Catholics—both lay and clerical—in Israel, the West Bank, Gaza, and Jerusalem were Palestinian, identified with the Palestinian cause, and were strongly opposed to any change in the status quo as long as Palestinian and Israeli interests were in conflict.

Pope John Paul II had been consistent in upholding that half-century history of unwavering Vatican support for the aspirations of Palestinians. But the Vatican's political positions in relation to Israel evolved along with the global and regional realities that opened up the opportunity for the historic 1994 Israeli-Palestinian peace agreement. The Soviet Union was collapsing, and the Gulf War had reconstituted relations between the Arab world and the West, which opened up the possibility for regional peace. If the Palestinians and the Israelis were talking to each other, why shouldn't the Vatican join in the dialogue? It was in this context that the Holy See formally moved to establish official ties with Israel as well as with the Palestine Liberation Organization. On February 15, 2000, just one month before his visit to the Holy Land, Pope John Paul II balanced the agreement between Israel and the Vatican by signing a Basic Agreement between the Holy See and the Palestine Liberation Organization. The most controversial passage in the agreement concerns the future status of Jerusalem, which both sides claimed as their capital. The ownership of Jerusalem was among the most emotionally charged issues awaiting resolution in a peace plan. After Israel captured predominantly Palestinian East Jerusalem in the 1967 war, it annexed East Jerusalem and tore down the barbed wire and checkpoints that divided the city, declaring Jerusalem the "eternal, and indivisible capital" of the Jewish state.

The Vatican-PLO document challenged Israel's claim to Jerusalem as its capital by declaring "an equitable solution for the issue of Jerusalem, based on international resolutions." The document stated, without mentioning Israel by name, that "unilateral decisions and actions altering the specific character and status of Jerusalem are morally and legally unacceptable." This wording was not significantly different from the position on Jerusalem held by virtually the entire international community, including Israel's chief ally, the United States, which did not recognize Jerusalem as the official capital of Israel. This is why foreign embassies are in Tel Aviv, not Jerusalem.

The United States maintained that official diplomatic recognition of Jerusalem as Israel's capital would come only at the end of the peace process, after the two sides had resolved the status of Jerusalem. The agreement's reference to a prohibition against "unilateral decisions" echoed the language used in the peace agreement Israel had signed with the Palestinians. But nevertheless, the Israeli government was furious about the Vatican-PLO agreement, especially about the passage related to the future of Jerusalem. And it was in this heated political environment that the pope prepared for his journey.

Just before the pope arrived in Jerusalem, I was invited to meet with the Rev. David Jaeger, a Franciscan friar and Vatican lawyer who had drafted the Holy See's agreements with Israel and the PLO. I waited for him in the lobby of the Notre Dame Center in Jerusalem, an elegant nineteenth-century Catholic monastery that had been turned into a hotel and convention center. Jaeger strode toward me, a whirlwind of words and energy. He used his shoulder to hold a mobile phone to his ear and spoke loudly in Hebrew while he simultaneously fumbled with the *corda,* or rope, of his traditional brown Franciscan habit and then cinched it tightly around his considerable girth. He clicked off the mobile and then began ordering a taxi in Italian at the front desk. Then he told me in English, "Okay, we have exactly fifteen minutes."

Father David may well be the first and only Israeli-born Jew to become a Catholic priest. His father was a diplomat for Israel in Latin America, and as a boy Jaeger often lived abroad. During his travels as a young man, he was greatly influenced by the message of the Catholic church, and he chose to convert, entering a seminary and eventually undergoing ordination to become a priest. He quickly became one of the Vatican's top lawyers. To me, he represented the perfect embodiment of the Byzantine complexities of the Holy Land in the year 2000—a Jewish priest representing the Vatican on both sides of the Israeli-Palestinian fault line.

"What the church has done is to exert itself on the universal nature of Jerusalem as the locus of a religious and cultural heritage that is of concern to all humankind. Therefore the aspects of the universal significance of Jerusalem must be anchored in a legal provision on the plane of international law," he said. "Both of these agreements are very similar statements which have a great deal to say about the meaning of Christianity. In the preamble to both, the article stated most emphatically is the one concerning freedom of religion and conscience. This is the meaning of 'witness,' in the Christian sense. Since to witness requires freedom, the Christians become agents for freedom. This is what the church is about. Our work on the legal agreements is to make a change in the status of Middle East Christians from tolerated subjects whom we have to somehow keep on the reservation into free and equal citizens. If they are free and equal, then they will not leave."

I was surprised to learn that Father David did not share my concern about the diminishing Palestinian Christian presence and in fact was annoyed by the campaign that some concerned church officials in Jerusalem were trying to build around the issue of emigration, which for decades had been encouraged by the church. Since at least the 1970s, though, there had been an awareness within the Vatican of the need to stem the tide before the living community of the church was gone altogether. The Catholic Church had provided universities, subsidized (and in many places free) housing, and virtually every incentive it could think of to keep the local Christian population in the Holy Land. The Notre Dame Center was one such enterprise, a beautiful old building that had been refashioned as a pilgrimage hotel and convention center. It was also a kind of Catholic public works project, offering local Christians jobs as waiters, cooks, and hotel administrators. But Father David was among a minority within the Catholic hierarchy who regarded these efforts as suspect. He referred to them at one point as a kind of "welfare state" and an attempt to keep local Christians "on the reservation." He was a firm believer that the Christian community would have to decide for itself that it wanted to stay, and that the church should focus on fostering within the community a personal and spiritual commitment to the Holy Land. He saw the pope's pilgrimage as a resonant way to build that conviction among the dwindling Christian population.

. . .

On March 22, 2000, Pope John Paul II journeyed to Bethlehem to begin what he called "the heart of my pilgrimage." There, the pontiff celebrated an outdoor mass in Manger Square.

Yasser Arafat, sitting in the front row in his signature olive-green military fatigues and kaffiyeh, was almost unable to contain his joy at playing host to the pope in Bethlehem. Arafat was beaming amid the trappings of statehood that came with this papal visit, reflecting its significance for the emerging Palestinian state and for Arafat's place in history.

Arafat's wife, Suha, was also there. She had been born Christian and had converted to Islam when she married the Palestinian leader. A circle of Christian Palestinians who know the inside story of her sudden and surprising wedding ceremony in 1994 say that Suha had a difficult time with her conversion. Islam does not require conversion for a woman "of the Book" (as Christians and Jews are referred to in Islam) who marries a Muslim man. But it is expected socially that such a woman will convert, and it was a political necessity that Suha do so, given her husband's position in the Arab world. When Suha married Yasser, she knew she was marrying the cause. (Still, those who know her say that she remained emotionally very attached to her faith, especially after the birth of their daughter.) Suha wore a black dress with a veil. She held Arafat's arm throughout the mass, helping him follow the order of worship, the readings from the Bible and the responsorial psalm printed in the program handed out before the service. She repeated the prayers in English as Arafat sat silent. Suha had brought a small black Bible of her own, carrying it into the service under her arm.

Arafat has always been attentive to the Christian minority within the Palestinian community, and some officials of the Palestinian Authority have criticized him for coddling the Christian minority in a way that causes their ostracization from the larger group. Arafat seems to have a genuine concern for the diminishing local Christian presence as well as a shrewd understanding of Christians' importance to his own political, diplomatic, and fund-raising missions throughout the Western world. Arafat has been attuned to the resonance of Bethlehem and Jerusalem during his frequent trips to France, Italy, and America. On these trips, whenever he spoke of a Palestinian state with Jerusalem as its capital, he evoked the images of Jerusalem's church spires along with the Dome of the Rock. When he spoke in Arab countries, the church spires were more often left out and the Islamic requirement to protect Al-Quds was stressed.

At the end of the mass, Arafat was so excited that he broke all Vatican protocol and bounded up the steps of the outdoor stage that served as the altar. He hugged the pope and kissed his hand, and turned and smiled in the direction of a thick forest of cameras mounted on tripods to the left of the stage.

The pope soon left Arafat and the crowd and the cameras and quietly shuffled into the Basilica of the Nativity, descending the steep stone stairs worn smooth through the ages by pilgrims, to the stone grotto where a gold star on a marble floor marks the place where the infant Jesus was born. For twenty minutes, with only candlelight and a Bible as companion, the pope remained in solitude and contemplation. Then he emerged from this stone womb into the light of the earthly, crowded, and poor city that is modern Bethlehem.

He visited the Deheisheh refugee camp, making his way through streets scrawled with pro-Palestinian graffiti and strewn with litter. Deheisheh is part of a network of camps, from the West Bank to Jordan and Lebanon, in which some 1.5 million refugees uprooted by the wars of 1948 and 1967 still live in squalor and wretched conditions. "Your torment is before the eyes of the world. And it has gone on too long," the pontiff said, speaking in a schoolyard packed with refugees from the camp and teenagers who had climbed the low-lying buildings that surrounded it to catch a glimpse of the pontiff.

The words should have resonated among this Palestinian crowd, but Arafat had failed to provide a translator from English to Arabic. The Palestinian television station also failed to provide translation, and the powerful statement of solidarity was lost to those who needed to hear it most. It seemed a depressing but somehow fitting scene for a Palestinian leadership (including the PLO's head of refugee affairs, Assad Abdul-Rahman, who made a long speech) that had long been accused of exploiting the suffering of its refugee population for its own nationalist, political cause, and of doing little to alleviate their plight. The refugees listening were roughly pushed away from the pope by Palestinian troops. Frustrated Palestinian teenagers who had waited to hear the pope were tired of being pushed, and began to shove the Palestinian police back. Not long after the pope's motorcade left, violence broke out. In a spontaneous burst of anger directed against their own police, the youths began rioting. For the foreign press assembled for the visit, it was a new vision of the West Bank—Palestinian youths throwing stones at Palestinian police. The Palestinian street was swelling with anger at Arafat and increasingly impatient with the failures of the peace process. This anger was just beginning to push its way to the surface in a way that was starting to worry the circle of advisers around Arafat.

In the following days, the pope continued his journey through the land. He conducted a mass at the Basilica of the Annunciation in

Nazareth, before the largest gathering of his trip. Some 70,000 believers came together on the hills overlooking the Mount of Beatitudes. The pageantry of the event—beginning with the pope's grand entrance, through a crowd waving national flags and banners of welcome, into a natural amphitheater overlooking the Sea of Galilee—seemed lifted from another century, or perhaps from one of the pope's much-loved European Cup soccer matches. The crowd chanted in unison, "John Paul II, we love you!" Among the flag-wavers were tens of thousands of college students from France, Germany, and Poland. There were clusters of immigrant workers from the Philippines and Nigeria, who lived in Israel serving as nannies and house cleaners and cheap labor, and who were helping to replenish congregations emptying through emigration. There were congregations of pilgrims from Mexico and Costa Rica and South Korea carrying banners announcing the names of their churches. American pilgrims had flown in from Detroit and Denver, Boston and Boise. Fully half of the crowd, more than 30,000 people, were members of an international Catholic movement known as the Neo-Catechumenal Way, which emerged in the slums of Madrid a quarter century earlier and is flourishing in Europe and Latin America. The movement, a politically conservative, evangelical wing of the Catholic Church, advocates adult catechism and baptism, and service to the poor.

The crowd of pilgrims speaking English and French and German and Portuguese and waving their national flags was leavened with a sprinkling of several thousand Palestinian Christians. The Palestinians were mostly Israeli citizens from the villages of the Galilee. A small number were traveling on special permits from the West Bank and Gaza. Most were Roman Catholics, largely from the Melkite community in the Galilee. There were also a few Greek Orthodox and Anglican groups. A large percentage of Palestinian Christians who had come from the West Bank and Gaza were seeing the Galilee for the first time. They had been prevented from visiting the region before, they said, by the system of Israeli permits and the humiliating searches of all Palestinians traveling past the military checkpoints that separate the West Bank and Gaza from the interior of Israel.

Shehade Didas, 28, a Greek Orthodox Christian from Jerusalem, said the Israeli police had confiscated a large Palestinian banner that he had tried to bring to the ceremony. Other Palestinian youths also complained that their Palestinian flags had been taken. In a field ringed by a fence of Israeli flags, these few thousand Palestinians were swallowed up in a sea of French flags and German flags and American flags, yet were not permitted to fly their own.

It was difficult to avoid the mud on this hillside where Christ once preached the Beatitudes. A cluster of six young Palestinian Christian women from Bethlehem University were seated on a green garbage bag, which they had laid down. They just couldn't stand any longer, they said. They were yawning and exhausted as they listened to the pope's sermon echoing out over the hillside in English. If they were tired, it was easy to understand why. They said they had been told by the Israeli authorities that they would have to leave the Palestinian checkpoint at 11 P.M. the night before in order to ensure, given security measures, that they would be at the site of the outdoor mass by the appointed hour of 6:30 A.M. It was roughly a three-hour drive from Bethlehem to Korazim, the village in the Galilee where the mass was held. So they had dealt with about four hours of searches of the bus by Israeli soldiers and delays at the checkpoint. For all six of the students, it was their first time ever traveling to the Galilee.

Shereen Ghannam, 22, a Roman Catholic from Bethlehem who was studying education, said, "It's our land. We have not been able to see it. Why?" She wanted to know if I thought any of the other Americans and Europeans in the crowd understood the restrictions she was under as a Palestinian, or the difficulty of life under occupation in the West Bank.

A group of Americans from Denver sat only a few blankets away. The Americans were more prepared for the mud, with thick camping tarps, and clad in their L.L. Bean and EMS rain parkas and their Timberland hiking boots. They had that warm, healthy, Colorado glow and invited me to share some trail mix as I sat down to talk to them about the pope's visit. It turned out they were all followers of the catechumenist movement and members of Denver's St. Louis parish. There was a programmed quality to their spirituality that seemed far from the Catholicism I knew. Theirs was more evangelical and more literalist, and had none of the mystery and metaphor of the more traditional, ethnic church that I knew from the Boston archdiocese. Peter Waymel, 22, like many American college kids, was thoroughly absorbed in what the trip meant to him personally. He said, "This is part of a process of living in the dimension of the cross, like, a growing process as we study and learn and live Christianity as an adult. You know?"

So a question about Palestinian Christians knocked him a bit off kilter. "Well, like, we haven't really looked at the politics here. I mean I didn't know there was a real problem with the Christians here. Are they actually Palestinian or are they, like, American or Europeans who live here?"

Not everyone in the group of young people was as disoriented about the reality around them. LeAnne Gechter, 23, a college student in Denver, said she and several friends had accepted an invitation from a Palestinian Catholic priest to travel to Jifna, a Christian village in the West Bank, located along a Roman road where tradition holds Mary and Joseph stopped on their way from Nazareth to Bethlehem. "All my life I saw the news on television and the image is always Palestinians fighting and shouting. The image was always that they were Muslim and different. I don't know, not like us. But here we were celebrating the Word with this community who were so welcoming. I learned a lot. It changed the way I see things here."

. . .

The pope's pilgrimage rolled on from the Galilee back to Jerusalem, where the most emotionally powerful moment in the pope's visit would take place. The papal motorcade climbed the roadway named after Theodor Herzl, to Yad Vashem, Israel's Holocaust memorial. The way into the memorial is lined by two rows of carob trees and is known as the Avenue of the Righteous Gentiles, named for the non-Jews who risked their lives to save Jews from the Nazis. The papal motorcade stopped before the Hall of Remembrance, a mausoleum like structure made of great slabs of basalt and fronted by a heavy black iron gate. The pope entered the hall, which was lit by the somber, flickering glow of "the eternal flame" that burns in a broken bronze vessel. The walls are built of boulders, and the cold, gray cement floor gives the place a sepulchral ambience. The ceiling slopes upward to a rectangular hole reminiscent of the apertures through which the gas poured into the asphyxiation chambers, and of the chimneys of the crematoriums where the bodies were burned. In the center of the hall is a flat stone mosaic of the names of the twenty-two largest death camps. And in recessed niches in the hall lay the ashes collected from death camp crematoriums, including the largest ones in Poland. This hall is more than a memorial; it is an enduring, twentieth-century symbol of the Jewish people and the state of Israel, the place where foreign dignitaries begin their visits to the Jewish state. The pope entered alongside Israeli prime minister Ehud Barak.

The pope listened to poignant remembrances of survivors. The mournful cry of a cantor prayed for the souls of the dead. At one point the pope seemed overwhelmed and appeared to wipe away a tear. "In this place of memories, the mind and heart and soul feel an extreme need for silence. Silence in which to remember," the pontiff said in the flickering glow of the flame. "Silence because there are no words strong enough to deplore the terrible tragedy of the Shoah."

This visit was the raw, physical encounter between the pope and his own haunting memories of the horrors of Nazi persecution of the Jews in his native Poland. Some of the hundreds of thousands who died in Polish death camps had been his childhood friends and neighbors; several of the survivors now sat in the audience, listening to the man they remembered as Karol Wojtyla. "I have come to Yad Vashem," he said, "to pay homage to the millions of Jewish people who, stripped of everything, especially of their human dignity, were murdered in the Holocaust. More than a half a century has passed, but the memories remain. . . . No one can forget or ignore what happened. No one can diminish its scale."

This was a crowning moment of the pope's devotion to interfaith healing and dialogue. But it was a dialogue conducted over the heads of the Palestinians. Most understood the need for it and respected it, but it was not a conversation the Palestinian people felt they were party to.

Well before World War II, Zionist pioneers began streaming into Palestine in large numbers. Some came seeking refuge from rising anti-Semitism in Europe, and others, to fulfill the dream of returning to the land of Zion. But in the aftermath of World War II, the mass immigration of European Jews into Palestine began to impose demographic and economic pressures on the native population and displaced many. Muslim and Christian Palestinians, who opposed the United Nations' partition of their homeland into Arab and Jewish territories, considered the Jewish state a colonialist project. They sensed that America and Europe, wracked by guilt over their failure to act sooner to stop the Holocaust, were turning a blind eye to injustices to Palestinians that a Zionist state would institutionalize. These Palestinian concerns were largely ignored by the United Nations, and Britain eventually withdrew from Palestine, permitting the state of Israel to be established. For the pope to focus on the Holocaust was, from the Palestinian nationalist perspective, effectively to avoid the moral questions involved in the present-day reality of the Palestinian-Israeli conflict—particularly, the profound question of the Palestinians' right to self-determination. The opportunity for the Holy See to gain a measure of moral authority by recognizing wrongs done to the Palestinians was lost in the overwhelming drive to acknowledge Christian Europe's responsibility for the Holocaust.

Palestinians' frustration with this reality sometimes translated into dismissal or denial of the Holocaust. I heard this expressed in hateful ways by young Palestinian Christians listening to the pope's message on the muddy hillside of Korazim (the biblical *Korazin* or *Chorazin*), a village that had infuriated Jesus for failing to understand his message and resisting conversion. There I spoke with James Kajjo, 26, a college-educated Roman Catholic from Jerusalem who ran his family's printing company. Even as the pope was celebrating mass, Kajjo told me, "Hitler was a good man. Look at what they did to raise up their country under him." I suggested he take a minute to talk to some of the German youths who were present at the gathering, and get their understanding of the evil committed during the Holocaust. Kajjo replied, "What do you want me to do? Cry? Because I can't. . . . What did Palestinians have to do with the Holocaust? Why should we pay the price?" I asked Kajjo how those thoughts squared with the message of the pope on this pilgrimage, and he shot back, "The pope will go back to Rome, but I am going to have to keep living here under occupation."

I had over my years as a reporter heard less crass but equally dismissive statements about the suffering of Jews in the Holocaust from Palestinian religious and political leaders, Muslim and Christian alike. On the eve of an interfaith conference to be led by the pope, Jerusalem's leading Muslim cleric gave a stunning example of this. Sheikh Ikrima Sabri, the grand mufti of the Al-Aqsa mosque, told a correspondent for the Italian newspaper *La Repubblica* that Israel had exaggerated the death toll of the Holocaust to garner international sympathy. "Six million? It was a lot less," Sabri said. "It's not my fault if Hitler hated the Jews. Anyway, they hate them just about everywhere."

These comments, which he repeated the next day to the Associated Press, provoked bitter responses in Israel and condemnation throughout the world. They cast a pall over the pope's interfaith meeting, and made it glaringly obvious just how much work remained to be done on the Muslim-Jewish side of the Holy Land's interfaith triangle. At the interfaith meeting, which took place at the Notre Dame center, just outside the walls of the Old City, the pope sat on a stage with the Ashkenazi chief rabbi Meir Lau to his right and the Muslim sheikh Taysir Tamimi to his left. At one point in the evening, Lau made a statement asserting that the pope's presence in Jerusalem confirmed Israel's sovereignty over the Holy City. Sheikh Tamimi was furious, and unleashed a tirade against Israel, at the end of which he walked out. On this occasion, the pope's determination to encourage interreligious dialogue could hardly be seen as anything more than a depressing failure. A news photograph from the meeting captured the spirit of this event, and perhaps a very human side of the pope. In the photograph, the pope, flanked by the rabbi on one side and the sheikh on the other, was covering his ears and looking distressed, as if he just couldn't take any more.

After the pope had completed his pilgrimage, a kind of growth industry sprang up for interfaith dialogue—what one Israeli derisively called the *dialogistas,* a collection of clerics and scholars who gather in one conference after another. They are mostly Christian and Jewish, and, sadly, very infrequently Muslim. They are also typically Israeli and Western, and almost never Palestinian. I have seen this pattern in so many interfaith conferences, even at the most enlightened forums. It is as if the Christian-Jewish dialogue takes place in a void, leaving out the indigenous Christians of the land. These Palestinian Christians have a different agenda, and, less encumbered by the history of the Holocaust, they are stridently persistent about more recent injustices, perpetrated by Israel.

In a letter headed "Concerning Pilgrimage to the Places Linked to the History of Salvation," the pope reflected on the meaning of his journey:

> The Great Jubilee is not just a series of ceremonies to be held but a great interior experience to be lived. External factors make sense only in so far as they express a deeper commitment which touches the hearts of people. . . . The pilgrimage to the holy places thus becomes a highly meaningful experience. . . . The Church cannot forget her roots. Indeed, she must return to them again and again if she is to remain completely faithful to God's plan. I therefore extend a warm invitation to the entire Christian

community worldwide to set out spiritually upon the path of the Jubilee pilgrimage.

I had set out on my own pilgrimage of sorts—following the path of Jesus's life, chronicling the modern realities and conflicts and efforts toward peace in the Holy Land in the year 2000. I little suspected then how this journalistic mission and the encounters I had with others along the way would change me, my attitudes toward my faith, and my views of the land and of the place of Christians and Christianity within it.

II

The Birth

The birth narrative of Jesus, as told in the Gospel According to Luke, begins in Nazareth, a poor, forgotten hamlet in ancient Palestine struggling under the Roman Empire. It was isolated—about ten miles off the Via Maris, the great trade route that linked Damascus with Gaza and Egypt, stretching from the Jordan to the Mediterranean. Mary was a young girl, no more than 15 years old, and betrothed to a local carpenter named Joseph. They were most likely illiterate Jewish peasants

In this spot on the distant fringe of the Roman Empire, Mary would have been brought up strictly in the Jewish tradition. Archaeological excavations reveal that the population of Nazareth in that era would have been no more than 150.

The Nazareth of Mary and Joseph was a harsh and solitary place, but although off the beaten path, it was still attended to by the Romans. Nazareth was, in this sense, an occupied village, and its residents lived under the heavy burdens of Roman rule and taxation. In the dreary reality of this village, Mary was retrieving water at a well when, Luke recounts, the angel Gabriel appeared and announced to Mary that she would bear a son, that his name would be Jesus, and that he would be "called holy, and the Son of God." This event later became known as the Annunciation.

IV

Nazareth

THE ANNUNCIATION

. . . God sent the angel Gabriel to Nazareth, a town in Galilee . . .

The angel said to her, ". . . You will be with child and give birth to a son,

and you are to give him the name Jesus."

LUKE 1:26–31 (NIV)

AN UNWAVERING SIREN pierced the air for a long minute. Then silence descended—a thick, impenetrable quiet that blanketed the streets of the modern Israeli community of Natzerat Illit (Hebrew for Upper Nazareth). On the sidewalks, people stopped in their tracks. At traffic intersections, cars and buses and trucks pulled over. Men and women and children alighted, and stood outside the vehicles as if at attention. At the town's cemetery, a stream of several hundred people pooled around the tombstones, having placed flowers there, pausing in prayer at the eternal flame that flickered in the afternoon sunlight. This was the full spectrum of Israel—young mothers with children in strollers, policemen in uniform, soldiers clad in green fatigues, construction workers still dusty from building sites, nurses from a nearby hospital dressed in scrubs, school children in matching white T-shirts, secular Russian immigrants, and members of the ultra-Orthodox Lubavitcher community. All of them were frozen in an intense reverence.

Remembrance Day was commemorated this way every year in Upper Nazareth, as in every other community in Israel. In every development town, every kibbutz, every moshav, and every city the same somber hush descended at the graves of the fallen, the same mournful chanting of the prayer for the dead. The entire Jewish state comes to a halt for this two-minute national reflection on the sacrifices made for the creation of Israel, and on all the wars fought since then for its preservation. It was always overwhelming to see the collective devotion, and the intense nationalism, of this country at this moment. It was May 9, 2000, Israel's fifty-second Remembrance Day.

After sunset on Remembrance Day, the somberness gives way to joyous celebrations of Israeli independence. Blue-and-white flags emblazoned with the Star of David flutter from the balconies of apartment blocks and the antennas of cars. Families head out for barbecues and picnics. Towns celebrate with parades and gala festivities. And as night fell on this particular Remembrance Day in Upper Nazareth, fireworks burst in the skies overhead, trailing off in a shower of blue-and-white sparks against the darkness.

Upper Nazareth was built in the early 1950s. Israel had captured and then annexed Nazareth after the 1948 war against the Arabs. Upper Nazareth was built as a settlement for Jews in the region of Galilee, which before the war had been a patchwork of overwhelmingly Muslim and Christian Palestinian Arab villages and towns. Today, Upper Nazareth was a planned community of wide streets, modern housing blocks, a huge shopping mall, and the sprawling construction of new neighborhoods. It occupies a high ridge looking down on the old Nazareth, which lies in a basin, across a deep canyon.

The biblical town of Nazareth clings to a slope of the Galilee hills. It has been likened to a wasp's nest—a sun-baked, brownish-gray hive of narrow, crooked streets and concrete houses stacked like cells atop each other. With a population of nearly 70,000, Nazareth is home to the largest concentration of Arabs living as citizens within the state of Israel, and it is the center of the Arab Christian community in the Galilee.

Though there is no wall or coiled razor wire or military checkpoints between modern, Israeli Upper Nazareth and old, Arab Nazareth, a formidable barrier separates the two. There are virtually no Jews in Arab Nazareth, which is roughly 70 percent Muslim and 30 percent Christian, whereas Upper Nazareth is overwhelmingly Jewish, with a few pockets of Israeli Arabs, almost all of whom are Christian. Only a small minority of the Israeli Jews of Upper Nazareth have any regular interaction with the Israeli Arabs of Nazareth. The two groups do not typically share the same schools, they infrequently work at the same firms or job sites, and they rarely mingle socially.

Down in the crowded streets of Nazareth, the shrill and unwavering siren blast that marked Remembrance Day brought on a moment of quiet tension—even seething resentment. None of the Israeli Arabs stopped on the street to honor it. Within the standard school curriculum, Israeli Arab children were required to prepare for the national holiday by studying Israeli history, drawing Israeli flags, and, if they chose to, joining in school assemblies and parades to commemorate the day. But the Israeli Arab students were drawn into the commemorative events half-heartedly at best, and many parents kept their children home from school on the days leading up to the holiday. Most Israeli Arabs referred to Independence Day as "Al-Nakba Day"—*al-Nakba* being Arabic for "the catastrophe," as Arabs refer to the 1948 war. More than 700,000 Arab refugees fled or were forced out of their homes in the course of that war, and those who stayed eventually became citizens of the new state of Israel. In recent years, though, the category *Israeli Arab* has grown controversial, as many members of this minority within Israel (about 20 percent of the country's population) feel that the term denies their heritage as Palestinians. It was becoming increasingly common for Israeli Arabs to call themselves "Palestinians living within the state of Israel."

Not surprisingly, on this Remembrance Day there were no Israeli flags fluttering from the antennas of Israeli Arab cars in Nazareth. The siren blast could be heard echoing down from Natzerat Illit, but the workday went on as usual. Some Arabs, or Palestinians, simply sat and sullenly stared. Others continued on their way with an air of defiance, seemingly stepping a bit more deliberately in a hastened pace as the siren wailed. Two narratives, two peoples—one the victor and the other the vanquished: the uncomfortable reality was never clearer.

. . .

On the outskirts of Nazareth, just before the Jezreel valley and its wide, flat fertile plain, the road came upon an open field—once the working farmland of the Palestinian village of Maalul. This was the site of intense fighting in 1948, as Israel cleared a path to take Nazareth causing the Palestinians of Maalul to flee their village. They were never permitted to return. On the morning of the fifty-second anniversary of the start of that war, about twelve Palestinian families who had been uprooted from Maalul and since lived in Nazareth were just beginning to gather for their annual picnic on the grounds of their ancestral village. Each year they laid down blankets and fired up barbecues. Most were employed by Israeli companies and kibbutzim, and so they had a two-day vacation for an Independence Day that was not their own. Instead, they commemorated "Al-Nakba" by telling their children of a time when this was their village and of the war in which they lost it.

After Israel declared its independence on May 14, 1948, following the Arabs' rejection of the U.N. partition plan of November 1947, the first Arab-Israeli war broke out almost immediately. Nazareth's inhabitants were fairly comfortable in the assumption that if partition did occur, a city so holy to Christendom would clearly be part of Arab Palestine. After all, this was spelled out on the map that had accompanied the U.N. partition plan. Nazareth therefore became an early refuge for those displaced by the sporadic fighting that had taken place before May.

In April 1948, when the Jewish fighters of the Irgun (the militant underground resistance organization led by Menachem Begin, a future Israeli prime minister) took control of the port city of Haifa, many Palestinians fled inland to Nazareth. Soon thereafter, fighting erupted in Tiberias, on the Sea of Galilee, and the Jewish forces of the Haganah (the largest of the Jewish fighting forces, out of which the Israeli army grew) began blowing up Arab homes there. The departing British troops sent buses to Tiberias, telling the fearful residents that the British could not guarantee their safety. The residents were transported to the neighboring state of Transjordan or into Nazareth.

Many fled, out of the fear that still lingered from the accounts of the massacre at Deir Yassin, an Arab village on the outskirts of Jerusalem. On April 9, 1948, fighters with the Irgun and guerrillas from the Stern Gang (named for its leader, Avraham Stern) invaded the village and committed some of the worst atrocities of the war. Estimates of the number of dead vary significantly. Official accounts claimed as many as 250 died; some Arab and Israeli revisionist historians have put the number closer to 100. There is little dispute, however, that a massacre was committed here. Women and children and in some cases whole families were murdered. There were allegations of rape, of the men of the village being paraded before a gauntlet of gun butts, and of the Jewish forces spitting on and cursing the Arabs before executing them. Three days after the Deir Yassin massacre, Arab forces attacked in reprisal, ambushing a convoy of Jewish settlers on its way to Mt. Scopus, where the Hadassah Hospital and Hebrew University are located. In the attack, 75 Jews—almost all of whom were either hospital staff or academics—were killed. The crowd of

Arab fighters that encircled the convoy shouted the reason for their act of revenge: "Deir Yassin!"

The Jewish village of Givat Shaul neighbored Deir Yassin. It was one of the more bitter ironies of this land that the old Palestinian village is now Givat Shaul Mental Hospital, the same one where I had visited with the psychologist Bar-El, who treats Christians suffering from "Jerusalem Syndrome." I had been to the village earlier with a Palestinian survivor from Deir Yassin, Ayesh Zeidan. He was 14 when the Jewish forces attacked his village and he ran barefoot into the night to save his life. Now he was in his mid-sixties and living in the West Bank town of Ramallah. I walked with him through his former village, past what were once elegant and spacious homes made of the beautiful old yellow limestone from a nearby quarry, where his father had worked. He remembered what life was like before the war, before all the killing. Many of his relatives and friends were killed that day. He told me that the village was once a monastery and that the Arabic word *deir* actually means "monastery." He remembered that there had been a few Christian families in the village when he was a child, but they had all left before 1948. The image was surreal—a Palestinian refugee walking through the fog of his own history as the twisted and distorted faces of the mentally ill peered out at him from the arched windows and terraces of an old, hand-hewn stone building that was once his family home. Bar-El's office, he told me, was on the foundation of one of the family homes. When the hospital's security guard discovered we were walking on the grounds, we were asked to leave. The only Palestinians who were allowed at Givat Shaul Mental Hospital were the poorly paid hospital attendants from Jerusalem. They changed the bedding and bathed some of the severely mentally ill patients, or occasionally pushed them in wheelchairs through the remains of the old village that was now synonymous with "Al-Nakba."

The 1948 Deir Yassin massacre, although swiftly condemned by the Haganah, touched off a wave of panic among Palestinians. Many fled their villages, believing they would return when the fighting was over. Others left because military and political leaders on the Arabic Voice of Palestine radio broadcasts were urging them to get out of the way; the war would be easier to carry out without civilians interfering with their offensives. Still other inhabitants of Palestinian villages and towns were simply forced out by the fighters of the Yishuv, as the emerging Jewish state was called.

Egypt, Syria, Iraq, and Jordan fielded armies that, on paper at least, seemed superior to Israel's in weapons and air power. But they were ill-led, and the Israelis were undaunted. Israel was able not only to hold the 5,400 square miles originally allotted to it by the United Nations but to expand its new state by 2,600 square miles, or nearly 50 percent. In June and July of 1948, Israeli troops converged for a military operation to overtake the Galilee. Between July 15 and July 18, Israeli armed forces quickly occupied Saffuriya, Mujeidil, Maalul, and a number of other Galilean villages. Maalul, southwest of Nazareth, was considered critical, because it allowed the Jewish state to connect the isolated kibbutz of Kefar Hahoresh with the land in the Jezreel valley that the state largely controlled. Saffuriya put up some resistance, but it was quickly crushed by a series of Israeli air attacks that left the fighters scurrying to the orchards and hills surrounding the village. The people of Mujeidil and Maalul surrendered largely without opposition, believing that they would soon be allowed to return to their homes.

Nazareth was one of the larger Arab population centers taken by force in 1948. Faced with annexing a Christian town so revered to the Christian world, David Ben-Gurion, Israel's first prime minister, ordered the military commanders to prepare a special occupation force with strict orders not to destroy or desecrate Christian religious sites. One brigade commander explained: "The conquest of Nazareth had a political importance. . . . Because of its importance to the Christian world—the behavior of the Israeli occupation forces in the city could serve as a factor in determining the prestige of the young state abroad."

Despite the Israeli leader's cautious approach to Christian Palestinians, the liberties lost and the fear and uprooting were the same for Christians and Muslims alike. Arabs of both faiths became refugees, pushing northward into Lebanon and Syria, southwestward into Gaza, and eastward into Jordan—726,000 in all. Of those, some 60,000 were Christians—that is, more than 35 percent of the total Christian population in Palestine prior to May 1948.

Before the end of the year, the United Nations General Assembly would pass Resolution 194, the first of twenty-eight different U.N. resolutions to affirm the right of the Palestinians to return home. Yet it was never implemented and would remain at the core of the conflict a half century later. The Israeli government has countered that the "right of return" should also apply to Jews who were forced to flee

Arab countries. Even then, most Israeli politicians, left and right, consider granting a "right of return" suicidal for a Jewish state—since its Jewish identity depended on ensuring the majority of the population was Jewish. The return of the Palestinian refugees would tip that balance. Many of these Christian refugees later emigrated to the Americas and Europe.

Some 150,000 more Palestinians—the vast majority Muslims—became known as internal refugees, having been uprooted from their towns and villages and forced to crowd into cities within the newly established Israel. As many as 20,000 ended up in Nazareth, camping out in the monasteries and churches and schoolyards of the local Christian community and tripling the population overnight. They lived in tents and in shacks fashioned out of scraps of wood and corrugated tin. They rented the homes of those who were fleeing, or stayed with relatives and friends. In the months after the war, it became clear that the demographic makeup of the historically Christian city of Nazareth had suddenly and irreversibly shifted from a 60 percent majority of Christians to a 60-percent Muslim majority. Middle-class Nazarenes, predominantly Christians, now found themselves cut off from their jobs in Haifa, Acre, and Jaffa, largely due to travel restrictions on Palestinians as well as to their replacement in the governmental bureaucracy by Jews. Farmers and laborers, predominantly Muslims, were uprooted from the fields they had harvested and the quarries they had worked for generations. Unemployment soared to well over 50 percent.

In the refugee camps outside Israel and in internal exile as well, Muslims and Christians were bound even more closely together as a Palestinian community by their tragedy. As neighbors, they joined in the joy of one another's religious feast days and family weddings and they shared the sorrow of funerals. At Mary's Well in the center of Nazareth, there was a tradition of marking crosses in henna; the Muslims would often mark the crescent of Islam as a way of showing reverence to Mary. The common culture included language, music, and food. Christians served date-filled cookies at Easter; Muslims, at Id al-Fitr. Pancakes filled with walnuts, cinnamon, and sugar were served at the Christian feast of Epiphany and during the Muslim holy month of Ramadan. The phrase Muslims and Christians alike used to describe their interfaith relationship fell naturally from their lips: "We are all brothers here."

. . .

The extended Bisharat family had for two generations gathered in the fields of Maalul every year on Al-Nakba Day. They were making coffee on an open fire and serving homemade pita bread dipped in olive oil and sprinkled with *zatar,* a local herb similar to thyme. Odeh Bisharat was surrounded by his wife and children, sitting on a log and ready to talk about why they came every year to this spot. They were Melkite Christians, but they were quick to point out that they saw no difference between the plight of Christians or Muslims when it came to "Al-Nakba." The suspicion ran deep in Nazareth that Israel and the West sought to divide Muslims and Christians, and any questions about Christians in this part of the land were typically met with raised eyebrows and often a lecture about how Christians and Muslims were brothers. The Bisharats and in fact most Arab Christians were comfortable only when their history was viewed as part of the larger dispossession of all Arabs.

"This is our village," said Odeh, who was in his early 40s. "My father was born here and he took us here when we were growing up. So I take my children. We have to know our history. The children have to know this is their homeland, and they have to know that one day they will have the right to come back. There is no difference in the way the Muslims and Christians suffered during the war. Our Muslim neighbors in Maalul were removed from their homes just as we were."

We had barely gotten past the introductions (and the two or three tiny cups of coffee that have to come before any serious talk can begin in a traditional Palestinian family), when a camera crew descended upon the picnic. They had come from Israeli television's Channel One, led by a producer named Riad Ali. With sunglasses, hair slicked back, and dressed all in black, Ali described himself as an "Israeli Arab." He worked on a freelance basis to report on his community and explained that he was trying to capture what "the average Arab and the average Israeli are doing on this day." I moved out of camera range, and asked my translator to fill me in on the interview. I was amazed at how practiced and precise the family's responses were.

"Fifty years ago," Odeh began, "my grandfather started this habit of coming here to the village of Maalul on this day. This was his village. And now this is the fourth generation who is continuing to come here." With that, he ruffled the hair of his young son. Odeh's brother Issa, a lawyer in Nazareth, then spoke up, and the camera shifted to him: "We do not teach our children to hate Israel, only to know what their right is and that their land has been taken away from them. They can respect the independence of Israel. But just like the Jews remember after two thousand years what was taken from them, we will never forget what was taken from us." He put his arm around his 12-year-old daughter Nardeen, and asked her, as if in a catechism, "Who used to live here, Nardeen?" "My grandparents were born here. This is my homeland," she said. Her father nodded his approval. Just then the tape ran out. As the cameraman apologized and quickly changed tapes, the producer asked them to repeat the last sequence. Issa picked up right where he had left off. He put his arm around his daughter again, and repeated, "Who used to live here, Nardeen?" It seemed that this branch of the Bisharat family had well learned its part in the drama.

The whole encounter lasted no more than eight minutes. As the television crew disappeared, so did the television smiles of the Bisharat family. They settled down on the blanket with more coffee. In a conspiratorial tone, they explained that for the last three years, different Israeli television camera crews had come to their picnics. Each time the TV crew had interviewed the family. And not once, as far as they could tell, had a story about Maalul ever aired on the nightly news.

The fact that the interviews had never aired in the past was an important reflection of the deep denial by the Israeli public about the impact the war of 1948 had on the lives of 700,000 people who had now, two generations later, become more than 3 million, according to U.N. estimates. A fuller version of history has been slow in entering the mainstream media outlets, especially the more conservative, government-run Channel One. As it turned out, Channel One did air a piece on Maalul. It did not run on Independence Day but the day after, and it characterized the Maalul residents as those who wish to "dwell on the past," contrasting them with another set of Arabs "more focused on the future," who celebrated their Israeli identity. The broadcast carried the patronizing feel of American coverage of race relations in the south around 1955. But at least the residents of Maalul were beginning to have their voices heard on the nightly news, which was more than had happened in the previous half century.

That there was a rehearsed sense of suffering among some in the Palestinian community did not mean that there was not also a genuine sadness at the injustices of 1948. Sitting off by himself on a rock under the shade of a pine tree was an elder of the family, Shafiq Elias Bisharat, born in Maalul in 1925. He was resting before his yearly walk up the dirt road from the fields to the narrow paths of the old village—or, at least, what was left of it. I offered to drive him. We bumped our way up the steep dirt path until it became impassable, and from there we walked into what remained of the town.

First we passed the Muslim cemetery, where weeds grew over toppled tombstones. Shafiq stopped to remember a few of the family names that could barely be made out on cracked and broken gray granite. "We were one soul," he said. At weddings it was traditional, he said, to have not one best man but two—a Muslim and a Christian. Now the cemetery was divided by barbed wire fencing, which circles the perimeter of an Israeli military site where the army had installed a missile battery to protect a nearby airport. Through the thicket of barbed wire and past a ten-foot-high pile of wooden ammunition crates, Shafiq pointed to the Christian cemetery, the headstones just visible above the overgrown grass. Shafiq said most of his ancestors were buried there but he had not been permitted to visit their graves for fifty-two years.

The path led to the remains of a mosque at the old entrance to the town. Its doors had been torn from their hinges, and the stairway leading up to the entrance had crumbled. A large section of the roof had fallen in. Graffiti were scrawled in Arabic on the walls: "We will return" and "Get out, thieves."

Another hundred yards up the path stood what was once the village's Melkite church. The Melkites are a breakaway Eastern Orthodox sect that accepts the primacy of Rome. They preserve most of the Orthodox tradition and the Byzantine liturgy but combine them with Roman Catholic traditions. This church, with its massive stone walls and vaulted ceiling, had been built in 1933. In more recent times, the stained-glass windows had been looted or broken out. The lintel over the front door—a relief sculpture of a cross set in a rising sun—was cracked. The stairway was smashed and crumbled underfoot.

Inside, the church's tile floor was covered in at least six inches of cow manure. A Bedouin tribe had used the church as a barn for years. Despite protests from the former residents, they said the Israeli army base and the nearby kibbutz had granted them permission (either that, or the Israelis chose to look the other way). In the hot midday sun, the stench of manure was almost unbearable. In one corner, the blackened pieces of Israeli army ammunition crates had been used as fuel. The stucco walls were covered in graffiti. Birds flew in and out of the open windows and the huge crevices in the crumbling masonry of the ceiling. A ceramic iconostasis, where icons are traditionally placed—in Orthodox tradition, dividing the inner sanctuary from the rest of the church—was covered in a gray layer of bird droppings. A cross at the center of the altar was cracked and broken in half. The children of the Palestinian families who returned to this site were running in and out of the church, and their voices bounced off its cavernous walls.

Two of Shafiq's sons, Marwan and Taysir, had just arrived, and several of Shafiq's grandchildren were adding their voices to the chorus of children playing, shouting, and laughing. "In all my dreams, I see myself back in this town. It was a life that you cannot imagine, a time of absolute happiness," said Shafiq, standing in the shadows of the crumbling church. "I feel there is a continuity when I hear the children of this generation come here. I hope that they will not live with only the dreams. I hope it will be a reality that they return someday," he added.

Taysir, accompanied by his two young children, had the day off from his job in an Israeli chemical processing plant in Haifa. Less dreamy than his father, he was of a newer, more pragmatic generation just trying to get by within the confines of life as a person with a Palestinian heritage and Israeli citizenship. When I asked him about returning to his ancestral land, he replied, "No, it will not happen. This is important for us as history now. But only as history. We would be foolish to come with a dream of returning."

Shafiq headed down the narrow paths of the village to the place where his family home once stood. It was barely possible to make out the boundaries of the old village from the overgrown cactus plants along the perimeter, which villagers had planted as a natural fencing. What once had been homes were now collapsed mounds of hand-hewn stones lying in an overgrown field. The Israelis, shortly after the war in 1948, had bombed and later bulldozed the entire village. Shafiq stopped at one heap of stones and a cracked slab that was once the floor of his parents' home. He walked to a crumbled, circular foundation built around a well just off to the side of the footprint of the former home, pried open a wooden covering over the twenty-foot-deep well, and stared down. "I dug this well with my own hands. It took me two years, and I had just finished when the war broke out," he said, as his grandchildren threw pebbles at a black snake squirming through the rocks at the bottom of the dry well. "We had nothing when we left here. We had to build ourselves up from nothing," he added.

As was the case in many villages in the Galilee, the history of the titles to the land in Maalul was a complex and tangled tale of real estate holdings during the British mandate and before, under the Ottoman Turks. A Lebanese Christian family, the Sursocks of Beirut, who were essentially absentee landlords, in 1922 apparently sold some five hundred acres of the Jezreel valley, which encompassed Maalul and several other villages, to early Zionist settlers from Europe. A 79-year-old descendant, Lady Yvonne Sursock Cochrane, told me the complicated family tale of real estate one afternoon in her home of faded elegance in a still bombed-out section of downtown Beirut. The land in the Jezreel valley, Lady Yvonne said, was bequeathed to the family under the Ottoman Empire by the sultan as a kind of royal trust. In a strict legal sense, she explained, it was not clear under Ottoman laws that the Sursocks held title to the land or had the right to sell it, since there were existing farming villages on the land. She remembered that it was her uncle, Georges Sursock, a wild man and ne'er-do-well, who signed for a sale of the property to pay off his debts "for gambling and for women," as she put it. His ownership of the land was bitterly contested by other family members, and she insisted that he had no right to auction the land without approval of the other family members. Over several decades, family members, including Lady Yvonne, filed several complex and ultimately unsuccessful lawsuits. Eventually, the title Georges had sold became part of the holdings of the Jewish National Fund (JNF), which had been founded in 1901 to buy and develop land in Palestine with contributions from the World Zionist Organization.

Officials of the British mandate contested the legal basis of the land purchase and other similar land deals that were taking place at the time. They argued that whole networks of villages could not be uprooted as the result of questionable deals. They suggested that the land be leased to the villagers, an idea that the JNF rejected. (To this day, the JNF leases its land only to Jews.) Finally, in 1946, the mandate courts worked out a deal by which the JNF would receive approximately 1,100 acres in Beisan, about twelve miles south of the Galilee, in exchange for the return to the villagers of Maalul and others in the area of their less valuable and less extensive holdings. Then the war broke out.

At the time, Shafiq was 23 years old and living in his parents' home. The village of Maalul managed to escape much of the fighting in 1948. Early on, the Zionist pioneers of the nearby Nahal Settlement, with whom Shafiq always maintained good relations, came to them and promised that they would not be targeted.

But then the Haganah set up an ammunition post next to the village. Early in June, fighting put Maalul between the Arab Legion forces and the Haganah. Families began to trickle out of the town, seeking refuge in Nazareth. Shafiq's parents left, but he stayed behind for a few days longer. Eventually it became impossible to remain in the cross fire. In mid-July, ten members of his family took refuge in a shack fashioned out of scrap wood and a corrugated tin roof on the outskirts of Nazareth. They figured they would eventually return home. But soon after the Israelis entered Maalul, they destroyed its houses and everything inside. The year after the war, the Israelis said they would permit the villagers to go back, but not to farm the land, which despite the earlier agreement under the British mandate had been expropriated for a kibbutz. Since their homes had been leveled, there was virtually nothing to return to, and the families rejected the offer. In effect, Israel took the land in Beisan as well as the land around Maalul, claiming legal ownership of both.

The Bisharat family were now what became known as "internal refugees." For nearly ten years they lived in the shack. Shafiq and his father had to abandon their traditional livelihood as farmers, and they took whatever work they could find in construction. Shafiq also worked briefly as a cook at the government's camps for Jewish immigrants. These immigrants were being provided with housing on land that had once belonged to Palestinian families.

The circle of shame and humiliation could be vicious. Once Shafiq had earned enough money, he too rented a house from the Israel Lands Authority that had belonged to a refugee family, on the outskirts of Nazareth. It was hard for him not to think of the house as somehow haunted.

In the early formation of the state of Israel, the JNF became a quasi-governmental agency. Huge tracts of land that Israel had captured during the war were sold to the JNF. In addition, Arab homes and property—owned by Arab families who had been dispossessed and prohibited from returning—were also turned over to the JNF and ultimately fell under the control of the Israel Lands Authority. Thus were the property lines blurred between what the JNF had purchased from willing Arab sellers and land that it had nominally bought from the Israeli state, which had captured it in war. Such sales of captured land were illegal under international law. And thus did the land of dispossessed Arabs become the property of the Jewish state, and subject to the bylaws of the JNF, which explicitly prohibited its land from being leased to non-Jews. With an estimated 93 percent of the land within Israel controlled by the state in this way, inherently discriminatory land policies were institutionally enshrined. Legal challenges to this control of land were only beginning to be launched in 2000.

The bitter history of these land acquisitions and the destruction of the villages such as Maalul that once dotted this landscape is now largely hidden from view. The crumbling stone foundations and toppled structures often had pine forests planted around them by the JNF in an effort to hide the destruction. Such is the case in Maalul, where the remains of the village are no longer visible from the road.

As we walked down the path through the shadows of the pines, I noticed a wooden plaque nailed to one of the trees, which bore an inscription in English and in Hebrew: "This forest is in the name of Dr. Gertrude Luckner for her appreciation in her help in saving Jews in Germany. *—Jewish National Fund.*" Luckner, I later learned, was born in 1900, to a Christian family in Liverpool, England, and was taken to Germany as a child. A scholar with a doctoral degree from the University of Frankfurt, she was active in the German association Krist, and through her connections with the German Catholic Church she managed to help Jews to escape Germany. On March 24, 1943, returning to Berlin from a mission to help Jews escape, she was arrested by the Gestapo and sent to the Ravensbruck concentration camp. After the liberation, frail and ill, she devoted her remaining years to helping the victims of Nazism and working toward greater understanding between Jews and Christians.

This plaque's location in the middle of this forest communicates something profound about the modern history of this land, something essential for understanding the Israelis and the Palestinians. The collective guilt of the Western world over the Holocaust loomed, just like this clump of JNF-planted pines hiding Maalul, over wrongs carried out in the name of building a Jewish state. Many Israelis are insulted by the notion that feelings of guilt for the Holocaust played a role in founding their state. They feel that such a view dismisses their historical connection to this land, and the heroic efforts of the early pioneers of Zionism. Yet most historians agree that the world's sympathy after the Holocaust had great bearing on the U.N. decision to partition Palestine. I wondered how a woman so dedicated to fighting injustice as Dr. Luckner would feel about the destruction of Maalul, and about a forest planted in her name that was there in part to hide the uncomfortable reminder of an injustice.

As we headed back to the roadside picnic spots, I saw that more family groups had gathered. Amid the parked cars of picnickers, I noticed a white Toyota festooned with Israeli flags. I wondered who these people were. Palestinian Israelis who were proud of their citizenship? Or perhaps newly arrived Israeli immigrants from Russia, unaware of the historical fault line they had chosen as a picnic spot? It turned out that they were a family of Romanian descent, a couple with children in their mid-20s and a cousin. Yosef Bernstein, the 52-year-old patriarch of the group, didn't want to talk to us: "It is a holiday. We are just a family. We don't want to talk politics."

Four teenage Palestinian boys were just showing up in the surrounding fields, riding double and bareback on two beautiful Arabian horses. The horses, sweating in the sun, cantered through the field. I pressed again, politely, and Bernstein declined again, and somewhat nervously explained, "I did not realize this was an old Palestinian village. It just looked like a nice field to have a picnic."

I nodded in agreement and looked around at the fields, and then asked him if he realized that Independence Day meant something vastly different to the Palestinian families picnicking around him. He surveyed the families and asked, "Were they evacuated, or did they leave by themselves?"

I told him that they say they were forced out by the fighting and then their village was destroyed by the Israeli troops, which effectively prevented them from returning. He shook his head and said he was genuinely surprised to hear this side of the story. He seemed a very decent man. After a pause, he replied, with a slight edge of indignation, "At least they were not taken to camps and killed."

This statement was like opening a door to a long, dark hallway. Either you walked in or you did not. Conversations in Israel are often like that, the weight of history crushing down on even casual discussions. When you do walk through the door, there is a gravitational pull that often draws you in farther and faster than you expected. You have to have plenty of time to listen if you begin such conversations. I ended up speaking with Bernstein and his family for several hours.

Romania had supported the Nazis during the invasion of the Soviet Union, and in exchange had been given an area in the southern Ukraine known as Trans-Dniestria. In October 1941, approximately 200,000 Romanian Jews, including Bernstein's entire extended family, were transported to Trans-Dniestria in cattle cars. During the journey, with no food and water, an estimated 130,000 died. The 70,000 who remained alive included Bernstein's parents, who would also survive years in the camps of Trans-Dniestria and were able at the end of the war, finally, to flee Eastern Europe for sanctuary in the newly formed state of Israel. Of the 9 million Jews who lived in Europe before World War II, only 3 million survived. One million of them came to Israel.

"This is my Independence Day. I know that if I were living in Romania today, I would still be spat on as a dirty yid. Do you know what a pogrom is? These happened in Romania. There were crowds with pickaxes who smashed shops. This is my Independence Day from all that," Yosef said. "This is my nation, and as a Jew you feel that and you are very proud of it."

Yosef is a manager of a canning factory at a nearby kibbutz, and he said that he works with many Palestinians there. "I know Arabs. I know how they look at us," he said. "But they do not want to know our history, they do not ask me what happened to my family. We all have stories. We all have pasts."

As he said this, I noticed that the Palestinian teenagers were galloping their horses closer and closer to his picnic site, the sound of the horses' neighing and the teenagers' laughing engulfing the Bernstein family's holiday retreat. We had drawn attention to the family, and there was some low-level intimidation going on from the Palestinian side. It seemed to be getting a bit more menacing, as if the Palestinian teenagers were trying to frighten the only family with Israeli flags fluttering from their car. I noticed that without saying anything Yosef's wife was beginning to pack up their lunch and slowly load up the car.

"Maybe this was not the right place for us to come today," said Yosef.

The Bernsteins' car left the field, kicking up a trail of dust as it headed back out onto the main road in the late afternoon. One of the teenagers on horseback galloped alongside them as they left. I was about to leave, myself, when one of the men I had met earlier in the morning motioned me over and offered me a cold beer, which seemed like a good idea.

Silman Faraj, a 33-year-old marketing expert who works for an Israeli company targeting the "Arab sector," was sitting in a folding lawn chair and slowly smoking apple-scented tobacco in a *nargila* (a traditional Arab water pipe) and sipping beer. He lived in Upper Nazareth now with his four-year-old daughter and his wife, whose grandfather had been born in Maalul. He ended up in the Turkish neighborhood, he explained almost apologetically, because the overcrowded city of Nazareth had virtually no available apartments, and the few that came onto the market were exorbitantly priced. But every year on "Al-Nakba Day," he leaves Upper Nazareth, sensing an uncomfortable tension between him and his Israeli Jewish neighbors.

"Every other day of the year we can get along, but this is one day not to try to go into politics," he explained. "It's just too much for everyone to handle, so I think we all know to stay away from it."

Faraj described himself as "an Arab, Palestinian Christian living in Israel." But the soul of him, he said with a smile, was "marketing."

I asked him what he meant.

"Marketing is everything," he said, and then repeated the phrase again with practiced intensity, as if giving a sales pitch. "Marketing is everything."

"Look around you, look at the flags, the moment of silence. The way the Israelis have marketed this victory commands respect. I may not agree with the history that it celebrates. But I have to admire the way they have marketed it. The same is true with Holocaust Remembrance Day. They have made the whole world aware of their suffering. And if the Palestinians could ever do that, we would not be in the situation we are. We should be in awe of what the Israelis did, not resentful of it. It is all effective marketing. And we need to be better at that."

It took me a minute to focus my thoughts on just how offensive this line of thinking was, especially after the several hours of conversation I had just finished with the Bernsteins. Faraj was cavalierly dismissing one of the darkest periods of history as a marketing plan by the Jews to get their own state. Had he ever talked to someone like the Bernsteins, I wondered? Then I asked him, and he quipped in a voice that conveyed his annoyance at the question, "Yeah, I've been to Yad Vashem."

I was surprised by how quickly his point of view, which seemed so practiced and so polished when we discussed marketing, descended into a crass and ugly denial of the Holocaust. By the end of our conversation, Faraj was insisting that many more Palestinians had been killed by Israelis than Jews killed during the Holocaust. He was adamant that that there was no difference between the Jewish state's persecution of Palestinians and Nazi Germany's genocide of Jews. When I confronted him with just how preposterous this view of history was, and presented the countervailing facts, he became more infuriated. Just as quickly as the late afternoon sun had slipped away, the conversation had darkened into the primal hatreds between the two people. This hatred was always lurking just below the surface, pent up and ready to erupt, even more than a half century after the war. As night fell over the Jezreel valley and the old village of Maalul, the Palestinian family groups became silhouettes clustered around the burning embers of their fading campfires.

. . .

In this land, perhaps more than any other place in the world, history shapes the present. Not just the history of the twentieth-century Arab-Israeli conflict, and not just the Holocaust, but thousands of years of history and ancient claims to biblical land.

From the bell tower of the old St. Gabriel monastery, on the highest hill overlooking Nazareth, the topography that has shaped this history stretches out in all directions. A climb up the narrow, winding staircase of the stone tower in the former monastery (now a hotel for pilgrims) leads to a perch under a cast-iron bell. Birds nest in the rafters. In every direction lies a dramatic view of the Galilee and the city that is its capital.

The Nazareth Hills form a broad, limestone ridge that runs east to west at 300 to 500 meters above sea level, south of the Galilee. These hills, their companion valleys, and the open plains have been silent witnesses to so much history of invasion and conquest and power. From the vantage of the bell tower, Nazareth itself looks like a basket filled with cement and stone. Chaotically built houses are piled atop one another at seemingly impossible angles. Among these precarious stacks are narrow, winding streets that crookedly traverse the town.

The imposing Basilica of the Annunciation presides at the center of it all. It is a modern structure of clean, vertical lines and imposing blocks of masonry that symbolize permanence and portray the strength and confidence of the modern Roman Catholic Church. Dedicated by the Vatican in 1968, the basilica preserves the outline of the remains of the twelfth-century Crusader church that stands within it. And within that Crusader church are even more ancient ruins of shrines from the Byzantine era that were built to commemorate the cave that, according to Catholic tradition, was where Mary was visited by the angel Gabriel, with the news that she would have a child and his name would be Jesus.

Beyond the clutter of modern-day Nazareth, the view opens up to the northeast onto the green, rolling hills that lead to the Sea of Galilee. In the distance are the distinctive "horns of Hittin," twin peaks of a mountain between which the road from Nazareth to the Sea of Galilee passes. It was here in 1187 that the decisive battle was fought between the Christian Crusaders and the Muslim armies led by Saladin. The European armies of the cross approached their mission largely without regard and usually with great disdain for the indigenous Christians who lived in the communities clustered around these religious sites. The Europeans were there for the conquest of sacred land, and not for the liberation of locals. Some of the indigenous Christians, in fact, sided with the Muslims against the West, and the tales of the Crusades contain stories of legendary Arab Christian warriors who stood with Saladin's army.

The church spires over Nazareth—including the bell tower in which I was standing—also tell a history, one of Christian renaissance in the nineteenth century, when the expanding European powers vied to exert their influence over the Holy Land from Jerusalem to Nazareth. The French built Catholic monasteries, the British established Anglican cathedrals, the Vatican constructed basilicas and a vast network of Catholic schools, and the Greek Orthodox struggled to compete by building more churches and social clubs. The colonialism of the churches is critical to the way Christianity is perceived in this land. The Anglican Bishop Riah Abu el-Assal, who is from Nazareth, said, "Colonialism does not occupy land only, but also infiltrates the spirit and the mind."

The Episcopal Church, known in the Middle East as the Anglican Church, was a classic example of this phenomenon. The Anglican Church was centered in St. George's Cathedral of the Episcopal Church of Jerusalem and the Middle East, which was established in 1841, in an attempt to create a worldwide Protestant union with Jerusalem as its center. But the bishopric also had large landholdings and churches and schools in Nazareth. The Anglican tradition in the Holy Land was steeped in the late century fervor to bring Christianity to the Jews of Palestine. In keeping with this history, its first bishop was a former Jewish rabbi who had converted to Christianity. In 1905, it was among the first of the established churches to "indigenize" its leadership, forming the Palestine Native Church Council, which promoted a self-governing congregation. The Anglican community set out to build educational institutions with rigorous standards of excellence. It also established two large hospitals in Gaza and Nablus. Its power and influence grew after World War I, under the British mandate, and a large number of Palestinian Christian families left their Orthodox and Catholic traditions to join the Anglican church. Some of the most prominent Palestinian Christians hail from this tradition, including the legislator Hanan Ashrawi, the scholar and commentator Edward Said, and Hanna Nasser, the president of the Palestinian university Birzeit. These leaders were shaped and repelled by the church's elitism—and, some would argue, by its inherent colonialism.

The Palestinian Anglicans, although at times treated with colonialist contempt by the British during the mandate, adhered closely to the British Anglican traditions, including the prayer books and the "cathedral talk," always in the King's English. Bishop Riah remembered that there were some "who even insisted on taking high tea at 4 P.M. Greenwich Mean Time." But in the decades since the end of the mandate, the number of Anglican Palestinians has dwindled dramatically. In Nazareth, no more than 250 were left by the year 2000.

Bishop Riah pointed out that the pervasive and suffocating influence of colonialism had had a particularly negative impact on his church: "I think this has had a great effect, deliberately or otherwise, in shaking confidence of Arab Christians in their own Arab identity. They were taught that the English way, its traditions, and its people were more competent. The same was true of the Greek Orthodox and Roman Catholic churches. And it had a debilitating effect on Palestinian Christians, and led many, I believe, to emigrate to the West, which they had been taught to revere by a hierarchy that was Western."

However, it was not Anglicanism but Zionism that the Arabs saw as a more powerful form of European colonialism—even though to Jews the movement was simply a new assertion of their identity and a return to the land of Zion. They came to work the land and live out a communal dream. They did not occupy themselves with erecting architectural monuments to God or to imperial glory but with the more practical purchase, settlement, and cultivation of land.

The physical presence of the Zionist movement could be seen at the higher end of the cascading ridge of the hills, in the Israeli development of Natzerat Illit. Utilitarian, high-rise blocks of urban housing, and the dull symmetry of suburban stucco walls and red tile roofs, stand out against the burbling chaos of old Nazareth. This is the landscape of modern Israel, as if someone has lifted tract homes from southern California and plunked them down in the crowded towns and quaint Arab villages of the Galilee.

Dan Rabinowitz, an anthropology professor from Hebrew University, believes that the differences between these two communities complicate Israel's quest to fashion a Western-style democracy in the Middle East. He explained: "You can see how the Israeli government designed Natzerat Illit to completely surround and ultimately constrict Nazareth. This was a very carefully designed policy that began in the very earliest years of the Jewish state, after the war of 1948."

Natzerat Illit has a population of 50,000 Israelis, the majority of them Romanian and Russian Jewish immigrants from the former Soviet Union. It is one of many towns in which new immigrants are resettled and guaranteed various opportunities for housing, education, and work.

"Lower Nazareth," as the Israelis call the original town, is hemmed in by the newly built Israeli highways, industrial parks, and housing developments that accommodate these new Jewish immigrants. Not surprisingly, with nowhere to grow, old Nazareth is significantly overcrowded. Whereas Upper Nazareth's population of 50,000 is spread over roughly 9,000 acres, old Nazareth has a population of almost 70,000 crammed into fewer than 4,000 acres. Natzerat Illit receives more than U.S. $50 million annually from various agencies of the Israeli government for its population; Nazareth receives about U.S. $40 million—half the amount Natzerat Illit gets, on a per capita basis. Even that is an improvement over 1983, when Upper Nazareth received nearly three times more than Nazareth per capita. One example of such inequity has been the unequal disbursement of funds by the religious affairs ministry's budget, of which only 1.5 percent is allotted to Israeli Arabs (who make up 18 percent of the population)—most of which goes to the Muslim majority. Christians, says Bishop Riah, end up with "a pittance." Even an official of the ministry conceded, "Obviously it is unfair, and has been unfair for too long."

Government incentives to businesses also are unequal. In Upper Nazareth, the Israeli government has zoned 1,750 acres for industrial use, providing a network of roads, water and energy infrastructure, and has reduced tax rates to create jobs. In Nazareth, the government has refused to permit more than 17.5 acres for industrial use; and unemployment has climbed steadily.

The inequality that exists between predominantly Jewish Upper Nazareth and Arab Nazareth is mirrored across Israel, and from the Arab point of view this systemic discrimination undermines the legitimacy of Israel's governmental authorities. In virtually every Arab village and town, the Arab citizens of Israel face significant discrimination in access to land resources, land rights, and land use in the interests of their communities. Consider the following statistics:

- Arabs make up 18 percent of Israel's population but own only 3.5 percent of the land in Israel.

- Over half of the land that was owned by Arabs in 1948 has been expropriated by the state of Israel.

- Arabs are effectively blocked from acquiring or leasing land in some 80 percent of Israel's territory—land that is controlled by Jewish rural regional councils, which prohibit sales to non-Jews.

But there were signs of change, too. In 1998, the first Arab justice was appointed to the Israeli Supreme Court. In 1999, an Arab beauty was selected as Miss Israel, for the first time in the contest's history. And in March 2000, the Supreme Court issued an important ruling that challenged, albeit in a limited fashion, the Israeli government's allocation of state-owned land to communities that bar non-Jewish residents. The Court reconfirmed that "equality is among the fundamental principles of the state." The petitioner, Adel Kaadan, was tired of living in the crowded, neglected Arab town of Baqa and wanted to move to a pleasant new Jewish suburb known as Katzir, which had been built on state-owned land under the control of the Israel Lands Authority. But the Katzir municipal council had excluded Kaadan from buying property in the town because he was not Jewish. Even though the High Court ruled that the council's decision was discriminatory, Kaadan was still being blocked from building his home by a wall of bureaucracy the town had constructed in front of him. The narrow ruling had virtually no impact on the systemic discriminatory policies of the Israel Lands Authority.

. . .

The highway that leads to Upper Nazareth is wide and open; traffic flows freely into the Israeli development town, past the shopping malls and factories and into the housing developments with their neatly groomed courtyards and grassy parks where children play. I was on my way to the home of Salim Khouri, a Christian Palestinian who in 1981 became a pioneer in Upper Nazareth, building a home in an outlying neighborhood called Al-Kurum ("The Vineyard"). This sliver of land, largely owned by Palestinians, had not been expropriated by the growing municipality.

The Khouri home was an attractive, modern, split-level structure that housed Salim on one side and his son and daughter-in-law on the other. Salim's home was filled with classic Christian kitsch. There was a 3-D poster of the Last Supper and a plastic statue of the Virgin Mary with a tiny light bulb that glowed inside it. Salim, born in 1942 to a Melkite family, had a child's memory of the war in 1948 and what it did to his family and his native village of Kana. The village, only a few miles from Nazareth, was where tradition holds that Jesus performed one of his earliest miracles, turning water into wine at the wedding of a poor couple.

Salim told me the history of Natzerat Illit. The community was begun in 1957, he said, when several hundred Israeli settlers moved into trailers that were parked on the highest ridge overlooking old Nazareth, clustered around a military observation post that kept a close eye on the Palestinian population below. Factories were built to employ the new Jewish immigrants from Central Europe, North Africa, and South America. They were still functioning today—among them the Elite chocolate factory; Kitan, a textile mill operated by the Histadrut, Israel's trade union federation; and Ta'as, a branch of Israel's military industry. Like the housing, the jobs were available only to Jewish immigrants. The Arab population was excluded, principally by requiring Israeli military service as a prerequisite for employment or a subsidized apartment.

Properties taken from Palestinian refugees, whom the state of Israel called "absentees," were controlled by a real estate conglomerate known as Amidar—which in Hebrew means "my people dwell"—under contract to the Israeli housing ministry. Under the terms of the Absentee Property Law of 1950, the state acquired control of all the land and physical property left behind by those who were expelled from or fled their homes during the 1948 war. The "absentee" status applied also to those who remained in the land as internal refugees, including the families from Maalul, and others I had met, from Tiberias, who were uprooted from their homes and never permitted to return. In the surreal parlance of the Israeli land bureaucracy, these families were regarded as "present absentees."

This seizure of land through military conquest, and its perpetuation by a subsequently created web of laws and state policies designed to control ownership, is not a strategy unique to Israel. It is at least as old as America's Western frontier and as modern as the Serbs' "ethnic cleansing" in Bosnia and Kosovo. Yigal Allon, the commander of the Jewish military forces in the Galilee in 1948 and later a deputy prime minister, actually used the phrase "cleansing" to describe the expulsion of Palestinians from the Galilee. Officially, the construction of Upper Nazareth was part of the third stage in Israel's drive to "Judaize Galilee," a policy endorsed by the Knesset in March 1949. Despite careless comparisons often made between these efforts by Israel and the dispersal of different ethnic groups in the Balkans, it is essential to underline that the killing and intimidation and forced expulsions of populations in the former Yugoslavia were far more vicious and bloody than methods used by Israel.

And even with this expropriation of land and the legal edifice built to maintain it, Jews remained a minority in the towns and villages heavily populated by Arab Christians and Muslims throughout the Galilee. The Israeli preoccupation with the "Arab threat" in the Galilee was revealed in a secret document leaked to the media in the mid-1980s. It was written by Yisrael Koenig, then the director of the northern region of Israel's Ministry of the Interior, and outlined a strategy for combating the Arab presence in the Galilee and altering the demographic balance in favor of Jews. The plan included a massive disbursement of government funds for the construction and expansion of Jewish development towns around the Arab communities, combined with the limitation of government funds to the Arab villages. Funds to large Arab families would be reduced; the number of Arab employees in Jewish-owned businesses would be restricted; Arab students would be encouraged to go abroad and not permitted to return; and tax assessments on Arabs would be enforced rigorously. Koenig has since retired to Upper Nazareth, an aging and surly man who will not speak to reporters.

Like most gifted young students growing up in the 1940s and 1950s, Salim Khouri had been encouraged by the church to consider the priesthood. For several years in elementary school he received training in that direction, and he was eventually invited to go to Rome for further studies. But Khouri's father wanted him close to home. In the early 1950s, Israel was under a military government, and the movement of Palestinians was tightly controlled by military laws dating from the British mandate but now enforced by Israel and applying only to Christians and Muslims. Special permits were needed to travel anywhere; there was no public transportation; and those who could not afford private transportation often did not go on to high school. In 1959, the Israelis began providing exceptional students with transportation to Nazareth, and Khouri was lucky enough to be the first in his family to attend high school. He graduated at the top of his class in 1963.

He landed a job out of high school as a clerk in the Arab-Israeli Bank, jointly owned by the Israeli government and wealthy Christian Arab financiers. In 1970, he was accepted to the business school at the Israeli government-funded University of Haifa. He worked in the bank in the day and took classes at night, and received his degree with honors in 1973. In 1975, he was named manager of the central branch of the bank in Nazareth, and in 1980, he was promoted to regional manager. Khouri's life was prospering within Israeli society; but it was at this point that he found himself hemmed in by the restricted housing market in Nazareth. He wanted to buy a home for his wife Odet, his two sons, and his daughter that was spacious and private. Nothing was available in overcrowded Nazareth; so in 1981, he bought a home in the Al-Kurum neighborhood of Natzerat Illit.

Al-Kurum began essentially as an accident, when the Israeli municipality transferred predominantly Palestinian-owned land from agricultural to residential zoning in 1980 without formally appropriating it. This occurred during a severe economic slump in Israel that sent the housing market in Natzerat Illit into a nosedive. Because of the lack of space in Nazareth, housing boomed for Palestinians in Al-Kurum, catching the Israeli authorities by surprise. By 1989, two hundred Palestinian families had moved into the neighborhood—almost all of them Christian, well educated, and economically self-sufficient. For years, however, they had been frustrated taxpayers, treated like second-class citizens—with no sewage system, limited water, bad roads, and no garbage collection.

At the Arab-Israeli Bank, Khouri had seen redlining of bank loans firsthand and was an adamant critic of the practice. His outspokenness ultimately brought pressure from management, leading to his resignation. The Israeli authorities also resented his attempts to improve municipal services in Al-Kurum. But in 1989 he was elected to the Upper Nazareth city council, and he would be reelected three times. He now wanted to work within the system.

Another prominent Arab politician representing Upper Nazareth was Azmi Bishara, a member of the Israeli parliament and a Greek Orthodox Christian. Bishara had moved to Upper Nazareth in 1998. He and his wife Rana had their first child in 1999 and were expecting a second in 2000. Bishara wanted to settle there, but he could sense underlying resentment and hatred from many of his Jewish neighbors, displayed in many little ways. Rana, who was from East Jerusalem, would be greeted in the supermarket with cold stares. She would not be invited by the other new mothers to walk with their babies in the park. She felt isolated and alone in the community. The couple soon began spending more time at their second home in East Jerusalem. Neither Salim nor Bishara had any inkling that this largely dormant racism would erupt later, in the year 2000.

Despite some of these uncomfortable realities of racism, Salim, on a local level, and Bishara, on a national level, provided evidence of at least limited inclusion of Arab representatives within the Israeli system of governing. Critics dismissed them as Palestinian Uncle Toms, but supporters held them up as Nazareth's answer to Andrew Young. For many Jewish and Arab citizens of Upper Nazareth, the presence of Khouri and Bishara was a true sign of democracy, and one they pointed to with pride.

But a considerable number of other Jewish residents of Upper Nazareth saw the two men's presence as evidence of a dangerous Arab intrusion into the collective, exclusive enterprise of a Jewish state. A vigilante group known as MENA (a Hebrew acronym for "Defenders of Natzerat Illit") had become notorious for spewing anti-Arab vitriol and warning Jews against selling any property to Arabs. MENA's influence had flamed out since its heyday in the 1980s, but Khouri said the raw bigotry of some Israelis toward Arabs occasionally still bled into daily conversations, even on the local council. Councilman Avraham Maimon, an Orthodox Jewish member known for his strident views, delivered one angry outburst: "The worst Jew in the world is still better than any other. God tells us this." Few in the room besides Khouri objected, although quite a few rolled their eyes.

The personality of Natzerat Illit is embodied in its no-nonsense mayor, Menachem Ariav, who is commonly known as "the Sheriff" and is seen by his Israeli constituents as a lawman who can keep the natives under control. As one Israeli councilman told me: "He knows how to handle the Arabs. He knows their mentality, and knows that they need to be shown force. It's the only way they understand." But some distinction is made between Muslims and Christians. A prominent real estate agent in Upper Nazareth, who sold many homes to Palestinian Christians in the Vineyard and profited handsomely in doing so, put it this way: "We fear the Arabs, but there is a lot less fear of Christians. Well, I mean, they are Arab but they are different. . . . They are more European, more modern, more of the intelligentsia. They are of a higher income. Of course we prefer them."

. . .

Driving down from Natzerat Illit, I thought about Mary's Well, about how it is metaphysically the life source of the beginning of Christianity. As I had learned while exploring Nazareth over the years, there were actually two wells by that name in Nazareth: one located behind the Greek Orthodox church—where the Orthodox community believes the original well that served the ancient village was located—and one at the center of town, which dates back only three or four centuries.

In the cavernous Church of the Annunciation, also known as the Church of the Archangel Gabriel, I had met a bowed and nervous couple who were the caretakers of the church and a crypt—the original Crusader-era chapel, around which this eighteenth-century Greek Orthodox church had been built. Inside the crypt is the well believed to be the site of the Annunciation, the spot where the angel Gabriel came to Mary as she was fetching water. The couple, Aisam and Rose Farji, came every day to the church, to direct the flow of dozens of tour buses laden with pilgrims. They worked diligently to keep votive candles stocked in the shrine. They dutifully cleaned up after the buses left. And they sadly watched their own Christian community wither away. I had gotten to know them a bit over the years.

"We are disappearing," Aisam, 56, told me. "It breaks our hearts."

Most of his extended family, he said, had moved to the United States. But he had a heart condition and had been told by his relatives that life was too hard in America, and medical insurance too expensive. He was better off in Nazareth, with the full coverage offered by Israeli medical insurance, they told him. As we spoke, a group of about fifty Italian tourists with matching yellow sun hats led by an Israeli tour guide entered the church, their footsteps echoing around us. Aisam looked nervous, as if they were unruly visitors who were entering his home and might perhaps break something.

Aisam was always extremely uncomfortable talking to me, worried that he and his wife and family could somehow be penalized by the Israelis or harassed by the local Muslims if they spoke to a journalist about the difficult and diminishing existence that Christians had in Nazareth. Aisam and Rose embodied a meekness that defined so many of the Arab Christians I had met. They simply endured, quietly, humbly, and unthreateningly doing their tasks in the church and going unnoticed by the tourists, to whom they felt as if they were invisible. Rose told me that their daughter recently was driving the family car, which had a crucifix dangling from the rearview mirror, and was stopped by a gang of Muslim teenagers who smashed the windshield and called her "an infidel." This was an uncharacteristic encounter in a community that prided itself on tolerance, Rose sought to assure me. But she said it also reflected a change she could feel in Nazareth, a rising tension between Muslims and Christians that worried her.

I left Aisam and Rose to walk down the hill to see the other Mary's Well. Old black-and-white photos of the city often featured this town-center well with women gathered around it washing clothes or balancing water buckets on their heads to bring back up the steep hills. The scenes were as they would have been in the time of Mary and Joseph, and remained much the same until the early 1970s. The women gathering at the well seemed to bring you closer to experiencing Mary's life than did the dark, devotional setting of the shrine near the church.

The communal well, with its distinct octagonal shape, was the municipal logo of the city. Nevertheless, a decision had been made in the late 1990s to tear down the centuries-old arched structure and to replace it with a larger limestone fabrication in the same shape but more modern-looking. The modern look was calculated to make the well seem less biblical. This, the thinking went in the Greek Orthodox community and among some of its political leaders, would encourage tourists to visit their church and its well. But when the city built the new well, the design was poor and the water did not flow naturally into it. It was dry. This was not the only botched renovation. The square around the well was refurbished for the expected rush of pilgrims that never came during the millennial year 2000. The renovations uncovered archaeological remains dating back to the Roman period; but when city officials tried to encase them in glass so that pedestrians could view them from above, the poorly designed frames splintered, making it impossible to see anything.

As a result, the Greek Orthodox church got its wish, and tourists indeed were redirected to its own well. There, however, another local scandal erupted, involving the water source. The water flowing into the church well, it turned out, was actually emanating from the Israeli water grid and not the ancient springs. Caught in the scandal, local politicians offered the suggestion that perhaps the water became holy when it entered the church. Few in the Greek Orthodox community accepted this municipal blessing on the water. The springs that offered water to Mary and Joseph bubble somewhere deep beneath the surface of modern Nazareth, but the municipal well has run dry.

I couldn't help but think of Mary's Well as the perfect metaphor for the Christian community in Nazareth, which is also gradually drying up—a community sweating under the burdens of an economic and social system deliberately weighted against them, steeped in intolerance, thirsting for justice, while a salt sea of Christian tourists sweeps in and out of their town in a great and indifferent tide.

Mary and Joseph left Nazareth for Bethlehem. According to Luke's gospel, they set off on their journey, presumably traveling by donkey through the Galilean hills, down the Jordan River valley, and across the Judean desert to the small town of Bethlehem. They had been ordered to go there, it is written in Luke, by the Roman government, which was conducting a census.

In Luke's gospel, we see the Holy Family as a young couple, poor and powerless. Mary was a pregnant teenager. Like families all over the world who live in poverty, they were being put through a great inconvenience by government bureaucrats whose seemingly arbitrary dictates (in this case, occasioned by the need for a census) were often issued with little regard to the way they might alter people's lives. This was the kind of social injustice, the hard life of the disenfranchised, that was at the center of Jesus's teaching and ministry.

The Holy Family ended up in Bethlehem and were forced to sleep in a manger, which in those times would actually have been a cave where shepherds sheltered their herds from the elements. It was there, in the manger, that Mary gave birth to Jesus.

V

Bethlehem

THE MANGER

And she gave birth to her firstborn, a son. She wrapped him in cloths and placed him in a manger, because there was no room for them in the inn.

LUKE 2:7 (NIV)

THE ROAD to Bethlehem begins at an Israeli military checkpoint. Soldiers with machine guns stand guard at a concrete bunker that marks the line separating Jerusalem from the Palestinian-ruled West Bank town of Bethlehem. The drive takes no more than ten minutes from our home in the neighborhood of West Jerusalem, known as the German Colony, with its outdoor cafés and wine-and-cheese shops and even a kosher Chinese restaurant (with takeout). It is a journey that crosses not just a threshold of sovereignty but a dividing line between two worlds. For reporters, who are among the few to regularly travel between these distinct Israeli and Palestinian realities, the checkpoint stands as a symbol of one of the more depressing facts of life here—the vast separation between two peoples trying to live in one land.

Along the two-lane road just before the checkpoint, orange plastic barricades funnel the traffic down into one lane. Yellow passenger vans, which serve as unlicensed shuttle buses, idle here, loading Palestinians who have permits to work in Jerusalem. It was common to see a few Volvos and Mercedes-Benzes with Palestinian Authority plates, belonging to the Palestinian elite, passing through the checkpoints. Trucks loaded with goods were stopped—some were turned back and others allowed through. It was never quite clear how these decisions were made, for the system that granted the Palestinian Authority the ability to hand out permits for shipping (which received final approval from Israel) had spawned a notoriously corrupt enterprise of Israeli-Palestinian partnered firms that controlled import licenses and effectively blocked any competitors. There were also dusty four-wheel-drive vehicles bearing the insignias of various nongovernmental organizations—a small international army of do-gooders under the banners of the United Nations, the Red Cross, CARE, World Vision, and literally hundreds of different agencies that provide services in the West Bank. On any given day, it was possible to behold a variety of holy men in their respective plumage—perhaps an Islamic sheikh from Hebron, or an Orthodox rabbi going to lead prayers at Rachel's Tomb, just beyond the checkpoint. And on this way to Bethlehem, where many of the representatives of the Christian denominations have patriarchates and churches and charities to tend to, there tend to be disproportionately large numbers of Catholic priests with their straight clerical collars and Franciscans with their brown robes, and Anglican ministers with their distinctive magenta shirts, and the Greek Orthodox, and the Copts, and the dozens of different denominations. The traffic builds as soldiers check papers and permits and identification. All the while, Israeli tour buses packed with Western pilgrims roll through a special lane, unimpeded and hardly catching a glimpse of the complexities of daily life for the occupier, the occupied, and all those in-between.

To the west of the checkpoint, Palestinian workers scurry up through rocky hills of terraced olive groves, on their way to jobs as dishwashers in restaurants, day laborers on construction jobs, or production line workers in factories. Since the beginning of the peace process in the early 1990s, Israel has required that Palestinians obtain special permits in order to work or travel in Israel. But tens of thousands of Palestinians skirted these rules every day in an economy of necessity tolerated by both sides. The Israelis hired the Palestinians for these jobs largely because the pay was too poor or the work too boring or too dirty to attract Israelis.

On a day in May 2000, I saw a Palestinian woman carrying a young child in her arms. She was wearing traditional dress, a long flowing blue cloak and a white head scarf. The way the cloth fell around her face and the way she held the baby looked timeless, even vaguely like the statue of Mary that stood just to the right of the altar in the parish church of my hometown in Massachusetts.

The woman was pleading with an Israeli border policeman to let her through. He took her identification card and gave a recognizable hand gesture in this part of the world, a clamping together of the fingers and the thumb—a nonverbal way of saying, "Wait a minute!" It can be presented softly and close to the waist or it can be thrust directly at one's face, depending on the tone intended. The soldier made it a dismissive gesture over his shoulder as he walked away with her documents. She stood on the side of the road, trying to comfort the baby, who was now crying.

A subtle language is at work here at the border, a mix of symbols and signs and gestures, and all of it is instantly interpreted by the Israeli border police. It was safe to assume that the Palestinian woman in traditional dress was Muslim, because Islamic culture imposes stricter requirements of dress on women than does Christianity; Christian women in the Arab world tend to wear Western-style clothing, which typically conceals less of the body than does traditional garb. A young Palestinian man with a beard is generally viewed with suspicion, as a potential Islamic militant. Older Palestinian men, especially those who favor sports coats and V-neck sweaters—a classic gentlemanly look carried over from the British mandate—are viewed as less threatening and usually allowed to pass. In general, Christian men are indistinguishable from Muslim men, and both are more often than not treated by Israeli border police with the same level of suspicion. But some border police had told me that they saw the Christians differently than the Muslims, as more educated and less threatening, and therefore they were usually passed through with little or no questioning. In any event, religious affiliation was also stamped on identification cards, whether issued by Israel or the Palestinian Authority. And Christians, especially women, often wore crosses on pendants. A Christian friend, Nuha, had once told me that there was, as she described it, "a language to how you wear the cross." For example, if she were shopping in the market where most of the produce peddlers were Muslim, she would tuck the cross into her blouse. On the streets of Bethlehem, she would wear it out. In Hebron, an overwhelmingly Muslim town, she would tuck it away again. It was a constant running dialogue with the symbol of her faith and what it meant in her homeland. She didn't like the fact that the Israelis were more lenient when they saw she was Christian. As a Palestinian, it bothered her. But there were times at the checkpoint, she said, when she just had to get through—or was in a rush—that she would reluctantly pull the pendant out and display the cross to speed things along.

Apart from checkpoint encounters and employment arrangements, there was very little daily contact between average Israelis and

Palestinians. Beyond the checkpoint lay even more formidable barriers of language and culture and history that set these two peoples apart. There were few friendships, and little in the way of socializing. Intermarriage was out of the question. They lived so close to each other, and yet they simply did not know one another.

The checkpoint had a schizophrenic quality to it. One day it could be a lenient and hopeful place, where the two sides were slowly learning to live together; the next day it might bristle with an undercurrent of tension, with the two sides gliding past each other, glaring. It was as if there was a confused, internal dialogue going on over the concrete barricades about whether Israelis and Palestinians were enemies in a conflict or neighbors striving for peace. But it was becoming clear that the leadership on both sides had failed to educate their people on the sacrifices necessary to achieve peace.

The boundary separating the Israelis and Palestinians was drawn in 1949. It was an armistice line, or "green line," that divided historical Palestine after the 1948 war. The West Bank and East Jerusalem fell under Jordanian control at that time, and the Gaza Strip, to the south, fell under Egyptian rule. In the 1967 Six-Day War, Israel captured these territories and then annexed East Jerusalem, declaring the newly united city its "eternal and indivisible" capital.

Five months after the war's end, on November 22, 1967, the U.N. Security Council passed Resolution 242, a cautiously worded document that had been formulated amid intense haggling. It called for "withdrawal of Israeli armed forces from territories occupied in the recent conflict" and affirmed that every state in the region had a "right to live in peace within secure and recognized boundaries free from threats or acts of force." In time, Resolution 242 became the cornerstone of the historic Israeli-Palestinian peace agreement. A "Declaration of Principles" by the two parties was signed on September 13, 1993, after secret negotiations in Oslo, Norway. But by 2000 it was becoming glaringly apparent that the document was too vaguely worded and too open to divergent interpretations to actually work. It had been hoped, at the time of the signing, that the vague wording would permit the process to get moving, build trust between the two sides and start them on the road to peace. At a ceremony in 1994 on the White House lawn, U.S. President Bill Clinton wrapped his arms around Yitzhak Rabin and Yasser Arafat, and the smiling confidence of the three men was an image for the history books. Now Rabin was gone, assassinated by an Israeli ultranationalist opposed to the peace process, and Clinton had narrowly survived impeachment and was in the final year of his presidency. Arafat himself was tremulous with age and various reported illnesses, including Parkinson's disease. The "peace process" itself was hopelessly deadlocked and teetering on the edge of collapse.

The idea of implementing the understandings between the two sides in a five-year staged process, and of postponing the more difficult issues until the end, had become mired in details, and the spirit was being drained out of the agreement. The problematic "final status" issues included the sovereignty of Jerusalem, which both sides claimed as their capital; the "right of return" of Palestinian refugees; the recognition of Palestine as an independent and sovereign state; the fate of the Jewish settlements in the West Bank; and the drawing of the final borders between the two states. Many deadlines had come and gone, and even the most basic steps of the agreement had not been completed, as both sides accused the other of violations and bad faith. The deadline within which these core issues were to be resolved was mid-May 1999, but that timetable proved overly optimistic. After Ehud Barak was elected prime minister of Israel in May 1999, he vowed to reach a peace agreement within one year; but now it was May 2000, and there still was no sign of a breakthrough.

Between 1994 and 2000, in slow, staged increments, Israel had redeployed its troops from approximately 20 percent of the West Bank. In this area the Palestinian Authority held full administrative and security control over the land and its people. Another roughly 18 percent was under shared control of the Israelis and Palestinians, with both sides "cooperating" on security (although Israel clearly had ultimate security authority) and the Palestinians having administrative responsibility. The remaining 62 percent of the West Bank and all of East Jerusalem was still under full Israeli military occupation.

In the West Bank, the land over which the Palestinians did have "full control" was an archipelago of towns and hilltop villages connected by roads that fell under Israeli control and on which Palestinian access was restricted. Nearly 90 percent of the Palestinian population lived within these isolated areas of either full or partial Palestinian rule; but to build a state and a self-sufficient economy would be impossible without the adjacent agricultural and industrial land and the vast and precious aquifers that existed deep under the limestone hills of the West Bank. Israel had essentially given the Palestinian Authority free rein to run their own schools and garbage collection and collect their own taxes; but it had not allowed them to create a contiguous state that could function on its own.

The Palestinian Authority also controls approximately 60 percent of the sandy strip of land along the Mediterranean coast known as Gaza, which is regarded as one of the more crowded and impoverished patches of land on this earth. More than two-thirds of the 1.1 million people who live there are refugees. The remaining 40 percent of Gaza is host to a network of Jewish settlements surrounded by Israeli military camps, with a population of just 5,000 Israelis. In neither the West Bank nor Gaza did the Palestinians control their own borders by land or sea. So there was no free trade to the east with Jordan or Egypt, two Arab countries with which Palestine shares a natural social and economic affinity. Everything had to pass through Israeli-controlled borders and customs. International commerce was constricted to the point of being nearly impossible.

By almost any economic index, things had gotten significantly worse for the Palestinians in the grueling seven years of the peace process. With some 120,000 Palestinians (or more than one-third of the workforce) relying on employment in Israel, repeated closures of the border by Israel had a devastating economic impact on Palestinians, according to data collected by the World Bank. Per capita income levels had been nearly cut in half. The closures, which were imposed on a sliding scale depending on Israeli assessments of security, rocketed unemployment from 11 percent to as high as 28 percent (and in some locales, such as Gaza City, as high as 40 percent). There was also significant underemployment among Palestinians, which combined to give the West Bank and Gaza an unemployment picture that was more dire than any of the other 57 economies analyzed by the World Bank's World Development Report published in 1999. One-fifth of Palestinians in Gaza and the West Bank lived in poverty, which under the World Bank's standard meant they earned less than U.S. $2 per day per capita. Israeli border checkpoints had also dramatically slowed the transfer of goods, and increased transaction costs had "contributed substantially to a reduction in the standard of living."

The strict closures were an Israeli response to a wave of suicide bombings by Islamic militants intent on destroying the peace process. A campaign of suicide bombings began almost immediately after the peace agreement was signed, and it reached a level of ferocity in 1996 that shook Israel and undermined the peace process. The Israeli leadership accused Arafat of having allowed the militant wings of the Islamic organizations Hamas and Islamic Jihad to flourish under his control—of essentially giving them a "green light," as the Israeli security establishment always put it.

In 1998, after Arafat began cracking down and arresting members of Hamas and Islamic Jihad, and after the election of Barak in 1999, there were signs of improvement in the Palestinian economy, and hope was rekindled. The closures became less frequent. But these gains were slow to take hold, and they hardly succeeded in bringing the economic situation back to the level it had been at in 1993. Hope was rapidly slipping away, and the word on the Palestinian street was that the situation would soon deteriorate. The suicide bombings had been thwarted; but the volatile mix of widespread anger and deep despair over the faltering peace process was approaching the flash point in the Palestinian community. The pressure continued to build as Jewish settlement in the West Bank steadily expanded.

Just to the east of the Bethlehem checkpoint was a construction site on a hill—a Jewish settlement on expropriated West Bank land, known to Israelis as Har Homa. The construction cranes were clearly visible, swinging steel girders into place, and the concrete mixers barreled in and out of the development with fresh loads for foundations. When completed, Har Homa would house 10,000. And just to the west was the sprawling settlement of Gilo, which already housed some 40,000 Israelis. These two settlements and the roads that connected them formed a wall along the southern end of Jerusalem, a link in the chain of some 140 Jewish settlements that dotted the West Bank. The barrier of roads and residential communities physically cut off Bethlehem, and the adjacent Palestinian villages of Beit Sahour and Beit Jala, from Jerusalem.

Bethlehem, Beit Sahour, and Beit Jala formed a "Christian triangle" in the West Bank, containing the highest concentration of the Palestinian Christian population. Roughly 30 percent of Bethlehem's 30,000 inhabitants were Christian; and Beit Sahour and Beit Jala, each with approximately 12,000 residents, were about 75 percent Christian. About two-thirds of all Palestinian Christians in the West Bank, Gaza, and Jerusalem lived in one of these three towns.

Driving into Bethlehem from the checkpoint, the road led past a United Nations refugee camp where thousands of Palestinian refugees still lived in cramped and crowded conditions, just as they did in dozens of camps in the West Bank and Gaza. It was easy to miss the squalor of the camp from the road, since the camp was tucked in behind a cluster of storefronts and its crude housing tumbled down a slope, out of view.

After this point, the road opened up into two lanes again and passed through the ramshackle city of Bethlehem, with its tacky souvenir shops and *shwarma* stands where lamb roasted on a spit. Jackhammers pounded and clouds of plaster dust swirled from the construction sites of new hotels and restaurants. One such site was the new Inter-Continental Hotel, built in the grand old Jacir Palace, once the home of a prominent and wealthy Christian family that has since emigrated. On this day, the workers were installing plate glass windows in the beautifully appointed palace built of Jerusalem stone and marble. The Inter-Continental, and local Palestinian investors, had sunk some $45 million into the project, which included a massive complex of 250 rooms, indoor gardens, and swimming pools. Throughout 1999 and the first half of 2000, Bethlehem seemed gripped by an almost messianic belief in the coming of millions of American and European tourists to celebrate the millennium, and the hundreds of millions of dollars in potential revenue they would bring with them. And of the dozens of new hotels and scores of shops and restaurants built to accommodate this expected burst of tourism, the Jacir Palace was the crown jewel.

Even in May, the skeletal outlines of the Christmas lights strung in the shapes of stars and candles and snowflakes and manger scenes were still hung across sections of Bethlehem. They go unlit at this time of year, but remain as a kind of suspended hope in a future season of great commercial promise. In the aftermath of the New Year celebrations and the visit of the pope, a quiet had settled over Bethlehem. The town had seen a steady stream of tourism, but the celebrated papal visit and the Easter holidays had not produced the numbers the restaurant and hotel owners were hoping for. At the Abu Shanab restaurant, a pleasant and popular place that served fresh, well-seasoned lamb, the proprietors (two brothers) told me they had only one customer on the day the pope visited—an American who dashed in and bought two bottles of mineral water and then left.

In his office at City Hall, Bethlehem's mayor, Hanna Nasser, told me that there was an air of failed expectations in the city, and investors were worried. With the tourists not coming and the peace process not moving forward, Christian Palestinian families, he confided to me, were continuing their slow and steady exodus. Nasser,

65, hailed from one of the oldest and most respected Christian families in the city, and he had watched this mass emigration all his life. Bethlehem's Christian presence, he said, had diminished from as much as a 95 percent majority in 1948 to no more than a third at the end of the millennium. The smaller towns of Beit Sahour and Beit Jala still had Christian majorities, but they too had suffered massive waves of emigration that had essentially kept the populations of these towns frozen at the level of 1948—even as the Muslim communities around them swelled with much higher birthrates and the Jewish population within Israel grew exponentially through immigration. Nasser estimated that in his own extended family, about 700 had emigrated and 200 had stayed.

"It is sad to see the Christian character of the place where the Lord Jesus was born disappearing," he said. "But why is this happening? Why are our Christian families leaving? It is pure economics. The historical fact that precipitated an exodus of Christians was the creation of the state of Israel. The Israelis have confiscated land around Bethlehem, much of it belonging to Christian families and institutions, to build Jewish settlements. And then the Israeli military used these settlements to close off our access to East Jerusalem. When they did this, they cut off the lifeblood of our economy. They know exactly what they are doing and exactly the impact it will have on our economy."

This was, of course, a politician speaking. The mayor was a political appointee of Yasser Arafat and could be expected to adhere to the political line of the Palestinian Authority. So his presentation of facts avoided previous migrations of Christians out of the Holy Land, including Bethlehem—migrations that had begun long before the modern state of Israel came into existence. The first big wave left in World War I, when Palestine was ruled by the Ottoman Empire. In fact, the Palestinian Christians living in Santiago, Chile; San Pedro Sula, Honduras; and San Salvador, El Salvador, are to this day still called *turcos*, which is Spanish for "Turks." Waves of emigration continued out of Bethlehem and other Christian towns in the West Bank under Jordanian rule, between 1948 and 1967, before Israel captured the West Bank from Jordan.

But certainly, thirty-three years of Israeli occupation had contributed to the flight, largely through economic policies that seemed intent on choking the Palestinian economy. The most visible example of this in Bethlehem, as Nasser pointed out, was the settlement of Har Homa. The settlement and the highways that connected it to similar settlements in the West Bank were part of Israel's explicit strategy to expand the municipal boundaries. Har Homa, which in Hebrew means "Walled Mountain," was built on a hilltop known in Arabic as Jebel Abu Ghneim. To the Palestinians, it was one of the most flagrant violations of the interim peace agreement, which had called for the two sides to refrain from unilateral actions that would change what were known as "facts on the ground." One of the bitter ironies of Har Homa was that now it was being built by Palestinian laborers who felt they had no choice but to take these jobs, which paid better than similar positions available in the Palestinian-ruled areas. For the roughly 1,200 laborers who depended for survival on the roughly $20 per day that they earned there, it was a desperately sad choice. Even more bitterly ironic was the fact that most of the lucrative contracts at Har Homa for marble, concrete, welding, trucking, and other materials and services subcontracted out by the large Israeli contractors were going to a network of powerful, politically well-connected Palestinian-owned firms. Some of the owners of the Palestinian companies cashing in on Har Homa and other settlements were purportedly members of the ruling inner circle of the Palestinian Authority. This was but one of many distressing examples of how a corrupt leadership undercut Palestinians' national aspirations. For many ordinary Palestinians who knew these facts, the leaders' sharp rhetoric against new Israeli settlements rang hollow.

Har Homa was being built on land that straddled Beit Sahour and Bethlehem. After the war of 1967, the land had been occupied and then annexed by Israel to Jerusalem. The pine forest that had covered the hillside before the construction began had been the last open space in Beit Sahour and Bethlehem and the last tract of developable land for the expansion of these tightly crowded communities. Palestinian legal advocates had fought in the Israeli courts to represent the original Palestinian landowners, a mix of Muslim and Christian families who held Ottoman-era deeds to the land. But establishing the legal validity of these historical deeds in the Israeli courts was a complex and tangled process that ultimately failed. The Israeli government approved the construction of the housing in Israeli courts, under Israeli land laws, despite violations of international law and numerous resolutions that prohibited settlement on occupied land.

The Banoura family was among the Christian clans of Beit Sahour that lost land to the construction of Har Homa. Michael Banoura was a 27-year-old graduate of law school whose passion for justice was ignited by the confiscation of his father's land. He met with me at the Beit Sahour town hall, where he wanted to show me the tax records on file and the topographical map that proved that his grandfather and his four great-uncles had each owned a parcel of land. And he showed me the records that indicated that the family had paid taxes to the Jordanian government from 1952 to 1967. He said the deed indicated that his great-grandfather had bought the land in 1921 for approximately 100 Palestinian pounds. The land, which had been subdivided into five lots, totaled approximately five acres. In tax records, the land was denoted as Umm al-Asafir, which means "Mother of the Birds." We drove out to the site, which was a beautiful, level pasture in a shallow wadi at the foot of the hill upon which the settlement was being built. A truck that bore the logo of a Palestinian firm hauled a load of earth from the construction site and dumped it on the pasture as we watched. This area was controlled by the Israeli Civil Administration, which had placed it under the jurisdiction of special military courts. These courts consistently ruled in favor of Israeli developers seeking permits for new settlement construction in the West Bank, which fit with the Israeli state's plan for continued expansion. However, ten Palestinian families—six of which were Christian (including the Banouras)—had filed a class action suit to block the construction of this particular settlement.

"It's our land, and it is taken from us, and we do nothing about it," said Michael. "The Israelis steal it and then our own Palestinian companies build on it. . . . I think Christians just aren't tough enough. They don't fight back. I think we should fight back, and that is why I became a lawyer. I know that land will be mine someday."

Settlement expansion like that at Har Homa has been carried out under Israel's left-leaning Labor and more rightist Likud governments, and it is clearly intended to create new "facts on the ground" in the West Bank. The strategy was to first plunk down trailer homes, then move in soldiers to protect the first pioneers, and then develop self-standing communities where only Israeli citizens lived. These would be surrounded by more military barricades, which would require the seizure of additional land. Much of the strategy in placing settlements was engineered and carried out by the retired Israeli general Ariel Sharon, through his cabinet postings under the governments of Menachem Begin and Benjamin Netanyahu. Sharon always carried rolled up maps of the West Bank and stressed these fortifications as not only necessary for Israel's strategic interests but also to ensure Israel's hold over the vast and precious aquifers in the West Bank, which provided Israel with roughly one-third of its water.

The Israeli policy of supporting the construction of new Jewish settlements in the occupied West Bank and Gaza was not born simply out of a need for more housing for Jews. There was plenty of open land to the west of Jerusalem, and vast reserves in the Negev and the Galilee that Israel was not bothering to develop. This was a policy designed to establish an Israeli foothold on what the settlement movement saw as land God promised to Jews. It was a policy carried out in the belief that once Jews were living there, it would be difficult, perhaps impossible, to make them move. There are few who would disagree that the policy was working, at least for now. Israel and its ally the United States, which did little to prevent the settlements, seemed blind in the first half of 2000 to just how much anger and despair the settlement expansion was causing among Palestinians.

The natural valley that extends from the southern end of Jerusalem into Beit Sahour and Bethlehem is an old pilgrimage route and is dotted with the archaeological remains of Byzantine monasteries and with various sites commemorating the birth of Jesus. One such site near Har Homa was the Church of Bir Qadisum, Arabic for "the Sitting Place." Tradition holds it to be the last place where Mary rested on her journey from Nazareth to Bethlehem. Located on the very site of the Har Homa construction is St. Paul's Hill, a Franciscan compound that contains the remains of a fifth-century monastery. Today, the crumbling stone walls of the monastery stand silent watch over the frenetic construction—cranes moving across the sky, cement mixers grinding away, jackhammers pounding—of the modern housing blocks that will be Har Homa.

Judith Green, an Israeli peace activist and a senior researcher at the Hebrew University's Institute of Archaeology who surveyed the West Bank hills so laden with these treasures of the early church, spearheaded an effort in 1996 to turn these lands into a kind of preserve of Christian archaeological sites. The idea was introduced to the Jerusalem municipal council and to the Roman Catholic and Greek Orthodox patriarchs; but it was promptly dismissed by the Israeli authorities and politely ignored by the Catholic and Orthodox church hierarchies, who apparently saw no political gain in challenging Israel's plans for new settlements and new roads.

"The fact is that what affects both Christians and Muslims in day-to-day life is the economic situation, and it is a desperate one here," explained Nasser. "We have roughly 30 percent unemployment and a per capita annual income below $1,000. That is why Christians leave. Muslims leave as well, but Christians historically have more links to the West, to North America and Latin America and Europe, so it is easier for them to find their way over there."

Israeli land policies have severely restricted Palestinian industrial and residential growth, and have had a devastating impact on Bethlehem's tourism-reliant economy. By limiting Bethlehem's potential for growth and effectively severing it from Jerusalem, Israel made it impossible for the Palestinian tourism industry to operate. Under the Palestinian Authority, Bethlehem had struggled to build in any vacant corner that could be found in the crowded tumble of a town. But the Israeli settlement chain took the most desirable land between Jerusalem and Bethlehem, Nasser said, where hotels for tourists would have been most conveniently located. The Palestinian tourism industry has fought hard to position itself; but through the years, Israel has engineered a near monopoly over tourism, and as a result, controls the lion's share of the industry. Total tourism revenue for 1995 was the equivalent of about U.S. $26 million in the West Bank and Gaza, compared to about $3 billion for Israel (not including $155 million in East Jerusalem). Among the most effective methods Israel has used to control the industry are the legal licensing of tour guides and the requirement that tour groups be accompanied at holy sites only by registered Israeli tour guides. In 2000, of the 8,000 tour guides registered by Israel, only 60 were classified as "Israeli Arab," and 48 were Palestinians from the West Bank—a smaller number of registered Palestinian tour guides than in 1967.

The Israeli tourism industry also has prevented Palestinian tour operators from traveling freely from Bethlehem into the other tourist sites in Jerusalem and to the north in Nazareth, thus shutting them out of the larger tourism market in the Holy Land. Israeli restrictions have severely inhibited the establishment of Palestinian tourist bus companies in the West Bank and Gaza. This in large part explains why the vast majority of Christians who visit the Holy Land come on Israeli package tours. These packages put them in Israeli hotels, feed them in Israeli restaurants, and bring them to Israeli souvenir shops. If they do take them to the Palestinian shops where wood carvings and olive-wood rosaries and decorative ornaments are sold, the Israeli tour operators typically take an unusually large commission—sometimes as high as 30 percent. Nowhere is tourism as political as in the Holy Land.

Israeli guides undergo a rigorous course as part of their certification. But several Palestinians who have been permitted to take the course say that it has an ideological bent toward describing the Jewish side of history in the Holy Land and skipping lightly over the centuries-long development of Islamic culture. It also requires fluency in Hebrew, which puts an added burden on Palestinians. The history of Christian sites is given relatively more attention in the Israeli guide course because of the large number of Christian tourists; but that history, too, is given relatively short shrift, some of the graduates told me, compared to the concentration on Jewish history. Most tour guides I met were professionals who tried to present a fair interpretation of history and commentary on the sites holy to all three faiths. I've heard many pilgrims tell me they were very happy with their Israeli tour guides. But there were also a lot of bad guides out there. Just about any day of the week, at holy sites in Bethlehem and Jerusalem, tour guides could be heard putting an Israeli nationalist spin on history—especially on recent history. Often these more ideological Israeli guides, probably out of their own ignorance of Palestinian society, plant seeds of fear in the tourists and advise them to see the sites and quickly move on out of the Palestinian-ruled areas and to be cautious of Palestinian shop owners. Such guides have created a climate of mistrust that has kept many Christian tourists from encountering Palestinians.

The mobility of Palestinian tour guides and Palestinian buses were two issues specifically addressed in the interim agreements of the peace process. But by the year 2000, common standards for tour guides had not yet been established. The two sides had not even met to discuss the criteria. This omission has effectively prevented the Palestinian-registered tour guides (except for a small number selectively approved) from operating in Israel; and the only buses allowed free movement there are still Israeli-owned.

The Palestinian sector of the Holy Land's tourism industry was historically run by Christian families. Israel's constriction of this industry therefore has fallen heavily on Christian-owned businesses. One firm that had survived these economic challenges was the Guiding Star Travel Agency in Beit Jala. Mark Khano, the second generation of his family to manage the 50-year-old business, was a graduate of Oxford University, but unlike many of his friends who were educated abroad, he brought his skills back home. He specifically sought out new markets, including the "Nativity Trail," which traces the path of Joseph and Mary from Nazareth to Bethlehem. It involved eight days of hiking and camping and what he calls "modern pilgrimage, which is layered with elements of political, spiritual, adventure, and ecological tourism." "The forces bearing down on this industry and all of the Palestinian economy are extraordinary," said Khano. "It is nearly impossible to survive without significant financial backing to ride through the hard times, a well-educated management, and the sheer force of will. And even then many of us are not making it."

The young, educated, and talented Palestinians who stay on, such as Khano, are the Palestinian economy's best hope. The peace process brought back some of those who had gone abroad to invest their efforts in the Palestinian future and to renew their connections to family roots. But by 2000, many were despairing at what the peace process meant. When I traveled through Bethlehem, I occasionally stopped in to see the Anastas family. On one such occasion, I met with Wa'el, the last son remaining in Palestine, who still lived with his mother in the family home. The home seemed quiet, in sharp contrast to all the commotion and joy that had filled it at Christmas in 1999, when members of the extended family had returned to their native city from all over the world to celebrate the holiday together.

Wa'el was an invaluable source of information, helping me better understand the economic forces bearing down on Bethlehem. His passion for economic theory was motivated in part by the loneliness he felt due to the disappearance of his brothers and sisters and so many of his friends and colleagues—as if solving the economic equation that had created their exodus would somehow bring him contentment. Wa'el had earned a master's degree at California State College at Sacramento, and had completed a thesis focusing on economic changes in the aftermath of the 1967 war.

"The economic conditions for the Palestinian people improved significantly under Israel," he began, "but the gains were artificial. What Israel did is to destroy the Palestinian agricultural sector, and then shift all of the farmers off of the land and into jobs in construction and industry where they could be a controlled workforce without any rights or ability to organize. The Palestinians became a low-paid workforce for the construction of Israel, its settlements, its schools, its factories. Then the Israelis dumped the Israeli agricultural products grown on the Israeli kibbutz, which served to deflate the prices and further destroy what was left of Palestinian agriculture. They also restricted the Palestinian export of goods, until finally the Palestinians were left with nothing except the olive groves, which required little in the way of labor and were often harvested by families for personal use. These are the forces that shaped our daily lives, and when I began reading the world's leading economists and piecing this together for myself, I wanted to return. I never wanted to leave Palestine, and I was drawn back home. And I was passionate about wanting to be part of a force for change."

Wa'el returned home from studies abroad in 1994 at the most optimistic moment in the peace process. Arafat was triumphantly returning to Gaza after twenty-eight years in exile. Wa'el took a job with the new Palestinian Authority, training the bureaucrats who would take their roles in the new government. But not long after Wa'el's return, his good feelings began to fade. He quickly realized that he did not want to work for the Palestinian Authority, having seen early on the chaos and corruption and compromise that were taking place. He instead became a program manager with the United Nations Development Project (UNDP), where he felt he would be able to contribute more effectively to the economic improvement of his people.

On one day in late May, after we had talked for a while, I noticed that a *humsein* was moving in. The *humsein* is a dry, yellowish wind stirred up in the desert, which blows into towns such as Bethlehem and Jerusalem, on the outskirts of the Judean desert, toward the end of spring. Wa'el covered his eyes against the wind and the fine dust that it carries with it and told me he was heading for the checkpoint for an appointment in Jerusalem at the UNDP offices. He was leaving himself two hours to get through the checkpoint, even though it was no more than a fifteen- or twenty-minute drive. Wa'el does not have a permit to take his car from Bethlehem to Jerusalem, and he feels humiliated every day, commuting to Jerusalem.

"The peace process has turned out to be a lie," said Wa'el, as he walked me out to our cars. "It took all of us a while to realize that, but once you do realize it, the future seems very bleak. I think all of us wonder what is going to happen. Every morning that some 19-year-old Israeli in a uniform demands my identification papers, I think about this. Everyone here knows there is a political storm coming, there has to be," he added as he shielded his eyes against the blowing wind, got into his car, and headed for the checkpoint.

. . .

The despair that so many Palestinians felt had become fertile ground for the Islamic movements Hamas and Islamic Jihad, which had seen a surprising increase in Bethlehem. Such movements reaped the benefits of the culture of intolerance—a culture that was beginning to be felt more acutely among Bethlehem's Christians than ever before. Many of the Palestinian Christian community's most educated and wealthy were leaving or thinking about leaving. However, many others, like Maryam Taljia, could not afford to emigrate. And for them, life was growing more difficult.

Maryam owned a small dry goods store just down the hill from Manger Square. Framed by a portrait of the Holy Family hanging on the wall, she sat leaning over an old cash register, which she opened every now and then to deposit a shekel (a coin then worth about U.S. $0.25) or two from children coming in to buy candy. She was bitter about life under the new Palestinian Authority, and furious about what she viewed as a growing bigotry toward Christians, evidenced by her Muslim neighbors. She said that during the violent clashes of the first *intifada,* she had closed her shop doors in solidarity with the PLO-declared strikes, as had her Muslim neighbors. During one violent demonstration, her 57-year-old husband had been caught up in the crowd and was beaten badly with an Israeli police baton. He never recovered from his head wounds, and he died two weeks later. Her sons had been arrested for taking part in various demonstrations. Having borne all that, she profoundly resented the way the sheikhs at a neighborhood mosque spoke of Jews and Christians as "infidels" in their sermons, which were broadcast on loudspeakers from the minarets. "Suddenly it is all about religion," she said.

Night was falling over Bethlehem. The evening call to prayer was coming on over the loudspeaker. Maryam was visibly annoyed by the volume of the muezzin, which stopped our conversation. She turned and flipped a switch on the wall behind the cash register, lighting up a six-foot neon cross that she and a half dozen other Christian families and shopkeepers had erected atop their roofs. "This is to say that we are Christians, that we are proud, and that we have been in Bethlehem for two thousand years," she said.

I wondered how these issues resonated among young Palestinian Christians, and so I headed over to the Bethlehem University for answers. The university had been founded in 1972 with direct support and funding from the Vatican, as part of an effort to stem the tide of Palestinian Christian emigration. The idea was to offer a solid academic institution open to local students of all faiths, so as to keep Palestinians from attending universities in America and Europe, where they tended to remain upon graduation. Now, three decades after the university was founded, the campus is nearly 75 percent Muslim. Christians complained to me of feeling confined by a rising Islamic influence among the student body. Hamas had become a strong force in student government, and its members were demanding that one of the classrooms be converted into a mosque. The Catholic administration of the university thus far had resisted, intent on preserving the Christian character of the school.

On a late spring afternoon, in the courtyard at the entrance to the college, the cultural breakdown was visible. Groups of Islamic young women were wearing head scarves and talking in a small cluster among themselves—a segregation of the sexes that was in line with their traditional Islamic culture. Circled around a water fountain, young Christian women in tight jeans and T-shirts and wearing gold crucifixes laughed and sipped coffee with young Christian men with jet-black hair and leather jackets, who also wore crosses. A group of intensely political, Islamist male students congregated on several benches in a far corner, talking about the upcoming student elections. The more secular students from the communist party (refashioned as the People's Party after the Cold War ended)—Muslim and Christian alike—were putting up cartoons lampooning corruption in the Palestinian Authority. These students in particular seemed to float freely between the cultural divisions in the courtyard. Even with their diverse cultures and ideologies, most Christians and Muslims got along well. They were friends and colleagues, and there was great esprit de corps among them, for the most part. Still, teachers and students said that they saw the Christians and Muslims increasingly pulling apart; and this surprised and worried them, because these two groups represented the future of a Palestinian state.

Amid this fraying of the social fabric, the campus was abuzz with the story of Rania and Nael. It had become a kind of postmodern fable about interfaith existence and the ways in which Palestinian society still clung to tribal notions of honor and shame. She was Christian. He was Muslim. And when Rania and Nael fell in love, everyone in their hometown of Beit Sahour knew there would be trouble.

Nael was a 27-year-old leader in the Popular Front for the Liberation of Palestine's Democratic Social Movement for Youth, where the political rhetoric was secular and where the community activists preached unity among all Arabs, Muslim and Christian. He was from a large and traditional farming family originally from Hebron, and he was confident and handsome and at ease with himself.

Rania was a 17-year-old high school student from a family shattered by an alcoholic father. Her father's extended Christian family were from a long line of respected merchants in Beit Sahour and Bethlehem. He himself worked as a plasterer when he was not in a drunken haze. Rania was a beauty with dark brown eyes and a disarming smile. Many of the young Christian men of the town had vied for her affections. In this community it was still common for a girl to be wed straight out of high school, and it was assumed that one of them would soon marry her. To Rania, Nael represented stability, groundedness; but perhaps equally important, he was forbidden her by the strict social norms of the Christian enclave of Beit Sahour—a community that in her eyes was full of hypocrisy and anything but Christian in the way it had dealt with her family's very obvious problems.

When she openly began dating Nael, young men in her extended family threatened to kill her if she did not break off the relationship. This reaction may seem outrageous to an American; but a strict religious tribalism, with an accompanying, deep sense of honor and pride, are at the center of Arab society. The price for casting shame upon your tribe, or by extension your religion, was severe. At a minimum, Rania knew that if she dated Nael—certainly, if she married him—she would be cut off from her family. In this part of the world, honor is everybody's business.

For the diminishing Christian population, the liaison between Rania and Nael was particularly sensitive because it raised the feared specter of conversion. With only 32,000 Christians in all of the West Bank, conversion to Islam could virtually erase Christian culture in a matter of one or two generations. This was the feeling expressed at Memories, a Christian-owned bar in Bethlehem where young people in their mid- to late 20s get together on Friday nights. There were, of course, examples of Christian-Muslim marriages throughout Palestinian society, but they tended to occur only among the highly educated elite.

I recalled a Christmas party I had attended at Memories in 1999. Loud Latin music blared, and many of the young Palestinians of the diaspora were in town, some of them speaking Spanish and French. There were also Palestinian Americans who had returned home with their families for the holidays. The emigrant crowd seemed more stylish and affluent, and an unspoken, mild resentment emanated toward them from those who had stayed behind. At one corner table, a group of women in their twenties, who lived in Bethlehem, were smoking cigarettes, drinking rum and Coke, and eyeing the dance floor. The conversation turned to Rania and Nael. Several of the women said the story was the talk of the town—not only because of its highly volatile mix of interfaith issues but also because it exposed a demographic reality that was a raw nerve for young Palestinian Christian women. They knew full well the stakes of marrying outside their faith, and most agreed they would never do so. But all of their reasons—traditional, cultural, spiritual—boiled down to the fact that they knew that such marriages almost never worked. However, the women also complained that there simply were not enough young Christian men to go around. Bethlehem, Beit Sahour, and Beit Jala were full of women in their 30s and 40s who had never been married. Too many of the good men emigrated to America or Europe, they said, and too many of those who stayed tended to have some kind of a problem that was keeping them there—a lack of ambition, a lack of funds, or an addiction to drugs or alcohol. For these single women in a traditional society, there was little social life and little opportunity to meet eligible and attractive men.

Making things worse was the fact that in Arab society men in their late 20s and 30s tend to marry women just out of high school or in their early 20s. "If you're not married by the time you are 30, it is over in Palestinian society," said Halla, a 30-year-old secretary. "And for Christian women, this is becoming an issue of whether our families will even continue their lineage. There are simply no Christian men."

An official from the World Bank, who oversaw various projects aimed at helping the Palestinians develop their economy and stem the tide of emigration, compared the situation of Palestinian Christians to that of "an endangered species" of wildlife. "At some point, it becomes mathematical that the species cannot survive if the women are not mating. I mean this is not an exaggeration for the Palestinian Christians, this is becoming a very real Darwinian reality," he said.

That is why the coupling of Rania and Nael was so potent in the

Christian community. Even the Muslim community, which was typically less absorbed by the issue, seemed to understand the damage that interfaith marriage could do to their relationships with their Christian neighbors. But Rania and Nael were married in a lawyer's office on Saladin street in East Jerusalem. The news of the marriage touched off a firestorm in Beit Sahour.

At one point, several hundred young Christian men gathered in the middle of the night in front of Nael's family home, where the couple were temporarily living. The men threw stones and one person in the crowd threatened to attack Rania and disfigure her face with acid, a gruesome form of retribution seen in other extreme "honor" cases in the Arab world. Eventually, Rania's family convinced her to go to a monastery in Bethany (Al-Ayzariyah), on the Mount of Olives, where young women who have "shamed" their families are taken in.

One of the angry young Christian men who had gathered outside Nael's home was Fadi Awad Bannoura. A thin, handsome, 23-year-old native of Beit Sahour, Fadi was a cousin of Rania's, but he was quick to point out that this was more than just a family issue. "This was a Christian issue," he said. "We Christians have a saying here regarding women who convert to Islam through marriage, 'Today it is one, tomorrow two, and by the third day they are all gone.'" He was whispering his thoughts to me while waiting to pick up his wife, Samara, 20, who was a student at Bethlehem University, in hotel management.

Fadi and Samara invited me to their home, where they felt they could talk more openly. They lived above the Bannoura family's olivewood factory, where Fadi fashions wooden crucifixes, sculptures of Jesus, and tiny crèches with figurines for the tourist shops in Manger Square, which resell them at a markup to tourists. The couple's livelihood thus is tied to the tourism industry, which ultimately is controlled by Israel. The powerlessness of their lives seemed to make them eager—even vengeful—in the enforcement of tribal customs over their community. "I think that she deserved to have the acid thrown in her face," Samara told me as she graciously offered sugar for my tea. "She made a mistake, she deserves it. If a Christian girl sees she can get away with it, then another one will try it, and the whole Christian community will disappear. I think it is sad that she is being made an example, but it is necessary."

Seeing my obvious shock at this statement, Fadi tried to explain: "The Christians of Europe and America should look at what is happening here. The world has no idea of how the Christians of this land are threatened by Islam, by the culture as it treats women, by the way in which they want to dominate the local Christians here. We cannot live in their Islamic society, and they do not want us to live in it. This is the truth here, everything else people tell you about brotherhood is only to sound nice. Of course there are some Muslims and some Christians who get along very well. But the truth is, Muslims are violent, they steal, they treat our women with disdain and rudeness, and it is very hard to live with them if you are not one of them."

Fadi's anger was obviously fueled by his deep frustration with his life and its limitations. Anger had soured into bigotry. The couple's rigidity reflected the sense that many Palestinian Christians have of having been backed into a corner, of clinging to a slippery foothold, in a land where their claim should have been as strong as anyone else's: the land where their faith began. It was easy to understand why some simply gave up and opted to leave. "The Christians of the West look at us all here as Arab, and they assume we are Muslim," he said. "Why don't they look at us as fellow Christians? Why don't they see that we live in the place where the faith began? Instead they look down on us all as Arabs and Muslims. This is the fact."

For almost a decade Fadi's family had tried to emigrate to the United States, working tirelessly through attorneys in California, where his uncle Elias had emigrated after going to college there in 1970. Elias owns a grocery store on Pleasant Hill in San Francisco, and, following the pattern of many immigrants, the family has tried to use Elias as a kind of grappling hook to bring in other family members to America. It was Fadi's dream to bring his wife to America and start a family there, leaving behind the tensions, turmoil, and intolerance in his homeland. He also seemed to want to free himself of his own growing prejudice, which he felt was shaped by the world around him. But the fact that Fadi was 21 (and therefore was not considered legally dependent) had prevented him from obtaining a visa. His family was leaving, but he and Samara would remain behind. He felt trapped.

Fadi brought me down into the shop to show me his work. He seemed to be producing more than he could sell. Busts of Jesus, and the crèche figurines, were lined up on shelves and tabletops and every available corner. Sawdust on the floor was piled at least six inches deep. The olivewood sculptures of Jesus's face were beautifully crafted. But I noticed that his carved Jesus always wore a crown of thorns and looked sad, lamenting, defeated. There was no Jesus in his glory. The carvings of the infant Jesus for the crèche scene were abstracted, with no detail of an innocent infant smile, no hint of the light he would bring to the world. Even the figurines of the shepherds in the crèche appeared despondent, almost mournful—an incongruous expression for a few local men experiencing the arrival of the messiah.

Fadi took me out to the yard, where piles of old olive branches that he used for his wood carvings were drying in the hot midday sun. He explained that the woodpile came from trees uprooted in the building of the Har Homa settlement. He had purchased the wood cheaply from the Israelis. To the west, we could see the construction cranes on the distant horizon, moving against the sky. I asked whether he saw any irony in the fact that the wood he used to make Christmas gifts for tourists was harvested from that same Israeli policy of settlement expansion that had enclosed his community and restricted its economy. But he didn't see it. When I tried to ask him again, he shrugged indifferently. It was a gesture that captured the noticeable lack of self-reflection that pervaded this part of the world. Fadi seemed to have little ability to make connections between the events that were happening around him.

Fadi stood in front of the olivewood pile and gazed eastward, out over the Judean desert. And then I noticed that his face bore the same despondent, mournful expression that he had carved so patiently into the wooden figurines of the shepherds overlooking the expressionless infant Jesus. I thought about all the Christian pilgrims who would buy his figurines and take them home in their suitcases, never knowing about Fadi and the real source of the despair on those shepherds' faces.

After Jesus was born, an angel appeared in the hills outside Bethlehem, according to the birth narrative in the Gospel of Luke. The angel came to a group of local shepherds guarding their flock at night, and the shepherds became the earliest witnesses to the light that Christians believe the infant Jesus brought to the world. There was an important message in the fact that the first to know of the birth of the Christ child were these rough-hewn shepherds. They were the everyman of ancient Palestine, the hard-working peasant class of a Jewish society under Roman rule, who would be the first to recognize the hope of salvation that this newborn wrapped in swaddling clothes up the hill in Bethlehem had brought to the world.

Today, the archaeological site known as Shepherds' Fields consists of two separately walled olive groves—one owned by the Greek Orthodox, and the other by the Roman Catholics. The Fields are viewed cynically by some as just another attraction established for the pilgrims who have flocked to the Holy Land through the ages. The fourth-century remains of walls and chapels in both olive groves, however, attest to the fact that the locations have been visited for a long time. Some biblical historians believe that this fact lends credence to the authenticity of the Fields; others maintain it is unlikely that these traditional sites have any true historical value.

VI

Beit Sahour

THE SHEPHERDS' FIELDS

An angel of the Lord appeared to them, and the glory of the Lord shone around them, and they were terrified. But the angel said to them, "Do not be afraid. I bring you good news of great joy that will be for all the people. Today in the town of David a Savior has been born to you; he is Christ the Lord."

LUKE 2:9–11 (NIV)

THE EARLY SPRING RAINS laid a carpet of yellow-green over the hills of the West Bank village of Beit Sahour. These terraced limestone slopes—saturated with runoff in April and May but returning to dry, rugged indifference by June or July—are associated with a two-thousand-year-old mystery. They were silent witness to an angel's visitation of humble shepherds guarding their flocks one winter night. As the shepherds wandered under a star-canopied sky—so the story goes—an angel appeared and announced the birth of the Davidic messiah promised by God, and then guided them to the spot where the infant lay. In the year 2000, Beit Sahour was the locale of a more modern mystery, and its inhabitants were once again guided by what could be considered either a prophetic message for their people or just a practical quest for justice.

This community of about 12,000—about 75 percent of whom were Christian—had played a critical role in the first Palestinian *intifada,* or uprising, which began in the winter of 1987 and 1988. Beit Sahour yielded its share of young rock-throwing *shebab,* just like any other West Bank town; but what set this small Christian enclave apart was that it was also an educated and relatively affluent community. Its residents wanted to participate in a revolt against the Israeli power structure that dominated them, but they wanted to do so in a way that fit within their cultural context, within their Christian faith. Out of this community, then, came a unique movement within the *intifada*—its truest and most effective and perhaps its only sustained campaign of nonviolent resistance.

Why Beit Sahour, one of the few Palestinian towns and villages that still had a Christian majority, was the only place to mobilize peaceful civil disobedience—as opposed to rock- and Molotov-cocktail-throwing mobs—was a riddle. The answers (several are possible) reveal interlocking truths about the local Christian presence and what its disappearance would mean for all Palestinians and Israelis alike.

Perhaps the most important factor at work was that Beit Sahour was a tight-knit community, where families had known each other through centuries and had assumed a vigilance about their town, protecting it from outside influences and guarding its character as the place of the "Shepherds' Fields." *Beit Sahour* in Arabic means "House of the Guardians," referring to the shepherds who protected the flocks. Nonviolence, too, requires a shared attitude of common guardianship, which provides the reassurance that those marching beside you will not suddenly pick up a rock and throw it (because the moment they do, everyone will be hurt by the act). The inhabitants of Beit Sahour were also relatively well educated and prosperous; at that time, the town boasted the highest number of advanced university degrees per capita of any locale in the West Bank. The town was also well known for its industrious and enterprising spirit, which had spawned many thriving, family-owned businesses, from textile mills and woodworking shops to bakeries.

But beyond these elements of class and culture, I wondered whether there was something inherently Christian about the nonviolent movement in Beit Sahour. The community leaders who organized it adamantly shook their heads "no" when I asked this question. In fact, these leaders, born Christian but secular in the way they lived—even tending toward a distinctly agnostic and communist ideology—felt that to even ask that question was to fail to understand them and their contribution to the first *intifada*. Yet some of the people who participated in their movement told me they felt that perhaps there was a thread that was *culturally* Christian. Others explained it more carefully as a pattern shaped by the influences of Western Christian thinking on secular democracy and its definition of the rights of the individual, which made the fabric of their society and the movement it produced different. Perhaps these people, who saw themselves as descendants of the first followers of Jesus, sensed that to define the movement as specifically Christian would have detracted from its power by separating them from their Muslim Palestinian neighbors, who also were fighting against the occupation. They knew that theirs was a voice within the protests, but not one that should be seen as shouting louder than the others, especially not in this land with its history of Western Christian rule in relation to Islam and to Judaism. In other words, they were influenced by Western Christian ideas through their church and its educational institutions; but they were Eastern enough to be suspicious of the practical application of these lofty ideals. They were not going to be suckers for one more Western attempt to divide and rule; to allow themselves to be separated from Muslims would be demographic suicide.

The fact that Israel set out determinedly to crush this nonviolent movement and that even the PLO attempted to undercut the movement's gains testifies to its extraordinary power. Why was a peaceful protest more threatening than rock-throwing to Israel? And why did the PLO leadership—then in exile in Tunis—see the leaders of the Beit Sahour movement as a threat to their control over the *intifada*? What was there in this Christian community's nonviolent approach that challenged the leadership on both sides?

. . .

In the spring of 2000, I visited Samir ("Sami") Kheir in his family's wooden furniture-making shop, a trade that dated back more generations than anyone could remember. Sami, who was in his early 30s and married, with two children, had lived all his life in the confines of Beit Sahour's Christian community, and had never traveled much beyond Bethlehem and Jerusalem. The history of his land was a part of him and a part of his Christian identity, but it was so woven into his daily existence that he didn't think about it much. He thought more of his brother Edmond, who was in St. Louis, Missouri, about the salary his brother was able to make in construction there, and about the pull he felt to leave this place for opportunities elsewhere. It saddened him to think of leaving, but he was as fed up with the grim reality of life during "the peace process" as anyone.

Sami was listening to the latest news on a radio sprinkled with sawdust in a corner of the workshop. Over the buzz of table saws, the

Voice of Palestine was broadcasting a report of new clashes between Palestinian demonstrators and Israeli troops. The protests were in reaction to the passing of the deadline for the final peace deal that Israeli Prime Minister Ehid Barak had promised when he took office one year earlier and in reaction to Barak's failure to release Palestinian prisoners still held by Israel.

Standing there, in the sawdust of his family's shop, Sami remembered the time when he had become caught up in the chaos and bravado and the tragedy and the hopes of the first *intifada*. The images and the memories all came flooding back from a day he would never forget, twelve autumns earlier.

On October 30, 1988, a black column of thick, acrid smoke from burning tires spiraled up into the air, as Beit Sahour's main street swelled with about two hundred Palestinian *shebab*. They were kids, most of them between 14 and 18 years old, dragging large stones and cinder blocks into the road to block Israeli armored personnel carriers. Israeli soldiers armed with Galil assault rifles were moving in on foot. They fired tear gas shells first, and then warning shots into the air. Yitzhak Rabin, who was then Israel's defense minister, had announced that his forces would combat the uprising with "force, might, and beatings." At one point, Rabin famously vowed to "break their bones." Beit Sahour had become a stronghold of resistance.

Sami, his brother Edmond, and their mutual friend Eyad Abu Saadah were teenagers then. It was a Sunday, and they were coming out of Beit Sahour's Greek Orthodox church, squinting in the morning light. Even before the *intifada*, church for Palestinian Christians was a tribal outing, a show of force for the big clans, as well as a profession of faith. It was about Arab tradition and honor as much as it was about religion. And during the uprising—a time when Israel was imposing military laws that forbade any public gathering of more than ten males under the age of 30—the importance of the church as a gathering of strength for the Palestinian Christian community was as central as it had ever been. The Greek Orthodox clerical hierarchy had hardly been supportive of the uprising; but the edifice of the church, the building itself, had become an important place where the congregation gathered for political action as well as for prayer.

Sami, Edmond, and Eyad were the best of friends and completely inseparable. Originally, this triangle of buddies had been a foursome. But the fourth, Edmond Ghaneim, 18, had been killed by an Israeli soldier three months earlier, and the grief and anger were still raw. To them, Ghaneim was a martyr. Their Muslim Palestinian brothers in arms had often looked down on the tiny Christian minority as a coddled, Western-leaning, educated elite that had not sacrificed enough in the street. They were seen as the spoiled children of a merchant class—unlike the rugged, poor farm families and construction workers of the traditional Muslim tribes of neighboring Hebron. Suspicions ran high among Muslims that Christians who tried to stay out of the conflict were collaborators. A Muslim faction of Arafat's Fatah organization had plastered the Christian neighborhoods of Beit Sahour with graffiti that read, "Where are the martyrs?" For all of the youth of Beit Sahour and especially for these three friends, Ghaneim's death was a bitter tragedy but also a proud answer to that question.

So that Sunday morning, when they heard in the distance the sound of Israeli soldiers with a bullhorn, ordering the crowd to disperse, their movement toward the protests was instant, involuntary, and inevitable. Together, they descended the main street of Beit Sahour into a neighborhood known as the Valley of Abu Saada, a tangle of streets and alleys that was the theater of most local clashes with Israeli soldiers.

Sami and Edmond jumped into the rock-throwing. Not Eyad. He carefully selected smooth, round stones that fit neatly into the leather sling with which he had become legendarily accurate. Ten- and twelve-year-old children also scurried around, picking up the Israeli-fired "rubber bullets" (the variant then in use was actually a steel musket ball about the size of a pinball, coated in hard plastic) and handing them to Eyad. He loaded them into his sling, savoring the idea of throwing them back at the soldiers.

His weapon, called a *mukle'a* in Arabic, was straight out of the biblical tale of David and Goliath. The sling was made of two simple leather straps with a pouch to load the stones. It was the perfect Holy Land weapon—local youth slinging stones against a giant enemy. (This was an ironic turnabout, in that the slingshot-wielding David had been an Israelite, and the giant Goliath, Philistine. The Philistines had invaded and settled ancient Palestine before the Israelites arrived; they fought the Israelites to maintain a hold over the land more than one thousand years before the birth of Jesus. It seemed almost as though the Palestinians and the Israelis had been assigned their roles in a modern reversal of the biblical tale.)

The Israelis began firing into the crowd—first with tear gas, and then with "rubber bullets." The soldiers were just loading live ammunition. Eyad shielded his eyes against the tear gas as he peered around a corner. Suddenly his left leg was knocked out from under him. He scrambled back into an alleyway and saw a small hole where a bullet had torn through his pants, near the left front pocket. A blotch of red the size of a quarter quickly formed around the hole. Eyad told his friends to keep on throwing stones, and he limped to a backyard of a house and lay down beneath an olive tree. When his two friends checked on him minutes later, he was slipping into unconsciousness. Unbeknownst to them, the bullet had entered near Eyad's groin, severed the femoral artery, and then angled sharply upward into his stomach, ripping through vital organs and causing massive internal bleeding. Edmond held Eyad's head. There was no way to get an ambulance to him. Eyad died about fifteen minutes later.

Edmond and Sami carried Eyad's lifeless body up the hill to the side entrance of the Greek Orthodox church. They needed to find somewhere to hide the corpse, because they knew the Israelis would try to retrieve it. Israeli soldiers had been seizing the bodies of victims and refusing to release them for days because the funerals had become rallying points for the youth and often triggered more explosions of violence. Typically, the Israelis allowed only small burial ceremonies, attended by no more than ten members of a family. Edmond and Sami had seen this happen with their friend Ghaneim's funeral, and it had enraged them. Carrying their dead friend several hundred yards was an act of honor as well as defiance. Eyad would have the proper burial of a martyr.

But they knew they couldn't keep him in the church. The soldiers would check there, and they didn't trust the Greek Orthodox priests —who were notoriously collaborative with Israel—to keep quiet. Instead, they carried the body another several hundred yards, to a house in a nearby neighborhood. Soon soldiers arrived at Eyad's house—led there, it was believed, by informants from the neighborhood. His parents, Maryam and Bishara, were in shock. They were told their son was believed dead. The Israeli soldiers began to ransack the house, looking for his body. Later, Edmond and Sami were joined by Eyad's brother Jack, and the three of them moved the body again to an old, abandoned stone home. They were exhausted from this macabre exercise of hiding the corpse. The afternoon was wearing on, and the body that they shouldered like a heavy wooden cross was beginning to leak fluids and to smell of death.

The boys were determined to keep the body hidden while the

mukhtar of Beit Sahour (a kind of mayor or tribal leader) pleaded with the local Israeli military commanders to permit the family to have a decent burial and funeral procession the following morning. After negotiations, the Israelis promised not to confiscate the body; but they insisted that only ten close relatives would be permitted to carry out the burial in the church cemetery, which must take place that very night. There could be no daytime funeral, not with tensions running so high. Either they produced the body now, or there would be arrests. Eyad's parents sent word to Jack and the two friends to bring Eyad's body home.

With flickering light from votive candles and a single flashlight, Jack and his father dug Eyad's grave while Israeli soldiers stood over them. Sami and Edmond remained in hiding, fearing that they would be arrested. A cluster of ten close relatives gathered and lowered the casket into the grave with rope.

Bishara turned to one of the local Israeli commanders, whose name was Udi. Furious and exhausted and overcome with emotion, Bishara broke down in tears and asked the Israeli commander: "How could you do this? How could you kill a young boy? He was just a boy."

Udi responded in Arabic: "This is not a game. Your sons cannot attack soldiers and expect us to do nothing. This is not a child's game we are playing."

The funerals of Edmond Ghaneim and Eyad Abu Saadah in Beit Sahour were followed by those of two more youngsters from Bethlehem and neighboring Beit Jala. By the end of the first year of the *intifada*, 311 Palestinians in all had been killed by Israeli security forces in the West Bank and Gaza. The daily news programs were filled with footage of chaos, violence, and mutual ferocity. But Beit Sahour stood out. Not because of its small army of teenage rock throwers, who diligently offered up their Christian "martyrs" just as Muslim towns and villages had, but because there was a new movement taking shape that was made up of middle-class adults carrying out a disciplined, nonviolent resistance to occupation. It came to be known as the Beit Sahour tax revolt.

. . .

Just up the hill from Sami's woodworking shop, Elias Rishmawi, 52, a father of four, was in the newly built warehouse of his private company Medipharm, the largest medical supply firm in the emerging

Palestinian state. It had been twelve years since the *intifada*, and Rishmawi was a wealthy and successful businessman within Beit Sahour's Greek Orthodox community. It was a beautiful spring day, and there was a warm, gentle breeze. But Elias still felt closed in, constricted and defeated. Despite his position in the community and his important business contacts with some of the largest pharmaceutical and medical supply firms in Israel, he was not permitted to make the ten-minute drive from his home to Jerusalem to meet with potential customers. The Israelis had caged Bethlehem and Beit Sahour, and Elias was growing increasingly frustrated not only with the Israeli restrictions but with the leadership of the Palestinian Authority. It wasn't only the Israeli-imposed closures that impacted his business but also the notorious corruption within the Palestinian Authority itself, and he was tired of it.

But when we sat down in his home and began to talk about the days of the *intifada* in 1988 and 1989, he seemed to light up. It was a hard time, but one that had radicalized him and in some ways empowered him as well as his community.

Back then, Elias was just beginning to see the fruits of twenty years of hard work as a pharmacist. In many ways, his experience reflected improvements in the Palestinian economic situation under Israeli occupation over that under Jordanian control. It was an irony of the Israeli occupation that it unified the idea of Palestinian nationalism, which had been fragmented before 1967, when Jordan controlled East Jerusalem and the West Bank, and Egypt controlled the Gaza Strip. When Israel took all of this land in the Six-Day War, ancient Palestine was in some sense reunified, albeit under Israeli rule; and this fact caused the dream of Palestinian nationalism to be reborn.

In June 1967, when the war broke out, Elias had been in Egypt, finishing his studies at the Alexandria School of Pharmacy. Like many Palestinians, he was unable to return home for several years—until the details of a family reunification application were worked out. Elias had no involvement in political activities and no interest in them, and so his application to the Israeli authorities was accepted. When he returned, he immediately set about to open the first pharmacy in Beit Sahour. It was located on a hilltop on the town's main street, near the Greek Orthodox church. Through fifteen years of hard work, the pharmacy became a lucrative business for him and his brother, and they were beginning to invest the capital into a medical supply company that would service hospitals and clinics as well as other pharmacies. Elias's mastery of English and his ability to communicate in Hebrew helped him establish contacts with some of Israel's most prominent pharmaceutical companies, and near the end of 1987 he secured a license as the sole Palestinian distributor for the largest Israeli pharmaceutical company at the time, Travenol.

"To have that account was a dream," he remembered. "And that is all I was thinking about then."

But just weeks later, the *intifada* broke out, and by January 1988 it was raging across the West Bank and Gaza. Elias, who had shied away from politics and had focused his ambitions on making his pharmacy successful, reluctantly found himself cast as one of its leaders.

Elias, like all Palestinians, closed his store in solidarity when the *shebab* started their demonstrations. At first, he did not see himself as part of the movement, and he figured that soon the protests would die down and everyone would get back to their lives. The *intifada* encroached on everyone in town, and soon Elias felt not necessarily a pull, but more accurately an accidental push, to get involved. It began when his neighbors asked him to join a "neighborhood committee," which would become Beit Sahour's core movement structure. The town was so intertwined along the lines of family and friends that politicians did not lead the neighborhood committees. Instead, the committees were organic, sprouting out of the local soil and forming almost spontaneously around people's different talents and expertise. There were committees to organize the young people; to plant vegetables and raise chickens and find other means of self-sufficiency from the Israeli economy; to organize the clerics of the different and notoriously bickering Christian denominations; and to oversee the provision of medical care. This last committee was the one in which Elias became involved.

"This was the real *intifada*," said Elias, reflecting back on that time. "It was grass roots, it was very local, and that was why it worked. It respected every individual's way to take part, and it allowed everyone to think of themselves as an individual hero. That spirit was very alive in Beit Sahour. It was also why Israel had such a difficult time penetrating the *intifada*, or even understanding its command structure. It was something that infuriated them and why we saw mass arrests in Beit Sahour. They didn't know what else to do."

A Palestinian Christian pacifist, Mubarak Awad, was widely credited with creating the wider foundation upon which Beit Sahour's nonviolent movement within the *intifada* was built. Awad, who had emigrated from Jerusalem to the United States along with his family after 1967, returned in 1982 to establish a Center for the Study of Nonviolence in Jerusalem. His father, a Greek Orthodox, had been killed by a stray bullet during the 1948 fighting, and his Pentecostal mother had raised him. His center hewed closely to the Quaker belief in pacifism. His ideas were popular, but he himself was viewed with some suspicion by Palestinians, who saw him as too Western and too Christian.

The Palestinian Christians were uncomfortable with such an overt attachment to religion, and many veered away from Awad and his ideas, seeing the whole enterprise as potentially divisive. But Beit Sahour's shopkeepers and merchants latched on to Awad's call for a revolt against the exorbitant Israeli tariffs imposed on the Palestinians. Under international law it is illegal to collect taxes on occupied land, and this standard became the basis of a broad revolt against personal income taxes in Beit Sahour. The merchants and store owners of the town also revolted against the Israeli-imposed value-added tax, or VAT, a 17 percent tariff on purchases of goods and services that was supposed to be paid monthly to the office of taxation under the Israeli Civil Administration. Any audit that proved store owners were skimming VAT was strictly punishable by incarceration or heavy fines—punishments imposed on Palestinians and Israelis alike. An important distinction, however, was that Palestinian violators were subject to military enforcement and legal jurisdiction. This was, in other words, militarized tax collection.

The argument for a tax revolt was certainly sound by the standards of American history. The Palestinians were paying disproportionately high taxes, even though their communities received municipal services that were vastly inferior compared to those in the Israeli communities across the green line. Roads, parks, and water and sewage facilities were scarce, and the infrastructure of the Palestinian towns resembled that in the third world, compared to that enjoyed by Israeli communities. Palestinians were not only upset about how the money wasn't spent but also about how it *was* spent. The West Bank Database Project, a Jerusalem-based independent research organization, found that tax revenues taken from West Bankers and Gazans, including income taxes, property taxes, and the VAT, were actually funding the Israeli military administration. Palestinians from the West Bank and Gaza who worked in Israel also were subject to withholding of roughly 20 percent of their earnings to cover national insurance payments; but they were not permitted medical treatment under the national health program. Their income tax contributions were transferred directly to the state treasury, and from there went to pay for the Israeli military presence in the West Bank and Gaza. It was worse than taxation without representation; it was taxation with occupation, and the Beit Sahourans didn't see the wisdom in underwriting their own oppression. They were also well aware that their movement carried echoes of the Boston Tea Party in proclaiming "no taxation with occupation."

Beit Sahourans protested by rejecting a primary instrument of Israeli control: their identity cards. These cards and a computerized database associated with them communicate detailed information about all Palestinians—their religion, family history, political affiliations, and any criminal arrest record. Perhaps more problematic, a system had been established in which the ID cards were needed for everything—to get through military checkpoints, to travel abroad, to drive a car, or even to walk down the street. If an Israeli soldier confiscated an ID card, which frequently happened, it essentially made life impossible for the Palestinian without the card. Since the card was the only documentation the Israelis recognized for residency rights, to lose it meant that a Palestinian could lose the right to stay in the land and might be forced out of the country. This happened to many Palestinians during the occupation. Israeli soldiers often threatened confiscation of an ID card in order to intimidate and humiliate Palestinians into following their orders. They used this tactic to force Palestinians to scrub anti-Israeli graffiti from public spaces, to clear protesters' barricades from the roadways, or to scale telephone poles and pull down Palestinian flags.

Beit Sahour's first major nonviolent action came in July 1988, when a group of more than five hundred residents gathered their ID cards together and ceremoniously returned them to the Israeli authorities. This was a unique and extraordinary act of defiance. And, as Elias remembered, it all happened rather spontaneously. At about 4:30 A.M. on July 7, Israeli Civil Administration authorities, backed by Israeli soldiers, stormed into the homes and businesses of several prominent merchants in Beit Sahour who had been resisting payment of taxes. The Israeli forces confiscated tax and inventory records in an apparent effort to build cases against tax resisters. Elias and several other shopkeepers met in the streets outside their stores and decided they should do something. Someone came up with the idea of gathering together IDs and returning them as a form of protest. Before noon they had collected more than five hundred IDs in the mayor's office in Beit Sahour. The plan was to deliver them to the Israeli authorities at the Civil Administration office in Bethlehem as a sign of protest. But the Israeli military commander had heard that demonstrators were gathering at the city hall, and he moved in with troops and ordered the people to disperse. At the time, about one thousand Beit Sahourans had assembled in the streets—mostly middle-aged and middle-class adults, along with several hundred *shebab* with kaffiyehs around their necks, some of whom carried slingshots tucked into their belts underneath their shirts. The *shebab* were excited to see the adults taking part in the *intifada*, and they were there to show solidarity and turn in their IDs.

The military governor met with Beit Sahour's deputy mayor, Khalil Kheir, who handed him the IDs in a cardboard box. At approximately 5 P.M., the military governor spoke on a bullhorn, ordering the Palestinians to collect their IDs and to disperse, and threatening them with arrest.

"We will punish the whole town," Elias remembered the Israeli military governor saying over the bullhorn.

Soon, more heavily armed units of soldiers began arriving in front of the Roman Catholic church just across from city hall. Again the military governor ordered the crowd to leave. The soldiers had lined up across the street and held their riot batons at the ready. Suddenly, a whisper moved through the crowd, "Everyone sit down!" And soon the hundreds of Beit Sahourans were sitting in the street outside city hall, refusing to move. Elias remembers speaking to the group and pleading with them, "Do not give them any reason to attack. Just sit down! We are not looking for a confrontation!" The crowd was disciplined, and the adult presence brought a calm to the protest. Even the *shebab* sat down on the street. There was not a rock thrown, as at least a dozen Palestinian eyewitnesses remember it. Then the Israeli troops moved forward with riot batons to disperse the crowd, and "all hell broke loose," in Elias's words. The soldiers fired tear gas and then "rubber bullets." Several people were injured. There was no time for the *shebab* to gather up stones to throw them, even if they had wanted to. The soldiers stormed city hall and arrested about twenty people. A curfew was immediately imposed over the town and announced on a loudspeaker. Elias, who had hidden in a neighbor's home for several hours, slipped back out onto the street and walked home. He felt certain that there would be no turning back the movement.

About two weeks after the return of the IDs, Sami's friend Edmond

Ghaneim was killed by the Israeli soldiers. Just two months after that, Eyad was killed. These deaths, and the mounting number of young Palestinian boys being sent to the hospital, were intolerable to the middle-class adults of Beit Sahour. They felt compelled to step up their actions in part so as to involve their children in what they felt was a more productive and nonviolent resistance against the Israeli occupation, as well as to channel their own rising sense of outrage.

As Elias remembered, the people of Beit Sahour were asking, "Is it effective for us to continue to sacrifice our children in streets where they are armed with rocks and the Israelis with assault rifles?" And perhaps more important, he added, they were asking, "Is it right to meet violence with violence?"

The tax revolt built momentum in the late autumn of 1988 in Beit Sahour, and soon there were more than fifty prominent owners of shops and factories refusing to pay the VAT. Elias was among them. On November 28, he was arrested in a raid on his pharmacy, along with three other pharmacists from the town. They were taken by force to a military court for a hearing, and were ordered to pay the equivalent of U.S. $6,000 in fines or face ten days in prison. They all held their ground and refused to pay the fines. The military court sentenced them to ten days at Israel's Bet Shemesh Maximum Security Prison, where these middle-class Palestinian merchants were tossed into group cells with hardened Israeli criminals. Elias remembered this as one of the more frightening moments of his life.

"In retrospect, I realize the Israelis understood that we were all Christian, all middle class, and this was an attempt to break into the structure [of the movement] and fracture it," he recalled. "They were betting that we would buckle, that we simply had too much to lose as businessmen and family men to go through with the arrest. But we did it."

Elias was released after ten days, on about $500 in bail. An Israeli friend, Yossi Cohen, whom he had met through his business contacts, came and paid the bail—an act of solidarity that Elias never forgot. The move infuriated the Civil Administration officials. When Elias came out of prison, he was politically awakened. "We suddenly felt like we were willing to risk everything we had worked for," he said. "We were very proud of it. What we were doing was ethical, it was peaceful resistance, and it fit with our faith as Christians and our understanding of democracy and the notion of no taxation without representation."

Throughout the end of 1988 and the beginning of 1989, the neighborhood committees and the commercial committees became more active in organizing the tax boycott and getting the word out to the media and to other activists. Although all of their coordinating actions were based on nonviolence, in March 1989 Defense Minister Rabin declared the popular committees illegal and issued a military order by which members of the committee were subject to a maximum of ten years' imprisonment.

As Elias became more deeply involved in the political actions, he was following a path of many Arab Christian thinkers before him. He was a contemporary representative of a long tradition of Arab Christians who through their education and their business contacts and their connections to the Western churches had become exposed to Western ideas of democracy and law. It had been a Christian womb, after all, in which the idea of Arab nationalism was first conceived.

. . .

The Christian influence in Arab nationalism dates back to at least the mid-nineteenth century. Indeed, many modern Arab analysts (most notably, Fouad Ajami, in his book *The Dream Palace of the Arabs*) credit the early emergence of the concept of Arab nationalism specifically to Arab Christian intellectuals. To Arab Muslims, Arabism and the religion of Islam were inseparable. But the Christians, if they were to be integral to the Arab awakening, had to define it along secular lines, as a form of nationalism. The struggle that emerged then between Muslims and Christians to define Arab nationalism continues along the same lines today.

Boutros al-Bustani, a mid-nineteenth-century scholar and a pioneering intellectual from Beirut, was among the first in a long line of Arab Christian thinkers and political theorists to bring structure and form to an awareness of "the Arab nation." Al-Bustani also contributed to the first translation of the Bible into Arabic, a critical development in Middle Eastern Christianity. His movement from language to politics showed how closely the two were intertwined. The translation of the Bible was evidence that Christians had long since adapted to the language of the Arab Islamic conquest. Arabic was the language of Islam; it had shaped the faith, and in turn was shaped by it. But Arabic had also become the language of the Middle Eastern Christians; the play between Arabic language and Islamic culture would largely define their identity. But in the nineteenth century, the notion of an "Arab culture" was only beginning to take shape.

Al-Bustani's thinking helped inaugurate a new Arab intellectual movement, which crystallized in George Antonius's 1938 work *The Arab Awakening*. Antonius, the son of a merchant family from Mount Lebanon, soon became active in defining the "Palestinian question." Antonius's writings presented to the world the Arab case against the accords that divided Arab lands between the British and the French after World War I. "*The Arab Awakening*," Ajami wrote, "was to be the manifesto of the Arab national movement." The movement was given a concrete political structure by Michel Aflaq, the French-educated Damascus thinker who founded the Ba'ath party, which espoused a unique brand of Arab socialist nationalism. The Ba'ath remain the ruling party in Syria and Iraq today.

Aflaq, Antonius, and al-Bustani all were Arab Christians, and their influence in shaping Arab nationalism is essential to understanding not only the 1988–1989 tax revolt in Beit Sahour but also the region's century-long struggle against the forces of colonialism. Many Christian Arabs, especially the Greek Orthodox and Greek Catholics, emerged from a heritage in which they struggled against Greek domination over their lives via the church hierarchy in Antioch, even as they relentlessly resisted the incursion of Roman Catholic customs, rituals, and theology. An effort in the 1920s to retain control of their own churches and regain huge land holdings and investments from the Greek Orthodox hierarchy came to be known as the Arab Orthodox Movement. It was anticlerical, anti-Western, and by extension anticolonialist (and occasionally Marxist) in its leanings. This rebellion against the Greek Orthodox hierarchy left many Arab Christians in a sort of politicized limbo. Although they identified themselves as Christians, they had become increasingly secular and anticlerical. Indeed, along this deep fault line that ran through the Orthodox church between Greek hierarchy and Arab laity, it was not uncommon for young, Western-educated leftists to make a total break from their church and plunge into a world of economics and revolutionary causes, including Arab nationalism. As Lebanese historian Kamal Salibi noted: "Arab nationalism as it came to exist in the Arab world after the first world war, was more of a romantic ideal than a political movement with precepts and a set program. Moreover it meant different things to its Muslim and Christian adherents."

On the level of local politics, most Christians in Beit Sahour were followers of the Popular Front for the Liberation of Palestine (PFLP), one of the major parties within the PLO. The PFLP had been founded by George Habash, a Palestinian Christian physician who had been radicalized by his experiences as a 1948 refugee from Lydda (Lod in Hebrew) and while working with poor Palestinian refugees after the 1948 war. Habash, one of the founders of the Arab Nationalism movement, was an extreme nationalist who espoused a hard-line Marxist doctrine. He was purportedly behind a spate of hijackings and bombings throughout the 1970s.

A number of other Beit Sahour residents were also loyal to the Democratic Front for the Liberation of Palestine (DFLP), an offshoot of the PFLP, founded by Naif Hawatmeh, a Jordanian Christian, after a doctrinal dispute with Habash. The DFLP called for struggle not only against Israel but also against conservative Arab regimes such as Jordan's monarchy. Habash and Hawatmeh were Greek Orthodox Christians by tribal affiliation, but it was their economic theories as Marxists and their passionate Arab nationalism that attracted their respective followings. They were seen as uncompromising, educated, and cultured. They were also legendary and sometimes bitter rivals of Arafat. But the ideas these two men espoused were far from the Christian theology of nonviolence. Both called for all-out guerrilla war against Israel and opposed any political solution involving an Arab compromise. The violent rhetoric and deeds of Habash and Hawatmeh often seemed over the top and out of context; it was almost as if these men had more to prove than other (Islamic) Arab leaders. Habash remained opposed to any political solution that involved a compromise with Israel, right up until the day he stepped down as head of the PFLP, late in 2000.

Despite the anticlericalism of the movement leadership, local priests and clerics who showed revolutionary zeal—especially those within the Roman Catholic patriarchate—became popular heroes. Several legendary gun-running clerics and priests are known to have participated in the revolution in historical Palestine. Beit Sahour's most beloved native son in this regard may have been the Roman Catholic priest Father Ibrahim Ayad. In 2000, Ayad was 90 years old and known to everyone as Abouna Ibrahim (Father Abraham, in Arabic). I visited him on several occasions at the monastery where he lived in Beit Jala, a beautiful old village of stone homes and church spires that clings to the steep hillsides. He greeted me in his black clerical vestments, a small man, stooped by age but with a radical spark in his eye.

As we sat and drank tea, he described the trajectory of his life: from the Ottoman era through the British mandate to 1948 and 1967, and through the civil war in Lebanon and the *intifada*. All through this history, Abouna Ibrahim trod a thin line between Christian theology and militant nationalism. During and after the 1948 war, Ayad was designated the Catholic liaison to the Palestinian Resistance Movement, which grew out of Palestinians' frustration, even desperation, at the indifference of the Arab world to their plight.

After 1948, Palestine was pulled apart in three directions: The largest piece was taken by the Jewish state; another piece, Gaza, was carted off by the Egyptians; and the West Bank and East Jerusalem fell under the control of the Jordanians. The Jordanian control was particularly unpopular, and by 1949, the Arab Palestinian population was bristling at what many saw as an opportunistic, expansionist land grab by the neighboring Hashemite kingdom of King Abdullah. In 1951, Abdullah was assassinated while entering Jerusalem's Al-Aqsa mosque. Along with eight other Palestinian activists, Ayad was arrested in connection with the shooting.

Eventually, a prominent member of the Muslim Husseini clan of Jerusalem was tried and executed for the crime, and Ayad was acquitted. He seemed to choose his words carefully when he denied that he had ever been "directly involved." "I despised the man, but I despise assassination as well," Ayad said. After the trial, Ayad was deported and eventually ended up in Lebanon, where he soon became a legend in the militant circles of the nascent Palestinian resistance. In the mid-1950s he was arrested for his suspected role in a foiled Palestinian plot to blow up the British embassy.

In 1964, a young man with a scruffy beard, Ray-Ban sunglasses, a black turtleneck, and a black-and-white kaffiyeh showed up at the Capuchin convent where Ayad lived in Beirut. His name was Yasser Arafat, and he had brought along his closest friend and colleague, Abu Jihad. The two men announced to Ayad the formation of the Fatah guerrilla organization, which would soon become the largest and dominant constituent group within the PLO. Arafat and Abu Jihad sought Ayad's advice and support, and requested his benediction on the newly formed militant resistance organization. "They were young people, I saw that they were serious," remembers Ayad, smiling. "I told them, 'With the blessing of God, I am with you.'"

Beit Sahour's tax revolt in 1988 was a fusion of this Christian intellectual stream that had shaped Arab nationalism, with the Christian veneer of militant rhetoric represented by Christians as prominent as

Habash and as local as Ayad. Given the violent rhetoric that issued from these two very different Christian leaders, it was hard to see any way in which the foundation of Beit Sahour's movement could be viewed as supported by a collective cultural understanding of Jesus's message of nonviolence. There are many different nonviolent traditions and modes of protest based on religious principles, of course—not just Christian but also Jewish, Muslim, Hindu, Buddhist, and others. The Beit Sahourans were not Christian pacifists in the same tradition as, say, Quakers or Mennonites. Theirs was a practical, strategic nonviolence based on the belief that tax resistance and turning in IDs were more effective ways of resisting occupation than throwing rocks. Their nonviolence was powerful because it exposed the occupation for what it was; that is why they were drawn to nonviolence. When I questioned them about it, they always hastened to point out that their protest tactics did not grow out of any religious conviction. But I wanted to dig deeper, to see whether there was a Christian culture in Beit Sahour that was more open to nonviolent resistance, and whether people there understood nonviolence in a way that their Muslim brethren did not. Beit Sahourans certainly were not sitting in church, nodding their heads to rousing sermons about turning the other cheek. But could it be that the framed pictures of Jesus in their kitchens and above the cash registers in their shops symbolized a radically subversive call for passive resistance—a call especially subversive in this desert culture, where social codes of revenge still prevailed?

Jad Isaac, a Palestinian botanist and Beit Sahour leader who helped spur the community action against taxation, affirmed that the revolt took hold in a Christian community partly because of the message of Christian nonviolence that was woven into the culture. But only as "a very, very small part," as he put it. "The media wanted Beit Sahour to be about Christian nonviolence. That is how they saw it. But in a way they were trying to make sense out of nonsense. The truth is, it was just a wild, chaotic time."

Jad identified with his heritage as a Greek Orthodox Christian but was stridently atheist. Such a self-view embodies the communal sense of religion in this part of the world, where Christianity defines a tribe, not just a faith. And this was why it was so common to hear adamant Palestinian secularists and atheists refer to themselves as Christians. The same was true, of course, of secular Jews and Muslims in Israel, who referred to themselves by the faiths into which they were born, even though they themselves did not necessarily adhere to or even believe in that faith. In this sense, religion here is a cultural point of reference—more a statement of where one comes from than a set of beliefs that defines who one is.

Isaac was still a community leader in 2000, through his Applied Research Institute, which tracked trends in the Palestinian community, encouraging Palestinians to harness their own considerable agricultural and scientific resources and create an independent economy less reliant on Israel. "What really happened here during the *intifada*," he commented, "was a community rose up against its occupiers, and they organized on a local level to do so. That is the real background to why it succeeded, to the extent that it did succeed."

Ghassan Andoni, a physics professor at Birzeit University and also a leader of the tax revolt, said that Beit Sahour's culture was very industrious, and therefore very pragmatic. "The community understood a challenge to occupation based on the principles of democracy and rights of the individual would be more effective, or effective in a different way, than violent street protests," he explained. "So all of these things were tied in to the fact that the community was Christian, but when you simply call it 'Christian,' you lose the meaning of it, you misinterpret what it really was."

Andoni was speaking to me in the office of his Palestinian Center for Rapprochement Between People, a movement that grew out of the tax revolt. The windows of the building look out over the Greek Orthodox church across the street, but the movement has nothing to do with the church. Andoni was raised in the Greek Orthodox tradition (although he would insist on calling it "Arab Orthodox"), and he wanted to be clear that not only were Orthodox clerics not supportive of the tax revolt but in some ways they actively sought to minimize its impact.

"You have to understand that the Orthodox clerics here are not the most well educated people of our community," he said. "They are chosen as clerics by the tribal rights of the prominent families in a kind of tribal electoral council. The church is really for children here. It is what I call 'children's faith,' meaning there is no theological or philosophical or political expression to it. It is the source of ritual and of tradition, but not where we look for leadership. We want our kids to go. That doesn't mean I go.

"The clerical leadership was not involved in our movement. They were more worried about their hierarchy, which you have to remember is not local. Their metropolitans and their patriarch, they are all

Greek. I have nothing against Greeks. They are okay, but they are not Palestinian. And their concerns are not our concerns. In a way, the church and its clerics in Palestine—not just the Orthodox but the Catholic and the Anglican—they are all colonizers.

"So when we came to the clerics for help, not only were they reluctant; there were times when they closed the doors on us when we needed to gather in the church or to ring the church bells to bring people into the street. They were all too worried about the special privileges the Israelis give them, and not wanting to do anything that would anger their Greek hierarchy."

Andoni's thoughts captured something I had repeatedly observed about the Christians in this land, something I knew he was not likely ever to admit: Arab Christians were reluctant to assert their Christian beliefs. They expressed beliefs clearly shaped through the teachings of Christian theology and the academic institutions, Western in their outlook, that the church built and funded through the centuries. But they did not want to have them categorized as such, and they were suspicious of anyone who tried to do so. Politicized Christian Arabs were consciously just as much part of an Islamic culture as they were of a Christian culture; and to embrace a Christian identity in too strenuous a manner would offend the Islamic and Arab part of their identity. So they constantly tempered their arguments in a way that turned the focus away from their Christian background.

Yet it was easy to see that seeping through Andoni's ideas were Westernized and Christian beliefs, formulations, and assumptions. They were colors and shadings of thought made more vivid when viewed against the broader canvas of Islamic culture of the Middle East. One simply didn't hear arguments for nonviolent resistance in the predominantly Muslim towns of Hebron or Nablus, or in the predominantly Muslim refugee camps. There were notable exceptions among individuals; but there were no broad-based community movements of nonviolence. The reasons for this were complex, involving economic and cultural and educational factors. But there was undeniably a religious component as well. Christianity stressed the power of nonviolence as a core spiritual message in a way that Islam and Judaism did not. Even though Islam and Judaism also have strong messages of tolerance and of trying to resolve conflict without resorting to violence, I found few rabbis or sheikhs who would disagree with the premise that the teachings of Jesus as revealed in the gospels placed a higher value on nonviolence than did the central teachings of the other two Abrahamic faiths.

The Beit Sahour resistance was unique in the *intifada* in yet another significant way: It invited the participation of the Israeli left and of Palestinian Christian women. These two groups were able to gather under the banner of nonviolence in a way they never could have in the violent street demonstrations with rocks and Molotov cocktails. Andoni's organization provided the vehicle for this broader participation, which included a contingent of lawyers, human rights activists, politicians, and even some rabbis from the left.

Veronika Cohen was one of the Israeli peace activists who crossed the divide, in solidarity with the Beit Sahourans, through the Rapprochement Center in the fall of 1988. For the first time in her life, Cohen had the opportunity to actually talk with Palestinians. This was a radical concept then, and one that in the year 2000 was still radical. She developed friends through the dialogue, and became convinced that what her government was doing was wrong. She worked tirelessly to stop it. "I began to really realize how it was in the interest of the Israeli government to portray the Palestinians as violent," Cohen recalled, "and here were these Palestinians in Beit Sahour inviting us in and talking and asking us to participate in their nonviolent resistance."

The most dramatic moment for her came when the Beit Sahour community invited her and a group of about seventy Israelis to the town to observe Shabbat, the Jewish sabbath, on a Friday night and then leave on Saturday after sunset. Several Beit Sahour families offered their homes to the Israelis to spend the night, and one family offered an unfinished building as the site of what would become a makeshift synagogue where the Israelis prayed. The Israeli activists would have to sneak into the town, which had been ruled a closed military area. And even when the soldiers discovered the group was there, it was after sunset on Friday, and under the religious rules on sabbath observance they could not be moved in vehicles. So they were permitted to stay until sunset on Saturday.

Cohen was unique among Israeli peace activists in that she was a "modern Orthodox" Jew, strictly observant of Shabbat and the dietary laws of Judaism. By contrast, the vast majority of Peace Now, the largest activist organization, were secular Israelis. So for Cohen the celebration of Shabbat took on a heightened significance.

For inhabitants of a Palestinian town at the political boiling point to invite Israeli Jews to stay and to pray in their homes was perhaps one of the more radical undertakings of the Beit Sahour peace movement. It broke many barriers. Not just those set by the Israeli authorities, but also those set by the Arab community and by the PLO leadership. Such actions were looked down upon by many Palestinian leaders, who viewed them as "normalization" with the enemy. The local sheikhs, especially, tended to view such efforts as signs of apostasy, and thundered against them in their sermons. Whether consciously or not, the Beit Sahourans had absorbed and were acting upon one of the most radical precepts of Jesus's ministry: the crossing of boundaries of religion, tribe, family, gender, and social caste with the goal of benefiting all and harming none.

Later, in November 1988, Cohen also participated in a service for peace that took place in the Greek Orthodox church. She too was crossing a big divide in accepting the invitation. Cohen was born in 1944 in Budapest, Hungary, and she and her parents had survived the Holocaust. After the war, they came to America and landed in Baltimore. She emigrated to Israel in 1979 with her husband and two children.

She vividly recalled the gathering in the church. She said she and the other Israeli participants had had to sneak through a graveyard in order to get past the soldiers, who most likely would not have permitted the Israelis to pass. She remembered the drone of Israeli helicopters hovering overhead, and the crackle of army radios calling in Hebrew for more troops. But what she remembered most vividly was that as an observant Jew and a survivor of the Holocaust, she had never sat in a church before. "This was a very special experience, but as a Jew I felt very uncomfortable being part of a Mass," she recalled. "It felt wrong on some religious level that I couldn't identify, but on the level of political activity I felt very good about being there. It was a very complex and very conflicted feeling.

"I have done so many actions as a peace activist, but the place that meant the most to me was Beit Sahour. It was a place where they stuck it out. . . . We had other dialogue groups, in Nablus and in Jericho, but this community-wide commitment to nonviolent resistance was unique. It was the only place in the *intifada* that it happened. When I would tell my Israeli friends about Beit Sahour, they would dismiss it. They'd say, 'Those are Christians, they aren't real Palestinians.'"

. . .

The Beit Sahour tax revolt did not expand to the rest of the West Bank. There was one overriding reason for its failure. The Israelis responded with a severity that starkly revealed just how much of a threat they considered a movement of nonviolence. American consultants to Israel had warned the government that civil disobedience, if it took root, was unstoppable. As long as the Israelis were up against kids throwing rocks, the use of force would be more acceptable in the eyes of the West. But as soon as Palestinian communities started submitting to mass arrests in peaceful demonstrations, Israel would fall on the defensive, more than it had already been, from the international community—especially if these peaceful protests included Israelis as well as Palestinians gathering in a place sacred to Christians all over the world, such as Bethlehem or Beit Sahour. So the government reacted swiftly and decisively and strategically against this movement. It had to be stopped.

They began by deporting Mubarak Awad, who was charged with fomenting a rebellion against the state. He appealed his deportation to Israel's High Court (the supreme court of the land). But Israel wanted neither a protracted legal battle nor more publicity for Awad. So the government instead successfully deported him on the technical violation that he had overstayed a three-month visa.

Israel then sent a clear message that the cost of expanding the tax revolt to other towns and cities would be devastating for Palestinians. "We will teach them a lesson," Rabin said. On September 19, 1989, the Israeli army entered Beit Sahour with hundreds of troops and imposed a strict military curfew. They cut phone lines and barred the press and the Israeli solidarity groups from entering. Beit Sahour was under complete siege. Soldiers went from house to house and business to business, confiscating truckloads of goods. An estimated $2 million worth of commercial equipment and personal property, including televisions, stoves, refrigerators, furniture, medicine from pharmacies, and factory machinery were taken by force to compensate for unpaid taxes. All of the produce and canned goods were stripped from the shelves of the main grocery store in town.

The family of Sami and Edmond Kheir, who had actively participated in the tax revolt, watched as their wood-furniture factory was invaded and stripped of all machinery and tools. Some forty merchants were arrested, and many were sentenced to pay a fine of U.S. $3,000 (in addition to back taxes) or to spend twenty months in jail for tax evasion.

For Elias Rishmawi, the price of activism was exorbitant. After his arrest, the authorities seized all of his firm's medicines, pharmacological stock, and supplies, which he estimated were valued at U.S. $130,000. He had won a court injunction barring the Israelis from seizing his assets without ten days' prior notice, but the Israelis seized the goods anyway, saying they would be held pending a hearing. Meanwhile, all of the medicines were placed in a steel shipping container and left in the hot sun at an airfield on the outskirts of Jerusalem. The intense heat destroyed the medicine and many of the medical supplies. When Elias returned from jail, he kept his pharmacy open seven days a week, as an act of defiance, even though its shelves were bare. This infuriated the local authorities. Eventually, the Civil Administration tax authorities, backed by soldiers, came to his pharmacy again. This time they said they were investigating his personal income tax. They ordered him to return to his home, where they seized the family's television, the dining room table, living room furniture, and even the children's desks from their bedrooms. The confiscated property was held at the airfield and auctioned off some months later. Elias was informed that his personal belongings had brought in the equivalent of U.S. $500—not even a tenth of their value by his estimation—to be applied against the roughly $80,000 that the tax authorities told him he owed.

On November 1, after forty-two days, the siege was finally lifted, but Beit Sahour defiantly continued its resistance, in part because it had no choice. It could not afford to turn back, given the exorbitant fines and back taxes that the Israelis were demanding. The town leaders announced a hundred-day general strike, and shops remained closed through February 1990 to protest the siege.

The Beit Sahour nonviolent movement was causing difficulties not only for the Israelis but also for Yasser Arafat, the PLO chairman. It came at a time when Arafat was trying to gain control of the *intifada* and to centralize its leadership throughout the West Bank and Gaza. Arafat felt that independent movements like the one in Beit Sahour could open the Palestinians to divisions and weaken the PLO's bargaining position in relation to Israel. Many other PLO leaders also were suspicious of the movement, seeing it perhaps as a Western-influenced plan to derail the momentum of the *intifada*. This suspicion was embedded in an important cultural divide, in which Muslims still saw Christianity as a bastion of the West rather than an indigenous faith with legitimate roots in the land of Palestine.

The PLO leadership was thus intent on derailing what was happening in Beit Sahour. Awad's offices in Jerusalem were broken into by PLO officials, and some of his supporters were personally threatened. There were allegations that the PLO (specifically, Arafat's Fatah party) undercut the Beit Sahour movement by sending in young supporters to throw rocks at Israeli troops whenever a large group of nonviolent protesters had gathered for peaceful demonstrations. The rocks inevitably provoked clashes with the Israeli troops, Awad said, and the atmosphere of nonviolence instantly evaporated. The allegations were never confirmed by other Beit Sahour activists, and they remain among the unanswered questions of that time.

Meanwhile, the PLO denied financial support and logistical help to Beit Sahour. In Jordan, the joint committee of the PLO met with prominent business leaders of Beit Sahour throughout 1988, and the word came back to the town that the PLO leadership in Tunis recommended against participation in the tax revolt. This was a confusing message, and to this day the leaders of the revolt are not sure whether the businessmen were directly told that by the PLO representatives in Jordan, or whether they interpreted certain conversations as a way to justify their willingness to pay the taxes and avoid the wrath of the Israeli authorities. Regardless, the effect was devastating, and the revolt unraveled as some businesses took on serious risks to participate in the tax boycott and others paid their taxes and stayed in business. By early 1990, the Beit Sahour tax revolt and the nonviolent movement it had helped inspire had been reduced to flickering embers. Arafat's PLO was successfully asserting control of the *intifada* through leaders more to its liking. Arafat and his leadership were in control and would remain obsessed with holding on to power into the year 2000.

A bitter irony was in store for the Beit Sahour activists when the Palestinian Authority took on limited self-rule of parts of the West Bank in 1994. As part of the interim peace agreement, the Israelis had listed Beit Sahour's unpaid taxes—totaling more than U.S. $5 million from about one hundred different companies—as a debt owed to the Palestinian Authority. So when the Authority established its tax offices, some of the leaders of the revolt were asked to pay these back taxes by Palestinian leaders newly appointed by Arafat, most of whom had come with him from Tunis. Only a few Beit Sahour shop owners paid their back taxes as ordered. A settlement was worked out whereby the Authority compensated business owners for losses they had suffered in the tax revolt. Some owners chose to apply their compensation against the back taxes they owed the Authority. But as Elias later told me: "It outraged a lot of us. It was insulting to what we had fought for."

. . .

One of the complaints that I often heard in Bethlehem and Beit Sahour during the spring of 2000 was that intolerance toward Christians was increasing within Palestinian society. I heard this from common people all the time—people like the shopkeeper in Bethlehem, with the neon cross, and many others. But such reports were always dismissed by the Palestinian leadership as outrageous lies, deliberate attempts by the Israelis to divide and rule. In 1998, David Bar-Illan, a key adviser to Israeli Prime Minister Benjamin Netanyahu, released a long list of purported acts of discrimination against Christians by Muslims in the Palestinian-ruled areas. I checked it out with Bassem Eid, an independent and respected Palestinian human rights worker, who researched the allegations. Eid concluded that Bar-Illan's report was based on nothing but "falsehoods and exaggerations." But from what I was gathering in the field, I could see that there were legitimate concerns about intolerance and discrimination among the Palestinian Christians, concerns that were being overlooked because of the charged atmosphere that Bar-Illan's reckless allegations had created. Indeed, many prominent Christian leaders—even one who was very close to Arafat—began to confide in me that although there was not necessarily discrimination in a legal sense, there was a growing apprehension on the part of the Christian minority about where they would fit in the overwhelmingly Muslim Palestinian Authority—especially to the extent that it was increasingly influenced by political Islamists.

Palestinian Christians cited fears of institutional discrimination at the hands of the Palestinian Authority, which had adopted Islam as its official religion. In shaping the "basic law" of the new authority, the legislators relied on *sharia*, or Islamic codes formed under former Jordanian and Egyptian administrations in the West Bank and Gaza. Specifically, Palestinian Christian leaders point to laws that prescribe the death penalty for selling land to Jews. This law was often interpreted by Palestinians in the street as preventing Muslims from selling to any non-Muslims, or "infidels"—a category that included Christians. This erroneous interpretation of the law had gained currency because of the preaching of radical Muslim sheikhs, who blurred the lines of distinction, referring to all non-Muslims as "infidels" in their sermons on the land laws. Some Palestinian lawmakers, including Hanan Ashrawi—a Christian and a prominent spokeswoman for the Palestinian cause—and several secular Muslims, had spoken out against the use of *sharia* as the basic law of Palestine, but they had lost the battle.

I was particularly stunned to hear about instances of discrimination against solidly nationalist families in Beit Sahour, including Maryam and Bishara Abu Saadah, the parents of the fallen Christian "martyr" Eyad. On the wall of their sitting room was a framed mosaic of plastic beads depicting the Virgin Mary. The Holy Mother looked down lovingly at a charcoal sketch of Eyad, positioned just below her on the wall. The drawing highlighted Eyad's earnest eyes, slight smile, the crucifix dangling from his neck, and his shoulders wrapped in a checked kaffiyeh. On this wall of family icons also hung a poster, mounted on a piece of polished wood, that depicts Eyad's mother, Maryam, standing on the pew of the church, her fingers raised in a victory (for peace) sign, holding a picture of her "martyred" son. Behind her, over the altar, is a prominently featured cross. The caption under the poster reads "Guardians of the Homeland." This poster was one of the more enduring images of the *intifada,* and an icon of Christian Palestinian resistance.

Eyad was one of some thirty Christian "martyrs" who died during the *intifada,* out of a total of nearly two thousand Palestinians—a number that was almost exactly proportionate to Christian representation in the Palestinian population. But those who had lost their sons in the violence—not only Christians but Muslims as well—had become deeply disillusioned by the year 2000. "Everything is corrupt," Bishara said bitterly. "The leaders of the Palestinians who lived in Tunis while we suffered now come home to steal from us here. The collaborators are now police officers, the car thieves are their deputies. But those of us who gave our sons have nothing."

Bishara had worked in construction for the Israelis for more than thirty years, laboring to build their settlements, but he had hurt his back and was now out of work, without any disability or retirement pay. He told me that he had tried to get work laying tiles in the construction of Arafat's opulent and enormous residence and guesthouse in Bethlehem, which is known by the locals as "the palace," but he was turned away. Only Muslims are getting work there, he complained. (Palestinian Authority legislators in Bethlehem, both Christian and Muslim, deny the allegations; but many Christians, like Bishara, believe that they have been discriminated against.)

Maryam said there had been great unity between Muslims and Christians during and before the *intifada,* but around the end of 1990 the language changed. It was just before the Persian Gulf War. Suddenly there was talk at the protest rallies "of how Christian martyrs are not equal to Muslim martyrs, because our sons were not part of the *jihad.*" She continued: "No one would dare say this to my face, but we heard things. . . . Well, we know why Eyad was martyred: to free this country from oppression. The Muslims believe it was to be taken to paradise, where they are given forty virgins. This is not our belief, these are not Christian beliefs. We believe in the nation of Palestine. Or at least we believed in the ideals. I don't know what we believe in now."

She pointed upward, at the poster of her in church at her son's funeral, and shook her head in disgust, saying, "We found out that the PLO was selling them for $200 a piece in America to raise money. They used the image of our son, and we were never given a thing. We were very mad."

"It has been sad to hear the language changing in Bethlehem," Maryam continued. "Even if you listen to the sermons at the mosques, they speak of Christians as 'infidels.' They say our belief in Jesus as the son of God is a blasphemy, that only Islam is the true religion. This is a humiliation to us, and we have heard it right there," gesturing in the direction of a newly built mosque. "I complained to the Palestinian Authority about this sheikh shouting that Christians are heretics over the loudspeakers at the mosque, shouting this here, where Jesus was born. They have no right!" Her anger seemed surprising after the quiet reverence with which she had spoken of her son. "I began screaming in the street about this, literally shouting in the streets against this sheikh, like a crazy woman. But we feel here like we are being pushed into a corner as Christians."

Sami Kheir, who had accompanied me to Eyad's family home, reflected on this as we headed back. "I can't help but feel we lost two friends for nothing," he said. "During the *intifada* we were all in the same fire. It was Muslims and Christians together. But when the Palestinian Authority came in after the peace process, the divisions surfaced. There was a time of excitement, but very quickly Muslims and Christians became divided. It became clear the leadership of the Palestinian Authority would be Muslim, the courts, the police, are all in the hands of Muslims, and we the Christians are expected to be a silent and humble minority. That's the way they want us.

"When the Muslims tell you we live as brothers," he said, "I always feel like asking them, 'Is this the way you treat brothers?'"

. . .

The Palestinian Legislative Council representative for the Bethlehem region, which includes Beit Sahour, is Salah Tamari. He is a large and powerful-looking man with blue eyes and the leathered skin of the Bedouin, Arab nomads to whom his extended tribe traces its heritage. The Tamari are the largest Muslim clan in the Bethlehem area, and like the Christians of Beit Sahour, they too see themselves as descendants of the shepherds who bore witness to the birth of Jesus. In fact, some of the Tamari were quick to point out that many of the Christians were actually from Crusader ancestry or Greek origin and that as Bedouins the Tamari were more likely to be of the same blood as the shepherds in the biblical story. All of these ancestral lines, of course, were lost to history. A truth of this land—which both the Beit Sahour Christians and local Muslims were reluctant to ponder—was that the biblical shepherds were more likely to have been Jews of the tribe of David.

Tamari told me that his relatives still tended their flocks on the rocky hillsides just outside of Beit Sahour. Many still kept guard over the sheep in caves and slept in tents beneath star-canopied skies of the desert, just as the shepherds of the Bible had done. "My pride and what enriches me is my connection to this land, to Bethlehem," he said. "As a Muslim, part of my faith is to believe in the message of Jesus. Along with that, I am born in the same city. There is a spiritual elation to that for Muslims."

As we spoke in his modest office, I noticed that the poster of Maryam Abu Saadah in church was prominently displayed on the wall just above his desk. It turned out that it was Tamari who had come up with the poster scheme that had so infuriated Maryam. Tamari was a controversial representative, and not much loved by the Christian community, which may have had an instinctive fear of his tough and extensive tribal base. Tamari was among Arafat's closest loyalists and had traveled with him throughout the 1970s and 1980s, from Jordan to Lebanon and then to Tunis. He was among the 10,000 "Tunisians," as the local Palestinians called them, who returned with Arafat to take up senior positions in the government. The Muslim and Christian Palestinians who had never left, like the leaders in Beit Sahour, greatly resented this.

Tamari was not born the son of a shepherd but of a restaurant waiter. He was Muslim, as his ancestors had been for hundreds of years. But he told me he had been baptized at the Church of the Nativity, in Manger Square. He explained that his mother had lost her first two children at birth, and she had prayed to God for a healthy child and made an oath, or *nid'r,* to Jesus that she would baptize the child if her prayers were answered. Christian baptism is a ritual that, Tamari told me, was not uncommon among Muslims of the Bethlehem area.

"I think it is one of the many ways in which you see the religious and cultural ties between Muslims and Christians that are the history of this land," he said. "And these examples are everywhere. You will find Muslims named Issa [the Arabic name for Jesus] on every street. As a child, I went to the Franciscan elementary school, as did most of my friends, whether Muslim or Christian, and we all wore the same black-and-white uniform. There were Muslim homes with pictures of St. George slaying the dragon, just as there were in Christian homes. We shared in our traditions and feasts. These are the images of Bethlehem for me, and they are always images of Muslims and Christians together as Palestinians and as Arabs. And I believe those images are still there today if you want to find them.

"If the Christians talk about discrimination in the new Palestinian state, I reject this. It is not true," Tamari continued. "But if they talk about a changing culture of Islamization, a more fundamentalist streak in our society, then I would say I am as alarmed about this as they are. Fundamentalism is an issue for Christians, Muslims, and Jews, no? For any of us who want to live with tolerance and pluralism this is a problem, not just Christians."

Arafat was acutely aware of this feeling of unease among Christians, and he insistently condemned religious intolerance of all kinds. For one thing, he knew just how crucial this issue was to his funding base. He had long cultivated Christian support for the Palestinian cause throughout Europe, and he frequently invoked the church spires of the Old City along with the minarets when he spoke of reclaiming Jerusalem as the capital of a Palestinian state.

Some Muslims even said that Arafat had coddled the Christian community, and engendered resentment as a result. Many Palestinian

Muslim leaders were quick to point out that several of Arafat's top advisers were Christian and that Arafat had appointed Christian mayors in Beit Sahour, Bethlehem, and Beit Jala. Local Muslims rightly claim that if a democratic election were held in Bethlehem, the Christian mayor would probably be unseated, because the town is at least 70 percent Muslim. Muslim leaders have also complained that Christians have been given preferential treatment with regard to obtaining the special permits required to travel beyond the Israeli checkpoint into Jerusalem.

Tamari said he was surprised to hear about allegations of discrimination against Christians, and he immediately dismissed these stories. "This is an old game of divide and rule," he said. "The Israelis have tried to play the Christian card and play up the divisions in Palestinian society. We saw this in prison during the occupation and certainly during Lebanon. The Israelis pitted the Christians against the Muslims, the Sunni against the Shiite, and any other divide they could find to strengthen their rule. Our main problem is occupation, it is not Muslim and Christian relations. Our main problem is the lack of jobs and the inability for a strong economy as long as the agreements of the peace process go unfulfilled by Israel."

Tamari stared indifferently as I told him about the young Christian woman who worked for the Voice of Palestine, who was told not to read Christian obituaries on the air and who eventually resigned because of what she felt was a discriminatory atmosphere created by her Muslim supervisors; the young man who worked for the Palestinian Authority, who was told he should not wear a crucifix because it would offend Muslims; and the dozens of Christians who said they were not given days off from work for the Christian feasts, whereas their Muslim colleagues enjoyed numerous religious holidays. Even after hearing a half dozen examples cited by solidly nationalist Christian families—two of which had even produced "martyrs"—Tamari remained suspicious and became increasingly impatient with this line of questioning.

"To take isolated cases and make this a reality is immoral," he said. "There is something more. There are Christians who are opportunists, who know that this is an Achilles' heel for the Palestinian state, and to advance their personal interests they say the PA is discriminating against Christians, with no regard of what that does to the image of our state."

The Holy Family fled Bethlehem and sought refuge in Egypt. Only one gospel writer, Matthew, describes this journey. Many biblical historians see Matthew's narrative of the Holy Family's flight into Egypt as an example of the author's persistent effort to try to square the story of Jesus with the prophecies about the Jewish messiah in the Hebrew Bible.

The historical setting was the reign of Herod the Great, whom the Romans had made king of Judea, in the land they called Palaestina. *Herod had been in power for more than a generation when Jesus was born. A king ordinarily would have had no reason to take notice of the birth of an infant to a peasant woman. But Matthew's gospel recounted that wise men came from the East and asked, "Where is the one who has been born king of the Jews? We saw his star in the East and have come to worship him."*

This news troubled Herod. He called for the wise men, who biblical scholars agree were probably best understood as either Persian or Babylonian priests expert in astrology. According to Matthew, Herod asked them where "the Christ" was to be born. They told him, "In Bethlehem in Judea, for this is what the prophet has written." Furious, Herod ordered the mass killing of all infant males under age 2 so as to prevent the prophecy from coming true. But before the massacre was carried out—as the story in Matthew goes—an angel appeared to Joseph and told him to take flight with the infant Jesus and his mother to Egypt.

VII

Egypt

THE FLIGHT

"Get up," he said, "take the child and his mother and escape to Egypt. Stay there until I tell you, for Herod is going to search for the child to kill him."

MATTHEW 2:13 (NIV)

CRIMINAL COURT for the Southern Region of Egypt is a depressingly modern and nondescript building. It stands at the center of a gritty industrial city named Sohag, which is built up along the western side of a bend in the river Nile, more than two hundred miles south of Cairo. Shayboub William Arsal was led into the courtroom in shackles and leg irons and seated at the defense table. Arsal, a Coptic Christian, stood charged with the killing of two other Christians, one of whom was his cousin, in the town of Al-Kosheh, a remote village some fifty miles farther south along the Nile.

Arsal, 38, looked thin and tired and unshaven. He wore soiled prison clothing and an expression of fear and desperation. Seated next to him was his attorney, Mamdouh Nakhla, who assured his client that justice would prevail, and did his best to conceal just how little faith he had in that actually happening. The three judges from the regional court, all of them appointed by the Egyptian minister of justice, filed in and took their places. It was June 3, 2000—judgment day for Arsal in the Al-Kosheh killings. He was facing a possible life sentence, perhaps even death, if convicted under Egypt's notoriously corrupt and brutal criminal justice system.

Al-Kosheh was a sleepy backwater that few in Cairo had ever heard of—that is, until the double murder of which Arsal stood accused. But it was not the act of murder itself that put Al-Kosheh on the map. Murder was not uncommon in Upper Egypt, a land where tribal feuds and questions of honor were often settled with violence. It is a place where the fiery Islamic militants of Gama Islamiya fought a raging insurgency—despite, or perhaps because of, brutal suppression by the Egyptian military from the early to late 1990s. The Gama Islamiya have periodically opened fire on Nile cruise ships and the ancient ruins of the pharaonic dynasties, trying to destroy Egypt's tourism-reliant economy. They've also gunned down Egypt's Coptic Christians, whom they brand as "infidels," painting a religious veneer over base extortion against wealthy Christian jewelers and landowners.

So the corpses of two men, shot in the back and lying face down in one of these hamlets, hardly seemed the kind of incident that could make Al-Kosheh the focus of the country's attention. The assumption was that it was just another tribal feud, another case of petty killing. But this murder case became much more than that, as it came to symbolize a reopening of old and deep wounds for Egypt's Coptic Christian minority. It was, as the Copts of Al-Kosheh saw it, a fulfillment of their ancient fears of persecution and discrimination at the hands of a Muslim society and a central government in Cairo that was indifferent to their plight. This murder case set the stage for what would become one of the more extreme cases of collective punishment by a notoriously brutal police force. And when the authorities tried to sweep the problem under the rug, the town of Al-Kosheh would explode into the worst sectarian strife Egypt had seen in decades.

On this day, appearing before the judges, Arsal broke down and cried. He pleaded: "I'm innocent! You know who the killer is. Everyone knows that I did not do this. This government has set a trap for me. You must see that."

. . .

On Saturday, August 15, 1998, the sun rose over a desert horizon in burning shades of ocher, ushering in the oppressive heat of another summer morning along the banks of the Nile. The world's longest river snakes its way up from the Sudan, swelling in the middle at Lake Nasser—formed by the Aswan High Dam in the southern reaches of Egypt—before splaying out into the vast delta north of Cairo. The Nile is the lifeblood of Egypt, and has been since the time of the pharaohs.

Nestled to the east, along a gentle curve of the river's banks sixty miles north of Luxor, is the remote agricultural town of Al-Kosheh. Though it may seem identical to the other settlements strung like beads along the river's slow, swirling waters, Al-Kosheh is one of only a handful of towns in Egypt with a majority Christian population. Egypt's Christians, known as Copts, have dwindled in number since the Islamic conquest in the seventh century A.D. Today the Copts are a small, embattled minority.

The Coptic Church is one of the oldest in Christendom, founded by Saint Mark the Evangelist, who was said to have arrived in Egypt in A.D. 60. All of Egypt's Christians are referred to as Copts, the Arabic term for all Egyptians before the Islamic conquest (a time when Egypt was 90 percent Christian). In its current usage, the word *Copt* indicates the original Christians of Egypt who kept their faith after most of the population converted to Islam. Followers of the Coptic Orthodox Church make up the vast majority of Egypt's Christian population today, although there are also Roman Catholic and Protestant denominations.

In the year 2000, Copts numbered less than 5 million, or about 6 percent of Egypt's population of 70 million. The Copts make up what is by far the largest population of Christians in any country in the Middle East, and they are not in danger of disappearing any time soon; but they are a continually shrinking presence, in terms of their proportion in the total Egyptian population. (Scholars and church officials estimate that in the early 1970s there were also 4 million Copts, the same number as today; but that number represented 12 percent of Egypt's population at the time.) This diminishing presence is mostly due to a lower birthrate, a steady flow of emigration, and a persistent level of conversion to Islam, mostly among young women and as a result of marriage to Muslims.

The Coptic Orthodox Church estimates that as many as one million Christians have left Egypt for the United States, Europe, Canada, and elsewhere in a steady stream over the last three decades. Every week at the embassies in Cairo, Egyptians, both Muslim and Christian, stand in line to apply for visas; but these lines contain a strikingly higher percentage of Christians than does the general population. Huge numbers of internal migrations also are taking place within Egypt. For more than a decade, Copts have been fleeing the southern region, which is steeped in a more traditional Islamic culture and in some places is controlled by militant Islamic groups such as Gama Islamiya. Copts are steadily migrating north to Cairo, fleeing not only the bleak economic conditions of Upper Egypt but also the violence perpetrated by Islamic extremists. Bustling, cosmopolitan Cairo offers Egypt's Christians—many of whom are merchants—greater economic opportunities , as well as the chance to integrate more easily into society. The trend of internal migration is dramatically evident in the southern governorate of El Minya, where the Coptic population has dropped from as much as 40 percent of the population in 1980 to less than 20 percent today.

In 1998, two-thirds of the 30,000 residents of Al-Kosheh were Christian, making this town a rare outpost of the faith. Yet it was there, in the tangle of alleyways and dirt roads and fields, in the sweltering heat of an August morning, that two bodies were found lying face down in a litter-strewn schoolyard. Both had been shot at close range in the chest, as evidenced by large exit wounds in the back.

The deceased men were both Christians. Samir Eweida, 25, and Karam Tamer Arsal, 27, were known as gambling and drinking buddies in Al-Kosheh's Coptic community. They rarely attended the early morning Sunday services. They rarely had steady work. They always seemed to be getting into trouble. Still, shock rippled through the produce markets, butcher shops, teahouses, bakeries, and bus stands as Al-Kosheh awoke to news that the two men had been gunned down the night before.

Despite periodic spasms of violence, Upper Egypt was known for its slow pace. This region was Egypt's equivalent to the American Deep South, and referred to as "Upper Egypt" only because the mighty Nile flows from south to north. For *saidi*s, as locals are called, life revolved around the river and cycles of planting and harvesting. But within this *saidi* culture, there were also class lines that had been shaped over many generations according to religious affiliation. The Muslims in Al-Kosheh still worked the land, harvested its produce, and sold vegetables and fruit from wooden kiosks set up along the main street. The Christians tended to have more education and more financial grounding, and they owned nearly all of the large shops, hardware stores, groceries, and pharmacies. A few also had large landholdings and employed Muslim laborers to tend their fields.

The police detectives' first assumption was that the murders were related to gambling. The victims had been seen the night before at one of the local teahouses, where it is customary for men to gather and play cards and dominos; the clacking of the ivory and black pieces slamming down on rickety wooden tables is one of the familiar sounds of life in an Upper Egyptian village. The night before, the Christian residents of the town said, Eweida and Tamer Arsal had argued with five Muslim men, apparently over a card game.

But there was another rumor. A young member of the Al-Karashwa family—the oldest and most prominent of the Muslim families in Al-Kosheh—had died a few weeks before, of apparent alcohol poisoning. The Muslim clan blamed Eweida and Tamer Arsal for his death, saying that the two Christians had poisoned him with the powerful home brew that they and their cousin Shayboub William Arsal had made of fermented sugarcane. This local beverage is a pinkish-colored raw alcohol with a high proof, and in large quantities it can be lethal. Shouting matches had broken out in the street, and the Al-Karashwa clan had threatened revenge against Eweida and Arsal. The more religious members of the Al-Karashwa clan saw the consumption of alcohol not only as a violation of the Islamic code but also as a kind of Christian-influenced demonism. Their story, steeped as it was in anti-Christian tones and as farfetched as it may seem to a Westerner, was entirely in keeping with the common patterns of local gossip in these southern Egyptian communities of largely uneducated farmers and field laborers. Primitive fears of evil spirits and witches' potions occupy the vast darkness at night in these little towns, a midnight blanket that stretches east across the Red Sea and west into the Sahara.

Far from the Al-Kosheh night, in the brightly lit offices of the sprawling centralized government bureaucracy in Cairo and its vast security apparatus, the government of President Hosni Mubarak was still stinging from the bad press it had received in the United States over the alleged persecution of Christians by Muslims in Egypt. The Coptic associations of America—claiming to represent 500,000 members of the North American Archdiocese of the Coptic Orthodox Church—were a powerful and shrill voice that often rose against Mubarak's regime and had fed the flames of media hype surrounding the purported persecutions of Christians. There had been a string of stories—most of them exaggerated—of church burnings and forced conversions by militant Islamists, all intended to create the impression that Mubarak's Egypt was overrun by Islamic intolerance. Mubarak did not want to be embarrassed any further by these Coptic Christian groups. He was worried about the powerful Washington coalition that had formed around the issue of religious persecution of Christians worldwide, from China to the Sudan and Egypt. The campaign was led by Michael Horowitz, an orthodox Jew and former top Reagan administration official who had been involved in the largely successful movement to push the Soviet Union to release Jews for emigration to Israel during the 1970s and 1980s.

This Washington machinery was pushing for passage of a Freedom from Religious Persecution Act, which had been introduced in the Senate by Arlen Specter, a Republican from Pennsylvania, and in the House by Frank Wolf, a Republican from Virginia. In the congressional debate, Egypt was frequently a target of criticism for its ill treatment of Coptic Christians. Over the summer of 1998, the House of Representatives had even dispatched to Cairo a conservative Republican congressman from New Jersey, Chris Smith, to look into allegations of persecution.

The proposed law called for the creation of a new ambassador-at-large post and an office within the U.S. Department of State to police religious persecution worldwide. It would also give the president power to take action against countries where harassment, imprisonment, and killings of religious minorities were taking place. The presidential actions could range from private condemnation to suspending foreign aid and imposing strict economic sanctions.

Egypt, a poor country deeply dependent on the $2 billion a year in foreign aid it regularly has received from the United States, was understandably concerned about this legislation and openly suspicious of its backers. Many of the Arab world's intellectuals and leaders, especially Mubarak, believed the drafting of the legislation had been orchestrated by the Israeli lobby in Washington, about whose considerable influence in the U.S. Congress Arab leaders were constantly fretting.

The Egyptian leadership saw the legislation as an effort to paint Egypt as a nondemocratic regime caught in the clutches of radical Muslim fundamentalists who were terrorizing Christians. They believed the Israeli lobby in Washington was intent on fostering divisions in Egypt, on alienating it from the United States, and on blocking U.S. aid. Israel and Egypt are in a perennial wrestling match for funds (they rank first and second, respectively, among the recipients of U.S. foreign aid), and the Egyptians are very sensitive to any perceived Israeli effort to reduce their share. Conspiracy theories have great currency in Egypt, and are expressed in the leading Arabic newspapers almost daily. And this broad conspiracy scenario surrounding the Freedom from Religious Persecution Act was sizzling in Egypt's media just as the news of the murders in Al-Kosheh broke.

Several Coptic clerics, Egyptian journalists covering the case, and human rights lawyers told me they believe that some order from Cairo came down to the local authorities that the case of the two

Christians found murdered in Al-Kosheh was not to become fuel for the fire of the "hidden hands" (as they were often referred to in the Egyptian press) that were trying to exaggerate a Christian-Muslim divide in Egypt. It seemed to many observers that this backwater police force's focus was less on solving the crime than on carrying out orders from Cairo that would ensure that President Mubarak would not be embarrassed by another story of sectarian strife or Christian "persecution." There was just too much money at stake for Egypt to allow this incident to be publicized by the international media.

On the morning the bodies were found, Egypt's security forces immediately moved in. Steel-plated troop transports of soldiers training automatic rifles rumbled down the dusty streets through the center of town. Police units in jeeps bumped along the narrower alleyways to the sound of crackling police radios. The search for suspects in the killings was on.

Despite the claims of the victims' families and of the local church leaders that the killing was the work of five quarrelsome Muslims, the local police—all of them Muslim—chose to pursue a different tack in their investigation. They began going door to door on a rampage of collective punishment against the Christian residents of Al-Kosheh. These tactics were all too familiar (the same police force had been notoriously brutal in suppressing the Islamic fundamentalist movement); but human rights workers agreed that this was among the most egregious instances they had seen in the country, and certainly the most dramatic for the Christian minority. Over the next three weeks, the police would arrest or detain for questioning as many as 1,200 Christians from the town. (A handful of Muslims were arrested as well, but promptly released.) Dozens of Christian men were forced to undergo "interrogations," which included beatings and torture. Several Christian women were threatened by the police with rape. Children, as young as infants, were torn from their mothers' arms, and at least one young child was injured in the process. This police brutality had one purpose, according to some human rights lawyers and church officials: to extract a confession that would become the basis for prosecuting a Christian man for the crime.

In early October, I headed for Al-Kosheh, accompanied by an Egyptian colleague and translator, Nadia Tewfik, and a photographer, Tom Hartwell. Our plan was to leave at dawn in order to reach Al-Kosheh by the first light of the next morning. The route to Upper Egypt begins on the outer edges of Cairo, at Maadi—the site where tradition holds that the Holy Family rested on their journey. The highway opens up about fifty miles outside the city, near the ramshackle town of Beni Suef, on the edge of the muddy banks of the Nile, and before long the images along the road become ancient, almost biblical. Young men plod along on donkeys. A farmer guides his handheld plow, pulled by an ox, slowly and deliberately tugging through the rich, fertile soil along the riverbed. A water buffalo fords a tributary of the Nile. Wooden waterwheels slowly turn, fetching buckets from the khaki-colored river. Women in long black robes and veils balance the filled buckets on their heads and turn toward home to cook dinner in mocha-colored, mud-brick homes. Men in the traditional kaffiyeh and cotton turban return from lush fields, with hand-hewn wooden pitchforks and hoes slung over their shoulders.

Icons of the Orthodox tradition always pictured the Holy Family on a donkey plodding past these ancient towns with rows of palms and mud-brick homes. And though we had not planned our route for this purpose, we were treading the same path that tradition held the Holy Family had traveled on its flight out of Bethlehem and into Egypt.

We journeyed farther, to a spot beyond Al-Qusiyah, near Deir al-Muharraq, the farthest point reached by the Holy Family, then past Asyut and into the region of Sohag. As we approached the small road that leads into Al-Kosheh, we were stopped at a checkpoint. Because we were traveling without the necessary permits from the Ministry of Information, we were taken to the local police station and questioned. We told the officials that we had an appointment with Bishop Wissa of the Baliana bishopric. Because of the late hour, we were permitted to go there to spend the night, but we were expected to leave in the morning. We were warned that we had violated the rules for journalists and that this would have to be taken up with officials in Cairo.

A covered blue pickup truck carrying six soldiers with machine guns followed us as we drove into the Coptic bishop's compound. The steel gates were padlocked, and a single bare bulb dimly lit the interior courtyard. We rang a small bell, and eyes appeared in a slit in the steel gate. The guard's eyes looked frightened—or perhaps just confused at the sight of the soldiers and Westerners. After we introduced ourselves, the guard, a small man in a *jalabiya* and a turban, with an antique-looking rifle slung over his shoulder, slowly opened the gate.

A man from the state security services hopped out of the blue pickup and attempted to follow us into the monastery. We asked him to wait outside, which he did. The troop transport idled at the gate all night, the police radios sputtering with messages. Here in Upper Egypt it was crystal clear just how much of a police state Egypt had become.

The place was consumed with worry. A nun, pacing, spoke breathlessly into a cordless phone. Several priests wearing thick beards and traditional black robes with conical hoods were conferring and seemed nervous, tired, and exhausted. Lights were on in a first-floor foyer adjacent to the office of Bishop Wissa, the top cleric for the Sohag region, which included Al-Kosheh. The bishop—who, as is the custom among Coptic clerics, uses only the first name he adopted at his ordination—had been a strong voice opposing the discrimination against Copts and the human rights abuses that had taken place during the murder investigation in Al-Kosheh. We were told that he had been ordered to report to the regional prosecutor's office in Sohag that morning and had not returned, even though it was now past 11 P.M.

Inside the monastery, we met with one of the church's chief pastors, Father Matteus, and a lawyer from the Egyptian Human Rights Organization, Mustafa Zidan, who had traveled from Cairo. They were surrounded by several traumatized residents of Al-Kosheh who had fled the town after being "interrogated." Some of them claimed they had been detained without charge, beaten, and tortured for days. Egypt is a state where people, especially the lower classes, live in fear of their police force. Together they told their terrifying stories about what had happened, knowing that in doing so they risked being subjected to further brutality by the local police.

Among the first to be arrested was Boctur Abu al-Yameen, 50. At 8 A.M. on August 15, he was picked up on the street in front of his home. The police alleged that his daughter, Haneyya, 15, was intimately involved with one of the victims, and that the father and his oldest son had killed the victim and his friend in a fit of rage.

He said the police placed a hood over his head and tied him, "like a slaughtered animal," to a wrought-iron window grate. They began beating him and threatening worse if he did not confess. The following morning, the police also arrested Boctur's wife, Helen; Haneyya; his other daughter, Amourra, 13; and his son Romani, 11. He claimed he could hear his wife and daughters and young son screaming in an adjacent room, as the police told him they would rape his daughters if he did not confess to the crime.

This went on for hours, he said, while his oldest son, Ayman, 20, who had traveled to Sohag to find a lawyer for his father, was returning home. When he arrived late in the afternoon, he found the family's house empty and was worried. Neighbors explained that the family had all been taken to police headquarters. When he got there, Ayman recounted, he found Amourra crying hysterically in the waiting room. Haneyya was bound to a chair in an interrogation room, and his mother was screaming at the police to stop torturing her eleven-year-old son. "It was like walking into hell," he said. Ayman was taken into an interrogation room, where he was asked where he and his father had been the night of the murder. He told them he had been at home with his father and the rest of the family. Then the beating and the torture began.

Ayman said he was blindfolded and forced to remove his clothing. He and several other eyewitnesses confirmed that in the corner of the room where most of the torture took place there was a machine that they described as similar to an old-fashioned teletype machine with a telephone crank. There were crude wires coming out of it. The police used the hand crank, they said, to turn up the electric current. The police officers attached the electrodes to Ayman's body, one on his toe and one on his penis, he said. He was tortured for one hour this way and then untied. He collapsed on the floor in pain, he said. He spent the next three days tied up in a small room next to a neighbor, Abdu Michael, an army conscript, who he said was "in miserable condition" from the beatings he had allegedly suffered.

"He [Abdu Michael] was begging me to confess that I had bought the weapon used in the killing from him. This poor soul was desperate, saying, 'Just tell them anything,'" recalled Ayman.

His mother, Helen, said: "I pleaded with them to stop the beatings and the torture. I swore by the Virgin Mary that we did not do anything, that none of us knew anything about these murders. The police laughed and said, 'What Virgin? What religion is this? You have no religion. Worshiping three gods and believing in virgins is not a religion.'"

Ayman and his father were held for thirty-four days. After two days in detention, the women and the young boy were released, but periodically throughout the following month, they were brought in again and beaten and threatened. On September 16, officer Mohammed Kotb signed a charge against Boctur for possessing an unlicensed weapon. Two days later, however, the charge was dropped and he and his son were released. When I spoke with them, rope burns from being tied up were still visible on their arms. They were thin, but their faces were swollen with bruises. A medical form that Ayman held in his hand attested to the fact that he had been "vomiting blood" and had suffered "extensive internal injuries."

This was just one family's account of the ordeal the town of Al-Kosheh suffered. The police also arrested dozens of family members and extended relatives of a man named Maurice Shukralla, whom they also "suspected" of the crime. The police who beat and tortured him never explained why he was a suspect. Shukralla, detained for three weeks, was tied "in the position of the cross" to a cell door and viciously beaten. Taking his fourteen-month-old son from his mother's arms and lifting the back of the child's shirt, Shukralla showed me a deep blue bruise the size of a golf ball, just to the left of the child's spine. He claimed that the police had done this when they pulled the child away from his mother and threatened to beat and rape her if she did not confess that her husband was responsible for the killing. "These are not police who uphold the law, these are animals," he said.

After four weeks of random arrests and beatings, the police narrowed the focus of their investigation to Shayboub William Arsal. He was officially charged with the killings, by the security forces of the Sohag governorate. The alleged motive for the killings was an argument over gambling debts. The prosecution's case was based on the statements of two men who the police claimed were eyewitnesses. But at the beginning of October, just days before we arrived at the monastery, the two witnesses had come to Bishop Wissa, saying that their "testimony" had been extracted by means of torture. Wissa helped them arrange a meeting with a lawyer.

One of the witnesses, Abdu Michael Mileik, 22, a soldier who had served in the security police forces of El Minya, hails from Al-Kosheh. After meeting with Wissa, he presented a new statement through the lawyer, saying that he was not present in Al-Kosheh on the night of the murder. The other witness, Yasser Shahed Allam, also gave sworn statements to defense attorneys that police had tortured him to extract his earlier statement and that the earlier statement was not true. In response, the regional prosecutor for Sohag indicted Bishop Wissa as well as the two witnesses on a litany of charges that included "obstruction of justice," "incitement," "changing truth as reported in official documents," and "making statements that harm national unity."

These trumped-up charges against Wissa and the two witnesses were still pending more than two years later. Technically, such offenses could bring the death penalty, but no one believed that was a real possibility. A hefty fine and several months in prison were more likely in this case, should the prosecution choose to move forward—which was considered unlikely. But the threat still loomed, and it had a chilling effect on those who might otherwise have dared to speak out.

Just after midnight, a car horn sounded in the courtyard outside. It was Bishop Wissa, and there was an audible gasp of relief that he and two other priests had been released from the police station. The nuns and priests and the human rights lawyer rushed to the doorway to greet them as they walked in.

Wissa was wearing a black silk turban and long black vestments with embroidered Coptic crosses of red and gold. A large leather cross hung around his neck—the sign of the Coptic clerical order. The frail, gray-bearded sixty-year-old had a warm charisma that was apparent the moment he entered the room. The priests and nuns kissed his hand, taking a sharp breath inward as their lips touched Wissa's skin. This is a traditional greeting by the Copts toward their parish priests, and clerics toward their superiors, that consciously evokes the gospel's mention of "true life from true life."

Once in his office, Wissa collapsed in the black leather chair behind his enormous desk and rubbed his head and eyes in exhaustion. The shelves of a glass case next to his desk were full of small plaster statuettes that depicted images of Christian suffering and bloody resilience: Jesus's face twisted in pain as he carried the cross; the Holy Family fleeing Herod's wrath on a donkey; Daniel in the lion's den; St. George slaying the dragon; bloody Lazarus emerging from the tomb. A clock, decorated with a portrayal of blood dripping from Jesus's crown of thorns, ticked past midnight.

Struggling to open a bottle of aspirin, Wissa began to recount the events of the day of his arrest and court appearance, and the ominous charges filed against him. "I am very dangerous, apparently," he said with a mischievous smile.

Mustafa, the passionate young human rights lawyer and the only Muslim in the room, carefully read the indictment against Wissa. "You will have to be very careful, Bishop," he said, with a look of deference and respect but also troubled concern. "They are charging you under the terrorism laws. They have now taken this to a very serious legal level."

"So they want me to shut up, to cower in fear," Wissa shot back. "I cannot sit here and say nothing with this injustice happening. Even if they charge me for doing that, I can't stop. You are not saying you think we should stop speaking out, are you?"

"No, I am saying please be careful, sir," Mustafa replied. "Please avoid confrontation in the next few days. This is not like 1981, things are getting much worse with our government."

Mustafa was referring to the last time Wissa had had this kind of run-in with the law. In a dramatic and unprecedented move in September 1981, President Anwar Sadat had ordered the arrest of 1,500 people, mostly Muslim sheikhs and vocal opponents to the government, who were perceived as a threat to his rule. The list included 22 priests and bishops. Wissa was among those taken into custody, and he ended up spending several months in prison.

Tangling with the government in Cairo was not new to Wissa, but it was exhausting. The fatigue and the sense of struggle were evident in his face, as was a deep sadness—perhaps at the fact that Christian-Muslim tensions that had long lain dormant were dramatically resurfacing.

We were shown to bedrooms in the monastery. The thick stucco walls provided a comfortable insulation from the summer heat and a heavy silence that was interrupted only by the sound of the troop transport idling and the faint clatter of a donkey hauling a cart down the street. I soon fell asleep.

At 6 A.M., with the first light of day, the sky was laminated with grays and purples, which were soon washed away by the searing summer sun. From my room, I could hear the rhythmic chanting of the priests' matins, the first prayers of the day. Later, at the start of the full Sunday mass for the congregation, Bishop Wissa walked the church swaying a censer that billowed clouds of incense, the congregation breathing in the ancient, holy smells of the Coptic tradition.

The congregation was segregated, with males on the right and females on the left. They were country people, the men dressed in *jalabiyas* and the women mostly clad in black with head veils. The stucco walls of the church were the color of wet sand and cracked in many places. The windows in the high reaches of the church were broken, and small birds flew in and out.

Above the altar was a classic Coptic depiction of the Pantocrator—the Eastern icon of Jesus Christ the King enthroned, exalted, and powerful.

The Coptic language used in parts of the prayer service is a direct descendant of the ancient tongue of the pharaohs. These Coptic incantations, exotic and elliptical, were echoing in the church just as the Muslim call to prayer began to blare from the loudspeakers positioned in the minaret of the mosque across the street. The minaret towers over the church and the loudspeakers are pointed downward toward the street, and the Arabic chant was all-consuming.

After the service, we took a local taxi with two of the Coptic priests out of the courtyard of the cathedral and somehow went unnoticed by the military guards stationed there throughout the day. The local taxi and the faces of the priests must have relaxed the soldiers manning the checkpoint, and we were able to enter Al-Kosheh, which we had been told by authorities was closed to members of the media without written permission from Cairo.

The streets in the Christian area were mostly empty and quiet. Doors on which Coptic crosses were crudely painted or drawn in chalk were tightly closed. The entrance to the Church of the Archangels, the largest of four in the town, was in a back alley, through a metal gate in a fifteen-foot brick wall fortified in the early 1990s, with the rise of Islamic militants. There was a watchtower at the entrance, from which a man eyed us, nodding to the priests. Inside the courtyard about one hundred people were milling about after Sunday services.

By that afternoon, the Christian families of Al-Kosheh had been assembled in the courtyard. Some four hundred angry parishioners clamored to tell me what had happened to them in police custody. The Egyptian press articles on Al-Kosheh had been censored, and they approached us with an eagerness that made us believe that this was their first opportunity to expose what had taken place. While they gathered, showing me and one another the bruise marks and cuts from what they said was torture, police security vehicles idled outside the gate. The church's own armed guards were posted at the entrance to the church to protect the parishioners, who still felt threatened after weeks of arbitrary arrest and police brutality. The air was thick with tension.

This was a village of farmers and merchants, and many of the complaints I heard were practical: for example, that during the six weeks of military rule in the town, commerce had stopped. Christian craftsmen, weavers, carpenters, and farmers were worried that their livelihoods would be devastated by the police tactics.

More and more people gathered to tell me their stories, and with each tale the crowd became angrier and rowdier. I sensed that this gathering could easily erupt into a riot. "The people are very angry. I am afraid we are going to let this get out of control. We need to leave," Father Matteus told us, as the police outside unsheathed riot batons and more military personnel appeared.

"The police want us to be afraid. They don't want anyone to know what is happening here," a man named Shawki Shenouda whispered to me just outside the church's gate. Shawki, 59, hurriedly told me how he had spent ten days in detention and had been tortured by the police. At this point we were ordered to leave by the military, which would escort us out of town. As we prepared to move down the narrow street, watched by fearful Christians peering out from cracks in doorways and from windows, Shawki clung to the window of the car, pleading, "Tell the world about the suffering here. Tell the world what is happening to us."

. . .

Coptic history is measured in epochs of suffering and martyrdom. According to the Copts' long-standing tradition, St. Mark the Evangelist "received the crown of martyrdom" on May 8, A.D. 68, in Alexandria, having been hunted down by a mob of Roman pagans on Easter and dragged through the streets. His corpse was to be burned, but a heavy rain came and doused the fire, as "nature would not permit disrespect to the body of the saint."

Even the Coptic calendar is based on suffering. The first year of history, as recorded by the Copts, begins with the *anno martyrum,* or year of the martyrs, in A.D. 303. This year marked the pinnacle of two decades of Coptic suffering under Roman rule, known as the Age of Martyrs. The massacres of Coptic Christians under the emperor Diocletian are legendary and still resonate in the minds of Copts.

When Constantine the Great issued the Milan Decree of A.D. 312 announcing that Christianity would be a recognized religion of the empire, the Copts were not suddenly free of oppression, nor did their resistance cease. They were only beginning a long fight to throw off Roman, and later Byzantine, rule. The height of this resistance would become known as the Great Tribulations. The Coptic Church rejected the doctrine of the dual nature of Christ—the claim that Jesus was both human and divine—and clung to the notion that only one, divine nature existed in the person of Christ. The Orthodox pejoratively dubbed those who believed in one divine nature "Monophysites," and such beliefs were ruled heretical at the Council of Chalcedon in A.D. 451. The Coptic Church rejected this theological ruling and broke away from the Orthodox mainstream. And the Copts suffered for their belief.

For these reasons, among others, the Copts welcomed the Muslim conquest in the seventh century and sided with the Arab armies against Byzantium. They hoped they would find a better life under Islamic rulers than they had under the Byzantine emperors. This is a period of history that the Copts frequently resurrect to remind their Muslim brothers in Egypt of a shared past that began in solidarity.

But Islamic rule did not mean an end to discrimination and suffering. Under Islam the Copts were forced to carry heavy crosses, even to wear bells on their feet, to mark themselves as the minority. A carryover of this practice, or a kind of defiant expression against it, exists today among Copts who discreetly profess their faith with a small blue tattoo, typically on the inside of their right wrist. The mark is intended as a symbol of permanent solidarity—as permanent as their faith in Jesus—that would make it difficult for any Christian who might choose to convert to hide his or her past.

As we drove out of Al-Kosheh on the long road back to Cairo, we passed through the province of Asyut. Nowhere has religious intolerance, and the exodus of Christians it has spurred, been felt more strongly than in this province, long considered the stronghold of the Islamic militant organization Gama Islamiya (the Islamic Group).

Asyut, a grimy industrial center, is Egypt's third largest city. About 20 percent of its residents are Copts. Amid row after row of depressing government-funded housing blocks and air heavy with pollution from factories, people had turned to the Islamic fundamentalist credo: "Islam is the solution." The message of militant preachers, such as Sheikh Omar Abdel Rahman, the blind cleric who would gain international fame as the spiritual inspiration for the 1993 World Trade Center bombing, had taken root in the poverty and despair that gripped this part of Egypt.

Just north of Asyut, in the town of Al-Qusiyah, we stopped to see Bishop Thomas, a refined and eloquent man in his mid-40s, who for years had helped his parishioners endure the indignities inflicted on them by Islamic militants, who seemed to surround them. He worked diligently at interfaith understanding and building bridges between the two communities.

In the traditional black vestments and long beard, the bishop welcomed us at the door of his residence. We stepped out of the hot midday sun and were invited into the cool, dark recesses of his library, where he invited us to share some mint tea. As it was being served, I asked him about the most obvious confusion a foreigner would have in understanding the Coptic situation in modern Egypt. Why do Copts defend their country at every opportunity, and deny that there are any problems? The Copts were, it often seemed, patriotic and generous to a fault. It was almost comical to hear them always begin discussions of Islamic-Christian relations with the same sentence: "The Muslims are our brothers."

He smiled politely and tugged at his beard flecked with gray. "It is part of Egyptian society to deny we have problems. When someone lifts up the carpet to show there is dirt, they are accused of being a traitor to the country. And there is nothing worse in Egypt than a traitor. That is just the way we are. I should play the same game with you and say we are living in harmony. The Muslims are our brothers. And there are, of course, levels on which that is accurate. The question is not one of brotherhood, but how you treat your brother."

Bishop Thomas had been born into the Cairene elite, the scion of wealthy textile industrialists, during a time when the Copts were no more than 10 percent of the population but controlled, by some estimates, nearly half of the nation's industry. In the mid-1950s and early 1960s, during the rise of pan-Arab nationalism and socialism under Gamal Abdel-Nasser, the economically prosperous Copts saw their businesses and factories nationalized. The bishop's family's textile mills were expropriated by the state in the early 1960s. He well remembered his family's humiliation and resentment, which at the earliest opportunity was translated into action: "My entire family has left. Everyone. Businessmen, engineers, doctors, all of them have left for the West," said Bishop Thomas. "But I refuse to go. I will die here. It is not because I am a nationalist; it is because I refuse to run away. It is because there is so much to do to help people here."

After Nasser died suddenly in 1970, Anwar Sadat came to power. His policies were marked by a deep concern for the threat from left-wing Nasser socialists, who saw him as softer and less charismatic than his predecessor. To confront this threat, Sadat encouraged the formation of Islamic groups and associations. He also released many militant Islamic leaders who had been in prison for years. This politics of religion resulted in Sadat's own death when the violent Islamic underground that his policies had benefited assassinated him in 1981.

At the trial of his assassins in 1981, a follower of Sheikh Omar Abdel Rahman described the secret *alim,* or religious guide, that the cleric had articulated for them regarding Copts. Rahman had decreed it legitimate to rob Christians in order to fund the purchase of weapons for their *jihad,* and he ruled further that the shedding of Copt blood was permissible. And so the militants targeted wealthy Copts. A spree of robberies of Coptic-owned jewelry stores was believed to have been aimed at financing the Gama Islamiya. Coptic store owners and industrialists also were forced to pay protection money. Copts who resisted were threatened with death or even killed.

The motivation for targeting Copts was neither purely theological nor simply financial. It was also political, since the Copts, as a substantial minority, were the guarantors of a secular government. And a secular, tolerant government was the last thing Islamic fundamentalists wanted.

The tide of Islamic fundamentalism, Bishop Thomas noted, had slowly, almost imperceptibly, invaded Egypt's daily life, creeping into the court system, the school districts, the media. On Egyptian television a popular Islamic leader, Sheikh Abdel Kafi, advised his followers not to shake hands with Copts, attend their weddings, or wish them a Merry Christmas. Kafi has since been kicked off the public airwaves, but Christians say they hear similar taunts, insults, and degradations broadcast over the loudspeakers of the minarets. The Copts have also had to endure the legal system's family laws, which are largely dictated by Islamic law, *sharia,* including strict social codes that (among other things) bar Christian men from marrying Muslim women and Muslims from converting to Christianity. The Copts live in a country where the constitution proclaims Islam the official religion, and where they are forced to carry identity cards that mark their status as a religious minority.

With their dwindling presence, Copts are increasingly marginalized politically and economically. None of the twenty-six governors appointed by the president are Copts. None of the presidents or deans at Egypt's universities are Copts. And with the powerful professional syndicates increasingly under the control of the fundamentalist Muslim Brotherhood, Copts in the professional class complain that they have been disenfranchised. Many have told me they feel like second-class citizens in a land to which they hold the oldest ancestral claim.

For Bishop Thomas and many of the Coptic clerics I met, the most immediate and troubling issues were the vast disrepair of their churches and the legal restrictions against building new ones. An Ottoman-era edict issued in 1856 and referred to as the Hamayouni Line prevents the building or repairing of any church without approval from the ruler of the government. Under this regulation, painting, plaster repairs, and even the installation of new benches must be approved by the president himself. Sadat was notorious for refusing permits, having issued only fifty during his tenure. In 1991, Mubarak issued a decree for the repair of a toilet in Mayiet Bara, in Munufiya province. "I don't know what kind of danger to the state repairing a toilet poses, but apparently there are security reasons for this," said Thomas, who oversaw twenty-one churches.

. . .

The Coptic community in each town has its own horror story.

Just down the road a few miles from Bishop Thomas's residence—a country road that winds through fertile fields of watermelons and sugarcane and a plantation of date palms—is the monastery Deir al-Muharraq, its heavily fortified walls rising out of a row of palms. Legend holds that the Holy Family stopped here and lived for some six months, and the land is thus regarded as sacred. The monastery is believed to have been established in the fourth century; and throughout the sixteen centuries since, there has been an annual *mulid,* or feast, at the Monastery of the Holy Virgin at Al-Qusiyah. The monks speak of dreams in which they see the Holy Virgin inside the walls of the monastery, and some report having had visions of her along the banks of the Nile.

In March 1994, the dreamy isolation and serene mysticism of Deir al-Muharraq were suddenly disrupted by an Islamic militant attack. Two monks who happened to be at the front gate and two lay people who were bystanders were gunned down in a hail of bullets from a passing car. Six years later, a monk quietly showed us inside the monastery, through the inner courtyard with its thick walls and its castellated keeps that had protected the community against invaders through ages. "You see, we have always been attacked," he said. "We have always had to live this way. It is our history."

Just ten miles from the monastery, heading north toward Cairo, is the village of Sanabu. In April 1992, the small village with its surrounding farmlands was the scene of a massacre of fourteen local Copts. All along the road back to Cairo were datelines of one atrocity after another. Among the worst was the one that occurred on February 12, 1997, in Abu Qurqas, a small town near El Minya. While a student prayer group was gathering in St. George's church, gunmen who police believe were Gama Islamiya militants opened fire, killing nine young people.

We returned to Cairo, arriving past midnight. The neon signs in Arabic pulsed above the buildings and the streets were crowded with pedestrians in the sultry late night air. The frenetic energy of Cairo was a refreshing change of pace after the slow backwaters of Upper Egypt.

In the groggy, hot Cairo morning, I began a series of meetings with human rights workers, academics, and government officials. As they accurately pointed out, Christians are not the only ones targeted by Islamic militants. Tourists, police officers, and prominent secular journalists and politicians have also been slaughtered on the streets and in their homes. Of the more than 1,300 victims from 1992 to 1997, 96 were Christian citizens. A disproportionately large number of the hundreds of police officers killed have been Copts, and of course most of the Western tourists gunned down were Christians. So the militancy has widely afflicted all of Egypt.

Throughout the 1990s, Mubarak's government had carried out a relentless crackdown on the militants, imprisoning some 20,000 Islamists. Human rights activists say thousands were illegally detained and tortured. But the crackdown had stanched the terrorist bloodletting. The militants were still able to commit sporadic and occasionally spectacular atrocities, such as the gunning down of 58 foreign tourists in the fall of 1997 at the Hatshepsut temple in Luxor. But generally, political analysts believed, Mubarak had effectively crushed the militant Islamic movement and destroyed the threat it posed to his regime.

In some ways the story of Al-Kosheh was the bitter legacy of that aggressive war against the insurgents; but in this case it was not the

Islamic militants but the government itself that had perpetrated the injustices. A violent police and security force had been given free rein to wipe out Islamists, and had exercised little or no self-control in the process. Extrajudicial murder, systemic use of torture, hostage taking, and collective punishment were among the grievances against the government recorded by Amnesty International, Human Rights Watch, and other prominent human rights monitoring groups. Yet in the ensuing news coverage, the Egyptian government went unquestioned when it said it had found no wrongdoing on the part of the police in Al-Kosheh. Officials said that the claims of torture had been exaggerated and that the police had arrested the right man for the double homicide. Some accepted this story; I did not.

My colleague Nadia helped me set up an interview with Osama el-Baz, chief of staff to President Mubarak, to probe further. His office was an opulent series of rooms filled with oriental rugs and Ottoman-era antiques. El-Baz typified the Cairene elite who were members of the Mubarak's inner circle, which was void of any Copts. He adamantly denied that anything had been amiss with the investigation in Al-Kosheh, or that there was any discrimination against Copts anywhere in Egypt. He even denied that there was a steady migration of Copts to the West. "Our statistics do not indicate a flight," he said, only "a very small difference in percentages" of Coptic emigration when compared to Muslim emigration from Egypt. When I asked whether the government's figures on migration and its census data on the Coptic versus Muslim population were available for research purposes, he replied, "They are with the Ministry of Interior. My understanding is they do not release the numbers."

El-Baz returned the conversation again to Al-Kosheh, insisting that the situation there had been exaggerated by the foreign media. He confessed that he had not visited Al-Kosheh himself, nor had anyone on his staff. But in a professorial tone, he spelled out centuries of Islamic rule in Egypt under which he said there had been a "proud history of religious tolerance."

"I confess that the Copts are claiming they are treated unfairly as a minority, but they are wrong," said el-Baz, flatly. "The incident was reported on a local level and we looked into the case. We have no interest in covering up if Christians are being tortured. We have no interest in doing that whatsoever."

An educated and genteel man, el-Baz had a way of looking at me when I pursued questions that he didn't like, or felt he had already answered—a look that could only be described as disappointment. "We have not deprived Christians of their rights," he sighed, placing his porcelain teacup in its saucer and giving me that look. "We don't even have the concept of a minority here. And legally speaking the Copts are not a minority. Let me ask you, can you walk through Tharir Square and pick them out as different? If you could, you could get into the slippery area of prejudice. But you cannot, and I can honestly say there is no prejudice in any form in this country toward Copts." El-Baz was right, of course, about not being able to distinguish a Copt by appearance. But he was overlooking the fact that typically Copt names are obviously Christian and thus an immediate giveaway. There were also the small blue crosses on the inside of their wrists.

El-Baz insisted that the only suffering the Copts had undergone was at the hands of the militants. And the military, he stressed, had taken severe measures to combat the militants. "Some of these fanatical bastards, who form a thin minority of this country, come in with fanatical ideas that are alien to our culture," he said of the Islamists. "They try to say that Copts should not be given full rights. They accuse the government of playing to the Copts to placate the West. There are people at the local level, a schoolteacher for example, who have these fanatic concepts in their minds. But the question is, what does the state do? Have we neglected the problem with the militants? Have we looked the other way? I don't think you could say that."

Just one week after my meeting with el-Baz, Hafez Abu Seda, the secretary general of the Egyptian Organization for Human Rights, was arrested and thrown in prison. He had just published a report on Al-Kosheh in which he sharply criticized the government for doing too little to respond to the atrocities there, and he was boldly speaking to the foreign media about the outrageous collective punishment and the allegations of torture. Abu Seda's critique included mention of the fact that innocent Egyptian Muslims had also been the victims of arbitrary mass arrest and systematic torture in the government's crackdown on militants. But his comments about the government's ill treatment of Copts—or more specifically, the way in which these comments were used abroad—caused the Mubarak government great discomfort.

The charges brought against Abu Seda were bizarre and clearly trumped up: from "receiving bribes from a foreign country" to "spreading reports" of police brutality against minority Copts, according to the early press reports in the government-controlled media. He was arrested at his home and dumped in one of Egypt's most notorious prisons. His head was shaved—typically an act performed only on common criminals and therefore deeply degrading, especially in Muslim culture—and he was left in solitary confinement for seven days.

Approximately two months after his release, I saw him at his office in Cairo. He showed me pictures of himself with his head shaved, and the record of indictment. Apparently the government had tapped into the EOHR's bank account through someone on the inside and had found a donation from a branch of the British government that promotes human rights work. This was apparently what the indictment meant by "foreign agents."

. . .

Abu Seda's arrest occurred in the very week in which the U.S. Senate was poised to vote on the Religious Freedom from Persecution Act. Supporters of the bill were stressing that Christians were the primary targets of government-sponsored persecution throughout the world, with China, the Sudan, and Egypt being leading cases in point.

Nina Shea, a Catholic and director of a program at the Washington-based Freedom House, had worked tirelessly to bring this issue to light. In her book *In the Lion's Den,* she wrote: "Millions of American Christians pray in their churches each week, oblivious to the fact that Christians in many parts of the world suffer brutal torture, arrest, imprisonment and even death—their homes and communities laid waste—for no other reason than that they are Christians. The shocking untold story of our time is that more Christians have died this century simply for being Christians than in the first nineteen centuries after the birth of Christ. They have been persecuted and martyred before an unknowing, indifferent world and a largely silent Christian community." Freedom House had been hammering this point across for years prior to the congressional vote. And in the weeks before, Shea's organization was blanketing the media with faxes about the plight of Christians in Egypt, and making Al-Kosheh the center of their campaign.

American Coptic organizations were also running full-page advertisements in the *Washington Post* and the *New York Times* about the persecution in Egypt in an attempt to influence U.S. lawmakers. (Their efforts were considered too strident, even by the Coptic clerics of Egypt.) "It's a declared war against the Christians," shouted Shawki Karas, head of the American Coptic Association, outrageously comparing the suffering of the Copts to that of the Jews in Nazi Germany.

Significantly, the Christian churches in the Middle East weren't buying Washington's sudden concern for their plight. The Catholic and Orthodox hierarchies in Jerusalem issued powerful statements of opposition to the legislation. And certainly the Copts, well versed in the West's use of divide-and-rule tactics throughout the centuries, were not willing to go along with this display.

In Egypt's secular circles, Muslim and Christian alike, the movement in Congress was seen as a thinly veiled attempt to cause divisions between Christians and Muslims. Abdel Monem Said, director of the Al-Ahram Center for Political and Strategic Studies, saw the Al-Kosheh story and the disturbing rupture between Christians and Muslims as stemming from economic disenfranchisement rather than religious differences. "The problem is between rich and poor," he explained. "The tensions between Christians and Muslims, and the exodus of Christians, reflects the failure of political, economic systems. Fundamentalism is connected to a search for identity, to economic disenfranchisement, much more than whether there are Christians here or not. Just look at the three governorates where the Copts have suffered, [El] Minya, Asyut, and Beni Suef. . . . This is also where 90 percent of extremist activity is. Now these are also the poorest governorates, the bottom three of Egypt's twenty-six districts. Do you think that is just a coincidence?"

In addition, there are many Copts among Cairo's secular elite. In the first half of the twentieth century, the sons of this elite were often sent off to Oxford and the Sorbonne before returning to Cairo to reap the fruits of their pedigrees. As Christians, they were favored sons under British colonial rule and handed steady jobs as civil servants and managers of industry. This helped them fare well in the world, but it also engendered Muslim resentment back home in Egypt. They were the scions of industry, but President Nasser's nationalization program changed that, inspiring a strong wave of emigration to the West.

One of the most prominent of this class who remained in Egypt was Milad Hanna. I had decided to pay him a visit. His home was in a venerable section of downtown Cairo, where lawyers and doctors and professionals live in orderly rows of three-story townhouses along a broad boulevard. One of his servants greeted me at the door and ushered me in. While waiting for Hanna to finish a telephone conversation, I browsed a bookcase lined with medals, proclamations, and framed certificates trumpeting the achievements of a man who for a half century has been Egypt's preeminent structural engineer, one of its most eloquent voices of tolerance, and certainly its most outspoken Christian politician. He had even done some time in prison, along with Bishop Wissa, for his political challenges to Sadat in 1981.

"So you've come from Al-Kosheh. Did you like my bridge?" he asked, surprising me with his booming voice. I realized he was referring to the massive, six-lane Nile crossing at Sohag, the seat of the province in which Al-Kosheh is situated, which he had engineered as a young man in 1954, after graduating from the Massachusetts Institute of Technology. The laborers who built the bridge had come largely from Al-Kosheh and other nearby villages, and to this day Hanna remembers the Coptic fathers and sons of that town working alongside their Muslim brothers from the other villages. This is the Egypt that Hanna loves, an ancient civilization uniquely blending Muslim, Christian, Arab, and African. "It has a Sunni face, Shiite blood, Coptic heart, and pharaonic bones," as he put it. "Most Muslims in Egypt recognize their heritage, they know that their great-great-grandfathers were most likely Copts. This is a very important factor in understanding Egyptian Islam. And it is a very important factor in understanding the hurt that something like Al-Kosheh causes. Not only to the Copts, but to the Muslims who want to think of their Egypt as being Christian in its roots, even if it is Islamic in the way it is flowering now."

. . .

After his release from prison, Hafez Abu Seda remained focused on the Al-Kosheh trial and convinced that Shayboub William Arsal had been framed. As Abu Seda assembled a case for the defense, he wondered what case the prosecution could possibly present. The evidence for the defense, he felt, was overwhelming. The prosecution's only two witnesses had recanted, and there were huge inconsistencies in the police investigation—enough to raise serious doubts.

In an interview with me that fall, Abu Seda was reflective about the future, and frighteningly prophetic. "This was a very vulgar and flagrant case of abuse. The longer the government covers up the problems and refuses to bring justice in Al-Kosheh, the more the tension is going to build. And we will see more violence there."

From December 31, the eve of a new millennium, through January 2, 2000, the town of Al-Kosheh erupted in the worst sectarian violence in Egypt's modern history. The first news reports did not even appear until January 3, a fragmented account that indicated a dispute between a Christian shopkeeper and a Muslim customer that had ignited into a street riot. The first reports were that twenty Christians had been killed in three days of shooting and rioting.

The massacre in Al-Kosheh made the front page in Egyptian newspapers. Headlines blared, most of them pointing to the involvement of "hidden hands" in the violence; but virtually every newspaper that used this phrase—and it was the overwhelming majority—failed to articulate what they meant by the phrase "hidden hands." I imagine they just assumed that readers knew they meant the West, the "Jewish lobby," the U.S. Congress, the American Coptic organizations, and every other hidden hand that they felt lurked behind so many events that changed their lives.

On January 4, I was on my way back to Al-Kosheh. But this time the military stopped our car. "I'm sorry, sir, this is regulation. This is a closed area," an officer said at the final checkpoint before Baliana. As usual, the Egyptian security forces were trying to keep the press out of Al-Kosheh. We were now in a kind of cat-and-mouse game. We told them it was late, we would sleep and leave in the morning—knowing that we would sneak out early, as we had done on our last visit, or at a minimum bargain with the authorities in the light of morning over coffee, when we might stand a much better chance of getting through.

Finally, we were taken to Bishop Wissa's front gate. Inside, Wissa and the priests looked exhausted. They had just completed the funerals of those killed in Al-Kosheh earlier that afternoon. "We buried seventeen today," said Wissa, explaining that three more bodies had just been found that would be buried the following day.

Wissa was smoldering. "But the president has intervened," he deadpanned, "and this means now the problem can be resolved. Yes, the president sent a minister, the minister of national development, to see us. So now we are very confident the situation is under control." It took a minute through translation for me to understand just how sarcastic a statement this was.

As we talked, the newly ordained priests were sitting on a couch facing us, studying a list of the deceased, which had just been retrieved from the morgue. Father Basillius adjusted his thick glasses and pulled the paper close to his eyes. Then he let the paper fall. Tears welled up in the corners of his eyes; behind the thick lenses the magnified droplets looked like small pearls that then rolled down his cheeks. There was a long silence, hushed voices of grief.

"Five of the victims are his relatives," Wissa explained several minutes later, after comforting the priest.

Fathers Basillius and Kirillus hugged each other and stared down at the ground. In the stillness of the night, there was the sound of a clock ticking, and once again the ubiquitous low idling of a police vehicle outside the steel gate of the monastery.

After a long silence, Wissa said, "Nothing was done. There was no correcting of the injustice. The police who tortured people were not reprimanded, an innocent man faces the death penalty, and now there is killing in the streets of Christians, which goes on under the eye of the police for three days. So long as there is no security or justice, things will get worse. We will be having more funerals in Kosheh."

The next morning the police permitted us to drive through Al-Kosheh but not to stop in the town. On the outskirts we could see the burned Christian shops, the smashed Muslim kiosks. The entrances to the town were sealed by armored personnel carriers. Dozens of police in riot gear and military troops in combat helmets were stationed at the entrance, and a small squad of six soldiers walked in a column through the main road entering town.

At the police station just a few miles down the road, Father Jibril and several eyewitnesses were gathering to voice complaints against the police for their failure to arrest those responsible for the looting and killing. Slowly we began to piece together what happened.

It was December 31, 1999, a day of overlapping religious calendars—the last Friday of the holy month of fasting known as Ramadan, and the beginning of the Christian celebration of the New Year that would mark two thousand years of the faith. It was late in the afternoon on Port Said street, a wide boulevard entering the town, lined by the well-established Christian merchants' shops and the struggling, ramshackle Muslim kiosks of street vendors.

The street vendors often aggressively sought to underprice the more established shops, and the Christians had won a court ruling that the street vendors' kiosks were illegal and must be dismantled. But the local police and legislators, all of whom were Muslim, refused to carry out the order, and Port Said street had become an economic and sectarian fault line. Christians considered the continued impunity of the kiosk vendors evidence that the Muslim government no longer respected their rights; but to many Muslims the kiosks represented a street-level economic challenge to the haughty Christians, who should know their place in a Muslim country.

It was in this context that an argument had erupted at 3:30 that afternoon at a Christian clothing store just off Port Said street. A Muslim woman told the owner, Rashid Fahim Mansur, that she was offended by his high prices. He erupted in anger and told her to leave. Some of the Muslim street vendors joined in the argument, accusing the Christian of insulting and pushing a Muslim woman. The argument raged for a while, but eventually things calmed down again.

From this point on, the details of the story depended on whether you were talking to a Muslim or a Christian. But as best as could be determined, a few Christian shop owners, furious that the police had not enforced the court ruling against the kiosks, began dismantling the structures themselves while the owners were at Friday sunset prayers. The Muslims, who had been gathering guns in their homes and shops to protect their kiosks, came to defend their stores, opened fire, and began looting Christian stores all along Port Said street. Christians complained that the local police did nothing to stop the Muslims from destroying the Christian property.

On Saturday morning there was a sullen truce as the Christians went about cleaning their shops, shocked at the violence of their neighbors. On Sunday morning, Muslims were repairing their kiosks as church services let out. A flood of Christians came into the street as they do every Sunday. Insults were traded. A fight broke out. Soon a man believed to be connected to a militant mosque in town was driving his car around town, loudspeaker blaring, encouraging Muslims to rise up against the Christians of the town, who he said were preparing for an attack. When the church bells tolled at noon, a rumor started in the Muslim community that it was a call to arms. (Actually, it was an extended ringing of the bells for a funeral.) Almost spontaneously, violence broke out in the streets, with sporadic gunfire being exchanged. The killing had started in earnest.

Gun-wielding Muslim men dragged Christian residents out of their cars, witnesses said. They stole herds of cattle and then shot the owners in the lush green pastures alongside the Nile, leaving them to die amid the dense rows of sugarcane and cornstalks. Then the Muslims began entering homes and killing people. Abdel Messih Mahrous and his daughter were shot in their house next to the Post Office. Buna al-Qoms was killed in her house near the canal. Eight men, mostly fathers with their sons, were killed in a field on the edge of town. Others were shot crossing the road, and one on a bridge. In all, twenty-one people were killed. Twenty were Christian, and one was Muslim.

"They were shooting people in the street. You could hear the yelling and the screaming, and you could see the Muslim men setting Christian stores on fire and rampaging," said Father Jibril, the Coptic priest who pastors the Church of the Archangel Michael in the town and witnessed much of the violence firsthand, from inside the church's gates.

Shamshun Michaeli saw his son Wa'el, 17, shot dead in front of him on the street on Sunday. Witnesses watched as Shamshun ran into the gunfire and held his son, screaming, in the street emptied by the shooting. Three days after the incident, Shamshun was still dressed in the clothes caked with his son's blood, which he had refused to remove even after the burial.

More than one hundred people were arrested and charged with having played a role in the violence. About half of those arrested were Christian, which further outraged the Christian community. The police, they claimed, were trying to paint the massacre as if it were a fight the Christians had lost, when actually it was a rampage in which a score of Christians were killed, many of them in their own homes. (All but a few of the thirty-five people injured were also Christian.) One of the first arrested was Father Jibril, who police claimed had been wielding an automatic rifle and had shot several Muslims on a bridge. Several Muslims had indeed been shot on a bridge, but witnesses to the shooting said that the shots came from a passing car of Muslims who had been targeting Christians. Jibril dismissed the charge as absurd, but it was never officially dropped, although the police could not produce a single witness, and human rights workers and journalists never turned up any evidence supporting it.

Al-Kosheh—no longer a sleepy provincial town but a landmark of sectarian strife—would take a long time to return to normal, and many residents believed relations would never be the same between Muslims and Christians. Already there was some sign of an exodus of Christians from the town. Many had left to move in with extended families in neighboring villages. Others had gone to the regional capital of Sohag or to Cairo. Many, especially the young people, said they would try to leave the country altogether and join the long list vying for visas to the United States or Canada—or anywhere but Al-Kosheh.

Meanwhile, human rights attorney Hafez Abu Seda left the country for a conference in France, having just been warned that he would be forced to stand trial upon his return. He remained in France, saying he would face trial but wanted to consult with attorneys before returning. While he was in Europe, a second EOHR report was issued on the killing spree in Al-Kosheh. It was a whitewash, deliberately playing down the sectarian nature of the rioting and the twenty-one deaths. EOHR president Abdel Aziz Mohammed said that the massacre was "not an example of sectarian strife" but rather a "natural phenomenon of a society with problems." An incredulous Egyptian reporter at the press conference asked him, "Do you understand that this could destroy your credibility?"

The government's policy of intimidation and repression had succeeded. The new investigator assigned by EOHR to the Al-Kosheh case, Mahmoud Kandil, 35, seemed passionless—more a bureaucrat than a human rights advocate. When I met him, I noticed that tacked to his bulletin board—among the black-and-white photographs of human rights victims—was a gold-embossed invitation from President Mubarak's wife to attend a gala celebration. So apparently there were rewards for not stirring things up any further in Al-Kosheh. When asked whether he was angry that his boss had been thrown in jail and that injustices continued to take place in Al-Kosheh, Kandil adjusted his glasses and calmly replied, "It is a different culture in Egypt. We don't use these terms. I try to put my emotions aside."

But others within Egypt, both Christian and Muslim, did rise up against the injustices. They railed against the government's inaction toward sectarian violence and its apparent determination to cover it up. Saad Edin Ibrahim, director of the Ibn Khaldoun Center, an independent think tank in Cairo, was among the government's public critics. He warned Egypt's leaders that to ignore the sectarian divisions was to guarantee that they would resurface again and again.

Ibrahim, a Muslim, was an expert on minority affairs in Egypt and had written extensively on the history and culture of the Copts. Along with others, he reminded the government that sectarian violence had steadily crested and fallen in waves over the last three decades since the 1972 church burning in the village of Khanka and the sectarian riots that ensued. Ibrahim and others consciously resurrected the

Khanka incident to remind the government of what they estimated were at least fifty major incidents of violence since then, and to put the Al-Kosheh story in perspective.

After the violence at Khanka in 1972, a parliamentary committee had been formed including renowned Coptic and Muslim figures. The committee presented solid recommendations on how to avoid further sectarian problems, but they were ignored. In February 2000, in the aftermath of the killing in Al-Kosheh, a group of prominent Muslims and Christians (some of whom had served on the original Khanka commission three decades earlier) formed a new committee and called once again for the government to implement the recommendations spelled out in the Khanka report, including constitutional and political reforms ensuring democratic and equal rights under the law; harsh penalties for religious hate crimes; an intense public awareness campaign in the regions where the violence had flared, to promote religious tolerance and brotherhood; the integration of Coptic history and the Copts' contributions to Egyptian civilization into the state's educational curriculum; and a standardization of all statutes governing the construction and restoration of religious buildings. The government this time chose not only to ignore the recommendations, just as it had thirty years before, but also to silence the critics.

Ibrahim was arrested on June 30 and held for more than a month in the Tora state prison, south of Cairo. The charges against him were similar to the trumped-up indictment against Abu Seda. The Ibn Khaldoun Center was raided by the state security forces, and several young staffers also were placed under arrest. In addition, various human rights reports, including one that Ibrahim's center had planned to publish, were censored by the government. The increasingly flagrant abuse of power by the state security forces seemed to be part of a broad effort by a jittery regime that was tired of the bad publicity it was receiving and perhaps nervous about the attempts by human rights leaders to monitor upcoming elections, which were widely viewed as a rubber stamp for the autocratic rule of Mubarak.

And amid this government clampdown, the justice system also had been grinding along, perpetrating what many Christian residents saw as the crowning injustice in the saga of Al-Kosheh: On June 3, 2000, after nearly two years of waiting, the man charged with the initial double murder in Al-Kosheh had his day in court. In the regional criminal court for the governorate of Sohag, Shayboub William Arsal appeared before the panel of judges who would present the evidence for the prosecution. Because Abu Seda was still in France, avoiding his own arrest, Arsal would not benefit from his aggressive representation. The job would be left to human rights attorney Mamdouh Nakhla, who did his best with the few resources he had. So despite the solid inconsistencies in the police reports and the recantations of the prosecution's two key witnesses—and even statements from the victims' families, that they believed Arsal to be innocent—the defendant was quickly and unceremoniously convicted of murder. The three judges admitted the first statements of the two key witnesses even though the witnesses had recanted, and this proved a devastating blow to the case.

"Arsal was poor and a petty criminal and therefore easy to convict, and the judicial system knew this, I believe," said Nakhla. "He was framed in this murder. Great pressure was brought to bear, that is what I believe. Why Arsal? Primarily because he is a Christian and they wanted to be sure that a Christian was convicted in this case."

Nakhla planned to file a motion for an appeal, and hoped for another chance to present the case. The next time around, he believed, he would have to go into the politics of the case and the intense pressure that he felt was brought to bear by the government, in order to establish a case that Arsal was wrongly accused. He would have to show that the Cairo government feared the negative publicity it would receive if the murder case fit within the framework of sectarian strife between Muslims and Christians. It would be a long shot, and he knew it. But he believed that was what had happened. The prosecution and government officials continued to insist that the right man had been convicted.

Arsal was sentenced to fifteen years of hard labor in prison, a relatively light sentence for homicide—but that fact hardly consoled him. He was led out of the courtroom and transferred to the Wadi Natrun prison, situated between Cairo and Alexandria. There he toiled in a work gang in the heat of the desert, digging irrigation trenches. The trenches will carry the water for the new residential community Mubarak envisions building in the barren wilderness of Wadi Natrun, which will house an overflow of Egyptians from other, overcrowded urban communities.

The Cairo government has washed its hands of the Al-Kosheh affair. No police official of Al-Kosheh or state security officer was prosecuted or even publicly reprimanded, despite the allegations of torture and police abuse and the human rights reports that supported such claims. There was little in the way of any genuine effort to publicly address the deep sectarian divide that had ruptured the social fabric of Al-Kosheh. There was no effort to develop a school curriculum that might inform the Muslim majority about the history of the Coptic Christians or their culture and their deep roots in Egypt. The violence was carefully swept under the carpet by the Cairo regime—to be left there, presumably, until the next eruption.

In the aftermath, the government proposed in the summer of 2000 that Al-Kosheh be renamed. In classical Arabic, the name *Al-Kosheh* translates into either "Place of the Dispersed" or "Place of Enmity." Either definition now seemed too aptly to describe the town; the enmity was obvious, and "the dispersed" is precisely what many Christians of Al-Kosheh had become after the violence. The regional council for municipalities in the Sohag governorate elected to rename the town Al-Salam, or "Place of Peace." To the Christians still living there, who had buried twenty members of their community after the rioting, the idea seemed surreal. Did government officials really believe that they could disguise what Al-Kosheh had come to represent by repainting a few road signs? On my return visit in late summer, I noticed that the signs pointing toward the town still read "Al Kosheh."

III

Jesus of Nazareth

The Holy Family returned to Nazareth, where Jesus came of age.

Mary and Joseph and the infant Jesus would have lived in one of the primitive dwellings, carved into grottoes, that can be seen today in excavations. The Holy Family were small-town Jews living in hard times. Their land was under a foreign conqueror whose culture had diluted their own proud heritage and ancient rituals, as many Jews at the time felt.

Little is known about Jesus's childhood and upbringing. Was he well educated and on his way to becoming a scholarly teacher? Or was he an illiterate peasant destined to become a Jewish sage? It is said in Matthew's gospel that Jesus was a "carpenter's son." In Mark, it reads a "carpenter." Since it was a time when sons followed in the footsteps of their fathers' craft, both statements were probably true. Some biblical historians believe that Joseph settled in Nazareth to work on a huge project—the rebuilding of the nearby fortified Roman city of Sepphoris by Herod Antipas, who inherited Galilee under the will of his father, Herod. Joseph was struggling to get any work he could, even if it meant building the occupier's fortifications—a humiliation perhaps not unlike that experienced by modern Palestinians who build Jewish settlements.

Biblical scholars concur that Jesus had at least six siblings: four brothers, who can be listed by name, and two sisters, whose names are unknown. His relationship with his family would tear at him, torment him, as he struggled to determine his own place in the world, his identity and mission. Which was the truer family: his disciples by faith, or his brothers by birth? Jesus was of a land where individuals defined themselves by their tribe and progeny, and he radically defied these notions, seeking to redefine "family."

VIII

Nazareth

THE FAMILY

He went to Nazareth, where he had been brought up, and on the Sabbath day he went into the synagogue, as was his custom. And he stood up to read. . . . "I tell you the truth," he continued, "no prophet is accepted in his hometown."

LUKE 4:16–24 (NIV)

THE ISLAMIC MOVEMENT pitched its tent on Mayor Ramez Jeraisi's dream. The bearded clerics, small-town political leaders, and numerous devout Muslim laborers and farmers who made up the political organization known in Israel as the Islamic Movement had forcibly taken over a vacant municipal lot in Nazareth. On it, they had erected a large green canvas tent, where they insisted they were going to build a towering mosque on a prized half-acre slice of real estate that lay directly in front of the Basilica of the Annunciation. And five times every day, hundreds of members of this movement gathered in the tent for Muslim prayers. Almost since the day he took office in 1994, Jeraisi, born into a Greek Orthodox Christian family, had envisioned the vacant lot as the cornerstone of "Nazareth 2000," which was to be a massive $100 million redevelopment project geared toward the millennial celebrations. He wanted to build a large plaza for Christian pilgrims and tourists from around the world—a much-needed open space for tour buses dropping off their groups, around which a cluster of shops and artist studios would be centered. His hope was to position Nazareth at the center of festivities on New Year's Eve 1999, as the world prepared to usher in the new millennium. What better location, he figured, than Jesus's hometown, for a celebration of two thousand years of the Christian calendar? But the Islamic Movement saw an opening in his plan to increase its political power. It raised objections, insisting that a mosque for the local Muslims should be built there, not a tourist site for Western Christians. This was municipal politics cast in religious terms. The ensuing two-year local political battle ultimately shattered Jeraisi's hopes and left Nazareth deeply divided along sectarian lines and struggling to hold on to Western tourists, who were intimidated by the rising tension and violence.

Jeraisi had been baptized in the Greek Orthodox Church, but his confirmed faith was in secular culture and socialism. His politics were those of the Israeli Communist Party, which operated on both the national and the local levels as an opposition of old-line leftist Jews and Arabs, a constant thorn in the side of Labor and Likud. Christians historically had been the driving force in the Communist Party's Arab Israeli front, and Jeraisi came out of this tradition. He was an efficient man, better at the mechanics of government than at projecting charisma and winning elections.

When he moved into the corner office in Nazareth's city hall, he found himself presiding over a populace with deepening class divisions. The Muslim farmers, fruit peddlers, and laborers were bristling at the power of what they saw as a wealthy elite of secular Muslims and rich Christians who ran city hall. Like similar movements elsewhere in the Arab world, amid increasing poverty, unemployment, and lack of hope, the Islamic Movement's political fortune flourished in Israel's struggling Arab communities like Nazareth. As it did, the old class divisions were increasingly redefined along religious lines. And at the center of the spiraling tensions and heated rhetoric between Muslims and Christians was Jeraisi—a modern man of politics, caught in a postmodern world of religious fundamentalism.

In late spring of 2000, I visited Jeraisi in his city hall office, just up the hill from the makeshift mosque. He sat behind a large desk, listening to my questions while diligently completing piles of paperwork. At the end of each question, he would look up over his bifocals, which typically rode low on his nose, and answer. On this occasion he seemed more worn down than during our previous conversations—almost resigned to the fact that the sharpening divisions in his community had taken on a momentum all their own and could no longer be reined in. It was as if the half century of separate and unequal treatment under Israeli rule had finally caused Nazareth to implode. In some ways it was surprising that this hadn't happened earlier. Jeraisi knew that the source of people's frustration lay in the disenfranchisement of their city at the hands of the Israelis; but he had grown philosophical about the inevitable clash it had produced between the Muslim and Christian residents of Nazareth. "For me, it is depressing," he said, looking out over his bifocals. "Members of this community so easily fall into the trap in the name of religion. The values are changing in Nazareth. Sometimes I think I am not from this generation. I belong to the past, not the future. It used to be that we were all like family here. Muslims and Christians were brothers. You should have been here then."

. . .

It was fate, not an election, that made Jeraisi mayor of Nazareth. He was serving as deputy mayor to the more charismatic Tewfiq Ziyad. Ziyad had been known as a poet—a man of swagger and passion—before he was elected the first Communist mayor of Nazareth, in 1975. But in 1994, Ziyad died in a car crash on a perilous, winding road near Jericho, where he had been attending a celebration of Yasser Arafat's triumphant return to Palestine after years in exile. Ziyad, a secular Muslim, had been a political force of nature for twenty years. He had modernized Nazareth and had made the city and his party, the Democratic Front of Nazareth, the political center of gravity in Palestinian politics in Israel. The Democratic Front was closely aligned with the Communist Party, which in the year 2000, after the collapse of the Soviet Union, changed its name to the People's Party. The goal of the Democratic Front and the People's Party was to challenge the bigger parties to live up to the promises Israel had made to all of its citizens, in what inarguably was the closest thing to a democracy in the Middle East.

After Ziyad's death, Jeraisi was sworn in as mayor by the city council. Almost immediately he took the first strategic steps toward achieving his long-term plan for the Nazareth 2000 project. Jeraisi initiated a newly cooperative relationship with the government of Prime Minister Yitzhak Rabin. At the time, he felt that Israel was on the threshold of a new relationship with its Palestinian minority. The historic Oslo peace agreement had just been signed, and there was new hope in the region. Nazareth had provided Rabin with key political support in his election victory in 1992, and now Jeraisi, just like any big-city ethnic politician in America, was expecting political benefits in return. Under Rabin, the patronage was forthcoming. Rabin made long-term commitments to pump unprecedented financial resources into the redevelopment of Nazareth, which had essentially been left by former Israeli governments in a state of disrepair, with bad roads, traffic nightmares, faulty sewers, and trash removal that in some parts of the town still relied on donkeys with saddlebags.

After Rabin's assassination in 1995, his successor, Shimon Peres, also eagerly sought to back Jeraisi's plan for "Nazareth 2000." But after Peres's defeat in the 1996 elections, everything changed. Virtually all of the city's ambitious plans were blocked, as the new conservative coalition government of Benjamin Netanyahu took great political satisfaction in sticking it to the Front, which had long supported the Labor Party. Jeraisi believed that the Jewish religious parties in Netanyahu's coalition also were making their reservations known about the Jewish state's funneling millions of dollars into the celebration of the year 2000, which they saw as a Christian event, tied to the Christian calendar.

Despite the diminishing chances of expanding Israeli government funding for Nazareth 2000, Jeraisi proceeded at full steam. A world-class musical extravaganza headlined by the legendary tenor Luciano Pavarotti was in the works, and the municipality was brokering the rights to the management of the event for $3 million, with a 10 percent commission on all ticket sales going to the municipality.

The centerpiece of the planned $100 million urban renewal project was to be a public plaza at the foot of the Basilica of the Annunciation. The plaza was intended to create a more welcoming atmosphere for what analysts were predicting would be a wave of millions of Western Christian tourists into Nazareth and the Galilee during the millennial celebrations and in the years that followed. The plaza would be a drop-off point for tour buses, which could then be quickly routed out of the clogged, cramped streets to wait while the tourists visited the shrine. It would be a place for tourists to mill about the gift shops at the foot of the basilica and to soak in the Arab culture of the city—the coffee shops, the wonderful smell of spices, the Arabic chatter.

But the mayor's political rivals in the Islamic Movement, who held four of the nineteen seats on the city council, seized on the plaza as a political issue. The Islamic Movement claimed that the new construction would necessitate the demolition of a nineteenth-century school building in which there was a small Muslim prayer niche. In a back corner adjacent to the lot there was also a small Muslim shrine to Shehab al-Din, a nephew of the legendary warrior Saladin, and a martyr in the battle of Hattin against the Christian crusaders. The movement's leaders claimed that the land fell under the control of the *waqf*, the Islamic trust that oversees all holy sites. The city leaders insisted that the plot of land was owned by the government. They produced city zoning maps that showed that the school and the shrine had previously been possessions of the Ottoman Empire and then the British mandate and were now under the ownership of the Israel Lands Administration. But the Islamic Movement persisted, saying that the site was originally *waqf* land and must be returned to the Islamic trust.

Since the city council had voted in favor of the plan for the plaza and it had the blessing of the Israeli government, Jeraisi gave the green light for municipal workers to tear down the Ottoman-era school in November 1997 to clear the way for construction of the plaza. The shrine to Shehab al-Din was left untouched, to be integrated into the layout of the new public plaza. But the supporters of the Islamic Movement were furious that the school had been torn down, and they stirred up unfounded rumors that the shrine was to be leveled as well. In December, tension reached a crescendo when the pounding of hydraulic drills cracked the foundation of the Shehab al-Din shrine. That evening, a group of supporters of the Islamic Movement stormed the empty lot, beat up several municipal workers, and took the land by force. On December 24, Christmas Eve, Muslim protesters gathered in the thousands to occupy the vacant lot and demand that a mosque dedicated to Shehab al-Din be built there.

Soon the Islamic militants had erected a canvas tent and crudely fashioned loudspeakers to the center pole—a makeshift mosque. Muslim architects began drawing up plans for an elaborate, towering mosque to be built on the site. The tent quickly became a stage—or perhaps more accurately, a circus big top—for a new theater of municipal politics. The protesters erected a billboard that featured an artistic rendering of the proposed mosque, showing its minaret—topped by a laser-lit crescent moon—towering over the Basilica of the Annunciation.

Salman Abu Ahmed, a city councilman and the local political leader of the Islamic Movement Party, had learned to play the tribalism game masterfully. As crowds circled around him at the tent, he would suddenly thunder forth with outrage in the name of Islam, to cheers and chants of *Allahu akbar!* ("God is great!"). He was a local populist in the making. His Islamic Movement had long been viewed with suspicion, not only by supporters of the Front but also by Israeli leftists who saw the Islamic party as a means for the Labor and Likud establishment to counter the local political power of Israel's Communist Party. In this carnival of political intrigue and conspiracy theories, Abu Ahmed was a midway barker.

Another tent-show character was the self-made sheikh Nazem Abu Slim, who had taken the pulpit at daily prayers in the tent and at the Friday noon prayer, which was attracting hundreds of faithful in the weeks after the land was taken by force. Abu Slim, a 35-year-old graduate of Ben Gurion University with a degree in biochemistry, had painted houses for a living until he took on the role as the imam of the tent-mosque. Donning a white knitted prayer cap and gray clerical vestments with yellow ribbing, he discovered a new vocation. He was joined at the makeshift mosque by Mohammed Nim'r Mahajneh, 57, a burly man with a thick gray beard, who intoned the call to prayer. Wearing a gray *jalabiya* and white headdress, and constantly clacking his Muslim prayer beads, he cornered me one day, roaring against "the Christian crusades" and pointing his finger at me. "The mayor and his Christians do not fear God. They tried to destroy a Muslim shrine!" he exclaimed. "The mayor and the West think they can bring their new Crusade here to Nazareth, but we will resist it. We will fight against these Crusaders to protect the name and the honor of the martyr Shehab al-Din."

One of the more intriguing characters to come under the tent was Danny Greenberg. He was a Likud Party operative who lived in the Lower Galilee and was responsible for developing the conservative party's "Arab portfolio." Likud had never found any natural constituency among Palestinian voters in Israel and had historically rejected any compromise on the territory of *Eretz Israel,* or the Land of Israel, which they believed included all of Palestine under the British mandate. But none of these ideological obstacles stopped Greenberg from trying to bring some Palestinian voters in Israel into the Likud fold—or more plausibly, from encouraging a boycott of Labor.

Greenberg saw his task as a matter of numbers: The Arabs constitute nearly one-fifth of Israel's population, enough to tip the balance in any election. But the Christians are such a small minority within this Arab voting block (about 10 percent) that no savvy street politician would want to appear to be taking sides against Islam if he hoped to court favor with the Arabs. In other words, Greenberg was willing to alienate the Christian Arabs by siding with the larger number of Muslim Arabs on the issue of the mosque. To him, it was just good politics. Greenberg's goal of convincing the Muslims to vote for Likud was a long shot. But he did succeed in getting them not to vote for Labor. Seventy thousand blank Palestinian ballots in the previous prime ministerial election had helped Netanyahu squeak past Peres with a razor-thin majority.

After Netanyahu became prime minister, Greenberg held secret meetings with leaders of Nazareth's Islamic Movement in which he encouraged the protesters to take over the tent and promised in return that security forces would not intervene. And indeed, the Israeli police did not intervene. Under Israeli land laws the police had to remove the Islamic Movement activists from the property within thirty days, or the activists would have a defensible legal claim to the land. The police never removed the protesters. Later, in response to questions about their inaction, police and government officials claimed that the seizure of the land had taken place during Ramadan, the Muslim holy month, and that it would have been too volatile a time to remove the protesters.

By January 1998, the Islamic Movement was preparing for a court battle and producing documents that it claimed established that the plot of land was *waqf* property. First they produced a *fatwa,* or religious ruling, from Jerusalem's grand mufti, Sheikh Ekrima Sabri. In response, Mayor Jeraisi rushed off to Jerusalem to prove to Sabri that the documents and maps he had been presented by the Islamic Movement had been altered to make it seem as if the former school and the surrounding municipal lot were included in the *waqf* land. After meeting with Jeraisi, the grand mufti issued an unprecedented overturning of his *fatwa,* and without specifically naming the Islamic Movement went out of his way to sharply criticize "those who lie to achieve their gains."

Within a week, the Islamic Movement had a new *fatwa.* This time they traveled over the Jordan River, to Amman, and presented their case to a Jordanian mufti, Said Abdel Hafif el-Hajawi, who ruled in their favor. Again Jeraisi chased after the Islamic Movement and brought his maps and documents to Amman, and again the mufti reversed his ruling, warning in equally ominous words that "those who lie are doomed to the fires of hell."

Despite these Islamic decrees against the building of the mosque, Greenberg kept pushing for it. He spoke on the Arabic service of

Israel Radio on March 2, expressing his support. It was a critical moment for Likud, which feared that the fractious and unruly coalition that Netanyahu had stitched together could come undone. The host of a news talk show asked Greenberg explicitly whether there was a bargain with the Muslims to give them a mosque in honor of Shehab al-Din as a quid pro quo for support to Likud. Greenberg denied the allegation but added: "This issue is in the media and gaining momentum, and now there is no way back. Anyone saying that things could be turned back to the previous situation is being misled."

"What do you mean, 'turn the situation back'?" the interviewer asked. "Are you saying that a mosque will be built?"

"Yes, there will be a mosque there. I am involved in this issue, they [the supporters of the mosque] have appealed to me several times, including the heads of the *waqf* in Jerusalem."

This tangle of political machinations and arcane Islamic decrees was too convoluted for average Nazarenes to follow. Like voters everywhere in the world, they tended to dismiss the details and believe what they wanted to believe. And all the supporters of the Islamic Movement cared about was that the schoolyard and the Muslim shrine had been reclaimed from the godless communists of city hall. The fight was consolidating the Islamic Movement's supporters. The number of people attending prayer services increased every Friday, and Councilman Salman Abu Ahmed was turning the services into weekly political rallies during the campaign prior to municipal elections in November.

Around the tent, the protesters had erected large placards and Islamic banners and had taken to turning up the volume on their loudspeakers during the call to prayer five times daily and the long, often fiery sermons on Fridays. They attracted menacing outsiders from neighboring villages in the West Bank and farther afield, some of whom were believed to be affiliated with Hamas. On any given day, one could see Western tourists cringing at the spectacle and scuttling away from the gift shops to the security of their air-conditioned tour buses. The economic impact of the simmering conflict on shop owners, Muslim and Christian, was devastating. Jeraisi filed a police complaint against the protesters at the tent, saying that they had no right to physically intimidate citizens, to present a hostile atmosphere to tourists, or to control the land through brute force. But the complaint was never pursued, and the case was closed. To Jeraisi, all of this was mounting evidence that there was a deliberate attempt by the

Israeli government, from the Likud Party leadership all the way up to the security and military establishment, to foment divisions between Muslims and Christians in Nazareth. Netanyahu's government repeatedly dismissed this claim.

The Islamic Movement successfully rode the wave of Shehab al-Din to election day. In the November municipal elections, the Muslim Unity Party picked up six seats, giving them a majority on the municipal council for the first time in a quarter century. Mayor Jeraisi was left with a fractured government in which he held the mayor's office but had no majority on the ruling council. The local government effectively ceased to function.

Jeraisi believed that Israel intended to create a municipal government that consolidated Nazareth and Upper Nazareth into one municipal entity. This, he feared, would undercut the political clout that Nazareth had developed in trying to secure the rights of the Palestinian minority within Israel. It was his worst fear that the Palestinian citizens of Nazareth—Christian and Muslim alike—would lose their voice in local matters, which would surely happen within a council dominated by Israelis from Upper Nazareth.

Jeraisi's fear was founded in part on the Israeli government's decision just a few years earlier to move the regional administrative offices and courts to a towering building in Upper Nazareth, effectively shifting all government responsibilities out of Nazareth. The new regional government edifice in Upper Nazareth, perched high on the ridge overlooking the old city, looked like an abstract interpretation of a Crusader castle, with its mock turrets and spires festooned with Israeli flags. Any resident of Nazareth who wanted to apply for a building permit or a marriage certificate, or to bring any matter to the local courts, even the religious councils where family court proceedings were heard, would have to travel across the valley and climb the steep hill that ascended to the modern castle of regional government.

After the elections, I visited Jeraisi in his office. Again I watched him poring over his paper work as I asked him questions. On this occasion he seemed particularly puzzled by the way the issues of religion had surfaced in Nazareth and shaped municipal politics. Why, he asked me, did reporters constantly refer to him as "the Christian mayor"? He gave a laugh under his breath that sounded more like indignation than amusement as he asked the question. He pointed out that he had devoted his entire adult life to the Communist Party and a secular, socialist ideology. His allies in the council were five Muslims and four Christians, yet the perception created in the media was that he was the Christian head of a Christian elite that ruled like lords over the largely Muslim city. Nothing, he said, could be further from the truth. He was proud of his heritage as a Greek Orthodox Christian, but prouder still of Nazareth's culture of cooperation between Muslims and Christians. He grew up, he said, never knowing whether friends and neighbors were Muslim or Christian. No one asked. No one cared. In his idealized view of the past, everyone got along.

Jeraisi's grandfather had been an Orthodox priest in the Galilee. As a boy Jeraisi faithfully attended services every Sunday, and his father still did. But when he reached college age, like many leftists in the Arab world, he drifted away from Greek Orthodoxy and instead focused on the struggle against colonialist oppression in Latin America, in Angola, in Cuba. Even when he married and began a family of his own, he did not, as some family men do, return to the church. He has three daughters, all of them in elementary school. His family celebrates the feasts at Christmas and Easter, but stops there. "I believe there is a God," he said. "I believe all of the prophets were revolutionaries in their time who tried to bring people human values. But the followers of religion, when they bring politics into their religion, have gone down a dangerous path. Religion is based on emotions and beliefs and it has a great force to influence people, and to appeal to the weakness of people, and it is very dangerous."

I walked from city hall to the tent, where a triumphant Salman Abu Ahmed stood in the shade, collaring every reporter he could find to continue the ranting that had brought him to power. On this day, I was the only one available. "Why do Christians want this specific piece of land?" he asked me, as his followers—farmers in wool caps, construction workers with plaster dust on their boots, and unemployed college graduates with thin beards—gathered in a cluster in the tent. "This is holy land, so why should they be entitled to build a tourist park? Build it somewhere else. The church owns a lot of land."

In fact, at city hall I had come across the minutes from a 1994 council meeting where Abu Ahmed himself had proposed that the land be used for a new municipal building. I asked him about his earlier position on the plot of land, just to see how he and his supporters would handle it.

"These are lies from the Christian mayor. All of them are trying to twist facts," said Abu Ahmed.

"Your signature was on the ballot. You voted for it, didn't you?"

As we dealt with the specifics, the crowd dispersed, and finally, with only a few supporters listening over his shoulder, Abu Ahmed replied: "Well, I didn't know it then. We had to do research to be sure this was *waqf* land."

"But it isn't *waqf* land," I replied. "The documents you have produced to establish it have been rejected by the muftis in Jordan and Jerusalem, right?"

Abu Ahmed ended the interview there, and returned to his crowd of supporters. I walked up Casa Nova street, past a string of tourist shops, and I met a 26-year-old Muslim shopkeeper who gave his name only as Sari. He was keeping an eye open for any tourists who might pass his street display of carved wooden crucifixes, plastic Virgin Mary dashboard ornaments, and glow-in-the-dark rosary beads. None came.

"The dispute has polarized things," he said, speaking in perfect English but very hushed tones, fearing that anyone who spoke out on the issue could be targeted. "Things have gotten very tense. It's not good for business."

All day, at coffee shops and bus stations and newsstands, Nazarenes seemed consumed with foreboding. Hassam, 29, a Christian accountant, said, "There is not open hostility, but there is a feeling of the society pulling apart."

Rev. Quirico Calella, an Italian Catholic priest who for twenty-three years had been the director of Terra Santa high school in Nazareth, said: "Christians here are living in fear. So many, especially the young men, prefer to simply leave. The reasons for decades have been economic hardship caused by Israel. But I think increasingly there is a sense of fatigue. They are tired of being caught in the middle."

Although Nazarene Christians are steadily emigrating, the numbers are nowhere near as dramatic as those in the West Bank. And there is a clear sense among the Christians of Nazareth, usually expressed privately, that given the history of warfare and dispossession they still would rather be under Israeli rule of law than Palestinian. The Israeli school system provides them a solid education, even if Arab communities complain that their schools suffer from more overcrowding and poorer services than those in Jewish communities. They also point out that the curriculum does not recognize the history and culture of the Palestinian people. But the preparation for and access to a college education at Israeli universities is a genuine bridge to opportunity for them, and one that the Palestinian citizens of Israel do not discount.

This was a point often stressed by members of the Israeli government. It was most stridently voiced to me by a man named Uri Mor, who for many years had served as the Christian affairs representative within Israel's Religious Affairs Ministry. The job had become a kind of hobby for Mor; his interest in the plumage of Christian clerics and the trappings of their ancient rituals and ceremonies carried a joyous curiosity not unlike that of an avid bird-watcher. His primary duty was to secure residency visas for bishops, priests, nuns, and lay members of charitable Christian organizations. This task required considerable acumen to navigate the bureaucracy of the Interior Ministry, which was sometimes under the control of the ultra-Orthodox religious parties and hostile to the Christian community.

Though Mor's responsibilities were directed primarily toward helping clerics from Italy and Greece and other Western countries who came to Israel, and thus had little to do with the indigenous Palestinian Christian community, he nonetheless took great offense at the suggestion that the government's economic and land policies were responsible for the emigration of Christians from Israel. "We have protected Christians," he told me. "The fact is, we have thousands of applications of [West Bank] Christians who want to become citizens of Israel. That is because they don't want to live under Arafat's government. They know what will be the future."

I asked him whether he believed the Christians within Israel and the parts of the West Bank still under Israeli control were afforded equal rights. "I will not say there are no problems," he replied. "But in general they have rights."

A vociferous complaint from Christian leaders has been the unequal disbursement of the Religious Affairs Ministry's budget. Although Arabs account for 18 percent of Israel's population and pay the same taxes as other Israelis, they receive only 1.5 percent of the funding. And with most of that small pool of money allotted to the Arab sector going to the Muslim majority, Christians end up with "a pittance," as Anglican Bishop Riah Abu el-Assa put it. Mor declined comment on the disbursement, and said he did not have exact figures on how much is allotted to Christians. But one ministry official conceded, "Obviously it is unfair, and has been unfair for too long."

. . .

In Upper Nazareth, a new community of Christians emerged in the 1990s, which made the religious equation there even more complex. These Christians were Russians who came as "Jewish immigrants" but who defined their faith as Christian. Nearly a decade after the breakup of the Soviet Union, the majority of Russian immigrants were Russians who had very little Jewish identity of their own. Most were simply seeking economic refuge from the chaos and collapse of the former Communist superpower. Under Israel's "law of return," they were granted Israeli citizenship if they had at least one grandparent who was Jewish. Of these Russian immigrants, about 20 percent considered themselves Christian, and a fraction of those were actually practicing Russian Orthodox Christians, who were beginning to show up in increasing numbers in places like Nazareth. (There was another Christian population of Israelis: the Messianic movement of Jews who embraced Jesus as the Jewish messiah. This fringe group, which had established a storefront church in the industrial zone of Upper Nazareth, included an estimated 10,000 members in churches from Jerusalem to Haifa.)

When I began asking about this phenomenon of Russian immigrants who were Christian in Upper Nazareth, very few Israeli Jews knew about it. And the few who did, didn't want to talk about it. But finally, through church connections among Arab Christians in Nazareth, I was told to find Abouna Dimitri, or "Father Dimitri," a Russian immigrant who came to Israel as a Jew even though he is a Russian Orthodox priest who had finished seminary and had been ordained.

After several days of searching the nondescript housing blocks of Upper Nazareth, I finally found Father Dimitri. As I walked up the steps that led into a little patio before his front door, his four-year-old son, Nicholas, with bright blond hair and blue eyes, and dressed only in a diaper and an unusually large silver crucifix around his neck, attacked me with a toy sword. On the front door was another large cross, an extraordinary image of Christianity in a Zionist development town.

Inside the home, Father Dimitri was dressed in his Russian Orthodox clerical robes and was finishing a phone call with a neighbor to arrange the baptism of a child just born to Russian immigrant parents, both Christian. On the shelves of a cabinet were small reproductions of various Russian Orthodox icons and a print of Tsar Nicholas II. Dimitri, 35, and his wife, Irina, 34, told me the story.

Dimitri's parents had come to Israel seven years earlier with his paternal grandfather, Michael, or Mordechai in Hebrew. Michael was a Russian Jew, although Dimitri never knew that when he was growing up, having been raised in the Russian Orthodox church, which was badly weakened during the Soviet era but existed nevertheless. In 1993, after the collapse of the Soviet Union, Dimitri's parents came as "economic refugees, not religious ones," he said, on an airline ticket paid for by the Jewish Agency. Dimitri and Irena followed two years later. They said that the Israeli officials never asked upon their arrival whether they considered themselves Jewish.

Some 300,000 of the roughly 1 million Russian immigrants are considered non-Jewish under religious law, which requires descent through a Jewish mother. If indeed 20 percent of these non-Jewish individuals consider themselves Christian, that would mean there are roughly 60,000 Christians living as citizens in Israel not counted in the total Christian population. Consider as well that only 100,000 Palestinian Christians live within Israel. The potential impact of immigration on the demographic fate of Christians in Israel then becomes clear. The Israeli attempt to bring more Jews to the Jewish state may end up—in a bizarre demographic twist—actually saving the Christian presence in the Holy Land.

But George Hintlian, the Armenian sociologist from Jerusalem, knew this new community and was not so convinced. He said, "This Russian immigration may have postponed the slow disappearance of Christianity, but not changed its course." He explained that the Greek Orthodox Arabs were reluctant to accept the Russians into the community, seeing them as too Israeli. After all, they lived on expropriated land and served in the Israeli army, and they did not speak Arabic. Several Greek Orthodox clerics said that many Russians are using Israel as a way station in emigrating to Canada, Europe, or the United States. But Christian immigrants have come to this land for many reasons, and through the centuries they have become part of its multicultured community. Armenians, Greeks, Crusaders, and missionaries from America and England came to Palestine, and many stayed on, becoming part of the multifaceted Christian population of this land. So why should the Russians not do the same?

Dimitri, with a mischievous smile said, "The Israelis made a mistake, I think. Perhaps they thought that Zionism was so strong, they would convert all the people to Judaism. But what happened is many Russians come to the Holy Land and come in touch with the land of the Bible and of Jesus, and they become pulled toward the Christian traditions, traditions they had seen somewhere in the back of their minds growing up. I don't know why this is happening. It is a spiritual thing, not a social phenomenon. There is definitely no benefit to saying you're Christian in Israel. In fact, many of the Russians are hiding this here and in Jerusalem.

"But the truth is, I think the Israelis just didn't expect this and they want to correct it now, so perhaps some people will be told to return if they say they are Christian. We don't know. We want to keep our traditions. What does Orthodox mean? It means straight by the book, it means traditions. The traditions are not part of the faith, they are the faith. We have to do this, we want to do it to keep our souls. But there are people who are afraid. They are afraid they will lose their jobs, that they could be sent back."

Dimitri and Irina were determinedly isolated from Israeli society. They had decided, for example, not to send their two children to the Israeli preschool and kindergarten, even though Irina works as an elementary school teacher in the nearby town of Afula. Dimitri said that he did not want to "confuse their religious upbringing" with the traditions of Judaism taught in schools of the Jewish state. Unlike many Russian immigrants, they refused to visit Yad Vashem. "In my religion the eternal flame is a vision of hell," said Dimitri, with a certain tone of contempt, "not something to be worshiped."

Orthodox Jews, through their powerful political parties, have raised strenuous objections to the immigration of Russian "non-Jews," saying that it threatens to undermine the Jewish character of the state and to dangerously dilute the religious lineage of the Jewish people. The rabbinical authorities are strict in not permitting those whom they regarded as non-Jews to be buried in Jewish cemeteries or to be allowed legally recognized marriages under Jewish law. Some even have gone so far as to say that their citizenship should be revoked.

"We are law-abiding citizens of Israel," Irina said. "But we ask that we have freedom to practice our faith."

Dimitri said that he had received a special ordination through St. George's, a Greek Orthodox church in Nazareth, permitting him to operate a mission and to perform the liturgy for a small congregation. He was allowed to do baptisms only if the child's mother was not Jewish. And he was entitled to perform other ritual functions, such as blessings at death and on new houses, which were very popular in the Russian community. Dimitri estimated that 1,500 of the roughly 5,000 Russian immigrants in Upper Nazareth would identify themselves as Christian. And about one hundred Russians, he said, attended services at the Greek Orthodox church in Nazareth, where Dimitri performed the service in Russian on Saturday, the Jewish Sabbath, since the Russians, like other Israelis, have to work on Sunday. "We pray to the Lord Jesus Christ to build a church in Upper Nazareth someday," he said.

Danny Cohen, a schoolteacher and former city councilman who has lived in Upper Nazareth almost since its foundation, reflects the larger, Jewish community of the town in his fierce opposition to building a church in Natzerat Illit. Cohen's family survived the Holocaust. His father worked many years in a forced labor camp in their native Romania. They lived for four months in transit camps in Cyprus before a boat named *The Diaspora* took them to the new Jewish state. He was only ten years old, but the trauma of the Holocaust is as real to him now as it was then. "I am an atheist, but I am a Jew," he said. "My nation is built on Judaism, the religion and the ethnicity of Judaism. If these people from Russia want to build a church, they are not Jews."

But couldn't they be citizens of Israel with a Jewish grandparent, who believe in Christianity? And shouldn't they be able to build a church if they so choose?

"Absolutely not," said Cohen.

It didn't take much questioning to access Cohen's deep distrust of Christianity and the symbols of the faith that he associated with Nazi Germany. The suffering of Jews, which he felt grew out of the culture of Christian anti-Semitism, came spilling out: "The movement that Jesus created butchered the Jews for two thousand years, and this is history, not religion. So whoever comes here from Russia and connects to this history and this religion is not one of mine. And certainly should not be able to build a church in my community.

"For 3 shekels and 70 agarot," he said, referring to the price of bus fare, "they can go down to lower Nazareth to any church they want."

. . .

I drifted back down to Nazareth's crooked cobblestone streets and met Nazem Abu Slim, the imam of the tent-mosque, at Motran Oriental Sweets, a small bakery and café across from the vacant lot. The tent sheikh was a second-generation Nazarene whose father had been an "internal refugee" after 1948. Abu Slim's father was 12 when his own father, a Muslim farmer from the village of Mejaidel on the outskirts of town, fled on foot to Nazareth and ended up taking shelter in one of the Catholic monasteries that provided food and shelter to the dispossessed. The village of Mejaidel had been destroyed by Israeli troops, and a new modern Israeli development known as Migdal Haamek was built over it.

Abu Slim embodied the frustrations of the second generation of this Muslim underclass that had arrived in Nazareth amid the chaos of war. He was educated in an Israeli high school and received his degree from an Israeli college. But when he set out to find a job in a chemical plant, his aspirations were immediately thwarted, as they are for many Palestinians with college degrees. The hitch for people like Abu Slim is that they were not accepted for jobs unless they had served in the Israeli military, and serving in the military, especially in the Muslim community, is tantamount to collaboration. (A small percentage of Christians had recently begun joining the Israeli military, but the choice had caused great divisions within towns and even within families.) Abu Slim's degree and hard work were worthless to him. The frustration pushed him toward Islam.

The leader of Nazareth's militant Islamic movement, Mahmoud Ghazali, had become radicalized in Israeli prisons in the 1970s and 1980s after being jailed for his political activity. In a magazine called *Ramadan's Flowers*, Ghazali had recently written that the Shehab al-Din tent-mosque stood as "a witness to the haughtiness of the rulers of Israel against the Muslim people in Palestine, and a reflection of the animosity directed against Muslims from groups calling themselves nationalists, the city council, the Front, and all other groups that use masks to hide their mercenary and hateful nature."

The stream of Islamic militancy that seemed to run through the clerics of Nazareth and some of the surrounding villages took a demonstrably different course than that of the West Bank's Hamas-linked Islamic movement. Back in July 1991, Hamas had issued a leaflet that defined the Koranic guidelines for relations between Christians and Muslims as follows: "Christians in Palestine are an integral part of the Palestinian people and its civilization. Christians have the same civil rights and duties as all Palestinians. We call on Christians to stay on the land and not surrender to the terrors of Zionism and the brutalities of occupation. We encourage them to participate in the struggle."

Exactly why Nazareth's Islamic militant fringe was so different (and so anti-Christian) is shrouded in mystery and political intrigue. Some church officials and political observers continue to think that Likud was orchestrating the tensions, believing that the Israeli right had much to gain from fomenting divisions between Muslims and Christians. One benefit would be to weaken the power of the Arab minority within Israel. But another benefit would be more subtle, these church officials and political observers believed. The conflict in Nazareth showed the world a stark image of Muslim intolerance. The footage of militants rampaging at the foot of one of the central shrines of Christendom sent a clear message to the world about another contested city—Jerusalem. The images provided a potent argument that the city holy to three faiths should never fall under the control of the Palestinian leadership, because the Islamic militants would threaten not just the Jewish presence but the Christian presence as well.

Abu Slim insisted that I needed to understand how revered Shehab al-Din, whose name translates as "Star of Faith," is in Nazareth's Muslim community. He was the beloved nephew of Saladin, the legendary leader of Muslim armies against the Crusaders in the twelfth century. Shehab al-Din and his brother Amr Din were both mortally wounded at the decisive battle of Hattin. They died and were buried in Nazareth. For generations, Nazarenes had attended the Ottoman-era school and made devotional visits to the tiny shrine of Shehab al-Din. Abu Slim believed that the "Christian West" had to understand that the reverence to this "martyr" was as valid a concern as a plaza at the foot of the site where the Catholic tradition holds that the "Son of God" was divinely conceived.

I asked for his response to the allegations that political powers in Israel had fostered this conflict and had used it—and indirectly, him—to foment divisions between Muslims and Christians. Surely there were thousands and thousands of acres of *waqf* land that the Israelis refused to relinquish, and land all over Israel and the former Palestine that was confiscated and never returned. I knew of abandoned mosques in Tiberias, Ein Karem, Haifa, and Acre, and many others elsewhere in what is today Israel. One mosque in a trendy Israeli port city had even been converted to a disco. So why in this one instance did Abu Slim think the Israelis would countenance a local group of Muslim militants seizing land and reclaiming it by force?

"We were serious and persistent in our demands," he replied. "They were forced to give it to us. They knew if this problem was not resolved, things will explode. We made this very clear. The Shin Bet [Israel's internal security service] came to me and they asked, 'If we don't give you the land, what happens?' And I told them this boiling up will turn not against Christians but against the Israelis. I told him we don't have weapons, or missiles. But we have our bodies and we will fight to death to protect this shrine."

So it came down to a plausible threat of violence, I asked?

"You could say this," he replied. "Yes."

. . .

That violence descended on Nazareth in a fury on April 3, 1999—Holy Saturday, on the Catholic calendar. It was a time when the Vatican was finalizing plans for the pope's visit to the Holy Land the following spring, and when Prime Minister Netanyahu was facing Labor Party challenger Ehud Barak in national elections scheduled for May. Ministers from three right-wing Israeli parties, all members of Netanyahu's coalition, had been canvassing for votes by promising to intervene in the Nazareth dispute in favor of the Islamic Movement. There were reports in the Israeli media of behind-the-scenes negotiations going on as well with Barak's Labor Party and the protesters in the tent. (The Islamic Movement was becoming well versed in the rules of Israeli politics, playing both sides against the middle.)

Nothing revealed this dynamic more dramatically than the sudden eruption in Nazareth that resulted in two full days of rioting, looting, and violence. There were conflicting accounts as to how it started. Muslims blamed a group of young Christians who had grown increasingly strident in their opposition to the presence of the tent and the plans for the mosque. And the Christians accused Muslim toughs, many of whom had come from other towns, of instigating the conflict and then orchestrating the rampage. No matter who started the rioting, the Christians bore the brunt of it. Nearly all of the shop windows that were smashed and the stores that were looted, up and down the length of Paul VI street, were Christian. Of the more than sixty stores affected by the rioting, only two Muslim businesses had windows smashed: a travel agency and the Nazareth Bus Company, both of which had been longtime political supporters of the mayor and the Democratic Front in city hall.

As supporters of the Islamic Movement and the protesters in the tent began to pour into Nazareth, terrorizing the Christian population and any secular Muslims who resisted them, the Israeli government officials did little to intervene. Footage was aired on Israeli television showing Israeli police standing with riot batons in their hands as looters devastated the city. Witnesses said they went directly to the police station and begged for protection but were told by the police that there was nothing they could do. At the center of the controversy was the commander of the Northern District of the Israel Police, Alik Ron, a notorious hard-liner in the eyes of the Arab community. People who telephoned the police were told to stay in their homes and not to go downtown or try to protect their property. This reflected an unusual passivity on the part of the Israeli police, especially Ron, who had never been shy about dispersing Palestinian protesters with tear gas and "rubber bullets."

Sufyan el-Ahmedi and his wife, Lamis Khouri, were watching from the balcony of their apartment in the predawn hours as gangs of Muslim men smashed the windows of Christian-owned stores. The crowd was turning over cars with crucifixes dangling from the rearview mirror and shattering the windshields with ax handles and rocks. All along Paul VI and Casa Nova streets, the narrow cobblestone pathway that leads to the basilica, the night was aglow with burning cars and the swirling blue lights of Israeli police vehicles.

Sufyan saw a man in a gray *jalabiya* and a white prayer cap wielding a sword and shouting "Allahu akbar!" Sufyan shook his head in disbelief as the Israeli police stood and watched.

Sufyan is Muslim. Lamis is Christian. They were newlyweds, and among a tiny minority of interfaith couples in Nazareth. They were from a part of Nazarene society that took great pride in a culture of tolerance among Muslims and Christians. Sufyan was head chef and co-owner of what was then the city's premier restaurant, El-Zaituna. They both knew the minute they saw the streets in flames and heard the triumphal shouting of Muslim militants as they burned Christian stores that the fabric that bound together Muslims and Christians, that bound together their two separate families, had been torn. Perhaps irrevocably torn. They were pretty sure right then that it would take a long, long time to heal the wounds in Nazareth.

The next morning, Easter Sunday on the Roman Catholic calendar and Palm Sunday on the Greek Orthodox calendar, the streets of Nazareth were in chaos. Mosques in Nazareth and throughout the surrounding villages had issued shrill announcements from loudspeakers, calling on the faithful to go to Nazareth to "protect the shrine of the martyr Shehab al-Din." By morning some two thousand Muslims had gathered in the public square surrounding the green canvas tent. Islamic clerics were thundering from the pulpit over loudspeakers against the Christian "infidels" and "the modern Crusaders of the West" who were behind the "godless Communist mayor" in his intention to "defile our holy shrine."

One Muslim leader who would not take part in the hysteria and the rabble-rousing was Ataf Fahoum, who hails from one of the oldest and most respected Muslim families of Nazareth. His family has been in control of the *waqf* of the White Mosque, the oldest mosque in the city and the heart of the Muslim community, since its completion in 1804. The trusteeship of the mosque was granted to Ataf Fahoum's ancestor Sheikh Abdallah al-Fahum by the Ottoman high commissioner in Nazareth, Suleiman Pasha. From 1970 to 2000, Fahoum had held the position of trustee, and he refused to issue a call to the Muslims at his mosque, seeing it as a dangerous incitement by misguided Islamic clerics who for short-term political gains were willing to sacrifice the long-established bonds between Muslims and Christians in Nazareth.

Instead, Fahoum, a distinguished-looking man of 70 with a thick head of silver hair, set out that morning with one of his oldest and closest friends, Assad Khaldoush, a Christian, to bring traditional Easter greetings to the Christian monasteries, the local parish priests, the bishops, and various old family friends. It was a custom he had carried out on both Orthodox and Catholic Easter Sunday for the last half century, and one that his father, the former mayor of Nazareth, had carried out for a half century before him, and so on through at least four generations of Fahoums.

This time some of the friends he ended up visiting were in the hospital, having been wounded in the rioting. So he went there first. He visited the teenage sons of an old Christian friend, Tewfiq Laham. The boys had been on their way to church when they were badly beaten by the mob. Dozens of other wounded Christians were lined up in the emergency room of the hospital that day, with heads bandaged and arms in slings. Fahoum made a point of checking on each one and offering his condolences for their sufferings and his blessings for Easter.

After the hospital visit, he tried to make his way through the throng of "troublemakers and thugs," as he referred to them, refusing to call them Muslims, who were stopping traffic on Paul VI street. Fahoum was driving a new Isuzu Trooper with his friend, Assad, who was wearing a crucifix. The crowd stopped the vehicle and Fahoum lowered his window only to be greeted by a sharp punch in his left eye. He refused to turn the car back, despite the angry crowd's insistence. The out-of-towners quickly learned that Fahoum was not only a prominent Muslim but the head of the *waqf* for Nazareth's oldest mosque. He was allowed to pass—but not without pounding on the windows and jeering from local supporters of the Islamic Movement, yelling that he had had failed to protect the shrine of Shehab al-Din. Some shouted that he was an "infidel" for, as they saw it, siding with the Christians.

With his eye swollen and his shirt covered in blood, he made his rounds to the convent of the Sisters of Nazareth, a French order of nuns; St. Joseph's parish church, run by the Franciscan Order; and the Greek Catholic "Synagogue Church" (believed to be the site of a synagogue where Jesus preached). He also visited with the Anglican Bishop Riah and a half dozen prominent families in the Christian neighborhoods of Nazareth. His first act in each case was to apologize to his Christian friends for what was being done in the name of Islam. They told him there was no need to apologize. They knew these people had nothing to do with Islam. But an unmistakable gloom, a sense that something had changed in Nazareth, had descended over the community.

As he watched television on Easter morning, Raed Hakim saw his shoe store smashed and burned over and over again. He could see that the Muslim pushcart vendors who worked in the courtyard in front of his store—people from whom he had bought produce and nuts and candy and with whom he had often chatted in the morning—were participants in the rioting. He had seen them metamorphose over the previous two years, growing beards and donning the white knitted skullcaps of political Islamists. The image of them rampaging the town was an image not only of religious divisions but of an unbridled class war.

Among them was Yahiya Sutre, 38, who ran a makeshift market on wheels, stocking everything from candy to transistor radios and cigarette lighters. His father was the first to start the pushcart business, selling cookies some thirty years earlier. A father of five, Yahiya was poor and had only a ninth-grade education. His father had been a young man when his family was forced out of their nearby village by the war in 1948. He is from a world far from the comfortable middle-class life of Raed, yet the two men had befriended each other. Joked with each other. Talked on occasion.

With a white prayer cap and a slight callus on his forehead from praying five times a day, Yahiya described the path that took him to a more religious life and brought him to be among the hundreds who were praying under the tent five times daily. He was proud that the vacant lot where drug addicts and alcoholics once hung out was now a place of prayer He said that by turning to the sheikh there, he had overcome his own problems with alcohol. He admitted that the emotion of the rioting had prompted him to use violence to defend the mosque. He felt terrible that Raed's shoe store had been looted, but he also insisted that he would use violence again to defend the makeshift mosque.

Raed knew of the tensions and resentments that seethed between Muslims, who were generally lower on the economic scale, and Christians, who were generally better off. But he never thought those tensions would erupt into violence.

Raed's shoe store was only a mile from his home, and he felt compelled to take a closer look at the damages; but he had been warned by his father and brother not to go without a police escort. When he called the police, they told him they could not help him. So he waited, watching the destruction in live updates on television. And when finally the looting and the burning had quieted down, he descended the hill to see the results for himself. Standing amid the shattered glass and the overturned shelves of his store, which had been looted of all its contents, he asked, "How could this have happened?"

. . .

The violence and intimidation in Nazareth began to extend beyond the vicinity of the tent. Mayor Jeraisi had been badly beaten twice, right outside his office at city hall. At his home, anonymous voices on the phone issued death threats and called him "Salman Rushdie," the author against whom a *fatwa* for death had been issued by Iran's Ayatollah Khomeini in 1989. The Israeli police had warned

Jeraisi that there were credible threats against his life, but he said they did nothing to investigate or prosecute the case.

In the aftermath of the rioting, Nazarenes began to clean up. Sidewalks were swept, windows were repaired, and insurance claims were filed. Some shopkeepers were even able to collect damages, since the rioting fell under a coverage category termed "an unforeseeable act of God." The divisions in Nazareth, though, were deeper and more bitter. Young Christian teenagers began wearing even larger crosses around their necks. Muslims had taken to calling the Christians "Serbs," a derogatory reference to the Serbian forces that had slaughtered Muslims in Bosnia and Kosovo. Sporadic incidents of fighting were breaking out. Meanwhile, the number of Muslims worshiping at the tent swelled upward of 1,500 for Friday prayers, with several hundred continuing to gather for daily services.

Back in his city hall office, Jeraisi learned that the event management company that had been planning the Nazareth 2000 festival had canceled the deal, fearing that violence would mar the festivities. In mid-April, the Israeli foreign minister, Ariel Sharon, went to the Vatican and assured the pope that no mosque would be built. The government, it seemed, was backtracking from the political games that had spiraled out of its control in Nazareth. Danny Greenberg had even been unceremoniously relieved of his Likud duties. "He [Greenberg] played a foolish game there. And he did it without authority. . . . He made them [the Islamic Movement] think they might gain something, but they are wrong if they think that," said Motti Zaken, an adviser on Arab affairs to Netanyahu.

Zaken dismissed the notion that Likud could ever work with the Arab sector in an election: "First of all, Muslims wouldn't vote for Likud even if we paid them. This is good for newspapers and conspiracy theories, but it has nothing to do with reality." He also dismissed the impression that Israeli police had tolerated violence by the protesters. "The police admitted that they were reserved, they wanted to let the situation calm down," he said. "And after it calmed down, they arrested seventy people. . . . The situation is very complex. There is political confrontation, demographic change, a religious tension. It is representative of what is going on in many parts of the world—in Bethlehem, in Turkey, in Lebanon, in Asia and Africa—a tension between Muslims and Christians, and it is growing. It is bigger than Nazareth. And we have always been in favor of reaching a compromise which both sides can live with."

That "compromise" came in late April. An interministerial committee appointed by Netanyahu ruled that the Islamic Movement could erect a shrine, but not a mosque, on one quarter (500 square meters) of the disputed lot of land. The remaining 1,500 square meters would be used for a plaza. The Christian community was furious, feeling that the Israeli government had in effect rewarded the violence and lawlessness of the protesters by granting them this space. The Islamic Movement also was unhappy that its demands for a mosque had not been met.

Jeraisi was worried that the crisis of municipal governance that had been caused by the dispute over the land might result in Israel's taking direct control of the municipality. So he decided to accept the compromise and hope that a new Israeli government under Labor would be elected and that a new deal could be struck with Ehud Barak. But after Barak's election, the Islamic Movement rejected the Netanyahu committee's decision, choosing instead to appeal to the courts for a ruling on whether the property was *waqf* land.

In October, the Israeli court ruled against the Muslims' contention that the land fell within the control of the Islamic trust. But events just then took a dramatic twist. The new Labor government, in the face of the court's decision and to the dismay of the Christian community, announced a new "compromise." They decided to permit the construction of a mosque and to expand the proposed site from 500 to 700 square meters. The Islamic Movement accepted the offer, and city councilman Abu Ahmed began publicly gloating that the Israeli government also would pay for the construction of the mosque.

Jeraisi and the institutions of the Catholic Church immediately suspected that the Labor government had cut a deal with the Islamic Movement for its support in the election. Once again, they felt, the interests of the diminishing Christian minority were being sacrificed to accommodate those of the political institutions of Israel and the larger community of Muslim Palestinians. The Barak government's interministerial committee tried to calm the Christians' fears by announcing that the plan also called for a small police station on the site and for an architectural design that would position the entrance to the proposed mosque in such a way that it would not interfere with the pilgrims going between the plaza and the basilica.

Jeraisi smartly walked away from the conflict, having decided that Israel had created a mess that he would happily leave them to resolve. And besides, there was someone else stepping into the arena with more clout and more money. The Israelis—both Likud and Labor—had wrongly assumed that by talking to Jeraisi they had been responsive to the concerns of the Christian community. But the Catholic Church was fuming at the government's diplomatic insensitivity in having failed to consult the church on the agreement. Wadie Abunassar, spokesman for the Assembly of Catholic Bishops, officially expressed deep regret that the Barak government had failed to consult with Christian church leaders in formulating its "compromise." The Catholic Church also expressed dismay that the promises made by Foreign Minister Sharon to the pontiff at the Vatican had been reversed in the current ministerial decision.

In a meeting with the U.S. Catholic bishops on November 10, Haim Ramon, an Israeli cabinet minister, characterized the decision as a "bad, but clever" compromise. The American church leaders were further angered by this characterization. International criticism of the Israeli decision was steadily mounting. In back channels, the Israeli government was apologizing to church leaders for what they admitted might seem an unfair decision, but they were also candidly stating that "the churches must reconcile themselves to political reality."

The Christian churches reacted strongly and in extraordinary solidarity. The patriarchs of the Roman Catholic, Greek Orthodox, and Armenian churches, together with the Franciscan Custody of the Holy Land, made a dramatic announcement. If the decision to build the mosque were not rescinded and the laying of a cornerstone of the mosque on November 22 went ahead as planned, the doors to all of the Christian sanctuaries in the Holy Land would be closed in protest for two days. The Syrian, Armenian, Coptic, and Anglican churches also lent their support to this demand.

When November 22 came, however, thousands of the mosque's supporters filled the plot of land in downtown Nazareth, and the cornerstone was laid. Abu Ahmed gave a rousing political speech that celebrated the efforts of those who had fought for the mosque. Abu Slim led the congregation in prayer. Muslim leaders lifted a green velvet prayer cloth off the marble slab, and as they unveiled the cornerstone, the Muslim crowd chanted, "With our blood, with our souls, we redeem you, Shehab al-Din."

Through office windows cracked from the Easter rioting, Amer Nijim looked out on the crowd. Nijim was a 40-year-old Greek Orthodox Christian and the manager of GB Tours, a travel agency specializing in Christian pilgrimage. "The saddest part of all of this is the deep divisions it has left behind," he said, clicking a lighter to a Marlboro and looking out the window. Night was falling now. Fireworks would soon light up the sky as Nijim and other Christians hurried home to avoid the Muslim street celebrations. On speakers set up outside a coffee shop, Arabic music blared the lyrics "Come, let Islam show you the way." Young men in the street shouted "Allahu akbar!" Nijim shook his head and said, "This used to be a place where everyone got along."

As threatened, when the cornerstone was laid, the church doors closed. It was a dramatic statement, an unprecedented form of protest in the history of the Christian churches. They were not alone in their criticism. Even Yasser Arafat's Palestinian Authority backed the churches in the dispute, as did the conservative Islamic kingdom of Saudi Arabia, which criticized the building of the mosque as a provocation and offered to pay for the construction of another mosque on any other site in the city. The Middle East has long produced strange alliances, but this dizzying tangle was particularly counterintuitive: the Palestinian leadership, which is predominantly Muslim, was siding with the churches, and Israel, with the Islamic militants.

But the closing of the doors was poorly handled by the Catholic Church. Although the Church's intent had been to send a powerful message to the world, a message evoking concern for the fate of Christians in the Holy Land, the images broadcast around the world cast the local church as villain. In one front-page photo, a man bowed his head in prayer at the locked doors of the Holy Sepulcher. In another, an Austrian nun, barred from the Basilica of the Nativity in Bethlehem's Manger Square, wept as a Palestinian policeman looked on.

The morning the church doors closed, I met John Gorman, a 64-year-old retired fireman from Queens, New York, and a parishioner from Our Lady Queen of Martyrs Catholic Church. He had come to the Holy Land for the first time, on a package tour, and he had his Irish up about the church closing the doors on his one day to see the Holy Sepulcher. "The doors should be open," he said, a red New York Fire Department cap pushed back on his head. "We are Christians here, and they shouldn't be punishing the Christian tourists who come. I don't see the benefit in that."

Israeli foreign ministry spokesman Aviv Sharon accused the Holy

See of playing "a time-honored game of pointing the finger in the wrong direction" in criticizing the Israeli government's role in the conflict. "It is strange that when there is a problem between Muslims and Christians, they blame the Israeli government," he added. The press coverage and public opinion, which had at first been strongly against the Israeli government's decision, suddenly swung against the church. Once again, the concerns of the local Christians would be overshadowed by the political blunders of a church hierarchy that was, for the most part, not of this land.

"It was like watching an accident in slow motion," a senior American Catholic official in Jerusalem told me, when I asked him why the Church had handled this so poorly. "The Church looked horrible, and all the power of the statement crumbled under the allegation that it was motivated by anti-Semitism. It was pure arrogance on our part, and we lost an opportunity to make a very important point."

In the summer of 2000, the canvas tent was lowered but not completely dismantled, as the Islamic Movement waited for its mosque to be built. The social divisions between Nazarene Christians and Muslims continued to deepen. The frustrations produced among Israeli Arabs by the economic and social discrimination against them continued to simmer. Nazareth, it seemed, was still a quarrelsome backwater, living under occupation and struggling to get along, just as it had been in the time of Jesus. Jesus's impatience with his hometown—its small-mindedness and its resistance to his message—came to mind. Despite all the idling tour buses for Christian tourists and the towering churches and basilica, the place seemed bereft of the tolerance and forgiveness taught by Jesus. I thought of the words of the apostle Nathaniel in the Gospel According to John, when he was told by Philip the news of the messiah from Nazareth. Nathaniel, who had not yet met Jesus, sneered, "Nazareth! Please. What good ever came out of Nazareth?" (John 1:46 [RSV]).

But the scripture that was even more relevant in Nazareth in the year 2000 was Jesus's struggle with his own family. In several passages in the New Testament, the gospels tell of Jesus's internal conflict between loyalty to his earthly family—Mary, Joseph, and his brothers in Nazareth—versus loyalty to his disciples in the Galilee and the growing family of believers in his mission. He struggled between the family of Judaism to which he belonged and the message of his ministry, which so many Jews viewed as an unforgivable abrogation of that faith. This was one of Jesus's most radical messages in the social context of his time, when the Mediterranean society was strictly based on kinship and on the family hierarchy. Family is a grouping to which one is irrevocably assigned. But Jesus negated this notion in favor of a radical redefinition of family as a community of faith that was open and equally accessible to all under God.

In the year 2000, the people of Nazareth were Muslim and Christian, and the people just up the hill, in Upper Nazareth, were Jews (except for a few Palestinian Christians and Russian immigrants who preferred to call themselves Christians). The Arab Nazarenes called themselves Palestinians, but they were citizens of Israel. The Israeli Upper Nazarenes called themselves Zionists, although some refused to call themselves Jews. The Palestinians were members of the communist-influenced Front and also devout believers in the Islamic Movement. The Israelis were Labor and Likud. It seemed that the year 2000 had brought an intense struggle within and among Nazarenes, between all of these overlapping identities. Especially for Muslims and Christians, a rupture had occurred in how Nazareth defined itself, and how the people living there defined themselves in relation to one another. Nazareth was grappling with its notions of family and community.

I returned one afternoon to talk with Raed Hakim and his young wife. They told me they were tired of the bitterness, tension, and looming violence that had descended over daily life in Nazareth. Family ties to the town were holding them there, but they were considering moving to America or Canada if they could secure visas. A sullen wall of silence had built up between Raed and Yahiya, the newly observant Muslim man who ran the pushcart store just outside Raed's shoe shop. I moved from the shoe shop to talk to Yahiya, and I noticed that the slight callus on his forehead from lying prostrate during prayers had grown thicker and more permanent. It now had the size and texture of a dried apricot. He said business had been good, and that he hoped soon to buy a store. When I began to ask about Raed, he said he was "too busy to talk about politics." He locked his kiosk, gathered up his prayer rug under one arm and a worn Koran under the other, and marched off as the Muslim call to prayer sounded over loudspeakers, echoing through the streets of Nazareth.

Jesus was baptized in the river Jordan. He had traveled there to see his cousin John, who had created his own messianic ministry in the desert wilderness. The terrain has changed little in two thousand years. It is still a chalky expanse of rocks and weeds, windblown and barren except for green rushes that rise from the riverbanks and sway back and forth in the dry breeze.

John the Baptist was an unbridled and unkempt wild man in a messianic age. Living on locust and wild honey, and clothing his loins in camel skin, this crazed nomadic preacher, with his apocalyptic warnings that "the Time has come," was both thrilling and horrifying to the multitude that followed him here. They came to confess their sins, to be spiritually cleansed with water, and to be prepared for the coming Time. Even though John was Jesus's cousin, it appears from the gospels that he did not see Jesus as the Messiah until he baptized him and saw the Holy Spirit descend on Jesus from above.

IX

Jordan

THE BAPTISM

"I am the voice of one calling in the desert,

'Make straight the way for the Lord.'"

JOHN 1:23 (NIV)

THE RIVER JORDAN flows through the Bible—an eternal source of life in the desert, an Old Testament setting for military conquest, and a New Testament promise of purity from sin. The Jordan and the flat plain through which it empties into the Dead Sea have been the setting for watershed events in the history of man's relationship with God. Here Abraham arrived in the Holy Land. Here God protected Lot while destroying Sodom and Gomorrah. Here Moses saw the Promised Land, and Elijah rode a "chariot of fire" into heaven. And here Jesus was baptized.

One would expect a river that has forged the human movement toward salvation to have a near mythic physical quality. The Jordan, at least as it exists in the mind's eye from reading the Bible and perhaps from watching the Hollywood epic *The Greatest Story Ever Told,* should have majestic banks with broad turns and cascading tributaries. The reality can only be described as disappointing. Crossing from the West Bank to the Kingdom of Jordan over the Allenby Bridge—a forty-yard expanse of rickety wooden slats named for the World War I British general Sir Edmund Allenby—travelers can see at a glance that this mythical river is in reality a slowly churning brown stream. Depleted from overuse by agriculture and industry, this stretch of the Jordan today trickles through dried, cracked banks strewn with litter.

On the west bank of the river, dark green Israeli military humvees with young soldiers cradling machine guns bump along dirt roads following the riverbank. Along the east bank, Jordan's tan versions of the same military vehicle make their way down a parallel road, bearing young Jordanian soldiers shouldering weapons. Fields of land mines have been planted all along the riverbed. They are surrounded by barbed wire fencing and marked with bright yellow signs in Hebrew, Arabic, and English, reading "Danger! Land Mines! Keep Out!" Israel and Jordan signed a peace treaty in 1994; but judging by the fortifications on both sides, there is still not much trust between them. Perhaps not surprisingly, this military presence has long made it difficult for generations of pilgrims to see the site where it is believed that Jesus was baptized.

In the Hebrew Bible and on Israeli tourist maps, the point along the river traditionally identified as the location of Jesus's baptism is Kasser el-Yehud, the Fortress of the Jews—whence Joshua led the assault against Jericho. Kasser el-Yehud is situated at a bend in the river, just north of the Dead Sea. The Israelis had captured this area from Jordan in the 1967 Six-Day War, and in the decades since, they had restricted Christian pilgrimages and prayer services to three specific periods each year. At the time of my visit in 2000, it remained a restricted military site, an Israeli security corridor within the pockets of Palestinian control around Jericho.

Clustered along the riverbanks at Kasser el-Yehud are a number of nineteenth-century monasteries and chapels, still standing on foundations that date back to the Byzantine era. These structures have been built and rebuilt over the centuries to repair the ravages of earthquakes, conquests, and time. Biblical historians say that these sites reflect a tradition of pilgrimage that was built up on the western side of the river simply as a matter of convenience. That is, most pilgrims throughout the centuries were coming from Jerusalem, and it was easier for them to observe the baptismal site from the west than to hire a boat and cross the river.

But the New Testament is clear in saying that Jesus was baptized in "Bethany beyond the Jordan," which most biblical historians agree indicates that John waded into the water with Jesus from the eastern bank. And in the last few years of the twentieth century, Jordanian biblical archaeologists revealed new findings indicating that ancient churches and Christian settlements once were located at Wadi al-Kharrar, a little more than one mile east of the river. The discovery was a dividend of peace. The area had been a Jordanian military post for at least thirty years, occupied by an infantry battalion's watchtower and ringed by land mines. But during the redeployment of Jordanian troops after the 1994 peace agreement, a tank had rolled over and exposed what appeared to be an ancient foundation and a mosaic tile floor. It took several years to clear the land mines, and then Jordanian archaeologist Mohammad Waheeb began his work. From 1996 to 1998, using biblical texts and the dating of archaeological artifacts, Waheeb found what he believed to be the baptismal site, on a small hill overlooking a thin patch of reeds that had sprouted around a natural spring.

A team of twenty archaeologists and one hundred laborers was brought in to excavate, and they eventually unearthed the stone foundations of three early Christian monasteries, a chapel, and three pools used to gather water from the spring. The structures, Waheeb believed, might date as far back as the third century. His estimate was based on the type of ceramic material used in an aqueduct leading to one of the pools and the type of mortar used in the construction of a monastery. Waheeb said that he had also found coins and pottery shards here that date to the first century—about the time of John the Baptist's ministry.

These findings, which may prove to be among the most significant in biblical archaeology in decades, made the site a frontier once again: not a military frontier, but a forward position in the battle between Israel and Jordan over the tourist trade, potentially worth hundreds of millions of dollars. And the two sides take this battle very seriously, because tourism ranks as a chief source of income for both. The Israeli-Jordanian rivalry for the baptismal site is a classic Holy Land struggle, with the Jewish state and a neighboring Muslim kingdom squared off over a sacred site in Christendom.

Jordan's minister of tourism and antiquities, Aqel Biltaji, quipped, "If people want to go to the West Bank of the Jordan River, we are not going to stop them. We are just saying they are in the wrong place." And Israel's Christian liaison, Uri Mor, responded, "How do they know he [John the Baptist] lived there? Do they have any proof? Pilgrims have been coming to the site at Kasser el-Yehud for generations now, and they're used to it."

This and similar bickering about the site was featured in a barrage of newspaper reports that preceded the pope's visit in March 2000, portraying a tasteless competition for tourist dollars that could leave even the most faithful feeling cynical. The notion that Jesus was baptized in the water, and the spirituality a Christian believer might feel on either side of the river, seemed lost in the Israeli-Jordanian squabble. But since it was a sure bet to draw Western tourists, Osama bin Laden—the Saudi financier of the terrorist network known as Al Qaeda—saw it as a perfect target for a bombing attack, one that would further his self-proclaimed war on the "Zionists and the Christian Crusaders." Jordanian officials broke up bin Laden's Al Qaeda cell in December 1999, just weeks before the turn of the millennium when the terrorists plot to attack a series of hotels catering to Western tourists at the baptisimal site and in Amman was to have taken place.

Biblical archaeology is often more of an interpretive art than a science, especially in this part of the world, where earthquakes, war, and the shifting sands of time have endlessly altered the landscape. But it is certain that this area is part of an ancient pilgrimage route leading through the Judean desert and Jericho and over the river to Moab, near Mount Nebo, where tradition holds Moses stood after leading the Israelites out of slavery in Egypt, when he first viewed the Promised Land. Although he never arrived in the Promised Land, Moses blessed the leaders of the twelve tribes of Israel and ordered them to go out and take the land of Canaan, believing that God had promised it to them. The place where the Israelites were believed to have forded the Jordan River into Canaan was at Kasser el-Yehud, about twenty kilometers west of Mount Nebo.

Since at least the fourth century, pilgrims would have taken this path to Nebo from Jerusalem, Hebron, and Bethlehem. On the way, they would have traversed steep, mountainous terrain past the city of Machaerus, where tradition held that King Herod Antipas imprisoned John the Baptist in a fortress dungeon before having him beheaded. From there, the road continues to wind upward, to the village of Madaba. And in Madaba, one of Jordan's earliest Christian communities, events took place that reveal the fate of Christianity along this ancient path of redemption. It is a story of how the Byzantine civilization ultimately crumbled and collapsed in the centuries after the Islamic conquest.

The town stood abandoned for centuries, until a strange circumstance of fate led to a resettlement there by three Christian tribes in the late nineteenth century. The history of these three Christian tribes in Madaba during the ensuing hundred years offers a unique glimpse into the relationships that have bound Christians and Muslims together in Jordan's tribal culture. It also illustrates how, through the processes of conversion and emigration, by forces both ancient and modern, the population of Christians in Jordan was eroded to a tiny minority.

Madaba's Christian community was among the oldest in Jordan. The faith was believed by historians to have gained a foothold here during the late Roman period, with accounts of martyrdom confirming the early Christian presence. In the Byzantine era, Madaba flourished. The city today sits atop the ancient remains of a dozen churches and chapels possessing the world's most elaborate and well-preserved sixth-century mosaics. The most famous, located in the Church of St. George, in the center of town, is the Mosaic Map of Palestine. Crafted around A.D. 560, the roughly 15-by-6-meter mosaic was originally composed of some two million colorful stone pieces carefully arranged to depict a uniquely detailed map of the ancient Holy Land. Only large fragments of the mosaic remain today. But they reveal a chart, oriented toward the east, with primitive but surprisingly accurate cartography and topography, featuring the walled city of Jerusalem, the Holy Sepulcher, Jordan River, Bethany beyond the Jordan, the Dead Sea, the Galilee, Jericho, Egypt, the Nile, and the Phoenician coast—tracing the path of the history of salvation in the Holy Land, from the narrative of the Israelites to the life and death and resurrection of Jesus.

Despite the Persian invasion and occupation of Syria in A.D. 614–629, and the emergence of Islam soon thereafter, Madaba, unlike many Christian strongholds in greater Syria, was not sacked or destroyed. There was a continuity between pre- and post-Muslim conquest, an important finding made by Italian Franciscan archaeologist Father Michel Piccirill—important because it contravenes the accounts of many Western and Israeli historians who have depicted the Muslim conquest as being led by armies of pillaging nomads sweeping in from the desert and destroying everything in their path. The Madaba mosaics, by contrast, indicate a peaceful transition. Still, there was some evidence of later destruction of the mosaics. In the Map of Palestine, the faces of two figures in boats on the Dead Sea were deliberately scratched out, presumably in the eighth century.

Possible explanations include the order from Muslim caliph Yazid II in A.D. 720 that all depictions of human images be destroyed as contrary to the tenets of Islam, or the ruling of Byzantine emperor Leo III five years later outlawing icons. The latter decree gave rise to the iconoclast movement, a reaction to a growing cult among monks seen as unnaturally devoted to images of saints. Equally plausibly, the defacement could have been the work of thieves.

The historical record on Madaba falls silent from the end of the eighth century to the early nineteenth century. Archaeological evidence indicates that at some point in the early Islamic period, probably during the latter half of the ninth century, Madaba's population shrank dramatically, to the point that the town virtually disappeared. Some suggest evidence of a series of earthquakes; others wonder if Bedouin tribes may have invaded the Christian stronghold and sent families fleeing over the Jordan to Jerusalem and Bethlehem. Throughout the next millennium Madaba appears to have existed as a kind of desert ghost town of toppled Roman columns, mounds of hand-hewn stones, and crumbling Byzantine churches, which had collapsed atop the ornate mosaics.

But because of its location along the King's Highway, Madaba was never forgotten by local tribesmen. The people of Al-Karak, a town some thirty miles to the south, would have passed frequently through the ancient remains on their way to Amman, even as the town gradually disappeared beneath the shifting sands of the desert. In the late nineteenth century, Madaba rose again with the in-migration of three Christian tribes from Al-Karak. According to oral tradition, in 1879 a dispute occurred between the Christian Azeizat tribe and Muslim Sarayra tribe over the abduction of a young Christian girl by one of the Muslim men in Al-Karak. In a tribal culture steeped in a primitive sense of honor and shame, this was an unforgivable insult to the family of the young girl and by extension to the entire tribe.

The oral tradition varies on what happened to the young girl and the man who abducted her. One version has the Azeizat family tracking both of them down in Nablus, across the Jordan, and killing them. Others say they simply disappeared. But no matter what happened, the incident caused an uproar in Al-Karak. The dispute was exacerbated by the fact that the two tribes were caught up in a wider battle for political control within the tribal council. As a result, in early 1880, three Christian tribes—first the Azeizat, and then the

Maayeh and the Karadsheh—pulled up stakes in Al-Karak and left in anger and disgrace over the incident. They traveled north along the King's Highway to caves on the outskirts of the fallen town of Madaba, where they remained for nearly a year.

What was left of Madaba was controlled then by the ruthless Beni Sakhr tribe of Bedouins. But with the support of local Ottoman authorities, who had been encouraging Christians to settle on land that was historically Christian, and through negotiations, which included an agreement to provide the Beni Sakhr with a percentage of the future harvest, the three Christian tribes reached an uneasy truce with the Muslim tribe. The Christians slowly began rebuilding Madaba, using stones from ruins of the once proud Byzantine city. In doing so, the tribes did considerable damage to the fragile archaeological remains—though, as many historians are quick to point out, they also contributed greatly to the flood of new discoveries.

Despite the relatively tolerant and at times even pro-Christian policies of the Ottoman Empire (e.g., allowing the resettlement of Madaba), the years leading up to World War I would be dramatically different for the local Christians as the Ottomans' oppression of non-Muslims intensified. And in the aftermath of the war and the dissolution of the empire, the League of Nations awarded Britain mandates over the territory that later became Palestine, Transjordan, and Iraq. At first Britain balked at granting independence to any of these lands; but the Arabian princes Faisal and Abdullah (sons of Britain's wartime ally, the sharif of the Hijaz) were allowed to set up partially autonomous kingdoms for themselves in the latter two territories. In May 1923, Britain recognized the emirate of Transjordan within the newly established borders. Abdullah continued to accept assistance from the British, which maintained its mandate over Transjordan, as he built his newly formed realm out of the desert expanse. On March 22, 1946, the agreements officially concluding the British mandate over Transjordan were signed. Two months later, Abdullah was proclaimed king of the newly independent state—the Hashemite Kingdom of Jordan.

When the British withdrew from their mandate of Palestine in 1948, Transjordan joined its neighbors in attacking Israel, the new Jewish state. When the fighting ended, Transjordan controlled "central Palestine," or what is today commonly referred to as the West Bank, and East Jerusalem. And in 1949, in recognition of its rule over both banks of the river, the kingdom changed its name from Transjordan to Jordan. About a half million Palestinian refugees who had fled or had been forced out during the fighting and could not return to their homes across the green line remained after 1948 as refugees in Jordan. By the year 2000, more than 60 percent of Jordan's 4.7 million citizens were Palestinian.

In 1951, just after Jordan annexed the West Bank, King Abdullah was assassinated at the Al-Aqsa mosque in Jerusalem, killed by a Palestinian radical. The king's grandson, Hussein, then only 16 years old, was standing next to him as he fell. Two years later, on his eighteenth birthday, Hussein was crowned king (because his father, Talal, suffered from mental illness). Under King Hussein, Jordan struggled through turmoil and violence and war and assassination plots to emerge as a modern, developed state.

In 1967, when Jordan lost the West Bank and East Jerusalem in the Six-Day War with Israel, a second wave of refugees flooded into the country. Today, one million people are registered by the United Nations as Palestinian refugees from 1967 who have never been permitted to return to the West Bank and East Jerusalem. Most are settled in the towns and cities of Jordan, but many still live in the squalor of refugee camps.

This influx of Palestinian refugees has been accompanied by a rapid decline in the percentage of Christians in Jordan's overall population. Christians represented as much as 13 percent of the future kingdom's population at the beginning of the twentieth century. Jordanian census data show that the number dwindled to 6 percent in 1961 and dropped further, to only 3 percent, in 1987, when the kingdom's Department of Statistics stopped publishing census data on the religious makeup of the country. Today, there are an estimated 80,000 Christians in Jordan, according to church officials, or about 2 percent of the total population.

In the year 2000, a man named Rocks Ben Zaid Azeizat was perhaps Jordan's longest-lived Christian. He was among the first born during the Christian resettlement in Madaba, his father having come from Al-Karak as a young boy with the first three tribes in 1880. Born in 1902, Rocks had seen much of the town's history unfold, and he was generally considered Madaba's town father, its historian, and its living link to the past. Dressed in a blue blazer and a white silk kaffiyeh, he appeared a benign mix of British colonial subject and Jordanian tribal chief. At the age of 98 years he had been forced to sell his home, a structure of hand-hewn stones that dated back to the early arrival of the tribes, and he was now living in Amman with his 75-year-old daughter, who took care of him. Sitting in his library surrounded by books on the history and politics of Jordan and photographs of him shaking hands with the king and the crown prince, Rocks told the story of Madaba.

"It was out of shame we left Karak. We could not trust that the Muslims would respect our women," said Rocks, his voice raspy with age.

When the three tribes came to Madaba, they were mostly Greek Orthodox Christians, and the first common structure they built was a chapel over the mosaic map they had discovered in the rubble. Archaeologists and explorers were just beginning to recognize the importance of the mosaics, which had aroused the interest of the Greek and Roman Catholic patriarchates in Jerusalem. In 1895, plans were made to turn the chapel into a larger Greek Orthodox church incorporating the mosaic map. The Church of St. George was duly built, and still stands today at the center of town.

The Azeizat tribe, however, was Roman Catholic, a conversion that had grown out of a dispute decades earlier, before the tribe left Al-Karak. In approximately 1850, the Greek Orthodox Church had passed over the Azeizat family in appointing the local priest. This deeply offended the family's pride and prompted the Azeizat to join the Roman Catholic rite so that they could continue their own lineage of priests. This story provides a classic mid-nineteenth-century example of how various Christian tribes splintered off from Greek Orthodoxy to Roman Catholicism, with the Roman patriarchate actively reaching out to bring more members into its fold and exploiting any divisions in the Orthodox community to do so.

Madaba's Roman Catholic Church of St. John the Baptist was founded in 1890. While the church was being built, the small Catholic community used a cave to the west of the town for its worship services. The Catholics had a harder time than their Orthodox neighbors in gaining the necessary permits from the Ottoman authorities to build a church, so construction was completed in fits and starts. The church, although incomplete at the time, was officially opened in 1913. In 1917, it was taken over for use as a military depot by the Ottoman forces, and it suffered extensive damage in their hands before the war ended in 1918.

The Ottomans stepped up pressure on Christian subjects during the war, suspecting them of siding with the European powers. Rocks was coming of age during this time, which was rife with tribal conflict and lawlessness. In 1923, he remembered, the Beni Sakhr tribe attacked Christian shepherds who were grazing their sheep on the outskirts of Madaba. Four members of Rocks's family were killed. The Christian tribes lost their herds and camels. Such attacks prompted many Christians to emigrate, especially those who traveled between Madaba and Aqaba and Jerusalem, who had a sense of a new world opening up for immigrants in the West. They left mostly for Latin American destinations at this time, although many also emigrated to the Christian communities across the Jordan in places such as Bethlehem and Ramallah and Jerusalem's Christian Quarter. Rocks hastened to explain the tribal violence: "This was not a Christian-Muslim dispute. The Bedouin invasions, as vicious as they were, came about because we had things that the Bedouin did not. They wanted our sheep and our produce. This was economic."

At this time, in the early 1920s, the Hashemite kingdom was just beginning to impose its order over the tribal culture that still ruled in the wilderness that surrounded the capital, Amman. For the Christians who stayed behind, the tribal culture often drew them to convert to Islam through marriage and through the resonant message of the faith. "Islam had its pull on the Christians of the desert," Rocks explained. "The man could marry as many as he wanted whereas Christianity demanded only one wife. Because the Christian community was always shrinking, it grew harder to find a Christian woman to marry. And the worship of Christianity depended a great deal on ritual and on a settled community. Islam was portable. And Islam was less philosophical and more practical than Christianity, especially in a desert culture. So Christianity was hard for some of the desert tribes, and they drifted away from it or never accepted it at all. To this day there are tribes in which some branches of the family are Muslim and some are Christian."

Such was the story of the Maayeh tribe, one of the three founding tribes of Madaba. Two distinct branches of the family tree emerged, one Muslim and one Christian. The Maayehs' story sheds light on the diminishing Christian presence in Jordan. According to one version of the story, two brothers and a sister from the Christian Maayeh clan fled Al-Karak and came to Madaba. The brothers' names were Salem and Suliman Maayeh. Their sister's name was Eida. A Muslim shepherd who lived outside of Madaba but who had very good relations with the Christian tribes there wanted to take Eida in marriage. The shepherd in turn offered the hand of his sister to one of the brothers. But should one of the Maayeh brothers accept the deal, according to Islamic law, that brother and his sister would have to convert to Islam.

Given the difficulty of finding a Christian bride in the middle of the tiny cluster of families that had gathered to rebuild the ruins of Madaba, Suliman accepted the deal. He gave his sister Eida to the shepherd, and he in turn took the shepherd's sister as a bride. He agreed to convert to Islam, but he laid down two very precise conditions. Suliman insisted on keeping the Christian name of Maayeh, and insisted that he continue to mark his sheep with the Christian cross, the way his tribe had done for generations. And indeed, in the latter years of the twentieth century, the Maayeh shepherds, almost all of whom were Muslim by this time, continued to mark their sheep with the cross. Setting out at the turn of the century to research this family, I decided to look into whether that tradition of marking the sheep continued.

In the spring of 2000, in a lush green wadi on the outskirts of Madaba, shepherds were grazing their flocks. The era of large Bedouin flocks was long past, but there in the rich, fertile soil soaked by winter rains, Ahmed Maayeh was herding a dozen sheep through a field. The sheep, newly shorn, chewed on field grass in the warm afternoon sun, the small bells around their necks clinking with each movement. None of the sheep had any visible markings. Ahmed explained that an Islamic ruling by a local sheikh had forbade the shepherds from branding their animals, and that over time most of the shepherds had found it easier to simply use dye to mark their sheep. But Ahmed, 39, part of the Muslim branch of the Maayeh, said he remembered as a boy that the ewes in his father's flock always carried the mark of the cross, a brand placed on the ear and often combined with a similar marking under the eye. "It is because our family was originally Christian," he said. "But for the history you have to speak with the *mukhtar.* He is the one who knows."

Nayef Hammad Maayeh, 72, was dressed in a white kaffiyeh and a black cape with gold ribbing, the traditional dress still worn occasionally by the elders of the tribes. He was surrounded by his extended family of sons and daughter and their children, and even a few of his great-grandchildren, who were running through the modest but sprawling house. The floors were covered by oriental carpets. One of Nayef's daughters brought in a tray with small cups of strong coffee.

My translator was Suha Maayeh, a young reporter from the *Jordan Times,* who had agreed to help me navigate Madaba and research its past. She had grown up in Amman, but her aunts and uncles and grandparents all hailed from Madaba, and many still lived there in the extended Maayeh family. The Muslim *mukhtar* warmly welcomed her as a family member (although she is a Christian), and made a great fuss about telling the story of her grandparents and listing the names of all of her relatives.

After recounting the story of the two brothers, the *mukhtar* boasted about how the Maayeh family members—both Muslim and Christian—continue to think of one another as family, attending the same funerals and weddings, mourning and celebrating together through the generations. The tale of the Maayeh family illustrates the preeminence of tribal affiliation in Jordan—and in much of the Middle East—over religious affiliation.

But the history of the Muslim and Christian Maayeh clan also reflects the steadily diminishing Christian presence in this part of the world. The brothers Salem and Suliman became patriarchs of two separate, Muslim and Christian, branches of the family tree. In the ensuing century, the Christian branch dramatically withered and the Islamic branch grew sturdier.

The Christian Salem and the Muslim Suliman began their families at the same time, around 1890. One hundred years later the Christian Maayehs in Madaba numbered about 700, and the Muslim Maayehs, approximately 4,000. The population of Madaba reflects a demographic change similar to what took place in the Maayeh family: A century earlier, Madaba had been almost entirely Christian, and until the mid-twentieth century, Christians still constituted about 80 percent of the population. But the vast majority of Palestinian refugees that came to the area in 1948 and 1967 were Muslim. They washed up like two great waves around Madaba, inundating the traditionally Christian culture. The migration of Palestinians dramatically changed the makeup of the town. In the year 2000 there were only an estimated 15,000 Christians in the governorate of Madaba, out of a total population of 130,000. The Christians were clustered in the cramped quarters at the center of old Madaba, whereas the Muslim population had settled in ramshackle neighborhoods and small villages around the town.

A desire to understand the reasons for this demographic gap between the Christian and Muslim populations brought Suha and me to the home of the tribe's Christian *mukhtar,* Fayez Maayeh, a 70-year-old, retired carpet weaver. The house seemed quiet and empty as we three sat visiting in the living room. Our host's wife was preparing Sunday lunch in the kitchen. Of the couple's five children, two had moved to America and two to Amman, and only one remained in Madaba. The quiet of the house was a sad contrast to the Muslim Maayeh *mukhtar*'s home on the other side of town, which was bustling with the activity of four generations.

Fayez, dressed in a blazer and a striped tie, was one of a long line of Maayeh men who crafted wool tapestries on old wooden looms—a long tradition in Madaba. But the job was physically taxing and did not bring in enough money to support his family, so Fayez bought a store that specialized in poultry, and this had been his living in the later part of his life. He was extraordinarily polite and gracious in welcoming us—especially Suha, whom he had not seen in years. After the two had caught up on news of their extended family, and on which cousins had left for Sydney and which for Dallas, his attention turned back to the Maayeh family trees. Many of the Maayeh had also been part of an internal migration that had brought the Christians, who tend to have a higher level of education and more professional jobs, into Amman, Jordan's modern capital. The Muslims tended to stay in jobs tied closely to agriculture and the rhythms of village life, in places like Madaba. Fayez explained: "The Christians are exiting primarily for economic reasons. The Christian schools and their teachers, the priests from Greece and France and Italy, expose them to the wider world. So they know the opportunities that are out there. Sometimes the opportunities lead to Amman, sometimes they lead to America. But almost always they lead away from Madaba." He said that the Christian family tree had shrunk also because Christians tended to have fewer children than do Muslims. "We are about 120 families, with an average of three or four children each. The Muslims are 350 families, with an average of eight or ten kids."

For many Christians who remained in Madaba, life was often hard. A neighbor and distant cousin of Fayez's, Michel Maayeh, 35, told us that he felt trapped, being unable to get a visa that would permit him to work in the United States, and struggling to survive in what he felt was a Muslim-dominated environment that marginalized Christians. After graduating from the university with a degree in engineering, Michel had soon landed a job with a local engineering office. But he left that job when he obtained a tourist visa to visit an uncle in Jersey City, New Jersey, having decided to pursue opportunities for work there. After he reached the United States, however, the prospect of living in America without a legitimate work visa was daunting, and Michel returned to Madaba. He said that for years he had been trying to get a job that would allow him to use his university degree, and he was consistently rejected. He believed this was due to discrimination. "They see by our names that we are Christian, and the attitude changes," he said. "The Muslims have taken over the municipality for themselves."

His frustration and sense of limitation grew out of an economy in Jordan that left all young men, Christian and Muslim alike, struggling to find work—especially for those who were educated and sought more professional positions. These young men faced bleak prospects and often had a difficult time finding a bride, given their economic status. Michel, for example, was the oldest of six brothers, aged 25 to 35, who still lived in their parents' home. The six brothers slept in two bedrooms, each containing three small beds that looked as though they dated from the men's childhood.

The brothers said that as devout Christians in a society permeated by Islamic fundamentalism, they had been thwarted professionally and socially. Life in the villages and towns of Jordan, they said, was becoming saturated with a religious intolerance that constricted secular Muslims and Christians alike. "I have watched this all happen in my lifetime," Michel said. "The Islamic movement coming into the mosques, and the sheikhs calling the Christians 'infidels,' and the pressures on the women of our families not to dress the way they want to dress, or to wear makeup. Islam has surrounded the Christians of Madaba and tightened in on them. It just gets tiring."

I decided to trace offshoots of the Christian branch of the Maayeh tribe in America, to find out why they had left and to assess how they are doing in their new land. I was given the name of Michael Maayeh, a native of Madaba who lived in a suburb outside Dallas. I called him from my office in Jerusalem and reached him on his mobile phone.

RICHARD SENNOTT

On a desert path to Bethlehem, this is the view of the Great Laura of the Greek Orthodox Christian monastery of Mar Saba, a last vestige of the Byzantine Empire shimmering in the early morning light. Only a handful of monks are left to carry on the ancient rhythm of life at Mar Saba where the desert fathers have contemplated the mysteries of good and evil in the barren landscape and chanted the divine office every morning for more than fifteen hundred years.

ASSOCIATED PRESS

On his historic pilgrimage to the Holy Land in March 2000, Pope John Paul II reached out across two thousand years of history to touch the Western Wall of the Second Temple, the holiest site in Judaism. This image will stand as a timeless icon of the pope's historic effort for reconciliation between Catholics and Jews.

TOM HARTWELL

In the Upper Nile town of Al-Kosheh, Egypt's Christians, known as Copts, sought refuge in a church courtyard as tensions between Muslims and Christians heightened. In January 2000, an outbreak of violence resulted in the death of twenty Christians in Al-Kosheh and surrounding villages, marking the worst sectarian violence in Egypt in a quarter century.

BRYAN McBURNEY

In Nazareth, Muslims prayed at a green tent on the site where they were demanding to build a towering mosque in front of the Roman Catholic Basilica of the Annunciation. A municipal conflict was suddenly cast in religious terms as the actions of the Christian mayor, the Vatican, Islamic fundamentalist parties, and Israeli political operatives all left the fabric of life among Muslims and Christians in Nazareth badly frayed.

BRYAN McBURNEY

One of at least three different sites along the Jordan River with rival claims as the traditional spot where Jesus was baptized by John. This site, known as Kasser el-Yehud on the West Bank of the Jordan, is a closed Israeli military site that is occasionally opened for religious processions such as this one.

RICHARD SENNOTT

Two Israeli fishermen pulling up their nets on the Sea of Galilee, where Jesus met up with his first disciples and told them, "I will make you fishers of men." It was in the villages along the northern edge of the lake that Jesus centered his ministry. Today there are no Christian communities left along the Sea of Galilee and no Christian fishermen working the water.

RICHARD SENNOTT

Father Jacob Willebrands, who the Palestinians call "Abouna Yakoub" and the Israelis call "Abba Ya'akov," walks near the stone chapel of the Laura Netofa. He founded this Melkite monastery in the Galilee more than thirty years ago. Since then, the octogenarian priest has carefully and lovingly cultivated both the land and a message of interfaith understanding.

STEPHEN WALLACE

The smoldering remains of Beaufort Castle on the morning after the Israeli military and their paid Lebanese militia, the South Lebanon Army (SLA), pulled out of the buffer zone they had occupied for twenty-two years inside Lebanon. The Crusaders had built the castle as a rampart against Islam. But in the year 2000, Islamic fundamentalist fighters of Hezbollah raised their yellow flag at Beaufort and claimed victory over Israel and its allied Maronite Christian-led forces of the SLA.

RICHARD SENNOTT

A view of Jerusalem's Old City with the Muslim shrine, the Dome of the Rock, and the Western Wall of Judaism's Second Temple. When Jesus stood on the Mount of Olives, lamenting that Jerusalem was not ready for peace, he would have had a clear view of the Second Temple. In the year 2000, the people of the land were left to lament again that Jerusalem was not ready for peace, as a Palestinian uprising broke out in part over who held sovereignty over the sacred ground that holds the Dome of the Rock and the remains of the Temple.

RICHARD SENNOTT

A priest of the Roman Catholic Franciscan Order, which holds responsibility at Christian sites as "Custody of the Holy Land," walks through the ancient olives groves of the Garden of Gethsemane. This was where Jesus was betrayed and arrested on the night before his crucifixion. The roots of these olive trees are said to date back two thousand years, and stand as a silent witness to all that has happened since the time of Jesus.

BRYAN McBURNEY

On October 6, 2000, a Palestinian youth gathered stones just outside St. Stephen's Gate to throw at Israeli soldiers on a declared "Day of Rage" in the Palestinian uprising, or *intifada*, against Israeli occupation. After tension around a faltering peace process built for years, the violence was set in motion September 28, when Israel's hard-right leader, Ariel Sharon, made a confrontational visit to the compound around the Dome of the Rock and asserted Israeli sovereignty over the disputed sacred space.

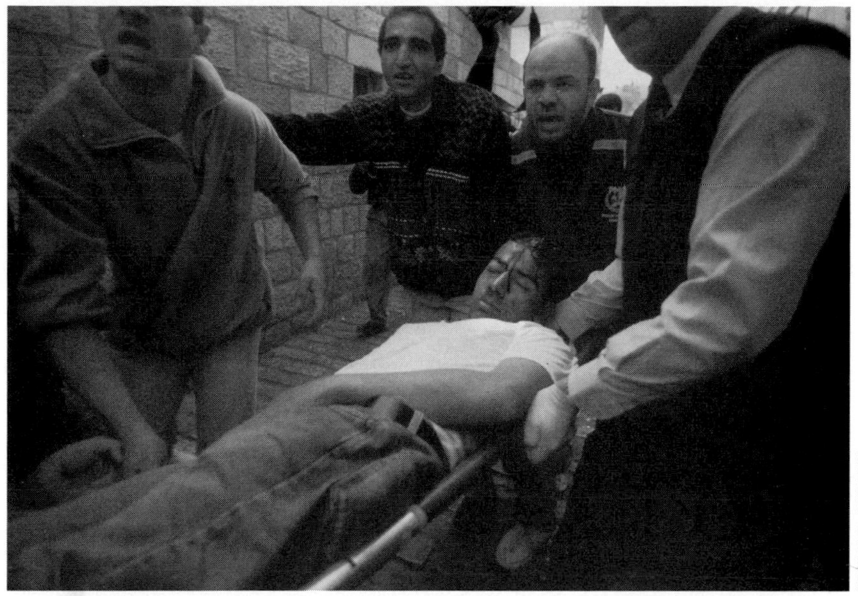

BRYAN McBURNEY

The Palestinian uprising that exploded in violence in the fall of 2000 continued to erupt well into 2001. The conflict claimed more than five hundred Palestinian lives and upwards of one hundred Israeli lives. In the fighting near St. Stephen's Gate on October 6, 2000, a Palestinian youth (*above*) who had been throwing stones was rushed to an ambulance after being shot in the head by Israeli forces. He later died of his wounds. The same day, an Israeli soldier (*below*) is rushed away after being wounded in a hail of rocks from Palestinian youths. He was treated at a hospital and released.

BRYAN McBURNEY

BRYAN McBURNEY

Palestinian Christians carrying a wooden cross on Good Friday enter the Church of the Holy Sepulchre after a procession along the Via Dolorosa, or "The Way of Sorrow," which marks the path that Jesus walked on the way to his crucifixion. The somber procession precedes the joyous Easter Sunday celebrations.

RICHARD SENNOTT

Anton Quliyoba on an ancient Roman path that tradition holds is the Biblical Road to Emmaus, where two of the Disciples walked in the presence of a man they thought was a stranger until they realized it was Jesus, and then he "vanished out of their sight." Today the road is in the West Bank Palestinian village of El-Qubeibeh and the Quliyobas are the last Christian family still living in the town.

He said he was out riding a bike on a sunny Saturday morning, and I could hear suburban America in the background, the sounds of children playing in the park and the Maayeh family dog barking as he ran alongside Michael's bike. It all seemed so far from the Middle East. We agreed I would call him later, when he would be at home. Thus began a series of conversations and e-mails.

At his christening he had been given the common Arabic Christian name of Michel, but in applying for his U.S. passport he had altered the spelling of the saint's name to the American English variant. He had been christened in the Catholic church in Madaba in 1944. At the age of 20, he left Jordan and headed for Dallas, to attend the University of Texas at Arlington. Though he had always believed that he would return to his native country, as he approached graduation Michael began to realize that his work opportunities at home would be limited. Most of his Muslim friends were returning to Jordan. They had had a harder time than he had in assimilating. Christian Arabs in the United States could easily join a local church community, and could date Christian American women without having to worry about the conflicts that can come with interfaith marriage. Because Michael had an older brother who had emigrated to the United States earlier, it was relatively easy for him to stay on and take U.S. citizenship, which he finally did. He was one of six siblings who eventually emigrated to the United States (out of a total of ten).

He had invested successfully in real estate, and he and his American wife of thirty years had had a comfortable income on which to raise their two children. They had a daughter in college at the University of Texas at Austin, and a son with a promising career at the Dell computer company. It was an American immigrant success story. He was wealthy enough to travel back to Jordan regularly to visit his cousins and old friends. He was well known and respected in the Maayeh clan, and he was seen as a kind of family ambassador to America.

Staying in touch was important to him, he said. He described a journey home in 1998 to attend the funeral of an elderly member of the Maayeh clan, one of his father's cousins. Michael joined the tribal families at a gathering at the Maayeh "guesthouse," a kind of informal clubhouse that was built for large family reunions, when the Maayehs from abroad came home. Michael watched the Muslim and Christian branches of the family mingling and consoling each other and telling stories over small cups of strong coffee. He was proud of the togetherness of the two sides of the family. But it seemed to contrast sharply with what he had heard from his young cousins and other Christians from Madaba, who had been coming in a steady stream from Jordan to Texas. They complained of a rising level of intolerance, of a sense of discrimination. "This is what the new immigrants are talking about," he said. "I think people used to come to America or to Australia or Canada for economic opportunity, but maybe now it is more because they feel they face discrimination. I think that is a big change in the last ten or fifteen years."

If the level of sectarian division had increased in Jordan, it was a trend that countered the enlightened leadership of the late King Hussein. His relationship to the Christian minority was part of what had made Jordan unique in the Middle East. King Hussein always embraced the Christian minority in Jordan as a community that was crucial to the well-being of his Islamic kingdom. Not only were the Christians a largely wealthy and educated class, but their presence in Jordan presented a challenge to the monarchy—a challenge that led to the development of some limited democratic institutions that have sought to guarantee subjects equal treatment under the law. That was the ideal, in any case, although it did not always work in everyday life.

Some Muslim Jordanians felt that the Hashemite kingdom doted on its Christian population, offering them disproportionate representation in the government and granting an unofficial, protected status to wealthy Christian business leaders. Under parliamentary guidelines, the Christians were allotted eight seats in the eighty-member legislative body. In other words, they held 10 percent of the legislature even though they represented only about 2 percent of the population. Through the decades, a disproportionate number of the king's closest advisers and top cabinet ministers had been Christian.

Some of King Hussein's affinity with Christianity may have come through marriage. Two of the king's four wives were Christians (although both converted to Islam prior to their marriage). His first wife, Antoinette Gardiner, was the daughter of a British lieutenant colonel stationed in Jordan. She was given the title Princess Muna. (The couple's firstborn son, Abdullah, took the throne upon his father's death.) Hussein's fourth wife, Queen Noor, was the American-born Lisa Halaby, the daughter of a prominent Washington family, and a graduate of Princeton. Their oldest son, Hamzah, was designated crown prince after Abdullah's accession.

The protection the crown has offered Jordan's Christians has been recompensed with great loyalty. And when King Hussein died in February 1999, Christian and Muslim families alike mourned his passing in an extraordinary outpouring of grief. My friend Rocks related a story to me that reveals much about the high esteem in which many Jordanians held their king.

In 1983, Rocks retired after sixty-one years as a teacher in the Roman Catholic school system. The Roman Catholic patriarchate, for which he had toiled at a low salary for his entire adult life, he said, never offered him a pension. As a result, he was left destitute and was forced to sell the family home in Madaba. When news of this reached the king, he dispatched his brother Hassan, who was then crown prince, to provide Rocks a pension of 200 Jordanian dinar (equivalent to about U.S. $300 a month), which since then has arrived at his doorstep in a fancy palace envelope every month. As Rocks finished his story, which had been filled with flourishes and details, both he and my translator were crying. For those of us who don't live in a kingdom, it all seemed a bit old-world and paternalistic. But to Jordanians, these stories that they tell over and over are part of Hussein's legacy.

The road from Madaba back to Amman cut through the patchwork of Jordan Valley farmland, where small flocks of sheep were grazing under the watchful eyes of their human guardians. Suha and I found ourselves stopping the shepherds to ask whether there were any crosses dyed in the wool or branded on the ewes' ears. It was an absurd and fruitless quest, and we finally abandoned it. Slowly the highway ascended to the outer traffic circles of Amman, and the landscape changed from rugged terrain to an urban jumble of McDonald's outlets, Internet cafés, and seemingly ubiquitous five-star luxury hotels. King Hussein was credited with having built this modern metropolis out of the desert wilderness that it was before 1948, aided by his brother Hassan, who as crown prince often acted as confidant and counselor as well as emissary.

Few dignitaries in the Arab world were more qualified to speak about the relationship among the Abrahamic faiths than Prince Hassan. He was in many ways the engineer who carried out his brother's vision of interfaith tolerance. Interfaith studies had been a passion for him almost all of his adult life—long before the catchphrase emerged in academic circles. In his youth, his academic mentor was the legendary Dominican scholar from Jerusalem's École Biblique, Father (Père) Tourney.

In 1967, when the Middle East was on the brink of war, Hassan was taking his final exams and preparing for graduation from Christ Church, Oxford. The Arab students on campus were "swept up in the political noise of the time," as he put it. The Israeli students were dutifully heading home for call-up. Amid the turmoil, Hassan maintained his focus on his studies, which included Hebrew and Aramaic. His "morals tutor" (a uniquely Oxonian mentoring position) was a Jew. One of his most senior advisers was the Christian Arab historian and fierce Arab nationalist Albert Hourani. Most of his friends were Christian. Hassan was far from home, and his brother advised him to stay there until the war was over. It lasted all of six days in June, but it devastated the Arab world and dramatically changed the political and geographic landscape.

Even after the humiliating defeat, through the late 1960s and early 1970s—at the height of Nasser's secularist, pan-Arab dreams—Hassan continued to pursue his passion for interfaith dialogue. This was at a time when "interfaith understanding" was not part of the vocabulary of the Middle East and certainly was never discussed in polite circles. Through the years, Hassan also developed expertise in more practical issues, such as the management of coveted water resources, and economic development. But his passion was still faith. He founded the Royal Institute for Interfaith Studies, and in 1995 he wrote a book titled *Christianity in the Arab World.*

Although he was a genuine scholar and a man with vision, Prince Hassan was unceremoniously pushed aside in the palace intrigue that unfolded around the time of King Hussein's death. He was a loyal brother and had believed for most of his life that he would inherit the throne. But when King Hussein entered the final stage of his battle with cancer in 1999, Hassan was stripped of the title of crown prince in favor of the king's oldest son, Abdullah. For Hassan this was a deeply hurtful and painful time. Hussein was not only his brother but a father figure and friend. My meeting with Hassan happened to fall just a few days after the first anniversary of King Hussein's death

The driver in the Mercedes limousine arrived in front of the Amman Inter-Continental Hotel to chauffeur me to the grounds of

Raghadan Palace, the royal residence, which occupies a series of hilltops overlooking Amman. In addition to the main residence, the compound includes a two-story office building that the prince had built to accommodate his staff.

Prince Hassan's palace was modest and tasteful. A small courtyard with a fountain led to the main entrance. Inside, the home was filled with antique Damascene chests and beautiful Persian silk carpets. We sat first in a living room of leather couches, warmed by a crackling fire next to which a silver platter of chestnuts had been placed. I told Prince Hassan I was searching for answers as to why Christianity hadn't taken firmer root in the land of Jesus. Hassan smoked a cigar as we began discussing the history of Christianity in the Middle East.

"If you talk about out-migration in terms of the Western Mediterranean, the Christian population under Muslim rule in the days of the caliphate is not one that witnessed an out-migration. In fourteen centuries of Muslim, Jewish, and Christian populations in this land, you would find that the Christian population did not actually dwindle. But I think that the post–Nicaean Creed schism between Byzantium and Rome clearly invited the growth of Western Christianity, so in a sense the political divide was a by-product of the first Crusade. In other words, it was the divisions within Christianity that first initiated the outflow. It wasn't Muslims who destroyed Byzantium, it was Christians who reoriented the focus and the demographic concentration of Christians in a 'safe and more acceptable environment.' So the question is not why didn't Christianity take firmer root here, but politically why it took deeper roots elsewhere.

"The most remarkable migration in the history of Christians from the Holy Land has been that of the last century. . . . This huge exiting of what is now over six million Arabs to Latin America, the vast majority Christian, began before the British mandate. They got on boats, thinking they were going to North America, but ended up in Latin America. This was the result of poverty, the breakup of the Ottoman state, the Great Depression, which affected us all globally, and the creation of the modern nation-states.

"Beginning with the British mandate, there was the encouragement of Christians associated with the Anglican and Catholic church to leave for Europe, there was a certain pull of moral authority by the Western churches. The local Christians looked to the Western churches as protectors, and to the Western churches as a point of reference for their identity. And so the result today is deeply troubling for the Middle East. You have more Christian Arabs from Jerusalem in Sydney, Australia, than you have in the whole of historic Palestine.

"I am not only concerned but saddened that this migration has taken place. How can you have plurality without the participation of the Christians in this part of the world? It is a very real question for us.

"I believe firmly that since the creation of the state of Jordan and the Emirates before that by my great-grandfather, there has always been an emphasis on inclusion. . . . I call it the Jordanian ethic. It is who we are."

Our conversation continued well into a long lunch and coffee. I persisted in questioning the prince about something I heard often from Arab Christians, that their faith just "wasn't tough enough," as one West Bank Christian put it, compared to Islam and Judaism. Indeed, it seemed that the whole message of humility in the Christian faith undercut Arab notions of pride and honor. After all, to live up to the scripture of turning the other cheek is not just foreign to tribal culture in this part of the world but is directly contrary to the culture.

"The Arab culture is strong on justice and vindication," Prince Hassan replied. "I think using the word *honor* is a mistake because I think it is associated in the religious context with false pride. *Justice* and *vindication* are better terms because they do not bring to mind the concept of martial honor, a notion of honor in the context of chivalry. And I do not think the Arabic cultural expression of justice and vindication had anything to do with the diminishing of Christianity, whether through emigration or conversion."

. . .

From the gardens of the king's palace, I departed for the border crossing between Jordan and Israel. The atmosphere at the crossing was never pleasant. The area was divided in two sections: One was for tourists from abroad; it was cleaner and provided a more streamlined process. The other was for Palestinians; it required a slower, more grueling process of verbal and physical examination. Palestinians—whether going to visit family members on the opposite side of the river, commuting back and forth between college, or traveling on business—often faced long delays and frequent humiliation. A Palestinian official sat at the customs window. Directly behind him, obscured from view by tinted glass, was an Israeli border official. The Israeli's silhouetted image asked the questions, which were repeated in Arabic by the Palestinian official sitting at the window. The Israeli was ultimately the one to decide who entered and who did not.

To many Palestinians this border crossing embodied the illusion of self-government. It was a depressing no-man's-land between the dream of Palestinian self-determination and the reality of Israeli occupation. Palestinians waiting on this line were often taken aside by the Israeli border officials and asked probing questions about their contacts in Jordan and in Israel. Frequently their bags were opened and unpacked while Israelis searched through them, leaving their personal belongings in a heap on the metal baggage tables. Occasionally, men and women were strip-searched. Many Palestinians described crossing the border as a degrading ordeal that they invariably dreaded. Israelis said it was a necessary part of life in a region where Israel's security was threatened every day by extremists. As I stood in line, I thought of Prince Hassan's differentiation of "honor and shame" from "justice and vindication," and just how much these deep codes of Arab culture were violated at this border crossing.

My friend and driver Usama waited on the Israeli side of the border while I was being processed. Soon we were winding through the desert toward Jericho in his black van—across the vast wilderness expanse where Jesus had wandered for forty days after his baptism, lost in meditation and prayer, and tempted by sin. A monastery soon came into view on the horizon. Carved out of the reddish-brown facade of a cliff believed to be the biblical Mount of Temptation, the desert monastery for centuries has sheltered a contemplative monastic order. Ironically befitting the year 2000, the first-ever Palestinian gambling casino had just been erected in the monastery's shadow, at the foot of the Mount of Temptation. At the Oasis Casino, which is managed by a European firm but financially controlled by prominent Palestinian officials (including Arafat and several of his key advisers), the management had hired mostly Palestinian Christians. Hundreds of Palestinians from Beit Sahour and Beit Jala relied on the casino for their paychecks. That was largely because Christians, unlike Muslims, are not forbidden by their faith to gamble or to serve alcohol. Christians here also tend to be better versed than Muslims in foreign languages.

Philip, a pit boss at a blackjack table, was a Christian from Beit Jala who spoke English and Spanish. I had met him on the night of the casino's grand opening. He estimated that more than half of the casino's Palestinian employees were Christian. The casino, he said, had become a leading employer in the villages around Jericho and deeper in the West Bank. (He estimated that two hundred Christians from Beit Jala alone were employed at the casino as waiters, bartenders, and card dealers.) It was not great work, he confessed, but for many it was the only option. "This is gambling and alcohol and a certain kind of people," he said. "There is not much honor to it. A lot of us would rather be doing different work; but this is what is available, if you want to make a living."

In the middle of the wilderness west of the Jordan River, the temptation to sin is as strong today as it was in the time of Jesus. Like the desert sands, however, the objects of human temptation continually shift; and the tempter now is a one-arm bandit, a roulette wheel, a prostitute, or the cheap vodka they serve at the Oasis. Riding with Usama on the way back to Jerusalem, I pondered why the desert was the setting in which all of the great prophets—Moses, Jesus, and Mohammed—were challenged and tested by God. Perhaps it was chosen because its terrain mirrored the harshness and indifference, the uncompromising nature, of Divine judgment?

These deliberations, of course, did not keep me out of the casino. I asked Usama to pull in—less for the gambling than for the cold beer. I am not much of a gambler, but the cool, air-conditioned bar was like paradise after the tense and hot border crossing. Inside there were vignettes rare in the Middle East: Israelis and Palestinians actually rubbing shoulders and talking to each other, sometimes even laughing, getting along. The tables were crowded with people from every walk of life in the Holy Land—even Sephardic Jews dressed in the traditional black costume with felt yarmulke, and Islamic women wearing headscarves. There were the shady and often corrupt Palestinian officials, in their cheap suits and dark sunglasses, and Russian Israeli mobsters with their open shirt collars and gold Star of David necklaces. There were tourists in sandals and shorts, trendy Israeli kids heavily into body piercing and spandex, and spoiled college kids from the wealthy Palestinian elite.

When I walked out of the dark, air-conditioned comfort of the casino and back into the blinding, searing heat of the desert, my wallet was $50 lighter. And on the drive through Jericho and up out of the desert, along the Jordan Valley, it often struck me that this was the same path that Jesus had taken at the end of his forty days of fasting and meditation, when he journeyed away from the stark and unforgiving terrain of the desert to the quiet, lush beauty of the Sea of Galilee.

After wandering in the desert, Jesus returned by way of Samaria to the Galilee. In the gentle, rolling hills that descend to the lake, one can imagine Jesus's life perhaps more clearly than at any other place in the Holy Land. It is the same watery expanse, the same shore, the same rocks, the same foliage of palms and thorns and wildflowers. Here Jesus began his active ministry by befriending a group of fishermen living in the village of Capernaum, on the lake's northern edge: Andrew, Simon-Peter, and Zebedee, and the latter's sons James and John. Along the shore, near a village today known as Tabgha, Simon-Peter and Andrew were casting their nets in the shallows as Jesus passed by. He had become acquainted with the brothers earlier, at one of John's meetings along the Jordan. Encountering them here, he invited them to follow him in his ministry.

On the southwestern shore of the lake, the fortress castle of the newly established city of Tiberias was visible. This was the power center of Herod Antipas, son of Herod the Great. News had come to Jesus that Antipas had had John the Baptist imprisoned in the Machaerus fortress, near Madaba, on the eastern bank of the Jordan. The teachings of John and his cousin Jesus were considered heretical by Jewish leaders and dangerously radical by the Roman imperial authorities. John would soon be beheaded.

Jesus settled into the community on the northern lakeshore, a refuge which would become the base for his traveling ministry.

X

The Sea of Galilee

THE MINISTRY

"Come, follow me," Jesus said, "and I will make you fishers of men."

MARK 1:17 (NIV)

AT DAWN, THE FOG was just beginning to lift from the Sea of Galilee. Fishermen, silhouetted in the harbor's mist, prepared their nets, folding and straightening them at the front of the boat. Egrets circled, waiting for the fishermen to begin work. Then the boat set out, cutting across the still water. On the lake's northern shore was Capernaum, where tradition held that Simon-Peter, Andrew, James, and John were living and working when they became the first disciples of the radical rabbi from Nazareth—Jesus.

On this day in late spring 2000, the fishermen directed the boat toward the northwest shore, where large schools of fish were drawn to the Tabgha springs, which originated somewhere in the nearby mountains. The whole scene seemed timeless and ancient, and if I squinted and looked out over the golden waters reflecting the early morning sunlight, the date palm trees waving along the shore, and the purple range of the Golan Heights perched in the distance, it was easy and pleasant to imagine life in the time of Jesus.

The moment didn't last long.

"Hey, give me a cigarette," said Nadav, breaking the morning silence. Nadav grew up on the Israeli kibbutz Ein Gev, which was on the eastern shore of the Sea of Galilee and which operated the largest commercial fishing port on the lake.

Gil, his friend who grew up with him on the kibbutz, threw him a long, sullen stare and said, "Fuck off, buy your own cigarettes."

Nadav and Gil were in their early 20s, sinewy and tan, both wearing olive-green army-issue fatigues cut off into shorts. Earlier in the year, they had completed three years of Israeli military service in the Golani brigade, including a three-month tour of duty in the war in Lebanon. They were crewing now under captain Yairi Freulech, a 46-year-old Israeli army veteran who had fought in the paratroopers unit in the Arab-Israeli wars of 1967 and 1973 and who also had been born on the kibbutz. The tough, no-nonsense skipper stood at the helm of the 50-foot vessel, a 1950 Israeli navy ship that had been converted into a commercial fishing boat, and barked orders at the two younger kibbutzniks.

Melanie Hanson, 22, with healthy American good looks and auburn hair twisted into a braid like a thick rope, made instant coffee in the galley. She was taking a semester off from Smith College to live in Israel. She was one of the kibbutz "volunteers," a group of wide-eyed Americans and Europeans who came to experience life on the collective farms that for so long had captured the mythic soul of pioneering Zionism. Certainly, the kibbutzim had been full of that idealism in the nascent Jewish state. But by the year 2000, life on a kibbutz had become a faded existence. Pioneering Zionist idealism had been replaced by post-Zionist cynicism. Most of the communal farms were tired, rusted, broken down, and in financial trouble. Ein Gev was the exception. It had maintained a healthy profit margin, albeit through tourism rather than fishing or farming. Ein Gev had a successful holiday village and a fish restaurant that catered to a steady stream of largely Christian tourists who come to see the holy sites related to the New Testament.

The men on this kibbutz boat, which was named the *Eitan* (after a naval commando from the kibbutz who had died fighting near the Suez Canal in 1973), were strong, hardened, and suspicious of glad-handing Americans. They were also aggressively secular. Nadav and Gil shot a glance at each other and rolled their eyes when I told them I was following the path of Jesus's life. They were the generation of the final phase of the war in Lebanon—the tail end of a twenty-two-year quagmire of occupation and guerrilla war casually referred to as Israel's Vietnam. Tattoos were mapped all over their bodies. Stretched across a canvas of skin that covered most of Nadav's back was a lion, the symbol of Jerusalem, climbing inside a Star of David. Gil had a spiderweb over his heart. They traded insults and cigarettes and exuded a practiced indifference around Melanie that made it obvious they were both vying for her attention.

Yairi, the captain, was from another generation, and had none of this practiced cool. He was stocky and focused. He sipped his coffee and kept his eyes fixed on the Optiquest, a high-performance fish finder. The depth gauge flashed over a liquid green computer screen. A sonar signal pulsed rapidly, like a heartbeat in ultrasound, as it tracked the movement of schools of fish beneath the water's surface. A large cloud of red and dark green on the screen indicated that the boat was in the middle of a school of fish, which the crew were hoping would turn out to be St. Peter's fish—a tasty, flat fish with few bones that is the best eating fish in the lake. And the namesake of the first apostle, Peter.

As I watched the three men position the hundred-yard-wide net from the deck, I thought about the long tradition of fishing along these banks, a history that stretched back two thousand years, to the times recorded in the Hebrew Bible, which like the New Testament contains numerous references to the practice of fishing on this lake. It occurred to me that these kibbutzniks probably resembled the Jewish fisherman who became Jesus's disciples—skeptical, focused on their work, but also humbled by the fatalism, even mystery, that comes with lowering nets into dark waters and depending for their livelihood on what the water yields. Simon-Peter was the archetype, with his exuberance, his aggressive self-confidence, and his impulsiveness and inconsistency. Toward the end of Jesus's life, Peter temporarily gave way to weakness and cowardice, although ultimately he fulfilled his role as "the rock" upon which the church would be built. His humanity shines through in the gospels. There was a profound difference between these modern Jewish fishermen and the apostles, however: The fishermen who lived around the lake at the time of Jesus were devoutly observant Jews, in sharp contrast to the aggressively secular kibbutzniks.

Nadav worked to keep the lines straight as Yairi steered the boat in a circle to spread the net, which fell like a purse around the fish. Melanie prepared the motorized winch system that would be used to pull up the net. This particular net was essentially a modernized seine, a type of dragnet often referred to in the New Testament and less frequently in the Old Testament. As the net was raised from the watery depths, the silvery shapes of the fish flashed in the sun. Gil dumped thousands of tiny sardines from the net into an ice-packed lifeboat, which was tugged behind the ship. The sardines were overabundant, and the take produced a profound look of disappointment in the crew. There were a few ten-inch buena fish that looked something like perch. And there was a thirty-inch silver carp, about which Yairi said, "Looks good, but it's a cheap fish."

Gil and Nadav sorted through the catch and threw back a few, including an ugly catfish—and in so doing, reenacted one of the central parables of the Bible. Jesus used the seine as a simile for the winnowing-out of spiritual imperfections that must precede the rule of heaven, saying, "Once again, the kingdom of heaven is like a net that was let down into the lake and caught all kinds of fish. When it was full, the fishermen pulled it up on the shore. Then they sat down and collected the good fish in baskets, but threw the bad away" (Matthew 13:47–48 [NIV]).

Sardines are a staple of the local diet today, as they were at the time of Jesus. Biblical historians believe sardines were the fish referred to in the "miracle of the multiplication" of loaves and fishes, recounted in all four gospels. The story begins with the gathering of crowds around Jesus as he preaches. Jesus tells his disciples that they should give the crowd something to eat. But at this stop along the Galilee shoreline, the food donations are meager. A boy offers them a mere "five loaves and two fishes." Jesus blesses the food before it is distributed, and it proves enough to feed a multitude of five thousand.

When I asked the fishermen about the life of Jesus and what they knew of it, Nadav shrugged and said: "I'm not religious. I know he had friends around here who fished. But I don't pay attention to all this Bible stuff." Melanie, who was born into a nominally Christian family in Bourne, Massachusetts, volunteered that she was "not really raised with any religion." In her six months on the kibbutz, she said, this lake's connection to Jesus had not really occurred to her, nor did it interest her. It had nothing to do with why she was there. Yairi didn't respond to the question but kept staring at the electronic fish finder and pointing to the fleeting clouds of red and dark green that indicated another passing school of fish. This technology took a lot of the mystery out of fishing. Had he been similarly equipped, Peter may not have been so overwhelmed by the miracle that occurred when, after a long day of coming up dry, he had cast his nets where Jesus indicated he should. In the parable recounted by Luke, Peter obeyed, and his nets came up full to bursting with fish. Who needs faith when they have a fish finder?

As we plied the morning waters and worked the deep holes and springs of the lake, I was surprised that we were the only fishing boat on the water. Of the four large commercial vessels belonging to the Israeli kibbutz, only one was in use on this day. I asked whether any Palestinian fishermen worked the water. Yairi looked up from the fish finder. "No," he said. "Arabs are not allowed." I had touched a nerve, and Yairi answered with an edge in his voice. As I would later learn, the Christians and Muslims who earlier had lived in the villages along the Galilee and in the city of Tiberias all had either fled (and never been permitted to return) or had been forced out during the war of 1948. "If you really want to know the history here, you should talk to Mendel Nun," Yairi added. "We are just fishermen, but he has studied the history and he can tell you what you need to know." He then went back to the fish finder, pulling hard on another cigarette.

The sun had risen directly overhead and was beating down on the boat. The crew came up with only three or four more catches of sardines, which would bring no profit at the market. The Israeli government paid fishermen to destroy the sardines they caught, so as to control the sardine population in the waters of Galilee. The crew decided to keep working, but agreed to let me off at the port before they continued. After disembarking, I headed straight for the home of Mendel Nun.

His cottage was set on the water's edge and shaded by eucalyptus and palm trees. From the branches he had strung scores of small, ancient stone net weights and sinkers that he had found along the lake. Nun (whose name means "fish" in Hebrew) is a living legend who has devoted his life to preserving and researching the history of the lake. He welcomed me at the door of his home, thin and still sturdy at nearly 80 years. He wore a faded, old canvas fishing hat, and his face and hands were weathered from working some sixty years as a fisherman.

The first wooden shacks of Ein Gev had been built in 1938, as Jewish organizations intensified their efforts to bring in new immigrants and build new settlements in Palestine. Mendel Nun was among Ein Gev's founders and the first to start its fishing industry. The kibbutz was situated within the area controlled by the British mandate, but directly neighbored the border with Syria, which was then under French mandate. Because it was situated on a strategic frontier, Ein Gev later became an important military outpost for the nascent Jewish state.

Sporadic fighting erupted between the Arab and Jewish forces in the area a few years before the 1948 war. Through it all, Nun kept working to develop the local fishing industry. The Zionist fishermen acted as an unofficial coast guard for Jewish forces, maintaining free passage over the lake, which at the time also was plied by many Syrian and Palestinian Christian and Muslim fishing vessels.

When Nun started fishing in 1941, the focus of the kibbutz was not on fishing but on clearing the land of shrubs and basalt rocks and preparing the soil for bananas and other crops. While that effort was proceeding, the fish from the Galilee were an important staple of the diet.

At that time the British mandate issued all fishing licenses. Jews had only 30 of the licenses, and Arabs, 200. "They were not so happy that we had started fishing," remembered Nun. "There were problems, and ships would trade gunfire in battles over the control of the fishing waters."

The political landscape was changing dramatically in the Middle East, but not the fishing techniques, which were the same ones used two thousand years before. The fishermen were still casting nets from the shore, and fishing at night with larger nets in the deeper holes in the middle of the lake. With the old, rope nets, they had to fish at night, because in the daytime the fish could see the thick webbing of the nets and would dart in the other direction. The night fishing was dangerous and difficult on a body of water known for sudden and often treacherous windstorms that could easily capsize a boat.

It was not until the early 1950s that the use of motorboats and synthetic fibers for netting radically changed the industry. Nylon netting, which was invisible, enabled the fishermen to work around the clock. By the 1970s, the use of sonar to find the fish was widespread, and these modern methods began to take their toll, greatly depleting the fish stock in the Galilee. Before 1948, Nun estimated that the average annual catch from the 170-square-kilometer lake was approximately 150 tons of sardines and 50 tons of St. Peter's fish. By the late 1960s it had jumped to 1,000 tons of sardines and 200 tons of St. Peter's fish. In the year 2000, the sardine catch had surged to 2,000 tons, but the St. Peter's fish had dropped off to less than 100 tons. In fact, the "miraculous draught" would be even more miraculous today, given the steady depletion of St. Peter's fish.

Nun, a secular Zionist who had a great respect for the traditions of the Galilee, approached the stories of the Bible with curiosity and healthy skepticism. They were, after all, fish stories. At times he disputed the gospels; at others, he supported the parables as well-grounded in the habits of the fish and the structures of the lake, which reflected his intimate knowledge of fishing in the Galilee.

Nun was a man with deep pride in the accomplishments of his country and the contribution his kibbutz made to building the state. But it was impossible not to notice that in his writings, interviews, and speeches to tour groups he had skipped rather lightly over what had happened to the Arab fishermen on the Galilee—especially the Christian Palestinian fishermen, whose traditional livelihood linked them to the apostles and the foundation of the faith. I had slept at the kibbutz that night, staying in a small cabin on the water's edge. I sat up late, reading Nun's short book *The Sea of Galilee and Its Fishermen in the New Testament,* in which I noticed that Nun had sketched the history of the Arab fishermen with a single sentence: "In 1948, the Arab fishermen, who had preserved the ancient tradition, left the area and with them the old methods faded away." Nun made it sound as though they had retired somewhere or moved on to better things.

Nun was a bit defensive when I told him I wanted to know more of the history of the Palestinian fishermen around the lake. But he was also level-headed, and he knew there was a painful narrative that he had avoided in his book. His first response was a direct statement of what he saw as the primary facts: "The Jews must control the fishing now. There are no licenses given to Arabs." From at least the 1920s through 1948, he explained, the fishing industry had been run by a Christian family from Tiberias, the Khouris. They worked in conjunction with a Jewish family from the nearby village of Safat, the Goldzweigs. The Khouris oversaw the Syrian fishermen and largely worked the fertile waters in the northeastern and northwestern corners of the lake. For their role in organizing the fishermen, the Khouris received 60 percent of the profit from the catch; and for providing the nets and boat, the Goldzweigs took 40 percent. The partnership, Nun said, was a model of how Arabs and Jews used to get along, working together and living side by side.

But during the fighting in 1948, the Khouri family, as Nun remembered it, fled Tiberias for Syria, and he presumed they still lived there. (Like other Arabs who left or were forced out by the war, the Khouris would not have been permitted to return.) The partnership was broken. Throughout the 1950s and 1960s, the lake was a flash point for conflict between Israelis and Syrians. There was continual shooting from the boats on the Syrian side, and return fire from the kibbutz—until the 1967 Six-Day War, when Israel captured the Golan Heights from Syria and secured control over the lake, a vital source of water. As a testimony of just how important this water source is, it remains a central issue in Syrian-Israeli talks aimed at establishing a peace agreement based on the pullout of Israel from the occupied Golan Heights. Israel has offered a pullout, but it refuses to withdraw from the shores of the Sea of Galilee. The two countries remain deadlocked—and technically at a state of war—over who will control water resources.

The lake's very survival is now in danger, given its historically low water levels, which in 2000 had slipped past the "red line"—the point beyond which authorities say water should not be diverted from the lake. But Israeli officials, pressured by the increasing demand for water combined with the decreasing supply, keep on pumping past the "red line" for agricultural and other purposes. The shoreline has receded so far that the lake is now surrounded by a huge expanse of dry, cracked earth and sun-baked rocks.

The lake's fishing industry has always been a source of political friction. Nun explained that the Israeli Ministry of Agriculture had never issued a fishing license to an Arab on the Galilee. In 1948, the Arabs had refused to register with Israeli authorities, for to do so was to recognize their authority over the lake. After 1967, when Israel captured the Golan Heights and Syria was no longer an immediate threat along the shore, commercial fishing licenses remained exclusively in the hands of Israeli fishermen. Today Israeli Palestinians are permitted anglers' licenses for fishing from the shore for sport, but they cannot use nets or fish commercially from boats. (In contrast, Arab fisherman have been allotted a set number of permits for commercial fishing in the Mediterranean ports of Haifa and Jaffa.) Nun said that the native Galilean fishing families had fled either to Syria or into Lebanon during the conflict that followed the declaration of Israeli independence. In 1949, after the war, the Israeli authorities offered to issue licenses to the local Arab population, but only if they came and registered as citizens of the state of Israel. The two countries that neighbor the Galilee, Lebanon and Syria, to this day do not recognize Israel's right to exist.

"We are not so confident, perhaps. We are not so sure, and we cannot be so generous as to let them back. Just a few months ago, Muslims tried to come to the mosque in Tiberias harbor. They want to recapture it. Policemen came and there was a fight," said Nun, then quickly shifted the subject back to fishing.

But not all of the fishing families went to Lebanon and Syria; many from Tiberias were pushed up into Nazareth. And in some of those Palestinian families, the traditions of the Galilee have been passed on to generations that have never been allowed to fish its waters. There were generations still weaving casting nets and selling them to Nun's kibbutz. I found two brothers, Moain and Nur al-Din Kharma, both of whom were born in the 1930s in Tiberias. They were on the rooftop of a nineteenth-century market in Nazareth, just off Casa Nova street with the Galilee nowhere in sight. But they had their nets spread out on the rooftop as if it were a working fishing port. The men sat on plastic buckets, their hands moving over the netting as they wove the nylon thread and placed the anchors and buoys on the throw-nets, just as their fathers and their grandfathers had done. They were accompanied by several other aging, dispossessed sons of fishermen from Tiberias. Nur al-Din, born in 1930, remembered the day in 1948 when he and his mother and father and eight siblings were forced to leave their home and their livelihood in the port of Tiberias. His father, Khader, owned three fishing boats on the lake; but they left everything behind when they fled to Nazareth, and they were never permitted to return or to reclaim their boats or fishing equipment. Nevertheless, they had continued to practice the craft of weaving nets, which had been passed from one generation to the next, and was still being passed down.

"The last time I was on the Galilee as a fisherman was fifty-two years ago," said Nur al-Din. "In the years before the war, Jews, Christians, and Muslims got along. There were enough fish for everyone. The port was lively."

I asked him about the Christian fishermen of the Galilee and what had happened to them.

"By 1948, most of the Christians were no longer fishing. Their hands had grown soft. They bought the fish from us and sold them in the markets. The Muslims were the only ones who really fished. We had the callused hands. The old Christians who were the real fishermen, they moved into the cities in the 1930s and a lot of them left for Europe and for America."

So for fifty-two years Nur al-Din had worked on this rooftop, weaving nets. Typically, he works several hours a day making one small cast net and then sells it to Israeli fishermen for a profit of about 25 shekels, bringing in roughly $6 a day. He had taught the trade to his son Hani, 36, who worked alongside him. Hani's was the first generation of Kharma men, as far back as anyone could remember, who had never fished the Galilee. The members of the older generation had left as teenagers and children, but they at least had memories of the water. Hani didn't even have that. He said he would not teach his sons, who were teenagers now, the skill of weaving nets; the family tradition would end with him.

Nur al-Din had applied for a commercial fishing license three times, and had been denied. When he pressed the government ministry to explain why he was denied a license, they said it was because he was not a resident of Tiberias. The same government that had forbade him to return to his home, which now houses a Russian immigrant family, refused him a license for fishing because he didn't live there.

The Galilee port city of Tiberias, where Christians, Muslims, and Jews lived together before the war, was now virtually exclusively Jewish. Most of the Christians and Muslims who left—the majority, fleeing the war, to Nazareth and Jordan—were never permitted to return. They are people like Afif Aliabouni, who was 10 years old when the British mandate authorities came to Tiberias in mid-April 1948 and told the Palestinians that they could not guarantee their safety from the Jewish forces and that it would be best if they sought shelter elsewhere. On April 17, units of the Yishuv's Golani brigade and the Palmah attacked the Old City of Tiberias with mortars and dynamite, causing a panic among the Christians and Muslims who lived there. The Aliabouni family, who were Roman Catholics, fled to the Sisters of St. Joseph in Nazareth and lived there for one year, then settled in whatever places they could find in Nazareth. The houses that they abandoned in Tiberias were transferred, as "absentee properties," to the Jewish state.

"We all suffered, Christians and Muslims alike," says Aliabouni. "Why is it any different for Christians? None of us have ever been allowed to return to our homes."

Aliabouni was right. Both Muslims and Christians were removed from the land. But wasn't he overlooking a particularly poignant historical development for Christianity? Wasn't it profound that Christians had abandoned the place where their savior had centered his ministry? Throughout my years of research along the path of Jesus's life, it consistently surprised me that the indigenous Christians were so eager to side with their Muslim neighbors in their nationalist sentiments, that even they did not attach particular significance to the fact that Christian life had vanished from the shores of a place so central to the teachings and the miracles of Jesus.

Israeli historians had long claimed that the local Arab population in what is now Israel was ordered to leave by the Arab Higher Committee, or that the mass exodus of Palestinian refugees was voluntary due to the demoralization of Palestinian Arabs, as one Arab city and town after another fell to Jewish fighters, who met with little resistance from often disorganized and poorly equipped forces. But a revisionist school of Israeli historians, with Hebrew University history professor Benny Morris in the vanguard, saw the depopulation of the area as a strategy "born of war, not by design," as Morris puts it. The expulsion of Arabs, especially in the Galilee, was complex. In fact, there was no discernible Israeli military policy; the force and brutality, or leniency and understanding, that were shown depended greatly on the local commander and on the local population. In this context the Christians, who tended to put up less resistance to Israeli military takeover of their towns and villages, often fared better than their Muslim neighbors; and in some cases, Arab Christians were permitted to stay.

Nevertheless, there was an early predisposition in the nascent Jewish state toward expelling the Arab population, and as it became more and more successful and could be done with surprising ease amid a growing wave of refugees, the Israelis saw great benefit in the policy. It took on a life of its own. As the *New York Times* reported on May 28, 1948, "Associated Press correspondents who toured battlefronts on the north and east with Israeli forces said the Arabs had been swept almost virtually clear of northern Galilee by an Israeli operation called 'The Broom.'" The purpose of the various operations in this area was to sweep the Galilee of its Arab population so as to keep control of the coveted water supply and fishing grounds. Many fled their homes, and they were never permitted to return.

In the operation to take the Galilee, one of the first towns to be captured by Israel was Beisan, about twenty miles south of the Sea of

Galilee. There was a tide of refugees from Beisan and a corridor of villages through the Galilee who were being pushed across the Jordan River into Transjordan or up into Nazareth. One of the refugees who came to Nazareth was Naim Ateek, who is today a canon of the Anglican Church and head of the Sabeel Ecumenical Liberation Theology Center. Ateek is one of the Palestinian Christian community's most respected theologians.

It was May 12, 1948, and Ateek—the son of a goldsmith, and one of ten children—was 11 years old. He remembers that Beisan—which had about 6,000 inhabitants, all of whom were Palestinian and most of whom were Muslim—put up no resistance. He watched the Jewish forces of the Haganah march past his front door and into the center of town. "We were simply taken over," he said.

Two days after the town was invaded, Israel declared itself a state and was recognized by most of the leading countries of the world. Beisan, which is now known by the Hebrew name Beit Shehan, lived under occupation for two weeks. On May 26, the military governor sent for the leaders of the town, which included Ateek's father. They were informed that Beisan was to be evacuated within a few hours. Ateek remembers his father telling the family that he had been told by the Israeli military commander that if they did not leave the town, they would be killed. His parents and his brothers and sisters frantically packed what they could carry, and met in the center of town as they were ordered to do. The residents were separated into Muslims and Christians. The Muslims were sent across the Jordan River, to the border of Transjordan. The Christians were loaded onto buses, driven to the outskirts of Nazareth, and dropped off at the roadside with their belongings.

"You cannot believe the wounds this caused, not just physically but psychologically," Ateek told me. "Borders were closed, families were torn apart, our community was completely uprooted. There was so much fear and anxiety and bitterness. We didn't yet realize that we would never return to our homes."

The circumstances under which the refugees left remain bitterly disputed. What is not disputed, however, is that the displaced Palestinians were never allowed to return. The morality of this strategy was hotly debated in the leadership of the newly formed Jewish state. There were liberal-minded leaders who saw such a policy as wrong and immoral, especially as it was being carried out by Jews, who had suffered so greatly from forced expulsions and depopulation. But others presented strong arguments that the return of the refugees would directly conflict with Israel's vital interests in securing a Jewish majority, settling Jewish refugees, and ensuring the country's internal security. On June 16, 1948, Prime Minister David Ben-Gurion told his cabinet: "I do not want those who flee to return. Their return must be prevented now because after the war, everything will depend on the outcome of the war—I will be in favor of their not returning even after the war."

For the outside world, the policy was never stated quite as harshly as Ben-Gurion had phrased it. Instead it was toned down and tempered for Western diplomats by the suggestion that it was a policy only "for the time being." In fact, the Israeli government in the year 2000 still stuck by this line as the two sides negotiated the "right of return" issue for the Palestinian refugees. By that time, the official number of registered refugees (and children of refugees) was greater than three million, according to the United Nations.

A walk around the Sea of Galilee today reveals the remains of a number of small villages and hamlets that were reduced to rubble, including Al-Mansura, Samakh, and Al-Samakiyya. Most of these villages were home to both Christians and Muslims. They are now either completely invisible, or recognizable only from piles of stones—all that remains of the ruined houses. Some of these villages are mentioned in the New Testament. Al-Majdal, on the western shore of the Galilee, is likely Magdala, mentioned by Luke as the home of Mary Magdalene. In 1948, Al-Majdal was a small hamlet of about one hundred residents, presumably all Muslim; but they abandoned their village in late April of that year, shortly after the fall of the large port town of Tiberias. Tabgha is the site of a fourth-century Byzantine church dedicated to the miracle described in the Bible as the "multiplication of the loaves and fishes." The name *Tabgha* is the Arabic version of the Greek name *Heptapegon* (Seven Springs), for the seven water sources that poured into the Galilee in that area. The church was probably destroyed by the invading Persians in A.D. 614, but the mosaics inside are still intact. Today, a complex of church buildings belonging to the German Benedictine order stands in Tabgha. The church was built in 1936 and the monastery in 1956. Before 1948, Tabgha was a fishing and agricultural village of about 300 Muslims and 30 Christians. It was depopulated and then destroyed by Jewish forces during Operation Broom. Only small piles of stones and crumbled walls were left, overgrown by cactus and sharp brambles known locally as "Christ thorns." The village land was now a grazing area used by the nearby Israeli kibbutz of Ginnosar.

Father Bargil Pixner, a German Benedictine priest who was regarded one of the foremost biblical historians in the Holy Land, lived at Tabgha. He had lovingly recorded his observations of this lake and the surrounding hills of wildflowers and thorns where Jesus had walked, calling his work *The Fifth Gospel.* Perhaps because of these writings, Pixner had been selected to accompany Pope John Paul II in a helicopter over the Galilee when the pope came to Korazim to celebrate an outdoor mass in March 2000. But it struck me as significant that Pixner's meditations on the landscape, so tied to the biblical narrative of Jesus, never mentioned any of the modern-day injustices that lay buried in the ruins around the edges of the lake and in the surrounding hills. Pixner told me he had been unaware of the remains of Palestinian Tabgha, just a half mile from where he had lived most of the previous thirty years. He looked disappointed when I asked him about the village—a subtle facial gesture that said, Don't go there.

Despite this oversight in his historical research, Pixner was indeed a brilliant biblical scholar. In the early spring of 2000 he invited me on a tour of the "Evangelical Triangle." It was a beautiful day to see this scenery, and we journeyed from Tabgha to Capernaum to Bethsaida to Kursi and to Hippos, tracing the ministry of Jesus around the lake. Pixner, in his early 60s, was guiding a group that included a German Lutheran theologian, a French Jewish historian of the earliest Judeo-Christian communities, an Israeli documentary filmmaker for *National Geographic,* a German journalist, and me. As we set off, the Galilee was bursting into green, and the shoots were just beginning to bloom with wildflowers. There were purple lilies, blood-red anemones, and pink cyclamens. At the base of the gently sloping hillside where Jesus gave the Sermon on the Mount, Pixner stopped to reflect on the significance of this rolling, gentle, green landscape in the message of Jesus. "The friendliness of this region has undoubtedly influenced the character of the Good News which Jesus proclaimed here," he said, smiling and surveying the land. This theme was central to Pixner's study of the landscape. As he pointed out, these gentle hills contrasted sharply with the harsh terrain of "the Old

Covenant, which had in the background the mighty Jebel Musa, Mount Sinai, with its rugged rocks of red granite and naked windswept cliffs, and therefore also has a much harsher tone to it than the Gospel which went forth from this mountain."

The Eremos hill was covered in an array of blossoms that shot up between the rocks in the fields and bathed it in beautiful color framed against a blend of green fields and gray rocks. The Palestinians refer to the hill in Arabic as "God's eye." It seemed perfectly fitting that a new message less harsh, less judgmental, and more forgiving would emerge from this pleasant hillside. This was the mountain of the New Covenant, the Mount of Beatitudes.

But as we journeyed, the beautiful spring sky quickly darkened, and a menacing wind from the east, known as the *sharkiya,* blew across the lake. This was exactly the kind of wind, Pixner informed us, that would have been blowing when Jesus saw his disciples struggling with their boat out on the lake, and, as the gospels declare, when he walked out upon the water to help them. Walking on water was certainly the most easily derided of all Jesus's miracles—or "deeds," as they were referred to on the Israeli tourist maps. An Israeli contractor who had seen a way to profit from this miracle was in the process of building a tourist attraction that would feature a Plexiglas walkway out onto the waters of the Galilee, to give Christian pilgrims the sensation that their Messiah must have felt. It ranked as the tackiest of all Israeli tourist enterprises planned for the year 2000; but apparently the contractor had been warned in advance how offensive the enterprise would be to Christians and had changed his plans. He had built a long dock for boat tours instead.

"Some laugh about walking on water, some believe it, but it is by far the most well known of the miracles of Jesus. It is the only one that the Israelis know. They come here and snicker," said Pixner.

The German newspaper writer for *Die Welt,* Paul Badde, stopped Father Bargil and asked, "Wait, do you believe that? Do you believe Jesus really walked on water?"

Father Bargil smiled and shook his head in affirmation. But he said nothing. The Lutheran theologian, Professor Wolfhart Pannenberg of Munich, Germany, cleared his throat and spoke up. "I believe that Jesus did many unusual things, but this one I am skeptical of," he said. "I believe it is a transmutation of the story of Jesus appearing over the Galilee after the Resurrection. There are theories, and I would support them, that the appearance of Jesus over the lake after Easter, which I do have faith in its occurrence, was transmuted into this story. This is the explanation I would offer."

French historian Simon Mimouni, who was in Israel studying at the École Biblique, later offered a very practical explanation. "Actually, I think the text has created a confusion," he suggested. "If you know the banks of the Galilee, you know you can walk out up to 150 meters into the water. The text says that the boat was blown back toward shore. And it says that Jesus walked on the water to help his disciples, well, I believe that meant he walked into the water. This seems like a very rational explanation that gets overlooked all the time."

We all turned our eyes toward Father Bargil, who just smiled broadly. The German journalist asked him again, "But you believe it happened?"

"Yes, I do," said Father Bargil, still smiling and adding, "I think he walked over the water, yes."

He looked gleeful in his belief as we walked on.

From the Sea of Galilee, I set out on the roads that led up into the villages in the surrounding hills to study the diminishing Christian presence there. One of the first Galilean villages that Jesus visited was Cana. In the biblical story, Jesus travels to Cana for the wedding of a young couple, who presumably would have been struggling to pay for the party. When the wine ran out, the Bible says, Jesus turned water in large earthen jars to wine.

I drove into the modern-day village of Kana on narrow roads made almost impassable by tour buses, and stopped in at the Melkite church, which was being invaded by a large group of American pilgrims with backpacks and water bottles and *Lonely Planet* guides. It was common for many Western tourists to come to renew their wedding vows at the so-called "Wedding Church" in Kana, and one such ceremony was taking place. A Franciscan priest from Ghana, who had been posted at the church by his order, the Custodians of the Holy Land, was trying to direct the tourists, saying, "Please, you must wait in line."

Up the street, at Elias's barbershop, a group of the town fathers were discussing a story that had appeared that day in the local Arabic newspapers, about an Israeli plan to expropriate land from Kana and other villages in order to expand Natzerat Illit. The move was stirring anger in the town—but not enough to stop the gents in the barbershop from playing their long-running game of gin rummy and listening to Arabic music on a beautifully preserved radio from the early 1940s. The chairs were classic 1930s antiques, white porcelain recliners with green leather cushions. The place seemed frozen in time, as did these Christian patriarchs of Kana, most of whom were the last members of their extended families remaining in the village. The rest had emigrated, mostly to Detroit and Los Angeles, which through family and community ties had become primary destinations for immigrants from Kana.

The town patriarchs pointed me toward Daoud Abu Daoud, an 86-year-old village elder who they said knew the history of Kana better than anyone. Abu Daoud was a mason by trade, and he had built many of the beautiful churches in the Galilee in the years before the war of 1948. After the war, much of his time was spent building the kibbutzim and Israeli development towns. He was a respected elder who had eight children, all educated and prosperous, and all still living between Kana and Nazareth. His family was unique in that it had not emigrated. He had instilled in his children a deep attachment to the land and a belief that younger generations should feel bound by duty to their roots as Christians and as Palestinians. Those ties, however, had weathered during decades of watching the Christian presence disappear.

Abu Daoud told me that before the 1948 war Kana had had a majority of Christians, at least 60 percent. And the Christians got along well with their Muslim neighbors. No longer, he said. The Muslims now accounted for about 85 percent of the 14,000 residents of the town. And if you looked into the school population, the statistics were even more foreboding. His son, who was an elementary school teacher, told us that of the 300 children enrolled, only 2 were Christian. And even in the Catholic and Greek Orthodox schools, the Muslims were a vast majority in the younger grades. (It was quite common for Muslims to send their children to Christian schools, which were considered superior to the public schools and offered a curriculum that was independent of the Israeli system.) In addition, the mosques in Kana had become a hotbed of Islamic militancy, and as a result tensions between Muslims and Christians were higher than they had been at any other time he could remember.

Abu Daoud reflected on the exodus: "This has been going on since I was a young man, a long, long time. The Christians left in large numbers during the British mandate. In the early years of the mandate, the British imported their own wheat, and the price of wheat fell dramatically. So many of the Christian farmers shifted out of farming into jobs as civil servants in the mandate, especially at the Haifa port and in Nazareth. Christians had learned other languages in the Christian schools, and so the British sought them to work for the mandate. This was the beginning of the change, and once they were no longer attached to the land, they sold their fields to Muslims, and later on it was also sold to the Zionists or seized by the Israeli government. The Christians once owned 90 percent of the land around Nazareth; now they own no more than 5 percent. And through all this the Christians received no support from the West. Where were Europe and America in all this? They were encouraging the Christians to leave. They were pulling them out of here."

He was sitting in a second-floor room with a large window overlooking the Galilee, and biblical shafts of sunlight were slicing through clouds in the hills behind him. He pointed out toward the horizon and named the surrounding towns where the Christian presence had dwindled and in many places vanished: "There's Umm el-Fahm, which has virtually no Christians left. There's Nain: no Christians left. There is Nahef, Al-Shajra. And there are towns like Eliaboun, which just ten years ago had more than half Christians and now has fewer than 25 percent. The Christians of this land are leaving. We are left only with the tour buses."

Although most left for economic reasons, the Christians in some villages were compelled to leave by the Israeli military. One of the most poignant and oft-told stories of this uprooting of the local population took place in the two Christian villages of Ikrit and Biram. In the fall of 1948, residents of the two villages were told to leave their homes and return in two weeks. Ikrit had a population of about 500, and Biram had about twice as many. The residents were never allowed to go back.

In Nazareth—roughly a one-hour journey from Ikrit and Biram—the former schoolmaster of Ikrit, Elias Yakoub, who was in his late 70s, told me the story. He was aging, but sharp and very precise in his recounting of events. After all, he had been telling the story for nearly fifty years. Israeli soldiers had marched into the two villages on October 29, 1948, and the villagers had surrendered peacefully. The elders of the village had offered them bread and salt, symbols of friendship. Two weeks later, however, the soldiers were given orders that the villagers were to be evicted, and they began removing the families from their homes. Yakoub remembered one commander in particular, who told the villagers they would be shot if they did not leave within twenty-four hours. The difference between Ikrit and Baram and other Galilean villages, he said, was that the residents were given a verbal promise by a regional officer that they would be able to return. And another significant difference was that the villagers of Ikrit and Biram fought their expulsion. They took their case to the regional military commissioner, but they were not allowed back in. The Israeli military argued that the area was of strategic importance because it was near the border with Lebanon.

In 1949, construction began on the government-funded kibbutz Biram, which was to be situated on more than one hundred acres of land that surrounded the Palestinian village of Biram. The villagers, many of whom had resettled their families in the neighboring village of Jish, decided to take their case to court. "We did not resort to violence," Yakoub told me. "We obeyed our Christian principles and fought through legal methods." The residents of Ikrit took their case all the way to the Israeli High Court, which ruled in favor of the villagers because the military authorities had never issued an official, written order for them to leave. But the authorities got around this decision by saying that they would issue a formal eviction order retroactively, which they did. On Christmas Eve 1951, Yakoub recounted, the Israeli Air Force carried out an aerial bombardment of Ikrit, leveling the entire village except for the small stone church. "We sat on a hilltop looking down as it happened, and crying," said Yakoub.

In Biram, the court case took two years longer. On September 16, 1953, the villagers once again prevailed in the Israeli High Court. Nonetheless, Israeli army officials immediately declared the area a closed military zone and barred the villagers from returning. The next day, the Israeli military leveled the stone homes in the village by aerial bombardment, leaving little standing except a few horse sheds and the two small stone churches that served the villages. In the early 1960s the government built Kibbutz Dovev in Biram and on an additional five hundred acres surrounding the village.

On Christmas, the Palestinian Christian families still attended services in the old stone churches that sat atop the barren hills, surrounded now by modern-style kibbutz housing. In July and August, the families gathered there to picnic and sometimes to camp out in the rugged terrain and to attend services at the church.

In 1999, an Israeli High Court judge ruled again that the families should be given a tract—only about 5 percent of the former land—on which to build new homes. The judge said, however, that his ruling should not be considered a legal precedent by the estimated 250,000 refugees from scores of other destroyed villages, whose cases, Palestinian land rights groups say, fall into the same category. More than a year later, the families of Biram were still waiting for the court's decision to be implemented. Meanwhile, new legal obstacles had been put in their way. Biram was now a national park, with a sign at the entrance that read "Biram Antiquities." There were, in fact, Roman ruins near the center of the rubble of the abandoned village. Israeli schoolchildren taken by their teachers to the site were taught about the remains of a Roman-era synagogue but not about the history of the Palestinian community that once had lived there. The Palestinians who had called this village home for hundreds of years had been edited out of the history of the land.

As the 1948 war ground on, Israel began to understand that its policies of evicting Palestinians and of destroying their villages were likely to evoke a backlash in the Western world if the victims were Christians, and so they focused more on the Muslim populations in the latter months of the war. A case in point is Eliaboun, a Christian Palestinian village whose residents were ordered out of their homes but were later permitted to return, whereas those who lived in nearby Muslim villages were not permitted to do so.

Fifty years later, the raw emotions of the war had faded in the Galilee, and a rising climate of tensions between Muslims and Christians seemed to be a more acute problem affecting the Palestinian community's daily life. As one Christian Palestinian explained, "The Israelis started a policy of divide-and-rule that pit the Christians against the Muslims. But now the Muslims carry out this policy quite on their own." A particularly powerful example occurred in the spring of 1998, in the village of Turan, which lay nestled in a flat agricultural basin that stretched between Eliaboun and Kana.

I first visited Turan shortly after violence had exploded there between Muslims and Christians on April 25, 1998, which was Good Friday. On the most solemn day of the Christian calendar, a group of nearly one hundred Muslim men had burst into the Milkite church, disrupting the services in progress. Clashes between the Muslims and young Christian parishioners who were enraged by the assault spilled out into the streets. A riot engulfed the town, and in the end, five Christian homes and seven Christian cars had been firebombed. A 23-year-old Christian art student, Sallah Sa'alame, had been stabbed to death in an ambush by a group of Muslim youths. (A local Muslim was eventually charged with and convicted of the killing.) Behind this spasm of violence were decades of resentment among Muslims toward the wealthier and more highly educated merchant class of Christians. The resentment had built up in more recent years and had crystallized into hostility, Christian leaders said, largely through the teachings of a militant sheikh who had taken control of one of the local mosques. In fact, an informal network of Muslim clerics who fueled intolerance toward Christianity by equating it with Western imperialism and Zionist aspirations had taken hold in the area around Turan. These clerics and their theological message were linked with the mosques of Umm el-Fahm, Kana, and other nearby towns.

The violence simmered throughout the year, and at various points I would stop in to visit the Rev. Basselius Khouri, pastor of the Melkite church in Turan, who had been a priest for a quarter century and whose father had been a priest in the same town for seventy years before that. In the fall of 1999, Khouri showed me two bullet holes in his kitchen window. Community leaders had tried to portray such incidents as episodes in an ongoing war between clans, but Khouri told me: "This is religious hatred, and Israel does nothing to stop it. We live in fear. We are left to fend for ourselves."

On a hot afternoon in the early summer of 2000, I again dropped in on Khouri, and we sat, sipping tea, in the shaded courtyard of his home. The violence had calmed down, he said, but the tensions had not. Christian families were talking of emigrating to America, he said, but in truth few had the ability to obtain the necessary visas or the conviction and resources to pull up stakes and start life over, far from their families and traditions. Even so, the Christian proportion of Turan's population was diminishing rapidly, as the Muslims had triple the birthrate. The Christians of Turan felt besieged and alienated from the Muslims in town, he said.

Khouri confided to me that his oldest son, Wa'el, 23, was among a growing group of young Christians of Turan who had taken the dramatic step of joining the Israeli military. This act had long been viewed by Palestinians—Muslims and Christians alike—as an unforgivable collaboration with the occupier. But as the Christians were backed into a corner in Turan and other villages and towns, Khouri said, young Christian men were joining the Israeli military, following the example of the tiny minority of Israeli Druzes—a notoriously insular and secretive sect that grew out of the Shiite branch of Islam. Fifteen Christian youths from Turan had joined up in 2000, he said.

"The Muslims call us traitors now," said Wa'el, who keeps his Israeli-issue rifle in the closet when he is home on leave from his military service. "We are not going to live in fear anymore. I think we realized that our future was more important than all the words of nationalism. You know the Muslims don't think of us as part of that nationalism, except when they need us. That's the truth. They talk about all this stuff against Israel and against occupation and collaboration, but they only care about fellow Muslims. We used to eat from the same plate, but now this town is torn apart. We [as Christians] have to do what is right for us now."

The decision of Christian youths in Turan to enter the military was not only motivated by the violence but also by economic considerations. After completing military service, they would have far greater job opportunities within the Israeli economy. After Wa'el rushed off, a green military duffle bag slung over his shoulder, to catch a bus to go back to his base, I asked Khouri how he felt about his son joining the military. "It is a very complicated feeling," he replied. "But I think he is making his own decisions, and I am proud of him."

In the shadow of biblical Mount Tabor stands the village of Nain. This is where Jesus is believed to have raised a widow's son from the dead. Through the centuries, the small hilltop cluster of homes had always been a Christian village. As recently as 1984, some three hundred Christians still lived there. By the year 2000, there was not a single Christian left in Nain. A Muslim woman surrounded by stray cats had taken up squatter's rights in a ramshackle house attached to the local church, which is dedicated to the miracle Jesus is believed to have performed here. She held a rusted skeleton key that opened the church to Christian tourists who happened to visit, and from whom she accepted small donations.

In broken Arabic, I asked the woman, "Where are the Christians?" She answered with one word, "America." The emptying Christian villages and the tides of tourists had made for a sad pilgrimage through a beautiful land. What was left was a dry, barren community of faith that seemed barely capable of clinging to its two-thousand-year-old roots. It had the decaying but somehow noble appearance of a gnarled, gray olive tree that no longer yielded fruit.

. . .

I had one last pilgrimage to make in the Galilee. Several acquaintances had spoken to me of an aging Christian sage named Abouna Yakoub, who lived in a remote monastery in the Galilee, and I set out to find him. I had been told simply to drive up into the small village of Deir Hanna and ask anyone to direct me to Abouna Yakoub. The first two men I stopped, both Muslim, not only told me the way but insisted on following me to the long dirt road. They were not just treating me with typical Arab hospitality; they seemed to feel a genuine respect for the stranger who was seeking Abouna Yakoub. The dirt road that led to the monastery wound through an olive grove and then up steeper terrain into terraced groves of apple and pear trees. I noticed right away how immaculately this land was tended. Every field was terraced with well-built stone walls. Saplings were carefully secured with string wrapped around stakes to support their roots.

At some point the road became too steep and difficult to navigate even with four-wheel drive, so I hiked the remaining kilometer or so. It was almost sundown, and I heard the murmuring of prayer coming from a rocky outcropping on the top of the hill. I approached the rock and noticed a wooden door that led into a cave, in which there was a flickering glow of candlelight. I sat at the entrance to the door and listened to the service. It was peaceful and beautiful.

When Abouna Yakoub (Abba Yaagov in Hebrew) emerged from the cave, he insisted that I stay for supper. At 82 years old, he was fit and bright-eyed and full of energy both physical and intellectual. He had been born in the Netherlands in 1918, and his full name was Father Jacob Willebrands. He was the hegemon of the Lavra Netofa, a monastery he had founded in July 1967. The most influential person in his life had been his father's cousin, Laetus Himmelreich, a Franciscan priest and biblical scholar who had many close Jewish friends all over Europe. This cousin used to speak at family gatherings and throughout his ministry about the Christians' close ties to the Jews—

which in the Netherlands of the 1930s, amid the rise of Nazism, was a significant and dangerous act. Himmelreich made such a strong impression on Willebrands that in 1936 Willebrands decided to pursue a vocation in the priesthood and join the Cistercian (Trappist) monastery of Our Lady of Refuge, on the Belgian frontier. But the quiet solitude of monastic life was suddenly and violently interrupted by the German invasion of the Netherlands in May 1940. The Nazis began detaining and deporting intellectual and religious leaders who spoke out against or had any ideas contrary to the Nazi regime. Included among those rounded up were 130,000 Dutch Jews. Father Himmelreich, along with many leading Dutch bishops, protested openly in churches against the deportations, and he himself was soon taken to the concentration camp in Dachau, Germany.

He was placed in a unit for Catholic priests, 250 of whom would be killed during the course of the war. Himmelreich was experimented on by Nazi scientists at Dachau. He survived the torture and was liberated in 1945, but he was left an invalid. Yet although old and frail, he expounded a powerful theology forged during his years in the Nazi concentration camp. Willebrands quoted Himmelreich as having told him, "In Psalm 117, Israel is the precantor who invites all the nations to the praise of God, and this really will start from now on." The frail Himmelreich wanted desperately to go to Palestine to "share the adventure of Jews returning to their homeland." He never made it; but Willebrands was inspired by his relative's message and took it on as his own life's calling.

As part of his vocation in the Trappist monastery, he was called upon to research the origins of monasticism. As he pursued this research, he was "more and more confronted with the Palestinian church and her monks," he said. "I discovered her great value and her perseverance for two thousand years under the most difficult circumstances." The idea began to stir in him of a passage from his Trappist order to the Melkite Church, which had existed in Palestine for two thousand years. The term *Melkite* comes from the Hebrew *melech,* which means "king." In the early centuries of the Christian era, the latter was a derogatory word used by Jews toward their coreligionists who embraced Christianity, Willebrands said. It presumably would have applied equally well as an epithet for those who followed the "king of the Jews"—as Jesus was mockingly dubbed at his execution—and those who followed the king of the Romans, Constantine. The

Uniate Greek Catholic (Melkite) Church was officially founded in 1724, after a split in the patriarchate of Antioch. One group continued as the Greek Orthodox Church of Antioch, under its own patriarch, whereas a different bishop was recognized by the Roman pope as the patriarch of the Greek Catholic Church. Although they have adopted some Roman Catholic traditions, the Melkites have maintained a Byzantine liturgy.

Willebrands knew that he wanted to begin a Trappist monastery in Palestine, but his superiors were not interested. He figured that if he could get approval from Rome to become a priest within the rites of the Melkite church, he could start a monastery that would be much more organic to the soil of Palestine. Trappists at that time were starting monasteries in Asia and Africa, but these monasteries were all "Trappist flower pots." He wanted a monastic order with a calling that would have roots in the community and that would flourish in the indigenous soil.

As he wrote in the typicon for the monastic order he founded, "We are an integral part of the local Catholic Melkite Church, which has been in existence here for two thousand years. We share their rich tradition, their joys, their sorrows and their aspirations. We are also the compatriots of those Jews who after two thousand years of exile have come back to their old homeland. With them we share a spiritual patrimony that is so great that we need brotherly dialogue to grasp all of its riches. We are impelled to do so, for centuries of Christian contempt preceded, and our generation has witnessed, the atrocities of the Shoah. At least since the time of the Crusades, a large part of the Palestinian population became Muslim. They too are well rooted in this country, and share with us a substantial part of God's revelation."

Thus he set out in 1967 to start a ministry of the Eastern rite that would both maintain loyalty to Rome and provide a spiritual touchstone for Jews and Muslims as well—a big challenge, in this part of the world. Willebrands's monastery was small, with only a handful of monks in residence, but he had developed close ties with the local community of Eliaboun, both Christian and Muslim. And thousands of Israeli Jews had visited his unique monastery. Busloads of tourists sometimes came to see the grounds and to hear his message, the aim of which was a healing of the rift between Catholics and Jews. Willebrands was emphatic about not trying to convert Jews to Christianity as part of his ministry, focusing instead on understanding the ways in which the Christian faith owed its origins to Judaism. He encouraged understanding among the faiths. As he put it: "Muslims and Jews on this land have collective souls. It would be wrong to try to work toward conversion."

Because in his view the Christian faith—and especially, much of Melkite ritual and liturgy—had come out of Hebraic traditions, Willebrands brought Hebrew liturgical elements into the service, placing a menorah on the altar and lighting traditional Sabbath candles. Some of the so-called messianic Jews—a relatively small underground movement in Israel that held to its Jewish tradition but embraced Jesus as the messiah—had come to Willebrands seeking kinship; but he had been resistant to their fellowship because they were strongly opposed to the established Roman Catholic and Greek Orthodox churches and had, in his view, "a very weak theology."

On the Palestinian side, Willebrands had made deep inroads into nearby communities. But it was not easy. "When I first came here, the Palestinians were very bitter about their experience," he recalled. "I think honestly now they are thankful to live within Israel, when they compare their rights and their standards of living to the countries around them, like Lebanon and Syria. Things are better now. They have jobs. They have universities they can go to. But the Israeli government has not treated them equally, so there are still problems. Deep problems. But overall it would be inaccurate not to stress that Palestinians living within Israel feel they have a clearer avenue to achieve full rights someday than most of their fellow Palestinians living under Arafat or living anywhere in the Arab world.

"We are a very advanced post within our church here," he continued. "Some of our local priests can be very closed off to our message. The lay people are much more open than the priests. The lay people work and go to school with Jews and have friendships and relationships. But the priests quite often stay in their village and do not go out and meet Jews. They become cocooned into their communities, where they gather up all the old prejudices. You hear the anti-Jewish statements all the time. But the truth is, Israel has also made many mistakes here from the beginning. If they had allowed equal rights, this would be a different place. I think the Israeli people still do not understand the anger that is here among the Palestinians who live among them."

It was late night now, and we were talking in a small room off the kitchen, over a glass of wine. The presence of the man was so soothing and so enlightened that I felt for the first time that I had come into touch with a true spirit of faith in the Christian community here, one that spoke of justice for Palestinians but also respect and genuine appreciation for Israel and what it had accomplished on this land. Abouna Yakoub's mission was firmly Christian but also revered Judaism as the root of Christianity, and welcomed Muslims as Abrahamic kin. When I said good-bye, he made me promise to visit him again. I went out into the darkness, using a cigarette lighter to find my way down the steep path to the Jeep.

As word spread of Jesus's ministry and the power of his healing miracles, Jesus and his disciples increasingly feared Herod Antipas. They were concerned that Antipas might deal as decisively and quickly with the popular prophet from Capernaum as he had with John the Baptist. So Jesus tried to avoid large gatherings, and traveled in the hills to stay ahead of his would-be captors.

He expressed bitter regret at leaving the Galilee, saying, "Woe to you, Korazin! Woe to you, Bethsaida! If the miracles that were performed in you had been performed in Tyre and Sidon, they would have repented long ago in sackcloth and ashes. But I tell you, it will be more bearable for Tyre and Sidon on the day of judgment than for you" (Matthew 11:21–22 [NIV]).

Moved, perhaps, by others' worries for his safety as well as by his own frustration with his ministry's lack of success in the Galilee, Jesus headed northward, to the Phoenician port of Tyre (in modern-day Lebanon). There his encounter with a local woman who pleaded with him to help her daughter moved Jesus to open his ministry to the Gentiles. Before this, it seems that he was reluctant to approach Gentiles and doubtful that they would understand his teachings, which were deeply rooted in the Jewish faith.

XI

Lebanon

THE GENTILES

Jesus left that place and went to the vicinity of Tyre.

He entered a house and did not want anyone to know it;

yet he could not keep his presence secret.

MARK 7:24–25 (NIV)

THE RAMPARTS OF BEAUFORT Castle loomed out of the low-lying fog. This massive twelfth-century fortress, an ancient outpost of European Christendom, commands the most strategic high ground in southern Lebanon. The powerful Litani River lies at its base; and its parapets offer a view that stretches from the Sea of Galilee to the Mediterranean coast—a panorama of the route that Jesus would have traveled to reach the port cities of Tyre and Sidon. This coveted strategic ground has been fought for through the ages by one conquering power in the Levant after another. In the first light of day on May 24, 2000, Beaufort was still smoldering in the aftermath of the final chaotic pullout of Israeli forces from southern Lebanon the night before. As I approached the castle, smoke and the smell of gunpowder were heavy in the air—the same, familiar scent of war that had lingered about the courtyards and hallways and revetments of the fortress for nearly a thousand years. As I stood there, I tried to imagine the Crusaders with their heavy armor clanking and their swords and shields clattering, manning catapults against the armies of Islam and then retreating, taking what they could and laying waste to the rest. The aftermath of their defeat, I thought, must have looked like this.

The Crusaders had built Beaufort Castle as a line of defense against an Islamic invasion from Damascus. It was manned by the Templars, the warrior monks who embodied the two great passions of the European powers of that time: war and worship. Saladin's Muslim army was the first to lay siege to the fortress, on his march to reclaim Holy Jerusalem from the European armies of the cross. Next, the Ottoman Turks held the fortress. And after the Ottomans' defeat in World War I, the French took claim, and the castle was yet again in Christian hands. It was the French in 1920 who created "Grand Liban," or Great Lebanon, carving it out of the Syrian territories over which they were given the mandate to rule after the defeat of the Ottomans. In 1943, the National Covenant was established, a power-sharing agreement that placed Lebanon firmly in control of the Christian Maronites—a community that took its name from a fourth-century monk and that later united with the Roman Catholic church, in the twelfth century. In Lebanon, the French established the first independent Christian government in the Middle East since the Crusaders. But by the early 1970s, the young Palestinian fighters of the PLO had flooded the neighborhoods of East Beirut and spilled into the towns and valleys of southern Lebanon. They penetrated the castle and held it for years, their guns and mortar launchers trained down on the Lebanese Christian militia positions below and at the Israeli communities of the Galilee. The Christian militias futilely launched mortars into the imposing fortifications of the castle. In June 1982, it was the Israelis who seized Beaufort, a pivotal foothold during their invasion of Lebanon, from which they would push all the way to Beirut. They pounded the Palestinian militias with American-made F-16 fighter jets while commandos ascended the steep escarpment leading up to the castle and fought a legendary machine-gun battle that forced the Palestinian militias into a hasty retreat. Within hours, the Crusader prize was in the hands of the Jewish state. Israel then formed an alliance in Lebanon with the Christian militias, controlling Beaufort for eighteen years, largely through its proxy, the South Lebanon Army (SLA), which was commanded by Lebanese Christian Maronites. Beaufort was the most critical Israeli and SLA stronghold in the central sector of Israel's security zone, where it was fighting the guerrilla forces of Lebanon's Hezbollah, or the "Party of God"—Shiite Muslim militants intent on driving the occupiers and their collaborators out of Lebanon.

Beaufort's history testifies to the Maronites' penchant for ill-fated alliances, first with the Crusaders, then with the French, and finally with the Israeli Defense Forces. All of these alliances had pitted the Maronites against the Arab Muslims, both Shiite and Sunni, and the

Druzes. In some sense the Israeli pullout was the denouement of that long history—the result of the Maronites' arrogance, and of the breakdown of their last unhealthy alliance with foreign powers, which the Maronites erroneously believed would allow them to cling to power.

Beaufort Castle was the most imposing symbol of Israeli occupation, and the one most laden with historical overtones for Hezbollah, which viewed the SLA and the Israelis as brutal and barbaric Crusaders. The road winding up to the castle was lined with concrete slabs known as "T-walls," as protection for the Israeli forces against Hezbollah's snipers and bombs. Inside the castle walls lay a military complex roughly the size of a football field that had been completely destroyed by the retreating Israelis, who wanted to leave nothing behind for the enemy. In a few places, the rubble was still smoldering and wisps of smoke coiled upward. Massive concrete bunkers were blown apart like collapsed cardboard boxes. Sandbags packed around the machine-gun nests were split open and spilling out their contents. Mountainous heaps of rubble and twisted thickets of steel support rods were littered with Israeli army documents and broken computers and tangled webs of communication-system wiring. A prison the Israelis had fashioned out of steel mesh lay crushed like a broken birdcage. A few stray dogs were picking through piles of food rations—broken boxes of cornflakes, crushed cans of beans, and burst tins of ready-to-eat kosher meals. The rubble left behind was just one more invading foreign empire's footprint left in Lebanon's soil. At the top of the highest turret in the castle, Hezbollah had hoisted its yellow flag, which depicted a fist raising a machine gun, over the central prayer of the Koran, "There is no God but one God." The flag snapped in the morning breeze.

In this chaotic pullout, the Israeli Defense Forces were abandoning the SLA and the Maronite towns and villages of southern Lebanon that had been the Lebanese militia's base. In the Maronite strongholds of Marjayoun, Qlaya, and Dibil, people were anxious about what would happen to them at the hands of Hezbollah. A sense of foreboding had gathered force in the months before the Israeli pullout. But amid that anxiety, there was one SLA commander who seemed to embody what was left of a fighting Crusader spirit. He was the one who was trying to hold it together, to assure his Maronite neighbors that the Israelis would not leave them behind and that their families would remain on the same land that their beloved St.

Maron and Jesus himself had trod. He was Akel Hashem, the top field commander of the SLA.

. . .

Akel Hashem always carried his piece of the cross. It was an ancient sliver of wood enclosed in a gold locket that dangled from a chain around his neck. He believed it was a remnant of the "true cross" upon which his savior, Jesus Christ, had been crucified. It had been presented to him by the Greek Catholic Archbishop of Haifa, Maximus Salloum, for gallant service as a protector of the Christian faith, and it came with a plaque from the Vatican attesting to its authenticity. Every day, as Hashem set out into the war zone of southern Lebanon, he carefully tucked the locket beneath his Israeli-army-issue flak jacket. The 48-year-old father of four always told his wife that this splinter from the cross was better protection than any flak jacket. Alongside the locket on the same chain was a medical medallion with his initials and blood type—"A.H., B-negative." Hashem felt he needed all of these multiple layers of protection—the kevlar vest, the blood supply, and ultimately the cross. He had too many enemies not to.

To the government of Lebanon in Beirut, Hashem was a collaborator with the enemy. The highest court in Lebanon had sentenced him in absentia to life in prison for treason. Hezbollah openly had called for his assassination, having branded him a national traitor and an enemy of Islam. The Syrian government, with its 30,000 troops stationed in Lebanon and its vast network of spies and operatives, also reportedly had marked Hashem for death. Hashem had already narrowly escaped at least five direct assassination attempts. Thanks, he believed, to that sliver of wood.

Hashem saw himself as a citizen soldier, a farmer, and a Christian who throughout his life had protected southern Lebanon from the threat of what he would define as foreign influences—Syria, Iran, and the Palestine Liberation Organization. In different ways and at different points in the past quarter century, each of these groups had exerted its influence over Lebanon. Following the popular axiom of the region—"The enemy of my enemy is my friend"—the threat they posed to Hashem made him an inevitable ally of Israel.

There was a glaring internal contradiction in Hashem's worldview, in that he wanted to save Lebanon from foreign influences but was siding with Israel to do so. But his ability to rationalize this particular contradiction was greatly aided by monetary incentives. Israel paid Hashem and his 1,500 SLA militiamen in U.S. cash dollars every month, and Hashem was said to have made a fortune from this alliance. The mercenary aspect of it revealed perhaps the true essence of Lebanon, a place of complex motivations, with a culture of shadowy deals; a land where politics and money, government and commerce, foreign invaders and local hires had mingled since the time of the Phoenicians.

In April 1975, the fragile balance that held together the demographic mosaic of Lebanon—Muslim, Christian, and Druze—was shattered when gunmen attacked Maronite worshipers at a Sunday church service in a Beirut suburb. In response, Maronite Christian militias attacked PLO headquarters; and the war was on. One year later, Christian militias massacred Palestinians—including some Christian families—in the refugee camps at Karantina and Tel el-Za'atar. The Christian militias wore oversized crosses and Nazi-style army helmets, and they taped icons of the Virgin Mary and of St. George the Dragonslayer to their Israeli-issued machine guns, ready for "cleansing" Palestinians from Lebanon. The Palestinian fighters responded with equal barbarity, invading the coastal town of Damour, killing hundreds of Maronite Christians, and even scattering bones from the Maronite cemeteries there. These events initiated a savage cycle of violence that steadily gathered in destructive force over the next fifteen years, eventually claiming some 70,000 lives.

In the first part of the war, from 1976 to 1982, Akel Hashem was head of intelligence in the Israeli-backed Army of Free Lebanon, in the south's bitter and brutal campaign against at least a dozen PLO factions, including Yasser Arafat's Fatah and George Habash's PFLP, which had controlled much of southern Lebanon since the late 1960s.

In many ways, Hashem's twenty-five-year relationship with the Israeli Defense Forces traced the history of the Jewish state's military involvement in southern Lebanon. But Israel's yearning to exert control in Lebanon had begun long before. Since at least the mid-1950s, Israel had had its eye on Lebanon. Some prominent Israeli leaders actively supported an invasion to set up a puppet Christian government in the south. Israel's intentions in Lebanon first came to light in 1979, when the posthumous memoirs of Israel's former prime minister Moshe Sharett were published despite persistent efforts by the

Israeli government and military to censor it. The book was Israel's equivalent to the Pentagon Papers.

In his memoirs, Sharett reprinted a letter from David Ben-Gurion, dated February 27, 1954, in which Ben-Gurion had written: "Perhaps now is the time to bring about the establishment of a Christian state in our neighborhood. Without our initiative and our energetic help it will not come about. And it seems to me this is now the *central task* or at least *one* of the central tasks of our foreign policy."

Just three months later, Israeli Defense Minister Moshe Dayan would second the idea, according to Sharett's diaries: "According to him [Dayan] the only thing necessary is to find an officer, even just a Major. We should either win his heart or buy him with money, to make him agree to declare himself the savior of the Maronite population. Then the Israeli army will enter Lebanon, will occupy the necessary territory, and will create a Christian regime which will ally itself with Israel. The area from the Litani [River] southward will be totally annexed to Israel and everything will be all right."

The Israelis' saw their first opportunity in 1976, when the Maronite-Palestinian conflict split the ranks in Lebanon's army. Hashem stayed in southern Lebanon to organize what would become the Christian-led forces there. In Beirut and to the north, the Muslims of Lebanon were in control, and they were generally more sympathetic to the Palestinians who had been uprooted and dispossessed by the creation of Israel in 1948. They also harbored deep resentment against the Maronite Christians' hold on power through the National Covenant and their tight control of the economic engines that generated the wealth of Lebanon.

In the now split army divisions, Muslim commanders in Beirut were isolating Christian forces in the south and trying to force them to submit, cutting off their water and electricity. The Israelis saw the plight of the southern Christians in isolated pockets along the border as an opening for them to create an alliance. They began by offering jobs to the Christians across the border in Israel and opening their ports for a flow of goods to the Christians in the south. The economic connections followed the opening of "the good fence," a special gateway between southern Lebanon and northern Israel—a passage availed to those who had proven their willingness to work with the Israelis. When the Israelis moved into the south with direct humanitarian assistance to the Christian population, they arrived with a military presence as well. Within a short time, they had put a stop to cross-border attacks by Palestinian guerrillas and were laying the groundwork for an occupation of southern Lebanon that could be adjusted in scale and intensity as needed. The Israelis trumpeted to the world their protection of the Lebanese Christians and played up the Western Christians' "abandonment" of their coreligionists, who had been cynically sacrificed to oil interests. When Israel's Likud Party leader Menachem Begin came to power in 1977, he especially stressed this theme.

By this time, the Lebanese Christians were rushing headlong into Israel's arms. In March 1978, Israel invaded Lebanon, sending a massive movement of tanks and armored personnel carriers and divisions of soldiers over the border and directly past the United Nations forces, which were completely overwhelmed by the offensive. The Israelis had set out on a new and controversial policy of "preemptive strike," vowing not only to carry out direct reprisals for cross-border attacks by the PLO but also to search out and destroy any other targets they deemed threatening. Four years later, after Begin's reelection, the new defense minister, Ariel Sharon, became the chief architect of a no-holds-barred militarism—some would say adventurism—in Lebanon. On June 4 and 5, 1982, Sharon led a ground invasion force accompanied by punishing air strikes deep into Lebanon. Israel dubbed it Operation Peace for Galilee, and stated its intention as the establishment of a twenty-five-mile-deep demilitarized zone. Israeli fighter jets equipped with advanced U.S. technology and missile systems quickly destroyed eighty of Syria's old Soviet-made aircraft—about one quarter of its air force. On June 11, a humiliated Syria agreed to a cease-fire. Two days later, Israel surrounded West Beirut and its population of roughly 500,000 Palestinians and predominantly Muslim Lebanese, initiating a siege that would last seventy days. Throughout the summer, Israel carried out massive shelling of PLO bases, and at times waged indiscriminate attacks on the civilian population, in a relentless campaign to finally force the PLO to flee Lebanon. This was a brutal campaign that went far beyond Israel's stated objectives, and it was harshly criticized in Washington, but it worked. American envoy Philip Habib brokered a withdrawal agreement, and at the end of August thousands of the PLO's guerrilla forces left by boat and by road for Tunis. Even as the withdrawal was being carried out, the Christian politician Bashir Gemayel was elected president of Lebanon. He was the son of Pierre Gemayel, founder of the right-wing Lebanese Phalange party, which was inspired by the Phalange youth movement that originated in Nazi Germany in the 1930s and in totalitarian Spain. Despite the Gemayel family's connections to this dark past, Israeli officials believed that Gemayel was their best bet for achieving Israel's longstanding ambitions in Lebanon. But less than one month later, on September 14, the Phalange party headquarters was bombed, and Bashir Gemayel was found dead in the rubble.

Revenge was swiftly and massively exacted by the militant Christians of the Lebanese Forces. The Israelis urged them on, insisting that terror cells operating out of the Palestinian refugee camps in West Beirut were responsible for the bombing. Two days after the assassination of Gemayel, the Israeli-allied Lebanese Christian militias massacred upwards of 800 Palestinian refugees, including men, women, and children, in the Sabra and Shatila refugee camps. (Palestinian witnesses placed the death toll above 2,000, but accurate numbers are unavailable.) There were reports of infants' limbs having been hacked off and of crosses having been carved into the flesh of victims. All of this unfolded as the Israeli troops surrounded the camps. Israel's own official and independent investigation, the Kahan Commission, established that Israeli commanders and troops knew what was going on inside the camp and did nothing to stop the slaughter. Sharon himself was held indirectly responsible for the unspeakable atrocities and was forced to resign as defense minister.

The horrific Israeli campaign to expel the PLO from Lebanon had strengthened the hand of a new enemy—Hezbollah. Iran's Shiite Islamic revolution was only a few years old then, and the Shiite Muslims of Hezbollah would be among the most eager regional importers of the anti-American and anti-Israeli fury of the Ayatollah. The world was introduced to Hezbollah in 1983, when the group purportedly took part in the truck bombing of the U.S. Marine barracks in Beirut, in which some two hundred forty American servicemen were killed. Hezbollah gained further notoriety with a series of kidnappings of Westerners in Lebanon in the mid-1980s.

Over the next two decades, with the Israelis occupying southern Lebanon and the Syrians and Iranians vying for power in the rest of the country, Hezbollah became an important and respected social movement that sought to improve the lives of poor, disenfranchised

Shiite Muslims. Its leaders also established a disciplined guerrilla army, with a core of no more than five hundred fighters, whose strategic strikes against Israel were by the mid-1990s wearing down one of the most powerful armies in the world. With nightly television news images of the casualties and heart-wrenching funerals at Israel's military cemeteries, a movement was being galvanized in Israel to pull out of Lebanon. In 1999, Ehud Barak was elected Israeli prime minister, in large part on a campaign promise to pull Israeli troops out of the quagmire by July 2000.

To Akel Hashem, Barak's vow meant a future bloodbath for the Maronites in southern Lebanon. As Israel's self-proclaimed withdrawal date approached, Hashem sought to calm the nerves of the Christian families in his neighborhood. A unilateral Israeli withdrawal, in the absence of a regional peace agreement, would leave the SLA fighters and their families even more dangerously exposed to retaliatory attacks by the Hezbollah guerrillas. There were reports that the Israelis were building a community in northern Israel to house Lebanese exiles who feared for their lives if they remained. The SLA soldiers were bitter, feeling that they had been betrayed by all sides. Only Hashem kept them from giving way to despair.

By 2000, Hashem's SLA forces were no longer made up solely of Christians. A large number of Shiite Muslim fighters were among them as well. They constituted the lower ranks of the militia, earning about U.S. $400 a month in a desperately poor region where war had left few options other than mercenary work. Senior officers made as much as U.S. $700 a month. All of them were paid in cash by Israel, and if "the zone" heated up, they occasionally received overtime pay. Hashem, his SLA colleagues said, was paid far more than any of his soldiers. In fact, some estimated that he had amassed millions of dollars in French bank accounts, thanks to his special skills, which were invaluable to Israel (such as fluency in Hebrew, a unique esprit de corps as commander on the ground, and a willingness to kill the Lebanese). The nominal commander in chief of the SLA, General Antoine Lahad, was 70 years old and living in a Paris apartment, far from the conflict. Lahad was not a native of the south, which further alienated him from the ground troops. Hashem was not only a native son but earned the loyalty and respect of the troops every day by wading with them into the fray.

Hashem, tall and charismatic, was popular not only among the

Christians but among the Shiite and Sunni Muslim SLA members as well. But even with this kind of interfaith camouflage, few would argue that the SLA's leadership was anything but Christian—and specifically, Maronite Catholic. Those who led the SLA believed they were fighting for the soul of Lebanon. They saw Hashem as the last remaining bulwark of the Maronite Christian ideal of Lebanon. Their Lebanon.

A Western diplomat in Beirut scoffed at this self-perception of the SLA as classic Maronite propaganda: "The SLA is not inherently Christian, it is only inherently Lebanese, which is to say, on the take. The Israelis paid them more than anyone else was willing to, and offered them protection. That is why the SLA is with Israel; the rest of it is delusional." Perhaps. But it was still the way the Christian-led SLA rationalized its collaboration with Israel. And Hashem was quite convincing about his belief in preserving Christians in Lebanon—and by extension, Muslims and Druze as well—from the influence or dominance of Syria and Iran. The Christians of the south saw Hashem as their savior; he was all they had left

On Sunday, January 30, 2000, Hashem attended the funeral of an elderly resident in the village of Dibil, where Hashem was born and still lived. He made sure he was there for every funeral and baptism in the town that he had sworn he would never leave until the day he too was buried. He had even built a new cemetery for Dibil, with a space reserved for his own grave, to make the point. That Sunday, after the funeral, Hashem descended the winding road from his hilltop villa to a farmhouse he owned, set amid fertile fields soaked by winter rains and still a few months away from planting. His wife, Layya, was at home, preparing a meal that she would later bring down to the farmhouse. Hashem was going to the shed to gather logs for the wood stove, but he never reached the woodpile. When he was just a few steps away, he was blown apart by an explosion, the first in a series. Hezbollah guerrillas on a nearby hillside detonated the sequence of bombs with a remote control.

The guerrillas, who had taken to videotaping their operations, had clear footage of the attack, one of their most precise and decisive assassinations in the sixteen-year resistance. On the videotape, the sound of the guerrillas rejoicing at the direct hit could be heard. Hezbollah knew that the tape of the assassination would be played and replayed from Beirut to Tel Aviv to New York, on every nightly news broadcast. And they were right; the footage became symbolic of a turning point. As did the footage of the following day's parade of Hezbollah supporters, rejoicing in the streets of their stronghold in the southern suburbs of Beirut and passing out baskets of candy to celebrate Hashem's death. These images were deeply troubling to the SLA. Panic was setting in among the troops. Even some of the most committed SLA men could see the writing on the wall. When Hashem died, so did South Lebanon Maronites' faith in the future.

At Hashem's funeral, thousands of mourners, including senior Israeli military officials, packed into the small church in Dibil, for a mass presided over by Maronite Catholic bishop Maroun Sader, who blessed the fallen commander in a glowing eulogy, describing Hashem as a "Christian martyr" who had "fought and died to preserve the Christian heritage of Lebanon, something he believed in his whole life." But even as the bishop spoke, Hezbollah guerrillas were ambushing three soldiers of the Israeli Defense Forces. They had stepped up their operations. Within one week of Hashem's funeral, the names of five Israeli soldiers had been added to the casualty list, along with those of five SLA soldiers. Dozens were wounded in the escalating violence. The scenes on Israeli television of soldiers diving for cover and trying to evacuate the wounded were hauntingly reminiscent of Vietnam, stark images of the limitations of the legendary Israeli military, and painful reminders that it was time to get out.

Even for a journalist, travel to Lebanon from Israel at this time was an exercise in war's absurdities. When I set off in late February 2000, a month after Hashem's death, I was forced to travel southeast first, in order to head northwest. The direct route—straight up the northern coast of Israel into Lebanon—would have been about a three-hour drive. But the border was a war zone, and I couldn't just walk in from enemy territory. The typical route for journalists based in Jerusalem was to cross the Jordan River to Amman, and then to catch a flight over Syria to Beirut. I would head south from there.

Any physical indication that I was coming from Israel could have been grounds for deportation from Lebanon—and for that matter, from many other Arab countries, including Syria, Iraq, and the Gulf states. So I conducted a bizarre cleansing ritual en route. First, I took all the Israeli currency out of my wallet and shed my Israeli press identification cards, as well as all receipts and business cards containing Israeli addresses or Hebrew writing. Second, I threw out my Israeli toothpaste and shaving cream. Third, I removed the batteries with Hebrew writing from my tape recorder and shortwave radio. Fourth, I switched to my "Arab world" business cards, listing an office address in Cairo. Fifth, I deleted all files with Israeli datelines from my laptop computer. Last, I made sure I had packed what is referred to in the trade as a "clean passport." This was a backup U.S. passport that I used only in the Arab world, because any stamp of entrance to or exit from Israel likely would result in interrogation and perhaps deportation. In Lebanon, it was illegal even to speak on the phone with someone in Israel, never mind to enter the country with an Israeli visa. The whole ridiculous procedure captured the essence of the modern Middle East and the unrelenting paranoia with which much of the Arab world views Israel. It seemed to me that the old enmities would never die, even after a half century of Arab-Israeli conflict. Israel was still deeply isolated from its neighbors, except Jordan and Egypt; and even on those two borders it was a cold peace, at best.

My journey from Beirut into "the zone" began with a stretch of highway that, of all roads from Beirut, was perhaps the most densely mined with bombs, as our driver Boutros reminded my translator and me. The explosive devices were usually packed inside imitation rocks made of plastic, which could be found in Beirut garden stores, where they were sold as casings for pool and patio lights. They were most commonly detonated by a remote control. These bombs had proven Hezbollah's most damaging weapons in its guerrilla war against Israel and the SLA. An overturned and burned-out carcass of an Israeli armored personnel carrier on the side of the road was a fresh reminder of that.

Boutros's old, beat-up Mercedes with its cracked windshield wound deeper into the craggy folds of southern Lebanon. The road cut cleanly along the border of Israel, near the settlement of Metulla, directly overlooking the red tile roofs and white stucco of its orderly homes with their small lawns, and its neatly laid-out streets. The northern Israeli community was no more than three hundred yards away, and all I could think of as we drove by was that from here Israelis were easily within pistol range. We passed an Israeli farmer on a tractor tilling the soil on an adjacent kibbutz, and we were close enough that I could see that he was wearing a New York Yankees cap. From this vantage point, Israel's security zone made sense, starkly revealing just how high the stakes were in protecting this area from any armed groups carrying out cross-border attacks.

As the road climbed upward into the western sector, toward Dibil, the ruins of what had been a Palestinian village appeared on the roadside—slabs of concrete collapsed in upon each other and rebar sticking out at crazy angles. What was left of the cement window casings had been chewed up by heavy-caliber machine gun fire. The few standing walls were punched and pockmarked by mortar fire. We entered Dibil and found the home of Hashem's family, which was still in mourning. An Israeli armored personnel carrier adorned with black bunting was parked in front. SLA soldiers stood guard outside. The sound of a choir practicing at the nearby church was momentarily drowned out by the dull roar of an Israeli fighter jet cruising high overhead. Hashem's widow greeted us in the foyer, surrounded by her two teenage sons and Hashem's six brothers. The sprawling home was decorated with French settees and high-backed chairs and antique chests cluttered with delicate French Colonial figurines. On the wall at the entry was a gallery of pictures of Hashem with high-ranking Israeli generals, prime ministers, and with the Maronite patriarch Sfeir. Layya led us to a sitting room.

Dressed in a black but fashionably styled outfit, she perched on a Parisian antique couch and clutched a small silk throw pillow to her chest as she spoke. "He was a pillar, a Christian pillar supporting Lebanon," she said, her eyes red. "He is gone, and people feel lost and do not know what to do. In Beirut, Christians do not have freedom of expression to say what they think. They live as a minority, they act as a minority, they are afraid to assert what they believe. So when Hashem died, Christians in Beirut felt a loss as well. They cried silently because they hoped that liberation for them might come from here in the south."

Layya explained that Hashem had refused to even think of leaving Lebanon. Since his death, she confessed, she had begun preparations for a possible move to Paris, or perhaps Sydney. But she said Hashem had clung to the belief that the Israelis would pull out their troops only within the framework of a regional peace agreement with Syria and Lebanon, an agreement that would grant those who served in the SLA leniency, if not amnesty.

Sitting next to Layya was their oldest son, Elias. A freshman at Israel's Haifa University, he already had one foot out of the country. I noticed that around his neck he wore the gold locket that his father had always carried. The piece of the cross had somehow survived the blast and had been passed on to him by his mother. He twisted the pendant self-consciously, watching his mother and listening intently to his uncles as they assessed the future of southern Lebanon.

Akel Hashem had been the second oldest of seven brothers—all of them loyal soldiers in the SLA—who now sat clustered in chairs and couches around the living room. Each was dressed in nearly the same outfit—black turtleneck, silky dark blue bomber jacket, heavy black boots, and tight jeans—as if the brothers intuitively had created a uniform for their own family militia. They explained that the Hashems had come to southern Lebanon two hundred years earlier, from a northern village in the rugged peaks of Mount Lebanon. Three members of the clan had been killed by Palestinians during fighting in the 1970s. But even apart from these war-related deaths, the Hashem men had been slowly disappearing for decades through emigration. The brothers estimated that at least one-third of the extended family (about three hundred individuals) had emigrated to America or Europe since the start of the civil war in 1975. The other large Christian clans of Dibil had an even higher rate of emigration, and some families had left Lebanon altogether. But the Hashem brothers were considered fierce fighters, and they would be loyal to the end.

The brothers wanted to show me the cemetery where Akel was buried. They had used heavy steel plates to weld his crypt closed after Hezbollah's spiritual leader, Sheikh Hassan Nasrallah, threatened in a speech broadcast over the radio to dig up Akel's grave so that his body could not be laid to rest in Lebanon.

Joseph, the oldest brother, said: "They want us to leave, they want to be rid of the Christians. But we have an obligation here. This is the land where Jesus walked, this is where Christianity began, this is where the Maronite faith began fifteen hundred years ago. This is not something we wanted to say in front of Layya, but we will not leave without a fight."

Less resolve was evident among the other residents of Dibil. A young couple who lived near the church, Tony and Najat Nassif, invited me into their home. They looked exhausted, and explained that they had been kept up all night trying to comfort their two frightened toddlers during a series of Israeli air raids that had pounded the nearby hills. Tony was a teacher in a public school, and his employer was the Lebanese government. But, as he put it, "Everyone here is in the SLA in one way or another." As we spoke, Tony's uncle Yakoub Nassif, Dibil's parish priest for forty-five years, stopped in. They sat drinking tea, huddled around an electric heater as the late afternoon sun began to fade. Father Yakoub explained that in the 1960s there had been 4,000 people in the parish. Now there were no more than 1,500. About half, he said, had emigrated. The families left in waves, some as early as World War I. When civil war broke out in 1975, a huge wave crested and crashed down on foreign shores. When the Israeli invasion came in 1982, still another exodus occurred. And now another hemorrhage was under way. Many others had migrated internally, to Beirut, to get away from the fighting and the dire economic situation. "Those who have left dream of coming back, but realize that it will not happen. And those who are in Beirut are in depression about the situation. The Christians here feel trapped," he said.

Tony politely waited for his uncle to finish, and then said: "If we could leave now, we would. Our children were screaming and crying from the bombing last night. There is no work. The Hezbollah militias fire their guns in celebration at night at the death of our friend and neighbor Akel."

His wife, Najat, said: "Last night I went to bed clutching rosary beads and praying through the bombs and watched the sun come up to the sound of the muezzin. We can't live like this." She added that her sister and brother-in-law had finally gotten out, after years of trying. They had moved to Dallas and were hoping to bring Najat and her family there as well. For now, Tony and Najat clung to that hope. They did not want to retreat to Israel, because it would more than likely mean that they could never return to Lebanon. They were hoping to hang on in southern Lebanon until they could make an orderly exit to Texas. Our conversation ended when Najat's sister telephoned from the United States. She was checking to see how they were faring, having heard news reports of the escalation of violence.

"The Christians who have any ability to leave, will leave," Tony said as he walked me back to Boutros's car. He was speaking more bluntly, now that he was out of earshot of his wife and young son. "The weak Christians will convert to Islam. The strong Christians will know that their only way out may be death. This situation is coming. Not for us, but for our children. I believe that."

Back in Beirut, I visited Simon Karam, former Lebanese ambassador to Washington. Karam hailed from Jezzine, a Christian burg in southern Lebanon that had been under Israeli occupation until June

1999. Karam was generally considered one of the most eloquent political analysts in Beirut, a thinker who approached issues with a sweeping view of history, an open mind, and a yearning for a Lebanon free of all foreign influence—an unpopular stance, in the current, Syrian-dominated Lebanese power structure. Karam was fond of saying, regarding Syria's using Lebanon for leverage in its negotiations with Israel, "Lebanon should be at the table, not on the table."

Karam was a Maronite by religion but not by politics. This was an important distinction. Karam did not share in the cultural arrogance of the Maronite political parties, in their open elitism, and often racism, toward the other groups in the country, as though they were Phoenicians looking down on the Muslims or the Arabs. (The Maronites typically set themselves apart from Arab culture by stressing their links to Phoenicia, the ancient coastal city-state they believed was the source of Lebanese civilization—although there is no historical evidence that Lebanon's Christians are any more "Phoenician" than are its Muslims.) Karam believed that in the aftermath of the civil war, the Christians of Lebanon had reached a fateful point in their history.

"The closing of the twentieth century marks an ending of a Lebanon where Christians had a preeminent place, where their freedom was ensured and their prosperity was engendered," he said. "It is the end of an experiment in history, an experiment in which Lebanon would be a nation where Christians within an overwhelmingly Muslim Middle East would have their own place. In the ultimate collapse of this experiment, the Christians themselves are to blame for many things, but not everything.

"For hundreds of years they had been successful in preventing empires from leveling this unique existence, their Christian face in a Muslim world, their links to Europe and the Vatican. They resisted the Mamluks, the Ottomans. The Christians were shrewd enough to always enlist Western powers to help them, and this worked. But at a great cost in the way those around them viewed them.

"I would say their own failure of leadership was their ultimate shortcoming. They did not know how to rule. And when the Christian right in this country took on the Palestinians, they opened the door to the wolves. No longer was it a European call for help, but an invitation to neighboring powers Israel and Syria, which had little concern for their notion of a Christian state."

. . .

Amid the ravages of civil war, the Christians fled Lebanon in the largest numbers. During the fifteen years of fighting, from 1975 to 1990, 850,000 Lebanese Christians fled the country, according to an official at the Lebanese Ministry of Foreign Affairs, about 160,000 of whom emigrated to France and about 150,000 of whom settled in the United States. The rest were scattered among Canada, Australia, and Latin America. In the 1990s the rate of emigration did not slow down. In fact, it accelerated for both Muslims and Christians, according to Boutros Labaki, a professor at St. Joseph's University, who has tracked the emigration patterns. In 1996, 190,000 emigrated; in 1997, 152,000; and in 1998, 173,000.

As for how many Christians were left, none knew the number with any precision. The last government census in Lebanon was completed in 1932. This fact shows how explosive population figures are in this country made up of some sixteen vying sects—truly a collection of minorities. As Farid Khazen, a political science professor at the American University in Beirut, put it, "Every group needs its own lies." The 1932 survey counted the Christians as 51.2 percent of the population; but the current World Fact Book (published by the U.S. State Department) states that Christians now make up an estimated 30 percent of Lebanon's 3.7 million inhabitants. Lebanon's Christian leaders say this estimate is too low, whereas Hezbollah leaders say it is too high. Even church officials, notorious for inflating the numbers, privately concur that no more than 1 million residents, or about 28 percent of the country, are Christian. Lebanese academics increasingly use the figure of 25 percent.

The Christians' loss of political power, and of their demographic claim to that power, is partly of their own making—a direct result of their having greedily clung to the reins of government throughout the 1960s and 1970s. Their unwillingness to share power ignited a war with Muslims—a war that the Christians lost, although in the process they committed some of the most unspeakable atrocities. Christian militias also fought viciously among themselves in the final months of the war. Most Christians would say that the Palestinians had started the conflict, not the Christians; but few would deny that it was the Christians who lost it. The loss, however, is also Lebanon's: The Christian exodus has been unrelenting, and it has drained

Lebanon of many of its best minds—many of its most gifted professionals, its skilled laborers, its wealthiest bankers, and its most promising young students.

The Christians left in larger numbers than the Muslims because they could afford to and because over the generations they had developed closer ties to the West through religious-based school affiliations and extended family trees that had branched out into Europe and America. Their exodus, combined with higher Muslim birthrates and a concerted government policy of assimilating hundreds of thousands of Muslim immigrants, has dramatically altered Lebanon's demographic landscape. At the time of my visit, there were also some 300,000 Palestinians, virtually all of them Muslim, still living in U.N. refugee camps in Lebanon, along with 1 million Syrian workers.

By the year 2000, the fragile balance that had so tenuously held together Lebanon's population of Christians, Sunni and Shiite Muslims, and Druze was threatened. What was once a clear Christian majority fully in charge of a wealthy country had become an embattled minority that feared an unstable future. Christians worried that Lebanon's once robust free market economy would never be resurrected, and that Beirut's unique prewar character as a secular society and cultural melting pot was being destroyed by Hezbollah's social intolerance.

Hezbollah had become a powerful political force within postwar Lebanon, and the largest party in the Lebanese parliament. In the years since its founding in 1982, Hezbollah's mission had expanded from resisting Israeli occupation to establishing an Islamic state. One of Lebanon's leading historians, Kamal Salibi, a Christian, said that Hezbollah's mix of social justice and resistance strongly appealed to Muslim youths. This, he added, was why their movement was feared not only by Christians but also in almost equal measure by secular Sunni Muslims, who, he said, were "terrified by the emergence of Islamic clericalism." He continued: "They have an umbilical attachment to the Christians as the preservers of secular government, and more importantly, a secular way of life. The secular Muslims say, 'Don't leave us alone against this monster that threatens our lives, our ability to have a drink at a bar, to watch movies, to have a culture we want.'"

Farid Khazen of the American University in Beirut said that Hezbollah and other non-Christian political parties had diluted the Christian role in a power-sharing formula established under the Taif

Agreement, which had ended the civil war. That agreement had spelled out that Christians must hold exactly half the seats in parliament and have a permanent claim on the presidency. The rest of the legislative body, and the country's prime ministership, were the domain of the Muslims. The Muslim parties effectively shifted executive power to the prime minister's office. Then they redrew electoral districts to prevent any powerful Christian politicians from emerging. It was, Khazen says, "what you would call good old-fashioned gerrymandering." As a result, Christian seats fell into the hands of weak candidates loyal to Syria, which effectively controlled the country with the compliance of the Lebanese government and military. Christian boycotts of the flawed elections compounded the problem, as Hezbollah consistently made a strong showing, and secured a power base in Beirut's southern suburbs. The December 1999 election of a Christian president, the popular General Emile Lahoud, exemplified this new reality, said Khazen. At first, the Christians saw him as their political savior, but he soon came to be widely viewed as just another Syrian puppet.

The Christians' loss of power was also evident in the Ministry of the Displaced, where the money for those displaced by the civil war was disproportionately doled out to Muslims and Druze, even though the Christians had a higher rate of displacement and had lost more land during the conflict. Worse yet, the government official who controlled the portfolio of the Ministry of the Displaced was the Druze leader and former warlord Walid Joumblatt, who had been a sworn enemy of the Christian militias during the war. From the Christian point of view, the man responsible for their displacement was now denying them the fair level of funding to rebuild their lives. "The Christians have clung to their role in business, academic institutions, and medicine. But in politics, they are losing. And they are losing dramatically," says Khazen. "Will this political marginalization erode Lebanon's uniquely pluralistic society? My sense is, it will."

As the Christians left, they took their money with them. There had been an estimated $5 billion in Christian capital flight from Lebanon since the war—capital that had at least doubled in value since then. Many economists believed the country would have to regain the confidence of the Christian business and banking elite—and the capital they had exported—if it was to successfully rebuild after the war's devastation.

. . .

Carved into a steep cliffside of the mountains overlooking Beirut was the seat of the Maronite patriarchate. A French-style courtyard led to a long gallery of lush oriental carpeting. At the end, seated in a red-satin high-backed chair and wearing silk vestments, was the Maronite patriarch Nasrallah Boutros Sfeir. As the Maronites' political influence has waned, the church has become the center of the community's political cohesion. The overstated French decor made the Maronites' waning power somehow more painfully obvious.

The Maronites had been greatly influenced by French missionaries in the nineteenth century. And after World War I, when the French mandate carved out a state for the Maronites in Lebanon, they became more French than the French. The Maronite elite spoke mostly French, typically using Arabic only to speak to the hired help. They built French schools. Those who could afford it shipped their children off to university in Paris. The Maronites fashioned their Lebanon as a kind of French province within the Middle East.

But the Christian sect had been founded as a form of cult worship around the teachings of the bearded fourth-century sage St Maron. They were branded heretics by the Byzantine church because of an eccentric Christology that set them apart from the accepted teaching on the "true nature" of Christ, as the church in Constantinople defined it. The persecution they faced for their beliefs was plainly brutal, and the Maronites retreated from Syria into the unapproachable granite ridges and valleys of Mount Lebanon. For centuries they dwelled in the Mount's impenetrable gorges and cliffs, defending themselves from their enemies—first the Byzantine imperial forces, and then the Islamic conquest. The huge monasteries they carved into those cliffs now are largely empty, except for a few rugged but aging monks and frail nuns. When the Crusaders stormed across the land from Europe on their way to Jerusalem, the Maronites aligned themselves with these barbaric armies of the cross. This event marked the beginning of their affinity with the West. In the twelfth century, the Maronites accepted the "primacy" of the teachings of Roman Catholicism and established a connection with Rome that would eventually bring them officially under the aegis of the Vatican, making them the first of the so-called Uniate churches within the Catholic fold.

"The Christian church has been here from the dawn of Christianity," said the patriarch Sfeir. "But what we see today is very sad for us. We see the Christian majority shrink to a minority. We fear it will shrink even more. The Christians have no confidence, no trust in the future. Many Lebanese would come back if they trusted the situation. These are very wealthy and very important people for the strength of this country. We have to find a way to bring people back."

The flight of Lebanon's Maronites was recognized by the Vatican as a profound issue for the future of the Catholic Church in the Middle East when the civil war ended in 1990. Rome convened a unique synod on Lebanon and spent seven years paving the way for a historic visit by Pope John Paul II in May 1997. The council created a dialogue for reconciliation between Christians and Muslims, which church officials saw as the first step to rebuilding the country and stanching the outflow.

The pope's pilgrimage to Lebanon reinvigorated the Christian community, which had felt shunted to the margins. The highlight of the pilgrimage was a papal mass that drew some 500,000 people in a country of less than 4 million. In his 194-page Apostolic Exhortation, *A New Hope for Lebanon,* the pontiff issued a challenge to the Maronite community, especially the youth, to be "the recipients of the message of renewal your Church and your country need." The document did not allow self-pity by the Christians but called instead for a spiritual renewal, which would have to occur before any political or social renewal would be possible. The document surprised the Greek Orthodox and Muslim communities, not to mention the Maronites themselves, by speaking in favor of the Catholics of Lebanon strengthening their solidarity with the rest of the Arab world. The pope cautioned against a faith that had become "tribalized" and encouraged the Maronites to examine their historical reliance on the West. This bold document was a road map for Maronites and for all Middle Eastern Christians seeking to find their way out of despair.

Mohammad Samak was one of the most instrumental Sunni Muslim participants in the Vatican synod that had preceded the pope's visit. When I visited him in his office, he was head of the government's Christian-Muslim committee for dialogue and a senior aide to Prime Minister Rafik al-Hariri. Samak articulated the concerns felt by many Muslim leaders about the diminishing Christian presence: "Christians are more financially versed and richer than Muslims. They have more experience in banking, and they have better connections to and understanding of the free market. When they leave and turn their back on Lebanon, they do great damage to this country."

His conclusion was blunt. "We will need each other to survive," he said.

. . .

On May 23, 2000, the Israeli occupation of southern Lebanon disintegrated. Within twenty-four hours of the chaotically executed Israeli retreat, the SLA forces collapsed. The first domino fell in the largely Shiite central sector of the security zone—an event that had been predicted years before by many Christians in the SLA. But even they had not foreseen the surprising rapidity with which the Shiite members of the Israeli proxy militia would turn themselves in to Lebanese government authorities to face prosecution as collaborators. The Shiites' mass defection from the SLA guaranteed the force's demise. The Christian leaders of the SLA fled across the border to Israel, where most were preparing to emigrate to France, Canada, and the United States. The Christians who stayed behind in their villages in southern Lebanon hid in their homes and feared the worst.

The next morning, I was with a group of Western journalists documenting the precipitous collapse. We drove into the zone behind a group of Hezbollah fighters who were jump-starting abandoned Israeli bulldozers and clearing the road of blockades that the retreating SLA and Israeli troops had set up. And as we pushed into the small villages, thousands of people lined the roadsides, cheering their "liberators." The Hezbollah guerrillas had been caught by surprise by the rapid SLA retreat and were in no position to wage a coordinated attack on the withdrawing troops—an act they had vowed to carry out for months. The ammunition dumps the SLA had ignited before leaving were still exploding in the early morning light.

We drove several miles down the road, through Shiite Muslim villages, creeping along behind a tank with a dozen Hezbollah soldiers piled atop it. One of them was waving a huge Hezbollah banner. Another yellow flag was hoisted on the gun turret. They were chanting, "God, oh God, victory to Hezbollah!" The Shiite Muslim villagers standing in clusters along the roadside were pelting the tank and our car with rice and flower petals, the customary Lebanese greeting for victors. (Ironically, the Israeli invading forces had been welcomed in this fashion by the Maronites two decades before.)

When we arrived at what had been the SLA headquarters in Marjayoun, the scene was like something out of the film *The Road Warrior.* Guerrilla fighters from Hezbollah, and the less-disciplined militiamen of the Shiite Amal (*Amal* means "hope") organization, were rushing around, collecting abandoned tanks, heavy-caliber machine guns, armored personnel carriers, rocket-propelled grenade launchers, warehouses of ammunition, and machine guns. Five men in black fatigues and black leather baseball caps were loading all the firepower they could find into an old T-55 Russian tank festooned with yellow Hezbollah flags. Gunfire crackled around the former headquarters as several other men in green fatigues shot open the locks on warehouses and began carrying out ammunition crates for heavy machine guns. Another man was lifting an artillery gun and its mount into the back of a pickup truck. Within a half hour, I counted more than two hundred guerrillas and militiamen loading up on heavy weapons. Others were picking through the offices of the former military leaders of the SLA, rifling through documents and ripping computers and televisions out of wall sockets to be loaded onto trucks and old, beat-up cars outside. An SLA poster of Akel Hashem, with the words *Dead Man* scrawled in black ink across it, had been half ripped from one office wall

Abu Jafar, a 37-year-old supporter of Hezbollah, was loading two machine guns and boxes of ammunition into a rusted Toyota with a yellow Hezbollah flag attached to the antenna. "This is the happiest day in Lebanon's history," he said. "The Israelis have never lost a war in fifty-two years, and now they are tasting defeat, thank God, to Hezbollah." When asked about the Christians' fear of Hezbollah reprisals, he replied: "If they are collaborators, they should turn themselves in. If they are not collaborators, they have nothing to fear."

But they are very afraid for the future, I told him.

"No, no, no. This is Israeli propaganda. We are the same. We are brothers. We are like this," he said putting two callused fingers together and not even flinching as he shouted over the explosions around him. "For twenty-two years the Israelis have told the world that we are divided, and none of it is true."

All around us, the mob was growing. People were looting everything they could get their hands on—army blankets, sweaters, sleeping bags, backpacks, helmets, ammunition canisters, television sets, refrigerators, typewriters, food rations. Teenagers were draping themselves in machine-gun belts and firing off rounds in the air. We drove farther down the road, past the square at the center of town, where Hezbollah supporters had just toppled the bronze statue of Saad Haddad, the Maronite army major who had founded the SLA.

By late morning the narrow roads in southern Lebanon were completely jammed with jubilant supporters of the Hezbollah and Amal militias. Horns blared triumphantly as beat-up cars with flags fluttering from their antennas crawled through the rugged, dramatic landscape. Thousands of cars were parked along the road leading to Beaufort Castle. Lebanese families, most of them Shiite, were flocking to Beaufort for a close-up look at what had been a hated and feared symbol of Israeli occupation. Now the fortress was theirs.

From Beaufort we headed south, to the Shiite village of Khiam, crawling through buildings chewed down and pocked by heavy-caliber machine gun fire. Khiam had been the address of the most notorious prison of the Israeli occupation. Human Rights Watch and Amnesty International, two of the world's leading human rights monitoring organizations, had issued scathing reports on Khiam prison, calling it a place where "torture is endemic." Stories had trickled out through the years of systematic torture, of extrajudicial killing, rape, and arbitrary arrest and detention. Israel had long denied its involvement at the Khiam prison; but just several months before the pullout, it had admitted in an Israeli Supreme Court case that Israeli officers had trained SLA officers there in "methods of interrogation." Akel Hashem had been one of those responsible for what went on in Khiam. In an interview with Israel's leading newspaper, *Ha'aretz*, in October 1999, Hashem had been quoted as saying: "If I were to tell you that there are no beatings going on there, I would be lying. They conduct interrogations the way they should be done. If someone made a mistake, he is interrogated in the proper manner, a bit of force, a bit of fear. It is an investigation, right? . . . If someone conceals an explosive charge or fires on an IDF convoy, how can you get information out of him? By asking nicely? By giving him a cup of coffee? There are many ways to get the truth out of a person."

The night before, after the Israeli pullback and SLA collapse, the

Shiite residents of Khiam tentatively, nervously began to gather outside the prison. They didn't know how many SLA soldiers might still be inside, guarding its walls, or whether they might try to open fire. The crowd began gathering by the hundreds and chanting "Allahu akbar!"—"God is great."

Inside the thick concrete walls and barbed wire of the prison, the inmates responded with chants of "Allahu akbar!" About ten nervous SLA prison guards, all Maronite Christians, came to the front gate with their weapons drawn and ordered the crowd back. The guards said that if they were allowed to exit safely, no one would get hurt and everyone would have free access to the prison. The crowd moved back. The SLA guards pulled their vehicles cautiously through, and then tore off to collect their families and head for the Israeli border.

Using sledgehammers, pickaxes, metal chairs, and anything else they could get their hands on, the Shiite residents of Khiam broke open the locks of the prison's fetid cells. A Hezbollah camera crew was on hand to document this scene. This was Hezbollah's Bastille. And the Maronites were the ancien régime, running for their lives.

The morning after the liberation, many of the former inmates—some of whom had been imprisoned since 1986—were still on the scene, waiting for their families to retrieve them. Thin, battered, and thrilled to be free, they became tour guides of the gruesome prison chambers and interrogation rooms. Khader al-Goul, who had spent eight years in the prison, led a tour of Hezbollah sheikhs, Lebanese citizens, and Western reporters through the maze of cells and dark passageways. In the hallways hung soiled blue hoods that had been placed over the inmates' heads during questioning and beating. Scattered on the ground were handcuffs, leg irons, wooden batons, and wire whips that had been used in "interrogation" sessions. "This is cell number 2. This is where the torture occurred," he said. "It was the worst of the interrogation rooms."

Deeper into the concrete labyrinth of the prison, the smell of urine and excrement became overwhelming. The plastic buckets the inmates had used were full to overflowing. He stopped at cell number 10. "This is where Bilal Salman was killed," he said, holding up a cigarette lighter to illuminate the darkened hole—a concrete box with no ventilation, measuring roughly five feet by five feet.

Throughout the tiers of the prison, the inmates' tattered belongings were lying about. Old, ripped clothing hung from a line between the rows of triple bunks. A backgammon table. A scattered deck of cards. Egg cartons fashioned into shelves. Prayer books. Scraps of paper. The walls were scratched with graffiti and drawings and verses of the Koran. In the administrative offices, Israeli-issue plastic riot shields were piled in a corner. There was also an SLA roster of twenty-five guards, twenty-two of whom had obviously Christian names.

Al-Goul, a Shiite Muslim and guerrilla fighter for Hezbollah, said he hoped the prison would be preserved exactly the way it was. "I'd like to show the world what happened here," he said.

. . .

The homes along the streets looked empty as we drove farther up the road, to the Maronite Catholic church of Qlaya. Only an occasional elderly woman peered out from behind a window curtain. The town was noticeably void of men. Before 1975, 15,000 Christians had lived in Marjayoun and Qlaya, a number that had dwindled to about 6,000 in more recent years. After the pullout, no more than 1,500 residents were left. The only Maronite males over age 14 who were still in Qlaya were the two dozen who had gathered in the courtyard of the church. The bishop of Tyre, Maroun Sader, who had eulogized Akel Hashem as a "martyr," had just arrived in a car with two armed men accompanying him.

The small gathering in front of the church followed the bishop into the rectory and clustered around him, sitting on sofas and chairs in a semicircle. The men were angrily clamoring and complaining. One of them shouted, "Hezbollah is stealing everything it can get its hands on!" Another stood up, saying, "Tell us, Father, is this an agreement with America, Syria, and Israel, to have all the Christians leave here for the Muslims?"

This last statement sprang from a conspiracy theory, patently paranoid, that was circulating in the south. I heard it often as I chronicled the end of the Israeli occupation. But I had a hard time following the logic. Essentially, this theory held that the U.S. government, since the time of Secretary of State Henry Kissinger, had worked in conjunction with Syria and Israel to rid Lebanon of the Christian presence and thereby bring stability to the country. It was a notion that brimmed with the megalomaniacal imagination of the Maronites, which sought an easy, cohesive explanation for the decades of war, American intervention, and back-channel diplomacy in Lebanon. And when this gentleman vocalized the suspicion, the crowd of men nodded in agreement and clamored even louder for an answer.

Bishop Sader, dressed in the distinctive Maronite black vestments with magenta piping, struck the tile floor with his staff and demanded silence. The men obeyed. "This is not an international conspiracy," he lectured. "But it is clear we as Christians are paying the price for this long, international game that has been played in our homeland. The point is, we must not leave. If those who fought with the SLA surrender themselves, they will be treated with mercy and—"

He could not finish the sentence, as the room exploded with protests.

"There is no mercy in Islam for Christians! Hezbollah does not know mercy," said one man. "And why should we trust the government to show mercy when they do not even send troops to protect us?"

More uproar. The bishop banged his staff again.

"We have been through much worse in our history. We can live through this. But we must find a way to bring those who have left back to their homes. If they do not come back, then what is our future? We have to be strong right now."

The bishop and the clerical hierarchy he represented were pretty much all that the Christians of southern Lebanon had left. There were no political leaders to protect them in the aftermath of the civil war. What little power they still had was consolidated in the church. This fact was brought home as I watched the bishop calm down the town residents, and later, broker a deal by telephone for an increased presence of Lebanese Army soldiers in the area to prevent looting and violence.

Sensing the fear in the community, the parish priest, Father Mansour Hkayem, canceled the services for Sunday, May 28. For the first time in the history of the hundred-year-old church, the bells did not ring at 10 A.M. Even when the church was in danger of being hit by shells in the civil war, the clergy had never canceled services. A huge chunk of stone punched out of the facade provided evidence of the real danger in those days in 1976, as Father Mansour himself remarked. He recounted how the congregation was in full attendance the very Sunday after the shelling, which had shattered the stained glass, toppled the ceramic icons, and sent chandeliers crashing to the ground. The plaster inside the church was still cracked, and large chunks hung perilously over the pews. It looked as if the whole ceiling might come crashing down at any minute—but that was how it had been for the past twenty-four years.

In response to the villagers' fears, Hezbollah dispatched one of its senior political leaders, Mohammad Raad, to the church. A skilled orator, Raad was the embodiment of Hezbollah's transition from a military force to a political party. Raad came to the church out of what appeared to be a very genuine effort at reconciliation. He said that Hezbollah wanted to work with the Christian community to rebuild southern Lebanon for the Shiite, Sunni, and Christian populations alike. About fifty parishioners crowded around him as he spoke.

Afterward, they said they were unimpressed. After all, just a few days earlier, they had heard Hezbollah's spiritual leader, Sheikh Nasrallah, thundering over the radio about the Christians who had chosen to stay behind and fight, that Hezbollah would "go into their beds at night and cut their throats." The Christian villagers sensed a hint in Raad's statements that they would be treated as *dhimmi,* as an alien minority within an Islamic framework of governance. They had always feared that Christians would be shunted aside in the absence of the Lebanese Army and amid the political ascendancy of Islamic fundamentalists. What they had feared now seemed to be materializing. Why should they need a Hezbollah politician to protect them? Where was the Lebanese government? Was this intended as a message to them that the new face of the Lebanese government was the face of an Islamic fundamentalist?

Shaker Khouri, 30, who had been blinded at age 10 when a Palestinian shell was fired into his home, was one of the few men still in the village. He was still there, he said, because he was not able to serve in the SLA due to his disability. "We don't want Hezbollah talking to us, we want our government talking to us," he said, standing in front of the empty church. "Why isn't the government of Lebanon here? Everybody knows the answer why. It is because Syria has told them not to come, and they do what they are told. They want us to be in fear here. They want the Christians to leave.

"I am the only one left in my family. All of them have gone to Israel—my brothers and my brothers-in-law. All gone. The Salemeh family, Nahara family, Mezher, Rizik, Daher, Farah, all of these families have disappeared from Qlaya except for a few elderly people. This is a history, our history, our Christian heritage in the land where Jesus lived that is gone. One more village, completely gone."

But Father Mansour refused to accept that notion. He believed there was a way to convince the parishioners who had fled to Israel to return. The only way to do this, he thought, was to show them that Hezbollah's offer of reconciliation was genuine. The church hierarchy seemed willing to put its faith in this gesture, and in this spirit Father Mansour ordered the church bells rung at 1:30 P.M. that Sunday. The 10 A.M. mass had not been canceled, he said, only postponed. After about fifteen minutes of vigorous bell-ringing by an elderly gentleman who pulled on the frayed rope of the church bell with stern determination, a group of about eighty parishioners had gathered at the front of the church. Father Mansour emerged from the rectory in his vestments and announced that it was time for mass. Usually, a total of 600 were in attendance at the two Sunday services.

In a back row, an old woman in a hand-crocheted sweater was crying, her sobs echoing in the empty church. Suleiman Haj, 80 years old, leaned on a weathered wooden cane as he walked into the church he had attended all his life, and shook his head. "There is no one left," he said.

Inside the church, Father Mansour delivered a sermon that was simple and direct. "Jesus told his disciples, 'Be not afraid.' He told them if you have faith, you have nothing to fear. 'Be not afraid.'"

After the mass, I spoke with Father Mansour as we drank coffee in a back room of the rectory. "They came with a message of reconciliation, and we, as Christians, should admire that, and respect it," he said. "This congregation needs encouragement to see that. They feel very lost right now."

The sadness of Qlaya's disappearing Christians stood in stark contrast to the sense of vindication among the Shiite Muslims of Khiam. It was particularly jarring to have come directly from Khiam to Qlaya, where many of the SLA guards and interrogators at the notorious facility had lived. I asked Father Mansour about the sins committed in the cells of Khiam by some of his parishioners.

"No. No. They were good to the inmates," he said, staring straight ahead with a confident gaze. "I was in that prison, there was nothing bad there. The chief interrogator, Jean Homsi, lived in this village. He has fled, of course. They would have killed him if he stayed. But he is a very good man. He is Greek Orthodox, but I know him very well. I asked him, 'Do you torture them?' And he told me they did not. He told me that maybe the Israelis do that, but not the Lebanese."

There was a long silence as the priest gauged the look on my face and on the face of my Lebanese translator, who also had just returned from Khiam. Father Mansour seemed to downshift his denial. "What choice did they have? They were part of a system," he said, the sentence trailing off. Whatever it was that they had done, the leaders of the SLA feared that they and their families would be killed for it.

Qlaya was not the only ghost town. In Akel Hashem's hometown of Dibil, nearly every house was shuttered and padlocked. Hezbollah militiamen had broken into Hashem's villa the first day of the Israeli pullout. They took away several cardboard boxes, neighbors said, presumably filled with documents. When I saw the Hashem home four days later, it was padlocked, and through a window I saw that although some of the furniture had been turned over, the family's belongings did not appear to have been looted or ransacked. I drove down the hill, toward the church, to check on the young couple I had visited several months earlier, Tony and Najat Nassif, but their home was padlocked as well. An elderly woman next door told me through a crack in the door that they had gone to live with their relatives in Dallas. Even the church was empty and locked. Father Yakoub had left for Beirut for several days but was expected to return. Once again, Dibil's Christian population had suffered another hemorrhage. The few who remained now estimated that the Christian community, which had shrunk from 4,000 to 1,500 over the previous generation, numbered no more than 500.

. . .

We headed back to the coast and the port city of Tyre, where Jesus had stayed for a time. The fishermen with weathered hands, repairing nets in their wooden boats, seemed as ancient as the Bible. From Tyre, it was a two-hour drive north along the coast to Beirut, where I had my first meeting to assess the Israeli pullout and what it meant for Christian Lebanon with the editor of *An Nahar,* an Arabic daily newspaper that was arguably the most independent voice in a region where independent voices were few. It was founded in Beirut in 1933, under the French mandate, and had remained in the hands of the Tueni family through three generations. The family was Greek Orthodox by tradition, but the paper's editorial line throughout the years of the French mandate, the struggle for independence, World War II, and the salad days of the 1950s and 1960s, before the civil war broke out, was adamantly secular and fiercely determined in its defense of Lebanon's interests and the Arab world's wider struggle against colonial rule.

In some ways the different ideological leanings of the Tueni family's three generations reflected the changes over time within Christian Lebanon. The founder, Gebran Tueni, had been a pro-Syrian, pan-Arab nationalist who fit solidly into the mold of Greek Orthodox Arab thinkers such as Michel Aflaq and George Antonius. He died in 1947, just one year before Israel announced its independence and the dreams of Arab nationalism began to crumble. Years of bitter infighting and corruption followed among the Arab movement's leaders, attended by a string of humiliating military defeats by Israel.

His son, Ghassan Tueni, was an erudite, Harvard-educated newspaperman whose leanings were nationalist but who was suspicious of Syria's aspirations in Lebanon. His suspicions had only deepened during the civil war. He was popular in Beirut, as he had all the charm and cosmopolitan flare for which the city in the 1960s had been renowned. Ghassan's son Gebran had joined an anti-Syrian faction of the Lebanese Forces during the civil war and had been forced into exile. In 1993, he returned. By 2000, after a quarter century of war in Lebanon, the 40-year-old Gebran said he understood all too well what he called "the lie" of Arab nationalism. He summed up nearly a century of history this way: "Arabism was invented by Christians against the Turks, then used by Arab Muslims against the Christians."

Gebran's was also the first and most courageous voice of public opposition against Syria's continued presence in postwar Lebanon. His brash demeanor, his directness, and his frank advocacy of a continued Christian role in Lebanon prompted some to view him as sectarian and divisive. *An Nahar* published a special issue in January 1998, headlined "Halt the Exodus of the Christians of the Orient." Some critics in Beirut's academic elite dismissed Gebran as a reactionary against the previous, well-reasoned generations of his family—a kind of postmodern, tribal Christian. But Gebran believed that Lebanon's vibrant culture and its future as a secular democracy were profoundly threatened by the outflow of Christians. He lashed out against the West—especially America, and more recently Canada—

for doing little to prevent it. He said that in the mid-1980s, U.S. embassy officials were urging Lebanese Christians to board boats stationed off the coast of Lebanon, telling them that they would be given safe passage to Canada and accepted as citizens there. And more recently, the Canadian embassy in Beirut had outraged Tueni and other leaders of the Christian community by advertising the services of immigration counselors, promising Canadian citizenship to any Lebanese who was willing to make a capital investment in Canada of CAN. $200,000 or more.

"I refuse to run these ads," he said. "They are unbelievable. Here we are fighting against the brain drain from Lebanon, fighting to hold on to our human and financial resources, and Canada is trying to lure them away with a price tag. Unbelievable!

"Every state in the Middle East has a national religion, which is, of course, Islam. Lebanon is the only country in the Middle East that has not declared Islam its national religion. This is a miracle in the year 2000. We are all connected within a confessional state. And because of this, we are the only state able to maintain pluralism and some sense of tolerance. Look at Egypt. It is anything but a republic, and anything but democratic. Look at Jordan, and you find the same story under a king. We know very well the story in Syria and the Gulf States. My belief is that if the Christians continue to leave, there will be no Lebanon left."

. . .

I was staying at the Phoenicia Intercontinental Hotel, once one of the grandest hotels in Beirut. That was before it became a prized machine-gunners' nest in what became known as "the battle of the hotels" during the early years of the civil war. The rival militias traded control of the Phoenicia and the modern high-rise Holiday Inn, both of which straddled the green line near the port in Beirut. In the end, the hotels had been so heavily riddled by heavy-caliber machine gun fire and mortars that they were barely standing. In the late 1990s, as part of a massive project by the Solidiere company to rebuild downtown Beirut, the Phoenicia had risen from the ashes of war. Just one month before the Israeli withdrawal, in April 2000, the Phoenicia reopened its doors to show off its restored beauty.

From the sixth floor of the hotel, visitors could look out over the

St. George Beach Club and the Mediterranean, or down at the pool, which was elegantly tiled in blue-and-green mermaids and dragons. A small orchestra played classical music for a charity ball attended by wealthy Maronite couples decked out in tuxedos and long evening gowns. There was a low murmur of chatter and clinking wine glasses—like wind chimes—under the soft orchestral strands. And then suddenly, a stream of traffic turned the corner. Car horns blared. Hoarse voices screamed triumphant chants in Arabic, "Allahu akbar!" It was a parade of tens of thousands of Hezbollah supporters, flooding the main street in front of the Phoenicia. Dilapidated cars and motor scooters were festooned with bright yellow Hezbollah flags snapping from their antennas. Some drivers leaned out their windows, waving Hezbollah banners and large posters of Sheikh Nasrallah. The orchestra came to a discordant halt. The clinking of glasses and the chatter stopped, too. The well-dressed Maronite crowd leaned out over a balcony that looked down on the rowdy and exuberant street scene.

The moment seemed to capture the true sense of what was really troubling the Maronites at the end of this conflict. It was less dramatic than the earlier, shrill predictions that the Christian collaborators of the SLA would be slaughtered by Hezbollah. That had not happened, nor would it happen in the weeks and months that followed. There had been no widespread looting by Shiites—another fear of many Christians. Something less dramatic yet more profound had happened to the Maronite community. The victory over Israeli occupation had left Hezbollah on the verge of surging political power, and this, everyone understood, heralded the finale of the Maronite vision of Lebanon. It was captured in a new phrase that had entered the political lexicon: *al-ihbat al-masiheh* (Christian disenchantment). What that phrase meant in reality was that the European-style, classical orchestras would now be rudely interrupted by the rising clamor of political Islam. Their elegant power and their prestige were evaporating amid the throng of Muslims in old, broken-down cars with Hezbollah flags. The whole Western-influenced notion of a "greater Lebanon"—which the Christians thought was theirs—had been taken up by Shiite fundamentalists, who were now running away with it. The wealthy Maronite elite represented Lebanon's past, and the impoverished and devout Shiite masses, its future.

. . .

I returned to Israel after the pullout and set out to find the family of Akel Hashem. I had been told that they were staying at a hotel in the northern Mediterranean coastal town of Naharia and were preparing to emigrate to Sydney.

It turned out they were at the Carlton, a four-star hotel where Hashem had often met with Ariel Sharon and Yitzhak Rabin, at some of the fateful turning points in the Lebanese-Israeli conflict. Over coffee in the lobby, Layya Hashem informed me that the hotel bill for her extended family, about one hundred people in all, was being paid by the Israeli government. Their status as refugees with room service made them uncomfortable, she said, especially seeing the thousands of other SLA families scattered in tented communities, in kibbutzim, and in third-rate hotels throughout northern Israel. The Israeli government, she said, would also be paying for the move to Sydney and a new house there.

Layya, her two teenage sons, and her 10-year-old daughter would be leaving the next morning for Ben-Gurion International Airport, where they would catch a flight to Cyprus and then to Australia. I had caught them just in time. Several family members were heading to Germany and a handful to Canada, but most were going to the land down under. Only one elderly aunt and uncle had stayed behind in Dibil. They would be the only Hashems left in the village. It looked like the end of the family's 200-year history in the town and its 1,500-year history as Maronites in Lebanon. "If Akel had lived to see this, it would have killed him," said Layya, sipping her cappuccino.

She seemed disconsolate as she told me how senior Israeli commanders had informed the family on May 22 that the pullout was imminent. She had packed a suitcase and a large album of photos of her husband through the years, and then drove across the border at Rosh Hanikra and down to Naharia. The seaside village and its ancient port lie well within the ancient boundaries of Phoenicia. Even though Naharia had become Israeli territory, it still held a part of the family's Lebanese heritage. But none of that seemed relevant to Layya. She barely smiled when I mentioned it. She was still dressed in black and was carrying a dog-eared paperback French edition of Fyodor Dostoevsky's *Memories from the House of the Dead.*

"Akel believed we would never leave Lebanon," she said. "He told us the Israelis would never leave those who fought alongside them. I believe that would have been true if he had lived. Maybe there will be a peace agreement, and then we will return home. That is our hope now. I just cannot imagine Dibil and Qlaya and Marjayoun will be abandoned, and the churches left empty."

After traveling in Phoenicia, Jesus began the journey back with his disciples. They crossed through Caesarea Philippi—part of what today is known as the Golan Heights. It was here that Matthew attested to Jesus's vision of impending death in Jerusalem. From that point on, the biblical narrative pointed Jesus toward preparing himself and his disciples for the day when he would shoulder the cross. He left for Jerusalem before Passover, lodging near the city, on the Mount of Olives.

On what Christians refer to as Palm Sunday, Jesus would have ridden the foal of a donkey, conscious of its imagery and in keeping with Jewish prophecies of the humble arrival of the messiah. As he "drew near and saw the city," it is said that he wept. On this ancient path today there stands the Catholic chapel of Dominus Flavius (The Lord Wept). Jesus held that in rejecting his teaching, the city would be rejecting its own salvation. And he warned that someday the city and its great Temple would be nothing but ruins. This episode, retold in the Bible, is known as the Lament.

When Jesus approached the city, he of course would not have seen a mosque or a church anywhere on the skyline—only the imposing Second Temple, with smoke curling up from its sacrificial fires. The Temple priests embodied the Sadducean hierarchy that Jesus felt had strayed from the message of the God of Israel, his God. In the eyes of Jesus, his death on the cross would be the last sacrifice necessary for human salvation. In this sense Jesus was part of the battle for the meaning of the Temple Mount—a struggle between man and God that has never really ended, and that flared up dramatically in the year 2000.

XII

The Mount of Olives

THE LAMENT

As he approached Jerusalem and saw the city, he wept over it and said, "If you, even you, had only known on this day what would bring you peace—but now it is hidden from your eyes."

LUKE 19:41–42 (NIV)

YEHUDA ETZION sat on a folding lawn chair amid the whitewashed graves of the Jewish cemetery on the Mount of Olives and looking down on Jerusalem's Old City. In the middle of that cramped maze of stone lay one open expanse of land—the compound known to Jews as the Temple Mount and to Muslims as Haram al-Sharif, the Noble Sanctuary—lined with pine and cypress trees and flowing bougainvillea.

Along the southern wall of the Noble Sanctuary stands the Al-Aqsa mosque. *Al-Aqsa,* "the farthest place"—refers to the farthest sanctuary Muslims believe Mohammed reached on his nighttime journey from Mecca. This central Jerusalem mosque routinely attracts tens of thousands of worshipers for the traditional Friday prayers. At the center of the sprawling plaza is the Dome of the Rock, the crowning jewel of Jerusalem architecture, its golden dome shimmering against the ancient gray stones of the ramparts of the Old City. Built two generations after the Islamic conquest, and completed in A.D. 691, the dome was Islam's first major sanctuary. Its base is a perfect octagon that circumscribes the rock from which Muslims believed the prophet Mohammed ascended to heaven. Archaeologists believe that the First and Second Temples were built on the same spot, and that the innermost chamber of the Temple, the Holy of Holies, rested on this rock. In building their mosque atop the remains of the Second Temple,

Muslims gave physical expression to their belief that Islam was the completion of God's message, a message imperfectly revealed in Judaism and Christianity.

But that was not how Yehuda Etzion saw the Dome of the Rock. "It is a desecration, an abomination for the Jewish people, and it must be removed," he said, squinting at the view in the scorching sun that burned overhead on a July morning. Jerusalem was listless, whispering with heat like a fire burning in the stones that baked this ancient capital. "For the Jewish people to find redemption, it will have to be removed," Etzion repeated. A tall and lumbering man with a reddish complexion, copper-colored hair, and a beard flecked with gray, Etzion did more than just talk about "redeeming" the Temple Mount from the Muslim shrine; he had actually tried to do it. He had been arrested in 1984, after Israel's security police uncovered a plot by his underground religious Zionist group to secure explosives sufficient to destroy the Muslim shrine and thus usher in what he believed would be an era of redemption. Experts on religious extremism and the Israeli judges who heard the case against Etzion calculated that had they fulfilled their plan, this act also would have ushered in a war that united not just the Arab world but the entire Muslim world, from Mauritania to Indonesia, against Israel.

Etzion was an extremist of the farthest fringe to emerge from Gush Emunim, the movement that began in the 1970s to build Jewish settlements in the belief that God had given the land to Jews. In 1978, Etzion's radicalism was hardened by the Camp David summit during which Jimmy Carter, Menachem Begin, and Anwar Sadat resolved that Israel would return the Sinai to Egypt in return for a signed peace agreement and recognition by Egypt of Israel's right to exist. What seemed to some a historic achievement was to Etzion an unforgivable act of betrayal on the part of Begin. And as his radicalism sharpened further in the early 1980s, Etzion developed a fierce belief that Judaism's Temple must be rebuilt where it had once stood, even if that meant blowing up the Dome of the Rock. "Determinist believers say that we have to wait for God," Etzion told me. "We believe we have to do the maximum that we can do, to see the Dome of the Rock and Al-Aqsa destroyed. This was robbery of the Jewish people at a time when we were so weak. . . . We are not weak anymore."

In 1980, this underground movement put its plans to destroy the Haram al-Sharif aside for a while. They set out instead on a bombing campaign to avenge the death of six yeshiva students who had been shot by Palestinian militants. They maimed the Palestinian mayor of Nablus and wounded the mayor of Ramallah with devices rigged to explode when they started their cars. Four years later, they were planning an even bigger bombing of a Palestinian bus when Israel's domestic security service, Shin Bet, moved in and arrested them. Three who were convicted of murder served seven years each, and Etzion was out in five. Etzion remains unrepentant, even if his methods have—as far as anyone can tell—been modified.

On a plaza set among the rows of graves in a Jewish cemetery on the Mount of Olives, Etzion had just finished setting up a canvas tent, where he was beginning a hunger strike to protest the latest Camp David summit, and what he saw as yet another betrayal in the Maryland woods.

In the second week of July 2000, Barak and Arafat were invited by Bill Clinton to the same quaint cabins at the American presidential retreat where Carter, Begin, and Sadat had had their breakthrough twenty-two years earlier. Clinton and his team had hoped that these quiet surroundings and their connection with history might inspire the two sides to seize the moment and reach agreement on a final peace that would end the fifty-two-year Israeli-Palestinian conflict.

By the summer of 2000 it had become glaringly clear that the Oslo agreement was on its last legs and could well collapse. Clinton, approaching the end of his second term in office, eagerly sought to finalize a deal, and pushed the two sides to tackle head-on the most powerful and emotional issue of the "final status" negotiations: sovereignty over Jerusalem, which both sides claimed as their capital. Clinton and his advisers must have believed that all of the other complex issues—the "right of return" of the more than three million Palestinian refugees; the fate of some 140 Jewish settlements that housed 200,000 Israelis in the West Bank and Gaza; and the allocation of critical water resources—could somehow be worked out, if only the mystical quest for Jerusalem could be resolved on paper.

Israeli press reports indicated that Barak was offering a withdrawal from "95 percent of the West Bank." This, it turned out, was not the case. The framework of a deal that would offer close to 95 percent of the West Bank in a staged process of several years was being discussed, and would take more shape at a subsequent round of negotiations in the Egyptian resort town of Taba in January. Nevertheless, the media obsession with these percentages was misleading. First of all, they were based on Israel's definition of the West Bank, which did not include large blocks of settlements which lay within the West Bank but which Israel claimed were now within their redrawn boundaries of Jerusalem. In addition, it did not include huge tracts along the Jordan River valley and the Dead Sea. According to Palestinian estimates, the figure the Israeli negotiators were offering to return was closer to 70 percent of the West Bank and the land was not contiguous. One Palestinian negotiator at Camp David explained why the Palestinians would not accept the Israeli offer this way: "You could argue that in a prison the inmates control 90 percent of the area. . . But if the other 10 percent represents the locks on the cells, the corridors and the watch towers. . . then the whole area is still in the control of the prison guards."

The Palestinian leadership insisted, furthermore, that to talk in percentages was to obfuscate what they felt was the core of the Oslo accord, which was that both sides would comply with U.N. Security Council Resolution 242, mandating withdrawal of Israeli forces to the pre-June 1967 boundaries in exchange for peace and recognition of Israel's 1948 borders. The Palestinians felt that they had already made a historic compromise in accepting only slightly more than 25 percent of historical Palestine, and they were unwilling to compromise further.

Still, the fact remained that Barak had gone further in his proposal than any other Israeli prime minister had ever gone before toward meeting Palestinian demands, and he had done so at a huge risk to his political future. According to the Israelis present at Camp David, he was talking about dismantling a large number of Jewish settlements in the West Bank, though not all of them. His most dramatic proposal, according to officials present at the talks, was a formula for sharing Jerusalem that would have granted the Palestinian Authority sovereignty over large parts of East Jerusalem and administrative rule over others. Barak also reportedly had proposed a formula for "extraterritorial sovereignty" to enable the Palestinians to control the Haram al-Sharif, much in the way a government holds sovereignty over its embassy in a foreign country. Another Israeli proposal was that the Palestinians would have sovereignty over the Noble Sanctuary and its mosques, and Israelis would have sovereignty over the Western Wall and the land beneath the Noble Sanctuary, where the remains of the destroyed Temple lay. The set of positions put forth by Barak indicated a genuine attempt to reach an agreement, a bold step forward that was certain to be met with cries of treason by the religious extremists in Israel but that Barak was confident he could sell to his people. It seemed likely to the Israelis and Americans that Arafat would at least present a counteroffer, if he could not accept some form of the terms on the table.

It all seemed so rational. But what Barak and the other secular leaders of Israel never seemed to grasp was that they were not dealing with rational elements—whether within their own society or within Palestinian Muslim society—when it came to assigning ownership of a plot of land so pregnant with prophecy and so tied to the Abrahamic faiths' yearning for redemption. Clinton and his team were equally blind to the power of these forces. The land of the Temple Mount/Noble Sanctuary was something the Jewish and Muslim religious leaders, particularly hard-liners, were not willing to compromise on, for they considered any such compromise a betrayal of God.

"What is happening at Camp David is a disaster, a catastrophe for the Jewish people," said Etzion, his face reddening with anger, his blue eyes glaring. "There is no leader in the history of Judaism who has willingly given up the heart of the Jewish people." As we squinted in the blazing sunlight at the Dome of the Rock, two large shadows suddenly fell over us. Etzion turned and covered his eyes to look up at the silhouettes that stood just behind us. "Nice view," said the larger of the two shadows, a man in his early 40s, with an intense expression and closely cropped hair. "For some it is nice, and for some it is the worst view in the world," said Yehuda, smiling, as he recognized the man. The shadow was one of the top commanders of Shabak, the domestic intelligence arm of the Israeli government. He was responsible for investigating Jewish fundamentalist militants within Israel and abroad, a group that Shabak had dangerously ignored prior to the assassination of Yitzhak Rabin. The commander had been involved in the investigation that had led to Etzion's prosecution, and he had kept a close eye on him ever since.

Etzion launched into his reading of the Camp David talks as the fateful beginning of a war in the Middle East that would ultimately be fought over the sacred space that lay before us. "How will you be judged when we are all under the rubble?" Etzion asked the Shabak man. "Well, if that happens, we'll all be together under the rubble, won't we?" he replied, in the soothing, rational, relaxed Hebrew of secular Zionism. "We are facing tough days. What happens is not in our hands. Some will be happy and some will be less happy."

. . .

Jerusalem—as both a sacred space and a nationalist symbol—was at the core of the Camp David talks in July 2000, where three political leaders represented three national aspirations and three monotheistic views, all directly related to Jerusalem. Camp David set the "heavenly Jerusalem"—the higher ideal of the holy city, the city of peace—against the "earthly Jerusalem," or the practical reality, the living city of torment and joy and devotion that Israelis and Palestinians, Jews and Muslims and Christians, so jealously coveted and sought to control. Camp David was seen by many as vivid proof that these two Jerusalems were inextricably bound together in a divine narrative.

For fundamentalist believers of all three faiths, Camp David was the point where the plot thickened, where they moved to the edge of their seats to see what would happen next. Etzion embodied an ultra nationalist, messianic sense of Jewish eschatology. And in the Noble Sanctuary, there were plenty of Muslims railing against any surrender of full sovereignty over Al-Aqsa, some of whom were so extremist as to see it as the trigger for Islam's own "End Times" scenario. In the Islamic eschatology, a false messiah, who will be a Jew, will conquer the world. But in the end, Jesus—whom they call Issa—will return to defeat this false messiah in a battle near Jerusalem, after which Jesus will slay all the swine, smash all the crosses, and proclaim Islam the world's sole faith. As the Israeli journalist Gershom Gorenberg observed: "The vision startles because we know these characters, yet they are transformed. At the world's end, the believers of three faiths will watch the same drama, but with different programs in their hands."

The Christian evangelical crowd that flowed in and out of Jerusalem embraced their own vision of how Camp David fit into a coming apocalypse. And in concentric circles, or layers, around these literal interpretations of scripture were the more established, mainstream views of each faith, in which Jerusalem tended to be viewed in a much more metaphorical sense, with the emphasis on its symbolic significance rather than its role as the stage for the End of Days.

Etzion represents a tiny fringe of perhaps several thousand Israelis who believe in an active restoration of the Temple. The Christian

Zionist movement that supports them has a more worrisomely large and rapidly growing following. But the overwhelming majority of observant Jews believe that the restoration of the Temple is up to God. Their role in life is to follow God's law, and to wait until that moment is revealed. To them, the Temple Mount is a metaphor of Jewish life, buried under layers of civilization and destruction. Its restoration symbolizes the time when all Jews will live by the commandments of the law. The Torah, not the Temple Mount, is the center of Judaism.

An even wider segment of the Israeli population—perhaps a majority—who define themselves as somewhere between "traditional" and "secular," see the Temple Mount as an archaeological fact of Jewish history but a distant theological concept that holds little or no meaning in their lives. For them, the Temple Mount stands, above all, as a national symbol of the triumphant, some would even say miraculous, victory in 1967, which brought about the return of Jews to the Old City after two thousand years of exile and exclusion. In sum, the Temple Mount matters; but in daily life they are more likely to be concerned about the national basketball rivalry between Hapoel Jerusalem and Maccabi Tel Aviv, or pending reserve duty in the military, or which local Internet provider has the most competitive rates. And this is the worldview in which Barak, a secular kibbutznik, had been raised.

Arafat, who cast himself as a traditional Muslim, was ultimately the secular leader of a very secular PLO. Arafat did not preside over a democracy, as did Barak and Clinton, but he still needed to pay attention to public opinion on what was commonly called "the Palestinian street." If he was not to be overthrown or even killed, he needed to stay in tune with the feelings of the vast majority of traditional and devout Muslims who made up the Palestinian people. And he knew them well enough to know that the Dome of the Rock, more than any other landmark, symbolized Arab Muslims' honor and dignity and yearning to redeem themselves from what they saw as humiliating defeats by Israel in 1948 and 1967. The Dome of the Rock had become the symbol of Palestinian nationalism, as well as a symbol for all of Islam. Arafat had stated clearly that he had no authority to relinquish the Muslim claim to the Dome of the Rock, making sovereignty a nonnegotiable point. The surprise expressed by Barak and Clinton and their advisers when Arafat remained steadfast on this point revealed their ignorance of Arab culture and their hubris in having failed to consult with Jerusalem's religious leaders (Muslim, Jewish, and Christian) on this issue.

It fell to Bill Clinton to put forth the Christian viewpoint. Clinton—a Southern Baptist with a profound sense of spirituality that could resonate from a pulpit as thunderously as any preacher he would have heard in his Arkansas youth—knew his Bible; and it seemed that on some level that spirituality provided him with the stamina he needed to continue what was seemingly a hopeless mission. His speeches seemed to reflect a view toward peace in the earthly Jerusalem that was close to the celestial way in which the teachings of Jesus presented the Holy City, not as a place to be coveted and fought over but as a concept of peace on earth—the New Jerusalem, as it was referred to in the New Testament. Shlomo Ben-Ami, who was then Israeli foreign minister, told me in an interview many months after Camp David: "That the whole peace process in Israel, in the Holy Land, had for Clinton something of a religious meaning, I do not have any doubt whatsoever. All of his involvement, all of the depth of his commitment, revealed that the man was not motivated by political considerations alone. . . . There clearly was a drive of a man there who believes in God and saw the spiritual meaning of all this."

But despite Clinton's Christian background, the reality was that on this issue the indigenous Christians and their church institutions were not included in the debate. That the Palestinian Christian presence was so small was certainly an important factor, but a deeper dynamic also was at work. Christianity had historically attached little significance to the Temple Mount/Haram al-Sharif, for the message of Jesus held a different notion of the relationship between "land" and what was regarded as "sacred." Jesus's theology expressed the idea of spirituality over place—a teaching that was captured in his lashing out at the money changers in the Temple, whose activities he felt detracted from the sacredness of this place. Over the centuries, Christendom (which hardly showed any understanding of Jesus's teaching on land) defined itself on some level against the Temple Mount, seeing its destruction as evidence of Christian ascendancy over Judaism. Throughout the late Roman and Byzantine era, in fact, Christians expressed this perception by using the Temple Mount as a trash heap.

But if Christianity's relationship to the Temple was characterized by a mean-spirited triumphalism, the history of Christianity's relationship to Jerusalem, the Holy City, was a different story. Jerusalem was of profound importance to the Christian world's community of churches, and especially to Christians living in that city. It was where their savior, Jesus, had preached to his disciples and articulated his vision of the kingdom of God. It was where Jesus had been crucified, had died, and had risen again in fulfillment of the scriptures. And so the fact that the established Christian churches in the Holy Land had no voice in the debate over the future of Jerusalem did not go unnoticed. In its agreements with Israel and with the PLO, the Holy See had spelled out understandings that both entities would respect the right of all faiths to worship. And in so doing, the Vatican had also clearly stated that it would not intervene in the final status negotiations over Jerusalem. But local church leaders, the Roman Catholic patriarch among them, were concerned about the developments at Camp David. For the time being, however, the Vatican remained conspicuously silent.

During the summit, the heads of Jerusalem's three largest Christian denominations—the Greek Orthodox patriarch, the Roman Catholic patriarch, and the Armenian Orthodox patriarch—expressed this concern in a letter addressed to Clinton, Arafat, and Barak. They formally requested that representatives of the churches be permitted to attend. "We trust you will not forget or overlook our agelong presence here," the clerics stated. "The rich tapestry of this land is made even richer and more precious with this continuous Christian life, witness, and presence alongside the two other Abrahamic traditions of Judaism and Islam."

One of the proposals that was reportedly considered at Camp David was a division of the Old City, with the Palestinian Authority taking administrative control of the Muslim and Christian quarters and Israel maintaining control of the Jewish and Armenian quarters. Leaders of the Christian community strongly opposed the separation of the Armenian and Christian quarters, saying that they were "inseparable and firmly united by the same faith."

The Christian churches never had a chance to be heard at Camp David. Despite President Clinton's charm, his pleading, and then his outright anger at Arafat's refusal to accept Barak's proposal on the West Bank and Jerusalem, the Camp David talks broke down without an agreement on the morning of July 26. Specifically, the process came to an impasse when Arafat and his chief negotiator, Saeb Erekat, refused to accept even the idea that the Temple Mount had existed in the place now occupied by the Dome of the Rock—a completely irrational denial of the Jewish claim to this sacred space, not to mention a huge body of historical and archaeological work. The talks had collapsed on the issue of Jerusalem.

. . .

One of the reasons for the failure to reach agreement at Camp David II was that the leaders there were largely tone-deaf to the spiritual harmony of Jerusalem, which was sung, albeit in different pitches and keys, by the three faiths. In contrast, at Camp David I, Jimmy Carter, Anwar Sadat, and Menachem Begin all carried a "genuine spirituality and commitment to their faith," according to Krister Stendhal, a former dean of the Harvard Divinity School, who followed the difficult negotiations closely and at one point in the process corresponded with Carter. Carter was a born-again Christian who boldly and openly professed that his faith shaped his life and his commitment to justice, and therefore his presidency. Sadat, still struggling to emerge from Nasser's shadow and put his own stamp on Egypt's top government office, turned to Islam and appropriated the descriptive epithet "the believer president." He walked a fine line, embracing Western values but also resolutely expressing his faith, encouraging Islamic family law, and supporting Islamic organizations on campuses. (Ironically, the Islamic movement later spawned the militant extremists who became his assassins.) Begin, too, embraced religion as part of his political program in a way that made him popular among Israeli conservatives and that brought the growing religious Zionist movement into the Likud fold. Begin not only employed biblical notions of *Eretz Israel* in shaping his land policies but also relied on the Hebrew Bible as the source of his yearning to make peace with Egypt. In addition, perhaps the purely political nature of the main issue at the first Camp David summit—possession of the Sinai desert, rather than of the coveted core of Jerusalem—permitted the leaders more easily to reach an agreement adorned with religious language, because Sinai did not evoke the strongly partisan religious sentiments Jerusalem did. In the Camp David II negotiations on Jerusalem, the power and emotion of religion in many ways became the center of discussion—and the point of impasse.

The leaders who met at Camp David in 2000 were motivated less by a genuine reliance on faith than by their need for what one might call political redemption. For Barak, the summit was a quest to secure a final peace plan and thereby fulfill a campaign promise. He hoped it might galvanize the country in a way that would keep his fragile coalition government from being toppled by the conservative and religious factions in the parliament, which were outraged at the concessions he was said to be offering, especially regarding the division of Jerusalem under Israeli and Palestinian control. For Arafat, the journey to Camp David was a more cautious pilgrimage. He saw no need to rush, but he also realized the hourglass was running out on his promises to declare an independent Palestinian state. He needed to deliver some tangible results in a "peace process" that had as yet brought Palestinians little redress. At the time of this summit, the Palestinian Authority had full control over no more than 20 percent of the West Bank and 60 percent of Gaza; essentially, Arafat ruled what many observers likened to the Bantustans in South Africa under apartheid.

For Clinton, the Camp David summit came at a time when he was yearning for public redemption from a presidency dragged down by what could be called, simply, sin. If anything could exorcise the memory of his scandalous actions in the Oval Office, it would be peace in the Holy Land, and an agreement by which the three Abrahamic faiths finally could live together in harmony—at least in Jerusalem. But Clinton's hard work failed. The effort was too much of a rush job, and any religious zeal he may have brought to it looked, in the end, like a failed shot at cheap grace.

The Israeli peace camp (exemplified by the movement Peace Now), for its part, was messianic in its drive to achieve a lasting peace, although that drive was not grounded in religious faith. In the aftermath of the collapse of talks at Camp David, hope mingled with despair. Hope was evoked by the fact that for the first time the two sides had openly discussed how to resolve the issue of sovereignty in Jerusalem—the first step toward a final deal. But many also feared that this process was hopelessly deadlocked, even fatally flawed. The Israeli left was stunned at Arafat's refusal to accept what they felt was the best offer Israel could afford to make. The burning, dry heat of August made the resultant malaise that much harder to endure.

It was at this time that I paid a visit to Yehuda Amichai, Israel's poet laureate—the Jewish state's Robert Frost. He had had a battle with cancer, and his health was frail. In the soft light of late afternoon, he looked out over the pink bougainvillea that embellished his balcony, down onto the Old City's gray ramparts at Jaffa Gate. On the paths below he saw Orthodox Jews in black hats, Palestinian kids pushing vending carts, tourists with their camera bags, and a Franciscan cleric trudging up the hill in his brown robes and sandals. Amichai, a student of human interaction, was watching the contact—and the lack of it—between two peoples and three faiths in one city. He was a staunch Zionist and an early supporter of Israel's Peace Now movement. I had come to him for a fresh perspective on the collapse of Camp David and Jerusalem's future, to get away from the political analysts and the ideologues and hear the poet's view. I wanted to know whether he was hopeful.

"'Hopeful' means nothing," he replied. "'Hopeful' is too big a word. I have cut it down to little hopes," he said. "I walked every little corner of Jerusalem. I walked every little corner of hope. And somewhere in there, that's where peace will come from."

One of his most enduring poems is titled "Jerusalem." At the end of this long, hot day, he read it aloud to me:

On a roof in the Old City
Laundry hanging in the late afternoon sunlight:
The white sheet of a woman who is my enemy,
The towel of a man who is my enemy,
To wipe off the sweat on his brow.

In the sky of the Old City
A kite.
At the other end of the string,
A child.
I can't see
Because of the wall.

We have put up many flags,
They have put up many flags.
To make us think they're happy,
To make them think that we're happy.

Amichai knew Jerusalem as well as anyone, and I had long wanted to ask him about the steady erosion of the Christian presence in the city, and what that meant to the city's future. He nodded in recognition at the question and then described the sadness he felt when he walked Jerusalem's Old City and saw the empty churches, "the thin funeral processions," the mostly elderly women with their crucifixes, and fewer and fewer children. He told me that the Christian Quarter had seemed more real years ago, and the senses picked up on it. The church bells still ring; but he said he believed "there was less incense in the air," wafting from the censers of the Orthodox.

"I have seen this in my lifetime," he said. "For Jews, the Christians have brought so much bloodshed here in the past. That is the history, and that is not easy to forget, nor should it be forgotten. But the Christians were more, much more than that to Jerusalem. The Christians always brought to this barren place art and music. They were always the best at that. Now the real culture is gone, and the Christians we see are just tour guides and big buses of people from Korea and Kansas. That is not real culture."

I told him about the bleak estimates of the shrinking Christian presence in Jerusalem, and he was surprised. "It will not be Jerusalem without the Christians," he said. "Are the numbers really that low?"

Less than two months after our visit, on September 27, 2000, Yehuda Amichai died. He was 74 years old. On the very day of his burial, events were set in motion that would make Jerusalem's "small corners of hope," as he had described them, much harder to find.

. . .

Enter Ariel Sharon, wearing black Ray-Ban sunglasses and a big smile. In the early morning of September 28, the legendary Israeli hawk lumbered onto the plaza of the Western Wall, weight shifting from side to side, like a wrestler in the ring. Sharon, the retired general who as defense minister had led the invasion of Lebanon in 1982, was now the leader of the opposition Likud Party. He stopped and turned to ascend an ancient ramp to the Mugrabi Gate of the Temple Mount. He was surrounded by security guards and flanked by about one thousand heavily armed Israeli border police and special forces. This looked more like a siege than a political visit to a holy shrine.

Sharon smiled as he greeted the press corps, with reporters yelling questions at him and the photographers' cameras going off like automatic gun fire. Sharon seemed to relish the attention. This was exactly what he wanted—a photo opportunity at the Temple Mount that would shore up his position on Israel's tumultuous political landscape.

Sharon's most immediate political goal was to steal the spotlight from former Israeli Prime Minister Benjamin Netanyahu, who had just been cleared of corruption charges and was returning to Israel from abroad, expecting to reclaim the leadership of the Likud Party. Netanyahu was, at this point, considered the party's best candidate for the coming election campaign against Barak. But Sharon was intent on holding on to the party reins, for he understood that Jerusalem, and Barak's ill-fated attempt to divide it, would be the key to victory. Even though many Israelis viewed Sharon as far too hawkish and retrograde in his view of the Palestinians, nonetheless Sharon knew that Barak was finished.

When asked why he was there, Sharon told reporters, "Because as a Jew I have the right to be here, and because we want to clearly exert our sovereignty over the Temple Mount." Palestinian leaders for days had been warning the Israeli government—Arafat even made a direct appeal to Barak—not to permit the confrontational visit by Sharon. Sharon was the Israeli leader most reviled in the Arab world for his role in the invasion of Lebanon and the massacres at the Sabra and Shatila refugee camps. His presence at this tense moment was almost certain to ignite emotions that had been heating up over the rival claims to Jerusalem.

Sharon saw himself as a warrior for Jerusalem. He had fought and had been wounded in the battle to break the Arab siege on Jerusalem in 1948. And after 1967, he had engineered a ring of Jewish settlements around Jerusalem to protect Israel's grip on the Holy City. In the early 1980s, he acquired a home in the center of the Muslim Quarter of the Old City and surrounded it with Israeli soldiers and security personnel. He erected a massive steel menorah that looked more like military hardware than a sacred instrument of religious observance, and unfurled a twenty-five-foot-long Israeli flag. His home was a statement—not a residence. Sharon rarely stayed there, preferring his ranch in the Negev.

Sharon carried all of this history with him onto the Temple Mount that morning, and the Arabs there greeted him with outrage. "Murderer, get out!" shouted Palestinian Muslims, lined up to defend the Haram al-Sharif, where in one corner there was a small shrine to the Palestinians killed at Sabra and Shatila. One Palestinian worshiper held a handwritten sign in English that said, "You murdered innocent women and children!" Furious Muslim clerics decried Sharon's incursion into their holy site as a desecration, and one that would be avenged. Palestinian leader Yasser Arafat described Sharon's act as "very dangerous" and said that Arab and Islamic nations should "move very fast" to protect the shrine.

After touring the grounds, Sharon descended the ramp and allowed the crowd of roughly one hundred reporters to swarm him, pushing and elbowing and shoving microphones in his face. "I come here with a message of peace," he said. "I came here to the holiest place for the Jewish people, to see what happens here. This is our holy place. . . . There will be problems if Jerusalem is divided as the prime minister wants. Many problems will be caused here."

At one point, Sharon used the phrase, "The Temple Mount is in our hands," a conscious echo of the legendary radio report from the Israeli brigade commander Motta Gur after Israeli paratroopers had completed the capture of the site in the 1967 Six-Day War. At that moment in 1967, Israel had repossessed the sacred core of Judaism and the hope for redemption. And at that moment, Palestinians and other Muslims lost sovereign control over this icon of their faith, which would come to symbolize their spiritual yearnings. As author Karen Armstrong has observed, "Jerusalem stood most powerful as a symbol to those who no longer felt they possessed it."

But Sharon's provocative reiteration of that famous radio announcement was actually a betrayal of the spirit of Israel's reunification of Jerusalem in 1967. The way Israel had conducted itself in the Old City was widely viewed as one of the Jewish state's more enlightened political moments. Rather than exult over the capture of the Temple Mount in 1967, Defense Minister Moshe Dayan moved quickly to order the Israeli flag removed from the Dome of the Rock, and sat down with the Muslim religious authorities to assure them that they would continue to administer their holy site. Israel would control security around the mosque.

After the victory in 1967, Israel's chief rabbis and sages immediately decreed it forbidden for observant Jews to pray on the site, since to do so required ritual purity. A plaza was cleared for Jews to pray at the Western Wall, and the Israeli religious leadership instructed the faithful to pray at the wall and to trust God to restore the Temple when the hour of redemption was at hand.

That had been the status quo ever since.

The spirit in which Sharon—who was adamantly secular, but on this day wore a blue yarmulke—strode into the compound flouted that fragile status quo for distinctly political purposes. He was using the sacred space of the Temple Mount as a purely nationalist symbol. And inevitably, the visit provided the spark that ignited a conflict in which nationalist and religious overtones were mingled. Only minutes after Sharon walked out of the compound, a first wave of stones was hurled by Muslim worshipers at the police at the Mugrabi Gate. Then came tear gas and the crackle of gunshots as police fired at the crowd with steel pellets coated in hard plastic, which the Israeli army called "rubber bullets." The violence had been set in motion.

As the clashes erupted, Sharon remained unperturbed, surrounded by security personnel as he made his way out of the plaza. I walked with him, ignoring the pushes and shoves from his security guards, and asked him how he responded to those who saw his visit as a provocation.

"It is a provocation to visit our holy site? Why?" he asked sharply.

Why Sharon was permitted such a visit was a troubling question, and one that the leaders of Barak's government had difficulty answering. Barak and his cabinet ministers insisted that they could not stop Sharon or any other Jew from visiting a site that was sacred to Judaism. Ben-Ami, who also served as public security minister under Barak, claimed that "intelligence reports" had indicated that Sharon's visit would not result in violence.

If his characterization was accurate, then the Israeli security establishment was alarmingly ignorant of the passions aroused by such religious symbols, and of the deep fear many Palestinians have of the powerful Jewish state, which for more than three decades has kept a firm grip around the sanctuary. They must also have been ignorant of Muslim suspicions about the growing Israeli subculture that seeks a more active role for Jews in rebuilding the Temple (and by logical extension, destroying the Dome of the Rock). Yet, to understand the enormous risk of violence, one would not have had to look far into history. In 1929, when a group of Zionist Jews raised a flag and sang the anthem *Hatikvah* at the Western Wall, these acts touched off a wave of violence that the British mandatory government could not control. The Jewish community in Hebron was set upon by Muslim rioters who went from house to house, murdering and looting. Sixty-seven Jews, including a dozen women and children, were killed. At the end of nearly two weeks of disturbances, 133 Jews and 116 Arabs had been killed in the violence. But there was even fresher historical evidence of the powder keg that the Temple Mount represented. In 1990, when a fringe group known as the Temple Mount Faithful attempted to lay a symbolic cornerstone for the "Third Temple," a rumor spread on the Haram al-Sharif that the Israeli government was preparing to rebuild the Temple. Rioting broke out, and Israeli forces killed 20 Palestinians. In 1996, the decision by the Israeli government to open a door to a Roman-era tunnel that ran along the Western Wall resulted in more rioting, and then clashes throughout the West Bank and Gaza, that ended with the deaths of 70 Palestinians, including police and civilians, and 16 Israeli soldiers and border police.

On the morning of Sharon's visit, the clashes were comparatively moderate. A handful of Israeli riot police were wounded, only two of them seriously. At least three Palestinians were hospitalized for gunshot wounds from the "rubber bullets." Four other Palestinians, including two senior government officials, were beaten with riot batons. But the Sharon visit would be remembered as the event that set in motion a deadly cycle of violence.

However, to say that the violence was caused by Sharon's visit would be inaccurate. There were much more profound issues behind the anger of Palestinians, including the continuing expansion of Jewish settlements in the West Bank, and the severe economic hardships endured by the Palestinians while the peace process limped along. Many Israeli analysts believed that the Palestinian Authority, after rejecting Barak's offer at Camp David, was seeking to use the violence as a tool at the bargaining table. They believe Arafat orchestrated the violence. Nevertheless, Sharon in many ways personified the grievances Palestinians held against Israel, and his visit at the Muslims' holy shrine was inarguably a match held to a short fuse.

. . .

The day after Sharon's visit, tens of thousands of Muslims flooded the Old City to attend Friday noon prayers at the Al-Aqsa mosque. The sermon of Sheikh Ekrima Sabri, the grand mufti (the chief Muslim cleric in Jerusalem), thundered out over loudspeakers. His words were spiked with hateful rhetoric, with preachings against "the infidels" and Koranic references to the treachery of Jews. That evening was also the beginning of Rosh Hashanah, the Jewish New Year, and Jews soon would be making their way to prayers in the Old City at the Western Wall and to synagogues throughout Jerusalem.

When the Muslim prayer ended, shortly after 1 P.M., the vast majority of worshipers made their way home. But several hundred angry young men did not leave, having been whipped up by the cleric's words. They began gathering stones and then launching them at Israeli police in the Western Wall plaza below. The police quickly moved on the Noble Sanctuary, responding first with tear gas and then with "rubber bullets" and live rounds. Then, accompanied by other Israeli forces, the police stormed into the Al-Aqsa compound itself. Rioting erupted inside the compound and outside the gates of the Old City.

Meanwhile, on the other side of Jerusalem, Jews were preparing to celebrate the New Year—a holiday that traditionally is observed in tranquillity, meditation, prayer, and the singing of psalms. It is a time for atonement and reflection. Nonobservant Jews typically used this holiday to rest and to get together with family. To us it seemed that our neighbors and friends were blithely ignoring the violence that was gathering around them. It was a beautiful Friday, without a cloud in the sky.

By sundown, a total of 4 Palestinians had been killed and 100 wounded in what was retrospectively seen as the first day of a new *intifada*. At St. John's Eye Hospital, a lone surgeon removed seven eyes damaged by "rubber bullets." One man from Hebron who had lost his right eye in the first *intifada* lost 65 percent of his sight in his left eye from a stun grenade. The old Christian medical institutions like St. John's, which was funded by the Ancient Order of the Knights of Malta, and the other neighborhood hospitals, such as nearby Augusta Victoria, were stressed beyond their limits. On Saturday the violence continued to escalate; 12 more Palestinians were killed and 500 more wounded. Among the dead was a 12-year-old Palestinian boy named Mohammed al-Dura, who was killed in his father's arms, by cross fire in Gaza. The event had been captured on videotape and was later broadcast worldwide, providing visual evidence of what human rights groups described as an excessive use of force by the Israelis. The image came to mean more than that, however; it symbolized the seemingly unstoppable descent to violence, the feeling of watching a horrible car accident in slow motion. As if there was nothing anyone could do to stop the senseless killing, the loss of innocent life—not even a father holding his son in his arms.

In the week that followed, the numbers of dead and injured mounted steadily. Funerals in Gaza and Ramallah became massive rallies of rage, fueling more clashes and more killing. On the morning of Friday, October 6, the Palestinian factions of Fatah and Hamas joined forces—a fusion of secular and Islamic fundamentalist movements—and declared a "Day of Rage." They handed out leaflets urging Palestinians to storm Israeli checkpoints and gather for noon prayers at the Al-Aqsa mosque compound to "liberate" the sacred ground from the Israelis. Israel moved quickly to close the border between the West Bank and Jerusalem and ordered the West Bank sealed until the Monday night following Yom Kippur, the holiest day on the Jewish calendar. By noon, about ten thousand Palestinian worshipers had made it through the heavy Israeli security cordon and gathered at the mosque for prayers. The crowd was about one-quarter its usual size, but it was an angry gathering from the start. The Muslim clerics delivered a fiery sermon, broadcast by loudspeakers from the minaret—a sermon that was seemingly designed to fan the flames of religious fervor among the faithful.

In the aftermath of the prayer service, the Israeli police showed restraint as a first volley of rocks were thrown at them by Palestinian youths inside the compound. But soon hundreds of young men were gathering up stones and hurling them over the western rampart of the compound and down on Jewish worshipers at the Western Wall. The Palestinian security forces had either failed to keep the youths back, or had not even tried. Within a half hour, hundreds of Palestinian youths—in what witnesses saw as a highly orchestrated action—were throwing rocks down on Israeli police near the plaza of the Western Wall.

This time, Israeli forces responded immediately with "rubber bullets." The echoing bang of gunshots at the Muslim shrine further inflamed the crowd, and an even heavier barrage of rocks rained down. A Muslim cleric could be heard on a loudspeaker, appealing to the youths to stop: "This is a holy place. Do not give the occupiers an excuse to storm our beloved mosque." But inside the compound, the cleric was being shouted down by a group of Palestinian women, their heads covered by the traditional chador, who were chanting, "With our blood and with our soul, we will sacrifice for Al-Aqsa!"

Most of the fighting that day would be focused around St. Stephen's Gate. This gate is remembered by Israelis as the site of the key battle in 1967 that led to the capture of the Old City. Inside the gate, a narrow street leads to the first station of the cross on the Via Dolorosa, and to the Ecce Homo arch. This storied portal, ironically, bore the name of the first Christian martyr, Stephen, who had been killed by stoning.

A Watch 2000 security camera at the Israeli police station in Jerusalem's Old City was gazing down over Al-Aqsa's northern wall, into the compound. The camera periodically swiveled at an angle, to view the interior of St. Stephen's Gate, recording what had become the most intense day of rioting thus far. The Israeli police officials at headquarters were monitoring the Day of Rage as it was building, focusing in on the rock- and Molotov cocktail–throwers. Suddenly the camera lens trembled, and a face appeared, half hidden by a kaffiyeh. The eyes stared straight into the lens of the Israeli security camera. This *shebab* had climbed the pole on which the camera was mounted, and now was shouting, "Allahu akbar!" straight into the camera. Then, with a softball-sized rock, he smashed the thick glass that protected the camera lens. From inside the Watch 2000 command center in the Old City, the Israeli police captain watched as a wide crack formed across the screen—and still the blows rained down on the camera. The police cameras had become a symbol of Israeli control in the Old City, and the youth was now attacking that symbol with a chilling ferocity. The rock slammed down on the lens again and again, until finally the glass splintered and the screen went black. When an Israeli police captain showed me the footage some weeks later, I thought this was what it would look like to be beaten to death with a rock. The eyes above that kaffiyeh burned with something beyond despair, beyond anger. A deep, almost primal hatred between Arabs and Jews had surfaced, or resurfaced, in the autumn of 2000.

After being pinned down on the Via Dolorosa between the Israeli soldiers' shooting and the Palestinian *shebab* throwing rocks, several reporters and I sought refuge in the Basilica of St. Anne, just inside St. Stephen's Gate. We climbed a set of stairs in the monastery and from the rooftop watched the conflict down below. From there, it was possible to see the whole battlefield—the northern rampart of the Haram al-Sharif and the stretch of cobblestone from St. Stephen's Gate up to the Ecce Homo arch and the first station of the cross.

We watched as the *shebab* furiously stoned a small wood frame police station tucked inside the archway of St. Stephen's Gate, where a half-dozen Israeli police were holed up. Now the Palestinian youths were trying to break open the locked door. Israeli troops moved in with full force, shooting live ammunition and "rubber bullets" to clear the street. The rioters fell back, but several were seriously wounded and had to be dragged off on the shoulders of their fellow *shebab,* screaming in pain, and bleeding as they went.

Israeli police shot open the lock to the door and freed the officers trapped inside. In the power vacuum left after the police evacuated the building, the Palestinian youths surged forward again, claiming control of the gate and smashing the windows and doors and computers inside the police station. They ripped down the neon Israeli police sign, and then set the station on fire. Thick, black smoke billowed out over the chaos. This infuriated the Israeli police, who moved closer to the rock-throwers (now numbering in the thousands) who had taken control of the Haram. Hundreds more had seized a plaza and a parking lot directly in front of St. Anne's. Priests peered from windows of the monastery, and then quickly pulled the steel shutters closed when the gunshots came.

We moved down from the rooftop and watched the rest of the action from a first-floor grated window that looked directly out on the Via Dolorosa. From this street-level perch I watched as several Israelis—apparently members of an elite division of the police known as the antiterrorism squad—pushed forward, passing by only ten yards in front of me. One soldier, with a packet of L&M cigarettes tucked in the camouflage mesh atop his helmet, charged the rioting youths, firing live rounds. Another soldier, a "spotter," ran alongside "L&M," pointing at what looked to be a boy of no more than 14, and said in Hebrew, "Right there, get that one."

"L&M" appeared to be aiming higher than the legs—flouting official Israeli military guidelines. From where I was watching, directly behind the officer, it looked as if he was aiming at the youth's head. He missed. Palestinian emergency medics who had been caught in the cross fire were hiding behind a wall nearby. At one point, Israeli soldiers, surprised to find them there, instinctively swung their rifles in their direction. The medics, dressed in white coats spattered with blood, threw up their hands and shouted in Hebrew, "No! No! No! Medics!" Then a burst of heavy gunfire was directed at a group of teenagers on the frontline who had been among the few throwing Molotov cocktails. No more than forty yards from Ecce Homo, a 14-year-old Palestinian boy was suddenly knocked off his feet and lay on his back as a pool of blood collected around him on the cobblestones. His friends rushed to grab him and put him in one of the waiting ambulances. He had been shot in the head, apparently by an Israeli sniper. Palestinian hospital officials later confirmed that a live round had killed him. Six other *shebab* were wounded in the burst of gunfire, two of them seriously. Emergency medical teams ferried the wounded on stretchers inside the Al-Aqsa compound, where they were treated at a makeshift field hospital. The seriously wounded were loaded into waiting ambulances that rushed them out through St. Stephen's Gate to nearby hospitals.

All day long, the rock-throwers were supplied with wheelbarrows full of rocks the perfect size for throwing from somewhere inside the Al-Aqsa compound. After several hours, the battle subsided, and I ended up sitting in the courtyard of the monastery of the White Fathers (the French Catholic order that runs St. Anne's), talking with Father Franz Bouen. He was a strong proponent of interfaith dialogue and a respected voice for reconciliation in Jerusalem, having lived in the monastery through more than three decades of violence and upheaval. "The struggle has a religious dimension now," he observed, "and I am afraid of what that is going to mean for the future for all of us here. This will not be an easy fire to put out."

As we sat together on a bench, the sound of birds picking at dates in the trees above mingled with the crude taunts of the *shebab* at the Israeli forces and an occasional pop of gunfire just outside on the Via Dolorosa. Bouen added: "It is a madness. There is no sense to it. But that is always the way in acts of war. I can understand rage, even when it explodes, but in this situation I cannot find meaning. I don't see what either side is going to achieve."

I asked whether he thought that the Israeli-Palestinian conflict over Jerusalem and its overlapping sacred space increasingly was defined as a Muslim-Jewish conflict, one that factored out the Christian presence altogether. The Temple Mount/Noble Sanctuary stood at the core of local Jews' and Muslims' faith, but the Arab Christians seemed to have a more complex relationship to the sacred space. Virtually none adhered to any eschatology at all related to the Temple Mount. The fundamentalist belief that the physical restoration of the Jewish Temple is a prerequisite for redemption and the Second Coming is most common among the evangelical Christians of the West and is rarely encountered in the more conservative, institutional churches—the Lutherans, Anglicans, Catholics, and Greek Orthodox—that predominate in the Palestinian Christian community.

On the contrary, the Palestinian Christians' attitude toward Haram al-Sharif is shaped by the Arab and Muslim culture that surrounds them. They view the Muslim shrine not only as sacred ground for their Islamic brothers but also as a potent symbol of Arab culture and Palestinian nationalism—just as the Holy Sepulcher, the Via Dolorosa, and the magnificent abbeys, monasteries, and churches adorning the Jerusalem skyline are also sacred and symbolic to Christians.

Yet in some ways the Muslim shrine could also be viewed as a direct confrontation to the Christians, an in-your-face message that Islam had triumphed over Christianity, just as Christianity earlier had claimed triumph over Judaism. The Arab Christians who visited the Dome of the Rock had only to look up to see that many of the marble pillars are carved with ornamental crosses—a reminder that they most likely were taken from Byzantine churches ransacked after the Islamic conquest. And it would be difficult to miss the large inscription, in beautiful Arabic calligraphy, wrapped around the drum-like base of the dome, which reads in part: "Oh, you People of the Book, overstep not bounds in your religion, and of God speak only the truth. The Messiah, Jesus, son of Mary is only an apostle of God, and his Word which he conveyed unto Mary, and a spirit proceeding from him. Believe therefore in God and his apostles, and say not Three. It will be better for you. God is only one God. Far be it from his glory that he should have a son."

"The voice of the Christians is weak," said Father Bouen. "It is as weak and as small as the population of Christians. But it is also weak because we have no demands, as Christians, to any of this space. The only demand our community has is as Palestinians, but it cannot be connected to the faith because the message of the faith is precisely opposed to such demands. So we are on a completely different footing, or we have a completely different approach than the other two faiths on these matters of sovereignty. . . . We are somewhere in between the Palestinian cause and the calling of the Christian faith. We have to live somewhere in between."

But there was a group of Western Christians in Jerusalem who didn't feel that way. In mid-October, at the height of the bloody and still escalating crisis, the Jewish festival of Sukkoth—also known as the Feast of Tabernacles or the Ingathering—took place. The seven-day feast was traditionally observed by the building of *sukkot,* or small palm-thatched booths, commemorating the quickly assembled quarters that Jews were forced to build during their wanderings in the wilderness. The holiday is a time of family and neighborly get-togethers in the *sukkot,* most of which are erected on terraces or in backyards of Jewish homes. The feast in October 2000 seemed an almost surreal contrast to the violence that was gathering force in the territories, but it was also a remarkable expression of the endurance of the Jewish people and their traditions through thousands of years of history.

About 15,000 Christian Zionists, mostly from America and Europe, flocked to Jerusalem for Sukkoth in 2000, defiantly ignoring the U.S. State Department's travel advisory and eager to show their solidarity with Israel in the face of the brewing conflict. At the Jerusalem Convention Center there were many rousing speeches suggesting that the End of Days was at hand. One of the most stirring came from Sister Gwen Shaw, president of the End Time Handmaidens and Servants International, which had established a worldwide network of Christian Zionists who believe that the creation of the state of Israel, and the ingathering of Jews there, are stages in God's plan for redemption. There were bus tours to Jewish settlements, headed by David Wilder, the spokesman for the Jewish community in Hebron—a place where tensions had soared between Arabs and Jews. Some six hundred Israeli soldiers were stationed in Hebron to enforce a curfew and siege on the 35,000 Palestinians of the town's center so that the 400 Israeli settlers would have freedom of movement. Dore Gold, who had served as a foreign policy adviser to former prime minister Netanyahu and who was a close political ally of Sharon's, was on the lecture schedule with a talk titled "A Crucial Moment for Israel." The speeches and healing sessions and performances resonated with a sense of the impending fulfillment of divine prophecies. As the International Christian Embassy of Jerusalem stated in its guidebook for the event, "Incredibly, God has used Israel as a vehicle for ushering in His redemptive plan within the bounds of time and called us all before time for an after-time purpose!"

With millions of evangelical Christians around the world forming close connections with the religious right in Israel, it is no longer possible for mainstream Christian denominations to dismiss the movement as a fringe phenomenon. The Israeli right wing has found it extremely profitable to deepen its embrace of the Christian Zionists, as tens of millions of dollars pour in to fund Temple restoration organizations, Jewish settlements, the continuing absorption into Israel of Jews from Ethiopia and the former Soviet Union, and a variety of social programs in Israel. A Chicago-based organization, the International Fellowship of Christians and Jews (IFCJ), raised some $30 million in 1999–2000, and its founder and president, Rabbi

Yechiel Eckstein, was in Jerusalem during Sukkoth to present a check for $12 million to the United Jewish Appeal, making the IFCJ the latter organization's largest single contributor.

The evangelical Christians' fervent support of Israel is said to be rooted in scriptures that call for an understanding between Christians and Jews, and to be based on a spiritual and material debt owed by Gentiles to Jews. But the funds raised by American evangelical icons such as Jerry Falwell, Pat Robertson, and Chuck Colson have been earmarked exclusively for the goals of Zionism—revealing the theology to be distinctly political. The Palestinian Christians have been overlooked by the Christian Zionist preachers and their fund-raising campaigns. To the extent that these organizations have contributed to the Jewish Agency's efforts to bring in and settle more Jews, these campaigns not only overlooked the Palestinian Christians but arguably contributed to policies that displaced them—in this particular case, from Gilo to Upper Nazareth. An equally troubling aspect of this Christian Zionist enterprise is the crass nature of the exchange—cash in return for redemption. The Israeli religious right has accepted millions of dollars from Christians who believe their donations toward the ingathering of Jews in Israel are intended to hasten the return of Jesus. In this divine program of final redemption, these evangelical Christians believe, Jews must accept Christ's kingdom or suffer God's wrath on earth.

I asked Eckstein about his organization's indifference to Palestinian Christians. "Well, we do work for Christians in China and in Sudan, where there is persecution," he replied, "but not in Israel. We don't do anything specifically for Arabs."

On October 16, in the Western Wall plaza, thousands of observant Jews carrying palm fronds in symbolic thanksgiving to God for the harvest were coming through the metal detectors. Among them was a small cluster of about two hundred members of the Temple Mount Faithful, who began to assemble directly in front of the ramp that leads up to the Mugrabi Gate and into the Temple Mount/Noble Sanctuary—the same gate by which Sharon had entered the Temple Mount grounds nearly three weeks earlier. The leader of the Faithful, Gershom Solomon, had been around a long time. He was a thin man who walked with a limp and who preached a strange secular Zionism couched in religious rhetoric. His theatrical efforts to "restore the Temple" had triggered the riots in 1990. Though Solomon had little support in the Israeli Jewish community, he was a big crowd-pleaser to the Christian Zionists, scores of whom were gathering. They held Bibles and listened with serene smiles as Solomon approached the Israeli police who blocked the gate. He demanded to be allowed to enter this "holy ground" in order to "replace" the Islamic shrines with the Third Temple. The Israeli cops didn't budge. Someone handed Solomon a microphone, and he began to lecture the crowd: "Look at what is happening around you. Wake up! Jewish people, do not give into Arafat. He is a war criminal. This belongs to the Jewish people. The Temple Mount is ours. The Temple must be rebuilt!"

As I moved through the crowd, I was not surprised to see many of the evangelical Christians I had met the year before, at the turn of the calendar to 2000. They were still here, still brimming with expectation of the End of Days. Ed Daniels from North Dakota was happy to see me, and immediately informed me that the conflict raging in the West Bank and Gaza was "such an exciting time for us!" He was almost breathless with his End Times zeal. "There is going to be a war!" he told me. "All of the nations on earth will come against Israel. Look at the U.N.—so eager to condemn Israel for defending itself against the terrorists. The only nation still blessed is the U.S. because it favors Israel. You see, Charlie, that is why you as an American are blessed. This is why you are here, Charlie. You are representing Boston. God will hold back his wrath against Boston just because of your presence."

All I could think of was how Ed—a follower of the deported Brother David—had been forced to hide from the Israeli police in order to avoid being kicked out of his home in the Mount of Olives the year before. The security forces considered him a member of the Christian underground that they feared would commit mass suicide or cause general panic in the streets of Jerusalem on December 31, 1999. And now here he was, talking—or actually, shouting—about wanting to destroy the Dome of the Rock and touch off a regional conflagration. "We love the Arabs, but they are controlled by demonic powers," he added, in his dry Dakota monotone. "But this is all coming together now, and the Temple is going to be rebuilt. Now is the time, brother!"

And so Jerusalem stood once again at a turning point in its history, its inhabitants pondering the significance of the events unfolding around them. To those who, like Ed, viewed the city as the staging point of the last battle before a messianic age of redemption, the events were a thrilling fulfillment of prophecy. To those who saw the city as a living community torn apart and suffering, the gathering storm of conflict seemed somehow inevitable. To those who believed that Jerusalem stood as a symbol of peace, its desecration with the crude graffiti of violence was deeply depressing.

On the streets of the West Bank and Gaza, the violence continued to rage, gaining in momentum as each new funeral stirred the coals of hatred and fanned the flames of militancy. The Palestinian Christians seemed, more than ever, to have been relegated to the sidelines. The *shebab* had already anointed this campaign with a distinctly Islamic name: the "Al-Aqsa *intifada*."

IV

The Passion

Jesus and his disciples gathered for what would be their last supper together. Most had no idea that they would soon part ways. It was the Thursday after Jesus had arrived in Jerusalem, and they, like Jews everywhere, were preparing for the Passover seder. Seated with his disciples at the table, Jesus spoke of the bread and the wine as his body and blood, and told his followers to remember that he would be present with them in these symbols. Whether they interpret Jesus's statement in concrete, physical terms or metaphorically, Christians all over the world believe that at this moment Jesus was offering himself in sacrifice for the salvation of the world. From the beginning of the church, Christians have assembled to reenact the disciples' breaking of bread and drinking of wine together—thus incorporating the "body" and the "blood" of Christ.

Jesus knew the hour of his death was near. He retreated from Jerusalem and went down into the Kidron Valley, to the Garden of Gethsemane, which lay along the base of the Mount of Olives. There, Jesus knew, one of his disciples would betray him. Yet he stayed in the garden all that night, struggling inwardly to accept his fate, to endure the pain and suffering that the morning would bring. It was there that Jesus revealed his humanity, his fear, anguish, and worry over his impending death. In the biblical locution, this was the Agony.

Today the Garden of Gethsemane is in the care of the Franciscan Custody of the Holy Land. The ancient olive groves still stand. Biblical historians and archaeologists believe the gnarled old roots of these trees date back to the time of Jesus. Walking among the trees was for me among the most genuinely tactile experiences of my trek along the path of Jesus. There were no churches, no chapels, no museums circumscribing the ground. There was no glass case through which to view the sacred space. There was just earth and roots and trees, ancient and gray and yet still bearing a healthy harvest of olives every year.

XIII

The Garden of Gethsemane

THE AGONY

"My soul is overwhelmed with sorrow to the point of death; stay here and keep watch." Going a little farther, he fell to the ground and prayed that if possible the hour might pass from him.

MARK 14:34–35 (NIV)

THE CNN CAMERA crew was setting up lights in Hanan Ashrawi's office while she fielded a phone call from the Associated Press. The CNN producer fixed a microphone to Ashrawi's lapel as she finished the call. Then the lights clicked on, the camera rolled, and Ashrawi straightened in her chair. She focused her thoughts and began one more television interview in what had become, on some days, a nearly hourly series of appearances on CNN and the BBC and the other major networks around the world, as the crisis surged out of control in October 2000. After Yasser Arafat, Hanan Ashrawi was perhaps the most recognizable spokesperson for the Palestinian cause in America and Europe. With her well-reasoned points of view, her passion about the injustice of Israeli occupation, and her dignified presence, Ashrawi had first come to international prominence in 1988, when she cut a striking figure on a televised meeting of Israelis and Palestinians on *Nightline,* moderated by ABC's Ted Koppel. Over the years, her voice as a woman, a mother, an academic, and a Palestinian Christian resonated throughout the Western world.

On this day, Ashrawi described the clashes between Israeli forces and the stone-throwing *shebab* as "popular demonstrations" that were being "put down with excessive force by the Israelis" against "a defenseless people." She pointedly did not use the phrase "the Al-Aqsa *intifada,*" but rather described the events as "the *intifada* for independence." Ashrawi's choice of words made the uprising sound so much more reasonable, secular, and appealing to the West than "the Al-Aqsa *intifada,*" with its shadings of a religious conflict between Muslims and Jews. She cast a Westernized veneer over the *shebab,* painting their conduct as a dignified popular resistance, akin to America's civil rights movement. She was dismissive of the gunfire coming from the Palestinian militias as "young men shooting from their homes without orders." Her skill in recreating the perception of this *intifada* was precisely why Arafat had relied on her for so long to represent the Palestinian cause to the Western world.

But in private Ashrawi was sensing by late fall that this *intifada* had spun out of control, and she feared it could descend into lawlessness. Despite her own secular leanings, she told me in later interviews that she did realize then that a powerful part of the emotion driving this uprising had everything to do with the volatile mix of nationalism and religion within a traditional Muslim culture. Using the phrase "the *intifada* for independence" on the American television networks was a wish, a hope, a yearning, perhaps—even if it was increasingly not the reality on the street.

Ashrawi's efforts to wrap this *intifada* in a package presentable to the West by focusing on nationalist aspirations rather than religious conflict were in keeping with her stance as a Palestinian Christian. In some ways, the Palestinian cause, as presented to Americans through their television networks and newspapers, is actually a Christian Palestinian view of the struggle—confidently Arab and nationalistic and assuredly not Islamic in tone. Like another Palestinian Christian advocate of the cause—Edward Said, the Columbia University professor and well-known author—Ashrawi always focused on the problems that she traced to violence from the Israeli side, including the occupation, the excessive use of force, the economic siege, and the social despair. But before I came to Ashrawi's office, never once had I heard the current uprising called "the *intifada* for independence," on any street, in any part of the West Bank or Gaza. And in the Arab world, the street doesn't lie. It was "the Al-Aqsa *intifada.*" Language mattered, as did the fact that the central organizing structure of this uprising was the Islamic and National Forces, local coordinating groups that consisted mainly of leaders from Fatah and Hamas—a marked contrast to the previous *intifada*'s "popular committees," which were made up of local Muslim and Christian community leaders.

After the signing of the peace agreement in 1994, Arafat appointed

Hanan Ashrawi to several important cabinet positions (including the ministry of higher education) in the newly forming government of the Palestinian Authority. Unlike many Palestinian legislators, she remained tough and independent. She resigned in 1998 from the cabinet because of, as she put it, "issues of corruption, human rights and accountability." But she retained her seat on the Palestinian Legislative Council and was now heading the Palestinian Initiative for the Promotion of Global Dialogue and Democracy, an institute that she had founded, and she remained as eloquent and assertive in her defense of the Palestinian nationalist cause as she had always been.

Even by the second or third week of this uprising—whatever one called it—Ashrawi understood quite well that this conflict was nothing like the first *intifada*. In the first week, it was characterized by a spontaneous outpouring of Palestinian anger at occupation; but that was soon replaced by a "low-intensity conflict," a guerrilla war, with most Palestinians, both Christian and Muslim, being civilians caught in the middle. There was only limited opportunity for them to participate in this armed uprising against Israeli occupation. At a deeper level, it was becoming clear that the anger in the streets was directed not only at Israel but also at the Palestinian Authority, at its corruption, and at the flawed peace agreement that Arafat had signed, which had never been implemented.

Ashrawi knew that this *intifada* had been, in her words, "a long time in the making." As she later told me: "Anyone who was watching the situation could see this coming. I was telling everybody, 'We don't know when and where it will explode, but it will explode.' The Palestinian Authority had done nothing to cushion this, to try to address the anger. So we, frankly, we didn't know whether it would be an implosion or an explosion, or both."

Many months before this *intifada* started, Ashrawi had expressed to me a sharp criticism of Hamas and of its influence in shaping the Palestinian Authority's basic law, especially the use of Koranic law and the adoption of Islam as the national religion. She had stood up against this, along with several secular Muslim legislators, but she had lost the battle and was now resigned to it all. "It seems fundamentalism is the language of the day," she observed, "and unfortunately there are people in our society who want to echo the intolerance of the Jewish fundamentalists in Israel."

As the conflict sharpened along religious lines, Ashrawi seemed to grow even less comfortable than she had been in the past with questions about her own religious background and to what extent it may have helped shape her views. The first time I interviewed her, in 1998, she expressed suspicion of anyone who wanted to talk about her Christian background, and she offered only reflexive answers to such questions. The answers were given with a spark and flare, like the lighter she touched to one cigarette after another: "The fate of the Christian community is indivisible from the destiny of the Palestinian people as a whole. . . . Occupation does not discriminate on the basis of religion."

At that time, Ashrawi explained to me that her spiritual background and moral education were influenced less by her mother, who was a devout Christian, than by her father, who was a confirmed agnostic and committed socialist and humanist. In her autobiography, *This Side of Peace,* she dispensed with her Christian background in one paragraph. The word *Christianity* does not even appear in the index. She bristled at the suggestion that her crisp and proper English, her reasoned points of view, and her life of political activism—even her understanding of nationalism and passionate belief in women's rights in a male-dominated society—emanated from the Western-influenced institutions that shaped her education, virtually all of which were Christian in their foundation. She was educated at the Friends' Girls' School in Ramallah, a Quaker institution founded by missionaries in the nineteenth century. From there she attended the American University in Beirut—the Harvard of the Middle East—which had been founded in 1866 as the Syrian Protestant College. These Christian educational institutions were imbued with a Protestant missionary zeal to foster the Arabic language and cultural heritage as well as the Western values of democracy and nationalism.

Another educational institution dear to Ashrawi's heart was Birzeit University, where for many years she had been the head of the English department. Founded by the Nasser family, prominent Anglican Christians, it was the pride of the Palestinian intellectual elite. It stood as a symbol of hope, high on a windswept hill in the village of Bir Zeit, outside Ramallah.

It was within the walls of these institutions and within the supportive structure of her family and her marriage that Ashrawi prepared herself, as a woman in a patriarchal Arab world, to step into a leadership role. "It is true," she said. "Christian women were able to be more active because they were raised in a more liberal and more open culture and family structure. Christian women had more access to education, to social work, to political activity, and this was true going back to the days of the women's union started in Bethlehem [in the 1940s], and which my father supported. This is one of the truly sad and disturbing elements of the disappearance of the Christians, that it will affect women's standing. There are of course many Muslim women who are leaders as well, but these role models and the culture that supports them is very important for women to have."

But the culture of tolerance and inclusiveness that Ashrawi so cherished in Palestinian society and in the first *intifada* went untapped in the first weeks and months of this *intifada.* Ashrawi knew this, and up to a point she acknowledged it, during interviews some months later. She knew that this conflict was veering in a direction that alienated the people it needed most, the community organizers and the educated elite, women and artists, who could redirect the struggle away from the angry masked gunmen firing on Israeli settlements and back to the ordinary Palestinian people and their legitimate yearning for independence. The leaders of the educated and largely secular elite were not going to pick up stones, and they didn't tend to carry guns. But in the fall of 2000, they remained silent—perhaps deliberately so. In the crisis atmosphere, there was no room for criticism of Arafat, or the Palestinian Authority, or corruption, or human rights violations, or the lack of freedom of speech. By filling the streets with stone-throwing youths, Arafat's Fatah organization left no place for demonstrations that might have challenged Arafat's leadership.

In the months that lay ahead Ashrawi would emerge as one of a handful of leaders trying to steer this *intifada* toward nonviolence, toward a nationalist movement that could be more inclusive and possibly more effective. This task would prove extremely difficult.

. . .

In the autumn of 2000, the violence never let up, and I found myself criss-crossing the same path that I had been traveling all year. The path of Jesus's life and ministry—in Bethlehem, Nazareth, the Galilee, the Mount of Olives, and Jerusalem—was now engulfed in a spasm of killing. At many of these turns in the road, the popular expressions of the Israeli-Palestinian conflict, the language in the street, was taking on a new tone. The real issues between the two sides were still matters of occupation and land, self-determination and economics, and limited water resources. But the fact that the eruption of violence emanated from the sacred core of Jerusalem—the Noble Sanctuary and the Temple Mount—cast a religious light on this conflict. The conflict was no longer between Palestinians and Israelis but between Muslims and Jews. The dwindling number of the Palestinian Christians made them largely irrelevant to the current cycle of violence. The Christian community was a disintegrating cultural interface between Islam and Judaism, a buffer that had finally been worn so thin that it had no effect.

The rising clamor of religion could be heard in the funeral processions of the "martyrs," which became mass marches, even assaults, on security checkpoints, where Palestinian youths would confront Israeli soldiers with stones. The chants along the way were not just the same old nationalist slogans of Fatah. New choruses had been added. One of the most common was *Khaiber! Khaiber! Ya Yehud! Jayesh Mohammed sawfa ya'oud!* ("Khaiber! Khaiber! All the Jews! The army of Mohammed will return!"). The chant referred to a passage in the Koran in which the Jews of Khaiber, a village near Medina, had made a peace settlement with Mohammed and then violated the agreement and attempted to kill the prophet. Throughout the 1980s and 1990s, this chant was shouted at the funerals and rallies of the Islamic fundamentalist groups such as Hamas and Islamic Jihad. Few of the secular crowd from the PLO knew their Koran well enough to understand the reference.

If the sources of the conflict were to be depicted through thermal mapping, the Temple Mount/Haram al-Sharif would appear in a glowing red mass, as the burning core. But there would be other concentrations of energy and heat that would appear as swirling masses around a coordinate of religious shrines throughout the West Bank. In Bethlehem, it was Rachel's Tomb, the traditional holy site revered for the biblical matriarch. In Hebron, a town deeply divided between the local Palestinian community and a small enclave of Jewish settlers, fighting raged around the Tomb of the Patriarchs, a site holy to Jews, Christians, and Muslims as the burial place of Abraham, Isaac, and Jacob. And in Nablus there were fierce gun battles at the Tomb of Joseph, a small Ottoman-era building that had been reconfigured by nearby Jewish settlers as a shrine.

All of these shrines were coordinates in a sacred landscape where Israeli Jews and Palestinian Muslims—and their collective memories and identities—were placed right up against each other. They had become junctions of hatred, dangerous intersections of differing interpretations of biblical history and archaeology and scripture and, ultimately, of who had ownership rights to the land. Under the Israeli occupation, soldiers had been stationed at these sites as guards, and thus the sacred spaces had been militarized. Since the first redeployments mandated by the peace process, Israel had maintained pockets of sovereignty around the sites and had kept a military presence amid the largely Palestinian-ruled towns. Jewish worshipers saw the soldiers as protection for those who wished to visit the shrines, whereas Palestinians saw them as one more reminder of a lingering Israeli occupation. At these points it seemed the nationalist struggle between Israelis and Palestinians was a holy war between Jews and Muslims—a conflict in which Christians were pointedly left out.

. . .

One of the hottest flash points in the early phase of the fighting was Rachel's Tomb, in Bethlehem. The biblical matriarch Rachel was revered as the wife of Jacob and the mother of Joseph and Benjamin. Jews, Christians, and Muslims throughout the centuries had considered the reputed site of her grave holy. More than a tourist attraction, the tomb was the locus of daily devotions for observant Jewish women from nearby settlements in the West Bank. These women prayed to Rachel for fertility, healthy birthing, and the safety of their children.

The clashes at the site, heavily guarded by Israeli forces, were drawing up to one thousand *shebab* each day for a deadly cat-and-mouse game of stone-throwing at the Israeli border police and soldiers positioned around the cinder block walls of the tomb. The soldiers stationed in a watchtower above the tomb were targets of hailstorms of baseball-sized rocks that would slam against the steel framework of the tower and at times crack the heavy Plexiglas windows. Israeli snipers were positioned on the walls surrounding the tomb, across the street in another observation tower, and in an abandoned building that also fell within the Israeli-controlled pocket.

The stone-throwing here was a highly ritualized affair in the first few weeks of the Al-Aqsa *intifada*. The *shebab* rolled burning tires up to create a front line of thick, heavy smoke, and then they inched forward, using metal dumpsters or the burned-out bodies of old cars to shield themselves and to get within range to throw rocks and Molotov cocktails. Typically, the first response from the Israeli soldiers was to fire tear gas, followed by "rubber bullets" and then live ammunition. But what made the rules of engagement in this *intifada* different was the presence of Palestinian gunfire. Palestinian militias, and sometimes Palestinian policemen in uniform, were positioning themselves in buildings and just off the main road and firing on the Israeli forces around Rachel's Tomb. This changed the dynamic, and the Israelis were quick to respond with bursts of automatic weapons fire. At the daily Israeli military briefings, reporters were told that the Israeli troops returned fire only on the sources of fire. But to those watching these street battles it was clear that the young Israeli soldiers were given a great deal of discretion and routinely fired indiscriminately into the crowd, killing many young Palestinians—including children who had been caught up in the chaos. Although rock-throwing is not a form of peaceful demonstration, international and Israeli human rights groups questioned whether Israel's "shoot-to-kill" response was appropriate.

One of the youths who was killed at Rachel's Tomb was 13-year-old Muayad Jawarish. Like all Palestinian children his age, Muayad had been watching the street clashes for three weeks on Palestinian television. The government-run station was drumming up emotional support for the popular uprising and casting the young demonstrators as the heroes of a battle for independence. The footage was cut in a way to mix images of Israeli soldiers firing with images of young boys on stretchers. The grainy footage was paired with sad, mournful Palestinian songs of independence and "steadfastness" and images of the Dome of the Rock. Unlike the Palestinian participants in the *intifada* of 1987–1992, those in 2000 had control of their own television and radio stations, and those who had satellite dishes could also watch the Qatar-based station *Al-Jazera,* the Arab world's answer to CNN. And with all of this jingoistic coverage bombarding Palestinian homes with images of heroism, just about every Palestinian kid wanted to take part in the Al-Aqsa *intifada.*

Muayad's mother, Iman, had told her oldest son to stay away from the clashes. But on his way home from school, just after 2 P.M. on October 8, the street demonstration was building into a fury. Muayad's friends stopped to watch the action but were too far back to take part. Molotov cocktails, fashioned out of Coke bottles and gasoline-soaked rags, smashed against the Israeli security post and ignited in a blaze near the Israeli soldiers. Suddenly there were gunshots. Everyone began running for cover.

Within seconds, Israeli snipers positioned on the roof of Rachel's Tomb and in the abandoned building across the street opened fire. Muayad and his friends ran for cover along with the rest of the crowd, heading toward an open field off the main road. A high-velocity bullet struck Muayad in the base of his skull. Older youths stopped and carried him out of the line of fire and lay him down, the blood gushing out of the back of his head, soaking the book bag on his back. He was breathing, but barely. An ambulance rushed him to Beit Jala's Al-Hussein Hospital, which had been founded by a Swedish Christian group in the nineteenth century and had become the central emergency facility for Bethlehem during the *intifada.* Surgeons tried unsuccessfully to remove the bullet that had lodged in Muayad's brain. He was pronounced dead at 8 P.M.

The next morning, five thousand Palestinians gathered for his funeral, including hundreds of his young classmates and friends. Fatah leaders marched alongside the open wooden casket in which Muayad lay wrapped in the Palestinian flag. Masked gunmen, presumed members of the Fatah Tanzim militia, brandished weapons. His mother, her face soaked with tears and distorted by anguish just barely visible under a black veil, cried out when the casket was brought into the family home for her viewing before burial: "My son! My son! They killed my son! God give me strength!"

Muayad had become a martyr. Posters of him were plastered on shop windows and telephone poles and street signs all over Bethlehem. They told the brief details of his short life and carried the heading, "Martyr of the Al-Aqsa *Intifada.*" Photographs of Muayad dressed in his school uniform with a thin tie and wearing a slightly mischievous smile made him look more like what he truly was—just a kid in the wrong place at the wrong time.

After the first nine weeks of fighting, 300 people had been killed, 275 of them Palestinian. Of those 275, one in four had been under age 17. Of the several thousand Palestinians who had been seriously wounded, approximately half were under age 17, hospital officials and human rights workers estimated. Hundreds more had been permanently disabled by high-velocity rounds that had shattered the bones in their not-yet-fully-grown legs, or by "rubber bullets" that had taken out eyes.

That children were dying in violent clashes around a holy site dedicated to a biblical matriarch who was believed to protect children was bitterly ironic. The biblical matriarch Rachel, who had died after giving birth to Benjamin, was a sympathetic figure whose beauty was renowned and whose tragic loss was commemorated in verse and in the writings of the sages. The tradition that identified her tomb in

Bethlehem began with events retold in the book of Genesis. The site also is mentioned in the Gospel According to Matthew, in the story of Jesus's birth and the flight of the Holy Family into Egypt. When the children of Bethlehem were slain by Herod, according to Matthew, an Old Testament prophecy was revealed at Rachel's tomb (Matthew 2:17–18):

Then what was said through the prophet Jeremiah was fulfilled:

"A voice is heard in Ramah,
weeping and great mourning,
Rachel weeping for her children
and refusing to be comforted,
because they are no more."

. . .

I headed north from Jerusalem through the West Bank to Nablus, to get to yet another sacred tomb that had become ground zero in a running firefight. Throughout October, I had been covering events daily with my colleague Said Ghazali, the *Boston Globe*'s Arabic translator and researcher. Said was a seasoned Palestinian reporter who had worked with the Associated Press and other Western news organizations for more than thirteen years, covering the Israeli-Palestinian conflict, and we traveled together just about every day throughout the fall.

It took roughly one hour and a half to drive to Nablus, to the tomb of Joseph, the son of Rachel and Jacob. In taking this route into the land referred to in the Bible as Samaria, we were roughly retracing the path Jesus would have traversed in his visit to the Samaritan woman at Jacob's well. We were in the same region described in Luke's recounting of the "Parable of the Good Samaritan." The road was treacherous during the *intifada.* Stone-throwers often would pop up from behind turns in the road and attack cars (including mine). Palestinian gunmen were shooting at the passing cars of Jewish settlers, which were distinguishable by the yellow Israeli license plates and the fact that Jews tended to drive newer models. Several Jewish settlers and Israeli reservists had been shot and killed along the road. The disintegration into lawlessness had prompted Jewish settlement "security forces" to ply the road in Jeeps and pickup trucks, carrying out their own vigilante attacks on Palestinians. The settlers had taken to setting up roadblocks at night, stopping and searching Palestinian vehicles at gunpoint. One of the people they stopped on the night of October 9 was Father Ibrahim Hijazin, a Catholic priest from Ramallah, who was returning from Nablus. The settlers, he said, ordered him out of his car. He showed them his Vatican laissez-passer, a permit allowing Catholic clerics to travel through checkpoints; but they smashed the windshield of his car anyway, before allowing him to continue on his way.

A few days before, on one of our journeys along this road, Said and I had been admiring the beauty of the landscape during the olive harvest. Palestinian families were clustered in the groves, picking the ripened green and black olives that would then be pressed into oil. We stopped to talk to one family we saw by the side of the road, thinking it might make a nice feature article, in contrast with all the violence we had been reporting. But as soon as we stopped, it became apparent that this family was in distress and shouting about some ordeal. It turned out that Jewish settlers from a particularly militant nearby settlement known as Rachelim had just held the family at gunpoint and threatened their lives. Three generations had been picking olives, the women batting the trees with sticks and the men gathering the olives that rained down onto tarps and putting them in sacks that were then loaded into saddlebags on a donkey for the trek home. But the settlers, the family claimed, had come and ordered the older relatives to run, and had forced the young men to lie down at gunpoint while they cut open all of the sacks of olives and dumped them on the road. Then they confiscated the family's tools, the coffee pot, and the picnic lunch that had been laid out on a blanket. The family said this all happened in full view of the Israeli soldiers who guarded the settlement, and that they did nothing to stop the settlers. "They even stole the donkey!" said Abdel Khader Matia, a man in his late 50s, who at this point seemed on the verge of tears. The women were screaming hysterically as everyone tried to tell us what had just happened. The Matia family dispatched a young member to the house to retrieve the Ottoman-era deed that they said proved ownership to the land, where their family had picked olives for generations. At first I thought the family was exaggerating, especially about the donkey. But the incident, if accurately described, was a deeply disturbing vignette of how the settlers had been routinely intimidating Palestinians in the West Bank. We didn't always have time to figure these situations out. It wasn't a story that would necessarily make the paper. But on this day, with this family, Said and I ended up involved. We drove about 200 yards to the front gate of the heavily fortified Rachelim settlement, and sure enough, there was a gray donkey with red saddlebags, exactly as the Matia family had described. The donkey was tied to a gun tower just inside the grounds. Without saying a word to the Israeli soldiers, Said and I untied the donkey and led it out through the gate. We were immediately surrounded by soldiers. "What is this?" a soldier barked in Hebrew. I answered in English, "I am taking this donkey back to that family," pointing to the family gathered on the road down below.

I showed the Israeli soldiers my Israeli government press credentials and told them who I was. I noticed them eyeing Said over my shoulder, with their fingers on the triggers of their M-16 assault rifles. I positioned myself very deliberately between them and Said and asked the soldiers for an explanation, and why the settlers were permitted to do this. The soldiers—mere teenagers who seemed by their demeanor and hairstyles to be liberal, secular, Tel Aviv youths—brought out a sergeant, no more than 25 years old, to talk to me. He confirmed that what the Matia family had told us was accurate, but said there was nothing he could do. "We have no orders for this," he said. I asked him then, What if Palestinian gunmen held a Jewish settler family at gunpoint and stole their belongings? Presumably they would have had orders then to react.

He stared straight at me and said nothing. I told him I wanted his commanding officer's name and that I wanted to file a complaint and be sure it was put on the record. As I unleashed this unabashedly American indignation on him, I noticed that he was nodding his head in agreement. Then one of the other teenage soldiers spoke up in broken English, saying: "This is good to do. You are right. These people here were wrong. They have no right for this." It was a scene that captured just how fed up many of the rank and file in the Israeli military were, with risking their lives to defend a tiny fringe of militant, ideological settlers. I had been all too prepared to blame the soldiers, but it seemed that they didn't like the situation any more than I did. It was just a glimpse of how complicated all this was.

We brought the donkey back down the hill to the family. A bit later, the sergeant returned their belongings to them and apologized for the incident. Said and I drove away, and Said finally broke the tension by saying we had now formed the PDLF, the "Palestine Donkey Liberation Front."

. . .

Amid all the random violence and shooting and the increasing air of lawlessness on the West Bank roads, Western journalists had taken to taping two big letters to the windows of their vehicles: *TV*, which had somehow become the international symbol of the media. The letters were intended as a message of neutrality to the jittery young Israeli soldiers and to the Palestinian snipers and rock throwers. But there was no guarantee that they would provide immunity. The *Boston Globe* invested in two $400 flak jackets with ceramic plates and Kevlar lining that Said and I hoped lived up to the manufacturer's promise to stop even a high-velocity bullet. We carried them with us, but wore them infrequently—at least, until several colleagues (including a CNN reporter, an AP photographer, and a French freelance) ended up in the hospital with gunshot wounds.

In many ways, the dangers on this road were as old as the path itself. Even at the time of Jesus, the rugged wilderness of Samaria was known as a refuge of brigands. The road led to the town of Shechem, as it was referred to in the Hebrew Bible and is known today in Israel, or Nablus—the name the Romans gave the area when it was a colony within the empire, and the name maintained by modern Palestinians. It was here that Jesus had his talk with the "Samaritan woman," according to John's gospel—one of the more human moments of Jesus's ministry. He was tired and thirsty and his disciples had gone into town. So Jesus sat down at Jacob's well. A Samaritan woman came to draw water, and Jesus asked her to give him a cup. The woman was surprised that such a learned rabbi would ask her, a Samaritan, for anything. At that time, Jews despised the Samaritans, who were considered heretics. Samaritans followed the Torah but did not worship at the Temple Mount, having built their own Temple on Mount Gerazim, which they believed was the true location of Abraham's binding of Isaac. At the well, Jesus told the Samaritan woman, "Whoever drinks of this water will thirst again, but whoever drinks of the water that I shall give them will never thirst." When the disciples returned, they wanted to know why their teacher was talking to this Samaritan, and Jesus used the occasion to teach of universal kindness and the "new covenant," the opening up of the word of God to everyone, including the Samaritans. In the year 2000, a small community of several thousand Samaritans still lived in the hills outside Nablus. The modern Samaritans still celebrated Passover with the sacrifice of one lamb per family, a ritual carried out in accordance with the strict prescriptions of Moses.

When we arrived at the entrance to Nablus, a vicious firefight was raging between masked Palestinian gunmen hiding in an olive grove and Israeli forces firing from armored Jeeps at a checkpoint just before the line that divided the Israeli and Palestinian sectors of the town. Nablus was a hot spot in the early phase of the Al-Aqsa *intifada,* in part because the young son of the governor of Nablus had been killed there during a clash between Palestinians and Israeli soldiers. The Palestinian *shebab* had joined forces with the police of the Palestinian Authority in seeking revenge, and on one of the days we were there, eight Palestinians, including two policemen, had been killed.

Inside the town, a tank could be seen, positioned on a hill—the biblical Mount Ebal, a barren, rocky point referred to in scripture as the mount of curses. Another tank was stationed on Mount Gerazim, a lush, green hill referred to as the mount of prayers. The tank guns from these two positions were trained down on the Palestinians of Nablus, who lived on a series of ridges in a basin between the curses and the prayers. On the main street in downtown Nablus was Joseph's Tomb. About 500 yards away was a Byzantine-era Greek Orthodox church that marked the traditional site of Jacob's well.

Inside Joseph's Tomb, a unit of Israeli soldiers was holed up and taking fire from Palestinian gunmen, an indecipherable mix of Palestinian police and Fatah Tanzim militiamen mostly dressed in civilian clothes, intent on "liberating" the tomb. Machine guns mounted on the Israeli tanks were firing to provide cover for the soldiers in the tomb, who were there ostensibly to protect students at nearby Od Yosef Chai yeshiva, a religious school affiliated with some of the more militant Jewish settlements in the area. The yeshiva students had already been safely evacuated, but the Israeli forces had been holding their ground—which, just as at Rachel's Tomb, was a pocket of Israeli sovereignty within the Palestinian-ruled town. Nablus's Palestinians saw the tomb as a last vestige of occupation and had focused their fury on it, pelting the structure with rocks and Molotov cocktails. Some masked youths could be seen scaling a wall near the tomb and hurling a large canister of gas, like the kind attached to outdoor barbecue grills in America, which ignited like an incendiary bomb, engulfing the roof of the stone building that encased the tomb. Shots were fired into the tomb as well.

It was horrifying to think about what the Israeli soldiers trapped inside must have been going through. A 20-year-old Israeli border guard named Madhet Yosef was killed in the fighting, in large part because Palestinian demonstrators and gunmen had kept the Israeli military from evacuating him to a hospital. Yosef bled to death inside the tomb. In the Israeli parliament, criticism was mounting as members questioned the military wisdom of allowing these soldiers to be sitting ducks.

Driving to and from Nablus, I was repeatedly struck by the poignancy of the conflict around the holy shrine to Joseph. Although fueled by religious fervor, the conflict evidenced a stunning lack of regard for the sanctity of the place. The street demonstrators claiming to be fighting for the tomb were actually destroying a shrine holy to Jews, Muslims, and Christians. The stone structure was an Ottoman-era building, which nineteenth-century pilgrimage accounts indicate had long been considered the place where Joseph's bones were taken by his family from Egypt, out of respect for his wish to be buried in the Promised Land. Perhaps partly out of anger generated by Israeli control of the tomb since the mid-1970s, the Palestinians had revised this tradition, and they commonly described the tomb's occupant not as the biblical patriarch Joseph but as some other Joseph who was a learned Muslim sheikh, the details of whose life were somehow unknown.

According to the Old Testament, Joseph was born to the lovely Rachel and was the favored son of Jacob. Joseph's brothers were jealous of his good looks and his standing in his father's eyes, and so they betrayed him. At first they intended to kill him; but they thought better of it, and decided instead to sell him into slavery. In Egypt, Joseph, who had the God-given gift of interpreting dreams, helped the pharaoh understand the meaning of his own dreams, and was then taken out of slavery and made governor of Egypt. When there was a drought in Canaan, his brothers ended up coming to Egypt for food. Joseph, despite his position of power, did not seek revenge on them. Instead, he secretly helped his brothers and then eventually revealed himself to them, and was reunited with them and his father. The same story is told in the Koran. The story was my favorite of all the narratives in Genesis, a great tale of what it is to be a brother, a story of forgiveness and ultimately of redemption.

On Friday, October 6, the Israeli forces withdrew from the tomb, having been promised by the Palestinian Authority that the shrine would be protected. But within hours, a Palestinian mob attacked the tomb in a frenzy of violence, blind to the message of the biblical patriarch to whom the shrine was devoted. Over the next twenty-four hours, the shrine was burned and torn apart by Palestinians, young and old alike taking turns in its destruction. Some used steel poles and pickaxes to loosen the stones, and as each stone tumbled to the ground, the crowd cheered. The Jewish sacred texts and devotional lamps inside were destroyed and thrown into a heap outside the tomb. A picture in the *Jerusalem Post* showed Palestinian youths gleefully bashing in a Star of David embossed on a door that had been ripped from its hinges.

The Israeli public was outraged at the desecration, and the Jewish settlers saw it as an omen of worse to come. The liberal former prime minister, Shimon Peres, slammed Arafat for not stopping the destruction and for permitting the agreement to be violated. Peres asked, If Arafat could not be trusted to serve as a caretaker of the tomb, how could he be trusted to control the overlapping sacred space in Jerusalem? The European Union, one of Arafat's more generous backers, sharply condemned "without reservation" the destruction of the holy site. Confronted by expressions of international outrage, Arafat issued orders for the shrine to be repaired.

. . .

The street clashes between Palestinians and Israelis spread like wildfire throughout October, jumping across the "green line" separating Israel from the West Bank and Gaza and blazing up in the Palestinian communities within Israel proper. In some cases there were even actual forest fires in which Arab citizens of Israel were suspected of torching the Jewish National Fund (JNF) pine groves, some of which had been planted over the remains of destroyed Palestinian villages. The JNF forest that loomed over the village of Maalul near Nazareth was set ablaze, blackening the Norfolk pines that had sheltered the Palestinian families gathered there for an "Independence" or "Nakba" Day picnic five months earlier. The damage in Maalul was not extensive, but the message was profound. A front-page banner headline in the *Jerusalem Post* called the upheavals the "Worst Civil Disturbances Since 1948." A quiet rage that had been building for years erupted in violent expressions of solidarity with Palestinians in the West Bank and Gaza. In fact, Israeli Arabs were now more insistent than ever on being referred to as "Palestinians living in Israel." Some of my Jewish neighbors in Jerusalem were furious about this, and insisted that if citizens of Nazareth and Umm el-Fahm wanted to be

Palestinians, they were welcome to leave their homes and live in the West Bank.

Suddenly, Israel was dealing with the *intifada* on two fronts, not only trying to control the situation in the occupied territories but also trying to quell massive disturbances among its own citizens. The Israeli Arab parties in the Knesset had become a growing political force in the country. They traditionally had supported the Labor Party, but they were furious with Ehud Barak and were threatening to join forces to topple his government. Azmi Bishara, an Israeli Arab Christian from Upper Nazareth and one of the nine Arab members of the Israeli Knesset, was among the leaders of this effort.

Violent expressions of rage crashed over towns in the Galilee, including Umm el-Fahm and Nazareth and Kana, where Arab street demonstrators were throwing up barricades of burning tires and boulders to block the roads, and engaging in violent, stone-throwing clashes with Israeli police. Coastal cities that had long been places of peaceful Arab-Jewish coexistence, such as Haifa and Jaffa and Acre, erupted in street fighting and rioting and raging ethnic conflict. The Israeli police and the military were cracking down hard on the Arab demonstrators—especially in the Galilee, under the controversial district police commander Alik Ron, who had been sharply criticized for doing little to stop the divisions between Christians and Muslims in Nazareth from spiraling into rioting in 1999.

There was also Jewish rioting against Arabs; but the official Israeli response to it was restrained, and in some places even seemingly complicit. In Tiberias, when Jewish youths attacked a mosque in the old town and set it ablaze, the mayor called their act "an understandable expression of anger." In Jaffa, crowds attacked stores that employed Arabs. Arab-owned stores in Haifa and Netanya were firebombed. In Tel Aviv's Hatikva neighborhood, Jewish rioters smashed the windows of Arab-owned cars, shouting, "Death to Arabs!"

The resurfacing of almost primal hatred between Arabs and Jews caught the Israeli establishment, the media, and especially the political left by surprise. The use of lethal force by the Israeli police against their own citizens shocked Israeli Arabs and unleashed more waves of anger. In October, thirteen Israeli Arabs were killed by Israeli police and military forces, hundreds were wounded, and hundreds more were arrested and detained. The state's discriminatory and exclusionary policies had long fostered the impression among the Arab minority that they were viewed as a security and demographic threat to the Jewish state; this impression now became a certainty. The police had reacted almost reflexively to the Arab demonstrators, as if they were a fifth column, an enemy within. In an October 6 survey reported by an Israeli newspaper, 74 percent of Israeli Jews polled said they considered the behavior of Israeli Arabs "treacherous." And 66 percent of Israeli Arabs polled said that if there was a broadscale conflict, they would show allegiance to the Palestinians next door rather than to Israel.

Perhaps the most dramatic demonstration of the polarization of Israeli Arabs and Jews occurred in Nazareth, on the night of Sunday, October 8. In Upper Nazareth, the synagogues were just letting out after services for Yom Kippur. Hundreds of Jewish residents of Upper Nazareth gathered in the streets and began venting their anger at the fact that Arab residents of Nazareth had been blocking roads with burning tires and rock-throwing mobs squaring off against police. For several days, the anger had been building. A Jewish mob carrying torches and hurling anti-Arab insults attacked several Arab homes in Upper Nazareth, including the new, elegant residence of Azmi Bishara, whose wife was eight months pregnant. Bishara and his wife were forced to flee. Leaflets in Hebrew claiming that "the Arabs are coming up here and harassing our women" were circulating in Upper Nazareth. The talk on the streets among young Jewish males, especially the new immigrants from the former Soviet Union, was that the Arabs were brazen in trying to pick up young Russian women at the Upper Nazareth mall and on the streets of their town. Even the mayor of Upper Nazareth, Menachem Ariav, usually seen as a tough but level-headed official, was making incendiary comments along these lines, saying, "We will not be the suppliers of sex for the Arabs. . . . Our girls seem to have become public property." The mayor, through the local newspapers, also made thinly veiled calls to action, saying that the Arab protesters blocking streets "must be put to a stop." The Russian-language newspaper *Index* was calling for a Jewish boycott of Arab stores.

In this climate, a group of some five hundred youths, mostly Russian Jewish immigrants, descended the steep hills of Upper Nazareth and began marching toward "the Canyon," where a shopping mall and a McDonald's had formed one of the few areas of common ground between Jewish Upper Nazareth and Arab Nazareth. Some of the young Russian men I had talked to had compared the Arabs of the Galilee to the Muslim Chechens whose uprising the Russian army was so brutally suppressing back in their native country. Many in the Jewish crowd were chanting, "Arabs out!" and "Death to Arabs!"

Natan Goldshmidt, a 17-year-old high school student from Upper Nazareth, was coming out of the Brit Shalom synagogue that night, and joined the crowd as it pressed down the hill. His parents were immigrants in the first wave from the former Soviet Union. Speaking of the Arabs, he told me, "They come to our city and they do whatever they want. They only understand force, and that is what we do, we show them force. This all they want to do is to fight. We cannot live with them."

Shira Elmalicach, 17, a blonde Russian immigrant living in Upper Nazareth, was also walking with the group. She echoed this commonly held perception of the Nazareth young men as sexually aggressive and rude, saying, "They touch you in the mall, and in the street. I don't hate them. But they are animals."

The Nazareth residents and city officials later claimed that the Upper Nazareth youths began throwing stones at Arab homes in the eastern section of Nazareth, shattering windows in the darkness. Arab youths quickly gathered in the streets to confront the Jewish crowd. Then a call for protection and *jihad* came from loudspeakers atop the minarets of several nearby mosques, bringing hundreds more Arabs into the street. The Israeli police arrived on the scene and began pushing the Jewish protesters back up the hill. Then they turned and fired tear gas on the Arab protesters, who by this time were also throwing rocks. It had become a full-blown riot. The Arab residents were furious that the police directed their force only at the Arab side of the rioting and not at the Jewish residents, who the Arabs felt had started the melee.

More Israeli forces were called in, and they began firing "rubber bullets." Having issued no prior calls for the protesters to disperse and no warnings, according to witnesses, the Israeli forces then switched to live ammunition. Israeli officials denied this, saying that no orders had been given to use live ammunition; but eyewitnesses, including emergency medical workers and high-ranking Nazareth city officials who were on the scene, claimed that the Israeli soldiers were firing "rubber bullets" and live ammunition from a position set up behind a series of metal dumpsters near the McDonald's. Amid the shooting, two Nazareth residents were killed and three others were critically injured. One of the two men killed, Wissam Yazbek, 25, was struck by a bullet in the back of the head as he, along with several city officials, tried to push the angry crowd back, away from the police.

I traveled to Nazareth to attend his funeral. Afterward I sat a while with the Yazbek family under a large green mourning tent set up near their home in an industrial corner of the city. The family members, many of them wearing the traditional Arab headdress, sipped coffee and smoked cigarettes and exchanged their version of events, venting their anger at the Israeli government and at the Israeli police force.

Hamdan Yazbek, Wissam's father, was a partner in an excavation company with an Israeli friend. He had made a good living, building roads in Upper Nazareth. He had sent his sons to Israeli high schools and colleges. He was born a decade after the 1948 war, but his parents told him the stories of "Al-Nakba." "My land is Palestine, but my country is Israel," he told me. "My son was a son of this country, of Israel, a Palestinian son of Israel, and this is why I am angry. I am angry that in every country police should be there to help people, to protect people. What kind of country is it, when it kills its own citizens like this?"

Among the mourners was Hamdan's Israeli partner and friend, a Russian Jewish immigrant from Upper Nazareth named Itzhak Rakovitch. They had worked together to pave many of the new roads in Upper Nazareth, and Hamdan had just been discussing with me the complexities of his position as both suffering from and economically benefiting from the sprawling Jewish community built on confiscated land. But in the end, Rakovitch was a friend. The two men hugged, and Rakovitch leaned close to Yazbek and said, "This was wrong. This should not have happened."

In the crowd of hundreds of mourners under the tent, I spotted Nazareth's mayor, Ramez Jeraisi. He was at the head of a group of Israeli leftists and intellectuals who had come to pay their respects to the Yazbek family and make at least some effort toward reconciliation—although many of the mourners thought their presence inappropriate. Jeraisi seemed to be carrying himself with a renewed sense of determination and purpose amid the violence. The current conflict was a tragedy for his community, but it had also served to bring Nazareth's bitterly divided Christians and Muslims back together. Arab Nazareth's infighting over the construction of the Shehab al-Din mosque seemed petty, in comparison to what had happened during these weeks in October. Shehab al-Din was knocked down to its proper context within the dramatically rising sense of alienation and anger felt by the Arab minority, Muslims and Christians alike, within Israel.

I went over to talk with Jeraisi. He emphasized that the street demonstrations were an "expression of rage against the inequality and oppression we live with," and not anger directed at the Jewish community, at Upper Nazareth. He said that all of the street demonstrations were directed against the police, and never against Jewish citizens—at least, that that been the case before the Jewish youths from Upper Nazareth descended on the Arab neighborhood and provoked a fight.

Jeraisi took the microphone and addressed the funeral gathering. His rhetorical demand for a national inquiry into the killings was met with nods of the head by the mourners. Then he turned his gaze to the Israeli intellectuals who sat clustered together in the white plastic chairs set up for the funeral. He said, "The point of beginning to heal has to be a recognition of responsibility on the part of the police. Anyone who is an Israeli who does not demand that is complicit in this crime."

His constituents under the tent gave him a round of applause, and I noticed that some of them were activists from the Islamic Movement who had been his political enemies in the Shehab al-Din mosque controversy. Christians and Muslims and Jews all were gathered under that one tent. It occurred to me then that although the mosque-tent had divided them, this mourning tent had reunited them—albeit temporarily. It was hard to discern anything good coming out of the violence of October; but it was nevertheless encouraging to see that Nazareth—or at least its Muslims and Christians—had been brought together again, albeit through suffering. And as I watched Jeraisi speaking before the crowd, I was struck by the fact that it was a Christian leader who had brought these people, these Arabs and Jews, Muslims and Christians, together as citizens who could share in their outrage and work together to correct the wrong.

. . .

Just a few days later, one of the defining moments of the Al-Aqsa *intifada*—certainly among its most barbaric—occurred in the West Bank town of Ramallah, the commercial and cultural center of Palestinian self-rule. The menacing air of mob rule had been gathering here like a storm. At 11 A.M. on Thursday, October 12, an angry army of *shebab* emerged from a mosque in downtown Ramallah after the funeral service of Khalil Samour, another rock-throwing teenager, shot by Israeli forces the day before.

Thousands of young mourners paraded through the streets. At the same moment, on the other side of Ramallah, the Palestinian police were apprehending two Israeli reserve soldiers in a Ford sedan who claimed to have gotten lost on their way to the post for reserve duty. The soldiers ended up at a Palestinian checkpoint, and in the charged atmosphere of suspicion and hatred, the Palestinian police took them into custody and were bringing them to the police station in downtown Ramallah.

Word spread on the streets that the soldiers were members of a feared and hated Israeli undercover unit. Israeli officials adamantly denied this, and the fact that the vehicle the soldiers were driving had Israeli license plates certainly made it hard to believe that they could have been part of any undercover unit. But the mob believed what it wanted to believe. It swarmed the police station and set fire to the soldiers' car. Dozens of angry *shebab* ripped the wrought-iron grating off the windows and climbed through. Twelve Palestinian police officers were injured while trying to hold the mob back.

The *shebab* set upon the two Israeli soldiers, beating and stabbing them to death. Footage by an Italian television crew showed the youths cheering and stomping and then unceremoniously throwing the corpse of one of the soldiers out of a second-story window. The video captured the youths dipping their hands into the Israeli's blood and then holding up their hands to a cheering crowd down below, which proceeded to beat the lifeless body. This was not just a lynching, it was a kind of primal release of hatred that left all of Israel, especially the left, speechless.

I arrived in Ramallah with Said approximately one hour after the killing, and the streets were crackling with tension. As we approached the center of town, Palestinian teenagers with automatic pistols drawn stopped our car and ordered us out. They searched through the vehicle, turning over my children's car seats and sifting through the toys and books piled in the backseat. They told us we could not go any farther, and we didn't argue. We left the car and walked toward the police station, in front of which a sullen and angry crowd was milling. The Israelis' torched car was still smoldering a bit farther up the street.

The lynching had taken place next to a school established by the Quaker Friends, which since 1901 had been a Christian missionary presence in Ramallah devoted to teaching nonviolence. The Quaker message clearly had not sunk into the mind of ninth-grader Khalid Hadithi, standing in the crowd, who said, "This will teach the Jews not to come to our land."

It took less than four hours for Israeli forces to exact revenge. Just before 3 P.M., Apache and Cobra attack helicopters appeared in the sky over Ramallah. The dull roar of helicopter blades sent the streets into a panic, as people ran in every direction for cover. An elderly woman had dropped a bag of vegetables that lay scattered in the street. A man sprinted to push a baby stroller inside a doorway for shelter.

And then there was a thunderous bang, and the police station was enveloped in smoke. Soldiers and police fled out the front door; a minute later came three more rockets, and the building was a heap of rubble. A warning call from the IDF had led to the hasty evacuation of the building, and only a handful of Palestinians were injured.

Amid the rubble of the police station, a poster of Yasser Arafat superimposed over the Dome of the Rock lay ripped in half. A Palestinian flag that had flown over the entry was shredded and had fallen. Col. Abu Awad Damra, commander of Palestinian leader Yasser Arafat's elite Force 17 paramilitary unit, pulled up in a green Land Rover and announced defiantly, "This was a fire cracker. We have no fear. We will turn Ramallah into a cemetery for the Israelis."

Over the streets of Ramallah, the attack helicopters hovered, poised for the next air strike. I had joined up with a Palestinian colleague and friend Nasser Atta, who was a producer for ABC News and had lived all his life in Ramallah. Nasser insisted that we travel with him for our own safety. We literally followed the helicopters from one attack to the next, through streets where people were rushing for cover. The radio in the car was tuned to Voice of Palestine, and Said was translating the broadcasts for me as we went. We were surprised to hear the announcers warning the Palestinians that more Israeli air strikes were likely, but pointedly omitting from their reports the details of the barbaric lynching of the two Israeli reservists. That event also went unmentioned in all subsequent reports. The only news Palestinians heard was that more "Israeli aggression" was imminent.

Suddenly, there was the ominous sound of the helicopters' rotor blades close overhead again, and then the chilling whir of missiles streaking through the sky. Just a few hundred meters away, three missiles slammed into the transformer and transmission tower of the

Palestine Broadcasting center. The car radio was now transmitting only an eerie static. Israel had intentionally silenced the source of the Palestinian Authority's official font of incitement, albeit only temporarily; the Palestinian government-controlled radio news broadcasts were shifted to a small commercial station transmitting from Bethlehem, and they were back on the air in a few hours.

As the air strikes intensified, we dashed into an apartment building and took cover in the home of a man named Ahmad Baker, 56, a professor of psychology. He looked down from his fifth-floor apartment, where he was huddled with his family, at the burning aftermath of the strike on the broadcast center, and said, "This is meant only to terrorize and humiliate. I hope the Israelis are very proud of themselves." He had not heard about the lynching that provoked these Israeli retaliatory raids until we told him.

The air strikes marked a turning point in the conflict, and suddenly it looked a lot more like war. There was swift international condemnation of the Israelis for taking such aggressive retaliatory action, and for targeting official buildings located in civilian neighborhoods. But what was equally disturbing was the absolute silence on the part of the Palestinian leadership. Not a single Palestinian politician or clergyman, Muslim or Christian, clearly and publicly condemned the murder of the two Israeli soldiers. The Palestinian police arrested none of the youths who had carried out the killing. (Over the next six months, however, Israeli undercover forces captured most of the ringleaders.)

At one point, earlier in the day, while we were standing in front of the Palestinian police station, I had wondered aloud why the Palestinian police were making no arrests, when clearly so many of the young men in front of the building were involved. Some actually had blood on their clothes. Said suggested that I keep my thoughts to myself if we wanted to get out of Ramallah unharmed. This conflict had descended into lawlessness.

In the subsequent days and weeks, the fighting would become a confusing mix of orchestrated rock-throwing clashes interspersed with sporadic gun battles. In Gaza and in Ramallah, I saw Palestinian gunmen open fire repeatedly. But what was puzzling was that they were firing not at the Israeli soldiers but into the air overhead. There seemed to be no intention to kill Israelis with this gunfire. It was almost as if the Palestinian forces, a melange of civilians and police, simply wanted to trigger an Israeli reaction. And, as they found out, that was not hard to do, as the IDF responded to each provocation with tank fire, heavy-caliber machine guns, and attack helicopters.

Hanan Ashrawi railed against what she considered a disproportionate Israeli response. But she was horrified as well by the killings themselves, even if that point was not well expressed in her interviews for television. As October wore on, she could see more clearly where this conflict was headed. She watched the television footage of the Palestinian gunmen from the Fatah Tanzim and the Hamas brigades marching in Ramallah and in Gaza, their faces masked with black hoods, their arms raised in the air, clutching machine guns. She watched the crowds torching cardboard replicas of the Jewish settlements in the West Bank. At one Gaza rally for Hamas, there were even small children costumed as suicide bombers. This was a parade of hatred and militancy that was marching in step with widespread despair, and heading directly toward disaster. Ashrawi was not yet voicing these thoughts—not publicly; she was staying on message as a Palestinian nationalist in her television interviews. But months later, she confided to me that she and other Palestinian leaders saw this *intifada* as having been "hijacked," in her words, by "people hiding behind masks."

"Extremism breeds extremism, absolutism breeds absolutism, violence breeds violence, and that has become the language of the day," she said. "This *intifada* was different. The Israelis were no longer in our streets and in our homes. The occupation was different, and the fight against it became different. The confrontations were at the entrances and exits of our land which the Israelis controlled. Suddenly people were using guns from residential areas, knowing that they were not inflicting any damage on the Israelis and knowing that they were inviting massive Israeli responses. I worry about that. . . . We should never mask our faces. We have nothing to hide. Our Palestinian identity is nothing to hide."

To further complicate the situation, the Al-Aqsa *intifada* seemed to have been an expression of anger not just against Israeli occupation but against the Palestinian Authority leadership as well. Arafat was being pressured by Israel and Washington to call for an end to the violence. The question was whether Arafat *could* control the situation. Arafat's entourage of advisers and ministers and officials who had come with him from exile in Tunis to run Gaza and the West Bank were notoriously corrupt, building mansions and business empires (some with Israeli partners) for themselves but leaving the Palestinian street as destitute and desperate as ever. By ignoring Arafat's calls to stop the violence, the street seemed to be rebelling against this corrupt regime as well as against the Israelis.

It was an opaque conflict, weaving together strands of religious struggle between Muslims and Jews, Palestinian resistance to Israeli occupation that verged on low-level guerrilla warfare, and internal rebellion within Palestinian society. But one aspect that seemed clear amid all the confusion and uncertainty was that the Palestinian Christian minority was fated to be irrelevant at best, or at worst, a target for Islamic fundamentalists.

. . .

The first case in which Christians were targeted amid the *intifada*'s rising Islamic militancy occurred in Gaza, where the Christian community numbered only 3,000. They were all that remained of the Christian presence in a city where Byzantine ruins lay everywhere beneath the teeming refugee camps and urban sprawl. The Christians of Gaza had long been in the restaurant and hotel business, in part because their religion does not prohibit the sale and consumption of alcohol. In the increasingly restrictive atmosphere of Gaza's Islamic fundamentalist culture, the Christians and the establishments where they served cocktails to officials of the Palestinian Authority became targets of protests.

On October 3, angry crowds of Hamas activists, fueled by the fiery speeches of a sheikh at the Islamic University, began threatening to burn down several of these establishments. They didn't follow through. But ten days later, the mobs returned with torches. They burned the Windmill, an elegant, Christian-managed hotel, which had been a favorite of Western diplomats, the well-connected inner circle of the Palestinian Authority, and foreign correspondents visiting Gaza. They torched the home of Abu George, a well-connected Palestinian Christian businessman who held the license to import alcohol to Gaza. And they torched at least four other establishments, including the home of Khalil Sayegh, who with his children had sold cold beer from a large refrigerator in a storage area of the house where they had lived for fifty-one years. The Sayegh family was among the oldest Greek Orthodox clans in Gaza, with an ancestry in the region dating back to the fourth or fifth century. They were prosperous, compared to the deep poverty in which many in Gaza lived. On the afternoon of October 13, a Friday, a mob came out of the mosque near the Islamic University after a prayer service, chanting in Arabic, *Kufar! Kufar!* ("Infidels!") and "It is our joy to burn the dens of alcohol!"

And with this, hundreds of young men—some of them brandishing torches—descended on the home. The children fled at the urging of the Palestinian police, but Khalil stayed behind. He was severely beaten by the crowd and dragged out into the street. The mob ransacked the house, smashing the supplies of beer and wine and ripping pictures of the Virgin Mary and the Holy Family off the walls. They piled the family's religious items—rosaries and crucifixes and icons and bibles—in a heap and set them ablaze.

Arafat was furious. His senior aide Ramzi Khouri, who is a Christian, tracked the family down within hours of their ordeal and promised to repair their fire-ravaged home and to pay for an apartment for them until they could return. The sheikh who had instigated the crowd with his anti-Christian sermon was arrested on charges of incitement. This and similar attacks were seen, by those who knew the internecine workings of Gaza politics, as a direct and unusually brazen challenge by Hamas to Arafat's rule. The militants within Hamas knew that such a confrontation would embarrass Arafat in the eyes of the Western world—whose approval, they believed, Arafat too eagerly sought. The attacks may have been aimed more at Arafat's inner circle than at Christians.

"Now Arafat is taking care of us, but what of the future?" said Samia Sayegh, 27, Khalil's oldest daughter. "What is happening here? Maybe these fundamentalists will kill Arafat and fulfill their wish to make this an Islamic country. They have changed the way we get along with our Muslim brothers. They have caused divisions. I don't know if we can live here anymore if we want to keep our lives."

This incident in Gaza was an isolated case of Islamic militant rage against Palestinian Christians, and Arafat had responded to it aggressively. But it nevertheless contributed to a pervasive feeling among many Christians, not only in Gaza but in the West Bank and in Jerusalem, too, that they were not part of this "Al-Aqsa *intifada*." On the street level, the uprising had become a fusion of nationalism and Islam, alienating Christians and leaving them vulnerable to attack as "infidels."

The high priests of the Sanhedrin charged Jesus with blasphemy, saying that he had proclaimed himself the messiah. Then Jesus was sentenced to crucifixion by Pontius Pilate, the Roman procurator in the province of Judea and the only one authorized by Rome to rule in capital punishment cases. On Friday, Jesus was beaten by the Roman soldiers who guarded him. A crown of thorns was placed on his head in mockery of the "king of the Jews."

When Jesus shouldered the cross, he was most likely setting out from the praetorium, where Pilate would have issued his ruling. Biblical historians believe the praetorium was at the entrance to Jaffa Gate, near what is today called David's Tower. But tourists have long accepted the traditional pilgrimage route, established in the fourteenth century, which locates the praetorium closer to St. Stephen's Gate. Either way, it takes imagination to envision the path leading outside the city walls. Jesus would not have been stumbling along cobblestone streets, but more likely, climbing over hard, rocky terrain to the steep outcropping of skull-shaped boulders known as Golgotha, where he was to be crucified. It doesn't perhaps matter so much where the "true" path was, if pilgrims choose to see the last steps of Jesus as a message, a metaphor, an embodiment of suffering and ultimately of redemption.

That path today is known as the Via Dolorosa, the "Way of Sorrow."

XIV

Jerusalem

THE VIA DOLOROSA

At the sixth hour darkness came over the whole land until the ninth hour. And at the ninth hour Jesus cried out in a loud voice, "Eloi, Eloi, lama sabachthani?"—which means, "My God, my God, why have you forsaken me?"

MARK 15:33–34 (NIV)

HEAVY FIRE THUNDERED across Jerusalem. Dug in on the southernmost edge of the Holy City, two Israeli tanks were shelling the predominantly Christian Palestinian village of Beit Jala, near Bethlehem. These were the IDF's dreaded fifty-ton Merkeva tanks with 105-mm guns. Their laser range finders and computerized firing systems were locked onto the rooftops and windows of residential buildings that IDF officials said were sources of Palestinian machine gun fire coming into the nearby Jewish settlement of Gilo, which was located within the Israeli-defined boundaries of Jerusalem. Inside the tanks, the greenish glow of the computer screen displayed a view of Beit Jala through a nightscope. The imposing structure and silver dome of the Greek Orthodox Church of St. Nicholas stood out clearly amid the cluster of homes. Between the homes one could see the crosses atop the spires of at least three other churches, as well as two minarets. The IDF soldiers had been warned to target their fire carefully; the IDF could not afford the international outrage that would result from blowing up a church next to the birthplace of Jesus, or a mosque, for that matter. The Palestinian gunmen on the other side—Muslim members of the Tanzim—knew this. They were using the Christian village for cover in their fight against the Zionist occupation.

Beit Jala was caught in the middle.

It was Sunday, October 22. For five days, Israeli forces and Palestinian militias had been trading machine-gun fire in a battle that began after an Israeli border policeman was critically wounded at his post in Gilo. The shooting of the Israeli policeman had shattered a U.S.-brokered cease-fire agreement reached on October 17 by Ehud Barak and Yasser Arafat in the Egyptian resort of Sharm al-Sheikh, on the Red Sea. On this Sunday the IDF was using tank missiles for the first time during the uprising in the West Bank, crossing a dramatic threshold. I could hear the recoil of the guns and the thud of the shells from the balcony of my home office in Jerusalem. I rushed to Gilo, making it in a matter of five minutes. I watched the battle from a perch near the Catholic-run Tantur Ecumenical Center, adjacent to the valley that separated Gilo from Beit Jala.

The Palestinian village was bathed in darkness after the IDF ordered the Israeli electrical company, which controlled all power grids in the West Bank, to pull the plug. Phosphorous-tipped tracer bullets lit up the sky over the valley as the Israeli soldiers and Palestinian gunmen traded fire. Attack helicopters hovered overhead and launched flares over positions in Beit Jala from which periodic bursts of light exploded—fire from Palestinian gunmen. Then came another powerful bang, and the bright red light of a guided tank missile streaked through the sky and slammed into a stone building on the other side, and flashed into flame. The attack helicopters then fired several missiles at a marble factory that lay in an olive grove at the bottom of the valley, punching an enormous hole into the side of the building.

These rumblings of war—tanks, attack helicopters, and the rattle of gunfire—had not echoed over Jerusalem since 1967. The fighting on this day had nowhere near the intensity of the Six Day War, nor was it by any stretch of the imagination a regional conflict. But it served as a warning to both Israelis and Palestinians that the Al-Aqsa *intifada* was teetering on the edge of all-out conflict.

If it did come to that, the battle at Gilo–Beit Jala starkly illustrated the incongruity of the two sides fighting. If the Palestinians threw stones, the Israelis answered with "rubber bullets." If they hurled Molotov cocktails, the response was sniper fire with live ammunition. If the Palestinians fired into a settlement, the Israelis employed tank shells and helicopter-fired missiles.

There were 30,000 Palestinian police and security troops and several small militias armed with assault rifles and machine guns. Some of the forces had even been trained by the CIA as part of the interim peace agreement, which allowed the Palestinians to develop their own security. The Palestinians had no heavy weapons apart from a few machine gun–mounted armored personnel carriers—freshly painted Soviet-era relics that were rolled out for military parades in Gaza. Still, this policing structure had the trappings of a small army. In the shadows of Gaza and the West Bank, there were also fringe militant wings of Fatah, and the Islamic organizations Hamas and Islamic Jihad, which had considerable experience in bomb making. In Gaza an effort seemed to be under way to mimic Hezbollah's hit-and-run tactics and its use of roadside bombs.

The Palestinian forces were lined up against the IDF, generally regarded as one of the most powerful military forces in the world. Backed with billions of dollars annually in U.S. military assistance, the seemingly invincible IDF had almost mythic status in the history of contemporary warfare. But at the age of 52, it was beginning to grapple with its own shortcomings, as had become apparent during the pullout from Lebanon. And now the IDF seemed to be facing a new phenomenon in the West Bank and Gaza—a Hezbollah-style guerrilla movement (much closer to home but lacking Hezbollah's discipline, training, and foreign backing).

The morning after the tank shelling, I drove into Beit Jala to assess the damage. Four homes had been extensively damaged, but there were no injuries. The Nazal family, however, told me of a horrifying night in which one missile had come perilously close to killing them. Suhair Nazal, 28, a Palestinian Christian woman, looked exhausted and frazzled. The night before, she had been rushed to the hospital for hysteria and shock, and now she was sweeping up rubble from the damage to her home. A tank missile had punched through the stone wall and crashed into the bedroom of her 4-year-old son George. The child had been sleeping there until the gunfire awoke him, and she had moved him just minutes before the missile landed. She showed me the path of the missile, which had made a three-foot hole through the outer, stone wall and then a smaller hole through the plaster bedroom wall, and had slammed straight into the washing machine—less than two feet from the door of the back room where her family had sought refuge. No one was hurt, but Suhair still seemed shaken. Stuffed animals and toys blackened by the explosion were scattered on the floor of her son's bedroom. A framed picture of the Virgin Mary holding the infant Jesus lay in a heap of broken glass. When I met the family, they were packing up food from the house and preparing to move in with relatives on the other side of town, out of the line of fire.

Suhair's husband, Samer, was a waiter at the Oasis Casino in Jericho but had not been able to work for a month. The casino, which employed more than two hundred Christians from Beit Jala, was considering closing down, having suffered huge financial losses in the first month of fighting and having taken some direct fire. Later the IDF would dig tank trenches around Jericho and completely seal off the town. In the coming months, the casino and the new hotel complex built alongside it would be shelled by tanks, shattering their plate glass windows and overturning their gaming tables. But for now, Suhair was focused on the rubble of her own home and the ordeal her family had just suffered.

"This is terror. They want us to live in terror," she said, as she busily packed food into boxes and dusted plaster chips from stuffed animals. "I don't know who fired first, all I know is that a tank shell came into my child's bedroom. This is not a bunker, this is a house. The Jews don't want peace."

. . .

In the valley between Gilo and Beit Jala, the Palestinian-ruled West Bank runs up close alongside the Israeli-carved boundaries of Jerusalem. Separated by eight hundred yards of gently rising olive groves, the two hilltop communities stand almost shoulder to shoulder. The Palestinians see Gilo as one more illegal settlement in the West Bank. Israelis see Gilo as a neighborhood of Jerusalem. Two months earlier—in the summer of 2000—a peace deal had seemed within grasp, as if the two sides were going to physically reach out and take each other's hands across this valley. But now the seemingly narrow strip of land had widened into an abyss, as the two sides looked out across the olive grove and saw the enemy. Each side was retreating into its own narrative of suffering and blaming the other, not just for the current round of violence but for the whole fifty-two years of conflict.

Viewed from Beit Jala, the concrete housing blocks of Gilo are a jarring interruption in the landscape. The older residents of the West Bank over the decades had seen scores of acres of land in Beit Jala and in the nearby villages of Mahel and Sur Baher confiscated by

Israel, or in some cases appropriated after being purchased from residents who had been pressured into selling their land for a fraction of its worth. (Palestinians who did sell were viewed as collaborators and as such most land deals were done secretly.) The Palestinians of Beit Jala watched as olive groves were cut down and hillsides were gouged out by bulldozers to make room for the sprawling development that now housed 40,000 Israelis, all of them Jewish, and many of them immigrants. Construction of Gilo started in 1971, as part of a long-term, gradual strategy of building Jewish settlements in occupied East Jerusalem and the West Bank, to form concentric circles around Jerusalem.

Beit Jala, a beautiful village of hand-hewn stone homes that fit gracefully into the landscape, was long considered a peaceful Palestinian community with relatively warm relations with its Israeli neighbors in Gilo. But for Beit Jala residents, Gilo still stood as a symbol of occupation and dispossession. Along Iraq street, which offered the most commanding view of Gilo, families gathered on front porches, talked with neighbors, and surveyed the damage to homes from the nighttime shelling. Windows everywhere were blown out; and the water towers that many Palestinians had atop their homes were punctured by Israeli machine gun fire, causing flooding and water damage. Palestinian Authority police were stationed on street corners. Families were stacking sandbags in their homes.

In Gilo, Israelis walked along a wide promenade and examined the Israeli tank positions just below. When the shooting on Gilo began, the army had begun digging in. Military cranes lifted ten-foot concrete barriers into place—the same tombstone-shaped forms the IDF had used for protection in south Lebanon. IDF units also prepared sniper nests in the rocky escarpment just above the valley. Just like their Palestinian neighbors, Gilo residents were fortifying their homes and an elementary school facing Beit Jala with sandbags.

The Palestinian AK-47 rifles could barely hit targets in Gilo, and there had been no civilian injuries there during the nights of shooting—just a few shattered windows and a lot of jangled nerves. Aviva Nur-El, a schoolteacher who had lived in the settlement for twenty years and had raised three daughters there, described the horror of the gunfire at night, not knowing where the bullets were coming from or where exactly they were going to hit. The immediate human instinct was to flee; but she and her husband and daughters were determined not to do that. They would huddle together in a back room of the apartment, listening to radio reports of what was happening, until the shooting fell silent and they could go to bed for another night of tossing and turning.

"I never thought I would see this," she said, over the rumble of a military tractor that was fortifying two tank positions in front of her home. "We used to have friends in Beit Jala, we used to go there and walk the streets. Now they shoot at us. We can't live like this. They don't just want the West Bank. They want everything—Jaffa, Haifa, Akko [Acre]. They want everything, and they want to push us into the sea. I used to be optimistic about peace, but now I am not."

Said Ghazali, my interpreter, accompanied me. He was getting uncomfortable stares from the Israeli residents of Gilo, who didn't understand why a Palestinian was walking their streets. (It always surprised me how Israelis and Palestinians could distinguish each other even though their features were generally quite similar.) Some openly stopped Said and asked him why he was there. But Nur-El, whose parents had been born in Egypt, was polite and relaxed with Said and spoke a bit of Arabic. Said asked her if she really wanted peace, and she nodded her head in agreement. And then he asked if she wanted peace badly enough to return the confiscated land on which Gilo had been built.

"No. We will never leave," she answered. "My parents were forced to leave their homes in Egypt in 1949, and that is how we came to Israel, as refugees. My husband's family was forced to leave Iraq. And now we are staying. We are not moving an inch, even if they want a war. If this is what they want, we will give it to them."

It interested me that she was so direct and honest with Said and able to converse with him as a person, although she always referred to Palestinians as "they" and "them." To her, Said was not part of that reality, over there in Beit Jala, even though that was where his sister and many of his relatives lived.

At noon, church bells rang out across the valley. Walking down Iraq street, we came across a man named Jamil Muslat. He wanted to show us the top floor of his home, an elegant nineteenth-century building, in which a four-foot-wide hole had been blasted by an Israeli tank missile. He pointed to the gaping hole in seeming disbelief, and said, "Look at this! They used a tank to blow up a bedroom."

The Israelis later insisted that the house had been the source of machine-gun fire. Muslat conceded that gunmen had been firing from the neighborhood the night before, but not, he insisted, from his home. But he just as quickly said, "I would welcome them if they wish to use our home as a place to fire. We are part of the resistance." Muslat was one of the tens of thousands of day laborers on construction jobs in Israel who had been forced to sneak across the border daily to get to work. But now even that was impossible, and he was unemployed. He had spent several years working in construction at Gilo, he said, digging foundations and pouring concrete slabs.

Inside the house, Muslat and several of his brothers and friends sat down in a circle on cushions on the floor, inviting us to join them. As we drank coffee and smoked a water pipe, evening crept in on us, and the shooting started. Sporadic gunfire from Beit Jala was answered by the roar of Israeli attack helicopters circling overhead. I thought about getting my flak jacket from the backseat of my car, but it would be awkward to put on a bulletproof vest while our hosts were sitting unprotected in their own home. Such was the etiquette of conflict reporting.

Like the Nur-El family, Muslat and his brothers said they would never leave. They, too, had been refugees in the war in 1948, having been expelled from their village, near what is today the Israeli town of Beersheba. "They blew up my father's home in 1948, and we became refugees, and we came here," said Muslat. "Then they occupied this land. And now they are bombing my home again. No, this time, we will never leave. The only politics I have is that we should get our land back. That is the deal—land for peace. We didn't get the land, so there will be no peace. We support Fatah and we support Hamas and we support the resistance. It is time to fight."

Everywhere in Beit Jala, I encountered seething anger toward the Israelis for their confiscation of Palestinian land and homes, and for the ongoing dislocation of life. Beit Jalans were furious at the collective punishment Israel meted out in Gaza and the West Bank, through a siege that severed workers from their jobs inside Israel and restricted the transfer of goods, further crippling an already struggling Palestinian economy. Some 120,000 Palestinians who worked in Israel, like Muslat, were now out of work. Unemployment levels in Gaza and the West Bank surged to 45 percent, a fourfold increase. The World Bank estimated that 32 percent of Palestinians saw their standard of living plunge below the poverty line—which means they were struggling to get by on something like $2.10 a day. That represented a 50 percent increase in poverty since the beginning of the conflict.

In this atmosphere of despair, the rage of Palestinians—Muslim and Christian—toward Israel quickly boiled to the surface in front-line communities such as Beit Jala. A more muted anger, directed at the Palestinian Authority militias, was expressed by the village's Christians, who felt that the militias were using the village as cover for an attack on Gilo. The Christian residents saw the gunmen as outsiders, albeit from nearby Muslim villages, whose actions seemed ill-considered. They were behaving like local toughs with guns, opening up on Gilo and thereby bringing retaliatory fire onto Beit Jala, putting civilians in danger—especially the wealthier Christian families who lived on the hillside. Such sentiments were always cautiously phrased and accompanied by the request that I not quote the speaker by name. Beit Jala's 8,000 Christians were afraid that such statements would be seen by their 4,000 Muslim neighbors as a betrayal of the Palestinian cause, and that they would be branded as collaborators—which in the current atmosphere could mean death.

This internal tension was reopening a long-hidden fissure between the Christians and Muslims in Beit Jala. The Christians were mostly middle-class shopkeepers and educated professionals who had lived in Beit Jala for generations and who had a lot to lose. They were the last remnants of families decimated by emigration. Most Muslims were laborers who had hustled to get work on Israeli construction crews, where the hard work and poor wages engendered resentment. Most also came from families that had been refugees in 1948, and many had only recently made it to Beit Jala from the nearby refugee camps and had huge extended families eager to join them. Beit Jala's Muslim population was also dramatically increasing through soaring birthrates, whereas the Christian population had stagnated at the level of a half century earlier. The resultant overcrowding in Beit Jala was exacerbated by Israeli land policies that had caused the village to shrink in size over the decades. Before 1967, Beit Jala had occupied 13 square kilometers; by 2000, it had been reduced to only 4 square kilometers, even though its population had increased by 50 percent.

The Israelis were keenly aware of the existing divisions between Muslims and Christians. Israeli military officials had been briefing reporters on the notion that the Christians of the town were angry that attacks by Muslim militias had put their community in the line of fire. In an October 25 statement, Major General Giora Eiland of the IDF said, "The Tanzim is using buildings in Beit Jala as cover for attacks on Jerusalem. The gunmen position themselves near churches, with the hope that Israel's response will damage a church, thus setting the Christian world against Israel. This is a cynical and deliberate method to involve a population that is not interested in conflict."

A front-page headline in the *Jerusalem Post* that same day blared "Christians Fleeing Beit Jala." The story that ran under it claimed that hundreds of Christian families were leaving the Bethlehem area with the help of foreign embassies because of the recent violence. The *Post* also reported that dual nationals, both Christians and Muslims, were being assisted by the Israeli Foreign Ministry in getting out of the West Bank and Gaza, but that 70 percent of those leaving were Christian—a vastly disproportionate number, given that Christians accounted for less than 2 percent of the Palestinian population.

"Hundreds of families have left," Shlomo Dror, a spokesman for the Israeli military coordinator for the West Bank, was quoted as saying. He also said Israeli officials feared that Palestinian Christians might become targets of attacks if they were heard criticizing the Palestinian Authority. "We are talking about families who lived in Bethlehem, Ramallah, Gaza, Tulkarm and other places who were assisted by many embassies. . . . The majority of Arab Christians yearn for peace."

The military commanders' statements were exaggerated and pointedly ignored the fact that the majority of Muslims also "yearned for peace." Israeli officials' claims that Christians were being "assisted by many embassies" were never backed up by American and European embassy officials themselves. The Israelis were never able to provide any details. Still, it was undeniable that the Christians were feeling caught in the middle and that dozens of families had left and many others were planning to leave. But as soon as Israeli officials began to publicize that fact, the Palestinian Christian community became defensive and closed ranks with its Muslim neighbors. The Roman Catholic patriarchate immediately issued a sharp denial of the *Post*'s claims that Christian families were fleeing. Palestinian Christians were keenly aware of the danger of falling victim to what they saw as one more attempt to "divide and rule."

The Qassiyeh family's home stood directly in the middle of all this.

Nakleh Qassiyeh, a Greek Orthodox Christian, was from a family of masons, and he knew his stone. He had built his entire four-story house "stone by stone," as he put it, on the highest hill in Beit Jala, fashioning it out of "sweet mizeh," a type of limestone that he had specially selected from one of the finest quarries in Hebron. The neatly squared blocks of hand-hewn stone had a warm, almost pinkish color. Their thickness insulated the house against the penetrating sun in the summer months, and their outer sheen provided a strong resistance to water in the rainy season. Qassiyeh was 66 years old, and this was the homestead he wanted for his extended family. He and his wife were on the ground floor, and his children and their families lived on separate floors above them. It was a traditional Palestinian home, a communal living space in which grandparents, children, and grandchildren all lived together.

Qassiyeh also held on to the olive grove in front of the property, which cascaded down a steep hill to a bypass road that Israel had built connecting Gilo to other Jewish settlements in the West Bank. He said the Israelis had built the road on a piece of his land. After the construction was complete, Israel offered Qassiyeh 20 Jordanian dinars (about U.S. $30) per olive tree on roughly an acre of land near the southern end of the tunnel. The offer was brought to him by the Civil Administration via the *mukhtar*, or village leader. He refused it—not only because it was insultingly low but also because of the shame that fell on any Palestinian who sold land to the Israelis.

On Friday, October 27, Qassiyeh saw Fatah Tanzim gunmen setting up a position along a wall in the garden in front of his home. Having seen what happened the previous week to the homes where the Tanzim had set up operations, he asked them not to do this. "I pleaded with them," he said. "I told them there were fifteen children living in the house, and that if they shot from there, the Israelis would cut down my house with bullets. But there was a big man who told me to get inside my house and to be quiet. I think the Tanzim were using the Christian neighborhoods because they knew the Israelis wouldn't hit back as hard."

But that night the Israelis struck back plenty hard. Qassiyeh and his extended family fled their home as the sun set and the first rounds of machine gun fire started from the Tanzim gunmen. Within minutes, the Israelis were responding with tanks and helicopter fire. The entire northern facade of the Qassiyeh home was sheared off. Over the next few days, the top floor of the house was hit by roughly thirty tank-fired missiles.

One of the big questions at the time was who was organizing this shooting from the Beit Jala side. It seemed to be a kind of fly-by-night Fatah Tanzim operation, headed by a man named Hussein Abayat.

Abayat was a 37-year-old baker and weapons dealer from one of the four largest families in the Muslim Tamari tribe. At the time of the shooting, he was elusive, driving the roads in his Isuzu pickup truck from his native village of Hindazi, and then at night setting up a tripod for his machine gun in Beit Jala and Beit Sahour. The word was out that Abayat was intentionally using the Christian enclaves as cover for Tanzim operations.

Hussein Abayat was the son of a shepherd, a member of a tribe that had been buying and selling sheep in the Judean hills for centuries. In 1980, as a teenager, he joined Fatah, and he participated in the *intifada* in the late 1980s. He served several stints in Israeli jails for his political activity. By 1990 he was a member of the Tanzim, which in Arabic simply means "the Organization," but which would come to mean the unruly militias in Gaza and the West Bank that operated as armed wings of Arafat's Fatah party. He had seven children, one of whom had been born during the Gulf War and named after Saddam Hussein. For many years Abayat had worked in Israel, at a bakery in West Jerusalem, where he baked Iraqi-style bread over an open fire—a treat especially relished by Sephardic Jews who had emigrated to Israel from Arab countries. In 1996, with the Israeli implementation of border closures, he was unable to commute to that job and began to devote more of his time to his own bakery in Bethlehem, just behind Manger Square.

But where he made his real bread was in the lucrative black market in weapons, according to Palestinian sources and some family members. He'd buy 9-mm automatic pistols and Israeli-made Galil automatic rifles from Israelis motivated by greed, or in some cases, drug habits. Then he'd turn around and sell the guns at twice the price, to Palestinians. He had developed a huge arsenal over the years, including an Israeli-made heavy-caliber machine gun roughly four feet long, with which he proudly posed for photographs with ammunition belts strapped across his shoulders. (Israeli military officials said the weapons had most likely been stolen, not bought.) He also had been stockpiling ammunition for at least a year before the fighting broke out. His brother said he had about two hundred steel boxes clearly marked "IDF," which held tens of thousands of high-caliber bullets. In addition to his guns, he had another beloved collection: Rambo videos. And the influence of Sylvester Stallone on Abayat was pretty easy to spot. He had taken to dressing in black military pants and high-laced military boots. He wore a green army ammunition vest strapped down with an automatic pistol and several grenades. He also wore wraparound sunglasses and a black baseball hat. He was Fatah's answer to Rambo.

. . .

It was October 25. Said and I were in the car, on our way out of Beit Sahour, when gunshots erupted around us. Palestinian gunmen were firing on a ramshackle Israeli military base called Shidma, which stood on a hilltop near Shepherds' Fields. We were just passing the home of Sami Kheir, who I had gotten to know that year through documenting his life as a Christian Palestinian in the first *intifada*. We pulled over right there, and he immediately ushered us into the basement, where he and his family (his mother; his wife and their two young children; his older brother Issam; and several other relatives) were waiting out the evening's gun battle. As tea was served we could hear the light-weapons fire of the Palestinian gunmen, answered by the more distant bursts of heavy-caliber Israeli machine guns, and the sound of the helicopters moving in. We waited tensely. And then it came—the horrifying whir of the missiles before they struck with a deafening bang.

"This is not an *intifada,* this is a war," said Sami. "No one is taking part in this from Beit Sahour, except the Tanzim gunmen, and the ones shooting from around the homes are not from here. . . . They are Muslims from the Tamari clan. You know this man Abayat, and his brothers? These are the ones doing the shooting. They come here at night. The Christians can't object to this. We have to follow them. If we don't, we are labeled collaborators."

Sami's mother was angry about the Gaza cleric from Hamas who had been thundering on Palestinian television against "infidels" and who had led the mob to burn Christian homes and establishments that served alcohol. She had heard this preacher call the Al-Aqsa *intifada* "a war against Jews and Christians."

"Can you believe they are saying these things about Palestinians on Palestinian television? Do they know how much Christians in Beit Sahour sacrificed in the first *intifada*?" she asked sharply, as her sons tried to calm her down. She shifted her angry gaze back to the television footage of the day's funerals in the West Bank and Gaza, which was being replayed to the sound of Koranic verses.

Issam told me, with great bitterness, the story of his young cousin

Elias, who had been injured while throwing stones at Rachel's Tomb. The other youths were slow in getting an ambulance for him. As the family story went, one of the youths said, "No need to rush, he is Christian." The story sounded like an exaggeration, but it had become a kind of parable that held some greater truth for the family.

"Why are we not fighting?" Issam asked rhetorically, and then answered himself. "Because when Christians die, we are not martyrs. We are just rotten flesh. Listen to the *shebab* out there. They say, 'God will give victory to Muslims.' Just listen to them. God created us all equal, so why victory only for the Muslims? You know, the Israelis have created these divisions between Muslims and Christians for a long time, but now it is like the Muslims are doing it themselves."

I was surprised at the depth of resentment toward Muslims in a family with such strong Palestinian nationalist sentiments. But this would turn out to be a fairly commonly held sentiment among the Christian families I had gotten to know in Beit Sahour and Beit Jala. The residents under siege were highly emotional, and that had to be factored in. The first reaction was always to point the blame at Israel. But just beneath that reflexive anti-Israeli feeling, a layer of anger was accruing among Christians toward their Muslim Palestinian brethren.

Sami told me he had just heard the Atrash family, one of the leading Greek Orthodox clans in Beit Sahour, protesting about Abayat and his militia shooting from in front of their home. There were rumors that Abayat's gunmen had even pointed their weapons at several young men from the Atrash family and told them to leave the area, that they were carrying out a "security operation." The threat at gunpoint, in their own neighborhood, by their own forces, had infuriated the Atrash family and the Christian community. There was an argument in the street just before the gun battle fully erupted and everyone had to run for cover.

After the shooting died down, we drove to see the Atrash family. It was the first night of the winter rains, and the roads were slick; so we drove carefully up the steep hillside to the family's home. As we arrived, we saw the Atrash family arguing with Palestinian police officers dressed in green fatigues. The patriarch of the family, Yakoub Atrash, was yelling, "Why are they allowed to shoot from here? Why are they shooting from homes? Why are these people coming here, just because we are Christians?"

His home had been raked by machine-gun fire and the window casings had been blown out by several tank missiles. He lived in the home with his extended family—three sons and their wives and a total of five grandchildren. When the Israeli tank-fired missiles began crashing through the windows, the family dove for cover. His wife, Mary, who had suffered small cuts from the shattered glass and had gone into shock, was still at the hospital.

Then Girius Atrash, a relative and a Christian aide to Arafat, showed up. I had met him during the pope's visit in March, as Arafat had chosen him to handle the considerable task of diplomatic protocol for the papal entourage. American-educated and erudite, he was one of Arafat's most polished fixers. He was a good man by many accounts, but he was also someone who personified the clique of Christians from Beit Sahour that Arafat had surrounded himself with, personally handpicked to ensure loyalty. Arafat was keenly aware that he needed his own representatives in the local communities, but especially so in Beit Sahour, where the grassroots leaders behind the 1988 tax revolt had shown themselves to be fiercely independent, creative, and potential rivals to his authority.

Girius Atrash lived in a sprawling compound, still under construction, just around the corner. It too had been hit by Israeli tank fire. He was trying to calm his relatives down and intervene between them and the soldiers. He put his arm around his uncle Yakoub, and said, "The men were firing against orders. They should not have been doing it so close to residential homes. There are orders against this, and we will be sure that they are enforced."

"They come here because they want to put the Christians in the middle of this," complained Yakoub, lowering his voice now, speaking to Atrash and not the soldiers.

At this point, the Palestinian police asked to see our identification. There was a heavy atmosphere of suspicion, and they didn't like that we had been taking notes on this confrontation. They checked our press cards and then politely but firmly ordered us to leave. But we had had a revealing glimpse into the current *intifada*. There on the street, we had seen what analysts had been telling us—that this shooting was a direct challenge by local Tanzim militias to Arafat's rule. It was also a stark illustration of just how different this *intifada* was from the previous one, especially in Beit Sahour. This town had been unique in developing a grassroots resistance to Israeli occupation in the late 1980s. Young men like Sami's good friend Edmond had sacrificed their lives in street demonstrations. The leaders of the tax revolt, such as Elias Rishmawi and George Andoni and Jad Isaac, had risked their livelihoods and spent time in jail to uphold their commitment to civil disobedience against Israeli occupation. The Al-Aqsa *intifada,* a hit-and-run guerrilla operation by Fatah thugs from the villages on the fringes of town, was threatening all that they had striven to accomplish. Abayat and the other gunmen did not even know the residents of Beit Sahour, and they seemed to care little that their random firing on Israeli military positions was putting the whole community at risk.

. . .

The ride home that night was perilous. The crackling of gunfire erupted again at about 8:30, as we headed for the checkpoint. Said and I put on our bulletproof vests as we drove. We had passed through the checkpoint and were in West Jerusalem when I realized that I had forgotten to take off my vest. It felt embarrassing, even absurd, to be wearing Kevlar in West Jerusalem.

The distant rumbling of the battle could be heard if you listened from a balcony or a hilltop. But for the most part people were coming and going as usual. As I drove home, I saw a family coming out of a Chinese restaurant and laughing. Young couples were clustered together at a café, over late-night cappuccinos. The last showing at the Smaadar movie theater was letting out. And my wife, Julie, now almost eight months pregnant, called on my car phone and asked me to pick up some Ben & Jerry's ice cream on my way home.

I studiously avoided telling Julie the details of what was happening in Beit Jala and Beit Sahour, largely because she was hoping to deliver the baby at Holy Family Hospital in Bethlehem. That would require us to pass through the Bethlehem checkpoint, which was fast becoming a no-man's-land between Beit Jala and Gilo. I just kept hoping that things in the Bethlehem area would quiet down in time for the baby to be safely delivered.

I was home by 9 P.M. There had been more tank fire on Beit Jala and my two sons were awake past their bedtime. Our dog, a yellow Labrador named Maggie, was trembling from the rumbling of the tanks in the distance. Thunder and fireworks always had the same effect on Maggie. And so we told the boys the sound they heard was thunder. I read them *Peter Pan,* skipping the part about the cannonballs fired from Captain Hook's pirate ship.

The daily routine of covering the conflict and coming home to a family was jarring and depressing. I was quite literally commuting to work in Kevlar and making it home, most of the time, in time for dinner. I had covered a number of conflicts, including the Persian Gulf War and various ethnic and guerrilla wars in places like Kosovo, the Sudan, Latin America, and Belfast. But in those conflicts I had been just one of many foreign correspondents parachuting into hot spots and camping out in hotels until the story faded from the front pages. This was a war without room service. In the end, I realized that to be with my family fundamentally changed not only the way I worked but also how I viewed the violent and tragic events unfolding around us. This time I was part of a community trying to get through a time of great difficulty. I worried about my friend and translator in Gaza, Saud Abu Ramadan, and his wife and four young children, when I heard the shelling on the phone as I received a nightly update from him. I worried about my neighbor Paul's son, Nadav, whom I still thought of as the skinny 14-year-old kid in hightops that he was when I first arrived but who was now entering his training for Israeli military service.

Certainly my children did not suffer much, not compared to the ordeal that Palestinian families, like Saud's, were enduring on a daily basis in the West Bank and Gaza. I did not have the same fatherly worries as Paul, with his son going off to the army and the country on the edge of war. But like all husbands and fathers in such situations, I worried every day about Julie, about her pregnancy, about our two sons. There was a sense of guilt, of questioning. Why in the world was I putting my family in this situation? Should I send them back to Massachusetts, or should we be sticking together? I found myself telling Julie not to worry since the tank fire was "at least two miles away" and pointed in the other direction. In hindsight that was an absurd rationalization, but it was the kind of bizarre calculus that went into getting by in a situation like this.

And it wasn't just distant fighting; the specter of suicide bombing had returned to Jerusalem as well. We found ourselves becoming expert at stopping and listening closely to the sound of an explosion in the middle of the afternoon. The trick was to decipher whether it was a sonic boom from an Israeli fighter jet overhead, or a bomb. The secret to figuring it out was in the moments after the explosion. If you heard the engine trail of the jet, you went back to your conversation or your morning newspaper or playing with the kids. But if in that moment you heard police and ambulance sirens, it was time to drop everything. You had to figure out as quickly as possible where the bomb had gone off, by tuning immediately to Israeli radio and waiting for the dreaded beeper messages from the IDF that updated correspondents of carnage by the minute. And then you had to perform the horrible scramble of checking coordinates and daily routines to make sure your family was nowhere near it. We avoided going to the Jerusalem mall or any shopping centers for fear of bombs, and that ruled out "Fun, Fun," the boys' favorite kiddy park. We didn't even think about going to the Old City, which we used to explore on Sundays. Ramallah, where we went to see friends or have dinner, also was out of the question. When a bomb detonated in an alley just a few blocks from our son's school and killed two Israelis, I called Julie on my way to the scene and couldn't get through because the mobile phone network always jammed in those situations. Later I learned that they were all safely at home.

Even though we did our best to keep what was going on from our children, there were times when we slipped up. One afternoon when I was taking care of the boys, we were watching a videotape. At the top of the hour, I clicked over briefly to catch the news on CNN. When I noticed the boys studying the images of rock-throwing clashes in Gaza, I clicked back to the video, which was a VeggieTales cartoon version of David and Goliath. The boys put all this together somehow and picked up on the intensity of what was going on. They were suddenly obsessed with David and Goliath. They were dressing up with headscarves and whipping blocks in the playroom at imaginary Goliaths. When our three-and-a-half-year-old, Will, got mad, he started saying, "I'll throw a rock at you!" His little brother Riley would say, "Well, I'll shoot you!" I didn't know whether to curse Disney or CNN or my own carelessness.

One day in early November, Will's teacher found him uncharacteristically quiet and sad at school. When she asked him what was the matter, he replied, "Soldiers are trying to hurt my Dad." I realized he had probably overheard me in my home office the day before, having a heated conversation with the IDF spokesman about shots that had been fired at two colleagues and myself by Israeli snipers on the roof of a building in Bethlehem. The spokesman couldn't have known this, and my son could never have understood it, but I probably had overreacted to the incident because I knew that was the same path that I would navigate with my wife when she went into labor—if, that is, we were going to have the baby in Bethlehem. We had made the decision to have our baby at the hospital in Bethlehem before the *intifada*. Our reasoning at that time was sound: We liked the hospital and the doctor, and the Bethlehem hospital was closer to our home than was the Israeli hospital in Jerusalem. But with violence erupting around the checkpoint, I was starting to lean strongly against the idea.

A few days earlier, on November 1, I had driven to Bethlehem to meet with Jad Isaac, who had been part of the Palestinian negotiating team at Camp David. Isaac wanted to go over the maps of the West Bank he had been so meticulously putting together, to show me that the Israelis at Camp David had actually offered significantly less than the "95 percent" claimed in the media. He carefully laid out his overhead-projector transparencies illustrating how the Israeli offer would have divided the West Bank into canton states or "three and a half Bantustans," as he put it. What they had offered, he said, were noncontiguous parcels of land that would leave the connecting roads subject to Israeli checkpoints and make Palestinian self-determination, both economically and politically, impossible. In his mind, the collapse of the peace process was inevitable, and the conflict it had unleashed was going to intensify.

I intended to ask Isaac about the nonviolent movement and about how it had been derailed, especially now, when it was so needed. I wanted to know whether he thought it could be rejuvenated in the current situation, whether it wouldn't be a more powerful tool than the rock-throwing clashes and the Tanzim randomly opening fire at distant IDF positions. But, almost on cue, a round of gunfire exploded around us, cutting the interview short. From what we could gather, the firing was coming from Palestinian gunmen stationed in a nearby building, who had opened fire on IDF soldiers posted at Rachel's Tomb, only a few hundred yards from his office. The heavy-caliber Israeli machine-gun fire was rattling the windows and shaking the walls.

Isaac and I retreated to a back room and took cover. Having to shout to be heard, he said, "You want to talk about nonviolence? Listen to what is going on out there! Listen to that! We have no chance of trying to return to dialogue right now. This has taken on a course that has its own momentum."

Three straight hours of heavy gunfire followed. It began as a concerted attack on Israeli positions in Gilo from ten different Palestinian militia gunmen operating under the leadership of Abayat. The battle was coordinated from Bethlehem, Beit Jala, and the village of Al-Khader—the town of St. George, who was perhaps the most beloved of all the saints for Orthodox Christians, and a symbol of strength for Muslims as well. It was believed that St. George had been imprisoned in Al-Khader, and the Greek Orthodox monastery there was said to hold the chains that had bound him. The chains were relics, believed to be imbued with the power to heal mental and other illnesses. Abayat was in Al-Khader that day. Israeli official sources said that he had killed two Israeli soldiers on the tunnel road near Gilo. Coupled with the death of another IDF soldier in Gaza, this marked the worst day of IDF casualties in the conflict so far, and it spurred a more determined effort to get Abayat.

Eight days later, Abayat was assassinated by the IDF. Israeli security forces had been using Palestinian informants in the Bethlehem area for weeks, trying to establish the pattern of Abayat's movements. Over the years, the Israelis had developed a sophisticated network of informants. The ones they used to target Abayat were mostly teenagers and young men in their 20s who had been lured into collaborating by money, the promise of a work permit in Israel, or in some cases, sex. One of them was an 18-year-old Christian construction worker from Beit Sahour who had no more than a third-grade education. His family told me that he had been lured through sex to cooperate with the Israelis in locating Abayat. On Thursday, November 9, at 11:50 A.M., Israeli intelligence units confirmed that Abayat was in Beit Sahour, near a home that had been severely damaged by IDF tank fire the night before. Two IDF Apache attack helicopters moved into position and fired a series of at least three anti-tank missiles directly at Abayat's white Isuzu pickup truck, completely destroying the vehicle and immediately killing him. But the missiles also killed two women bystanders on the road. They were relatives of the owner of the home that had been shelled and had come to offer their support and help in cleaning up the rubble. Aziza Shaibat, 52, was a mother of seven, and Rahma Shahin, 55, was a mother of four. Eight other Palestinians were wounded, including a Palestinian Authority police intelligence official who had been driving with Abayat.

A leading Israeli newspaper columnist, in a front-page editorial the next day, described the weeks of shooting around Bethlehem that had preceded the assassination, and the assassination itself, as "a critical point, almost a point of no return." The words were prescient. Israel soon would unleash a policy of assassination (or "liquidation," as IDF officials referred to it). The policy, a return to Israel's darkest days of extrajudicial killing, met with harsh international condemnation. Nevertheless, in the months following, some twenty senior Fatah activists were assassinated in what the deputy defense minister, Efraim Sneh, called "hits" by Israeli forces. Fatah called for revenge, and Palestinian attacks escalated to a new level.

Soon after Abayat's assassination, I met with his brothers. Based on interviews with them and other members of the Tanzim who knew him, I was able to confirm that what we had been hearing for weeks about Abayat was true. He had been using Beit Jala and Beit Sahour as staging grounds for his attacks, primarily because they were where he could get a clear shot at Israeli troops. But, a brother confirmed, Abayat was also intentionally firing from the Christian enclaves because he understood that the Israelis would be more restrained in returning fire.

"He was aware of this. It was a military strategy," said his 28-year-old brother Naji, proudly showing us a family photo album of his brother posing with his arsenal of weapons. "The Israelis were killing children! So what if a house was destroyed. This is the way he thought when he was firing from Beit Jala. This is what he told us. The Christians offered him coffee. They were good to him and supported him to his face. But all the time they were complaining [behind his back]. They told their churches about this problem and then there was pressure on Arafat from the pope to stop the shooting. When the Christians complained, he was feeling that they did not want to sacrifice for the Palestinian people to defend themselves."

"But it's okay, we still love the Christians," he added, referring to the Christians as *dhimmi,* or a minority that needed protected status, and thus revealing the Islamic cultural paternalism that drove many Arab Christians crazy. "They are still our brothers," he said.

It was astounding that more of these Christian "brothers" in Beit Jala had not been killed in the fighting. Israeli forces were answering with heavier retaliatory attacks at the Tanzim gunmen who had picked up where Abayat left off. On Wednesday, November 15, Harold Fischer, a German chiropractor who had married a Palestinian Christian woman and lived in Beit Jala, was killed. The 68-year-old doctor, who was beloved in the neighborhood for the physical therapy he provided to many wheelchair-bound victims of the first *intifada*, had been on his way next door to try and help several neighbors who had been injured in an Israeli reprisal. I attended his funeral two days later at the Lutheran Church, at a mass presided over by the Lutheran Bishop Mounib Younan. In a rousing eulogy, Younan referred to the doctor as a "martyr." I was surprised to hear Younan, who was an inspiring leader and a strong voice for interfaith dialogue, resorting to such a loaded phrase, which was so nationalistic and seemed such a mischaracterization of the man's life and death. Wasn't Fischer just a good man and a professional healer trying to help people in a dangerous situation? Why did that make him a martyr?

The mourners marched through Beit Jala, the men bearing an open casket inside which lay the doctor's body wrapped in two flags, German and Palestinian. At the head of the procession was a banner with a rather confusing theology, which read, "Jesus Christ Will Not Be Crucified Twice In His Home Country, Palestine.—*PFLP*." An even more bluntly worded banner read, "Drop the Olive Branch, Raise the Gun." When the crowd reached the graveside, the Fatah leader in Beit Jala, Hassan Abed-Rabbo, turned on the microphone of a sound system that had been set up for him, adjusted the volume, and began his political speech, "All Palestinians—"

"Shwai, shwai!" Younan sternly interrupted him with a common Arabic admonition ("Slow down, slow down!"), demanding that the religious burial rites be completed before the political speeches began. Younan had his way—almost: Just before the casket was lowered into the freshly dug grave, Abed-Rabbo turned on the microphone again, and proclaimed: "All Palestinians need to know that everyone is a target. We are all in the same trench, Muslims and Christians. Dr. Fischer is a martyr for the Palestinian cause. . . ."

After the speech, seven Palestinian policemen in army fatigues fired a 21-gun salute. The honor seemed a risky tribute, since it easily could have provoked a response from the Israeli military positions at Gilo, which were within view of the graveyard. I wondered, too, why a German doctor—who according to his wife did not believe in guns or violence—was receiving Palestinian military honors. Apparently a dean of the Lutheran church in Germany who was attending the service recognized the incongruity of tone at the funeral and asked to have the last word. He said: "It is not God who makes the wars; it is mankind, and he does it against His spoken will. And I do hope the message is understood here: We have to fight for peace. What a terrible situation that a man who was trying to help others had to die for it."

. . .

In the days after Abayat's assassination, the conflict around Bethlehem had escalated to a new level of intensity. But on Monday, November 13, Julie had an ultrasound appointment with her physician, Dr. Nihad Salsa, at the Holy Family Hospital. We were getting very close to the December 3 due date, and we could not afford to miss the appointment. We headed from our home toward the Bethlehem checkpoint and were waved through the first post. Then, as we proceeded toward Rachel's Tomb, we were stopped. An Israeli border policeman with an M-16 drawn ordered us to go back.

I pointed to Julie's obvious condition and tried to explain to the soldier that we had been waved through the first post and that my wife was pregnant, and he said, "Go to hospital in Jerusalem! This is danger here now." He banged on the hood with the assault rifle and barked, "Y'allah!"—an Arabic command (meaning "Let's go!") that had found its way into the Israeli vocabulary.

It was hard to tell what the specific security concern was. It seemed from a distance that an Israeli bomb squad was checking a Palestinian car parked too close to an Israeli post. We wrapped the heavy flak jacket around Julie and turned the car around. As we headed back, we heard a loud explosion near Beit Sahour, several miles to the east, which we later learned was a helicopter missile attack. I called Dr. Salsa and told her that it looked like we would not be able to make it through. She had been living under the closure long enough to take it in stride, and she told us to come any time we could. But after we had waited a few minutes at the first post, the Israeli soldiers started waving cars through again.

We went ahead with the ultrasound appointment. The baby looked big and healthy. Afterward, we stopped at the Jacir Palace. It was empty and the kitchen was closed, but the manager insisted that we rest and have some orange juice. We sat in the beautiful environs of the renovated hotel and did our best to convince ourselves that the scare on the way in was not likely to happen twice. We were both trying to put each other at ease about everything that was going on around us. Then the waiter came to us and said quite politely, "Are you finished?"

Yes, we nodded, and thanked him.

"Well, it is probably best that you leave right away then," he said. "There is a very large demonstration coming down the street."

From the front door of the hotel we saw roughly three thousand Palestinians marching toward Rachel's Tomb, carrying banners and chanting Fatah slogans. We got in the car and left as quickly as we could, with the front row of the angry crowd in our rearview mirror. The first tear gas canisters were fired on the crowd just as we approached the next checkpoint, roughly a quarter mile down the road.

It was definitely time to rethink having the baby in Bethlehem. Close friends and family thought we were out of our minds for even considering it, and I was beginning to agree with them. But Julie felt very strongly about it. Our second son, Riley, had been born at an Israeli hospital in our neighborhood in Jerusalem, but that hospital was going out of business. The other hospitals, Hadassah Mount Scopus and Hadassah Ein Karem, were modern and well-equipped but massive and impersonal. They were also farther away than the Bethlehem hospital. Julie was confident in the doctor and the midwives. My opinion, of course, carried little weight in such matters. But we agreed to go to the Bethlehem hospital, with one caveat: if there were any sign of violence at the checkpoint, we would turn around and head straight to Hadassah Mount Scopus.

On December 8, at about 2 P.M., Julie went into labor. As planned, I called Father Michael McGarry at Tantur to get an update on the situation at the checkpoint, which he could see from his office. I also called our friend Gerry Holmes, the ABC News bureau chief in Jerusalem, who was working on a piece about Beit Jala. They both reported that it was a rare afternoon of quiet. We headed for Bethlehem. And we were pleasantly surprised to find that the Israeli soldiers at the checkpoint were the nicest reservists I had come across in the two months of the conflict. They ushered us through with great fanfare and wished us luck. One of them, a slightly overweight youth with wire-rimmed glasses and a warm smile, leaned into our car and offered his own quick blessing, "Good luck, baby! And may there be peace here in your lifetime." The hospital was a beautiful facility on the grounds of a nineteenth-century monastery. We walked back and forth in the warm sunshine, in the courtyard with palm trees and rose bushes, waiting for the heavy contractions. Because of the border closures, the hospital was nearly empty. Palestinian women in Hebron and outlying villages were delivering at local clinics or at home, the nurses told us. That night, only one machine-gun battle erupted, rattling the windows, and it lasted only about thirty minutes. According to the morning newspapers, no one was wounded.

On December 9, 2000, at 7:35 A.M., Gabriel Jerome Sennott was born in Bethlehem. He and Julie were both fine.

Gabriel's Palestinian Authority birth certificate listed his place of birth as "Bethlehem," and his U.S. passport listed it as "West Bank." Riley, who had been born in Jerusalem, had an Israeli birth certificate that listed his place of birth as "Jerusalem, Israel," and a U.S. passport that listed it as "Jerusalem, ———." Although no country was listed after the comma in the American document, the punctuation mark itself was laden with significance: it anticipated an imminent determination on the Holy City's sovereignty. So we had two sons born in biblical cities that were, at least at this point in history, not internationally recognized as part of any sovereign state. It seemed appropriate that both of these places so connected to redemption should remain outside of the parameters of the conflict that was raging in the year 2000 over national borders.

Beyond the issue of their birthplace, our sons' very identities contravened this ancient land's accepted notions of nationalism, ethnicity, religion, and tribe. All three were American citizens. But in this land where nationality was defined by religion, where did they fit? Because their mother was Jewish, they were Jews by Jewish law. Because their father was Christian, they were Christian within Arab tradition. Riley was a *sabra,* as Israelis called children born in Israel. And Gabriel could qualify for a Palestinian identity card. William was born in Newton, Massachusetts, and named after a beloved priest from my mother's side of the family, the Rev. William Morgan. The three boys shared a wonderfully complex set of identities that captured a hope that we as parents had for all our children: that they might live "in the in-between"—not a place devoid of religious values but a place that appreciated all faiths, giving greater weight to what they shared in common than to what divided them. I would hope that they would be proud of their Jewish identity as well as open to the teachings of Jesus in the New Testament. A considerable challenge lay ahead of us, in teaching our children about faith.

. . .

Christmas 2000 was filled with meaning for us, sometimes a little too much meaning. We both felt a little bit like we were trapped in a Hallmark greeting card. But the intensity of it all made it a time we would never forget. It had its fittingly absurd moments, like the day I went to the Christmas Land Toy Shop, just off Bethlehem's Paul VI street, to buy Riley a plastic Harley Davidson motorcycle—and ran straight into a Hezbollah rally. As I traded pleasantries with the Christian shopkeeper and wished her a happy holiday, five thousand Islamic extremists were waving the yellow flags of Hezbollah and the green banners of Hamas and shooting AK-47 assault rifles into the air. A sheikh screamed in Arabic: "Death to America! Death to Israel!"

But there were also moments that shone with the unique beauty and timelessness many associate with the Holy Land. On Christmas Eve, I took the two older boys to Shepherds' Fields in Beit Sahour. Riley kept pointing at Palestinian gentlemen in kaffiyeh and exclaiming, "Hi shepherd!" The Franciscan chapel there is situated just above a simple stone grotto—a rival to the Greek Orthodox cave with its Byzantine mosaic floor and its more ancient claim as the true location of where the shepherds were visited by the angel of the Lord. I had been showing the boys the oil paintings in the church and telling them the same story that they had just seen acted out in the Nativity play at Will's school. After the service, they couldn't believe it when on the road back toward downtown Beit Sahour we saw a real shepherd with his flock in the hills. We drove up a dirt road in order to catch him. He was hitting the branches of gnarled old olive trees with a wooden staff, knocking down olives for his sheep and goats to feed on. The sheep also grazed on tufts of grass that had sprouted up on the hard, chalky hills—the same hills on which an angel is said to have appeared to simple shepherds two thousand years before, announcing the birth of the messiah.

But just over the hills, in Bethlehem, the official Christmas festivities had been canceled. Religious observances for the birth of Jesus would still be celebrated at all of the churches—Roman Catholic, Greek Orthodox, Armenian, Anglican, Lutheran, and all the rest. But the scheduled events for "Bethlehem 2000"—concerts, choirs, art exhibits, parades, tree lighting ceremonies—all of which were supposed to lead up to Christmas and which had been planned for years in advance—were called off. The traditional Christmas lights strung along the public streets were left dark as a sign of protest. There was no Christmas tree in Manger Square. It was hard to feel Christmas cheer after three months of conflict, hatred, and killings.

Bethlehem's hotels and restaurants—most of them freshly renovated in anticipation of a wave of more than two million Christian pilgrims to the Holy Land—were empty. There was not a single guest in the 1,700 hotel rooms that Bethlehem had to offer. Well, actually, the 250-room, five-star Jacir Palace had one guest registered Christmas week, but he was a Dutch journalist covering the conflict. As one hotel manager wryly observed, "There's plenty of room at the inn."

In Bethlehem, the streets were hauntingly empty. The blinking Christmas lights in the windows looked forlorn. Gloom had descended over the town. A few days before Christmas, I spotted a lone tour group of about twenty-five Christians from Nigeria. Despite the long walk back to the checkpoint, they seemed thrilled to be in the birthplace of Jesus. I stopped one man, who said with a lilting Nigerian accent, "Bless you, brother!" When I asked him if he felt intimidated by the fighting, he answered, "No, we have plenty of that at home."

The same day, I noticed a hearty British couple crossing the checkpoint on foot because no vehicles were being permitted into what had been declared a closed military area. They seemed a bit tentative, but carried on anyway. The husband, Michael Honey, 62, and a lifelong resident of London, said, "It's not exactly a little town, is it? And not exactly a peaceful one! And, from what I can see, there aren't any wise men."

I went to the office of Nabeel Kassis, the Palestinian Authority minister of the Bethlehem 2000 project, which had been planning the festivities since 1996. "This is an absolute disaster," he said. "None of us could have expected this in our worst nightmare. We thought this would be the best year we ever had. There were life savings that were gambled on this, huge investments. I don't think the world realizes just what this has done to the economy here, and the impact it will have in the future."

But the obvious question was, why wasn't the Palestinian Authority doing more to control the Tanzim gunmen in Beit Jala and Beit

Sahour so as to avoid the disastrous and often excessive retaliations by the Israelis? It was a question to which Kassis had no answer. He was a bright man, one of Arafat's handpicked Christian elite. But sitting in his office on this day, he was consumed with depression, seeing years of careful work and planning collapse around him. And in this sense he was no different from the other Palestinians living in Bethlehem. He seemed defeated and at a loss for any explanation of what was happening.

A U.N. report estimated that the Palestinian economy was hemorrhaging roughly $9 million per day during the conflict, and roughly one quarter of that figure represented losses in the tourism sector. About 75 percent of the Palestinian tourism industry was in Bethlehem, and the overwhelming majority of those businesses were Christian-owned. So the disaster to the tourism sector fell particularly hard on the Palestinian Christians. Travel agencies and hotels and restaurants were closing on every corner. Even the Guiding Star Travel Agency, one of the premier agencies in Jerusalem, was forced for the first time in a half century of ownership to lay off staff. Mark Khano, the Oxford-educated son who had returned to his native Jerusalem to head the agency and contribute to the Palestinian economy, had packed it in and left for New York with his wife, who was attending graduate school there, and their newborn child. He was heartbroken, but he felt he had to leave, at least for the time being, for the sake of his family.

Michel Sabbah, the Roman Catholic patriarch of Jerusalem, announced that all of the celebrations for Christmas would be scaled down to reflect the grim reality of conflict and killing that surrounded Bethlehem. He released a statement that read, "We bear in our hearts and minds the pain of our own communities as well as that of all Palestinian and Israeli men and women of faith in our land."

The year 2000 marked a confluence of the calendars of the three different faiths of the Holy Land. It was not only Christmas time but also the feast marking the end of Ramadan, the Muslim holy month of fasting, and Chanukah, the Jewish festival of lights. But a dark pall hung over the land. Prayers were focused on ending the conflict and reinitiating the peace process, which Palestinian and Israeli leaders were working to do in talks with President Clinton in Washington. No one was ready to give up hope that a solution could be reached at the last minute and reverse the momentum toward war.

On my way across Manger Square, I stopped in to see the Giacamans, an old Bethlehem family descended from the French Crusaders who had come to Palestine as stone carvers for the cathedrals in the eleventh century and never left. After nine hundred years on the land, they considered themselves Palestinians. They owned a small factory and shop just off Manger Square, which was widely regarded as the place to find the finest carvings of olivewood and mother of pearl in all of Bethlehem The matriarch of the family, Warda, 79, who was still carving mother-of-pearl inlays for religious jewelry and rosary beads, said definitively, "This Christmas is the worst I have ever seen. It is worse than the war in 1948 and the war in 1967. At least during 1948, the British soldiers came in and bought things."

Jacques Giacaman, her 30-year-old grandson, told me that for the first time that anyone could remember in the family's long history, they had been forced to take out a loan to stay afloat. They had also been forced to lay off half of their staff, a total of twelve people—something they had managed to avoid even during the worst days of the first *intifada,* in the late 1980s. I had gotten to know Jacques over the years and had spoken with him on several occasions about the devastating effects of emigration on young, educated Christian Palestinians who remained behind, like himself. Of the thirty Palestinian Christians from his graduating class at the St. Lasalle Brothers' School, only two were left in Bethlehem. The rest had gone to live abroad. And now he said both of the last two remaining students, which included himself, were considering heading to America. He predicted that the events of 2000 would produce a wave of Christian emigration rivaling those in 1948 and 1967, leaving the Christian population in Palestine hanging by a thread.

Just before Christmas, I went to Beit Jala to see the Qassiyeh family, and found Ramzi, 35, a construction worker and second son of the owner of the home, digging through rubble on the bombed-out top floor. He was searching for a cardboard box that held a plastic Christmas tree, ornaments, and lights.

"Here it is!" he said as he pulled a string of Christmas lights, a few pieces of a plastic tree, and some shards of broken glass ornaments from under several feet of crumbled concrete wall. There was not much left of the top floor of the family's home. He dusted off the bent pieces of the artificial tree and set it up against the front steps of the house, which were covered in shattered glass from the windows. The family had fled their home in late October, seeking refuge from the conflict. Since then, they had been staying at the Millennium

Hotel, a 35-room facility built for the expected tourist boom in 2000. The hotel stood empty until necessity transformed it into emergency housing for about fifteen of the roughly two hundred families who had been forced to evacuate their homes in Beit Jala. Ramzi and his wife, Michelle, posed for a photograph with their broken tree against the backdrop of the bombed-out remains of the house. They began gathering up fragments from the thirty-two tank- and helicopter-fired missiles that had hit their house, planning to use them as ornaments on the pathetic tree. Some parts of the missiles were clearly stamped "Made in USA." Yakoub, 45, the oldest brother, said, "We just want to thank America so much for this present they have given us with their good friends the Israelis."

The Qassiyeh brothers had become a bit too practiced at sound bites. Several reporters gathered around them as they decorated the tree and posed for pictures. Their artificial tree, their rehearsed rage, and the broken missile fragments serving as macabre ornaments provided the perfect snapshot of Christmas in the Holy Land, 2000.

On the third day after he was crucified, Christians believe Jesus rose again in fulfillment of the scriptures. The day after the Resurrection, according to Luke, two of Jesus's disciples headed out to a village named Emmaus, approximately eight miles northwest of Jerusalem. Perhaps they were fleeing in fear of being apprehended by the Roman authorities for their connection to Jesus. Eventually, all of the disciples, except James, would emigrate in some fashion out of the Holy Land.

It was on the road to Emmaus that something mystical happened. The disciples were met on the road by a man. It was Jesus, Luke's gospel tells us, but the disciples were unable to recognize him. As they walked, they told this man the news that their messiah had risen. As the light of day faded and evening began to set in, the disciples implored the man to stay. As they approached the village, the man turned as if to go on, but then turned back and stayed with them. They sat together at a table, and as the man broke the bread, blessed it, and reached out to offer it to them, the disciples' "eyes were opened" and they recognized him as Jesus. But at that moment, he vanished from their sight.

XV

The Road to Emmaus

As they approached the village to which they were going, Jesus acted as if he were going farther. But they urged him strongly, "Stay with us, for it is nearly evening; the day is almost over." So he went in to stay with them. When he was at the table with them, he took bread, gave thanks, broke it and began to give it to them. Then their eyes were opened and they recognized him, and he disappeared from their sight.

LUKE 24:28–31 (NIV)

AT THE DAWN of the third millennium, it took the mystery of faith to believe that the people of the Holy Land could find the road back to peace. One effort to find that path began on a muddy track laid down by tank treads at the fortified entry of the Shidma Israeli military base. This IDF post was on occupied land—on the fringes of Beit Sahour, near Bethlehem, where Jesus was born, and within sight of the modern boundaries of Jerusalem, where Jesus died and Christians believe he rose again. It stood on a rocky hilltop in Judea or the West Bank, depending on whose language one chose. It was a no-man's-land between the emerging Palestinian state and its hopes for justice, and Israel and its yearnings for security. Shidma overlooked the Shepherds' Field of the New Testament.

The Shidma post was an old military camp established during the British mandate and held briefly by the Jordanian army before its defeat and retreat in the Six-Day War. Shidma was now an Israeli bunker. Marching toward it were a group of Palestinians from Beit Sahour, Israelis from Jerusalem, and Europeans and Americans. They were advancing in the name of peace and justice, in the first nonviolent demonstration after three months of conflict and a toll of casualties that was still rising daily. Beit Sahour had been one of the first stops in my journalistic pilgrimage along the path of Jesus's life, and it was where my wanderings through the Holy Land in the year 2000 would end.

. . .

It was December 28, and the marchers were led by Ghassan Andoni, the Palestinian leader whom I had met in researching Beit Sahour's role in the nonviolent movement of civil disobedience during the first *intifada.* I had been especially interested in the Palestinian Center for Rapprochement Between People, which Andoni had founded in 1990 and which had played a key role in the movement. A virtual cottage industry of institutes dedicated to "dialogue" had since sprung up; but the Rapprochement Center in fall 2000 was, by many accounts, the only institution where direct lines of Israeli-Palestinian dialogue were still open and functioning. Amid the violence that had convulsed the West Bank and Gaza and Jerusalem, there had been depressingly little in the way of nonviolent action to break the cycle of recrimination. Andoni had struggled, through the seven years of faltering negotiations around the Oslo agreement and then the descent back into conflict, to keep his center and its mission alive.

At the front of the procession, Andoni and his old friend Jad Isaac, another leader of Beit Sahour's nonviolent movement, walked with their arms locked together. They were the first to enter the gate of the military camp. Several Israeli soldiers emerged from a concrete bunker that was encased in sandbags and draped in camouflage netting. Speaking through a bullhorn, Andoni called on the soldiers to leave the post, but got no response. He then instructed the marchers, "Okay, move forward a bit. Just a bit." They shuffled inside the gate. The soldiers came nearer, visibly tightening their grip on their weapons. With such a small group, Andoni was able to maintain the calm discipline required for nonviolence. I saw him frown as a Palestinian teenager ran up a gun tower just inside the gate and tied a Palestinian flag to the top. A French activist in his 30s quickly climbed the tower and came back down with the teenager in tow. Andoni calmly brought everyone back in line.

Then he shouted something to the soldiers, who were slowly walking toward him, guns at the ready. This moment captured the power of nonviolence, as well as the huge risk involved in practicing it. The soldiers were tense, and it was not difficult to imagine them opening fire on this crowd, which was approaching the gate without authorization. Tension hung in the air. A quiet fell over the marchers—a summoning of courage, perhaps. Or maybe just fear. The conflict was laid bare, the injustice revealed as unarmed civilians confronted armed occupiers. Andoni waved a typewritten statement in his hand like a white flag. Then he read it aloud in English and rather theatrically. It urged the soldiers to leave the post and end their occupation. As he read the statement, I noticed one of the Israeli soldiers smirking and then casually walking down the road, relaxing his grip on his weapon. With remarkable ease, he slowly coaxed the crowd back outside the gate. The soldier accepted the letter from Andoni, and in Hebrew, told the crowd to leave, saying, "I thought you were against violence. . . . So go away, and there will be no violence."

The group was discouragingly small, including less than one hundred demonstrators. Nearly half were from a visiting Italian and French peace mission headed by Luisa Morgantini, an Italian member of the European parliament, who in 1989 had organized a human chain around Jerusalem that had been violently broken up by Israeli police. Ten were European and American expats from Jerusalem, four of whom I knew from Christian organizations. About two dozen Palestinian Christians were there, as well as about ten Israeli peace activists, including Veronika Cohen, who was making her first visit to Beit Sahour since the Israeli siege following the tax revolt in 1988, when she had observed the Sabbath there in solidarity with the town.

The event received little attention from the international media. Even the foreign desk at my own newspaper was uninterested. But to me the quiet power of the statement made that day dwarfed the thousands of Palestinian *shebab* throwing rocks that I had been witnessing day after day.

Andoni had chosen the Shidma base because it was as layered with the conflict's complexities as it was with layers of archaeology and history. Earlier that month, Israeli troops bulldozing a site for another tank installation accidentally unearthed what appeared to be tombstones. A subsequent, more careful excavation revealed a large Christian cemetery that dated to the early Byzantine era. This rare archaeological find provided Beit Sahour with a unique footing on which to call for the removal of the IDF post. The enterprising Andoni had seized the opportunity for a nonviolent protest urging the withdrawal of Israeli troops from the post—not only because it symbolized the hated occupation but also because it sat on Beit Sahour's sacred ancestral burial ground.

After delivering the letter, Andoni called upon the marchers to head back. "We have accomplished what we came here to do," he said. As they left, an Israeli soldier yanked down the Palestinian flag from the gun tower and tossed it into a metal trash container. The nonviolent protest may not have impressed the soldiers much, but it was a symbolic start.

Veronika Cohen was walking down the muddy path that led away from the military camp. As she observed the column of marchers, she said, "This is small. It's sad." And then she mused in an uncertain voice, "Maybe it's a beginning."

One Beit Sahouran who was pointedly missing from this march was Elias Rishmawi, the pharmacist who had been a leader of the tax revolt. When the returning marchers passed his home, I stopped in to see him. He told me that he had been watching the nightly battles between the Israeli soldiers and the Fatah gunmen set up around Beit Sahour. He was puzzled by the shooting. It was his impression that the Fatah Tanzim gunmen were consistently firing either into the air or at a spot at least one hundred meters away from the camp. He wondered exactly what they were trying to achieve. Was this intended to provoke Israeli retaliation on the community of Beit Sahour and win international sympathy, or was it truly a guerrilla operation? After watching for several weeks, he had concluded that it was the former rather than the latter. He came back to an existential question that applied to this *intifada* as well as the last one: Was it meant to change the situation, or merely to turn the world's spotlight back to a situation that remained unchanged?

Rishmawi was now a successful businessman, and like so many Palestinian businessmen he was suffering greatly under the border closures. Perhaps some of his anger came from the fact that he had more to lose in this conflict, or from wondering what his sacrifices in the last *intifada* had achieved. What made Rishmawi's financial plight more profound was that his losses were also the losses of the community at large. If he was unable to import medicines and medical equipment, then the hospitals and pharmacies would not be able to care for those who were ill or wounded in the fighting. Rishmawi deeply respected the work of his friends Andoni and Isaac, but he worried that the march could unintentionally provide a veil of legitimacy for the leadership of the current uprising, which he felt very strongly had no legitimacy.

"I want a homeland," he told me, "where human dignity is respected, where there is social justice; and if these criteria are not met [by the Palestinian Authority], then I have a problem. I cannot participate. I cannot be a part. It is true that Israel puts plenty of obstacles in our way. But the conduct and behavior of the P.A. has a very negative effect on the community. People do not feel a social or even physical sense of security, or a rule of law. They are afraid both of the lack of direction of their own leaders and of the Israeli response to those actions. It has degraded confidence in the [Palestinian] Authority.

"This is especially true here in Beit Sahour, where we are paying a price for the decisions that are not made by our own community. They are calling this the 'Al-Aqsa *intifada*.' I don't use that phrase, even though I see Al-Aqsa as a nationalist symbol and not just a religious one. First of all, by using the name 'Al-Aqsa,' they are only trying to influence the Muslim communities and a people who are very traditional and religious. I would hope that many of them would see through that. Call it whatever you want, it is not a mass movement. So more simply, they have no right to call it an *intifada* at all. The word *intifada* means literally 'a shaking off.' But it carries the meaning of a whole body working together to reject something. It carries the meaning of spontaneity and a collective. This is not an *intifada*."

Later that evening, after the march, I visited with Andoni in his small office in Beit Sahour, just across from the Greek Orthodox church—or "Arab Orthodox," as he always insisted on calling it. Andoni and I talked about the march's noticeably small numbers. He explained that one reason for the lack of community interest was that "the movement," as he called his efforts, had had to build itself up again from nothing. The leaders of nonviolence had invested their hopes in the peace process, and as a result their organizations and infrastructure, which had already been undermined by Arafat's PLO in the early 1990s, were inoperative during the seven years of the Oslo peace process. They had been lulled into believing that peace was just around the corner—that Oslo was the embodiment of their nonviolent movement. Trusting that the politicians would work out the details, Israeli and Palestinian peace activists had failed to keep up the hard work it would take to convince people that the risks needed to complete this peace agreement were worth taking. When events degenerated into violence in the fall of 2000, the peace activists were confronted with their error.

On the Palestinian side, Christian leaders in Jerusalem, Ramallah, Birzeit, and Beit Sahour were generally the first to try to reactivate a nonviolent movement. In Beit Sahour, they were doing it in a classically Christian Arab way, which was to mask, even deny, any Christian aspect to their efforts, casting them instead in nationalist terms. Andoni, for example, intentionally did not focus on the Christian archaeological angle during the Shidma march, or the obvious relevance of the Shepherds' Field at Christmastime, even though such overt associations might have attracted Western media attention. This was sacred Christian ground, but Andoni and his group of activists deliberately chose not to stress that fact, preferring, in the Christian Arab way, to subsume their Christianity into their nationalism. To give their protest a specifically Christian character, they felt, would have been to alienate the larger Arab and Muslim community to which they belonged.

Andoni gave me a wry smile when I asked him about this. He then told me with a sharp edge of indignation in his voice that he had invited clergy from all of the Christian denominations as well as the mosques in Beit Sahour to attend that march. Not one of them, he said, had decided to take part in the action aimed at raising awareness not only of the occupation but of the Christian burial ground. To him it was one more confirmation of the fact that the established Christian leadership—especially that of his own church—had little connection with the parishioners or care for their concerns. He seemed almost pleased as he told me this, as if it eased his guilt over his personal alienation from the Orthodox church and its Greek hierarchy.

However, if Andoni and others were correct in stating that their efforts at nonviolence had little to do with their Christian culture and nothing to do with their churches, then why was it that the first embers of a nonviolent movement would flicker once again in Christian Beit Sahour? Andoni's work in some way embodied the riddle I had long been trying to solve: whether there was indeed something unique in the Christian presence in this land—perhaps a belief in nonviolence, or a cultural affinity for nonviolence—that set the Christian Arab leaders apart from their Islamic brothers and their Israeli occupiers. I was still trying to penetrate the layers of religion, class, education, and culture that were wrapped around this question.

At the beginning of the year, I had viewed the Christians as a kind of buffer between Muslims and Jews, but several Palestinian Christian leaders bristled at the word "buffer." It implied neutrality, they pointed out, and the Palestinian Christians were not neutral in the struggle. So I reconsidered my view. I came to see the indigenous presence of the three faiths in the Holy Land in terms of an archaeological dig, a geological cut in which the layers of earth and the periods they reflect could be studied. There was Judaism in the bedrock; Christianity, a thinning layer of shale atop that; and then Islam, a thick crust of fertile soil. They all rested on one another, and were in some places marbleized together. But in this *intifada* it seemed that the geological layer between the bedrock and the soil was shifting, the shale was crumbling and giving way, and the landscape as a result was being broken up and eroded. If the contours of the struggle continued to take on a religious shape—Islam versus Judaism—the religious extremists on both sides would increasingly control the direction of the conflict, making it more prone to violent eruptions. This *intifada* had become an example of where this land could be headed without a Christian presence to recast the quest for justice in broader terms, to complicate the equation, to stabilize the surface, and keep it from being defined along stark religious lines.

If the struggle continued in this vein, the negative effects would be compounded. The Christian West would remain comfortable in its resignation, believing that the Arab-Israeli conflict between Muslims and Jews was insoluble and that Christianity had no part in it. Yet the Israeli-Palestinian struggle was at a turning point, a pivotal time when the Christians of this land could play a unique role. As a minority faith, Christianity could serve as an interface between the two more dominant faiths. During his visit in March, Pope John Paul II—particularly in his willingness to listen to the narratives of both sides—had modeled a Western Christian role. In his pilgrimage, he embraced the suffering of Jews in the Holocaust and showed respect for the history that had brought them home after two thousand years. But he also stood as witness to the dispossession of Palestinians, and supported their demands for justice.

Was there any way for Palestinian Christians to continue where the pope left off, or had their suffering driven from them all desire to speak out in behalf of peace and justice in their homeland? Or, perhaps even more tragically, had the brutal history of the previous millennium of Western Christianity, beginning with the Crusades and ending with the Holocaust, rendered the Christian voice inaudible to

Muslims and Jews? Was the living presence of Christians in this land thinning to the point where the voice was too faint to matter, even if it could be heard? The year 2000 came to a close with no end in sight to the fighting, and with these questions still looming large.

. . .

Islam and Judaism offer their own admirable theologies of peace and justice, and they have plenty of followers who see the practical value of nonviolence. But few biblical scholars and theologians I have met, whether Muslim or Jew, would disagree with the assertion that Jesus stressed nonviolence as a core of the faith in a way that Mohammed and Moses did not. And no political activist, Muslim or Jew, would contest the fact that the core leadership of the nonviolent movement among Palestinians—to the extent that there was one—was made up disproportionately of Christians.

Yet to others who lived in this land where violence and military might ruled, where terms were dictated from positions of strength, the Christian notion of pacifism might easily appear flawed or simplistic—even trite. Could Jesus's teachings, as ethereal as they often sounded, halt the cycle of violence? To answer that question, one must understand how Jesus practiced pacifism in the context of his time, within the many streams of Judaism that existed then, and in the brutal realities of this land. His pacifist teachings were not at all ethereal; they were tied directly into the thinking of Judaism's established sages and prophets, and they reemphasized an ancient tradition of teaching. They were thoroughly practical and creative responses to the oppression that he and his listeners faced.

Under the Roman occupation, crosses would periodically line the way into Jerusalem. These were not church steeples but public crucifixions, clearly intended to assert the military superiority of Rome and illustrate the fate of anyone who challenged its law and its order. Jesus knew the violence of occupation. Jesus knew, too, the retaliatory violence of the rebels of his day, the Jewish zealots, who saw themselves as fighters for freedom and against the tyranny and injustice of the Roman colonizers. The Romans viewed those zealots as religious extremists, terrorists who had to be controlled. Jesus also was well acquainted with the Pharisees and often criticized what he saw as hypocrisy in their adherence to religious legalism. He was wary of the collaborationist ways of the Herodians, who served as puppets of the

Roman emperors and carried out their policies. He knew the functionaries of Rome, who served as its tax collectors and its enforcers. He knew the wild messianism of the Essenes, who withdrew to live in the wilderness and practice contemplative prayer rather than dwell in what they viewed as the corrupt world of the Sadducees, the religious aristocracy that controlled the financial power base of the Second Temple. Jesus's message resonated within his own contemporary context, with a set of ancient realities (militancy, corruption, and collaboration) that are echoed in the Israeli-Palestinian conflict of today.

Jesus's message was that of creative resistance to oppression, against a power with overwhelming military superiority—a message that drew on all of the existing Jewish sources that were part of his life. His goal was to identify ways in which the powerless of his time and place—for the most part, Jewish peasants—could challenge the economic and social and political inequalities they faced in their daily lives. The most obvious, oft-quoted, and misunderstood axiom of Jesus's idea of pacifism comes from the Gospel According to Matthew: "But I tell you, do not resist an evil person. If someone strikes you on the right cheek, turn to him the other also" (Matthew 5:39). I heard this notion literally laughed at in the West Bank and Gaza, and snickered about in Tel Aviv and Jerusalem, by members of all three faiths, by politicians and peaceniks and plenty of reporters. It was generally viewed as ridiculously irrelevant in this land, and impossibly idealistic in general. But what exactly Jesus meant by "turning the other cheek" in the context of his time and in the context of his land has been reexamined by theologians and biblical historians, and their reinterpretations of Jesus's message seem very relevant to the conflict between Palestinian Arabs and Israelis.

To hit someone on the right cheek assumes that the aggressor has hit the person with the back of his right hand. In the ancient customs of the land, this was considered a deep insult; this was how the powerful struck the powerless, the way a master struck his slave, or a Roman struck a Jew. But a blow administered with an open hand on the left side of the face was a blow struck at an equal. The difference between the two types of blows was actually codified in Jerusalem's local law at the time according to some historians. A backhanded slap to the right cheek of a man's peer was grounds to sue for punitive damages. The fine for a backhanded blow to a peer was 100 times the fine for a blow with a forehand. If a backhand was delivered to an underling, however, there was no fine. So when Jesus said to offer the left cheek, by this historical interpretation he wasn't prescribing a blind, masochistic pacifism. He was telling his followers, effectively, "Confront the person offending you, forcing him to face you as an equal, but do not respond with violence in return." That, in the context of Jesus's time and the social and legal codes that existed then, was a radical act of defiance. It turned the tables, forcing the striker to accept the humanity and the equality of the one he was striking, even if he was not legally (or militarily, or politically, or economically) recognized as an equal.

But creative nonviolence was virtually impossible in the heat of conflict. At Rev. Ateek's Sabeel Ecumenical Liberation Theology Center, toward the end of the year, a group of a dozen American and European Christians and a handful of Palestinian Christians gathered in a circle to plan some nonviolent activity. There was despair among the Palestinians. Samia Khouri, a leader of the Palestinian Christian community, said, "Who's going to listen to the Christian world, which has been the source of so much of our troubles? Fifty years of rage can't be contained right now." A young Palestinian woman who was a student at Birzeit University said, "We are not defining violence correctly. The violence is not throwing stones, the violence is occupation." Ateek offered his thoughts, saying, "Most Christians, even if they are not committed to their faith, know that nonviolence is at the center of it. I believe that. The problem is, we don't have any clout. We don't even have the backing of the hierarchy of the church. But we have to try, we have to try to be leaders for a movement that will be across cultural and national and religious divides. But I think it has to begin from the Palestinian Christian community. And we will be surprised to see how many Muslims are with us."

Everyone in the room nodded their heads in agreement. But Rich Meyer, an American from the Mennonite Church, spoke up. He had been working in Hebron, trying to stand as a witness for the nonviolent resolution of conflict there, and at the end of the meeting he injected a sobering note of reality. "What do I think are the possibilities of nonviolence right now?" he asked. "I think it's like trying to teach a pregnant woman who is pushing and in pain, in labor, breathing techniques. She can't hear you. Those techniques have to be taught months ahead."

The violence had gathered its own ferocious momentum, and no one present thought it could be easily redirected. Further complicating the situation was a political hourglass that had been running down as the year 2000 ended. President Bill Clinton's term was up on

January 20, and it was fast becoming clear that his tireless devotion to the peace process was not shared by his successor, George W. Bush. Ehud Barak had taken considerable political risk at Camp David, and as a result his coalition government had collapsed, forcing him to call snap elections. Thanks to the Israeli public's outrage over the ongoing violence, Ariel Sharon was surging ahead of Barak in the polls. Yasser Arafat's popularity among Palestinians, in contrast, was strengthened by what the Arab world viewed as his steadfastness in rejecting the offer at Camp David. The violence, even if it could have been stopped by these leaders, was allowed to roll on, because it served their competing political interests. Palestinian leaders could have done more to crack down on the stone-throwers and stop the Palestinian gunmen from shooting, but they feared the rage that had been unleashed would turn against them if they did. Israeli leaders could have refrained from the disproportionate response of tanks and attack helicopters and tightened the often indiscriminate open-fire orders Israeli forces were given in the West Bank and Gaza; but they had to look tough if Barak were to have a chance at winning reelection.

On February 6, 2001, Israel elected Ariel Sharon prime minister, by the largest margin of victory in the Jewish state's history. The conservatives had mobilized to stop what they saw as Barak's unforgivable concessions at Camp David, and the center and the conservative side of Labor had joined them. As most pundits interpreted it, Sharon had a historic mandate to punish Arafat and the Palestinians for not accepting the far-reaching deal that Barak had offered.

The day he won election, Sharon—Israel's controversial warrior—marched to Gilo and stood there, surveying the Christian village of Beit Jala as if it were enemy territory. He vowed to voters that no one would dare threaten the residents of Jerusalem, and that the city would never be divided again, as long as he was prime minister. Sharon railed against the continuing violence that had killed an Israeli soldier the previous night at the Rafah checkpoint in Gaza. And that very day, there was a little-noticed funeral for this fallen soldier in the Israeli Arab village of Turan in the Galilee. Sgt. Rujia Salame, 23, became the first Christian soldier in the Israeli army ever to have been killed in the line of duty. The rites of burial at the Latin Catholic church in Turan were a testament to conflicted loyalties. There were Israeli military honors, of course. But the family—and the church—refused to drape the fallen Christian soldier's coffin in the

Israeli flag. The Muslims of the village sullenly stared at the Christian mourners as the funeral procession passed through town. The dead soldier was a cousin of the Khouris, the priest and his son whom I had met in Turan during the Muslim-Christian violence there that had prompted so many of the young men in town to join the military. They stood in somber silence at his grave and made the sign of the cross over themselves as his body was lowered into the ground.

Sharon formed a unity government, with Labor Party stalwart Shimon Peres as his foreign minister. It became clear that the sides were retrenching and that even a cease-fire agreement would be extremely difficult to achieve. Even by the most optimistic predictions, the negotiations that could lead to a final peace plan were a long way off, perhaps years away. It was in this context that some initiatives toward creative nonviolence began to take shape among Israelis and Palestinians. The Beit Sahour march on Shidma had tested the water, and now the movement would try to mobilize on a wider scale. Once again, they would learn just how difficult—and powerful—nonviolence was.

In March, at a sharp turn in the road in the West Bank village of Surda, a group of Palestinians put the notion of creative defiance against occupation to a test. The Israeli army had dug two six-foot-wide trenches along the main road through Surda, the road that connected Ramallah and Birzeit University. These trenches cut off students from the university, people from their work, families from each other. Hanan Ashrawi and Birzeit University's president Hanna Nasser led a march to protest this siege. About two thousand students, professors, professionals, and political leaders—Christian and Muslim—marched alongside a bulldozer to the Surda blockade. The bulldozer began clearing the cement barriers and filling in the trenches. Soldiers watched, seemingly puzzled as to how to handle the crowd. Palestinian marchers began clearing with their own hands the stones that the IDF had placed to block the road. Suddenly, about a dozen teenagers who had joined up with the marchers began throwing stones. Immediately the Israeli soldiers opened fire with tear gas, and then with "rubber bullets." The exchange of rocks for gunfire happened in a matter of seconds. But that was all it took.

As the clash started, Albert Aghazarian, an Armenian Christian from Jerusalem and a professor of history at Birzeit, stood in front of the rock-throwing youths and held up his arms to stop them. It was a moment of courage. He had quite literally put his life on the line by turning his back to the Israeli soldiers who were firing on the youths, and facing the youths with rocks in their hands. They didn't listen to his pleading to stop. There was another sharp crack of gunfire, and a Palestinian man was killed by a "rubber bullet" in the chest. The shots kept coming, and several dozen Palestinians were injured. This march had the numbers that drew the television cameras and the reporters, but it did not have the discipline of the relatively tiny Beit Sahour march.

Nevertheless, Surda was seen as a turning point, a new incentive for those who believed in nonviolent resistance to occupation. The road remained clear, at least for a few days. Hanan Ashrawi and the other Palestinian leaders at the march felt that they had accomplished something. But a struggle was under way within the Palestinian leadership, between the Fatah leaders who wanted to continue the violent clashes against Israeli forces and the Palestinian community leaders—Christian and Muslim—who felt that nonviolence was more effective. Fatah, along with Hamas and Islamic Jihad, issued fliers declaring that the following Friday another "Day of Rage." Ashrawi, meanwhile, planned another nonviolent demonstration in which musicians and artists would march on an Israeli checkpoint.

The second march remained nonviolent throughout. Ashrawi was buoyant. After the march, she told me, "It felt like the old days again." Ashrawi saw nonviolence in very practical terms: It was effective. Ashrawi was no pacifist—she had supported armed Palestinian struggle throughout the 1970s and 1980s—and she still believed that stone-throwing was "not violent, but a metaphor of stones against guns." "To not take this lying down is a human response," she insisted. "Why should Palestinians not have the right to confront occupation with resistance, just as France and England resisted in World War II?" Nevertheless, she felt that the tactics of the *intifada* had to shift, and that nonviolence was the only way of including a broader group of Palestinians in this uprising.

"Israel has the strongest army in the region; if you play by their rules, you lose," she said. "The only way you can disarm Israel is by not adopting its methods and its concept of power and subjugation. . . . If they dehumanize you, you mustn't dehumanize them. If they kill you, you mustn't kill them. I don't say that out of some sense of Christian charity, a sense of 'turn the other cheek.' I say that out of a sense of humanity. It is humanism, not Christianity."

But, I argued, wasn't that message precisely part of the teaching she had learned in the context of her Christianity? I was curious to know whether she could accept that her views might have been shaped in part by her Christian background. "Why can't it just be a humanistic message?" she replied. "Why does it have to be defined as my Christianity?"

Clearly it didn't. But so many Palestinian Christians, especially those in positions of leadership, shied away from and in some cases even rejected the idea that nonviolence and pacifism were grounded in the message of the religion into which they were born, which had its roots in this land. The constant effort to broaden these beliefs as a form of "humanism" rather than to employ them as a galvanizing force to bring together the other two faiths struck me as a dilution of their inherent power. The Palestinian Christians' efforts were undercut by their own insistent secularism within a society so deeply bound to the traditions and customs of religion. It seemed to me that Ashrawi and Andoni and others would be seen as stauncher in their convictions—in the eyes of many of their Muslim and Jewish neighbors—if they balanced their actions with an open expression of the way their ideas were grounded in their faith, or if they pushed their own churches to be more actively involved. Not to flaunt their beliefs as triumphant or superior, but to be aware of the way in which they were part of the tradition of this land of three faiths.

In Gaza, I interviewed Eyad Sarraj, head of the Gaza Community Mental Health Program and of the Palestinian Independent Commission for Citizens' Rights. He was a secular Muslim, born to a very traditional, religious Islamic family in Gaza. He smiled knowingly when I recounted my conversation with Ashrawi, whom he saw as an ally and friend. He was grinning, he said, because what she said was "so very Arab Christian." He continued: "Hanan can't say this as an Arab nationalist, but, as a Muslim, I can. Christianity's message of nonviolence is very important, and it is not there in Islam, and I believe it is not there in Judaism. I would honestly say that if I could choose a religion, I would choose Christianity and its ideal of universal acceptance, love, and forgiveness. It is all so beautiful. It is just so unfortunate that the history of Christianity has nothing to do with these ideas."

Sarraj had been outspoken in calling for nonviolence, believing it to be the only practical way for the Palestinian people to gain their rights and their independence. "What is needed is a Gandhi, or a Nelson Mandela," he had told the *Los Angeles Times*. This comment had gotten him detained for questioning by Arafat's security forces. Sarraj was a courageous man who had fought for years for human rights and justice, and had long preached nonviolence. He was clearly aware of the risks it involved.

Sarraj was also honest. He told me he could not get more than a handful of people together in Gaza who believed in nonviolence as a way to resist occupation. I asked him why he felt his call for nonviolent action was not heard in the overwhelmingly Muslim population of Gaza. Why was it that the handful of effective leaders of Palestinian nonviolence (with one or two notable exceptions) had been Christian Palestinians in the West Bank?

"It is not because Hanan or Hanna Nasser or Ghassan Andoni are Christian," he replied. "It is because they are educated, more exposed to the culture of the West. They have had lives or opportunities where they were allowed to breathe without occupation.

"We are a patriarchal society conditioned to revenge. That is true on every level of interaction in our community. We are asked in our culture and in our religion to defend our honor. It is shameful for a man to live without honor. And the Palestinian people feel such injury to their psyche from occupation, that their immediate reaction is to fight. They fight in a way that not only is violent, but in a way that says, 'Follow the leader.' There is no room for dissent, no room for discussion both in the cultural and religious parameters of our society. And the leaders use this to fly away with their rhetoric, violent rhetoric. Think about the words *Allahu akbar!* Think how many times you have heard that in this *intifada*. It is a cry for help, the utmost yearning for justice. It is a war chant, but one imbued with the power of God. And when you hear it, remember you are in a land of infidels, the land that does not accept the true message of its prophets, where religion is only used for politics. All of the messages of the prophets, Moses, Mohammed, and Jesus, are about peace, and to be kind to your neighbors, to show tolerance. If people really believed what religion said, people would not fight."

From the dust and despair of Gaza I traveled back to quiet, treelined King David street in West Jerusalem to see Rabbi David Forman, a Boston-born immigrant to Israel and a founder of Rabbis for Human Rights. For years he had worked tirelessly to oppose through nonviolent means what he saw as the injustice of occupation. His style of political action, backed by faith, had been developed in the civil rights movement in the Deep South in the mid-1960s and carried through the first *intifada* and now into the turn of the millennium, when he was expecting the birth of his first grandchild. To him, Judaism was "the longest-running liberation movement there was." But something had changed for Forman in this *intifada*. He was not going to the West Bank to participate in nonviolent marches. He was, frankly, afraid. The joint movement of Israelis and Palestinians had broken down, along with the bonds of trust between the two communities. It sometimes seemed that the only thing they now shared was the gunfire and the blame they shot back and forth at each other.

However, a younger member of Rabbis for Human Rights, Arik Ascherman, was still carrying the nonviolent movement from Israel into the line of fire in the West Bank. Ascherman asked Forman at some point why he was not joining him. Why, Ascherman wanted to know, was Forman willing to risk his life in the mid-1960s, for the right of black Americans to vote, but not now, for the right of Palestinians in the West Bank to possess their land? Forman had two answers. One was obvious—he was a father and soon to be a grandfather, and he didn't take the same risks he used to. The second was more troubling, and had to do with the fear that the raw hatred in the streets had made it too dangerous for Israelis to go into Palestinian areas, even in support of the Palestinian cause. "The blacks weren't trying to kill me in the South," Forman told Ascherman.

Forman was eloquent in expounding on the Judaic tradition of prayers for peace. But he also agreed that Jesus's teachings contained a more "pronounced" message of pacifism than he had found in Judaism, or in Islam as he understood it: "I think that is an important role the Christians play here," he said, "and an important message that the Christian faith has brought to movements in America and in South Africa and Latin America. Absolutely, I think that. Everyone who has worked in the peace movement here just has to look around a rally to see the Palestinian Christians provide leadership on this."

But what saddened and troubled Forman as a religious leader was how small these voices for nonviolence were in all three faiths. "The Christians who are supporting nonviolence, they are important, but represent a tiny percentage," he observed. "And then look at Sarraj in Gaza, with no following. . . . Look at our group, Rabbis for Human Rights—the truth is, we represent almost no one in Israel. None of us have large followings, and there is a reason for that. Religion has become nationalized in this land."

It was one of the more depressing realities of this land, Forman pointed out, that the religious establishment not only had failed to lead in the efforts toward peace but had even come to be viewed as working against such efforts. That had much to do with the fact that the religious movements—especially in Orthodox Judaism and Islam—were strictly limited in the political realm. The chief Orthodox rabbis of Israel and the head Islamic sheikhs of the Palestinian territories were appointed by and paid through their respective governments or affiliated political parties. The Christian priests, of all denominations, were not politically appointed or paid by any governments. But they had been compromised in a different way. The large Christian denominations received patronage from Greece (the Orthodox) and Rome (the Catholics), from England (the Anglicans), and from Germany (the Lutherans). In the international power politics of this Western backing, criticism was sometimes muted. In the denominations ruled locally by Palestinian patriarchs, such as the Roman Catholics, Anglicans, and Lutherans, the churches were often reluctant to voice opposition to injustices committed by Palestinians, for fear that they might be seen as undercutting national aspirations. The churches for the most part dwelled outside the politics.

The more direct financial link between the rabbis and the sheikhs and political parties within their governments had more substantially muted any faith-based initiatives and weakened their ability to bring the voices of their religious institutions into the equation of reconciliation. There was no question that both Judaism and Islam contained powerful messages of accepting "the other" and safeguarding sacred rights for minority religions to practice their beliefs. But the leaders of the clerical hierarchies in both faiths were often descending into the worst kind of bigotry and incitement against "the other." The situation was especially politicized on the Palestinian Muslim side, interfaith experts agreed; but there was also no shortage of examples of the leading Orthodox rabbis in Israel tailoring their theological pronouncements to fit political views, especially through crass anti-Arab diatribes.

Rabbi David Rosen, a president of the World Council on Religion and Peace, and a prominent rabbinical scholar who has been in the vanguard of interfaith dialogue, said the lack of leadership in the peace process on the part of the religious establishment (of the dominant faiths of Islam and Judaism) comes down to a "cultural mindset." The clerics of both faiths are too often isolated within their own communities, and have rarely met "the other" on "an even playing field," Rosen explained. In a land in which all sides see themselves as struggling minorities (Jews, as a minority in a hostile Arab world, and Palestinians, as a minority under Israeli domination), religious leaders too often have fallen back into insecurity and bigotry, despite the teaching of precisely the opposite in both Judaism and Islam.

In many ways, religion had been manipulated for nationalistic purposes in the eruption of violence in late 2000; and Rosen actively had sought to "manipulate [religion] again, if you will," for the purpose of achieving peace. "A conflict that has taken on religious tones will require a peace agreement that also has religious tones," said Rosen. "The religious leaders will have to become much more active before any solution can be found."

In Christianity, the problems with the local religious establishment have been different; but it too has failed to take an active role in working toward a peaceful solution to the conflict. The churches too often have supported one side against the other. The Catholic and Lutheran and Anglican churches, for example, have sided with their local parishes and fought against the injustices of occupation but have done little to reach out to the Israeli people as supporters of their cause, and in large part have been reluctant to participate in interfaith dialogue (with a few notable exceptions). The Protestant and evangelical churches too often have sided with Israel, due to their eschatological and political proclivities, and in the process have overlooked the injustices that have left Palestinians, including Christians, in despair.

The collective voice of moderate and traditional religious leadership—which represents the vast majority of both Palestinians and Israelis—was not being heard amid the deafening roar of secular political leadership and religious extremism on all sides. Yet these establishment religious leaders, and the moderating wisdom they could lend to the dialogue, held a key to ending the violence and reaching an agreement that would hold. This was especially true in the volatile core issue of the sovereignty over the Temple Mount/Noble Sanctuary, an issue that would ultimately have to be addressed in a new light before any true peace negotiations could move forward.

But even if nonviolence could stop the fighting and end the occupation, there would still have to be reconciliation—the Palestinians and Israelis would still have to recognize and resolve the injustices they had committed against one another, in order to live together.

. . .

The concept of reconciliation—the idea of forgiveness as a way to resolve conflict—has become a global phenomenon. At least in the abstract, "forgiveness" was being talked about everywhere at the end of the second millennium. It was a constant theme emanating from the Vatican, as the church seemed to be soul-searching its own history. A historic moment in that vein was Pope John Paul II's issuance of a formal apology to Jews and expression of "profound regrets" for "the failings" of members of the Catholic Church to do more to stop the Holocaust. The pope also issued an apology for the collective suffering and injustice that church teaching may have caused women.

In Washington, President Clinton had in 1999 apologized for America's use of slavery in the founding of the country. Clinton brought the idea of redemption also into many other areas of his political and personal life. He had made a public plea to Americans for their forgiveness of his sordid affair with White House intern Monica Lewinsky, a liaison that nearly toppled his presidency. Ironically, this scandal reached its boiling point at a critical juncture in the Israeli-Palestinian conflict and weakened his presidency at a time when he needed all of the strength of office to make the peace process work.

Forgiveness has even become an intellectual discipline at universities and institutes such as the John Templeton Foundation, an international organization devoted to exploring the borders of science and religion. Recent research in the medical field has shown that forgiveness can be good for your health.

Cultures around the world are increasingly embracing the notion that forgiveness is essential for coming to terms with a troubled past, and then moving forward. This is true of conflicts as diverse as the troubles in Northern Ireland and the mass killings in Cambodia, Guatemala, and East Timor, where haunting atrocities by brutal dictatorships have been unearthed. A movement is even under way to bring about reconciliation in the Balkans, where 200,000 were killed in the recent, decade-long conflict.

Nowhere has a collective search for reconciliation been more successful and more healing than in South Africa. Anglican Bishop Desmond Tutu, a Nobel Peace Prize laureate, was the spiritual founder and legal head of that country's Truth and Reconciliation Commission. From the pulpit of the TRC, he presided over a bold attempt at national healing by creating a forum in which victims of apartheid heard their former oppressors confess to torture and other injustices.

The perpetrators were inclined to honesty because of the commission's extensive research and documentation, and because they could be granted amnesty if they told the truth. Tutu proposed what he defined as "restorative justice" versus "retributive justice." "Restorative justice" would have to embrace a way for both sides, the powerless and the powerful, the majority and the minority, to regain their dignity and to be given an opportunity for redemption. "Retributive justice" would do little to heal old wounds, and might even open fresh ones. This had been proven after World War I, many historians would contend, when a retributive peace agreement only fostered the divisions that fomented World War II.

Back in early 1999, when Israel and the Palestinians were still inching toward implementation of the Oslo agreement, there was a glimpse—a warning, perhaps—that the agreement might be in danger of fitting that mold of retributive justice. Bishop Tutu had come to the Yakar Center for Tradition and Creativity, a liberal Jewish synagogue and religious center in Jerusalem, where he spoke to a packed congregation about the South African commission's work. His speech was punctuated by disarming humor; but his passionate and somber message about forgiveness as a precondition for peace was riveting. Tutu was sensitive enough to point out that South Africa, during its struggle, did not appreciate efforts from outsiders telling them how to reach justice. But he was also courageous enough to pose a question: "Look, we were able to do it. Why can't it happen here?" The congregation met this question with awkward silence. I had the sense that those listening knew the discomforting answer to Tutu's question. Although nothing was said at the gathering, afterward several in attendance insisted that the Israeli-Palestinian conflict was vastly different from the one in South Africa. So many comparisons had been made over the years between these two conflicts. The occupied West Bank and Gaza were frequently compared to the Bantustans in white-ruled South Africa. Some South African diplomats based in the region had even suggested that the economic separation and limited movement of the Palestinians were more restrictive than apartheid. Such comparisons, however, were ultimately unproductive.

To depict Israel exclusively as a colonizing power is to deny the history of the Jews, their connection to this land and their yearning to repossess it. To describe Arabs only as the indigenous majority is to deny that Arabs too were immigrants to this land, coming from the Arab peninsula with the Islamic conquest. Several Israeli leaders in attendance at the Tutu speech also pointed out that under apartheid, there was a clear villain—the white minority—and a clear victim, the black majority. In the Holy Land, Palestinians and Israelis both felt they were victims. So who was to forgive whom?

In addition, in South Africa, the oppressor and the oppressed were two peoples largely bound by one faith in Christianity. In the Holy Land, there are two peoples, Palestinians and Israelis, often separated by three different faiths. South African blacks had a strong tradition of communal justice; Israelis and Palestinians had no sense of it at all, and both cultures were geared toward revenge. Israeli Jews and Palestinian Muslims were the vast majority of those caught in this conflict. And their faiths—Judaism and Islam—fostered ideas of justice and forgiveness radically different from those fostered by Jesus's teachings.

In his own death on the cross, Jesus offered a radical notion of forgiveness that sought to alter the relationship between a tribe and its enemies, between the oppressor and the oppressed. Even as he hung dying, he said, "Forgive them Lord, they know not what they do." At the time of Jesus, the "peace process," to use today's term, was mired in mistrust and cycles of violence, just as it is now. Romans and Jews were wrestling with justice and peace. Jesus's insistence that occupiers, enemies, even his own killers, must be forgiven in order to break that cycle of violence is an idea as radical today as it was back then.

Whereas Islam and Judaism spell out preconditions for forgiveness, Christian teaching views the situation in reverse: forgiveness must come first, and reconciliation will open the way toward resolution of the practical details of getting along. Christian theologians in the Holy Land believe that the peace process will be doomed until each side is willing collectively to recognize the pain endured by the other, and then to forgive the other side for the pain inflicted on it.

Judaism and Islam place forgiveness largely under the governance of God. In contrast, the radical notion in Jesus's ministry was that forgiveness could and should be a way to bring the presence of God into human relations on this earth. This was most clearly expressed in the Sermon on the Mount, where Jesus stood on a Galilee hillside and taught a large crowd to value human reconciliation over false piety, saying, "If you are offering your gift at the altar and there remember that your brother has something against you, leave your gift there in front of the altar. First go and be reconciled to your brother; then come and offer your gift" (Matthew 5:23–24 [NIV]). Of all Jesus's teachings on forgiveness, this one seems the most practical and applicable to this conflict.

One of the few I found striving toward this human reconciliation was Yitzhak Frankenthal, a 50-year-old Israeli father whose son was kidnapped and killed by Hamas militants in 1994. Moved by this anguishing experience, he formed a foundation called Parents' Circle, which was dedicated to bringing together the families of bereaved Israelis and Palestinians. Frankenthal has a thick shock of gray hair that bulges out from beneath his yarmulke, and a face that would fit a man with a big laugh; but it seems tightened, remolded in sorrow. His life changed forever the day his 19-year-old son Arik was found dumped on the side of the road in a village near Ramallah. Arik, the commander of an Israeli tank unit, had been hitchhiking home when two Hamas militants abducted him. He resisted, shooting the Palestinian driver with his military-issue machine gun. Arik was then shot three times in the head.

After months of grieving, Frankenthal decided to devote himself to working full-time for peace, and since then his nonprofit organization has brought together some sixty-five other bereaved Israeli and Palestinian parents, bound by a desire to see the violence end, so that no other parent need lose children in this way, so that they themselves will lose no more children.

"I am not here for forgiveness or revenge but to stop the hatred and stop the bloodshed," Frankenthal told one meeting in Gaza, where he had brought parents together. "I am a realist. I think Palestinians and Israelis may never agree on what is justice. So what we need is not necessarily a just peace but a wise peace. We all have to be realists."

One of Frankenthal's Palestinian partners in the Parents' Circle was Ramadan Elizami, a 50-year-old mason whose teenage son was killed by Israeli soldiers in cross fire in Gaza. Elizami said he had sent his son, Ahmad, to fetch a load of cement in the family's donkey cart. Ahmad never came home. Standing in the sandy cemetery at his son's grave, Elizami said, "We should let the Jews live, and they should let us live. Them on their land, and us on our land. . . . The revenge will never stop if it keeps going. I cannot lose another son. None of us can afford to lose another son."

I frequently heard Frankenthal insist that his organization had nothing to do with forgiveness. "My message is, bring me back my son, and I will forgive you. But that is not possible, so let's figure out how we are going to live together. My soul will be okay if I do not forgive. We all need to use our brains, our practical common sense, not our souls and our spirits. And if we, as those who lost children, can get together to talk, then anyone can do it."

The truth is, Christianity has centuries of history in relation to Jews and to Muslims that is anything but forgiving, and they greet Jesus's message of forgiveness with understandable suspicion. To Jews, forgiveness sounds too much like forgetfulness. To Muslims, forgiveness sounds too much like giving up and relinquishing their claims.

It had become clear to me that the Christian notion of forgiveness had little resonance and therefore no practical applicability among the people of this land. To respond to Tutu's question of whether a South African–style reconciliation commission could work, the answer in most Jewish and Muslim corners is a resounding "no." Reconciliation here will be defined by Judaism and Islam, and it must be practical and clearly spelled out within the established political and religious traditions. Western Christianity's notions of forgiveness will have to give way to the more local sense of pragmatic justice. Justice will have to resonate from the people of this land alone; and they will inevitably face the same struggle and obstacles that Jesus did in trying to make their ideal of justice work within the local context and within the messages of their own faith. But still the Christian presence and the teachings of the faith had a role in the Middle East's search for justice and reconciliation.

. . .

During Easter Week 2001, the Old City was alive with the parade of faith, the carnival of religion, the tribal rites that were Jerusalem. On Good Friday, the day commemorating the death of Jesus on the cross, the streets were crowded with worshipers. There were Muslims returning from their Friday prayers, Jews on their way to the Wall for afternoon prayers, and Christians of all denominations processing along the Via Dolorosa. At one point I saw a Palestinian Franciscan brother, at least six feet tall and heavyset—whom a fellow Franciscan once had described to me as "local muscle"—literally directing the flow of spiritual traffic. He worked alongside the Israeli police to dam the rivers of Muslims coming from Al-Aqsa, so that a trickle of a Christian procession could pass by. Later I saw the big Franciscan redirecting some Orthodox Jews heading for the Wall, asking them to detour around a prayer service at the Third Station of the Cross.

The Palestinian Christians were conducting their processions, and sprinkled among them in the Latin Catholic service were hundreds of Philippine immigrant workers and African day-laborers who had entered the country on work permits. Mixed in with the Greek Orthodox processions were hundreds of Russian immigrants to the Jewish state who were actually Christian by faith. The Filipinos and the Russians provided a visual glimpse of new springs of demography welling up in the pool of pilgrims and seekers who had made up the local body of the church through the ages.

And amid this human stream I could make out, just barely, a crown of thorns amid a phalanx of Israeli policeman. Roman centurions in cheap plastic helmets and red rayon capes were yelling, "Come on, Jesus, move it!" Jesus, in this procession, was actually a fireman from a nondenominational church in Anaheim Hills, California. The centurions were also from the California congregation, members of which for twenty years had come to Jerusalem to carry out an annual reenactment of the drama. The fireman, Anthony Revilla, looked the part of the Western notion of Jesus, with his blue eyes, long brown hair, and unkempt beard, and the red paint simulating blood dripping from the crown of thorns.

One Palestinian Muslim woman in a veil, who was carrying produce for her Friday shopping and walking by this scene, didn't realize that it was all a reenactment. She muttered as she walked past the Israeli police, "Have mercy!" But most of the Muslim shopkeepers smirked knowingly at the sight, and my reporter colleagues snickered at the Californian Jesus heading toward a mock execution, surrounded by Israeli police in blue uniforms who seemed unaware of or unconcerned by the role in which they had been involuntarily cast. This was carnival Christianity, a kind of spiritual funhouse mirror from the West that made a mockery of the reality lived by the local community. This procession contained no more than five or six people, but there were at least thirty Israeli police forming a cordon around them, and at least twelve network television and news reporters swarming around the cheap and crassly choreographed scene.

The next day, Holy Saturday, was the biggest day of the year for Palestinian Christians, a day of tribal rites and public processions by the Greek, Armenian, Coptic, and Syrian Orthodox denominations and featuring the Ceremony of the Holy Fire. The Holy Sepulcher was packed with people holding bundles of 33 votive candles tied together like a torch, and waiting to light them with the Holy Fire. The procession rites began with the Greek Orthodox hierarchy filing into the Holy Sepulcher, and marching three times around the edicule, or tomb, where Jesus was held to have been buried. The procession was led by the heads of the 14 most prominent Greek Orthodox families, each carrying a banner representing one of the 14 stations of the cross.

Though this event marked one of the holiest moments on the Christian calendar, it was not at all somber. It was a rowdy affair, with chanting and sweating and yelling and pushing and ultimately chaos and finally celebration. In the back corner of the edicule, as happened every year, rowdy Syrian Orthodox teenagers from Bethlehem tried to break into the procession and were pushed back, because only the Greek and Armenian Orthodox and the Roman Catholics had the right to process in the Holy Sepulcher under the "Status Quo-Ante" agreements. The Syrian Orthodox took this as a challenge, something akin to a football match.

They were banging drums and climbing atop one another's shoulders, shouting an Arabic chant that was strangely similar to the one shouted at the funerals of "martyrs" of the *intifada:* "With our soul, with our blood we sacrifice for you, oh, Mary!" There was bitter disagreement between the Syrians and the Armenians over the ownership of the chapel of Joseph of Arimathea, a tiny cave in the back of the Holy Sepulcher. At one point the youths were pushing each other, on the point of blows, yelling and screaming. But this year the Armenians had brought in some hefty Armenian Orthodox immigrants from the former Soviet Union to help them, and the presence of the heavyweights brought a kind of détente. There were no open brawls, as there had been in years past.

After these raucous processions, the Greek patriarch and an Armenian bishop entered the tomb, which was then sealed shut with wax. Then, according to tradition, a new fire was kindled in the tomb and passed out through the holes on either side. The flame was passed from one torchbearer to the next until the dark, musty, Crusader-era church and all its Christians with all their petty divisions were illuminated in the warm light of flickering candles. Rising plumes of smoke, the ringing of church bells, and the thunder of church organs and cheers engulfed the Holy Sepulcher. The Holy Fire was rushed in a lantern to a plane waiting at Ben-Gurion International Airport and flown to Greece. Runners with lanterns also took the Holy Fire to Bethlehem and the Orthodox churches in the surrounding villages and towns of the West Bank.

This was the tribal Christianity that I had come to know on my pilgrimage and had come to understand as an expression of the faith in the eastern Mediterranean. It was part of its customs and its culture and its tribalism and its tactile spirituality. I was in the gallery with a group of Catholic priests, watching this ritual. The Catholic Church officially does not take part in the rite of the Holy Fire. A Franciscan in brown robes pointed down at what was supposed to be the mystery of the lighting of the fires, and said, "Right there, can you see the flame!" as he pointed to the lantern, supposedly unlit, as it entered the tomb. "See, they light it before it goes in!" he added. The Franciscans were, well, snooty about the Holy Fires. But they missed the point of the tradition, if they failed to understand and even embrace the tribalism of it, the way in which it was grounded in local custom and this land's belief in mystery, just as their own Christian faith was.

Later that afternoon, there was another procession and a completely different expression of faith. This was a march of peace activists trying to converge on the checkpoint in Bethlehem. About one hundred Israeli peace supporters gathered on one side of the checkpoint, carrying placards that read, "Occupation Is Illegal" and "No More Settlements" and "End Apartheid in the West Bank!" On the Palestinian side of the checkpoint were about fifty people, about half of whom were European, once again led by Ghassan Andoni and Jad Isaac. Both sides were prevented by Israeli soldiers from entering the checkpoints, which were separated by roughly 150 yards. Andoni and Isaac were both dressed in their Easter finest, and Abouna Ibrahim, the Catholic priest and militant Palestinian nationalist whom I had met earlier in the year, was marching with them. He was the only clergyman participating in the march, although dozens of Greek Orthodox clergy who were returning from the Holy Fires were freely allowed to pass the checkpoint in their black clerical garb. They walked by, puzzled by what was going on, but they didn't stop to inquire. One of them was carrying a lantern with the Holy Fire. He walked briskly as he tried to shield the flame to keep it from going out.

The Israeli and Palestinian leaders of the march were communicating by mobile phones across the physical divide that the Israelis had created. The leaders on the two sides wrested a concession from the Israeli soldiers to permit a small delegation to meet in the middle. There was a nice irony here: If Andoni and Isaac and their Palestinian marchers, the majority of whom were Christians from Beit Sahour, had said they wanted to pass the checkpoint because it was Holy Saturday, they would have presumably been permitted to do so. The Europeans and Americans who were there to support them could have passed any time they wanted. But Andoni and Isaac refused to couch their request in terms of religious observance, wanting to make a political point that they should be able to pass any day of the year. Just as they had done at the IDF post over the Christian cemetery at Beit Sahour, once again they were wrapping their march in secular, nationalist terms, even though its core intent was solidly Christian. They knew that press coverage of the march would appear on Easter Sunday, and that's exactly what they wanted.

The Israeli marchers had somehow persuaded the Israeli soldiers to allow a small delegation to pass and to meet up with the Palestinian marchers. But more and more Israeli marchers slipped through, and soon the soldiers couldn't hold back the Israelis without using force. The soldiers formed a line across the road, but the marchers kept moving, unthreateningly, nonviolently but lightly pushing, and eventually the soldiers' line broke. The Palestinian marchers could see this happening and were demanding that a delegation from their side be allowed through. Reluctantly, an Israeli soldier finally relented. But then the Palestinians did the same thing—they gently pushed past the soldiers. One soldier drew his rifle and pointed it at a roughly 20-year-old Palestinian, and I saw an Israeli peace activist immediately grab the young man's arm and walk with him. In the middle of the gauntlet between the two checkpoints, the marchers were united. They mingled together, hugging each other. Some Norwegian marchers started singing an out-of-tune rendition of "We Shall Overcome." A few Israelis sang along, with Hebrew accents; Andoni and Isaac were singing, with their Palestinian accents; and I noticed that the rest of the Israelis and Palestinians, who didn't know the words but understood the tune, were humming along.

There, in the spirit of that march was the presence of the living Christian church that I had been seeking. It was "the salt of the earth," as Jesus had said, that would leaven humankind. But just as salt was inseparable from the bread it was baked into, all of the ingredients of Christianity in this land—the tribal seasoning, the European and American flavor, even the dashes of carnival Christianity—were necessary in order to understand this land.

This was the "body of Christ" in the Holy Land.

As I watched Andoni and Isaac, I realized they weren't denying their Christianity by refusing to make their contribution in its name. They were being practical in applying their beliefs in a way that would not alienate the two other faiths with whom they shared the land and all of its spiritual claims, just as Jesus had come up with practical expressions of dissent. It was about being Christian, not asserting Christianity. I knew for sure they represented a voice in this land that would be sorely missed if it ever fell silent.

Sadly, the Christian presence seemed as imperiled as ever by the renewed conflict. Among the crowd of marchers were many with family names that were steadily dying out. The Palestinian Christians were watching more and more of their brothers and sisters and cousins emigrating to the United States and Canada and Europe. These were families with old names—Hazboun, Shomali, Saad, and Banoura. This was the bleeding of the body of Palestinian Christianity. A statistical survey carried out by the Latin Catholic patriarchate's Program Development Department had revealed that Beit Sahour's Christian community of roughly 8,000 was being hit by a "wave of mass immigration" that "imperils the continuity of the Christian presence." It was an ominous report for the Palestinian Christians, revealing that 51 percent of the respondents were seriously considering emigrating due to the economic and political instability created by the conflict. Even more ominous was the news that 40 percent of those seriously considering emigrating had already obtained visas and appeared to be on their way. Of this group, about 35 percent had visas for the United States. This would mean that some 1,800 Palestinian Christians could be pulling up stakes in Beit Sahour alone.

Although Beit Sahour was the only place where a systematic study had been completed, priests and political leaders in the Christian communities of Bethlehem, Beit Jala, Jerusalem, and Ramallah were reporting similarly distressing levels of emigration. The figures were alarmist in the sense that they did not reflect the fact that many might return if conditions improved. And, of course, the point should be made that Muslims were emigrating as well. But the situation was particularly dire for Christians, because so few were left that the very existence of a Christian community was in question. I stopped in to see Bernard Sabella, the Bethlehem university professor who had documented Christian emigration. This wave of emigration was undeniably massive, he said, larger and more threatening to the Palestinian Christian population in the West Bank and Gaza than any other since the 1967 war.

As the Christian Palestinian hemorrhage persisted, it threatened to drain the life out of a community that played a unique role in Arab culture under both the Palestinian Authority and the Israeli government. As the community shrank further, so did its ability to persuade the majority cultures and governments to adopt a more secular and more tolerant view. Those who believe that respect for diversity strengthens democracy view this as a tragedy. In a way, the thinning Christian population was a test of both the Palestinian Authority and the Israeli governments, a challenge to protect the rights of "the other" within national movements that defined themselves religiously. Without the Christians, the enlightened promises of tolerance and democracy could go that much more easily unfulfilled.

Whether Christians would endure in this land, whether they would continue to share in its future was a mystery, a parable as perplexing as the story of the disciples on the road to Emmaus.

A few days after Easter Sunday, I set out on the road that leads from Jerusalem to what is considered the traditional site of Emmaus. The way was lined with military checkpoints and two Israeli tank positions. My modern Israeli atlas named this as "Modiim road," and showed it winding its way between Jerusalem and Tel Aviv, the West Bank and Israel. The newly paved road, with its joint industrial area and its access to both West Bank villages and Israeli planned communities, was intended to exemplify the new Middle East. It had instead become synonymous with fear for Israelis, after a spate of drive-by shootings by Palestinian militants which had killed and wounded at least eight Israelis.

About eight miles from Jerusalem, the Modiim joins a smaller road, which leads to the Palestinian village of El-Qubeibeh. Since the days of the Crusaders, this village has been revered as the biblical Emmaus. Every year, on the Monday after Easter, a celebration has taken place there at the Roman Catholic church that has drawn Palestinian Christians from East Jerusalem and all of the villages and towns of the West Bank. During the service, a bread specially baked in Bethlehem is distributed to the congregation—recalling Jesus's breaking of bread with his disciples in Emmaus after his resurrection. A generation ago, thousands used to come from all over to attend the service. The number had dwindled over the years, and the turnout in 2000 was particularly heartbreaking. No more than twenty families showed up—largely because of the military restrictions on travel, but also because many families had left.

I had heard there was only one Christian family still living in El-Qubeibeh, and that with the current violence, they were thinking of leaving. Their departure would mean a break in the living presence of Christians in this town connected in the Catholic tradition to the site of the last physical visitation by Jesus. I had set out to find this family in the village . . . but then I got lost on the road to Emmaus.

At an intersection, a Palestinian man with an old Fiat Uno and a warm smile saw me struggling with a road map. He asked in English whether he could help. His name was Ali Jambour, and he worked for the British consulate. Ali, who was Muslim, offered to escort me to the village, and so I followed him. When we got there, he insisted on showing me the church and the beautiful grounds of the monastery, and he introduced me to the priests. He knew the history of the grounds, pointed out the cedar trees that came from Lebanon, and showed me the ancient paving stones that were all that remained of the Roman road down which the disciples probably had walked. Ali was proud of the Christian history of his village.

When I told him I was hoping to speak with the Christian family in town, he looked at me as though he were seeing a beautiful sunset, and said, "You know Anton? We are old friends, we were brought up together in this village." I tried to tell him that I had never met Anton, but he was already leading the way toward his house. On the way, he talked about the Christian population that had dwindled so dramatically in El-Qubeibeh and the surrounding villages and towns.

"This is very sad for us," said Ali, who was refined and educated and spoke English with a slight British accent. "The Christians have been such a part of this community, such a part of who we are as Palestinians. We have celebrated feasts and weddings and funerals together. And I have known Anton all my life, and I knew all of his brothers."

Anton Quliyoba was a 47-year-old taxi driver who was the oldest of six brothers. All five of his brothers had moved to the United States, and there was a rumor that Anton was thinking of leaving as well. We walked from the church up the hill to the Quliyoba home, where Anton's wife, Lucy, invited us in and dispatched their 12-year-old son to find his father. When Anton arrived, he and Ali hugged.

We sat on the couch, drinking tea and talking about all of Anton's family members—his five brothers, his sister, his mother—whom he had watched leave for Los Angeles over the years. The Quliyobas were the only Christians left in the village. In addition to Anton, there was his uncle Yakoub and his cousin Victor and several aunts who had never married (because the Christian men had disappeared). With the renewed violence and the resulting economic crisis, Anton confessed that he too was tempted to go, to seek out a better life and more opportunities for his children in America. But at least on this day, Anton was insisting that he would not leave. He seemed eager to assure Ali on this point, saying that it would be too hard to leave the land where his family roots had so long been planted, and where he had friendships that stretched over a lifetime.

"Don't leave us. In America it is too hard to live. You need too much money," said Ali, who had briefly lived in Louisiana but hated it, and who seemed doubtful that Anton had really made up his mind. "You should stay. This is your home."

And as Ali spoke these soft, coaxing words to his friend in the long shadows of the late afternoon, it was as if he were unconsciously echoing the disciples' invitation to the man they had met on the road from Jerusalem and had not yet recognized as Jesus: "Stay with us!" Although Ali's words to Anton were just one man's personal protest at the impending loss of a friend, they resounded in my mind as a timeless lament for the fragile, living presence of Christianity at the dawn of a new millennium, there on the road to Emmaus.

EPILOGUE

May 6, 2001
The Feast of St. George

ON THIS DAY, I sat down to find a way to end this book. I should have known better.

In the early morning, just as I was settling in at my desk with a cup of coffee, gunfire erupted in the distance. My wife Julie was with our three boys in our yard just beneath the balcony of my office. The gunfire was faint, a distant disturbance on an otherwise quiet Sunday morning. The children didn't even stop playing. Unusual to hear the fighting so early, I thought.

But I tried to stay focused on closing thoughts, what this pilgrimage meant to me. Why was I so struck by the emotion of watching the Christian presence diminish? What was the fate of this land without its indigenous Christian population, without its two thousand-year connection to the "Mother Church" of Jerusalem and to the Holy Land? These thoughts were all the more poignant because I was preparing to leave. After four years, my posting was up and I was to be reassigned to London over the summer. But beyond this, as a father, I felt it was time to evacuate my family from Jerusalem. The daily risks were increasing, and I was feeling a gnawing sense of irresponsibility in continuing to put everyone through all this for the sake of my work. Even more than the physical risks, I didn't want my sons to be surrounded by hatred. I didn't want them to learn about that, not at so young an age. I realized that I was ultimately making the same choice that so many people of this land—particularly, the Christians—had made throughout the cycles of conflict here since 1948.

But as a journalist, I couldn't quite believe that I was leaving the story behind just when it seemed so poised at the edge of historic events. But then again, this place always seemed to be teetering on that edge.

Such musings were interrupted by the morning's first burst of tank fire, the guns across Jerusalem once again. Birds scattered from the eskadinia tree in our yard. I came out onto the balcony of my office to hear it better. This time the children stopped playing. But not for long. They had become accustomed to the sound, or they had observed that our facial expressions hardly changed now, when the distant rumbling started. Julie looked up and spelled out the word so that the children would not understand what she was saying: "T-A-N-K, right?" Then there were bursts of gunfire from Palestinian Kalashnikovs. Julie said she thought they sounded as if they were coming from Al-Khader, or perhaps from the part of Beit Jala that overlooks the tunnel of the settler bypass road, approximately two miles away. The Palestinians' 7.62-mm bullets had a range of only 700 yards and typically could not reach the nearby settlement of Gilo, let alone (we had convinced ourselves) our backyard.

Then there were louder bursts of gunfire, which made me think the Palestinians were using heavier caliber bullets than usual. These were answered by sharp cracking sounds that I figured were the Israelis' tank-mounted Barrett machine guns firing .50-caliber bullets with a full metal jacket, which typically have armor-piercing tips. They were usually reserved for heavy firefights. Then the tanks boomed again. I grabbed my bulletproof vest and headed for our car. So much for concentrating on concluding the book. As I drove, I wondered when Julie and I had become so well versed in the sounds of the machinery and caliber of battle. And what had that done to us? And how, albeit on some subliminal level, was it affecting our children? What was going on in their heads at the moment when they stopped playing? Did they have any idea of the ugly reality behind those distant rumblings? How long would it take before they did?

The feast of St. George was to be celebrated in Beit Jala and Al-Khader that day. I had wanted to go but had made the decision to focus instead on my writing. Now, as I approached the Bethlehem checkpoint, I tried to picture the Palestinian Christian community of Beit Jala and the Muslim community of Al-Khader, preparing, as they did every year on May 6, to honor a figure who is part legend, part history. To the Christians, he was St. George who slew the dragon at the entrance to the city. To the Muslims, he was Al-Khader, the "Green One," who fought bravely on the side of God against injustice. I was certain the celebration would be canceled due to the battle that I could now hear outside the car window.

I had driven up through Bethlehem and the long way around, out of the line of fire, into Beit Jala, to meet with some of the Palestinian Christian families I knew there. The town's streets were empty. When I arrived, the gunfire was still sporadic on both sides.

In the old section of Beit Jala, Diana Mubarak quickly rushed me into her living room and scolded me for walking the streets while there was shooting. Her living room wall was barricaded with sandbags, which looked strange against the velvet curtains and the beautiful antiques. Her family home was perched elegantly, but now very dangerously, on the face of a steep hillside overlooking the valley that lay between Beit Jala and Gilo. I had gotten to know Diana over the previous month, having bumped into her at several funerals. In her mid-40s, she is a very smart, competent professional, the head of social work for the Palestinian Authority in Bethlehem. She comes from a prominent Greek Orthodox family in Beit Jala, and like so many of the Christian women there, she is unmarried.

Diana showed me three new bullet holes that had pierced one side of her home just hours earlier. It seemed an almost impossible angle of fire, from Gilo. It was a miracle, she said, that no one was hurt. She was surrounded by her extended family, a collection of sisters and nieces and cousins. I realized there were many more women than men. As I got to know these women, I was impressed that they were so accomplished, with advanced degrees in psychology and public health. They explained to me that most of the men in their family had emigrated, and that many of the women who had stayed on were not married. One of the women, Fairuz, told me how this day's battle had started. Early in the morning, she had been among a handful of Christians, mostly women, who had headed out in procession up to the Greek Orthodox church where it is believed St. George was imprisoned. On a ridge between Beit Jala and Al-Khader, gunfire erupted. It wasn't clear who fired first, she said. As I would later learn, a Palestinian Tanzim force headed by Mohammed Abayat, the cousin of Hussein (the Rambo-like figure whose life and death I had documented in Beit Sahour), was stationed there. Mohammed was the head of a militia that had taken the name Hussein Abayat Regiment and that was operating around Beit Jala. Israeli forces with armored personnel carriers and tanks were returning fire. Something triggered a dramatic gun battle, and Israeli tanks actually invaded Beit Jala briefly in the late morning. It was the first time in this *intifada* that Israeli tanks had invaded Palestinian-controlled territory in the West Bank—one more red line crossed in a conflict that was now in its eighth month. Already it had claimed the lives of more than 400 Palestinians, more than 75 Israelis, and 13 Israeli Arabs. Mohammed Abayat would become another name to add to the casualty count that day, and the second member of the Abayat tribe to die. Two young boys from Beit Jala, ages 6 and 12, were badly wounded in the cross fire. Amid the fierce fighting that broke out that day on the ridge, the Christian women who had been walking in the procession ducked into doorways for cover.

Fairuz was still shaken from the experience. She vowed that she would leave Beit Jala and go to live with her two children, who had already emigrated to San Diego, California. But she still had to convince her husband, she said. As these women of Beit Jala gathered for yet another night in the makeshift bomb shelter they had built in the basement of their home, all of them were talking about who was emigrating and who was not. The trip to the bomb shelter had become a routine in the preceding months; they would bring coffee and sweets and stay up through the shelling and the gunfire.

The sun was fading. Tank fire was thundering again and Diana winced at the sound of an Israeli shell hitting Beit Jala. "My God, how can they do that? Do they want us all to just leave?" she asked. The Beit Jala community was furious with the Israeli punishment of their community for the actions of the Palestinian militias. But they were also increasingly furious at the gunmen, most of whom were Muslims from the Abayat branch of the Tamari tribe. The Christians I had gotten to know were incensed that these Tanzim gunmen had put them in the middle of this fighting, especially because the Tanzim had driven a wedge between Beit Jala's Christians and Muslims that had never before been so deep. Through the months of conflict it had become clear that not only Christians but also Muslims in West Bank towns such as Hebron and Ramallah, where the seams between Jewish settlements and Palestinian communities had been torn by violence, were upset by the Palestinian militias' firing from civilian areas. Muslims and Christians alike felt that Arafat's Palestinian Authority was allowing chaos to rule, and in the process, jeopardizing their families. Beit Jala was unique in that it was the first community to organize a public protest and speak out against these Palestinian militias, and the first to hold meetings with senior officials of the Palestinian Authority. On several occasions, Beit Jalans had physically confronted the gunmen, and street fights had broken out. There was even a leaflet released, signed "the Christians of Beit Jala," which condemned the gunmen's actions. No one in the community ever came forward to claim authorship, and some strident nationalists in Beit Jala contended that it may have been a deliberate attempt by the Israelis to foment interreligious strife. But regardless of the mysterious leaflet's origins, most of the Christian Beit Jalans I interviewed were quite aware of very real divisions between Muslims and Christians that had arisen within their own community, and they were sad about it. The Feast of St. George might have been a traditional day of Muslim-Christian unity, but at least half the people in that bomb shelter felt there was something pulling them apart from their Muslim neighbors even if they also knew that the bigger divide was the valley that separated them from where the Israelis lived.

. . .

As I tried to piece together my thoughts about what I had seen in this journalistic pilgrimage along the path of Jesus's life, I realized that mine was a pilgrimage that had no ending, one that would continually turn in cycles of revenge and recoiling as it had from one century to the next and would continue long after I was gone. It had swept me up in its path for a time, as it had many chroniclers before.

Over this weekend, the report of an international fact-finding commission headed by former U.S. Senator George Mitchell was submitted to the Israelis and the Palestinians, laying out the conditions for a cease-fire and the resumption of peace talks. It was a tough but fair document—it pulled no punches on the Israelis' excessive use of force and the need for an immediate freeze on settlement expansion, but it also blamed the Palestinian Authority for doing too little to rein in the violence emanating from militant factions within the West Bank and Gaza. With all previous efforts to obtain a cease-fire having failed, Mitchell's report was greeted with what could only be called guarded pessimism. Within Israel, an independent commission was holding hearings on allegations of criminal conduct by the police and military in the killing of 13 Israeli Arabs in Nazareth and during the rioting that had swept Israeli Arab towns throughout the Galilee in the fall of 2000. These were raw wounds that only time—and justice—could heal.

And on the same day, Pope John Paul II was also back in the region, this time on a trip to Syria. He had arrived from Greece, where he had met with the Greek Orthodox hierarchy in an effort to reach a reconciliation between the bitterly divided churches; and in Syria he was planning to continue his interfaith pilgrimage by becoming the first pope ever to make an offical visit to a mosque. Bashar Assad, the young, untested Syrian president, heir to his father's brutal Ba'ath Party regime, greeted the pope by making an outrageous comparison between the suffering of the Palestinians and the crucifixion of Jesus. It was a clumsy and flawed statement that infuriated the Israelis—and Jews all over the world—who saw it as imbued with layers of anti-Semitism. Many Jewish leaders expressed disappointment that the pope had silently listened to Assad's skewed theology and not spoken out against it. The pope was also a pilgrim caught up in the vortex of this land.

Over the months since the year 2000 had ended, all of the stories that I had documented on my pilgrimage were still turning on the axis of conflict. After four years here, it seemed the only fixed point in the Middle East.

Although the Israelis had pulled out of Lebanon in May 2000, the border remained tense a year later, and many right-wing Israelis were beginning to see the pullout as a mistake. Just days after Easter, an Israeli soldier was killed near Sheba Farms, a disputed corner of the former occupied zone. (Hezbollah guerrillas had insisted—despite U.N. maps that stated otherwise—that Israel must leave this small pocket of land in order to comply with U.N. resolutions ordering their complete withdrawal.) Israel retaliated with an air strike on a Syrian observation post, killing three people. Members of the South Lebanon Army who had fled Lebanon earlier for Israel were still trying to get visas for other destinations, and the family of their fallen leader, Akel Hashem, had moved to Australia.

In Egypt, the ethnic strife between Muslims and Christians had subsided, but the underlying problems had not yet been addressed by the government. President Hosni Mubarak, who was positioning himself as a regional broker in the Israeli-Palestinian conflict, visited the United States in April and spoke out against Israel's policies of collective punishment and its excessive use of force. But even as he worked his way around Washington, the Coptic question kept dogging him, to his undisguised annoyance. In an interview with the *Boston Globe*, Mubarak was defensive when asked about the treatment of Copts. He stressed that Muslims and Christians were "unified" in Egypt and that "the chief of the Air Force is a Copt . . . and there are two ministers, of the economy and the environment, who are Copts." Indeed, in almost every statement, Mubarak's paternalism toward the Copts bled through: "We are leading a very normal life. I have a man who is looking after my private things—he is a Copt." Some of the president's best friends were Copts, he seemed to be saying, so how bad could their life be? Meanwhile, Mubarak's justice system had convicted Saad Ibrahim, the outspoken liberal Muslim academic who had dared to speak out against Mubarak's regime and the treatment of Copts in Egypt. He was sentenced to seven years in prison—a move that sparked outrage among international human rights activists.

In the United States, the church-led movement to highlight the diminishing Christian presence in the Holy Land seemed to be making some strides. The Holy Land Christian Ecumenical Foundation was one of several different Christian organizations becoming increasingly active in its efforts to find new and creative solutions to open American eyes to the problem. The Western churches were doing their own soul searching on this issue, acknowledging that for generations they had done too little, or perhaps too much in the wrong way, to try to keep Christians in the Holy Land. The Roman Catholic patriarch Michel Sabbah, who had been defensive about the notion of the diminishing Christian presence when I first met him three years earlier, was now converted to the cause of increasing the Church's awareness of this issue. He regularly toured the United States, appealing to Catholics for support in seeking a resolution to the problems fueling Palestinian Christian emigration. In the spring of 2001, the U.S. Conference of Catholic Bishops came out with a strongly worded statement, citing international law as the basis for its call to Israel to pull out of the occupied territories and to permit Palestinian refugees the "right of return."

The churches seemed to be maturing in their efforts to keep Palestinian Christians on the land, recognizing that a system of providing them with gifts of clothing, food, housing, schools, and even jobs had created a debilitating culture of dependence. Such pampering also had created a dependence on the West and had hurt the church's image among Palestinians and Israelis as an indigenous force. The secret to empowering the local Christian population and in stemming the flow of emigration, the hierarchy had come to realize, was to "Arabize" the church. The church must actively seek a role in helping this land find a way toward justice and reconciliation—the more so as the other forces involved seemed hell-bent on mutual destruction.

. . .

Meanwhile, the cycle ground on; there would be cease-fires and violations of cease-fires. There would be more negotiations and breakdowns in negotiations. There would be flare-ups in violence, followed by political crises. There would be hope that this land would avoid war, and despair that war was inevitable. As I drove home from Beit Jala watching tracer fire and missiles light up the night sky once more, I realized that the story of this book would never be over. The path of Jesus's life would always produce new stories of sorrow and redemption, of intractable conflict and yearning for peace, and of the constant movement of people and history along this age-old route.

The steady exodus of Christians was the story I had set out to chronicle on my pilgrimage, but along the way there was a personal change that had come out of this experience, a redefinition of my own faith, an understanding of how the Christians and Christianity fit into the history of this land. I had gained a much deeper sense of how Jesus himself was of this place, of its conflicts, of its sense of tribalism and progeny and their connection to the possession of land; and I now saw that his message rejecting those three overriding themes of daily life here were what made his message so challenging and potentially so powerful. I had come to learn about Jesus as a Jew, a rabbi preaching against occupation. His teaching could be claimed by both sides in this conflict, and also rejected by both at the same time. Judaism provided the roots of so many of his ideas of universal liberation and freedom and faith; and the Palestinians lived the life that Jesus did under the heavy boot of occupation.

I also had learned a lot about my own church, about Christianity and the sins it had committed against the other peoples of this land,

Jews and Muslims alike. And I had learned how little the Christianity I knew, the one I was raised in, had to do with this land. In fact it was intentionally remote and distant from this place. In this rugged, arid climate, Western Christianity was brittle and frail and therefore dying. Its roots were barely clinging to the rocky soil where the prophet of the faith was born and lived and died and was resurrected.

But there was something different now, a sense of despair among the Christians of the Middle East, a sense that this battle might well be the last one they could endure. Many of them wanted out. A few were determined to stay. Diana Mubarak was one of the latter. "I'm not leaving. This is my land," she said defiantly, even with the sound of gunfire in the background. "We've already given up too much."

Some, like Diana, were staying out of a conviction to remain on the land where their own history and the history of their faith began. Most were staying quite simply because they did not have the resources or the courage or the contacts to move. Whatever their reasons, I had come to believe that these Christians who did stay in the Holy Land had a unique, possibly even sacred role to play. As Palestinians, they had a great deal to contribute in shaping their national aspirations and their collective culture. As Christians, they had the implicit mission of preserving the two-thousand-year-old, living presence of the faith in their land, and of providing a nexus where Muslims, Jews, Israelis, and Palestinians could come together. Certainly as their numbers diminished, these roles were threatened. But this dwindling Christian presence, the ones who were holding on in this land, could be viewed as what Jesus called "the salt of the earth."

The Lutheran pastor in Bethlehem, Mitri Raheb, had explained to me the relevance of that biblical reference one afternoon in his church in Bethlehem, saying that even as salt dissolves, it adds seasoning to the bread. It is an essential ingredient. The body of the church was like leavening in the Holy Land, giving it its unique flavoring. Raheb had wisely cautioned me so many months ago and now I understood what he meant. He had told me, "You cannot come to this land trying to look for the salt, to separate it from the bread and measure its quantity. You will never find it, even though it is always there."

ACKNOWLEDGMENTS

DURING THE WRITING of this book, my wife, Julie Klapper Sennott, offered keen insights, clear perspective, and a calm spirit while I ran ragged on caffeine and adrenaline, trying to cover a conflict, write a book, and still be a father and husband. Through it all, she brought our new son Gabriel into the world and provided a sane and warm home for our family. Her selflessness and stamina saw us through a difficult, emotional, joyous, tragic, and above all memorable time in our lives together.

I would also like to thank my editors at the *Boston Globe* for their support and for allowing me some precious blocks of time as this book underwent dramatic change, becoming more ambitious and more deeply personal than I had first expected.

My agent, Esther Newberg, has my deep appreciation for seeing immediately that PublicAffairs was the right place for this book. PublicAffairs is an extraordinary refuge in the tundra of publishing for journalists and those who take nonfiction seriously. And I would like to thank Peter Osnos for his vision, and for allowing me to share in it. I would also like to thank the staff of PublicAffairs for putting up with the insane schedule of an author trying to balance the daily demands of his beat with delivering a manuscript as close to deadline as possible.

My PublicAffairs editor Paul Golob was a consummate professional in the way he tackled this book after inheriting it from his predecessor, Geoff Shandler. Geoff was invaluable in helping me shape the early drafts of the manuscript and even made his own pilgrimage to

Jerusalem to work directly with me. I'd like to thank both Paul and Geoff for staying committed to making the book better.

My brother Mark offered sound counsel. My brother Rick traveled to the Holy Land with his camera and his sharp eye for detail, and provided most of the photographs included here. I would also like to thank Heidi Levine, Bryan McBurney, Stephen Wallace, and Tom Hartwell for contributing photos.

Any mistake or error is, of course, my own. But I thank the many people who took time to help me avoid making them. Father Jerome Murphy-O'Connor deserves special mention. Many other friends and family members also offered to read the manuscript at various stages, and provided insights and questions that made it better. I am particularly grateful to William Orme, Gerry Holmes, Jennifer Ludden, Jeanmarie Condon, Joseph Lagan, Megan Crowley McAllister, Gershom Gorenberg, Father Athanasius Macora, Yehezkel Landau, Henry Carse, Drew Christiansen, Kees Hulsman, Bernard Sabella, Nick Blanford, Clay Scott, Mohamad Bazzi, Said Ghazali, Mike O'Connor, Larry Kaplow, George Hintlian, Vera Inoue-Terris, Dan Rabinowitz, Rabbi David Rosen, Nadia Tewfik, and Jack Levine.

NOTES

MOST OF THE MATERIAL for this book came from my firsthand experiences as a journalist covering events in the Holy Land in the year 2000. The idea grew out of a three-part series I wrote for the *Boston Globe,* titled "A Test of Faith in the Holy Land," which was published in January 1999. Most of the interviews and impressions and conversations included in the last three chapters (Part IV) came from my daily coverage of the conflict for the *Boston Globe.* Information for this section also came from daily coverage by the *Jerusalem Post* and the English-language version of the Israeli newspaper *Ha'aretz.* The conclusion was shaped around an essay I wrote for the *Boston Globe Magazine* on April 4, 1999.

Although I used the path of Jesus's life as a narrative theme and an organizational device, I completed a year and a half of research before my journalistic pilgrimage began. There were also six months of follow-up after the year ended, as I chronicled the fast paced developments of the Palestinian revolt against Israeli occupation that began in September 2000 and continued well into the summer of 2001.

Notes on Preface to the Paperback Edition

The preface relies on my reporting for the *Boston Globe.* Also subsequent interviews with IDF officials and Michael Aviad, the Israeli newspaper *Ha'aretz* and the detailed reconstruction of the siege in *Newsweek,* May 20, 2002.

Notes on Chapter 1: Pilgrimage

For the history of Mar Saba and the Byzantine period, see William Dalrymple, *From the Holy Mountain: A Journey Among the Christians of the Middle East* (New York: Henry Holt and Company, 1997).

For the history of pilgrimage, see Andrew Sinclair's *Jerusalem: The Endless Conflict* (New York: Crown Publishers, Inc., 1995).

The overcrowding in Jerusalem at the time of Jesus is based on my interview with biblical historian Jerome Murphy-O'Connor in October 1999.

History of the Crusaders and the slaughter of 30,000: Karen Armstrong, *Jerusalem: One City, Three Faiths* (New York: Ballantine Books, 1997), pp. 271–294.

Jesus in the Temple as a threat to the Temple establishment: Armstrong, *Jerusalem,* p. 143.

The divisions between the Sadducees and the Pharisees at the time of Jesus: David Flusser, *Jesus* (Jerusalem: Magnes Press, 1997), pp. 67–75.

On the seizure of Arab homes in Jerusalem after the 1948 war: Salim Tamari, *Jerusalem 1948: The Arab Neighborhoods and Their Fate in the War* (Jerusalem: Institute of Jerusalem Studies, 1999).

The 1914 figure on Christian population comes from Andrea Pacini, *Christian Communities in the Arab Middle East* (Oxford, England: Clarendon Press, 1998). The modern-day figure of "under 5 percent" is my extrapolation using Pacini's figure of 7 percent as a baseline and then downsizing the estimates based on more recent independent studies, especially in Jordan, Lebanon, and Egypt, which indicate a lower percentage of Christians than Pacini's work.

Christians constitute less than 2 percent of the total population in the Holy Land (Israel, West Bank, Gaza, and Jerusalem): This figure comes from official Israeli and Palestinian Authority sources.

Population figures for Jerusalem: The 1944 figure comes from Daphne Tsimhoni's *Christian Communities in Jerusalem and the West Bank Since 1948: An Historic, Social and Political Study* (Westport, Conn.: Praeger, 1993). The 2000 estimate comes from church records and my interviews with researchers on Christian population, including Bernard Sabella, Amnon Ramon, and George Hintlian.

Some scholars have questioned whether Christians truly represented a statistical majority in the fifth and sixth centuries: from author's interviews with historian Thomas Stransky of the Tantur Ecumenical Institute in Jerusalem, in June 2000.

It should be noted that some Israeli officials and American Jewish organizations have challenged the notion that the Palestinian Christian population in Israel is shrinking. They contend that the Christian population has increased threefold under 52 years of Israeli rule. But some population experts maintain that their statistical information is skewed because it relies on a statistical low point in 1949 (after tens of thousands of Christian Palestinian refugees had left who would not be allowed back in) and a statistical high point in 1994 (a year in which the Israeli census still included under the category "Christian" tens of thousands of immigrants to Israel from the former Soviet Union who listed their religion as Christianity).

Statistical information on Palestinian Christians by age and sex: "The Emigration of Christian Arabs: The Dimension and Causes of the Phenomenon," paper presented by Bernard Sabella to the Giovanni Agnelli Foundation, Turin, Italy, May 1995.

"Canaries in the mine": Judith Miller, *God Has Ninety-nine Names* (New York: Touchstone, 1996), p. 467.

Notes on Chapter 2: The End of Days

The Israeli police considered Brother David's group a "threat to public order" and believed they were planning a mass suicide: *Ha'aretz,* October 29, 1999.

After considerable diplomatic pressure, the Irish pilgrims were permitted visas for Easter 2000.

The history of millennialism in America comes from Gershom Gorenberg, *The End of Days: Fundamentalism and the Struggle for the Temple Mount* (New York: Free Press, 2000).

Different faiths can be tone deaf to each other's music: Gershom Gorenberg eloquently makes this point in *The End of Days.*

John the Baptist and Jesus growing out of a tradition of apocalyptic prophets: John Dominic Crossan, *Jesus: A Revolutionary Biography* (San Francisco: HarperSanFrancisco, 1995), p. 43. Thomas Cahill (*Desire of the Everlasting Hills: The World*

Before and After Jesus [New York: Nan A. Talese, Doubleday, 1999]) also explores this idea, although he presents Jesus as departing from and even transforming the apocalyptic traditions into something new and revolutionary.

Notes on Chapter 3: The Vicar of Christ on Earth

The Year of Jubilee, as it figured in Jesus's sermon in Nazareth: Osvaldo D. Vena, "The New Testament Understanding of the Biblical Jubilee," pp. 55–68 in *Holy Land, Hollow Jubilee: God, Justice and the Palestinians,* eds. Naim Ateek and Michael Prior (London: Melisende, 1999).

The Vatican document *Nostra Aetate* and the Vatican's historic reexamination of its attitude toward Judaism: from my interviews with Rabbi David Rosen and from his article "A History of Reconciliation: The Catholics and the Jews," *Jerusalem Post,* December 31, 1999.

Pope Pius X speaking to Theodor Herzl: from Rosen, "A History of Reconciliation."

Israel's annexation of East Jerusalem has never been recognized by the international community, including the United States.

Notes on Chapter 4: Nazareth: The Annunciation

History of the 1948 Israeli-Arab war and specific operations and movements in the Galilee: See Israel's revisionist historian, Benny Morris, *The Birth of the Palestinian Refugee Problem, 1947–1949* (Cambridge: Cambridge University Press, 1989). Thc historical and political background of Nazareth came largely from two excellent academic studies: Chad F. Emmett, *Beyond the Basilica: Christians and Muslims in Nazareth* (Chicago: University of Chicago Press, 1995), and Dan Rabinowitz, *Overlooking Nazareth: The Ethnography of Exclusion in Galilee* (Cambridge: Cambridge University Press, 1996).

Fighting around Tiberias and the Galilee: Emmett, *Beyond the Basilica,* p. 41, and Morris, *The Birth of the Palestinian Refugee Problem,* p. 71.

The death toll in the Deir Yassin massacre: Benny Morris, *Righteous Victims: A History of the Zionist Conflict, 1881–1999* (New York: Knopf, 1999), pp. 208–209.

Description of the Mt. Scopus ambush: based on Larry Collins and Dominique LaPierre, *O, Jerusalem* (New York: Touchstone, 1988), pp. 290–291.

In the 1948 war, Israel expanded territory allotted to it by 50 percent: *Political Dictionary of the Arab World* (New York: Macmillan Publishing, 1987), p. 48.

"The conquest of Nazareth had a political importance": Morris, *The Birth of the Palestinian Refugee Problem,* p. 201.

Approximately 60,000 Palestinian Christians emigrated in 1948: Bernard Sabella, "Christian Palestinians: A Modern Community in a Date with Democracy" (Bethlehem: Bethlehem University, Department of Social Sciences, 1999), p. 2.

Shift in Nazareth population from 60 percent Christian to 60 percent Muslim: Emmett, *Beyond the Basilica,* p. 47.

History of Sursock family: based on my interview with Lady Yvonne Sursock Cochrane on February 18, 2001 (translated by Kim Ghattas).

Narrative of the Maalul land deal: based on my interviews with families of refugees and with Mohamed Zeidan, president of the Arab Association for Human Rights, which has extensively researched land expropriation in the Galilee; and on Walid Khalidi, *All That Remains: The Palestinian Villages Occupied and Depopulated by Israel in 1948* (Washington, D.C.: Institute for Palestine Studies, 1992).

Jewish National Fund prohibited land from being leased to non-Jews: Meron Benvenisti, *Sacred Landscape: The Buried History of the Holy Land Since 1948* (Berkeley: University of California Press, 2000), p. 177.

History of the Anglican Church in Jerusalem: Rev. Riah Abu El-Assal, "The Birth and Experience of the Christian Church: The Protestant/Anglican Perspective," p. 131 in *Christians in the Holy Land,* eds. Michael Prior and William Taylor (London: World of Islam Festival Trust, 1994).

Figures on funding discrepancy between Nazareth and Upper Nazareth were derived from my interviews with Upper Nazareth councilman Salim Khouri and Nazareth mayor Ramez Jeraisi, and from data compiled by the Arab Association for Human Rights in Nazareth. The 1983 figure comes from David K. Shipler, *Arab and Jew: Wounded Spirits in a Promised Land* (New York: Penguin Books, 1987), p. 144.

Statistics on inequality between Arabs and Jews living in Israel: "After the Rift: New Directions for Government Policy Towards the Arab Population in Israel," published by an inter-university research team in Israel and submitted to then Prime Minister Ehud Barak, November 2000.

"Judaize Galilee": from Rabinowitz, *Overlooking Nazareth,* p. 7.

Notes on Chapter 5: Bethlehem: The Manger

Timing of the Roman imperial census: Several biblical historians have established that the census described in Luke's gospel actually was conducted a few years *after* Jesus's birth is believed to have taken place. Depending on one's perspective, these findings cast doubt either on the accuracy of Luke's account or on the traditional year-date of Jesus's birth.

Data on the economic effects of Israeli closures on the Palestinian standard of living come from "Development Under Adversity: The Palestinian Economy in Transition" (Ramallah, West Bank: World Bank/Palestine Economic Policy Research Institute, 2000); and "West Bank and Gaza Update" (Ramallah, West Bank: World Bank/Palestine Economic Policy Research Institute, 1999; 2000).

The Jacir Palace Inter-Continental Hotel: from my interview with the hotel manager in December 2000.

Regarding the Har Homa settlement: The Israeli legal system considers itself immune from international laws spelled out in the Geneva convention that prohibit the transfer of population to militarily occupied territories.

Israeli control of the tourism industry: from my interviews with owners of travel agencies; tour guides; and from "Development Under Adversity" (World Bank/Palestine Economic Policy Research Institute).

The number of Israeli-licensed tour guides who are Palestinian: from data provided to author by the office of Israel's ministry for tourism in Jerusalem, December 19, 2000.

That the only buses allowed free access were Israeli owned: from author's interviews with Palestinian tourism industry officials and owners of Palestinian bus companies; and from "Development Under Adversity."

Notes on Chapter 6: Beit Sahour: The Shepherds' Fields

The history of the Christian role in Arab nationalism: Fouad Ajami, *The Dream Palace of the Arabs: A Generation's Odyssey* (New York: Vintage Books, 1999); Kamal Salibi, *A House of Many Mansions: The History of Lebanon Reconsidered* (Berkeley: University of California Press, 1988); and Said K. Aburish, *The Forgotten Faithful: The Christians of the Holy Land* (London: Quartet Books, 1993). The Salibi quote is from *A House of Many Mansions,* p. 48.

Number of Palestinians killed in the first *intifada*: The Israeli human rights organization B'tselem reports 22 Palestinians killed by Israeli security forces in December 1987, and 289 in 1988, for a total of 311. In addition, 15 Palestinian civilians had been killed by Israeli civilians; 6 Israeli civilians had been killed by Palestinians; and 4 members of Israeli security forces had been killed by Palestinians.

"The Arab nation": Manuel Hassassian, "The Influence of Christian Arabs in the National Movement," speech, Bethlehem University, January 14, 1999.

About George Antonius: Ajami, *Dream Palace of the Arabs,* pp. 16–17.

Greek Orthodox Church's influence on Arab nationalism: Ajami, *Dream Palace of the Arabs,* pp. 33–34.

American consultants warned Israel about the power of nonviolence: from my interview with Mubarak Awad, May 5, 2000.

"We will teach them a lesson": Glenn E. Robinson, *Building a Palestinian State: The Incomplete Revolution* (Bloomington: Indiana University Press, 1997), p. 86.

Forty merchants arrested in the Tax Revolt; *Boston Globe,* November 2, 1989.

Beit Sahour's nonviolent movement presented a challenge to Arafat: Said K. Aburish, *Arafat: From Defender to Dictator* (London: Bloomsbury, 1998), p. 219.

The PLO denied financial and logistical help to Beit Sahour: Glenn Frankel, *Beyond the Promised Land: Jews and Arabs on the Hard Road to a New Israel* (New York: Touchstone, 1996), p. 65.

Arafat controlling the *intifada* with leaders more to his liking: Aburish, *Arafat,* p. 219.

Notes on Chapter 7: Egypt: The Flight

The courtroom scene and quotes from Arsal are based on my interviews with Mamdouh Nakhla, Arsal's lead attorney, in September 2000.

Precise figures for the Coptic Christian population in Egypt are impossible to come by. The Egyptian government does not release population statistics on religious affiliation. It was assumed in the 1950s that the Christian population was about 15 percent. In 1977, official government figures placed the Coptic population at 2.3 million, or about 6 percent of a population of 39 million. Coptic Church officials strongly disputed this figure as too low and cited church records that they claimed indicated the Christian population was as high as 18 percent, numbering almost 7 million, in the mid-1970s. Academics and researchers generally accept that the figure was probably somewhere in the middle, at about 12 percent of the total population, or slightly more than 4 million, in the mid-1970s. Twenty-five years later, most government and church officials agreed the generally accepted figure for the Christian population was holding steady at 4 million, or 5.7 percent of Egypt's population of 70 million.

Immigration statistics are notoriously unreliable because so many of the applications are for tourist and student visas, but once they are in the host country, those who have received such visas often stay on and apply for citizenship. The observations here are based on my interviews with staff at the American and Canadian embassies and on research by the Cairo-based journalist K. Hulsman.

Coptic diaspora: Otto Meinardus, *Two Thousand Years of Coptic Christianity* (Cairo: American University in Cairo Press, 1999). A leading authority on the history of the Coptic Church, Meinardus wrote: "The Coptic Diaspora during the second half of the twentieth century is undoubtedly the most significant demographic movement in the history of the Coptic Church. The exodus had already begun in the late fifties, then continued in the sixties, seventies and eighties on account of the re-pressive political and economic measures by the Egyptian government" (p. 129).

The description of the journey from Cairo to Al-Kosheh is based on my firsthand observations during several trips.

"The crown of martyrdom"; "nature would not permit"; and the history of the Coptic Church: Meinardus, *Two Thousand Years of Coptic Christianity,* pp. 28–29.

The ruling that the shedding of Copt "blood was permissible": Miller, *God Has Ninety-nine Names,* p. 53.

Regarding Sheikh Abdel Kafi: Miller, *God Has Ninety-Nine Names,* p. 7. Egyptian government officials noted in an interview with me that Sheikh Abdel Kafi was reprimanded for his comments in 1997 and is no longer permitted to make public addresses on government-run television.

Mubarak issued a decree for the repair of a toilet: Miller, *God Has Ninety-nine Names,* p. 53. This decree was modified in 1999, and these decisions are now made by Egypt's governors.

The chronology of events over New Year's weekend in Al-Kosheh is based on numerous sources, including my interviews with victims; the EOHR's February report; and various accounts in *Al Ahram* and the *Los Angeles Times,* and on National Public Radio.

"Do you understand this could destroy your credibility?": *Cairo Times,* March 1, 2000, p. 11.

The abuse of power by the state security forces: From transcript of Saad Eddin Ibrahim's interview with Freedom House on July 13, 2000.

Renaming Al-Kosheh: *Al Ahram Weekly,* January 20–26, 2000.

Notes on Chapter 8: Nazareth: The Family

The Islamic Movement as a means for Labor and Likud to deter power of Israel's Communist Party: Emmett, *Beyond the Basilica,* pp. 269–271.

Description of internal Israeli politics, especially of the role of the Catholic Church in opposing the construction of the mosque: Rev. Drew Christiansen, "Nazareth Journal," *AMERICA* [magazine], February 12, 2000.

The passages on Israeli politics going under the tent in Nazareth were informed by my extensive interviews with several Nazareth political officials, including sources at city hall and within the Islamic Movement. I also interviewed many Israeli government officials, including Likud operative Danny Greenberg (briefly, by telephone), who denied most of the allegations of divide and rule which were made against him.

Israel's politics of "divide and rule" in Nazareth: Rev. Drew Christiansen, "Nazareth Journal," *AMERICA* [magazine], February 12, 2000. The statement that "seventy thousand blank Palestinian ballots in the previous prime ministerial election helped Netanyahu squeak past Peres" comes directly from this article.

"The churches must reconcile themselves to political reality": Christiansen, "Nazareth Journal."

An unprecedented form of protest: Church officials said that the doors of some holy places were closed in 1990 to protest the takeover of St. John's Hospice by radical Jewish settlers of the group Ateret Cohanim in the Christian Quarter of Jerusalem's Old City. But other church officials said the doors were only briefly closed as a symbolic gesture, not for two days as was the case in 1999.

Jesus's notion of family: Crossan, *Jesus: A Revolutionary Biography,* pp. 58–59 ("Tearing the Family Apart"); and A. N. Wilson, "His Wondrous Childhood," in *Jesus: A Life* (New York: Fawcett Columbine, 1992).

Notes on Chapter 9: Jordan: The Baptism

History of Madaba: Patricia Mayno Bikai, ed., *Madaba: Cultural Heritage* (Amman: American Center of Oriental Research, 1996).

The historical record falls silent: Bikai, *Madaba,* p. 5.

Christians are about 2 percent of Jordan's total population: Hashemite Kingdom, Department of Population Statistics; and my interview with experts at Jordan's Center for Statistical Studies, headed by Mustafa Hamarneh.

The story of the Maayeh tribe: There are several versions of the story, and the details, especially the names, vary considerably. I have relied completely on oral tradition—on Rocks, and on my interviews with the modern Maayeh tribal chiefs, or *mukhtar*s, both Christian and Muslim—to tell the story of how the Maayeh tribe divided into Muslim and Christian branches.

The population figures for Christian and Muslim Maayehs: based on my interviews with Christian and Muslim *mukhtar*s of the Maayeh tribe, and my tracing of the two family trees.

Notes on Chapter 10: The Sea of Galilee: The Ministry

My understanding of the fishing and the weather patterns on the lake today and in the time of Jesus were shaped by Mendel Nun, *The Sea of Galilee and Its Fishermen in the New Testament* (Kibbutz Ein Gev: Tourist Department and Kinnereth Sailing Co., 1989); and on my interviews with Nun in his cottage on the edge of the Galilee.

Regarding the refusal to permit Arabs fishing licenses: During my interview with the Israeli agriculture ministry's Chaim Anjouni, on September 27, 2000, he said: "This may be a practical reality, but it is not a policy of the Israeli government. We stopped giving licenses three years ago because of the depletion of the stocks, so we are not issuing anyone licenses now."

Population figures in Tiberias: Israel, Central Bureau of Statistics, *Demographic Characteristics of the Population in Localities and Statistical Areas,* 1995, Publication no. 7, vol. A, p. 229. Total population in Tiberias is 10,127, of which 9,790 are Jewish.

Description of destroyed villages around the Galilee: Khalidi, *All That Remains,* p. 539.

"I do not want those who flee to return": Benvenisti, *Sacred Landscape,* p. 150.

"For the time being": Benvenisti, *Sacred Landscape,* p. 150.

Notes on Chapter 11: Lebanon: The Gentiles

Templars, warrior monks who embodied the two great passions of European powers: from Armstrong's *Jerusalem: One City, Three Faiths,* pp. 271–294.

For the history of Beaufort Castle and much of the general history of Lebanon's civil war I relied on Robert Fisk's *Pity the Nation: Lebanon at War* (London: André Deutsch, 1990).

The portrait of Akel Hashem is based on my interviews with Hashem's wife, Layya, and his six brothers, at the family home in February 2000; and on my interviews with senior South Lebanon Army and Israeli military officials who worked with Hashem.

The Israelis urged them on, insisting that terror cells operating out of the Palestinian refugee camps in West Beirut were responsible for Bashir's death and should pay: Jonathan Randal, *The Tragedy of Lebanon: Christian Warlords, Israeli Adventurers, and American Bunglers* (London: Hogarth Press, 1983), p. 14.

Bombing of the U.S. Marine barracks in Beirut: Hala Jaber, *Hezbollah: Born with a Vengeance* (New York: Columbia University Press, 1997), pp. 79–82. Jaber explains that Hezbollah never claimed responsibility for the bombing, although they supported the attack. My interviews with Western diplomats indicated that

Hezbollah was believed to be involved in the planning and the attack.

"Something he believed in his whole life" and the description of the funeral: based on my interview with Bishop Sader and several parishioners in attendance, February 20, 2000.

Lebanese Christian emigration: Carole H. Dagher (*Bring Down the Walls: Lebanon's Post-War Challenge* [New York: St. Martin's Press, 2000]) provides a thoroughly researched overview. On page 71 of her book, Dagher cites research by Ralph Ghodbane, published in a special issue of *An Nahar*, in January 1998. Christian emigrants, from 1975 to 1990, outnumbered Muslim emigrants by 3 to 1, but that trend seems to be changing. Now some researchers estimate that more than half of the emigrants from Lebanon are Muslim, and mostly Sunni. But of those emigrating to the West, Christians are still a majority. There are an estimated 1.5 million Lebanese Americans, more than 60 percent of whom are Christian. I also have relied on Boutros Labaki's analysis of the accelerated emigration of Christians from Lebanon. Labaki's figures are considered more reliable than others, because his data emanate directly from the Ministry of Interior, which is responsible for passport control of departures and arrivals in Lebanon. Labaki's data therefore provide a clearer indication of the emigrating population that may have left from Beirut for New York or Paris on a travel visa but stayed on, either with a resident visa or by eventually obtaining citizenship.

1996, 1997, and 1998 figures from: Lebanon, Central Bureau of Statistics, Statistical Bulletin, 1999.

Hezbollah as the largest party in the Lebanese parliament: *New York Times*, February 12, 2000.

How Christians fared within the Ministry of Displaced: In *Bring Down the Walls* (p. 85), Dagher describes how the Christian population was displaced by the war at a much higher rate than other sects. Dagher showed the displaced as a result of war amounted to nearly one fifth of the total resident population in Lebanon, 81 percent of whom were Christians and 19 percent Muslims. Most of the displaced originated from Beirut, where the heaviest fighting took place. Some 115,000 Muslims were uprooted from East Beirut, and about 175,000 Christians, from West Beirut and the suburbs of the city. Christians also suffered disproportionately severe losses of landholdings as a result of the war, either abandoning them or being forced by the situation to sell them off. This crippled the traditional agricultural economy of the Maronites. The overall Christian presence on the map receded from 70 percent of the total surface of Lebanon in 1975 to less than 30 percent by the year 2000.

Qlaya population after the pullout: This estimate is based on my interview with Shadi Masaad, head of the Lebanese government's Central Fund in the Ministry of the Displaced, on May 25, 2000.

". . . go into their beds at night and cut their throats": Sheikh Nasralla speech on Lebanese radio, May 21, 2000, trans. Kim Ghattas.

Notes on Chapter 12: The Mount of Olives: The Lament

The background of Yehuda Etzion and how he fits within a militant fringe of the Jewish settler movement in the West Bank came from Gorenberg, *The End of Days*. This thoroughly researched book also provided an overall sense of the apocalyptic strains within Judaism, Islam, and Christianity in relation to the Temple Mount/Noble Sanctuary.

The percentage of the West Bank that the Palestinians felt Israel was offering at the Camp David summit in July 2000: From my interviews with Jad Isaac and chief Palestinian negotiator Saeb Erekat.

The idea of two Jerusalems: Robert L. Wilken, *The Land Called Holy: Palestine in Christian History and Thought* (New Haven and London: Yale University Press, 1992), pp. 40–41. Wilken quotes a beautiful third-century midrash on the "Jerusalem above" and the "Jerusalem below."

Notes on Chapter 13: The Garden of Gethsemane: The Agony

The descriptions of Hanan Ashrawi during the conflict come from my interviews with her throughout that time period and from one extensive interview in April 2001, in which she reflected on the events of the Al-Aqsa *intifada*. Information on her background also came from her autobiography *This Side of Peace* (New York: Touchstone, 1995).

Information on all of the holy shrines involved in the conflict came from a variety of sources, including Gorenberg, *The End of Days;* Wilken, *The Land Called Holy;* and Jerome Murphy-O'Connor, *The Holy Land,* 4th ed. (Oxford University Press, 1998). I also relied, on occasion, on *NIV Dictionary of the Bible* (New York: HarperPaperbacks, 1989).

"Khaiber! Khaiber! All the Jews! The army of Mohammed will return!": *Khaiber* is a town near Medina in which, according to Islamic tradition, Jews conspired against the prophet Mohammed.

Notes on Chapter 14: Jerusalem: The Via Dolorosa

The history of Beit Jala and the population figures come from interviews with municipal officials and the Palestinian Legislative Council representative Bishara Daoud, as well as from other town residents. Some of the statistical information on population came from the Palestinian Academic Society for the Study of International Affairs in Jerusalem.

Notes on Chapter 15: The Road to Emmaus

My research into the history of Jesus's life again centered around Crossan, *Jesus: A Revolutionary Biography;* Wilson, *Jesus: A Life;* and Cahill, *Desire of the Everlasting Hills.*

I gained important insights into nonviolence and forgiveness from several long conversations with a former dean of the Harvard Divinity School, Bishop Krister Stendahl; Lutheran pastor Rev. Mitri Raheb; Harvard Divinity School professor Harvey Cox; Rabbis David Rosen and David Forman; and Muslim scholar Mitkal Natour, of the Inter-religious Coordinating Council in Israel; and from Simon Wiesenthal, *The Sunflower: On the Possibilities and Limits of Forgiveness* (New York: Schocken Books, 1997).

The sociological analysis of "turn the other cheek" in the time of Jesus: Daniel L. Buttry, "The Peacemaking Teaching of Jesus in the Sermon on the Mount," in *Seeking and Pursuing Peace,* ed. Salim J. Munayer (Musalaha, Jerusalem: American Baptist Churches in the United States, National Ministries, 1998).

World War I's retributive peace agreement only fostered the divisions that fomented World War II: based on telephone interview with Donald Shriver, former president of New York's Union Theological Seminary and author of *An Ethic for Enemies.*

The notions of Palestinian Christians as "the salt of the earth," and of being Christian rather than asserting Christianity: my interviews with Rev. Raheb.

INDEX

PUBLICAFFAIRS is a new nonfiction publishing house and a tribute to the standards, values, and flair of three persons who have served as mentors to countless reporters, writers, editors, and book people of all kinds, including me.

I. F. STONE, proprietor of *I. F. Stone's Weekly,* combined a commitment to the First Amendment with entrepreneurial zeal and reporting skill and became one of the great independent journalists in American history. At the age of eighty, Izzy published *The Trial of Socrates,* which was a national bestseller. He wrote the book after he taught himself ancient Greek.

BENJAMIN C. BRADLEE was for nearly thirty years the charismatic editorial leader of *The Washington Post.* It was Ben who gave the *Post* the range and courage to pursue such historic issues as Watergate. He supported his reporters with a tenacity that made them fearless, and it is no accident that so many became authors of influential, best-selling books.

ROBERT L. BERNSTEIN, the chief executive of Random House for more than a quarter century, guided one of the nation's premier publishing houses. Bob was personally responsible for many books of political dissent and argument that challenged tyranny around the globe. He is also the founder and was the longtime chair of Human Rights Watch, one of the most respected human rights organizations in the world.

. . .

For fifty years, the banner of Public Affairs Press was carried by its owner Morris B. Schnapper, who published Gandhi, Nasser, Toynbee, Truman, and about 1,500 other authors. In 1983 Schnapper was described by *The Washington Post* as "a redoubtable gadfly." His legacy will endure in the books to come.

Peter Osnos, *Publisher*